D0889954

Map Guide
to the
U.S. Federal Censuses,
1790-1920

Map Guide
to the
U.S. Federal Censuses,
1790-1920

William Thorndale and William Dollarhide

Genealogical Publishing Co., Inc.
Baltimore

Published by Genealogical Publishing Co., Inc.
1001 N. Calvert St., Baltimore, Md. 21202
Paperback edition 1992, 1993, 1995, 1997, 1998, 2000
Library of Congress Catalogue Card Number 87-80143
International Standard Book Number 0-8063-1188-6
Made in the United States of America

To Our Parents

Wilma Ann Lewis
Charles William Thorndale

Marjory Watkins Wiles
Albert Raymond Dollarhide

Contents

Preface

The *Map Guide* shows county outline maps at ten-year intervals, the old county boundaries being superimposed over the modern lines. These maps are designed for historians, genealogists, and demographers who use the name lists and statistics of the censuses, but will help anyone seeking some sense of county boundary changes. The maps begin with 1790, the earliest federal census, and end with 1920 in anticipation of the release of the name lists of that census in 1992. Thus there are maps for all federal censuses until the 1930 lists are released in the year 2002. The phrase "all federal censuses" needs clarification, since Congress sometimes encouraged states and ordered territories to take special censuses. A map has been included if the name lists went to Washington, as did the lists for 1885 and Minnesota 1857.[1]

The *Map Guide* also presents much background information on the censuses, this information being essential to researchers, as an example will illustrate. A scholar recently derided the 1860 Florida census because it enumerated only one Indian, a number that had "unaccountably doubled" to two Indians by 1870.[2] In actual fact, Indians not taxed were specifically excluded from federal censuses in 1860 and 1870. The *Map Guide*'s introduction summarizes such background information in (1) a history of census growth; (2) a precis of technical facts about each census, including dates taken and the number of copies made; and (3) a discussion of census accuracy. The actual questionnaires used in each census are not described, since that information is readily available elsewhere.[3] Not so readily available is the book's most useful supplemental information: a statement with each map of which county lists survive or are lost.

The accuracy of the enclosed maps comes from the territorial and state laws defining the county lines, an indispensable standard but one ambiguous at times. The appendix outlines various technical problems in identifying former county lines, a situation compounded by so few states having detailed studies of all their county boundary changes. The bibliography discusses aborted national projects and summarizes state by state the sources used for this present work. Lastly, an index has been included listing counties—modern and defunct—along with a locality code for finding each county on the state maps.

Aside from being census units, American counties are interesting in their own right. There seems to be no comprehensive list of all U.S. counties. Certainly the well-known compilations—those by Kane, Kirkham, and Everton—omit many defunct counties.[4] Of the roughly 3,250 counties that have existed, it is difficult to say which was the largest, since several once covered what are now whole states but were then mostly occupied by hostile Indians. The largest county today is San Bernardino in California, covering 20,117 square miles, four times the size of Connecticut. The smallest counties are Hawaii's Kalawao with fourteen square miles and Minnesota's defunct Manomin (1857-69) with sixteen square miles. By comparison, New York County on Manhattan Island covers twenty-three square miles and the District of Columbia sprawls over sixty-one square miles. So small was

Manomin that it bore the mocking name of Fridley's Farm in honor of its ruling family.[5] Kalawao, the former leper colony on Molokai, still exists after a fashion, the 1980 census reporting 144 inhabitants.

Initially created in Virginia in 1634 and in Massachusetts in 1643, the U.S. county has not received its historical due, such as being one of the pioneers' most vital tools in the westward movement. The county has been both a historical success and a survivor, supplying for most Americans in the eighteenth and nineteenth centuries their most accessible government. Even today, when the great majority of Americans live in incorporated urban areas, the county refuses to disappear, though some county/city consolidation is taking place, such as Marion County/Indianapolis, Indiana; Duval County/Jacksonville, Florida; and Ormsby County/Carson City, Nevada. Alaska alone has never had counties, since the extraction industries sought to curb local taxes by winning a requirement that Congress approve the creation of any county in Alaska Territory.[6] Only in New England does the county remain weak in competition with the rival town governments. But if Connecticut abolished county government in 1960, Arizona and New Mexico each created a new county in the early 1980s.[7] So the county, a leftover from the horse and buggy days, continues to function across nearly the whole nation, just as it did for the federal censuses from 1790 to 1920.[8]

*NOTES
1. The 1885 Dakotas have maps because the other 1885 enumerations have maps, although no evidence was found that the Dakota lists went to Washington.

---

*Abbreviations: GPO, Government Printing Office, and NARS, National Archives and Records Service.

2. Harry A. Kersey, Jr., "Florida Seminoles and the Census of 1900," *Florida Historical Quarterly* 60 (1981-82), 146.

3. Bureau of the Census, *Twenty Censuses: Population and Housing Questions, 1790-1980* (Washington: GPO, 1979); Val D. Greenwood, *The Researcher's Guide to American Genealogy* (Baltimore: Genealogical Publishing Co., 1973), pp. 154-63; National Archives, *Guide to Genealogical Research in the National Archives* (Washington: NARS, 1982), pp. 20-21; Arlene Eakle and Johni Cerny, *The Source: A Guidebook of American Genealogy* (Salt Lake City: Ancestry Publishing Co., 1984), p. 98. James Hansen notes (by personal correspondence) that *Twenty Censuses* contains no instructions for the 1860 census, thus duplicating the omission in Carroll D. Wright and William C. Hunt, *The History and Growth of the United States Census* (Washington: GPO, 1900). Hansen observes that the 1860 census, per its instructions to census takers, was the first to seek the German state/province of nativity for German-born persons, "Germany" being deemed insufficiently precise.

4. Joseph Nathan Kane, *The American Counties*, 4th ed. (Metuchen, NJ: Scarecrow Press, 1983); E. Kay Kirkham, *The Counties of the United States: Their Derivation and Census Schedules* (Salt Lake City: the author, 1961); George B. Everton, Sr., *The Handy Book for Genealogists,* 7th ed. (Logan, UT: Everton Publishers, 1981).

5. Mary Ellen Lewis, "The Establishment of County Boundaries in Minnesota," (M.A. thesis, University of Minnesota, 1946), pp. 7, 95.

6. The borough governments of Alaska's larger communities exercise some county-like functions but cover only a small part of the state.

7. La Paz County: Arizona Laws 1983, 36th leg., ch. 291, p. 1087; Cibola County: New Mexico Laws 1981, 35th leg., ch. 24, p. 76.

8. For instance, the automobile and the need for county mergers are linked in Warren A. Beck and Ynez D. Haase, *Historical Atlas of California* (Norman: University of Oklahoma Press, 1974), map 65; and Mrs. Dan "Peggy" Kirkbridge, *From These Roots* (Cheyenne, WY: Pioneer Printing & Stationery Co., 1972), p. 3.

Acknowledgements

Most of the research for this book was done at the LDS Genealogical Library, Salt Lake City, and the University of Utah's Marriott and Law libraries. We thank their staffs for so much help. Certainly this book would not exist if the Genealogical Library did not maintain its open-door policy.

Research was also done at the State Library of Massachusetts; the Connecticut State Library; the Geography and Map Division of the Library of Congress; the Cartographic Division of the National Archives; the National Cartographic Information Center, U.S. Geological Survey; the Tennessee State Library and Archives; the Alabama Department of Archives and History; the several libraries at the University of Texas-Austin; the Utah State Archives; the Washington State Law Library; and the M.G. Gallagher Law Library of the University of Washington. We owe special thanks for the extended assistance given by the Kentucky Historical Society (Mary Winter, map collections), the Georgia Surveyor General Department (Marion R. Hemperley, director) of the Georgia Department of Archives and History; and the Texas General Land Office (Herman Forbes, director of the surveying division).

Individuals and institutions helping by mail were John H. Long; the National Endowment for the Humanities; Robert J. Boroughf of Nevada; Robert S. Davis, Jr., of Georgia; Robert C. Anderson of Utah; Elizabeth Shown Mills of Alabama; Carol Wells of Northwestern State University of Louisiana; the State Historical Society of North Dakota; the Historical Resource Center of South Dakota; the Montana Historical Society; Larry Weathers of the Pacific County Historical Society, Washington; the Arizona Historical Society; the Arizona Department of Library, Archives, and Public Records; the Nebraska State Historical Society; the Golden Public Library, Golden, Colorado; the Colorado Historical Society; the Colorado Division of Archives and Public Records; the Florida State Archives; the Hawaii Department of the Attorney General; Virginia Hinton, Breckinridge Historical Society, Kentucky; and William E. Miller of Maryland.

The happiest sort of help comes from people who share one's research enthusiasms. We especially thank James Hansen of the State Historical Society of Wisconsin for volunteering his researches into the early censuses around the Great Lakes and in the 1790 Southwest Territory, and for describing some of the discoveries made by the archives staff of the SHSW in seeking Wisconsin county copies of the 1850-70 censuses. Hazel L. Bowman of Florida sent unsolicited information that proved how a statutorily-unchanged boundary could shift its interpreted location.

Craig Hanks, Rose Nerad, Bob Merth, Marcia Romero, Ralph Reed, Jeanne Tinker, Courtney McRill, and Barbara Hoyt at Sunshine Printing (Bellingham, Washington) were involved in map reproductions, typesetting, and coordination of production from the beginning of the project to the end. Evidence of their dedication and professionalism can be seen on every page and map.

The text has been read in draft by Frederick G. Bohme (chief, Census History Staff, Bureau of the Census), James Hansen, Arlene Eakle and Michael Tepper. We repeat the thanks already given to them several times before.

It is customary at this point in acknowledgements for the authors to accept responsibility for any errors that *may* still remain. With the *Map Guide* there is no doubt that errors remain undetected. Among the many thousands of boundary changes mapped in this book, there are certainly lines incorrectly drawn. We hope others interested in local history will be inspired by the uncertainties of local boundaries to research individual states and incidently correct our mistakes.

The ultimate thanks go to James Cumming of Seattle. He knew that two strangers a thousand miles apart had the same vague idea for a book of maps and he insisted they get together.

Introduction • Federal Censuses

HISTORY

The U.S. Bureau of the Census with its permanent, professional staff is a twentieth-century phenomenon.[1] The first six censuses, those from 1790 to 1840, were overseen by federal marshals under the lax supervision of officials in the national capital. The first Census Office began operation in Washington in 1850, but only temporarily, the office being disbanded after each decennial count and reassembled for the next. The Census Office became permanent in 1902.

The federal government managed to report the 1790 census in a pamphlet of fifty-six pages, but used 1,203 volumes to describe the 1970 data.[2] This publishing explosion partly reflects the nation's burgeoning population, which went from under four million in 1790 to over 200 million in 1970. Just as important were the growth of an ever-busy bureaucracy and the proliferation of questions, name lists, and special censuses. Researchers will find that the censuses differ substantially in size and content.

The first six censuses were similar in content, being authorized by the federal law of 1 March 1790 as mandated by the U.S. Constitution and modified by later acts.[3] These censuses all name only heads of families at their "usual place of abode" on some early day in June or August, while supposedly enumerating persons without a settled residence wherever they were on the census day. *Head of family* was defined for 1790 as the "master, mistress, steward, overseer, or other principal person" of a residence, including any free person living alone. All other people were noted only by tally marks in categories for age, sex, race, and slavery, except that the Constitution excluded from the census all Indians not taxed.

The U.S. marshals were responsible for taking the census. There was one federal district court and one U.S. marshal in 1790 in each state plus Kentucky and Maine. Population growth later caused the division of some states into multiple districts, but never did federal court districts cross state lines. The marshals appointed assistants to take the actual census in divisions to consist, as the 1790 act put it, "of one or more counties, cities, towns, townships, hundreds or parishes, or of a territory plainly and distinctly bounded by water courses, mountains, or public roads." While subdivisions within counties were authorized and used, such as New England towns, the instructions for census enumeration areas maintained the integrity of county boundaries. The major exceptions to this rule were in South Carolina for Orangeburg 1790 and Georgetown 1800 and in 1900 for some Indian reservations. The integrity of county boundaries can be seen in the census act of 1820, which stipulated that if a county straddled two federal court districts in a state, then the county was to be enumerated totally in the federal district containing the county's courthouse. The 1830 act directed that an enumerator's division "shall not consist, in any case, of more than one county."

The 1790 census act gave enumerators nine months from the census day to enumerate the people, to post copies of the statistics "at two of the most public places" in the divisions, and to send the name lists to the marshal. The marshal then had four months to send "the aggregate amount" of each census to the president, having deposited the actual name lists with the clerk of the federal district court. The clerk was "hereby directed to receive and carefully preserve the same." Further, the respective federal judges were required to submit the census returns to their grand juries for verification of compliance with the census law. These steps also governed the censuses from 1800 to 1840.

The requirement to store the 1790-1810 censuses in federal district courthouses undermines the repeated assertions that the burning of Washington in the War of 1812 destroyed many of the early census lists.[4] As just explained, only statistical summaries of the early censuses were supposed to go to the federal capital, so the name lists during the War of 1812 were presumably not in Washington but in such places as Boston, Philadelphia, and Nashville. Only in 1830 did Congress order the clerks of the district courts to send all the old census lists to the State Department in Washington.[5] An absence of inventories of the early census schedules collected by the State Department makes the matter difficult to clarify, but presumably most of the missing early lists were either lost before 1830 or not sent to Washington despite the 1830 law. It is certain that the 1820 lists for Michigan Territory remained, and still remain, in Michigan.[6] Probably the only name lists lost in the burning of Washington were those of the District of Columbia's 1810 census. The District gained its own federal court in 1802 and thus its 1810 census was the first taken separately from Maryland and Virginia.[7]

Collecting the old census lists at Washington in 1830 apparently came from a desire to recalculate and standardize the population statistics, which had heretofore employed the numbers sent by the marshals.[8] This growing interest in statistical studies also inspired the creation in 1839 of the American Statistical Association.[9] From the beginning, the Association took a close interest in the U.S. censuses. Its leaders lobbied for the notable changes seen in the 1850 census: Lists of each free person by name, age, and birth state (but slaves usually given only by numbers); a special mortality census of all individuals who had died during the year ending 1 June; the collection of names and information on farmers and businessmen in censuses of agriculture and industry; and the creation of an interim Census Office under the supervision of the U.S. Secretary of the Interior. These reforms reflected a hope that vital statistics could be sampled at decennial intervals and supply the first firm numbers about the nation's births, marriages, and deaths. For example, the 1870 population schedules asked the month of a birth or marriage occurring within the year, while a separate mortality schedule did the same for deaths.

Using the census to gather vital statistics proved an interim expedient and ultimately a failure, since informants were very inaccurate in remembering and reporting births and deaths. The 1900 mortality and population schedules, which sought the month and year of each person's birth, marked the culmination of this approach. State and city registrations of births and deaths proved far superior in accuracy, even if it took a couple of decades from the turn of the century before such registrations covered most of the country.

The U.S. marshals oversaw their last census in 1870, a census considered one of the worst ever taken.[10] The marshals were presidential appointees confirmed by the Senate, so the Census Office had no direct authority over them and little hope of instilling professionalism into the marshals' assistants, who in 1870 were far too few in number to take an adequate census. Such census takers were usually chosen for their party affiliations under the spoils system. In the South the pool of competent potential assistants was especially limited by the low pay and the repugnance that former Confederates felt for Republican marshals. Combined with the unsettled post-war populations, especially freed slaves, these various troubles made the 1870 Southern census "grossly deficient," as a head of the Census Office later put the matter.[11] A subsequent census report estimated that 1.2 million Southerners were missed by the 1870 census.[12] Not surprisingly, the 1880 census brought major reforms, most notably in using nearly five times as many local enumerators as in 1870 and in giving the Census Office direct control over their hiring.[13]

In the last decades of the nineteenth century the census became a tool of the era's expansionism, both externally in inventorying overseas possessions such as Puerto Rico and the Hawaiian Islands, and internally in counting Indians living on lands the whites might desire. The 1880 census was the first to authorize a census of Alaska, as far as was practicable, which turned out to mean a count of accessible villages and an estimate of the rest. The 1890 and 1900 Alaska enumerations were each touted as major advances over their predecessors in counting more and guessing less, a trend greatly helped by gold rushers opening the backcountry.

The 1880 census was also the first to authorize a census of Indians, at the discretion of the Superintendent of the Census. [14] The National Archives has microfilmed such special Indian schedules for a few reservations in California, the Dakotas, and Washington, but there are also other 1880 Indian census lists. [15] The constitutional prohibition against counting untaxed Indians was not violated by this or the 1890 Indian census, since these counts were done on special schedules and kept separate from the population totals used to apportion the U.S. House of Representatives. These enumerations should not be confused with those taken for the Bureau of Indian Affairs. With the 1887 Allotment Act, also called the Dawes Severalty Act, the federal government moved to dissolve Indian reservations by giving—from those reservation lands—a tract to each tribal member, a policy evoking the elaborate 1890 census count. [16] Starting with 1900, Indians were enumerated in the regular census.

Making the Census Office a permanent federal agency in 1902 did more than just increase its professional stature. A permanent staff was now available to collect annual statistics and conduct inter-decennial special projects, such as advising on the 1907 Cuban census and taking the 1907 Oklahoma census ordered by the president. The permanent office, which in the years before World War One gradually came to be called the Bureau of the Census (informally called the Census Bureau), was also in a position to make long-range managerial decisions concerning records. Two of the most important were the 1918-19 transfer of the 1850-80 non-population schedules to state and private de-

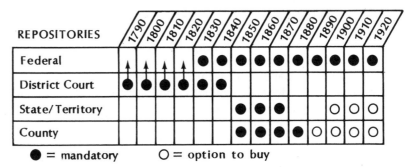

Mandated Census Copies

REPOSITORIES	1790	1800	1810	1820	1830	1840	1850	1860	1870	1880	1890	1900	1910	1920
Federal	↑	↑	↑	↑	●	●	●	●	●	●	●	●	●	●
District Court	●	●	●	●	●	●								
State/Territory							●	●	●			○	○	○
County							●	●	●	●	○	○	○	○

● = mandatory   ○ = option to buy

Figure 1. Mandated Census Copies.

Copies of federal census name lists went to the indicated repositories. The arrows indicate the 1830 ordered transfer of the federal district court copies to the U.S. State Department. The counties 1890-1920 received no automatic copy but had the option of buying their name lists at cost, an option almost never exercised, though such a list exists for 1890 Washington County, Georgia.

positories (there being no national archives) and the destruction of the paper copies of the 1900-20 population and non-population schedules. [17]

RECORDS

This section describes for each federal census 1790-1920 such basic facts as the census day, the sorts of censuses taken, and the required number of copies of each name list. (See Figure 1 for a summary of the number of copies required for each census year.) From the first day of the census—the *census day*—enumerators had some set period such as nine months or thirty days to go around their districts doing the *field count* of locating and listing everyone alive on the census day. Those persons who died before or were born after the census day were theoretically not counted. If the census taker enumerated an area several months after the census day, he was supposed to include all persons who lived in his division on the census day even if they had since moved or died, and to ignore all who had moved into the area after the census day. Obviously, such fine distinctions were unrealistic, opening the way to skipping or counting twice those people on the move around the census day.

Schedule means a name list enumerating the general population or such special groups as farmers, businessmen, Indians, or veterans. It excludes the early "social statistics collection," which was purely numerical. *Soundex* and *miracode* are phonetic indexes compiled in the 1930s for the 1880-1920 censuses to aid applicants in proving their age for Social Security. The codes use the same phonetic principles to bring together surname spelling variants but differ in the layout of their index cards. Both, for example, code Gilasby and Gillespie as G421. Coding instructions are widely available and are described, for instance, in Greenwood's *Researcher's Guide to American Genealogy,* the *Guide to Genealogical Research in the National Archives,* and Eakle and Cerny's *The Source,* all cited in note 3 of the preface.

When referring to U.S. marshals and federal district courts, it should be understood that for 1790-1810 the comparable official in the territories for overseeing the enumeration was the territorial secretary, or the governor if necessary, and the name lists were to be stored in the territorial superior or supreme court. In 1813 federal marshals were authorized for each territory and they then oversaw the censuses in the territories through to 1870.[18] The major congressional acts noted for each census are cited in the standard manner, thus "2 Stat. 564, 26 March 1810" means an act passed by Congress on 26 March 1810 and published in *United States Statutes at Large,* Volume 2, page 564.

1790 Enumeration: First decennial census. U.S. population of 3.9 million (3.2 million free and .7 million slave). Census day of the 1st Monday in August (2 August 1790), the field count due within nine months (1 Stat. 101, 1 March 1790). Of the two states late to join the Union, Rhode Island was to be enumerated within the set nine months (1 Stat. 129, 5 July 1790), but Vermont had a census day of the 1st Monday in April 1791 (4 April 1791), the field count due within five months (1 Stat. 197, 2 March 1791). South

Carolina's field count was extended to allow completion within nineteen months from the census day (1 Stat. 226, 8 November 1791). Census conducted by U.S. marshals under the direction of the president. Schedules: Population. Mandated Copies: One set, to the federal district court but in 1830 ordered sent to the U.S. Secretary of State. Remarks: No census was required in the Northwest and Southwest territories, but militia captains in the latter (which became Tennessee in 1796) took a count under the direction of the governor.[19] Kentucky and Maine, though respectively parts of Virginia and Massachusetts, had their own federal district courts and therefore their own enumerations. The surviving 1790 schedules were published in the early 1900s by the U.S. Bureau of the Census, with Virginia state enumerations 1782-85 partly substituting for the lost federal lists. The extant original 1790 lists are available as National Archives microfilm M637 in twelve rolls.

1800 Enumeration: Second decennial census. U.S. population of 5.3 million (4.4 million free and .9 million slave). Census day of the 1st Monday in August (4 August 1800), the field count due within nine months (2 Stat. 11, 28 February 1800). Census conducted by U.S. marshals under the direction of the U.S. Secretary of State. Schedules: Population. Mandated Copies: One set, to the federal district court but in 1830 ordered sent to the U.S. Secretary of State.

1810 Enumeration: Third decennial census. U.S. population of 7.2 million (6.0 million free and 1.2 million slave). Census day of the 1st Monday in August (6 August 1810), the field count due within nine months (2 Stat. 564, 26 March 1810), but extended to allow completion within ten months from the census day (2 Stat. 658, 2 March 1811). Census conducted by U.S. marshals under the direction of the U.S. Secretary of State. The U.S. marshals also conducted a census of manufactures under the direction of the U.S. Secretary of the Treasury (2 Stat. 605, 1 May 1810). Schedules: Population, manufactures. Mandated Copies: One population set, to the federal district court but in 1830 ordered sent to the U.S. Secretary of State; one manufacturing set, to the U.S. Secretary of the Treasury. Remarks: Extant 1810 manufacturing lists are scattered among the population schedules, their page locations given in Katherine H. Davidson and Charlotte M. Ashby, *Preliminary Inventory of the Records of the Bureau of the Census* (Washington: National Archives, 1964), pp. 132-34.

1820 Enumeration: Fourth decennial census. U.S. population of 9.6 million (8.1 million free and 1.5 million slave). Census day of the 1st Monday in August (7 August 1820), the field count due within six months (3 Stat. 548, 14 March 1820), but extended to allow completion within thirteen months from the census day (3 Stat. 643, 3 March 1821). Census conducted by U.S. marshals under the direction of the U.S. Secretary of State. Schedules: Population, manufactures. Mandated Copies: One population set, to the federal district court but in 1830 ordered sent to the U.S. Secretary of State. Remarks: The manufacturing census is on National Archives microfilm M279 in twenty-nine rolls.

1830 Enumeration: Fifth decennial census. U.S. population of 12.9 million (10.9 million free and 2.0 million slave). Census day of 1 June 1830, the field count due within six months (4 Stat. 383, 23 March 1830), but extended to allow completion within twelve months from the census day (4 Stat. 439, 3 February 1831). Census conducted by U.S. marshals under the direction of the U.S. Secretary of State. Schedules: Population. Mandated Copies: Two sets, to the federal district court and the U.S. Secretary of State. Remarks: First federal census to supply enumerators with uniform, printed forms for recording names.

1840 Enumeration: Sixth decennial census. U.S. population of 17.1 million (14.6 million free and 2.5 million slave). Census day of 1 June 1840, the field count due within nine months (5 Stat. 331, 3 March 1839), but extended to allow completion within eighteen months from the census day (5 Stat. 452, 1 September 1841). Census conducted by U.S. marshals under the direction of the U.S. Secretary of State. Schedules: Population (including military pensioners). Mandated Copies: Two sets, to the federal district court and the U.S. Secretary of State. Remarks: The census of military pensioners was taken on the population forms and compiled and published separately in 1841.[20] A census of industry was taken "in statistical tables" and survives in the National Archives.

1850 Enumeration: Seventh decennial census. U.S. population of 23.2 million (20.0 million free and 3.2 million slave). Census day of 1 June 1850, the field count due within five months (9 Stat. 428, 23 May 1850). Census conducted by U.S. marshals under the direction of the Census Office appointed by the U.S. Secretary of the Interior. Schedules: Free population, slave population, mortality, agriculture, industry. Mandated Copies: Three sets, to the county court, the secretary of state of the territory or state, and the U.S. Secretary of the Interior. Remarks: The federal government's copy of the non-population schedules was given to state and private depositories in 1918-19. The agricultural census covered farms with annual produce worth $100 or more; the industrial census covered businesses grossing $500 or more.

1860 Enumeration: Eighth decennial census. U.S. population of 31.5 million (27.5 million free and 4.0 million slave). Census day of 1 June 1860, the field count due within five months (per section 23, 9 Stat. 432, 23 May 1850). Census conducted by U.S. marshals under the direction of the Census Office appointed by the U.S. Secretary of the Interior. Schedules: Free population, slave population, mortality, agriculture, industry. Mandated Copies: Three sets, to the county court, the secretary of state of the territory or state, and the U.S. Secretary of the Interior. Remarks: The 1860 census was the first to ask for the state/province of nativity for German-born persons. The federal government's copy of the non-population schedules was given to state and private depositories in 1918-19. The agricultural census covered farms with annual produce worth $100 or more; the industrial census covered businesses grossing $500 or more. Known damaged population schedules include parts of the counties of Essex, NJ; Arizona, Bernalillo, Dona Ana, Rio Arriba, Santa Ana, and Valencia, NM Territory; Chenango and Columbus, NY; and Fayette, PA.

1870 Enumeration: Ninth decennial census. U.S. population of 38.6 million. Census day of 1 June 1870, the field count due within five months (per section 23, 9 Stat. 432, 23 May 1850). Census conducted by U.S. marshals under the direction of the Census Office appointed by the U.S. Secretary of the Interior. Schedules: Population, mortality, agriculture, industry. Mandated Copies: Three sets, to the county court, the secretary of state of the territory or state, and the U.S. Secretary of the Interior. Remarks: The 1870 census in the Southern states omits a great many persons. The federal government's copy of the non-population schedules was given to state and private depositories in 1918-19. The agricultural census covered farms with annual produce worth $500 or more; the industrial census covered businesses grossing $500 or more.

1880 Enumeration: Tenth decennial census. U.S. population of 50.2 million. Census day of 1 June 1880, the field count due within thirty days, except communities over 10,000 population due within two weeks (20 Stat. 473, 3 March 1879, as amended by 21 Stat. 75, 20 April 1880). Census conducted by the Superintendent of the Census (Census Office, U.S. Department of the Interior). Schedules: Population, mortality, agriculture, industry. Mandated Copies: Two sets, an abbreviated version to the county court and the original, full version to the Superintendent of the Census. Remarks: The federal government's copy of the non-population schedules was given to state and private depositories in 1918-19; its population schedules were distributed to non-federal depositories in 1956 after being microfilmed. The county copy was supposed to list just each person's name, age, sex, and color. A soundex index exists for all states and territories, but only for households with at least one child aged ten or under. The regular census omits Indians not taxed, but some special Indian schedules exist with a census day of 1 October 1880. Known damaged population schedules include parts of the counties of San Francisco, CA, and Suffolk, NY, and New York City.

1885 Enumerations: The census act of 1879 pledged the federal government to pay half the costs of a census taken by any state or territory in June or July 1885, if the format followed the federal census and if a set of all schedules was sent to Washington (section 22, 20 Stat. 480, 3 March 1879). Such 1885 censuses were taken by Colorado, Florida, Nebraska, and the territories of Dakota and New Mexico. Schedules: Population, mortality, agriculture, industry. Mandated Copies: Probably three sets, to the county court and the Superintendent of the Census per the act of 1879, plus a copy to the state or territory. Remarks: The National Archives lacks the Dakota schedules but has the others, and has

microfilmed its 1885 population lists. North and South Dakota have their respective halves of the Dakota census, with the South Dakota portion microfilmed on National Archives GR27, rolls 1-3.

1890 Enumeration: Eleventh decennial census. U.S. population of 63.0 million. Census day of 1 June 1890, the field count due in thirty days, except communities over 10,000 population due within two weeks (25 Stat. 760, 1 March 1889). Census conducted by the Superintendent of the Census (Census Office, U.S. Department of the Interior). Schedules: Population, mortality, agriculture, manufactures, Indians, Union veterans. Mandated Copies: One set, to the Superintendent of the Census. Local jurisdictions could buy a copy of their schedules at cost. Remarks: Various fires have destroyed nearly all 1890 schedules. Population schedules survive for 6,160 persons, all indexed.[21] The lists for Union veterans or their widows survive for part of Kentucky and all states alphabetically from Louisiana to Wyoming, and also for Washington, D.C., the Indian Territory, and some military installations.

1900 Enumeration: Twelfth decennial census. U.S. population of 76.2 million. Census day of 1 June 1900, the field count due within thirty days, except communities over 10,000 population due within two weeks (30 Stat. 1014, 3 March 1899). Census conducted by the Director of the Census (Census Office, U.S. Department of the Interior). Schedules: Population, mortality, agriculture, manufactures. Mandated Copies: One set, to the Director of the Census. Local jurisdictions could buy a copy of their schedules at cost. Remarks: Population schedules exist for overseas and shipboard military, especially in the Philippine Islands. A soundex index exists for all states and territories. By authority of Congress, the non-population schedules were destroyed unmicrofilmed, and the population schedules were destroyed in the 1940s after being microfilmed. Some Indian schedules, because the Census Office was unable to assign all reservations to specific counties, are placed at the end of state lists.

1910 Enumeration: Thirteenth decennial census. U.S. population of 92.2 million. Census day of 15 April 1910, the field count due within thirty days, except communities over 5,000 population due within two weeks (36 Stat. 1, 2 July 1909). Census conducted by the Director of the Census (Census Bureau, U.S. Department of Commerce and Labor). Schedules: Population, agriculture, manufactures. Mandated Copies: One set, to the Director of the Census. Local jurisdictions could buy a copy of their schedules at cost. Remarks: Population schedules exist for overseas and shipboard military. Soundex/miracode indexes exist for Alabama, Arkansas, California, Florida, Georgia, Illinois, Kansas, Kentucky, Louisiana, Michigan, Mississippi, Missouri, North Carolina, Ohio, Oklahoma, Pennsylvania, South Carolina, Tennessee, Texas, Virginia, and West Virginia. By authority of Congress, the non-population schedules were destroyed unmicrofilmed, and the population schedules were destroyed in the 1940s after being microfilmed.

1920 Enumeration: Fourteenth decennial census. U.S. Population of 106.0 million. Census day of 1 January 1920, the field count due within thirty days, except communities over 2,500 population due within two weeks (40 Stat. 1291, 3 March 1919). Census conducted by the Director of the Census (Census Bureau, U.S. Department of Commerce). Schedules: Population, agriculture, manufactures. Mandated Copies: One set, to the Director of the Census. Local jurisdictions could buy a copy of their schedules at cost. Remarks: Under the rule of seventy-two years of confidentiality, the 1920 population schedules should be released to the public in 1992. A soundex index exists for all states. By authority of Congress, the non-population schedules were destroyed unmicrofilmed, and the population schedules were destroyed in the 1940s after being microfilmed.

Overseas Enumerations: Federal censuses were taken for several overseas possessions not shown in the *Map Guide.* Such censuses for 1910 and 1920 survive in the regular decennial schedules. Whether some others are extant was not determined. In addition, the military schedules of the federal censuses 1900 and later cover various U.S. personnel stationed at some of these possessions. The dates shown below in parentheses are the years when the U.S. took formal possession of these places.

Guam (1898): Census in 1920.
Midway (1867): Censuses in 1910 and 1920 (both schedules filmed with Honolulu County, Hawaii).
Panama Canal Zone (1912): Census in 1920.
Philippine Islands (1898): Censuses in 1904 (Philippine Commission) and 1918 (Philippine Government).
Puerto Rico (1898): Census in 1899 (U.S. War Department, schedules destroyed), 1910, and 1920.
Samoa (1899-1904): Census in 1920.
Virgin Islands (1917): Census in 1917.
Wake (1899): Census in 1920.

COMPLETENESS

Much research is still needed to account for the various incomplete censuses. Some losses, though, are easily explained. Most of the 1890 schedules burned in a 1921 fire. The 1900-20 population schedules were destroyed after being microfilmed, but the filming in the 1940s was so primitive that significant sections of the films are illegible or decipherable only at considerable eye strain. There is no census for Hernando County, Florida, in 1860, because none was taken.[22] As for the missing three counties for 1850 California, the name lists never reached Washington.[23] Other fires damaged a few 1860 and 1880 population schedules,[24] as well as much of the 1870 Minnesota lists, for which Minnesota's state copy survives.

The summary given in the previous section on the number of copies mandated by each census act shows that only one master copy was made for each of the first four censuses, and those were called to Washington in 1830. Nearly all lost pre-1890 federal censuses are from this 1790-1820 period. The census acts of 1830 and 1840 mandated two sets of each name list, one going to Washington and one to the appropriate federal district court. The federal courthouse copies may still exist, as is the case for Vermont 1830 and 1840.[25] Whether other lists exist in such court records still needs to be determined.

Regarding losses in the 1850-80 censuses, Congress directed that each state 1850-70 and county 1850-80 get a copy of its own schedules, though there is no guarantee that these extra copies

Figure 2. Duplicate Census Entries.

The lack of ditto marks for some state-of-birth columns is in the originals, but two-letter state abbreviations are used here to save space. B/p= birthplace.

Pickens Co., SC

1. 14 Oct 1850 p. 413 #629

Name	Age	Sex	B/p
John Honey	49	M	SC
Aly	42	F	
Elias	23	M	
Malkin S.	21	M	
Neoma	19	F	
Sarah	17	F	
Clara	15	F	
Aly	13	F	SC
Benson	11	M	"
William	5	M	"
Robert	4	M	"
John	3	M	"
Mary Honey	25	F	"
Henry	5	M	"
Susan	3	F	"

29 Oct 1850 p. 439 #999

Name	Age	Sex	B/p
John Honey	50	M	SC
Elly	40	F	"
Elias	22	M	"
Macomb	20	M	"
Maomi	18	F	"
Sarah	16	F	"
Clara	14	F	"
Penelope	12	F	"
Benson	10	M	SC
Harrison	5	M	"
Robert	2	M	"
John	2/12	M	"
Mary Honey	25	F	"

St. Francis Co., AR

2. 17 Aug 1860 p. 503 #734

Name	Age	Sex	B/p
Isam Aldridge	37	M	AL
Pollie	30	F	"
Martha A.	15	F	"
Gustine	14	M	"
Henry	12	M	"
Ann	11	F	AR
Sallie	8	F	MS
Amanda	4	F	"

16 Aug 1860 p. 435 #319

Name	Age	Sex	B/p
Isam Aldridge	36	M	AL
Martha	14	F	"
Augustin	12	F	"
Wm H.	6	M	"
Ann	9	F	"
Sarah	7	F	"
Amanda	3	F	"

Menifee Co., KY

3. 10 Jun 1880 p. 681 #169

Name	Age	Sex	B/p	F	M
Buddie Igo	57	M	KY	KY	KY
Pheby	20	F	"	"	"
Berry	21	M	"	"	"
Shelt	13	M	"	"	"
Jane	11	F	"	"	"
Ellen	7	F	"	"	"
Josy	1	F	"	"	"
Nansy Igo*	16	F	"	"	"

Montgomery Co., KY

9 Jun 1880 p. 465 #88

Name	Age	Sex	B/p	F	M
Absolam Igo	46	M	KY	KY	KY
Phoeba	20	F	"	"	"
Greenbury	19	M	"	"	"
Shelby	13	M	"	"	"
Jane	9	F	"	"	"
Mary Elen	7	F	"	"	"
Josie	1	F	"	"	"
Alonzo Salliers*	17	M	"	"	"

* Boarder F & M = birthplace of father and mother

Claiborne Par., LA

4. 12 Aug 1870 p. 65 #118

Name	Age	Sex	Clr*	B/p
Green Holland	60	M	B	GA
Mary	45	F	M	GA
Zachariah	15	M	M	LA
Laura	13	F	M	AR
Lewis	10	M	M	AR

13 Aug 1870 p. 66 #136

Name	Age	Sex	Clr*	B/p
Green Holland	70	M	B	NC
Mary	40	F	B	GA
Zack	16	M	B	AR
Laura	12	F	B	AR
Lewis	10	M	B	AR

*Color

Wythe Co., VA

5. 18 Jul 1860 p. 899 #1349

Name	Age	Sex	B/p
George Jones	44	M	VA
Sarah	44	F	NC
Catharine	19	F	"
Calvin	16	M	"
Jane	14	F	"
George	11	M	"
Williams	5	M	VA

19 Jul 1860 p. 901 #1361

Name	Age	Sex	B/p
George Jones	45	M	VA
Sarah	45	F	"
Calvin	16	M	"
Margreat	14	F	"
George	11	M	"
William	6	M	"

Casey Co., KY

6. 22 Aug 1860 p. 492 #945

Name	Age	Sex	B/p
Cyrus Roberts	27	M	KY
Nancy	23	F	
Harrison	3	M	
Doran A.	2	F	
Joseph E.	3/12	M	

22 Aug 1860 p. 493 #948

Name	Age	Sex	B/p
Cyrus Roberts	30	M	KY
Nancy M.	25	F	
Harrison	4	M	
Dora A.	2	F	
Joseph V.	6/12	M	

Adams Co., IL

7. 13 Nov 1850 p. 295 #129

Name	Age	Sex	B/p
Joseph L. Sharp	45	M	TN
Malinda S.	45	F	SC
Neil J.	17	M	IL
Ewing S.	15	M	"
Illisume	13	F	"
Emily E.	10	F	"
Joseph G.	7	M	"

Fulton Co., IL

25 Dec 1850 p. 133 #120

Name	Age	Sex	B/p
Joseph L. Sharp	45	M	TN
Matilda	46	F	SC
Johnson	16	M	IL
Ewing	14	M	IL
Illisiania	12	F	IL
Eliza E.	10	F	IL
Joseph	8	M	IL

Hancock Co., MS

8. 27 Sep 1850 p. 63 #273

Name	Age	Sex	B/p
John Stewart	23	M	H. Co., MS
Mary Ann	19	F	"
Jourdan	1	M	"

30 Oct 1850 p. 77 #469

Name	Age	Sex	B/p
John Stewart	27	M	MS
Mary Ann	23	F	"
Jourdan	2	M	"

were always made or that they reached their intended recipients. Possibly a few missing federal name lists can still be replaced by surviving state or county copies, which a systematic inventory would reveal. Many state and county copies are certainly lost. The South Carolina State Archives has the 1870 state copy but not those for 1850 and 1860.[26] A check of many county inventories compiled by the Historical Records Survey (Works Progress Administration) suggests that most county copies are lost, especially for 1850 and 1860. That the state and county copies were assumed to be made and distributed seems verified by the Superintendent of the Census who, in reporting the 1880 returns, complained at length of the high cost of making extra copies. He also questioned letting people read their neighbors' confidential answers in the courthouse copy.[27]

Copying name lists brought inevitable miscopying. By the 1850-70 acts, the original list went to the county, presumably so the states and the federal government could receive the cleaner, later copies. But did the local census takers, who were probably political appointees, understand the instructions or choose to follow them? Wherever the copies went, they do contain transcription errors, as a genealogist discovered:

> I have personally found many discrepancies between the Federal and State copies themselves, and vast differences between them and the Originals [i.e., the county copies]! Whole names have either been changed or omitted. Ages have been copied wrong. Whereas, in the originals, the surnames of each family are generally written over and over again, in the copies the word "ditto" or its abbreviation "do" appear instead. When written over and over, a surname has much less chance of being written incorrectly! In one Federal entry, I find Rebecca Gey but "Grey" in the Original. In another Federal copy, Amanda Vandyke appears, but she is Amanda A. Vanslyke in the Original. Esther Hollinsworth of the original—the correct name—appears as Esther Hollenback in the Federal copy![28]

Copy errors are part of the larger subject of the general accuracy of censuses, which can be illustrated by comparing duplicate entries. Figure 2 presents eight such doubles where a family was enumerated twice in the same census. These are not horror stories selected for fright value; they are routine examples. Judging from such duplicate entries, age was the most unreliable information, though name, sex, and birth place were also subject to error or garbling. A person's age has a habit of changing every year. Today's custom of giving gifts makes family members very aware of each others' birthdays, yet this ceremony has been widespread only in the last hundred years. A person in 1850 reciting family ages to a census taker likely had an uncertain idea of family birth dates, was probably poor at arithmetic, and certainly found it difficult to state ages that changed every year for each person. Once civil registration spread among states and cities in the late nineteenth century, demographers could prove that vital statistics gathered in censuses were extremely unreliable.[29] The discrepancies in the duplicate census entries might also be attributable to different informants giving the information, including children or neighbors. Perhaps that explains why Isam Aldridge (No. 2, Fig. 2) appeared as a merchant in one entry and a school teacher in the other, the two entries being recorded a day apart.

Another facet of completeness is undercounts. Estimates of census undercounting before 1940 are not numerous, nor are they nearly so accurate as implied by numbers taken to a tenth of a percent. They do, however, suggest that the census takers missed a great many people. There have also been occasional overcounts. Enumerators were convicted of fraud for padding the Tacoma, Washington, census of 1910 by an extra 38%.[30]

Undercounts were far more prevalent. A comparison of the 1790 tax lists with the census for Mifflin County, Pennsylvania, shows that the census taker missed one in ten families.[31] Comparisons with the Boston city directories produced estimated undercounts in censuses of 8.0% for 1860 and 8.3% for 1890.[32] Such oversights are seen in two small areas in Strafford County, New Hampshire, that were enumerated twice in 1790. (Fig. 3, p. xxii). Why the Grafton County census taker crossed a few miles into Strafford is not known, though he did enumerate five other "locations" in Grafton and perhaps thought he had a charge to canvass such extra-town areas in the region.[33] Of the thirteen men shown in the duplicate entries that follow, only six appear on both lists, though perhaps Burbank Ardua and Jonathan B. Ordway were the same man:

Strafford County	Grafton County

Sterling's Location

Strafford County	Grafton County
Benja Heath	
Hugh Sterling	Hugh Sterling
Joseph Walker	Joseph Walker
Joseph Ardua	
Burbank Ardua	
John Wilson	
Paul Wentworth	
Joseph Ardua, Jr.	
John Ardua	

Stark's Location

Strafford County	Grafton County
	John Evens
	John Ordway
	Jonathan B. Ordway
	Joseph Ordway
	Joseph Ordway, Junr.
Samuel Starks	Samuel Starks
Archb Starks	

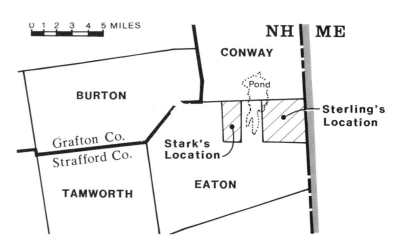

Figure 3. Stark's and Sterling's Locations, New Hampshire.

These two non-town areas in 1790 lay in Strafford County between the towns of Conway and Eaton.

Undercounting has become a very important matter in the last twenty years as billions of federal dollars go directly to local governments in proportion to their populations. Studies done on the last several censuses show that blacks are overlooked much more than whites. A comparison of 1940 Selective Service records with the 1940 census gave a national undercount of 2.8% for whites and 13% for blacks.[34] A panel helping plan the 1980 census found decreasing undercounts for the next three censuses:[35]

	Whites	Blacks
1950	2.5%	9.7%
1960	2.0%	8.1%
1970	1.9%	6.9%

Unprecedented efforts in 1980 to reduce the disproportionate undercounting of minorities did not prevent numerous law suits from being filed against the Bureau of the Census asking the courts to require urban population totals be adjusted upwards by some mathematical formula. The courts declined, accepting imperfection as part of the census process. Strangely, studies analyzing the 1960 and 1970 censuses reported a rural undercount larger than that of the cities.[36]

An ethnic undercount can stem from various racial, cultural, or language differences between census taker and population. An 1880 enumerator faced just this problem: "The men on this page [of the census] are all Italians just come over and it is very difficult to understand them. On the pay Rolls of the Rail Road Co. they are known by numbers instead of their names—they all lived in a Rail Road Car. I did the best I could with them."[37] A lack of empathy or trust on either side could cripple coverage by the enumerator and inhibit cooperation by a socially invisible group. The first U.S. census of New Mexico, that of 1850, has been termed a "massive undercounting" of the newly-conquered Mexicans.[38]

Age and gender also influence who may be overlooked. Infants were once significantly omitted, especially in the mortality schedules. Women have lower undercounts than men, since a settled residence increases chances of appearing in a census. Young bachelors were and still are the most undercounted segment of

American society. It should be no surprise that black males in their twenties, even in post-World War Two censuses, have undercounts approaching 20%.[39] It can also be predicted that California gold rushers were likely left out of the census in great numbers.[40] Similarly, census completeness was affected by whether the enumerator came in summer or winter to find people away on seasonal jobs or gathered in winter quarters, a seasonal pattern more applicable to men.

A special case concerns soldiers in the U.S. Army, especially in frontier forts. No rule dictated whether to enumerate them or not, at least in the nineteenth century. New Mexico's Fort Defiance in eastern Navaho country was not counted in 1860, but the commander of Fort Mojave on the Colorado River supplied an enumeration to spare the census taker a dangerous trip.[41] The 1860 Utah census has the strange situation of omitting Camp Floyd with about 275 men but enumerating the town near its gate. The pony express stations and towns all around are shown as having their post office at this invisible Camp Floyd.[42]

With the acute American sensitivity to race and its legal and social implications, a census in a slave state might be expected to get right at least the paramount fact of racial identity. Yet a study of 1,614 families in the 1860 census for Natchitoches Parish, Louisiana, found surprising mistakes: "In twenty-three cases, a well-known family of color was identified as white by the newcomer who took the census, while fifty-three white families whose ancestry was European with no African admixture were labeled 'mulatto.'"[43] That nearly five percent of the race entries could be wrong in a Southern slave area shows again the need to treat particular census entries with caution.

NOTES

1. Standard studies of the census are Carroll D. Wright and William C. Hunt, *The History and Growth of the United States Censuses, Prepared for the Senate Committee on the Census* (Washington: GPO, 1900), 56th Cong., 1st sess., Senate Doc. 194, serial 3856; A. Ross Eckler, *The Bureau of the Census* (New York: Praeger, 1972); W. Stull Holt, *The Bureau of the Census: Its History, Activities and Organization* (Washington: Brookings Institution, 1929); W.S.

Rossiter, *A Century of Population Growth from the First Census of the United States to the Twelfth, 1790-1900* (Washington: GPO, 1909); Katherine H. Davidson and Charlotte M. Ashby, *Preliminary Inventory of the Records of the Bureau of the Census,* National Archives Preliminary Inventory No. 161 (Washington: NARS, 1964). More popularized accounts are Hyman Alterman, *Counting People: The Census in History* (New York: Harcourt, Brace & World, 1969), and Ann Herbert Scott, *Census U.S.A.: Fact Finding for the American People, 1790-1970* (New York: Seabury Press, 1968).

2. Ian I. Mitroff et al., *The 1980 Census Policymaking Amid Turbulence* (Lexington, MA: D.C. Heath, 1983), p. xxiii.

3. U.S. Constitution, Art. I, sec. 2. For federal census acts, see section on "Records" in this introduction.

4. For example, the Genealogical Library, LDS Church, Salt Lake City, Utah, in its current (1987) guide to U.S. census microfilms, says the missing 1790 schedules were apparently "destroyed during the British attack on Washington during the War of 1812." The National Archives' *Guide to Genealogical Research in the National Archives* (Washington: NARS, 1982), p. 21, states: "The [1790] schedules for Delaware, Georgia, Kentucky, New Jersey, Tennessee, and Virginia were burned during the War of 1812."

5. 4 Stat. 430, 28 May 1830.

6. Davidson and Ashby, *Preliminary Inventory,* p. 100; Donna Valley Russell, ed., *Michigan Censuses 1710-1830 under the French, British, and Americans* (Detroit: Detroit Society for Genealogical Research, 1982), p. 101.

7. 2 Stat. 166, 29 April 1802.

8. Davidson and Ashby, *Preliminary Inventory,* p. 94.

9. John Koren, *The History of Statistics: Their Development and Progress in Many Countries* (New York: Macmillan, for the American Statistical Association, 1918), pp. 3, 7-8.

10. New York County, Indianapolis, and Philadelphia were enumerated twice in 1870. See, for instance, Robert G. Barrows, "The Ninth Federal Census of Indianapolis: A Case in Civic Chauvinism," *Indiana Magazine of History* 73 (1977), 1-16. In 1880 it was St. Louis that got a second count: Jeanette C. Lauer and Robert H. Lauer, "St. Louis and the 1880 Census: The Shock of Collective Failure," *Missouri Historical Review* 76 (1981-82), 151-63.

11. U.S. Congress, *House Executive Documents,* vol. 11, 51st Cong., 2nd

sess., pp. cxliii, serial 2840.

12. Census Office, *Compendium of the Eleventh Census: 1890,* pt. 1, Population (Washington: GPO, 1892), p. xxxvi.

13. Holt, *Bureau of the Census,* p. 25.

14. Usually "Superintendent of Census" but sometimes "Superintendent of the Census," the form used here.

15. Edward E. Hill, *Guide to Records in the National Archives of the United States Relating to American Indians* (Washington: NARS, 1981), p. 385. Schedules for other reservations exist, aside from those in the four volumes, such as South Dakota's Crow Creek Reservation and the Rosebud Agency. James Hansen (by personal correspondence) says the original 1880 census for the Menomonies is at the tribal headquarters at Keshena, Wisconsin. Davidson and Ashby, *Preliminary Inventory,* p. 30, note a manuscript volume in the National Archives that records which 1880 schedules were received from Indian agencies.

16. Census Office, *Report on Indians Taxed and Not Taxed in the United States* (Washington: GPO, 1894).

17. Davidson and Ashby, *Preliminary Inventory,* pp. 96, 101-02. The location of some of these non-population schedules 1850-80 is given in Eakle and Cerny, *The Source,* pp. 108-09. The National Archives is microfilming such schedules as it locates them.

18. 2 Stat. 806, 27 February 1813.

19. Clarence E. Carter, ed., *The Territorial Papers of the United States,* vol. 4, The Territory South of the River Ohio, 1790-1796 (Washington: GPO, 1936), pp. 49-50, 52-53, 69-70, 80-81, 105-06.

20. U.S. Secretary of State, *A Census of Pensioners for Revolutionary or Military Services: With Their Names, Ages, and Places of Residence Taken in 1840* (Washington: Blair and Rives, 1841; reprint, Baltimore: Genealogical Publishing Co., 1967).

21. National Archives, "Index to the Eleventh Census of the United States, 1890," microfilm M496, 2 rolls.

22. Census Office, *Population of the United States in 1860* (Washington: GPO, 1864), p. 54.

23. Census Office, *Seventh Census of the United States: 1850* (Washington: Robert Armstrong, Public Printer, 1853), p. 966; see also 10 Stat. 25, 30 July 1852.

24. Davidson and Ashby, *Preliminary Inventory,* pp. 101-02.

25. In Record Group 21, Washington National Records Center, Suitland, Maryland, as noted in National Archives, *Guide to the National Archives of the United States* (Washington: NARS, 1974), p. 88.

26. "Federal Census Records at the South Carolina Archives," *South Carolina Historical Magazine* 85 (1984), 253-54.

27. Census Office, *Compendium of the Tenth Census,* pt. 1 (Washington: GPO, 1883), pp. xxxv-xxxvi.

28. Harry Hollingsworth, "Little Known Facts About the U.S. Census," *The American Genealogist* 53 (1977), 11.

29. Holt, *Bureau of the Census,* pp. 52-53; Hugh H. Wolfenden, *Population Statistics and Their Compilation* (Chicago: University of Chicago Press, for Society of Actuaries, 1954), pp. 23, 32-67.

30. Holt, *Bureau of the Census,* pp. 58-59.

31. Raymond Martin Bell, *Heads of Families in Mifflin County, Pa., 1790* (Lewistown, PA: Mifflin County Historical Society, 1958), pp. 1-2.

32. Peter R. Knights, "A Method for Estimating Census Under-Enumerations," *Historical Methods Newsletter* 3 (December 1969), 7.

33. Bureau of the Census, *Heads of Families at the First Census of the United States Taken in the Year 1790: New Hampshire* (Washington: GPO, 1907), pp. 37, 100. Our thanks to Robert C. Anderson and John Brooks Threlfall for this example. For historical background, see Nellie M. Carver, *Goshen: South Conway, New Hampshire* (Portland, ME: House of Falmouth, 1971).

34. Alterman, *Counting People,* p. 279.

35. Panel on Decennial Census Plans, National Research Council, *Counting the People in 1980: An Appraisal of Census Plans* (Washington: National Academy of Sciences, 1978), p. 2.

36. Mitroff, *The 1980 Census,* p. 84.

37. Jean Rumsey, "Pity the Poor Census Taker!," *The American Genealogist* 60 (1984), 167. Very little has been written about the census takers themselves despite their crucial roles as pollsters and copyists. Their interpretation of the instructions naturally affected the sort of information recorded. For instance, James Hansen (by personal correspondence) reports instances in the 1860 and 1870 Wisconsin schedules where the recorded post office appears to be that of the enumerator, not the enumerated subdivision. Yet the multiple shortcomings examined in this "Completeness" section should not slight the difficulties surmounted by the census takers.

Here are statements by men describing their experiences in the backcountry (with some punctuation added):

1790 Morgan District, North Carolina, p. 173: "I have Been Closely Employd Since the 25 of December Last. One Other man has been Closely Employd Since the 6th of January; one other has been Employd Since the 12 of January; a third one Since the 1st of March and Two others A Week Each and all had Since to fall Behind. After Riding horses almost to Death. This is a True State of Facts. No one Man Can Number the People in the District of Morgan Going from House to House in 18 Months I Aver, and if there is no Provision to Collect the people in the Next Law, no man that understands will have anything to do with it."

1820 Hall County, Georgia, p. 156: "The difficulties were very considerable that attended taking the census, in the first place, the inhabitants are very dispersed, in the second place the country being but lately settled, there are but few roads, in the third place great part of the Country are very Mountainous, and in the fourth place it was, except in the oldest settled parts, difficult to get nourishment for either myself or horse, and often when got, had to pay very high, in the 5th place had often to travel a considerable distance through fields to get to the dwelling cabbins, often, and generally, drenchd in dew, particularly in August and September; and often had to walk many miles where it was so steep that I could not ride, or even set on my horse."

1870 Barton and Rush Counties, Kansas, p. 371: "I found the settlers on Walnut Creek near the west line of Barton County and I was not able to ascertain deffinitely if they were in Barton or Rush County. I also found two other settlers whom I had enumerated in the town of Elsworth, they having left their families at that place because of the fear of Indian difficulties, but had come out here with their horses & plows to prepare houses for themselves and eventually for their families. ... I traveled through this country with a strong escort of U.S. Soldiers to protect me from hostile Indians who roam at will over these prairies, which ought to be the home of our people in the over-crowded cities of the East."

1880 Lane County, Kansas, p. 13: "The People Mostelley Liv in Holes in the Ground—Espeshley in the N.W. Part of this County varley Porley Ventilated—hence you will find dustey Shedules as well as indistinct letters & figures."

38. Richard L. Nostrand, "Mexican Americans Circa 1850," *Annals of the Association of American Geographers* 65 (1975), 383; J.M. Blaut and Antonio Rios-Bustamante, "Commentary on Nostrand's 'Hispanos' and Their 'Homeland,' " Ibid., 74 (1984), 162-63.

39. National Research Council, *Counting the People,* p. 4.

40. Nostrand, "Mexican Americans Circa 1850," p. 383.

41. "Federal Census—Territory of New Mexico and Territory of Arizona," U.S. Congress, *Senate Documents* no. 13, 89th Cong., 1st sess., serial 12668-1; U.S. Census, New Mexico Territory, 1860, Arizona County, p. 182, National Archives microfilm M653, roll 712.

42. U.S. Army, Returns from U.S. Military Posts, 1800-1916, Fort Crittenden (alias Camp Floyd), Utah, June 1860, National Archives microfilm M617, roll 268; U.S. Census, Utah Territory, 1860, Cedar and Shambip Counties, National Archives microfilm M653, roll 1313.

43. Elizabeth Shown Mills, "Ethnicity and the Southern Genealogist: Myths and Misconceptions, Resources and Opportunities," in Robert M. Taylor, Jr., and Ralph J. Crandall, eds., *Generations and Change: Genealogical Perspectives in Social History* (Macon, GA: Mercer University Press, 1986), p. 96.

Sample Map

Explaining Format, Symbols, and Notes

(1) Counties in existence for the census are lettered in black. Modern lines that coincide with census lines will also be in black. Names and lines in white indicate modern differences from that census year.

(2) The twelve locality zones atop the legend bar are keyed to the book's index: "Fillmore...7." On this 1857 map, modern Brown **(2a)** in zone 4 is part of the much larger Brown of 1857 **(2b)**.

(3) Defunct county names appear in the index in italics with the years of their censuses. *"Pembina 1850-70....2"* in the index says Pembina, now defunct, can be found at zone 2 but only on maps from 1850 to 1870. Pembina is defunct because, as a note at Minnesota 1870 says, in 1878 it was renamed Kittson **(4)**.

(5) Dashed lines indicate various situations: (1) boundaries through water; (2) uncertain statutory lines; (3) special circumstances explained in the notes; and (4) county creations and land transfers on multiple-year maps. This last situation, not shown here, can be seen at South Carolina 1860-1870 and West Virginia 1880-1920.

(6) Inset maps clarify territorial lines, as do the U.S. maps starting on the opposite page.

(7) Asterisks indicate that explanatory information is given under "Notes" or "Census Availability."

(8) "Extant" at "Census Availability" means a census name list survives in manuscript or on microfilm. It does not mean that all of a county's census exists. Pages may be missing or illegible in "extant" schedules.

(9) "As part of" means the territory had different boundaries from the state of the same name.

(10) Some major Indian treaty lines mark the practical limits of counties and censuses. Most Indian cessions are not shown, especially for overlapping treaties, small tribes, and western states and territories.

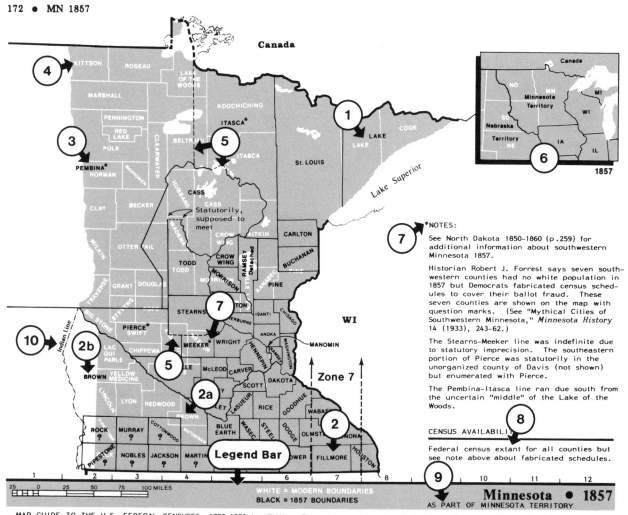

172 ● MN 1857

*NOTES:

See North Dakota 1850-1860 (p.259) for additional information about southwestern Minnesota 1857.

Historian Robert J. Forrest says seven southwestern counties had no white population in 1857 but Democrats fabricated census schedules to cover their ballot fraud. These seven counties are shown on the map with question marks. (See "Mythical Cities of Southwestern Minnesota," *Minnesota History* 14 (1933), 243-62.)

The Stearns-Meeker line was indefinite due to statutory imprecision. The southeastern portion of Pierce was statutorily in the unorganized county of Davis (not shown) but enumerated with Pierce.

The Pembina-Itasca line ran due south from the uncertain "middle" of the Lake of the Woods.

CENSUS AVAILABILITY

Federal census extant for all counties but see note above about fabricated schedules.

WHITE = MODERN BOUNDARIES
BLACK = 1857 BOUNDARIES

Minnesota ● 1857
AS PART OF MINNESOTA TERRITORY

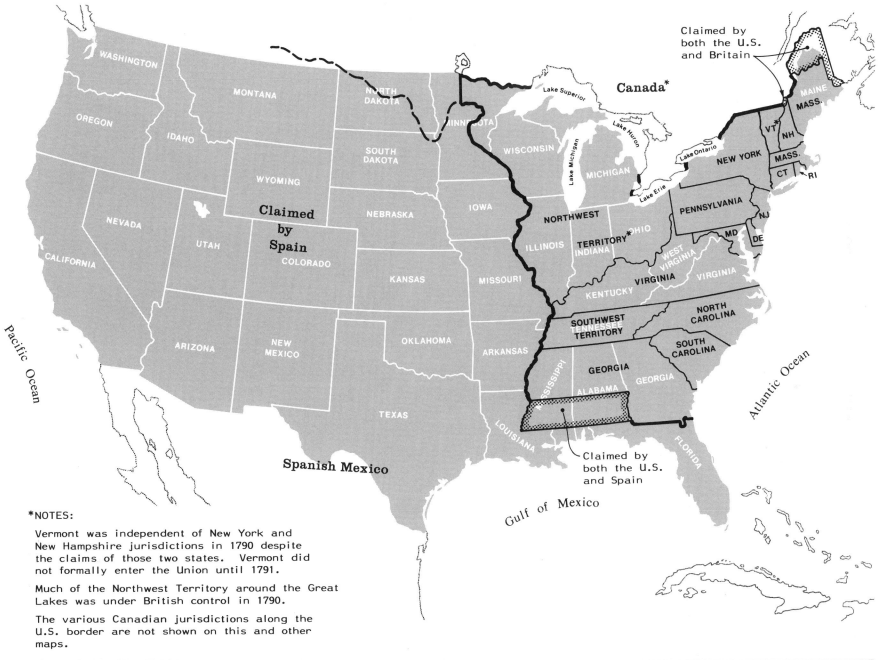

Claimed by both the U.S. and Britain

Canada*

Claimed by Spain

Spanish Mexico

Claimed by both the U.S. and Spain

Gulf of Mexico

Pacific Ocean

Atlantic Ocean

*NOTES:

Vermont was independent of New York and New Hampshire jurisdictions in 1790 despite the claims of those two states. Vermont did not formally enter the Union until 1791.

Much of the Northwest Territory around the Great Lakes was under British control in 1790.

The various Canadian jurisdictions along the U.S. border are not shown on this and other maps.

0   500   1000 MILES

WHITE = MODERN BOUNDARIES
BLACK = 1790 BOUNDARIES

United States ● 1790

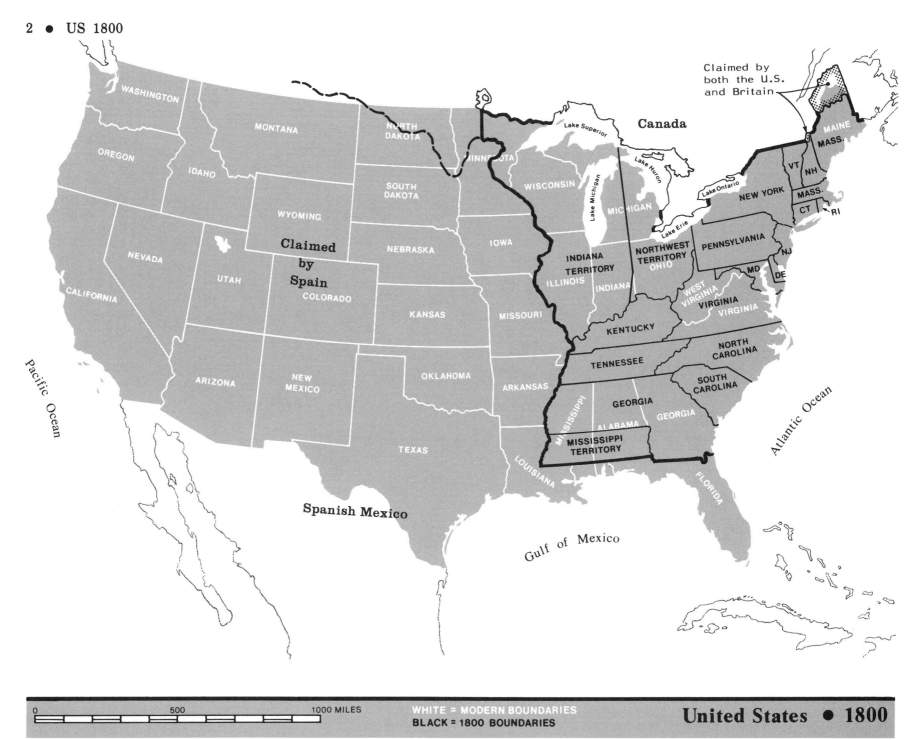

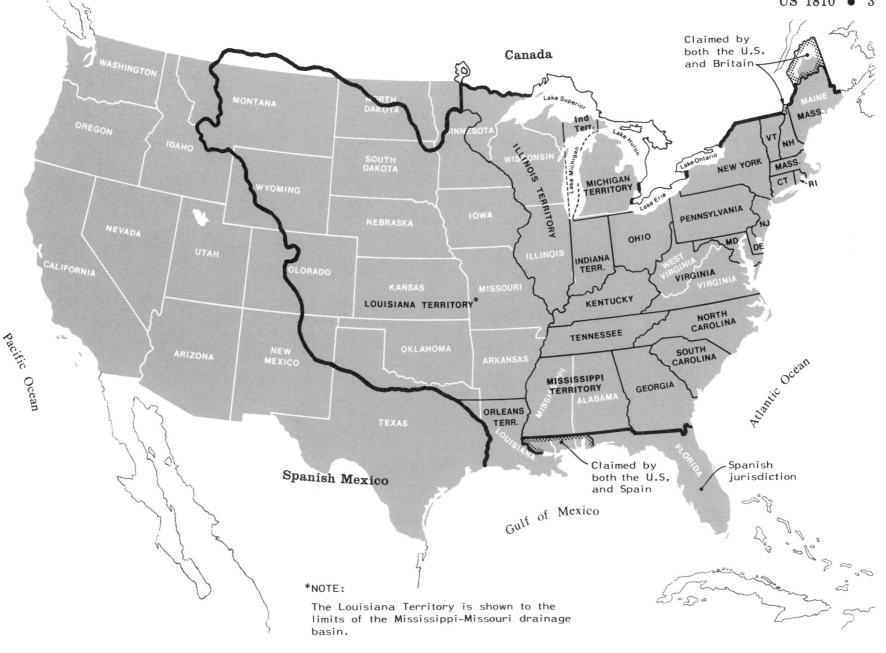

Canada

Claimed by
both the U.S.
and Britain

Lake Superior

Ind
Terr.

Lake Huron

Lake Ontario

Lake Erie

WASHINGTON

OREGON

IDAHO

MONTANA

NORTH
DAKOTA

MINNESOTA

WISCONSIN

MICHIGAN
TERRITORY

ILLINOIS TERRITORY

Lake Michigan

MAINE

MASS.

VT

NH

MASS.

CT

RI

NEW YORK

PENNSYLVANIA

NJ

MD

DE

SOUTH
DAKOTA

WYOMING

NEVADA

UTAH

NEBRASKA

IOWA

ILLINOIS

INDIANA
TERR.

OHIO

WEST
VIRGINIA

VIRGINIA

VIRGINIA

CALIFORNIA

COLORADO

KANSAS

MISSOURI

LOUISIANA TERRITORY*

KENTUCKY

Pacific Ocean

ARIZONA

NEW
MEXICO

OKLAHOMA

ARKANSAS

TENNESSEE

NORTH
CAROLINA

SOUTH
CAROLINA

Atlantic Ocean

TEXAS

ORLEANS
TERR.

MISSISSIPPI
TERRITORY

MISSISSIPPI

ALABAMA

GEORGIA

FLORIDA

Spanish
jurisdiction

LOUISIANA

Claimed by
both the U.S.
and Spain

Spanish Mexico

Gulf of Mexico

*NOTE:

The Louisiana Territory is shown to the
limits of the Mississippi–Missouri drainage
basin.

0   500   1000 MILES

WHITE = MODERN BOUNDARIES
BLACK = 1810 BOUNDARIES

United States ● 1810

MAP GUIDE TO THE U.S. FEDERAL CENSUSES, 1790–1920 by William Thorndale and William Dollarhide.   Copyright 1987, all rights reserved.

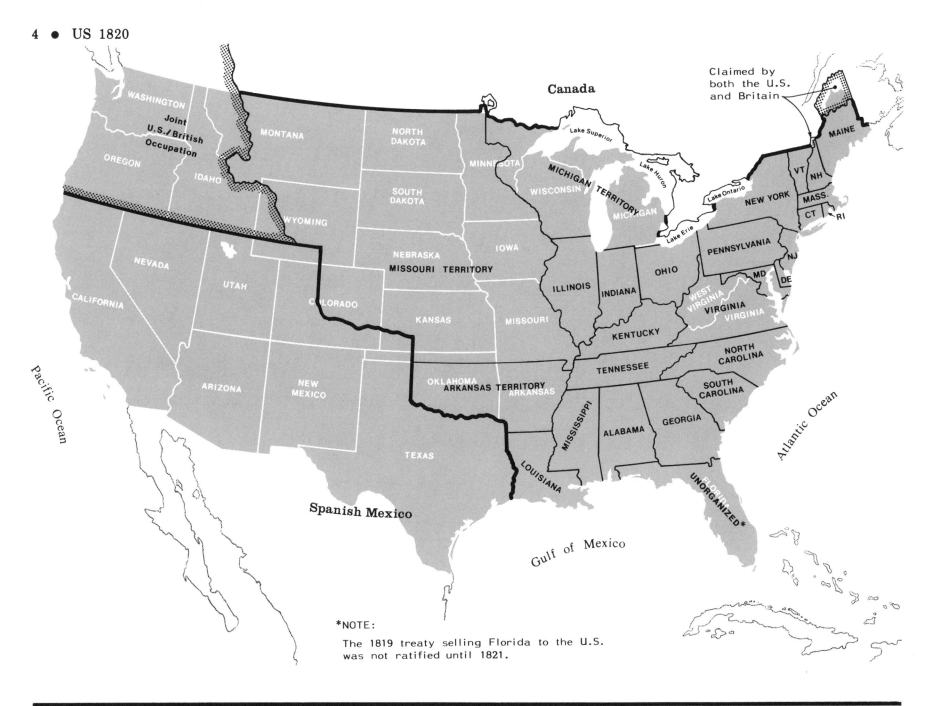

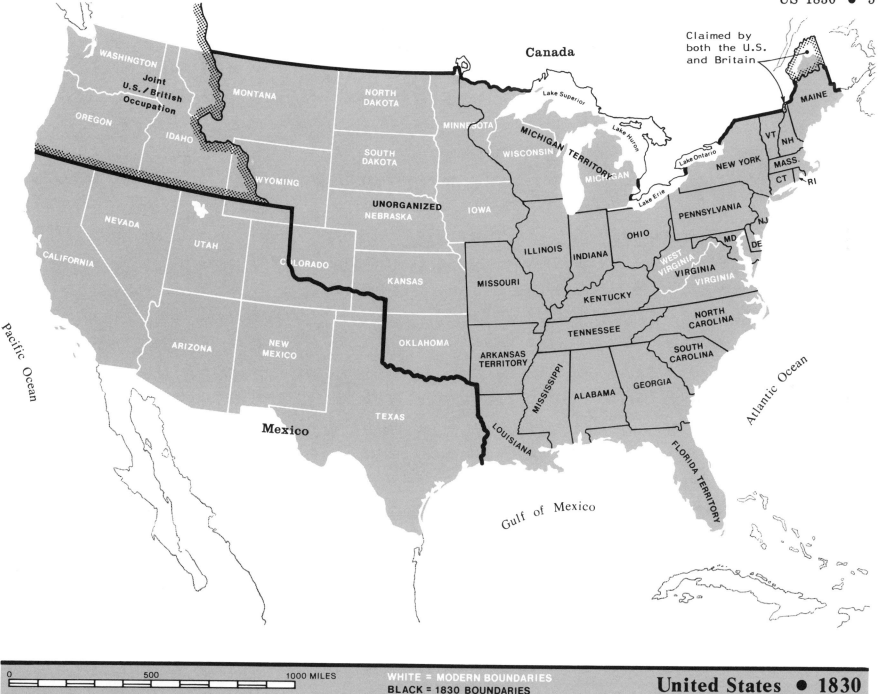

Canada

Claimed by
both the U.S.
and Britain

WASHINGTON

Joint
U.S./British
Occupation

OREGON

MONTANA

IDAHO

WYOMING

NEVADA

UTAH

CALIFORNIA

ARIZONA

NEW
MEXICO

COLORADO

NORTH
DAKOTA

SOUTH
DAKOTA

UNORGANIZED
NEBRASKA

KANSAS

OKLAHOMA

TEXAS

MINNESOTA

IOWA

MISSOURI

ARKANSAS
TERRITORY

LOUISIANA

Lake Superior

WISCONSIN

MICHIGAN TERRITORY

MICHIGAN

Lake Huron

Lake Ontario

Lake Erie

ILLINOIS

INDIANA

OHIO

KENTUCKY

TENNESSEE

MISSISSIPPI

ALABAMA

GEORGIA

MAINE

VT

NH

NEW YORK

MASS.

CT

RI

PENNSYLVANIA

NJ

MD

DE

WEST
VIRGINIA

VIRGINIA

VIRGINIA

NORTH
CAROLINA

SOUTH
CAROLINA

FLORIDA TERRITORY

Mexico

Gulf of Mexico

Pacific Ocean

Atlantic Ocean

0   500   1000 MILES

WHITE = MODERN BOUNDARIES
BLACK = 1830 BOUNDARIES

United States ● 1830

MAP GUIDE TO THE U.S. FEDERAL CENSUSES, 1790-1920 by William Thorndale and William Dollarhide.   Copyright 1987, all rights reserved.

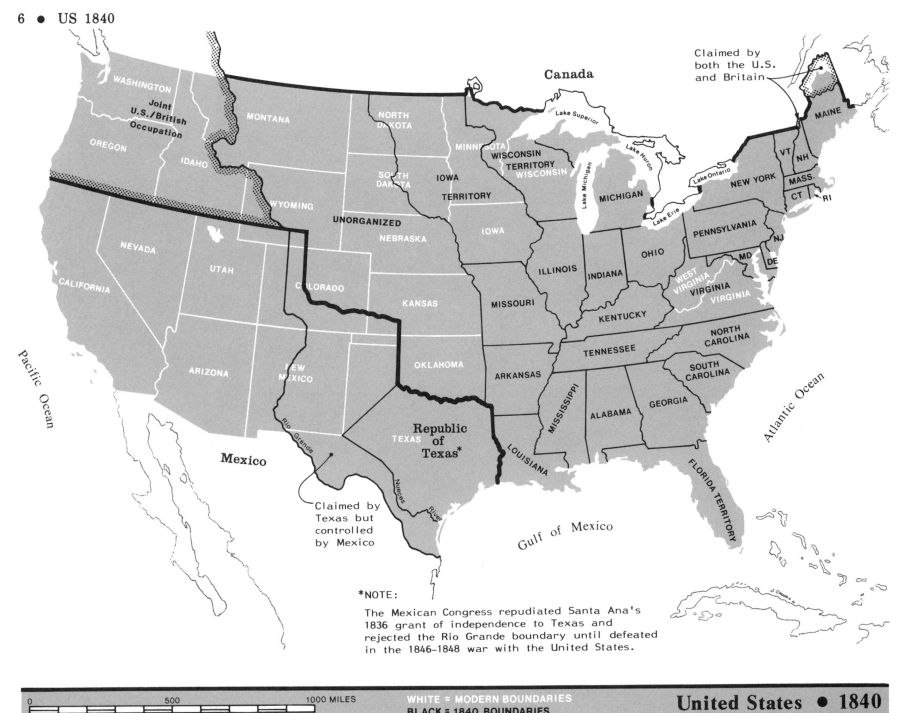

Claimed by both the U.S. and Britain

Canada

Joint U.S./British Occupation

WASHINGTON

OREGON

MONTANA

IDAHO

NORTH DAKOTA

MINNESOTA

WISCONSIN TERRITORY
WISCONSIN

Lake Superior

Lake Huron

MAINE

VT

NH

MASS.

CT RI

Lake Michigan

MICHIGAN

Lake Ontario

Lake Erie

NEW YORK

NEVADA

WYOMING

SOUTH DAKOTA

IOWA TERRITORY

IOWA

PENNSYLVANIA

NJ

UTAH

COLORADO

UNORGANIZED NEBRASKA

ILLINOIS

INDIANA

OHIO

MD

DE

WEST VIRGINIA

VIRGINIA

VIRGINIA

CALIFORNIA

KANSAS

MISSOURI

KENTUCKY

ARIZONA

NEW MEXICO

OKLAHOMA

ARKANSAS

TENNESSEE

NORTH CAROLINA

SOUTH CAROLINA

Rio Grande

TEXAS

Republic of Texas*

LOUISIANA

MISSISSIPPI

ALABAMA

GEORGIA

Mexico

Nueces River

Claimed by Texas but controlled by Mexico

Gulf of Mexico

FLORIDA TERRITORY

Pacific Ocean

Atlantic Ocean

*NOTE:

The Mexican Congress repudiated Santa Ana's 1836 grant of independence to Texas and rejected the Rio Grande boundary until defeated in the 1846–1848 war with the United States.

0   500   1000 MILES

WHITE = MODERN BOUNDARIES
BLACK = 1840 BOUNDARIES

United States ● 1840

MAP GUIDE TO THE U.S. FEDERAL CENSUSES, 1790–1920 by William Thorndale and William Dollarhide. Copyright 1987, all rights reserved.

0   500   1000 MILES

WHITE = MODERN BOUNDARIES
BLACK = 1850 BOUNDARIES

United States ● 1850

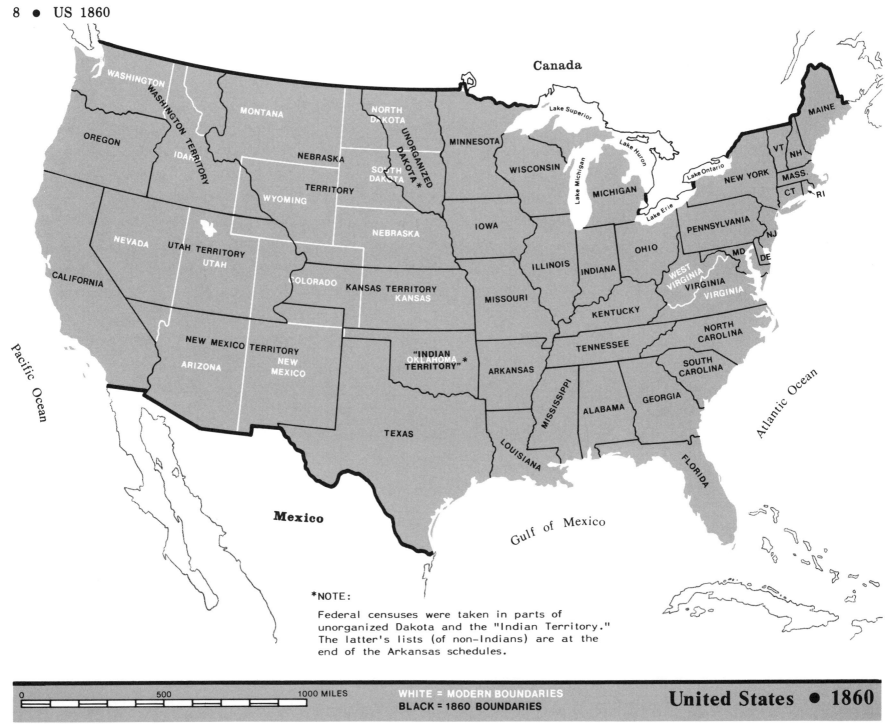

Canada

Lake Superior

WASHINGTON

WASHINGTON TERRITORY

OREGON

IDAHO

MONTANA

NORTH DAKOTA

UNORGANIZED DAKOTA *

SOUTH DAKOTA

MINNESOTA

Lake Huron

MAINE

VT

NH

NEBRASKA

WYOMING TERRITORY

WISCONSIN

Lake Michigan

MICHIGAN

Lake Ontario

NEW YORK

MASS.

CT

RI

NEVADA

UTAH TERRITORY

UTAH

COLORADO

NEBRASKA

IOWA

Lake Erie

PENNSYLVANIA

NJ

MD

DE

CALIFORNIA

KANSAS TERRITORY

KANSAS

ILLINOIS

INDIANA

OHIO

WEST VIRGINIA

VIRGINIA

VIRGINIA

MISSOURI

KENTUCKY

NEW MEXICO TERRITORY

ARIZONA

NEW MEXICO

"INDIAN OKLAHOMA TERRITORY" *

ARKANSAS

TENNESSEE

NORTH CAROLINA

SOUTH CAROLINA

Pacific Ocean

TEXAS

MISSISSIPPI

ALABAMA

GEORGIA

Atlantic Ocean

LOUISIANA

FLORIDA

Mexico

Gulf of Mexico

*NOTE:

Federal censuses were taken in parts of
unorganized Dakota and the "Indian Territory."
The latter's lists (of non-Indians) are at the
end of the Arkansas schedules.

| 0 | 500 | 1000 MILES |

WHITE = MODERN BOUNDARIES
BLACK = 1860 BOUNDARIES

United States ● 1860

MAP GUIDE TO THE U.S. FEDERAL CENSUSES, 1790-1920 by William Thorndale and William Dollarhide. Copyright 1987, all rights reserved.

NOTE:

Alaska was purchased from Russia in 1867.
The first American governor arrived in 1884,
but Alaska became a territory only in 1912.

WHITE = MODERN BOUNDARIES
BLACK = 1870-1880 BOUNDARIES

United States ● 1870–1880

MAP GUIDE TO THE U.S. FEDERAL CENSUSES, 1790–1920 by William Thorndale and William Dollarhide. Copyright 1987, all rights reserved.

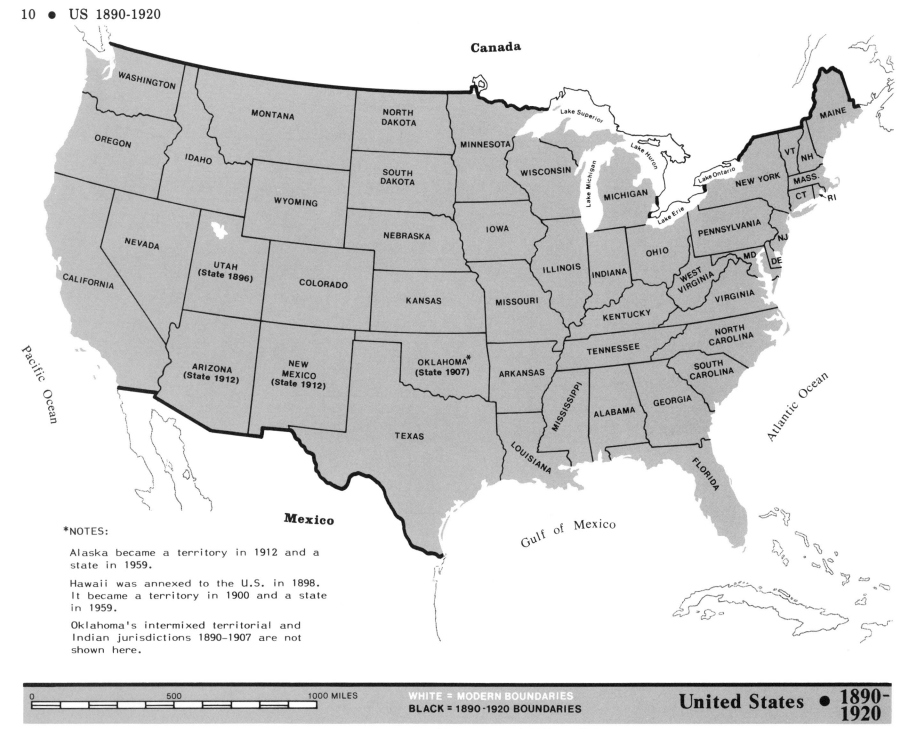

Canada

WASHINGTON

MONTANA

NORTH DAKOTA

Lake Superior

MINNESOTA

MAINE

OREGON

IDAHO

SOUTH DAKOTA

WISCONSIN

Lake Huron

Lake Michigan

MICHIGAN

VT

NH

Lake Ontario

NEW YORK

MASS.

WYOMING

IOWA

Lake Erie

PENNSYLVANIA

CT

RI

NEVADA

NEBRASKA

OHIO

NJ

UTAH
(State 1896)

COLORADO

ILLINOIS

INDIANA

WEST
VIRGINIA

MD

DE

CALIFORNIA

KANSAS

MISSOURI

KENTUCKY

VIRGINIA

ARIZONA
(State 1912)

NEW
MEXICO
(State 1912)

OKLAHOMA*
(State 1907)

ARKANSAS

TENNESSEE

NORTH
CAROLINA

SOUTH
CAROLINA

MISSISSIPPI

ALABAMA

GEORGIA

TEXAS

LOUISIANA

FLORIDA

Pacific Ocean

Atlantic Ocean

Mexico

Gulf of Mexico

*NOTES:

Alaska became a territory in 1912 and a
state in 1959.

Hawaii was annexed to the U.S. in 1898.
It became a territory in 1900 and a state
in 1959.

Oklahoma's intermixed territorial and
Indian jurisdictions 1890–1907 are not
shown here.

0	500	1000 MILES

WHITE = MODERN BOUNDARIES
BLACK = 1890-1920 BOUNDARIES

United States ● 1890-1920

MAP GUIDE TO THE U.S. FEDERAL CENSUSES, 1790-1920 by William Thorndale and William Dollarhide. Copyright 1987, all rights reserved.

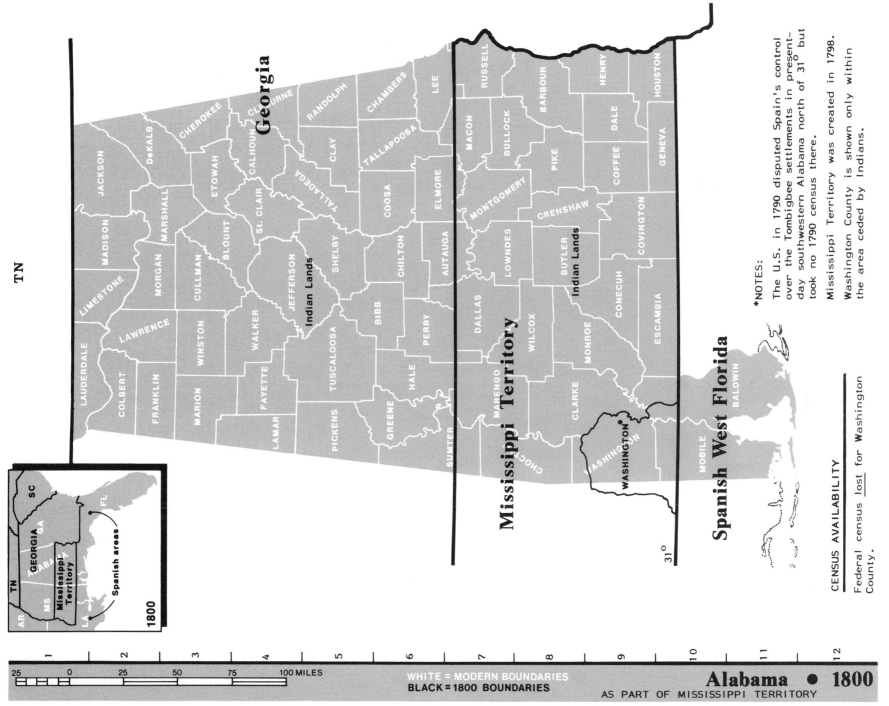

TN

Georgia

CHEROKEE
DeKALB
JACKSON
CLEBURNE
RANDOLPH
CHAMBERS
LEE
RUSSELL
BARBOUR
HENRY
HOUSTON
ETOWAH
CALHOUN
CLAY
TALLAPOOSA
MACON
BULLOCK
DALE
GENEVA
MADISON
MARSHALL
MORGAN
CULLMAN
BLOUNT
St. CLAIR
TALLADEGA
COOSA
ELMORE
MONTGOMERY
PIKE
COFFEE
LIMESTONE
SHELBY
CRENSHAW
COVINGTON
LAUDERDALE
LAWRENCE
WINSTON
WALKER
JEFFERSON
Indian Lands
CHILTON
AUTAUGA
LOWNDES
BUTLER
Indian Lands
CONECUH
ESCAMBIA
COLBERT
FRANKLIN
MARION
FAYETTE
BIBB
PERRY
DALLAS
WILCOX
MONROE
CLARKE
LAMAR
WINSTON
TUSCALOOSA
HALE
GREENE
SUMTER
PICKENS
CHOCTAW
MARENGO
WASHINGTON*
BALDWIN
MOBILE

Mississippi Territory

Spanish West Florida

31°

*NOTES:
The U.S. in 1790 disputed Spain's control over the Tombigbee settlements in present-day southwestern Alabama north of 31° but took no 1790 census there.

Mississippi Territory was created in 1798.

Washington County is shown only within the area ceded by Indians.

CENSUS AVAILABILITY

Federal census lost for Washington County.

1800

SC
FL
GEORGIA
GA
TN
ALABAMA
Mississippi Territory
MS
AR
LA
Spanish areas

| 25 | | 0 | 25 | 50 | 75 | 100 MILES |

WHITE = MODERN BOUNDARIES
BLACK = 1800 BOUNDARIES

Alabama ● 1800
AS PART OF MISSISSIPPI TERRITORY

MAP GUIDE TO THE U.S. FEDERAL CENSUSES, 1790–1920 by William Thorndale and William Dollarhide. Copyright 1987, all rights reserved.

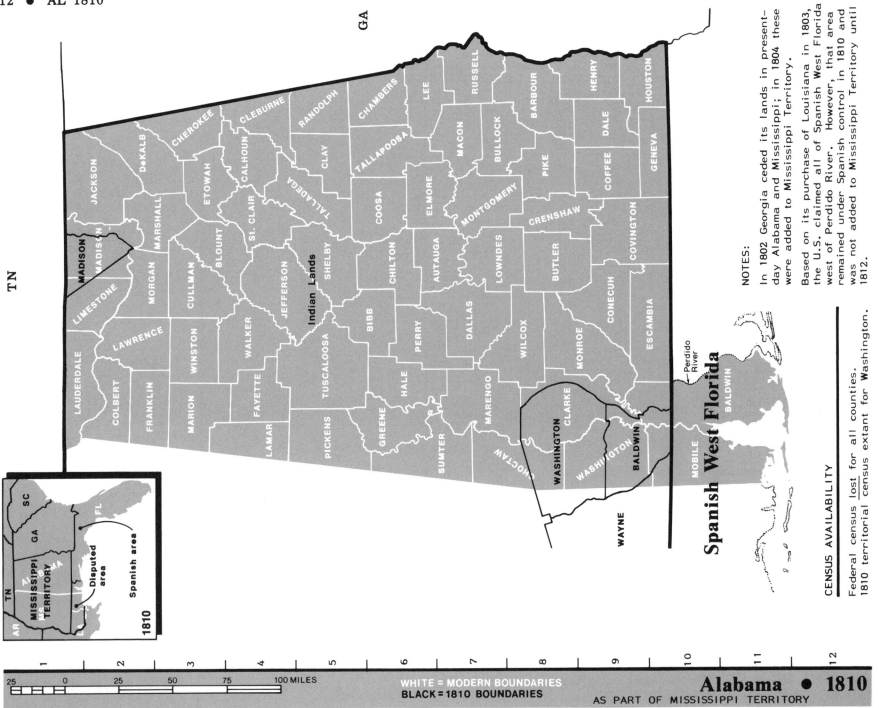

GA

TN

NOTES:

In 1802 Georgia ceded its lands in present-day Alabama and Mississippi; in 1804 these were added to Mississippi Territory.

Based on its purchase of Louisiana in 1803, the U.S. claimed all of Spanish West Florida west of Perdido River. However, that area remained under Spanish control in 1810 and was not added to Mississippi Territory until 1812.

CENSUS AVAILABILITY

Federal census lost for all counties. 1810 territorial census extant for Washington.

Spanish West Florida

MADISON

Indian Lands

Perdido River

WASHINGTON

WAYNE

MOBILE

BALDWIN

1810

Disputed area

Spanish area

25   0   25   50   75   100 MILES

WHITE = MODERN BOUNDARIES
BLACK = 1810 BOUNDARIES

Alabama ● 1810

AS PART OF MISSISSIPPI TERRITORY

MAP GUIDE TO THE U.S. FEDERAL CENSUSES, 1790-1920 by William Thorndale and William Dollarhide.   Copyright 1987, all rights reserved.

GA

TN

MS

JACKSON
JACKSON
DeKALB
CHEROKEE
CLEBURNE
RANDOLPH
CLAY
Indian Lands
CHAMBERS
TALLAPOOSA
LEE
RUSSELL
MACON
BULLOCK
BARBOUR
HENRY
DALE
HOUSTON
GENEVA
COFFEE

MADISON
MADISON
MARSHALL
COTACO*
MORGAN
MARION*
CULLMAN
BLOUNT
ETOWAH
CALHOUN
ST. CLAIR
TALLADEGA
COOSA
ELMORE
MONTGOMERY
MONTGOMERY
CRENSHAW
PIKE
HENRY
COVINGTON
CONECUH

LIMESTONE
LAWRENCE
BLOUNT
BLOUNT
JEFFERSON*
JEFFERSON
SHELBY
AUTAUGA
AUTAUGA
LOWNDES
BUTLER
BUTLER
CONECUH
ESCAMBIA

LAUDERDALE
FRANKLIN
FRANKLIN
WINSTON
WALKER
TUSCALOOSA
BIBB
CAHAWBA*
CHILTON
PERRY
DALLAS
WILCOX
MONROE
MONROE
BALDWIN

COLBERT
Indian Lands
MARION
FAYETTE
TUSCALOOSA
PICKENS
GREENE
HALE
GREENE
MARENGO
CLARKE
CLARKE
WASHINGTON
WASHINGTON
MOBILE
MOBILE
BALDWIN

LAMAR
SUMTER
Indian Lands
CHOCTAW

*NOTES:

Alabama became a territory in 1817 and a state in 1819.

Cahawba was renamed Bibb in December 1820.

Cotaco was renamed Morgan in 1821.

Jefferson and Marion are not on the federal government's 1820 population list. See note 7 in the bibliography for an explanation.

CENSUS AVAILABILITY

Federal census lost for all counties. 1820 state census extant for Baldwin, Conecuh, Dallas, Franklin, Limestone, St. Clair, Shelby, and Wilcox.

25 0 25 50 75 100 MILES

1 2 3 4 5 6 7 8 9 10 11 12

WHITE = MODERN BOUNDARIES
BLACK = 1820 BOUNDARIES

Alabama ● 1820

MAP GUIDE TO THE U.S. FEDERAL CENSUSES, 1790–1920 by William Thorndale and William Dollarhide. Copyright 1987, all rights reserved.

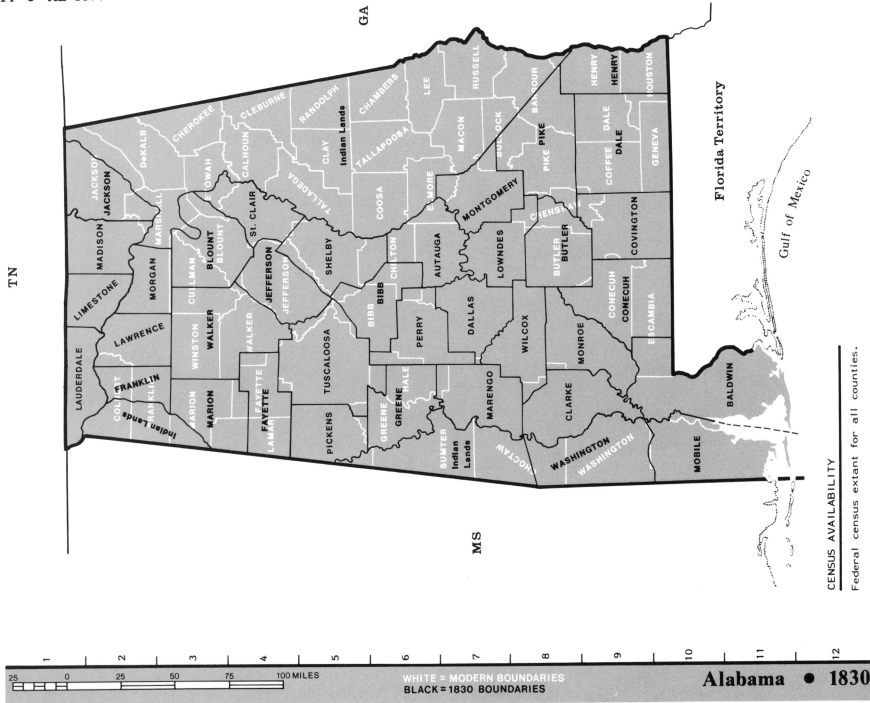

GA

TN

MS

Florida Territory

Gulf of Mexico

JACKSON
MADISON
LIMESTONE
LAUDERDALE
COLBERT
FRANKLIN
Indian Lands
MARION
LAMAR
FAYETTE
PICKENS
MARSHALL
MORGAN
LAWRENCE
WINSTON
CULLMAN
WALKER
DeKALB
BLOUNT
JEFFERSON
TUSCALOOSA
ETOWAH
St. CLAIR
CHEROKEE
CLEBURNE
CALHOUN
SHELBY
TALLADEGA
RANDOLPH
CLAY
Indian Lands
COOSA
BIBB
GREENE
HALE
PERRY
CHILTON
AUTAUGA
DALLAS
MARENGO
SUMTER
Indian Lands
CHOCTAW
WASHINGTON
CLARKE
WILCOX
MONROE
ELMORE
MONTGOMERY
LOWNDES
CRENSHAW
BUTLER
CONECUH
ESCAMBIA
TALLAPOOSA
CHAMBERS
LEE
MACON
RUSSELL
BULLOCK
PIKE
BARBOUR
COFFEE
DALE
COVINGTON
HENRY
HENRY
HOUSTON
GENEVA
BALDWIN
MOBILE

CENSUS AVAILABILITY
Federal census extant for all counties.

25 0 25 50 75 100 MILES

1 2 3 4 5 6 7 8 9 10 11 12

WHITE = MODERN BOUNDARIES
BLACK = 1830 BOUNDARIES

Alabama ● 1830

MAP GUIDE TO THE U.S. FEDERAL CENSUSES, 1790-1920 by William Thorndale and William Dollarhide. Copyright 1987, all rights reserved.

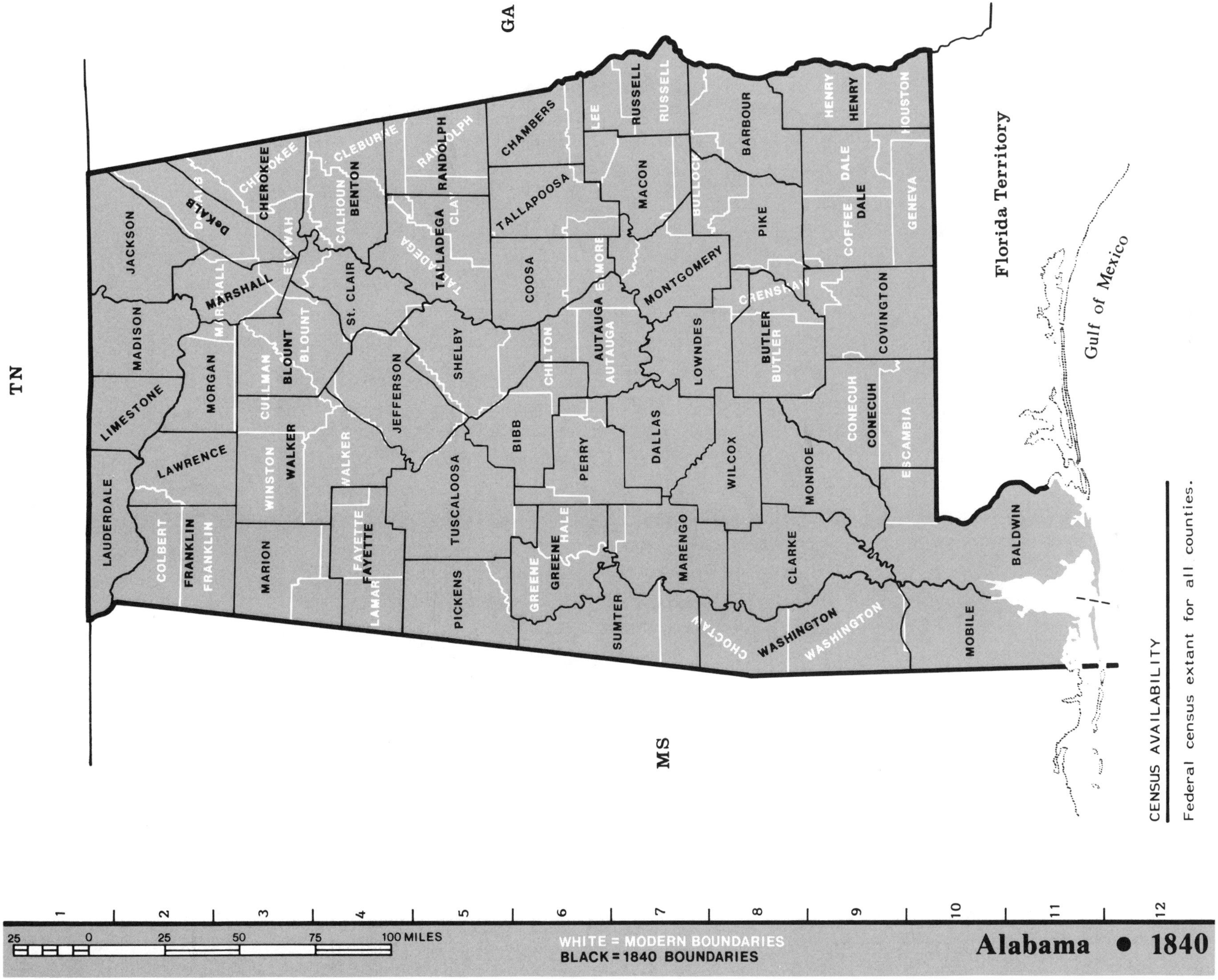

GA

TN

MS

Florida Territory

Gulf of Mexico

JACKSON
DEKALB
CHEROKEE
CLEBURNE
BENTON
RANDOLPH
RANDOLPH
CHAMBERS
LEE
RUSSELL
RUSSELL
BARBOUR
HENRY
HENRY
HOUSTON
MADISON
ETOWAH
CALHOUN
TALLADEGA
CLAY
TALLAPOOSA
MACON
BULLOCK
PIKE
DALE
DALE
GENEVA
COFFEE
MARSHALL
MARSHALL
St. CLAIR
TALLADEGA
COOSA
ELMORE
MONTGOMERY
LAUDERDALE
LIMESTONE
MADISON
MORGAN
CULLMAN
BLOUNT
BLOUNT
SHELBY
CHILTON
AUTAUGA
AUTAUGA
LOWNDES
CRENSHAW
BUTLER
BUTLER
COVINGTON
LAWRENCE
WINSTON
WALKER
JEFFERSON
CONECUH
CONECUH
ESCAMBIA
COLBERT
FRANKLIN
FRANKLIN
WALKER
BIBB
PERRY
DALLAS
WILCOX
MONROE
MARION
FAYETTE
FAYETTE
TUSCALOOSA
GREENE
HALE
SUMTER
MARENGO
CLARKE
BALDWIN
LAMAR
PICKENS
GREENE
HALE
CHOCTAW
WASHINGTON
WASHINGTON
MOBILE

| 1 | 2 | 3 | 4 | 5 | 6 | 7 | 8 | 9 | 10 | 11 | 12 |

25 0 25 50 75 100 MILES

WHITE = MODERN BOUNDARIES
BLACK = 1840 BOUNDARIES

Alabama ● 1840

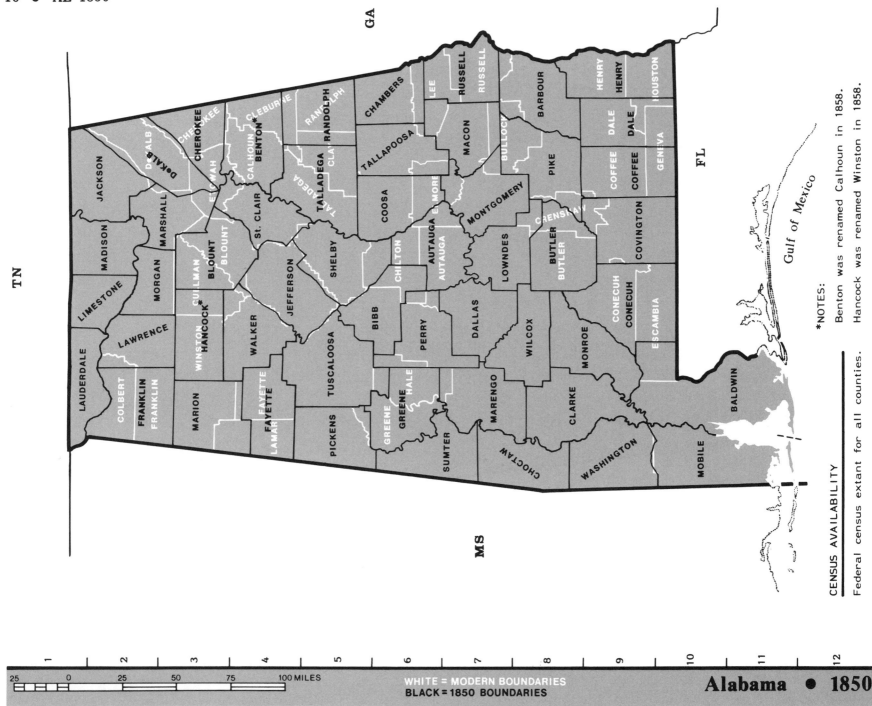

GA

TN

FL

MS

Gulf of Mexico

*NOTES:

Benton was renamed Calhoun in 1858.

Hancock was renamed Winston in 1858.

CENSUS AVAILABILITY

Federal census extant for all counties.

WHITE = MODERN BOUNDARIES
BLACK = 1850 BOUNDARIES

Alabama ● **1850**

25 0 25 50 75 100 MILES

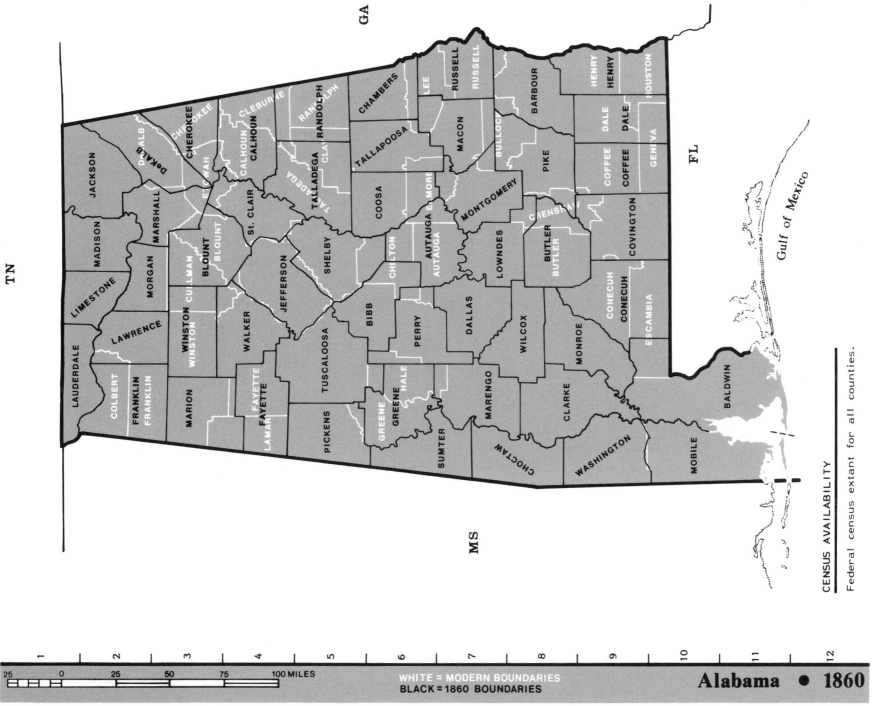

CENSUS AVAILABILITY

Federal census extant for all counties.

WHITE = MODERN BOUNDARIES
BLACK = 1860 BOUNDARIES

Alabama ● 1860

MAP GUIDE TO THE U.S. FEDERAL CENSUSES, 1790–1920 by William Thorndale and William Dollarhide.   Copyright 1987, all rights reserved.

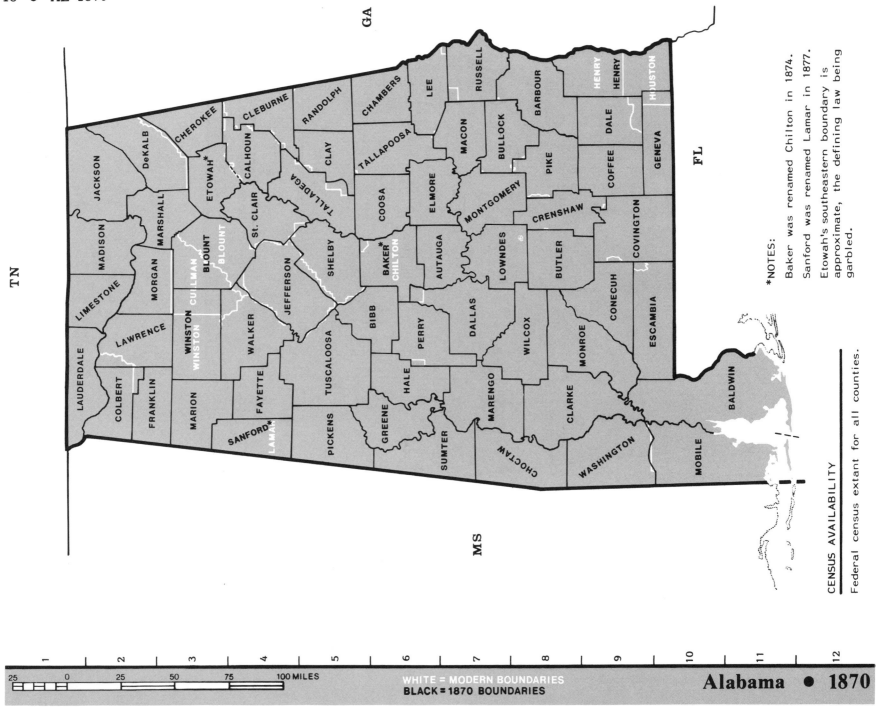

GA

TN

FL

MS

*NOTES:

Baker was renamed Chilton in 1874.
Sanford was renamed Lamar in 1877.
Etowah's southeastern boundary is
approximate, the defining law being
garbled.

CENSUS AVAILABILITY

Federal census extant for all counties.

100 MILES

25   0   25   50   75

WHITE = MODERN BOUNDARIES
BLACK = 1870 BOUNDARIES

Alabama ● 1870

MAP GUIDE TO THE U.S. FEDERAL CENSUSES, 1790–1920 by William Thorndale and William Dollarhide. Copyright 1987, all rights reserved.

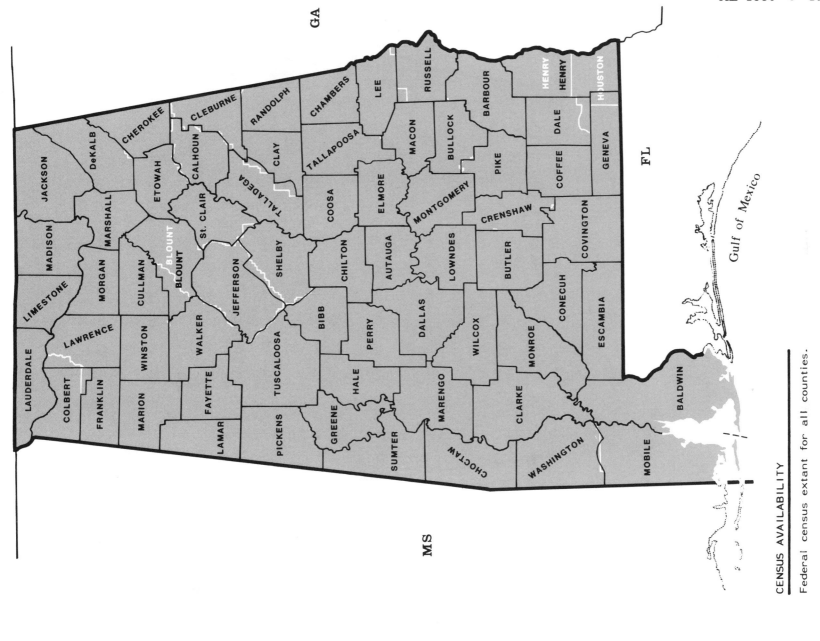

GA

TN

MS

FL

Gulf of Mexico

JACKSON

DeKALB

CHEROKEE

CLEBURNE

RANDOLPH

CHAMBERS

LEE

RUSSELL

BARBOUR

HENRY

HENRY

HOUSTON

MADISON

MARSHALL

ETOWAH

CALHOUN

CLAY

TALLAPOOSA

MACON

BULLOCK

DALE

COFFEE

GENEVA

LIMESTONE

MORGAN

CULLMAN

BLOUNT

BLOUNT

St. CLAIR

TALLADEGA

COOSA

ELMORE

MONTGOMERY

PIKE

CRENSHAW

COVINGTON

LAWRENCE

WINSTON

WALKER

JEFFERSON

SHELBY

CHILTON

AUTAUGA

LOWNDES

BUTLER

CONECUH

ESCAMBIA

LAUDERDALE

COLBERT

FRANKLIN

MARION

FAYETTE

LAMAR

TUSCALOOSA

BIBB

PERRY

DALLAS

WILCOX

MONROE

BALDWIN

PICKENS

GREENE

HALE

SUMTER

MARENGO

CHOCTAW

CLARKE

WASHINGTON

MOBILE

25 0 25 50 75 100 MILES

1 2 3 4 5 6 7 8 9 10 11 12

CENSUS AVAILABILITY
Federal census extant for all counties.

Alabama ● 1880

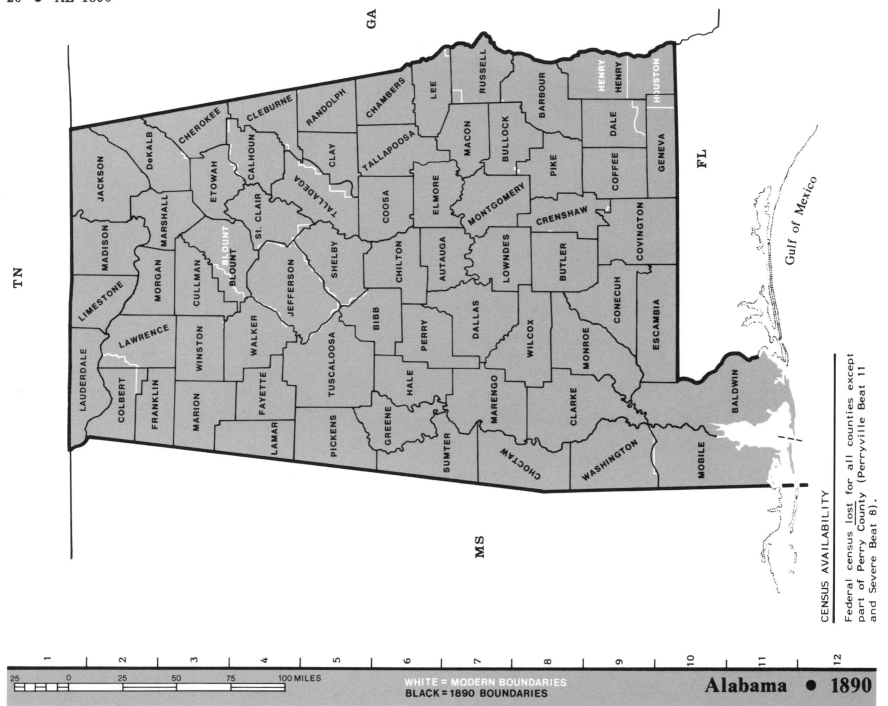

GA

TN

FL

Gulf of Mexico

MS

JACKSON

DeKALB

CHEROKEE

CLEBURNE

RANDOLPH

CHAMBERS

LEE

RUSSELL

BARBOUR

HENRY

HENRY

HOUSTON

MADISON

MARSHALL

ETOWAH

CALHOUN

CLAY

TALLAPOOSA

MACON

BULLOCK

DALE

GENEVA

LIMESTONE

MORGAN

CULLMAN

BLOUNT

BLOUNT

St. CLAIR

TALLADEGA

COOSA

ELMORE

MONTGOMERY

PIKE

COFFEE

LAUDERDALE

LAWRENCE

WINSTON

WALKER

JEFFERSON

SHELBY

CHILTON

AUTAUGA

CRENSHAW

LOWNDES

BUTLER

COVINGTON

COLBERT

FRANKLIN

MARION

FAYETTE

TUSCALOOSA

BIBB

PERRY

DALLAS

WILCOX

CONECUH

ESCAMBIA

LAMAR

PICKENS

GREENE

HALE

MARENGO

MONROE

SUMTER

CHOCTAW

WASHINGTON

CLARKE

MOBILE

BALDWIN

CENSUS AVAILABILITY

Federal census lost for all counties except part of Perry County (Perryville Beat 11 and Severe Beat 8).

25   0   25   50   75   100 MILES

WHITE = MODERN BOUNDARIES
BLACK = 1890 BOUNDARIES

Alabama ● 1890

1 2 3 4 5 6 7 8 9 10 11 12

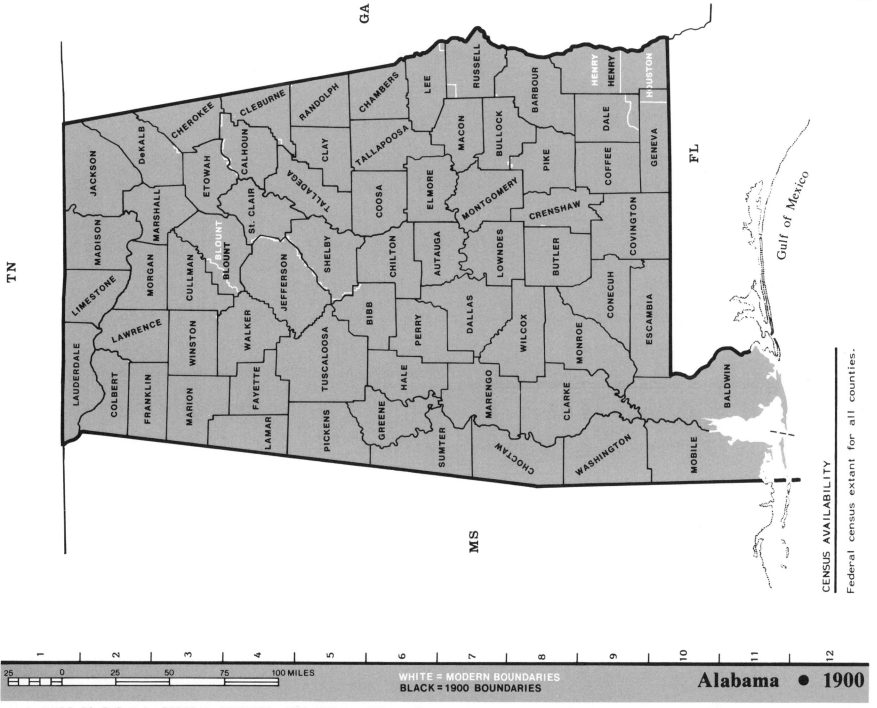

GA

TN

MS

FL

Gulf of Mexico

25 0 25 50 75 100 MILES

1 2 3 4 5 6 7 8 9 10 11 12

WHITE = MODERN BOUNDARIES
BLACK = 1900 BOUNDARIES

Alabama ● **1900**

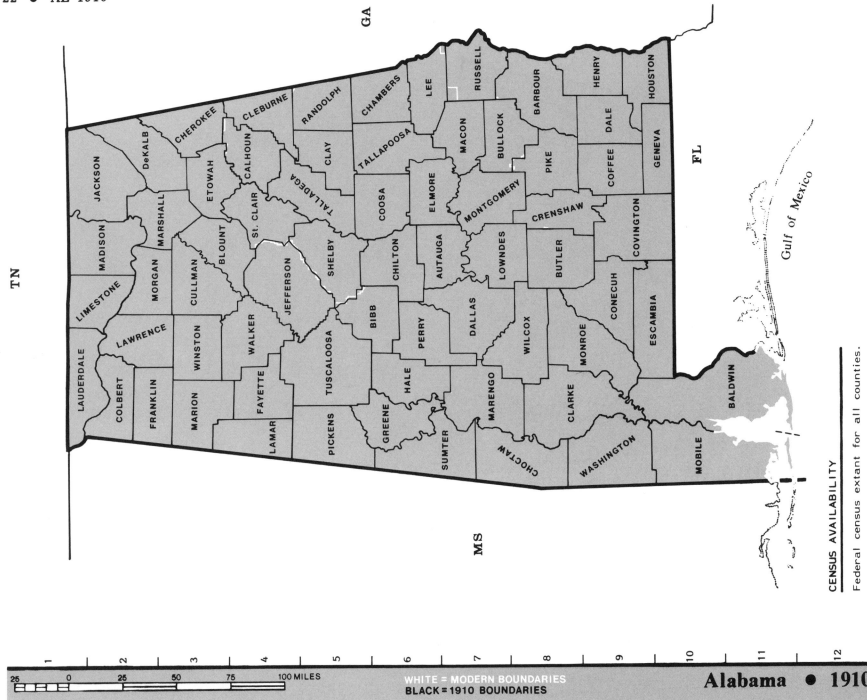

GA

TN

FL

Gulf of Mexico

MS

JACKSON
MADISON
LIMESTONE
LAUDERDALE
COLBERT
FRANKLIN
LAWRENCE
MORGAN
MARSHALL
DeKALB
CHEROKEE
ETOWAH
BLOUNT
CULLMAN
WINSTON
MARION
FRANKLIN
FAYETTE
LAMAR
WALKER
ST. CLAIR
CALHOUN
CLEBURNE
RANDOLPH
CLAY
TALLADEGA
JEFFERSON
SHELBY
TUSCALOOSA
PICKENS
BIBB
CHILTON
COOSA
TALLAPOOSA
CHAMBERS
LEE
RUSSELL
MACON
BULLOCK
ELMORE
AUTAUGA
MONTGOMERY
PIKE
BARBOUR
DALE
HENRY
HOUSTON
GENEVA
COFFEE
CRENSHAW
COVINGTON
LOWNDES
BUTLER
DALLAS
PERRY
HALE
GREENE
SUMTER
MARENGO
CHOCTAW
WILCOX
MONROE
CLARKE
WASHINGTON
CONECUH
ESCAMBIA
MOBILE
BALDWIN

CENSUS AVAILABILITY

Federal census extant for all counties.

WHITE = MODERN BOUNDARIES
BLACK = 1910 BOUNDARIES

Alabama ● 1910

25 0 25 50 75 100 MILES

1 2 3 4 5 6 7 8 9 10 11 12

GA

TN

MS

FL

Gulf of Mexico

JACKSON
DeKALB
CHEROKEE
CLEBURNE
RANDOLPH
CHAMBERS
LEE
RUSSELL
BARBOUR
HENRY
HOUSTON
MADISON
MARSHALL
ETOWAH
CALHOUN
CLAY
TALLAPOOSA
MACON
BULLOCK
DALE
GENEVA
LIMESTONE
MORGAN
BLOUNT
St. CLAIR
TALLADEGA
COOSA
ELMORE
MONTGOMERY
PIKE
COFFEE
LAUDERDALE
LAWRENCE
CULLMAN
SHELBY
CHILTON
AUTAUGA
CRENSHAW
BUTLER
COVINGTON
COLBERT
MORGAN
WINSTON
WALKER
JEFFERSON
BIBB
PERRY
DALLAS
LOWNDES
CONECUH
ESCAMBIA
FRANKLIN
MARION
FAYETTE
TUSCALOOSA
GREENE
HALE
WILCOX
MARENGO
MONROE
CLARKE
WASHINGTON
BALDWIN
MOBILE
LAMAR
PICKENS
SUMTER
CHOCTAW

CENSUS AVAILABILITY
Federal census extant for all counties.

WHITE = MODERN BOUNDARIES
BLACK = 1920 BOUNDARIES

Alabama ● 1920

25 0 25 50 75 100 MILES

MAP GUIDE TO THE U.S. FEDERAL CENSUSES, 1790-1920 by William Thorndale and William Dollarhide. Copyright 1987, all rights reserved.

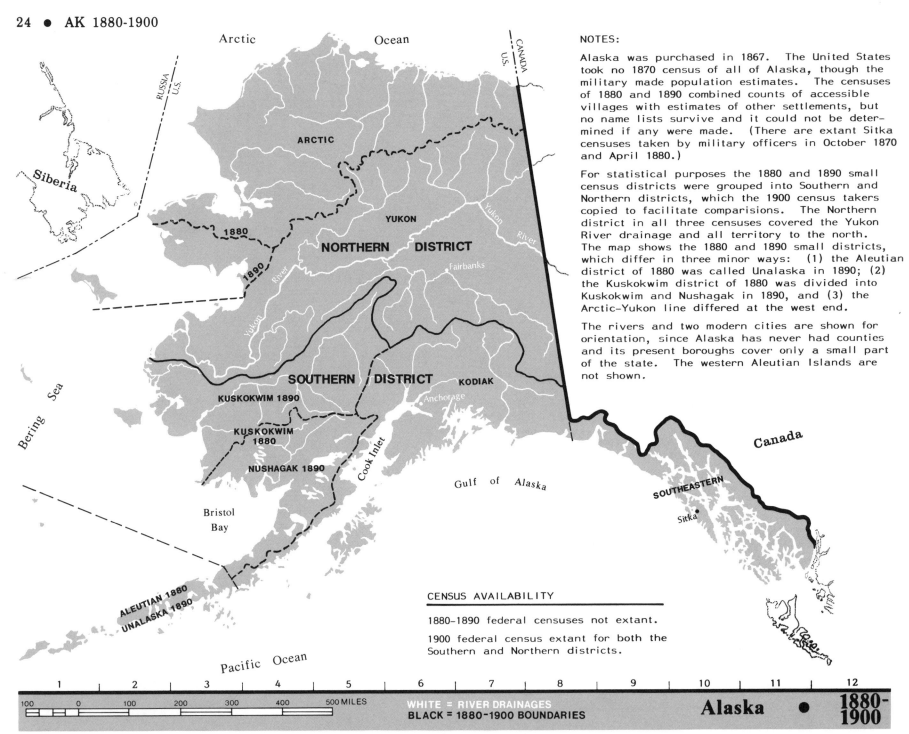

Arctic Ocean

RUSSIA
U.S.

CANADA
U.S.

Siberia

ARCTIC

1880

YUKON

1890
River

NORTHERN   DISTRICT

Yukon River

Fairbanks

Yukon River

SOUTHERN   DISTRICT

KODIAK

KUSKOKWIM 1890

Anchorage

KUSKOKWIM
1880

NUSHAGAK 1890

Cook Inlet

Bering   Sea

Gulf   of   Alaska

Canada

Bristol
Bay

SOUTHEASTERN

Sitka

ALEUTIAN 1880
UNALASKA 1890

Pacific   Ocean

NOTES:

Alaska was purchased in 1867. The United States took no 1870 census of all of Alaska, though the military made population estimates. The censuses of 1880 and 1890 combined counts of accessible villages with estimates of other settlements, but no name lists survive and it could not be determined if any were made. (There are extant Sitka censuses taken by military officers in October 1870 and April 1880.)

For statistical purposes the 1880 and 1890 small census districts were grouped into Southern and Northern districts, which the 1900 census takers copied to facilitate comparisions. The Northern district in all three censuses covered the Yukon River drainage and all territory to the north. The map shows the 1880 and 1890 small districts, which differ in three minor ways: (1) the Aleutian district of 1880 was called Unalaska in 1890; (2) the Kuskokwim district of 1880 was divided into Kuskokwim and Nushagak in 1890, and (3) the Arctic-Yukon line differed at the west end.

The rivers and two modern cities are shown for orientation, since Alaska has never had counties and its present boroughs cover only a small part of the state. The western Aleutian Islands are not shown.

CENSUS AVAILABILITY

1880-1890 federal censuses not extant.

1900 federal census extant for both the Southern and Northern districts.

| 1 | 2 | 3 | 4 | 5 | 6 | 7 | 8 | 9 | 10 | 11 | 12 |

100   0   100   200   300   400   500 MILES

WHITE = RIVER DRAINAGES
BLACK = 1880-1900 BOUNDARIES

Alaska   ●   **1880-1900**

MAP GUIDE TO THE U.S. FEDERAL CENSUSES, 1790-1920 by William Thorndale and William Dollarhide. Copyright 1987, all rights reserved.

Arctic Ocean

Siberia

RUSSIA
U.S.

CANADA
U.S.

Division 2

Division 4

Yukon River

Fairbanks

Yukon River

Bering Sea

Division 3

Anchorage

Cook Inlet

Gulf of Alaska

Canada

Bristol Bay

Division 1

Pacific Ocean

NOTES:

The absence of Alaskan counties led census takers to create enumeration areas for 1880–1900 and use judicial divisions for 1910 and 1920. The act of 1912 making Alaska a territory prohibited the creation of counties without the approval of Congress. None were ever created. Alaskan local governments function through incorporated cities, village governments, and various area–wide units such as judicial, election, school, recorder, and public utility districts. The modern Alaskan boroughs –– not shown on the background basemap –– can cover large areas but are not analogous to counties, since they have the legislative powers of municipal corporations and are not, as are counties, primarily administrative units of state government.

Alaska became a state in 1959.

CENSUS AVAILABILITY

1910–1920 federal censuses extant for all federal judicial divisions.

1   2   3   4   5   6   7   8   9   10   11   12

100   0   100   200   300   400   500 MILES

WHITE = RIVER DRAINAGES
BLACK = 1910-1920 BOUNDARIES

Alaska   ●   1910-1920

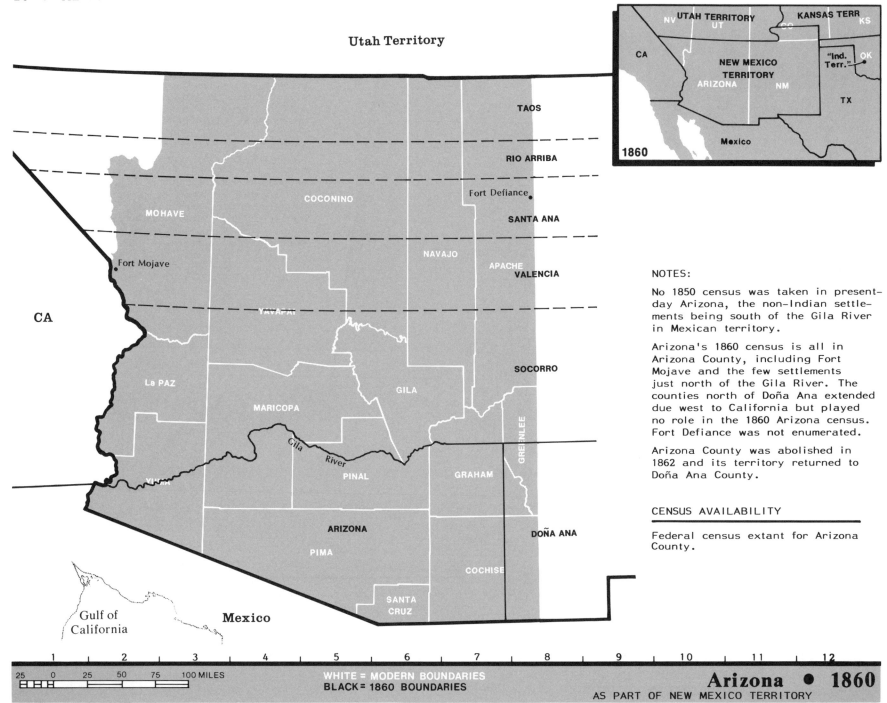

Utah Territory

TAOS

RIO ARRIBA

Fort Defiance

SANTA ANA

MOHAVE

COCONINO

Fort Mojave

NAVAJO

APACHE

VALENCIA

YAVAPAI

CA

SOCORRO

La PAZ

GILA

MARICOPA

GREENLEE

Gila River

YUMA

PINAL

GRAHAM

ARIZONA

DOÑA ANA

PIMA

COCHISE

SANTA
CRUZ

Gulf of
California

Mexico

NOTES:

No 1850 census was taken in present-
day Arizona, the non-Indian settlements being south of the Gila River
in Mexican territory.

Arizona's 1860 census is all in
Arizona County, including Fort
Mojave and the few settlements
just north of the Gila River. The
counties north of Doña Ana extended
due west to California but played
no role in the 1860 Arizona census.
Fort Defiance was not enumerated.

Arizona County was abolished in
1862 and its territory returned to
Doña Ana County.

CENSUS AVAILABILITY

Federal census extant for Arizona
County.

Inset map:

UTAH TERRITORY
UT

NV

KANSAS TERR
KS

CO

CA

NEW MEXICO
TERRITORY

"Ind.
Terr."

OK

ARIZONA

NM

TX

1860

Mexico

Scale:

1 2 3 4 5 6 7 8 9 10 11 12

25 0 25 50 75 100 MILES

WHITE = MODERN BOUNDARIES
BLACK = 1860 BOUNDARIES

Arizona ● 1860

AS PART OF NEW MEXICO TERRITORY

MAP GUIDE TO THE U.S. FEDERAL CENSUSES, 1790–1920 by William Thorndale and William Dollarhide. Copyright 1987, all rights reserved.

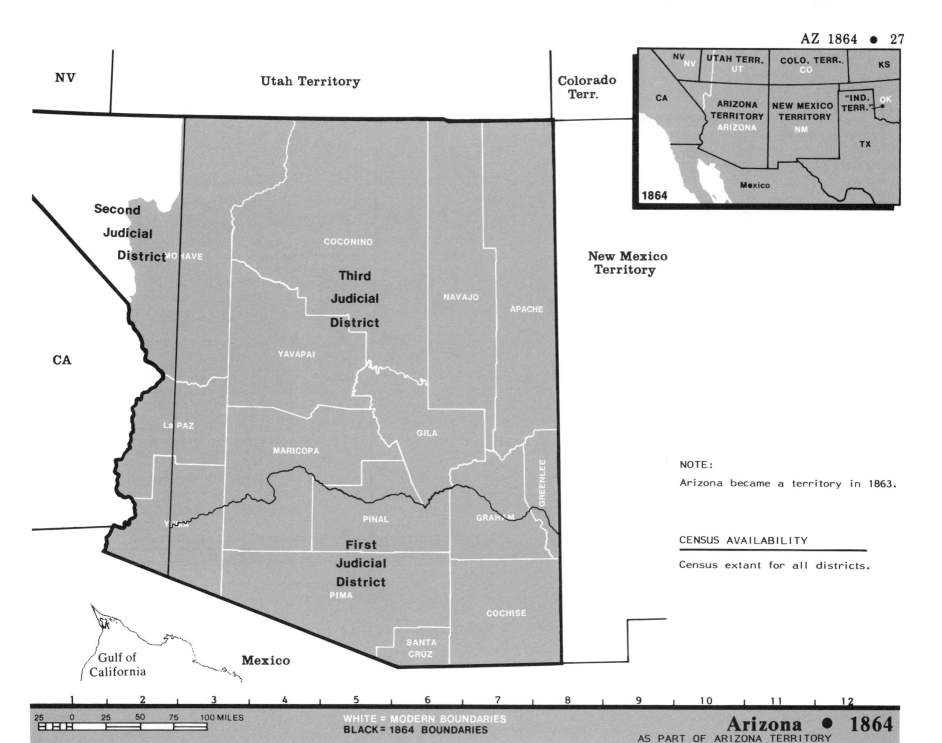

NV

Utah Territory

Colorado Terr.

Second Judicial District

MOHAVE

COCONINO

Third Judicial District

NAVAJO

APACHE

CA

YAVAPAI

New Mexico Territory

La PAZ

GILA

MARICOPA

GREENLEE

YUMA

PINAL

GRAHAM

First Judicial District

PIMA

COCHISE

SANTA CRUZ

Gulf of California

Mexico

Inset map labels:

NV NV

UTAH TERR. UT

COLO. TERR. CO

KS

CA

ARIZONA TERRITORY ARIZONA

NEW MEXICO TERRITORY NM

"IND. TERR." OK

TX

Mexico

1864

NOTE:

Arizona became a territory in 1863.

CENSUS AVAILABILITY

Census extant for all districts.

1   2   3   4   5   6   7   8   9   10   11   12

25 0 25 50 75 100 MILES

WHITE = MODERN BOUNDARIES
BLACK = 1864 BOUNDARIES

Arizona ● 1864

AS PART OF ARIZONA TERRITORY

MAP GUIDE TO THE U.S. FEDERAL CENSUSES, 1790–1920 by William Thorndale and William Dollarhide. Copyright 1987, all rights reserved.

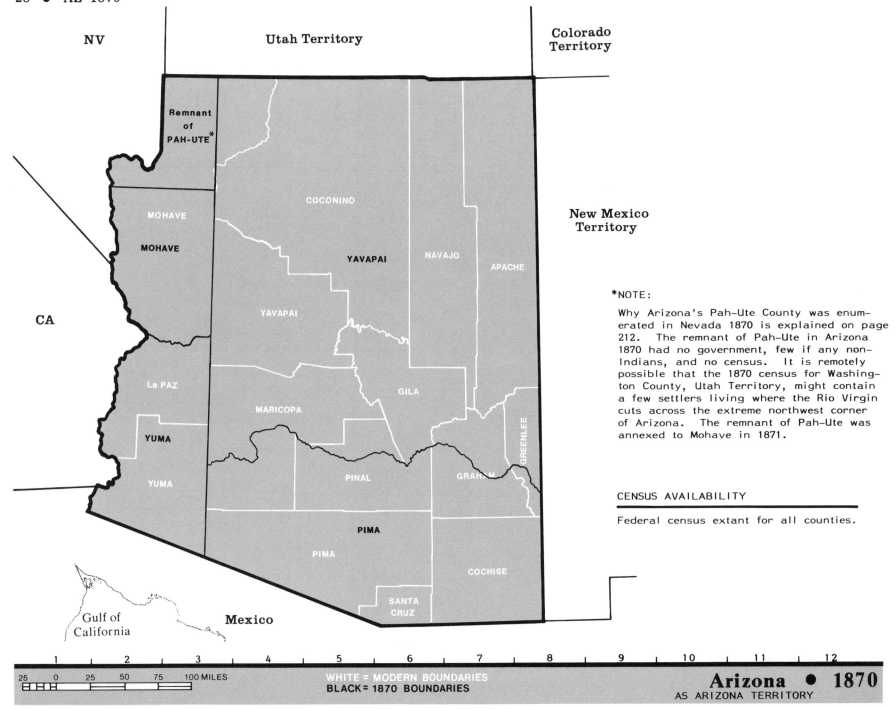

NV

Utah Territory

Colorado Territory

Remnant of PAH-UTE*

MOHAVE

MOHAVE

CA

La PAZ

YUMA

YUMA

COCONINO

YAVAPAI

YAVAPAI

NAVAJO

APACHE

New Mexico Territory

GILA

MARICOPA

GREENLEE

PINAL

GRAHAM

PIMA

PIMA

COCHISE

SANTA CRUZ

Gulf of California

Mexico

*NOTE:

Why Arizona's Pah–Ute County was enumerated in Nevada 1870 is explained on page 212. The remnant of Pah–Ute in Arizona 1870 had no government, few if any non-Indians, and no census. It is remotely possible that the 1870 census for Washington County, Utah Territory, might contain a few settlers living where the Rio Virgin cuts across the extreme northwest corner of Arizona. The remnant of Pah–Ute was annexed to Mohave in 1871.

CENSUS AVAILABILITY

Federal census extant for all counties.

| 1 | 2 | 3 | 4 | 5 | 6 | 7 | 8 | 9 | 10 | 11 | 12 |

25   0   25   50   75   100 MILES

WHITE = MODERN BOUNDARIES
BLACK = 1870 BOUNDARIES

Arizona ● 1870
AS ARIZONA TERRITORY

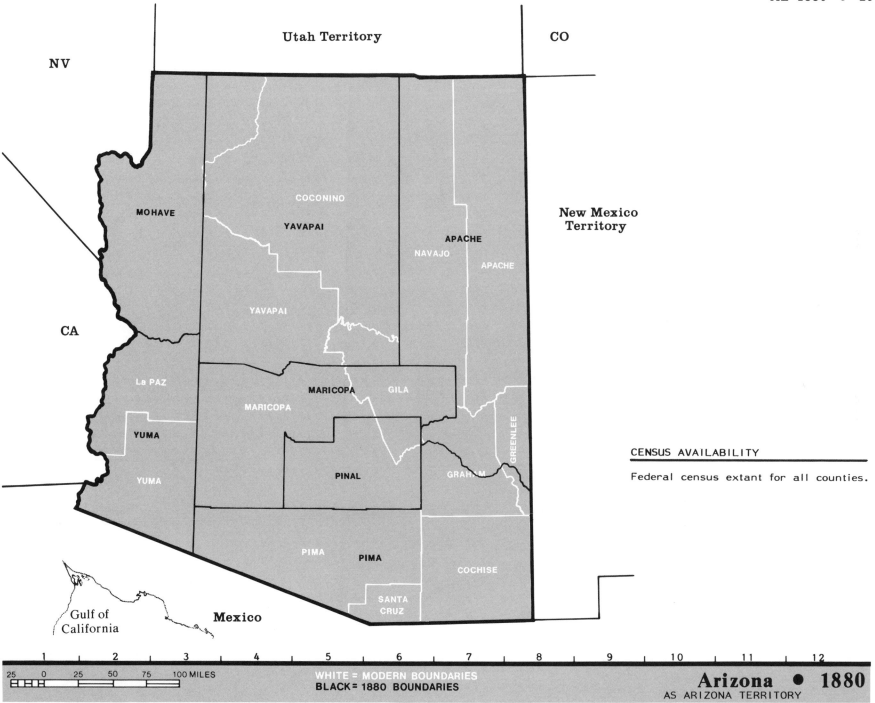

NV

Utah Territory

CO

MOHAVE

COCONINO

YAVAPAI

APACHE

NAVAJO

APACHE

New Mexico
Territory

CA

YAVAPAI

La PAZ

MARICOPA

GILA

MARICOPA

GREENLEE

YUMA

CENSUS AVAILABILITY

Federal census extant for all counties.

YUMA

PINAL

GRAHAM

PIMA

PIMA

COCHISE

Gulf of
California

SANTA
CRUZ

Mexico

| 1 | 2 | 3 | 4 | 5 | 6 | 7 | 8 | 9 | 10 | 11 | 12 |

25 0 25 50 75 100 MILES

WHITE = MODERN BOUNDARIES
BLACK = 1880 BOUNDARIES

Arizona ● 1880
AS ARIZONA TERRITORY

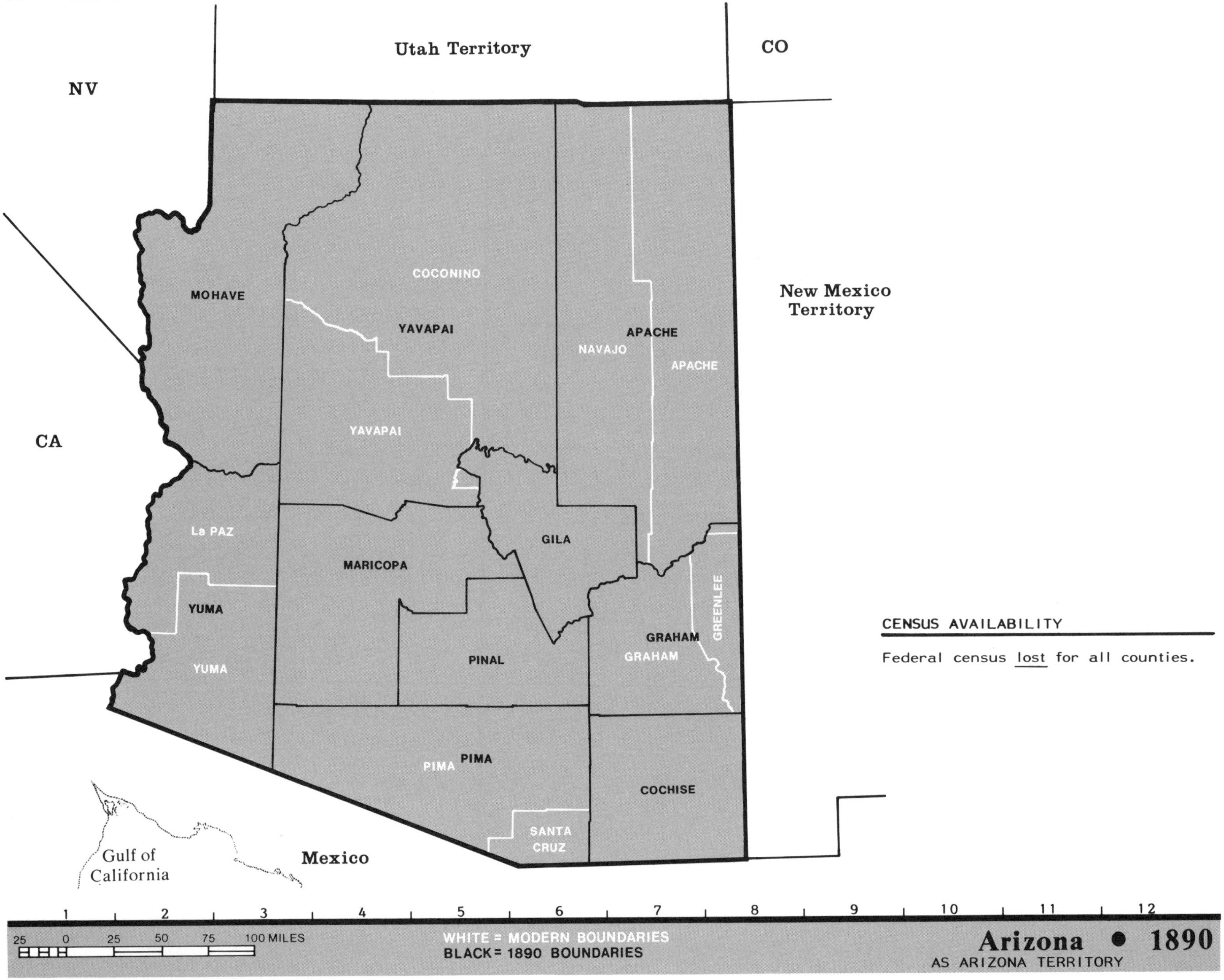

Utah Territory

CO

NV

NEW MEXICO
Territory

CA

MOHAVE

COCONINO

YAVAPAI

APACHE

NAVAJO

APACHE

YAVAPAI

La PAZ

GILA

MARICOPA

GREENLEE

YUMA

GRAHAM

GRAHAM

YUMA

PINAL

CENSUS AVAILABILITY

Federal census <u>lost</u> for all counties.

PIMA
PIMA

COCHISE

Gulf of
California

Mexico

SANTA
CRUZ

| 1 | 2 | 3 | 4 | 5 | 6 | 7 | 8 | 9 | 10 | 11 | 12 |

25 0   25   50   75   100 MILES

WHITE = MODERN BOUNDARIES
BLACK = 1890 BOUNDARIES

Arizona ● 1890
AS ARIZONA TERRITORY

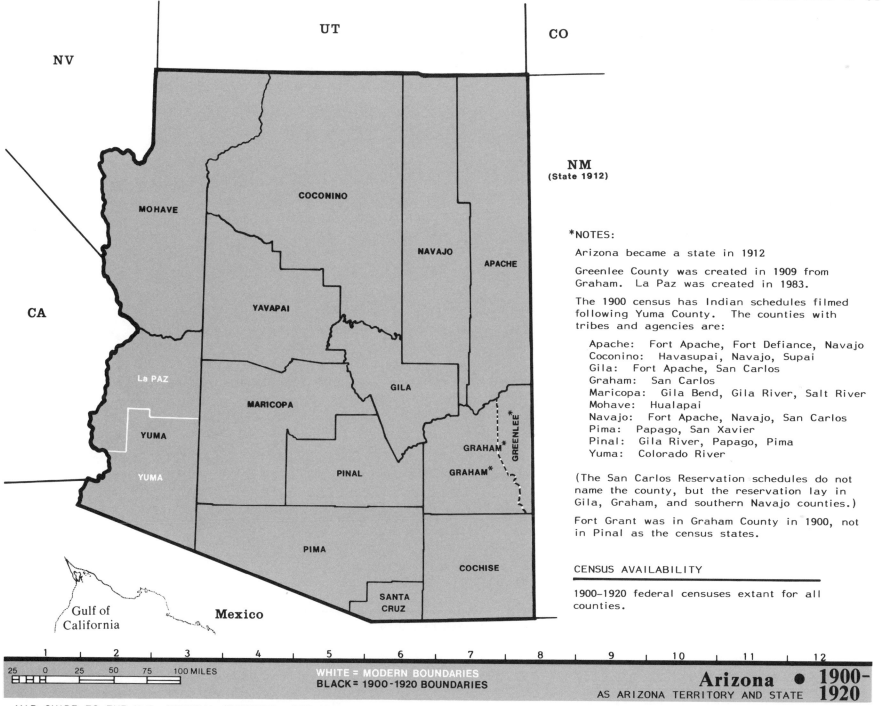

NV

UT

CO

NM
(State 1912)

MOHAVE

COCONINO

NAVAJO

APACHE

CA

YAVAPAI

La PAZ

GILA

MARICOPA

GRAHAM*

GRAHAM*

GREENLEE*

YUMA

YUMA

PINAL

Gulf of
California

Mexico

PIMA

COCHISE

SANTA
CRUZ

*NOTES:

Arizona became a state in 1912

Greenlee County was created in 1909 from
Graham. La Paz was created in 1983.

The 1900 census has Indian schedules filmed
following Yuma County. The counties with
tribes and agencies are:

Apache: Fort Apache, Fort Defiance, Navajo
Coconino: Havasupai, Navajo, Supai
Gila: Fort Apache, San Carlos
Graham: San Carlos
Maricopa: Gila Bend, Gila River, Salt River
Mohave: Hualapai
Navajo: Fort Apache, Navajo, San Carlos
Pima: Papago, San Xavier
Pinal: Gila River, Papago, Pima
Yuma: Colorado River

(The San Carlos Reservation schedules do not
name the county, but the reservation lay in
Gila, Graham, and southern Navajo counties.)

Fort Grant was in Graham County in 1900, not
in Pinal as the census states.

CENSUS AVAILABILITY

1900-1920 federal censuses extant for all
counties.

1   2   3   4   5   6   7   8   9   10   11   12

25 0   25   50   75   100 MILES

WHITE = MODERN BOUNDARIES
BLACK= 1900-1920 BOUNDARIES

Arizona ● 1900-
1920
AS ARIZONA TERRITORY AND STATE

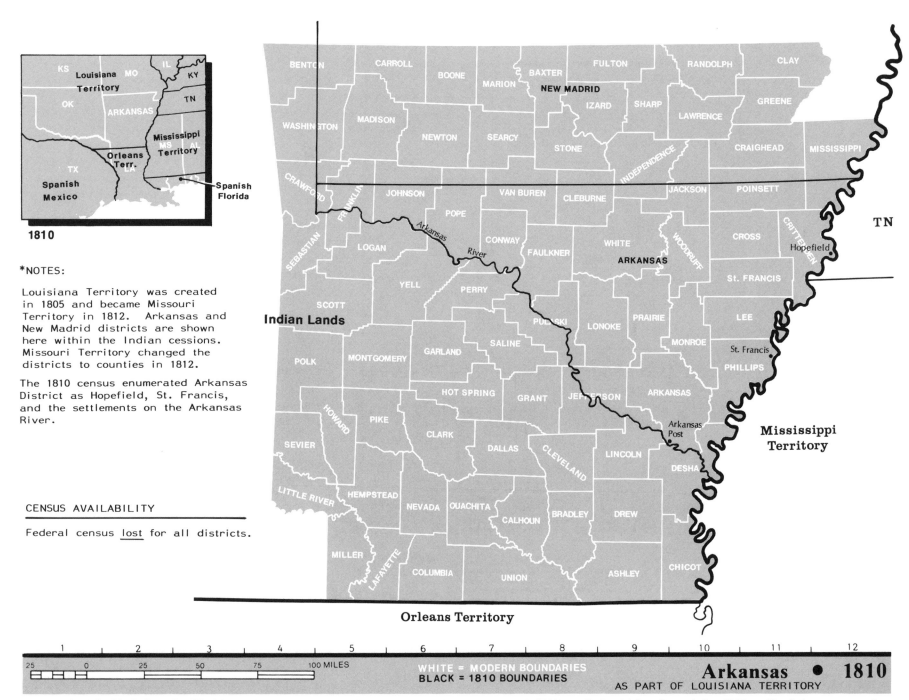

1810

*NOTES:

Louisiana Territory was created in 1805 and became Missouri Territory in 1812. Arkansas and New Madrid districts are shown here within the Indian cessions. Missouri Territory changed the districts to counties in 1812.

The 1810 census enumerated Arkansas District as Hopefield, St. Francis, and the settlements on the Arkansas River.

CENSUS AVAILABILITY

Federal census lost for all districts.

WHITE = MODERN BOUNDARIES
BLACK = 1810 BOUNDARIES

Arkansas ● **1810**
AS PART OF LOUISIANA TERRITORY

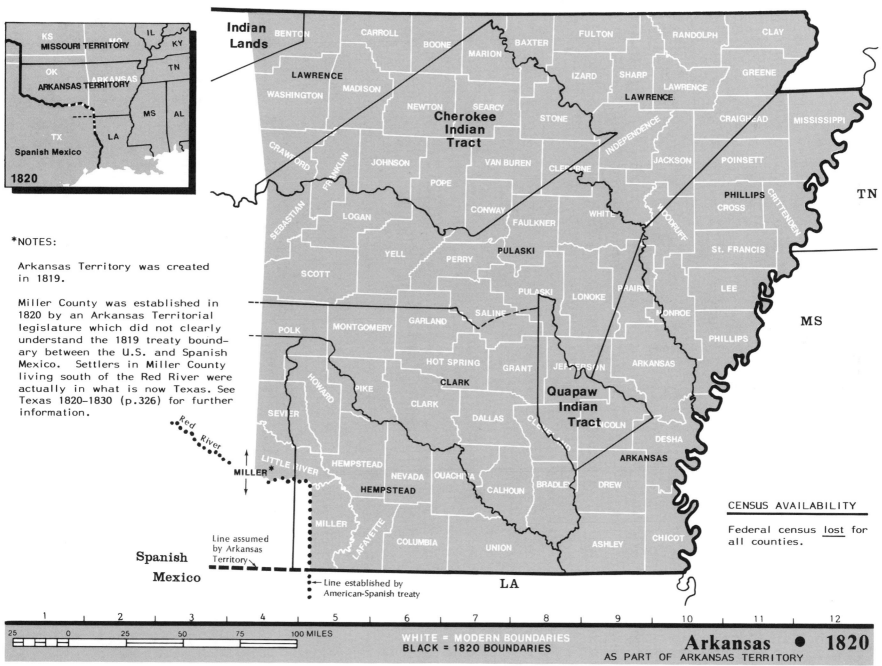

Missouri Territory

Indian Lands

*NOTES:

Arkansas Territory was created in 1819.

Miller County was established in 1820 by an Arkansas Territorial legislature which did not clearly understand the 1819 treaty boundary between the U.S. and Spanish Mexico. Settlers in Miller County living south of the Red River were actually in what is now Texas. See Texas 1820–1830 (p.326) for further information.

Cherokee Indian Tract

Quapaw Indian Tract

Line assumed by Arkansas Territory

Spanish Mexico

Red River

MILLER*

Line established by American-Spanish treaty

CENSUS AVAILABILITY

Federal census lost for all counties.

LA

MILES

Arkansas ● 1820
AS PART OF ARKANSAS TERRITORY

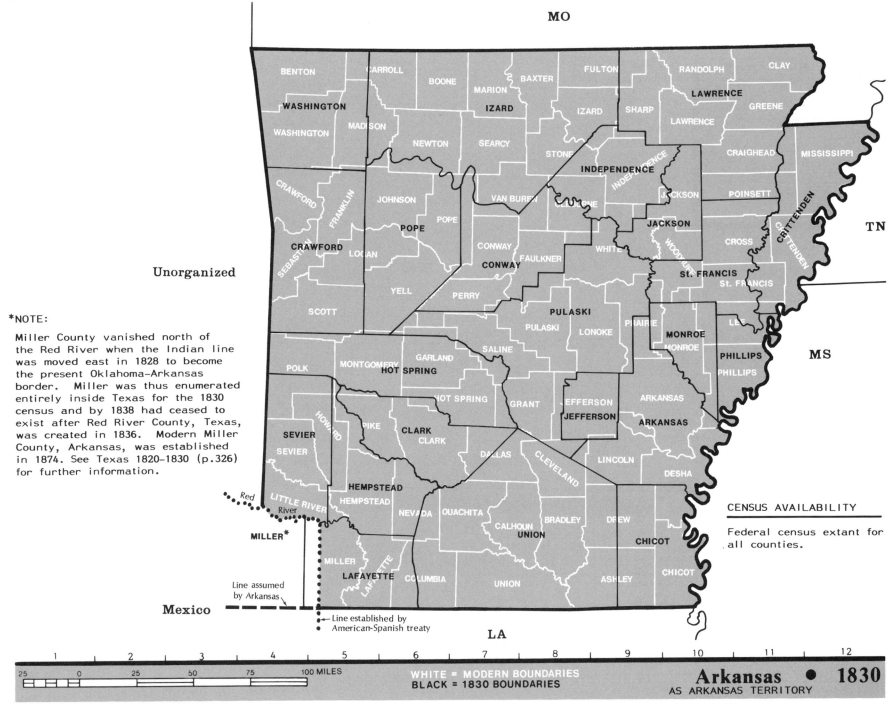

MO

BENTON

CARROLL

BOONE

BAXTER

FULTON

RANDOLPH

CLAY

WASHINGTON

MARION

LAWRENCE

IZARD

LAWRENCE

GREENE

WASHINGTON

MADISON

IZARD

SHARP

LAWRENCE

NEWTON

SEARCY

CRAIGHEAD

MISSISSIPPI

STONE

CRAWFORD

INDEPENDENCE

INDEPENDENCE

FRANKLIN

JOHNSON

VAN BUREN

JACKSON

POINSETT

CRAWFORD

POPE

CLEBURNE

JACKSON

SEBASTIAN

POPE

TN

LOGAN

CONWAY

WHITE

WOODRUFF

CROSS

Unorganized

CONWAY

FAULKNER

CRITTENDEN

YELL

PERRY

St. FRANCIS

ST. FRANCIS

SCOTT

PULASKI

LEE

PULASKI

PRAIRIE

MONROE

GARLAND

SALINE

LONOKE

MONROE

MS

MONTGOMERY

HOT SPRING

PHILLIPS

POLK

HOT SPRING

GRANT

JEFFERSON

ARKANSAS

PHILLIPS

PIKE

JEFFERSON

ARKANSAS

HOWARD

CLARK

SEVIER

CLARK

DALLAS

CLEVELAND

LINCOLN

SEVIER

HEMPSTEAD

CENSUS AVAILABILITY

Red

LITTLE RIVER

HEMPSTEAD

Federal census extant for
all counties.

River

NEVADA

OUACHITA

BRADLEY

DREW

MILLER*

CALHOUN

Line assumed

MILLER

UNION

CHICOT

by Arkansas

LAFAYETTE

COLUMBIA

UNION

ASHLEY

CHICOT

Mexico

LAFAYETTE

Line established by
American-Spanish treaty

LA

*NOTE:

Miller County vanished north of
the Red River when the Indian line
was moved east in 1828 to become
the present Oklahoma–Arkansas
border. Miller was thus enumerated
entirely inside Texas for the 1830
census and by 1838 had ceased to
exist after Red River County, Texas,
was created in 1836. Modern Miller
County, Arkansas, was established
in 1874. See Texas 1820–1830 (p.326)
for further information.

1	2	3	4	5	6	7	8	9	10	11	12

25   0   25   50   75   100 MILES

WHITE = MODERN BOUNDARIES
BLACK = 1830 BOUNDARIES

Arkansas ● **1830**
AS ARKANSAS TERRITORY

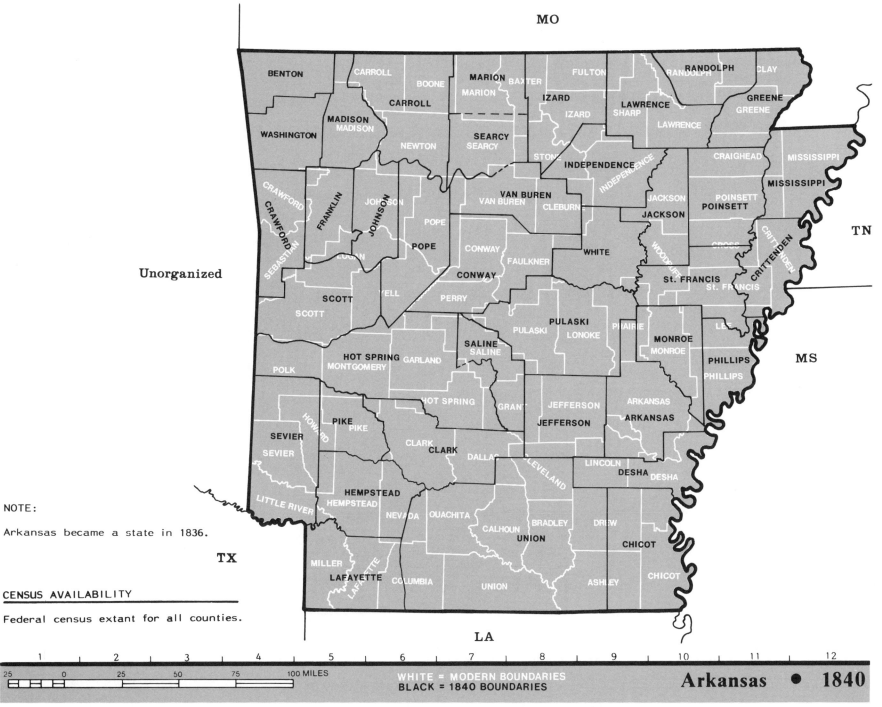

MO

BENTON

CARROLL

BOONE

MARION BAXTER

FULTON

RANDOLPH

RANDOLPH

CLAY

MADISON

CARROLL

MARION

IZARD

LAWRENCE

SHARP

GREENE

MADISON

CARROLL

IZARD

LAWRENCE

GREENE

WASHINGTON

NEWTON

SEARCY

SEARCY

CRAIGHEAD

MISSISSIPPI

STONE

INDEPENDENCE

CRAWFORD

FRANKLIN

JOHNSON

POPE

VAN BUREN

VAN BUREN

INDEPENDENCE

JACKSON

POINSETT

POINSETT

MISSISSIPPI

CRAWFORD

CLEBURN

JACKSON

SEBASTIAN

LOGAN

POPE

CONWAY

WHITE

WOODRUFF

CROSS

CRITTENDEN

TN

Unorganized

SCOTT

YELL

FAULKNER

CONWAY

ST. FRANCIS

CRITTENDEN

SCOTT

PERRY

PULASKI

PRAIRIE

St. FRANCIS

PULASKI

LONOKE

MONROE

LEE

HOT SPRING

MONTGOMERY

GARLAND

SALINE

SALINE

MONROE

PHILLIPS

MS

POLK

HOT SPRING

GRANT

JEFFERSON

ARKANSAS

PHILLIPS

PIKE

CLARK

JEFFERSON

ARKANSAS

NOTE:

HOWARD

PIKE

CLARK

DALLAS

LINCOLN

Arkansas became a state in 1836.

SEVIER

SEVIER

CLEVELAND

DESHA

DESHA

TX

HEMPSTEAD

HEMPSTEAD

NEVADA

OUACHITA

BRADLEY

DREW

LITTLE RIVER

CALHOUN

CHICOT

CENSUS AVAILABILITY

MILLER

LAFAYETTE

UNION

ASHLEY

CHICOT

Federal census extant for all counties.

LAFAYETTE

COLUMBIA

UNION

LA

| | 1 | | 2 | | 3 | | 4 | | 5 | | 6 | | 7 | | 8 | | 9 | | 10 | | 11 | | 12 |

25 0 25 50 75 100 MILES

Arkansas ● 1840

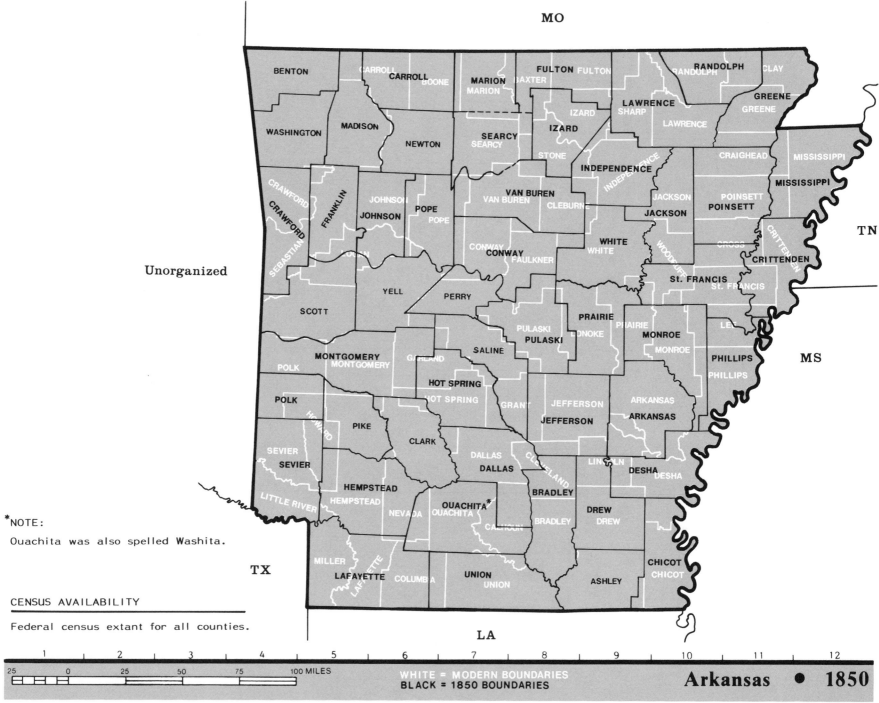

MO

BENTON

CARROLL
CARROLL
BOONE

FULTON FULTON
FULTON

RANDOLPH
RANDOLPH

CLAY

MARION
MARION

BAXTER

GREENE
GREENE

WASHINGTON

MADISON

NEWTON

SEARCY
SEARCY

IZARD
IZARD

LAWRENCE
SHARP

LAWRENCE

CRAIGHEAD

MISSISSIPPI

CRAWFORD
CRAWFORD

FRANKLIN

JOHNSON
JOHNSON

POPE
POPE

STONE

INDEPENDENCE
INDEPENDENCE

MISSISSIPPI

Unorganized

SEBASTIAN

LOGAN

VAN BUREN
VAN BUREN

CLEBURNE

JACKSON
JACKSON

POINSETT
POINSETT

YELL

CONWAY
CONWAY
FAULKNER

WHITE
WHITE

WOODRUFF

CROSS

CRITTENDEN

TN

PERRY

ST. FRANCIS
St. FRANCIS

CRITTENDEN

MONTGOMERY
MONTGOMERY

SCOTT

GARLAND

SALINE

PULASKI
PULASKI

LONOKE

PRAIRIE
PRAIRIE

MONROE
MONROE

LEE

PHILLIPS
PHILLIPS

MS

POLK

HOT SPRING
HOT SPRING

GRANT

JEFFERSON
JEFFERSON

ARKANSAS
ARKANSAS

POLK

HOWARD

PIKE

CLARK

DALLAS
DALLAS

CLEVELAND

LINCOLN

DESHA
DESHA

SEVIER
SEVIER

HEMPSTEAD
HEMPSTEAD

BRADLEY

DREW
DREW

LITTLE RIVER

NEVADA

OUACHITA*
OUACHITA

CALHOUN

BRADLEY

*NOTE:

Ouachita was also spelled Washita.

MILLER

LAFAYETTE
LAFAYETTE

COLUMBIA

UNION
UNION

ASHLEY

CHICOT
CHICOT

TX

CENSUS AVAILABILITY

Federal census extant for all counties.

LA

| 25 | 0 | 25 | 50 | 75 | 100 MILES |

1 2 3 4 5 6 7 8 9 10 11 12

WHITE = MODERN BOUNDARIES
BLACK = 1850 BOUNDARIES

Arkansas ● 1850

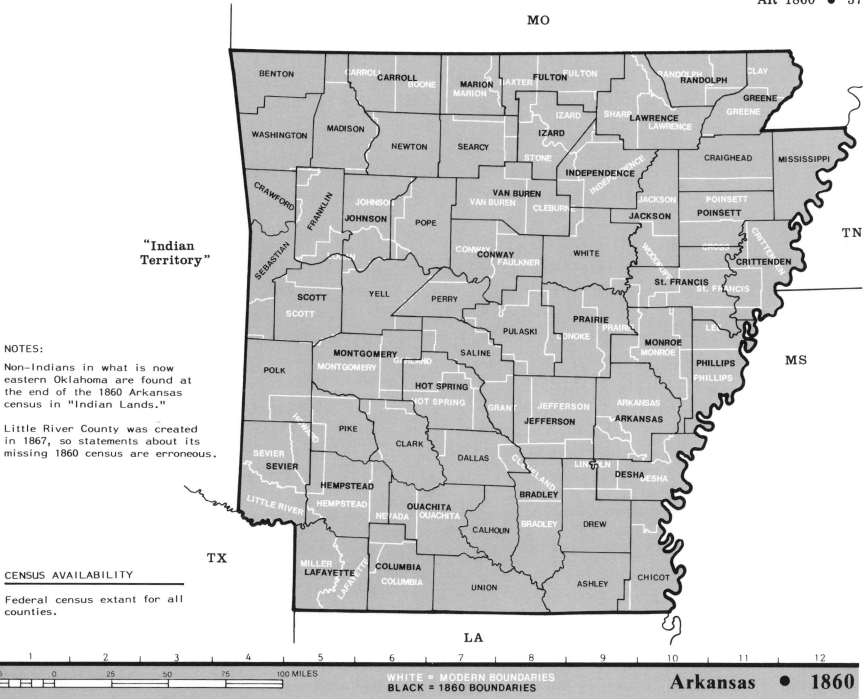

MO

"Indian
Territory"

TN

MS

NOTES:

Non-Indians in what is now
eastern Oklahoma are found at
the end of the 1860 Arkansas
census in "Indian Lands."

Little River County was created
in 1867, so statements about its
missing 1860 census are erroneous.

CENSUS AVAILABILITY

Federal census extant for all
counties.

TX

LA

BENTON, CARROLL, BOONE, MARION, BAXTER, FULTON, RANDOLPH, CLAY, GREENE, WASHINGTON, MADISON, NEWTON, SEARCY, IZARD, SHARP, LAWRENCE, STONE, INDEPENDENCE, CRAIGHEAD, MISSISSIPPI, CRAWFORD, FRANKLIN, JOHNSON, POPE, VAN BUREN, CLEBURNE, JACKSON, POINSETT, SEBASTIAN, CONWAY, FAULKNER, WHITE, WOODRUFF, CROSS, CRITTENDEN, SCOTT, YELL, PERRY, PULASKI, ST. FRANCIS, PRAIRIE, LEE, MONROE, POLK, MONTGOMERY, GARLAND, SALINE, LONOKE, PHILLIPS, HOT SPRING, GRANT, JEFFERSON, ARKANSAS, PIKE, CLARK, DALLAS, CLEVELAND, LINCOLN, DESHA, HOWARD, SEVIER, BRADLEY, DREW, HEMPSTEAD, LITTLE RIVER, NEVADA, OUACHITA, CALHOUN, MILLER, LAFAYETTE, COLUMBIA, UNION, ASHLEY, CHICOT

1 2 3 4 5 6 7 8 9 10 11 12

25 0 25 50 75 100 MILES

WHITE = MODERN BOUNDARIES
BLACK = 1860 BOUNDARIES

Arkansas ● 1860

MAP GUIDE TO THE U.S. FEDERAL CENSUSES, 1790-1920 by William Thorndale and William Dollarhide. Copyright 1987, all rights reserved.

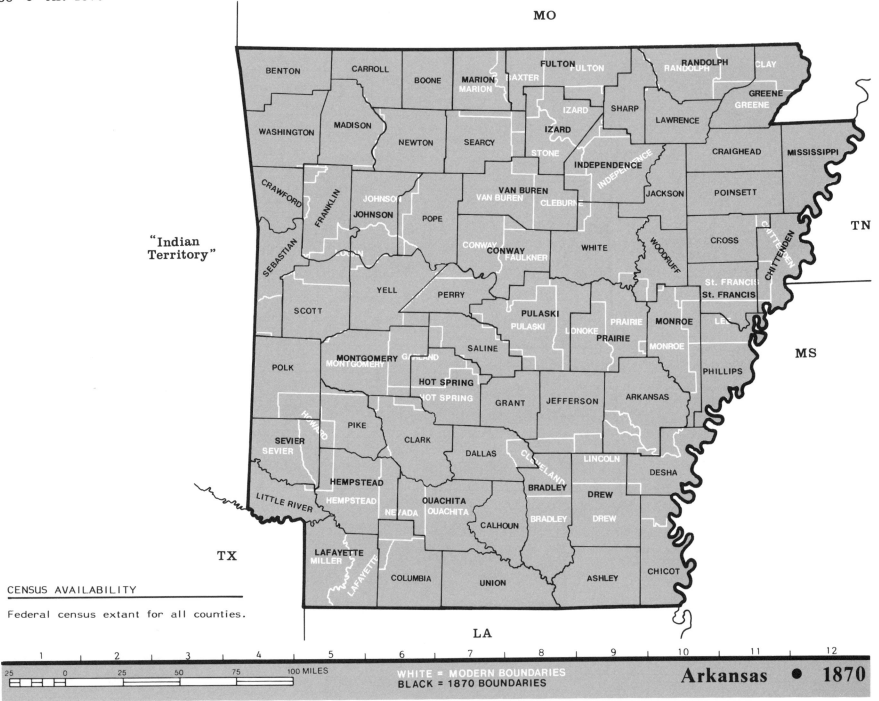

MO

BENTON   CARROLL   BOONE   MARION   MARION   BAXTER   FULTON   FULTON   RANDOLPH   RANDOLPH   CLAY

GREENE   GREENE

WASHINGTON   MADISON   NEWTON   SEARCY   IZARD   SHARP   LAWRENCE   CRAIGHEAD   MISSISSIPPI

STONE

INDEPENDENCE   INDEPENDENCE   POINSETT

CRAWFORD   FRANKLIN   JOHNSON   JOHNSON   VAN BUREN   VAN BUREN   CLEBURNE   JACKSON

"Indian Territory"

POPE   CONWAY   CONWAY   FAULKNER   WHITE   WOODRUFF   CROSS   CHITTENDEN

TN

SEBASTIAN   LOGAN   YELL   PERRY

SCOTT   PULASKI   PULASKI   PRAIRIE   MONROE   LEE   St. FRANCIS   St. FRANCIS

MONTGOMERY   MONTGOMERY   GARLAND   SALINE   LONOKE   PRAIRIE   MONROE   PHILLIPS

POLK   HOT SPRING   HOT SPRING   GRANT   JEFFERSON   ARKANSAS

MS

HOWARD   PIKE   CLARK   DALLAS   CLEVELAND   LINCOLN   DESHA

SEVIER   SEVIER   HEMPSTEAD   HEMPSTEAD   OUACHITA   OUACHITA   BRADLEY   DREW   DREW

LITTLE RIVER   NEVADA   CALHOUN   BRADLEY

TX

LAFAYETTE   MILLER   LAFAYETTE   COLUMBIA   UNION   ASHLEY   CHICOT

LA

CENSUS AVAILABILITY

Federal census extant for all counties.

25   0   25   50   75   100 MILES

1 2 3 4 5 6 7 8 9 10 11 12

WHITE = MODERN BOUNDARIES
BLACK = 1870 BOUNDARIES

Arkansas ● 1870

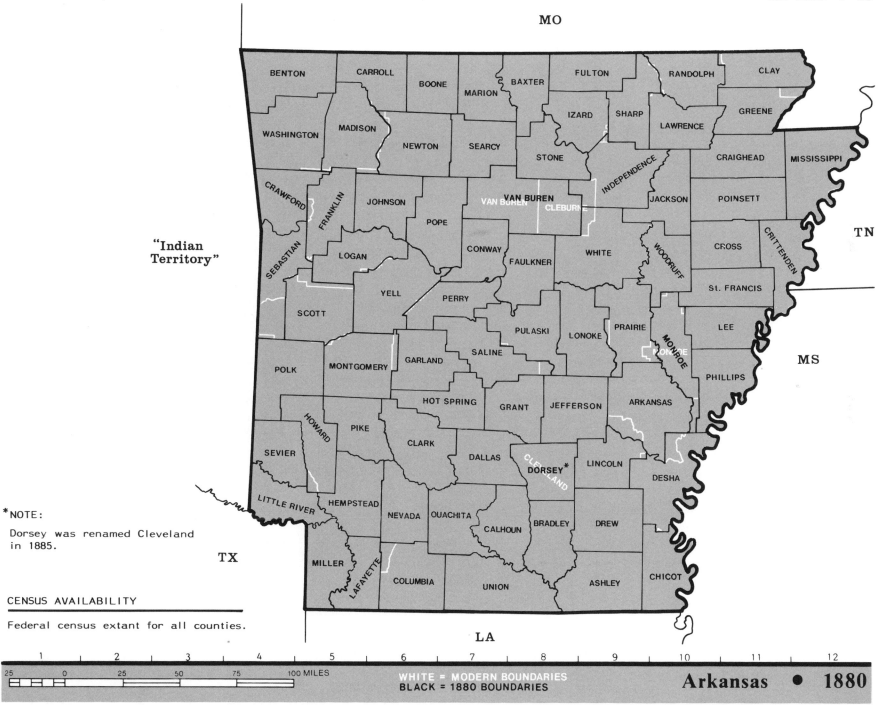

MO

BENTON | CARROLL | BOONE | MARION | BAXTER | FULTON | RANDOLPH | CLAY

WASHINGTON | MADISON | NEWTON | SEARCY | IZARD | SHARP | LAWRENCE | GREENE

"Indian Territory"

CRAWFORD | FRANKLIN | JOHNSON | STONE | INDEPENDENCE | CRAIGHEAD | MISSISSIPPI

VAN BUREN | CLEBURNE | JACKSON | POINSETT

TN

SEBASTIAN | LOGAN | POPE | CONWAY | FAULKNER | WHITE | WOODRUFF | CROSS | CRITTENDEN

YELL | PERRY | St. FRANCIS

SCOTT | PULASKI | LONOKE | PRAIRIE | LEE

POLK | MONTGOMERY | GARLAND | SALINE | MONROE | MS

PHILLIPS

HOWARD | PIKE | HOT SPRING | GRANT | JEFFERSON | ARKANSAS

SEVIER | CLARK | DALLAS | DORSEY* | LINCOLN | DESHA

*NOTE:

Dorsey was renamed Cleveland in 1885.

LITTLE RIVER | HEMPSTEAD | NEVADA | OUACHITA | CALHOUN | BRADLEY | DREW

TX

MILLER | LAFAYETTE | COLUMBIA | UNION | ASHLEY | CHICOT

CENSUS AVAILABILITY

Federal census extant for all counties.

LA

| 1 | 2 | 3 | 4 | 5 | 6 | 7 | 8 | 9 | 10 | 11 | 12 |

25   0   25   50   75   100 MILES

WHITE = MODERN BOUNDARIES
BLACK = 1880 BOUNDARIES

Arkansas ● 1880

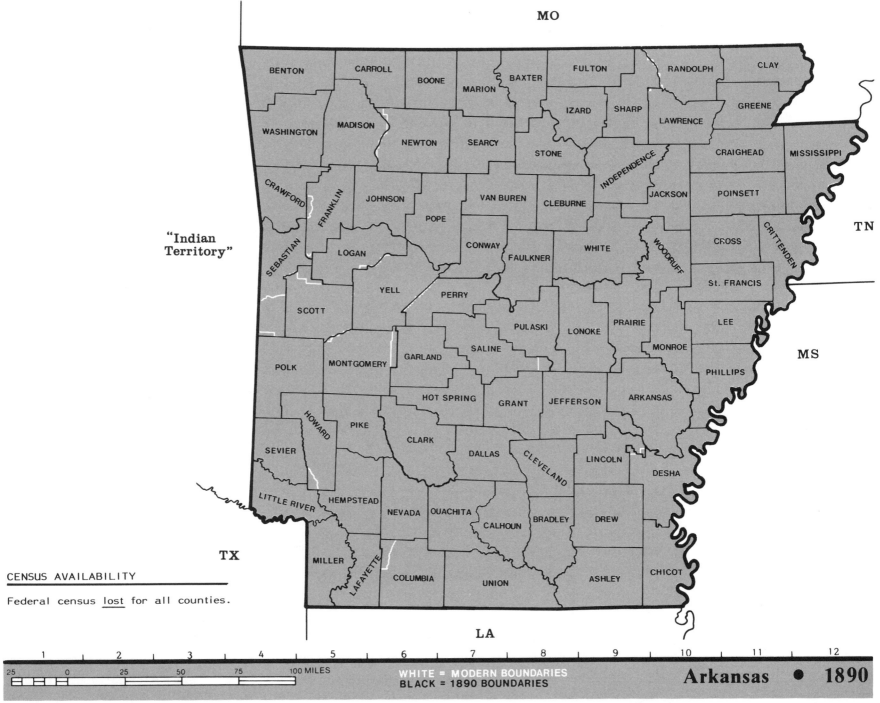

MO

BENTON CARROLL BOONE MARION BAXTER FULTON RANDOLPH CLAY

WASHINGTON MADISON NEWTON SEARCY IZARD SHARP LAWRENCE GREENE

CRAWFORD FRANKLIN JOHNSON VAN BUREN CLEBURNE INDEPENDENCE JACKSON CRAIGHEAD MISSISSIPPI

STONE POINSETT

"Indian
Territory"

SEBASTIAN LOGAN POPE CONWAY FAULKNER WHITE WOODRUFF CROSS CRITTENDEN

TN

YELL PERRY St. FRANCIS

SCOTT PULASKI LONOKE PRAIRIE LEE

POLK MONTGOMERY GARLAND SALINE MONROE

HOWARD PIKE HOT SPRING GRANT JEFFERSON ARKANSAS PHILLIPS

MS

SEVIER CLARK DALLAS CLEVELAND LINCOLN DESHA

LITTLE RIVER HEMPSTEAD NEVADA OUACHITA CALHOUN BRADLEY DREW

TX

MILLER LAFAYETTE COLUMBIA UNION ASHLEY CHICOT

LA

CENSUS AVAILABILITY

Federal census lost for all counties.

1   2   3   4   5   6   7   8   9   10   11   12

25   0   25   50   75   100 MILES

WHITE = MODERN BOUNDARIES
BLACK = 1890 BOUNDARIES

Arkansas ● **1890**

MAP GUIDE TO THE U.S. FEDERAL CENSUSES, 1790–1920 by William Thorndale and William Dollarhide. Copyright 1987, all rights reserved.

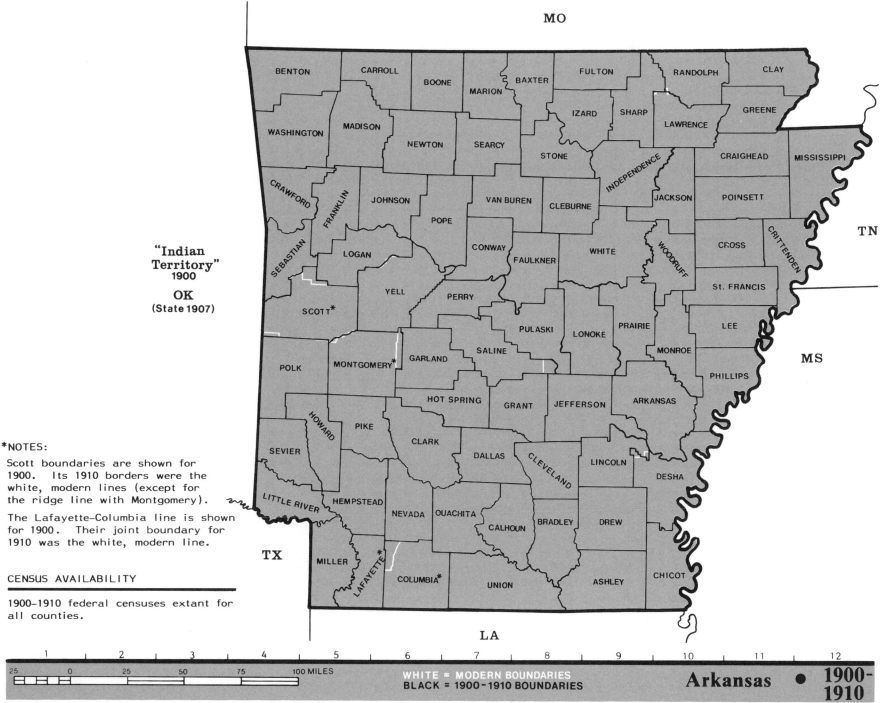

MO

BENTON
CARROLL
BOONE
MARION
BAXTER
FULTON
RANDOLPH
CLAY

WASHINGTON
MADISON
NEWTON
SEARCY
IZARD
SHARP
LAWRENCE
GREENE
STONE
CRAIGHEAD
MISSISSIPPI

CRAWFORD
FRANKLIN
JOHNSON
VAN BUREN
CLEBURNE
INDEPENDENCE
JACKSON
POINSETT

SEBASTIAN
POPE
CONWAY
WHITE
WOODRUFF
CROSS
CRITTENDEN

LOGAN
FAULKNER

YELL
PERRY
St. FRANCIS

SCOTT*

PRAIRIE
LEE

MONTGOMERY*
GARLAND
SALINE
PULASKI
LONOKE
MONROE

POLK
HOT SPRING
GRANT
JEFFERSON
ARKANSAS
PHILLIPS

HOWARD
PIKE
CLARK

SEVIER
DALLAS
CLEVELAND
LINCOLN
DESHA

LITTLE RIVER
HEMPSTEAD
NEVADA
OUACHITA
CALHOUN
BRADLEY
DREW

MILLER
LAFAYETTE*
COLUMBIA*
UNION
ASHLEY
CHICOT

TX

LA

TN

MS

"Indian
Territory"
1900

OK
(State 1907)

*NOTES:

Scott boundaries are shown for
1900. Its 1910 borders were the
white, modern lines (except for
the ridge line with Montgomery).

The Lafayette–Columbia line is shown
for 1900. Their joint boundary for
1910 was the white, modern line.

CENSUS AVAILABILITY

1900–1910 federal censuses extant for
all counties.

| 1 | 2 | 3 | 4 | 5 | 6 | 7 | 8 | 9 | 10 | 11 | 12 |

25   0   25   50   75   100 MILES

WHITE = MODERN BOUNDARIES
BLACK = 1900-1910 BOUNDARIES

Arkansas ● 1900-1910

MAP GUIDE TO THE U.S. FEDERAL CENSUSES, 1790-1920 by William Thorndale and William Dollarhide. Copyright 1987, all rights reserved.

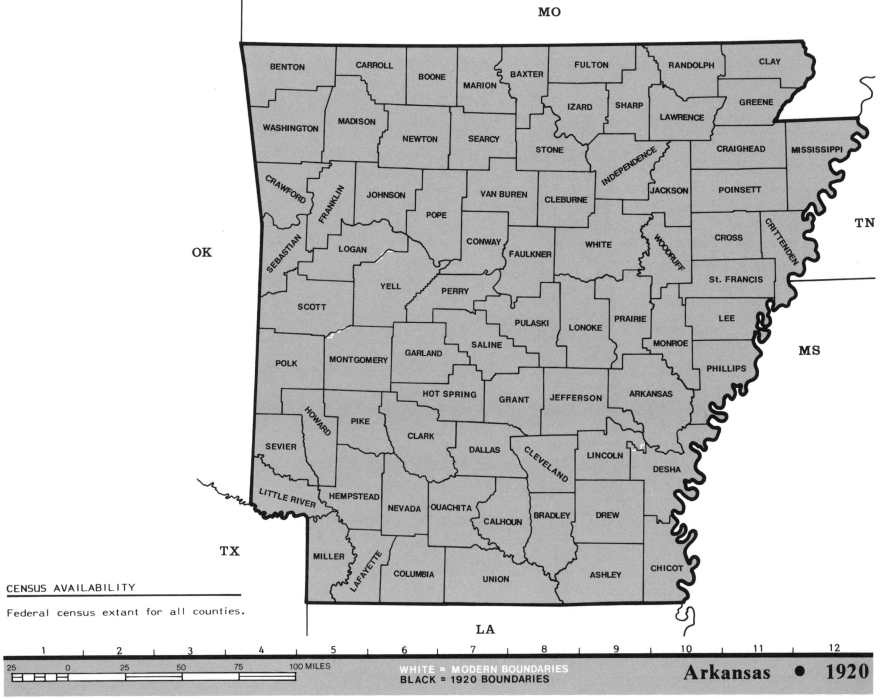

MO

BENTON

CARROLL

BOONE

MARION

BAXTER

FULTON

RANDOLPH

CLAY

WASHINGTON

MADISON

NEWTON

SEARCY

IZARD

SHARP

LAWRENCE

GREENE

STONE

INDEPENDENCE

CRAIGHEAD

MISSISSIPPI

CRAWFORD

FRANKLIN

JOHNSON

VAN BUREN

CLEBURNE

JACKSON

POINSETT

OK

SEBASTIAN

LOGAN

POPE

CONWAY

FAULKNER

WHITE

WOODRUFF

CROSS

CRITTENDEN

TN

YELL

PERRY

St. FRANCIS

SCOTT

PULASKI

LONOKE

PRAIRIE

LEE

POLK

MONTGOMERY

GARLAND

SALINE

MONROE

PHILLIPS

MS

HOT SPRING

GRANT

JEFFERSON

ARKANSAS

HOWARD

PIKE

SEVIER

CLARK

DALLAS

CLEVELAND

LINCOLN

DESHA

LITTLE RIVER

HEMPSTEAD

NEVADA

OUACHITA

BRADLEY

DREW

TX

MILLER

LAFAYETTE

COLUMBIA

CALHOUN

UNION

ASHLEY

CHICOT

LA

CENSUS AVAILABILITY

Federal census extant for all counties.

| 1 | 2 | 3 | 4 | 5 | 6 | 7 | 8 | 9 | 10 | 11 | 12 |

25   0   25   50   75   100 MILES

Arkansas ● 1920

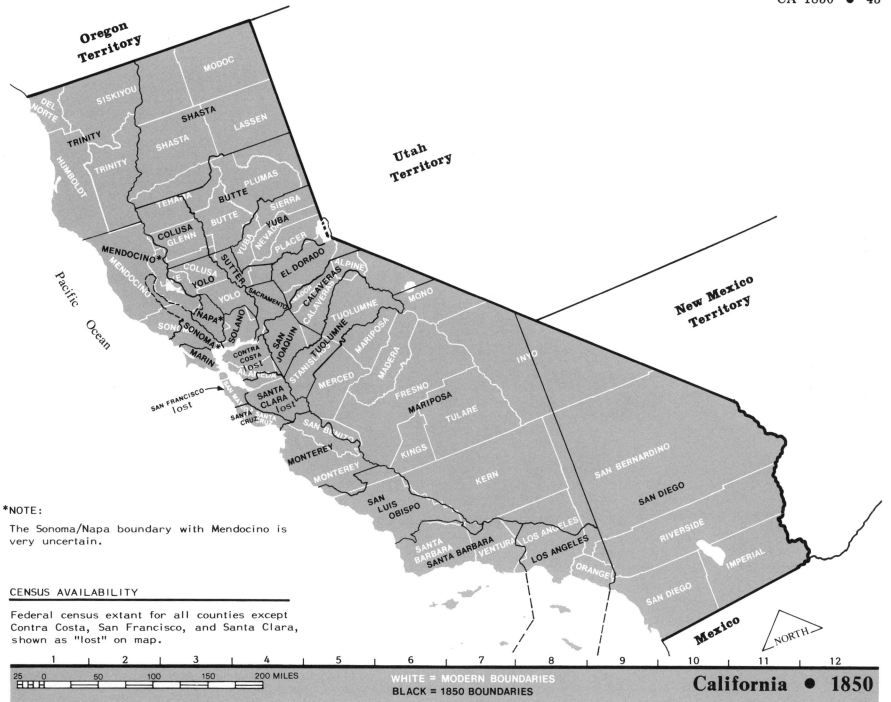

Oregon Territory

Utah Territory

New Mexico Territory

Pacific Ocean

Mexico

DEL NORTE

SISKIYOU

MODOC

TRINITY

SHASTA

SHASTA

LASSEN

HUMBOLDT

TRINITY

TEHAMA

BUTTE

PLUMAS

MENDOCINO*

COLUSA GLENN

BUTTE

SIERRA

YUBA

YUBA

NEVADA

PLACER

MENDOCINO

COLUSA

SUTTER

EL DORADO

ALPINE

YOLO

YOLO

SACRAMENTO

CALAVERAS

CALAVERAS

MONO

NAPA*

SONOMA

SONOMA*

SOLANO

SAN JOAQUIN

TUOLUMNE

TUOLUMNE

MARIN

CONTRA COSTA lost

ALAMEDA

STANISLAUS

MARIPOSA

MADERA

INYO

SANTA CLARA lost

SAN FRANCISCO lost

SAN MATEO

MERCED

FRESNO

SANTA CRUZ

SAN BENITO

MARIPOSA

MONTEREY

TULARE

KINGS

MONTEREY

KERN

SAN BERNARDINO

SAN LUIS OBISPO

SAN DIEGO

SANTA BARBARA

SANTA BARBARA

VENTURA

LOS ANGELES

LOS ANGELES

RIVERSIDE

IMPERIAL

ORANGE

SAN DIEGO

NORTH

*NOTE:

The Sonoma/Napa boundary with Mendocino is very uncertain.

CENSUS AVAILABILITY

Federal census extant for all counties except Contra Costa, San Francisco, and Santa Clara, shown as "lost" on map.

1   2   3   4   5   6   7   8   9   10   11   12

25 0   50   100   150   200 MILES

WHITE = MODERN BOUNDARIES
BLACK = 1850 BOUNDARIES

California ● 1850

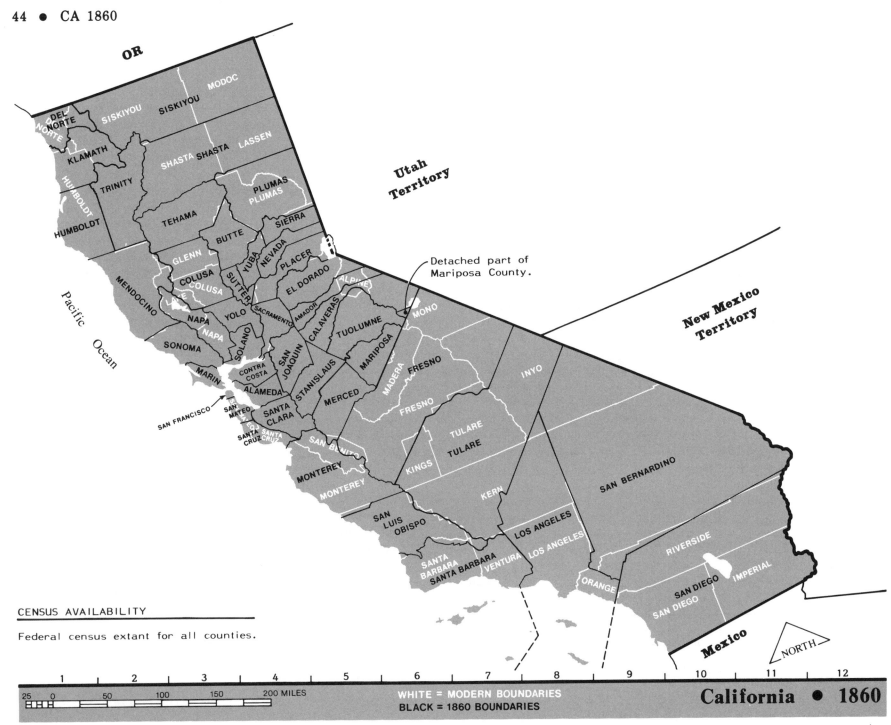

OR

DEL NORTE
SISKIYOU
SISKIYOU
MODOC

KLAMATH

HUMBOLDT

TRINITY

SHASTA SHASTA
LASSEN

PLUMAS
PLUMAS

TEHAMA

Utah
Territory

Pacific

Ocean

SIERRA

BUTTE

GLENN
NEVADA
PLACER

COLUSA
COLUSA
YUBA
SUTTER

LAKE

MENDOCINO

EL DORADO

ALPINE

Detached part of
Mariposa County.

NAPA
YOLO
SACRAMENTO
AMADOR
CALAVERAS

NAPA

SONOMA
SOLANO

MONO

TUOLUMNE

New Mexico
Territory

CONTRA
COSTA

SAN
JOAQUIN

MARIPOSA

MADERA

MARIN

ALAMEDA
STANISLAUS

FRESNO

SAN FRANCISCO
SAN
MATEO

SANTA
CLARA

MERCED

FRESNO

INYO

SANTA
CRUZ SANTA
CRUZ

SAN BENITO

TULARE
TULARE

MONTEREY

KINGS

MONTEREY

SAN BERNARDINO

SAN LUIS
OBISPO

KERN

LOS ANGELES
LOS ANGELES

SANTA
BARBARA
SANTA BARBARA
VENTURA

RIVERSIDE

ORANGE

SAN DIEGO
SAN DIEGO

IMPERIAL

Mexico

NORTH

CENSUS AVAILABILITY

Federal census extant for all counties.

| 1 | 2 | 3 | 4 | 5 | 6 | 7 | 8 | 9 | 10 | 11 | 12 |

25 0   50   100   150   200 MILES

WHITE = MODERN BOUNDARIES
BLACK = 1860 BOUNDARIES

California ● 1860

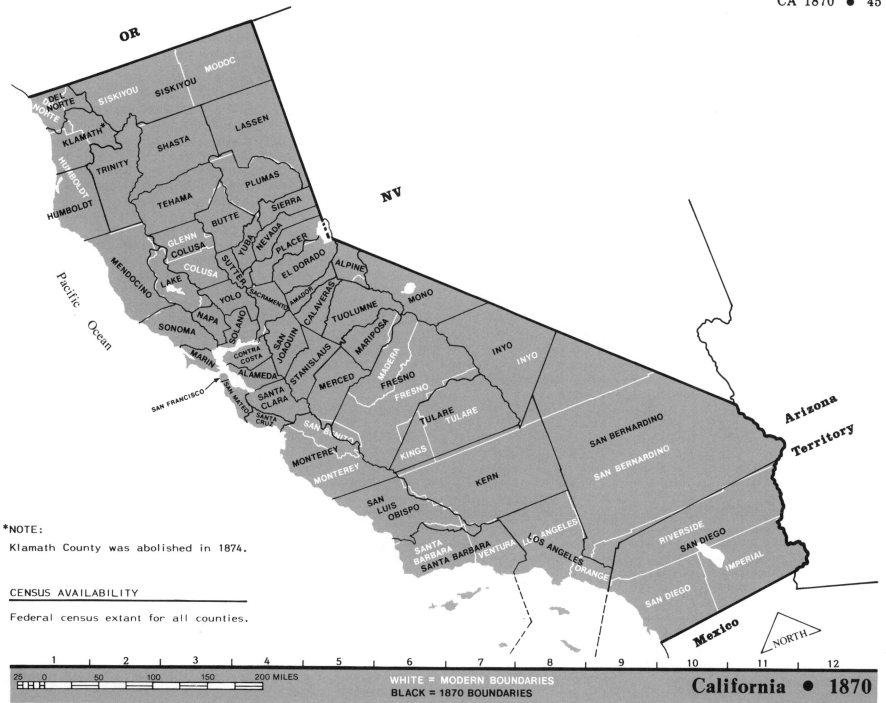

OR

NV

Arizona
Territory

Pacific
Ocean

Mexico

DEL
NORTE

SISKIYOU   SISKIYOU   MODOC

KLAMATH *

HUMBOLDT

HUMBOLDT

TRINITY

SHASTA   LASSEN

TEHAMA   PLUMAS

BUTTE   SIERRA

GLENN   NEVADA
COLUSA   YUBA

MENDOCINO   COLUSA   SUTTER   PLACER

LAKE   EL DORADO   ALPINE

YOLO   SACRAMENTO   AMADOR   MONO

NAPA   CALAVERAS   TUOLUMNE

SONOMA   SOLANO

MARIN   CONTRA   SAN   STANISLAUS   MARIPOSA
COSTA   JOAQUIN   MADERA   INYO

ALAMEDA   INYO

SAN FRANCISCO   SANTA   MERCED   FRESNO
CLARA   FRESNO

SAN MATEO

SANTA
CRUZ   SAN BENITO   TULARE

TULARE   SAN BERNARDINO

MONTEREY   KINGS

KERN   SAN BERNARDINO

MONTEREY

SAN
LUIS
OBISPO   RIVERSIDE   SAN DIEGO

LOS ANGELES   IMPERIAL

SANTA
BARBARA   LOS ANGELES

SANTA BARBARA   VENTURA   ORANGE   SAN DIEGO

NORTH

*NOTE:

Klamath County was abolished in 1874.

CENSUS AVAILABILITY

Federal census extant for all counties.

1   2   3   4   5   6   7   8   9   10   11   12

25   0   50   100   150   200 MILES

WHITE = MODERN BOUNDARIES
BLACK = 1870 BOUNDARIES

California ● 1870

MAP GUIDE TO THE U.S. FEDERAL CENSUSES, 1790–1920 by William Thorndale and William Dollarhide. Copyright 1987, all rights reserved.

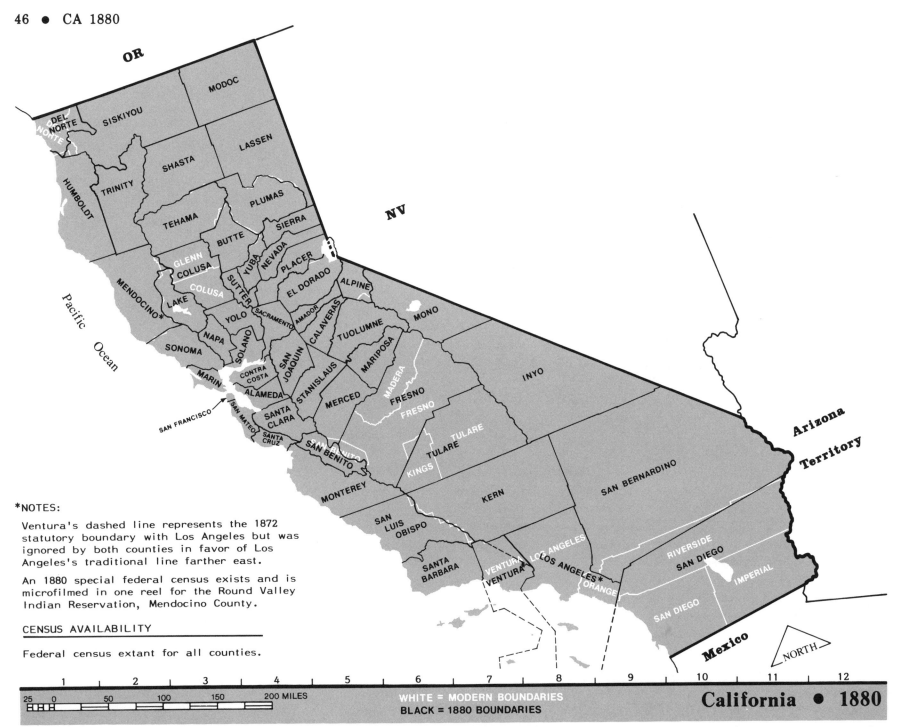

OR

NV

DEL NORTE
SISKIYOU
MODOC
LASSEN
SHASTA
TRINITY
HUMBOLDT
TEHAMA
PLUMAS
BUTTE
SIERRA
GLENN
COLUSA
YUBA
NEVADA
PLACER
COLUSA
SUTTER
EL DORADO
ALPINE
LAKE
MENDOCINO*
YOLO
SACRAMENTO
AMADOR
CALAVERAS
MONO
Pacific Ocean
NAPA
SOLANO
TUOLUMNE
SONOMA
CONTRA COSTA
SAN JOAQUIN
STANISLAUS
MARIPOSA
MARIN
ALAMEDA
MADERA
INYO
SAN FRANCISCO
SAN MATEO
SANTA CLARA
MERCED
FRESNO
SANTA CRUZ
SAN BENITO
FRESNO
SAN BENITO
TULARE
MONTEREY
KINGS
TULARE
KERN
SAN BERNARDINO
SAN LUIS OBISPO
VENTURA
LOS ANGELES
SANTA BARBARA
VENTURA*
LOS ANGELES*
ORANGE
RIVERSIDE
SAN DIEGO
IMPERIAL
SAN DIEGO

Arizona Territory

Mexico

NORTH

NOTES:

Ventura's dashed line represents the 1872 statutory boundary with Los Angeles but was ignored by both counties in favor of Los Angeles's traditional line farther east.

An 1880 special federal census exists and is microfilmed in one reel for the Round Valley Indian Reservation, Mendocino County.

CENSUS AVAILABILITY

Federal census extant for all counties.

1   2   3   4   5   6   7   8   9   10   11   12

25   0   50   100   150   200 MILES

WHITE = MODERN BOUNDARIES
BLACK = 1880 BOUNDARIES

California ● 1880

OR

MODOC

SISKIYOU

DEL
NORTE

LASSEN

SHASTA

HUMBOLDT

TRINITY

PLUMAS

NV

TEHAMA

SIERRA

BUTTE

GLENN
COLUSA

YUBA NEVADA

PLACER

MENDOCINO

SUTTER

COLUSA

LAKE

EL DORADO

ALPINE

YOLO

SACRAMENTO AMADOR

NAPA

SOLANO

CALAVERAS

MONO

SONOMA

TUOLUMNE

MARIN

CONTRA
COSTA

SAN
JOAQUIN

MARIPOSA

ALAMEDA

STANISLAUS

MADERA

SAN FRANCISCO

SAN MATEO

SANTA
CLARA

MERCED

FRESNO

INYO

SANTA
CRUZ

FRESNO

SAN BENITO

TULARE

TULARE

KINGS

MONTEREY

KERN

SAN BERNARDINO

SAN
LUIS
OBISPO

Pacific

Ocean

Arizona

Territory

SANTA
BARBARA

VENTURA

LOS ANGELES

RIVERSIDE

ORANGE

SAN DIEGO

IMPERIAL

SAN DIEGO

Mexico

NORTH

CENSUS AVAILABILITY

Federal census <u>lost</u> for all counties.

1   2   3   4   5   6   7   8   9   10   11   12

25 0   50   100   150   200 MILES

WHITE = MODERN BOUNDARIES
BLACK = 1890 BOUNDARIES

California ● 1890

MAP GUIDE TO THE U.S. FEDERAL CENSUSES, 1790–1920 by William Thorndale and William Dollarhide. Copyright 1987, all rights reserved.

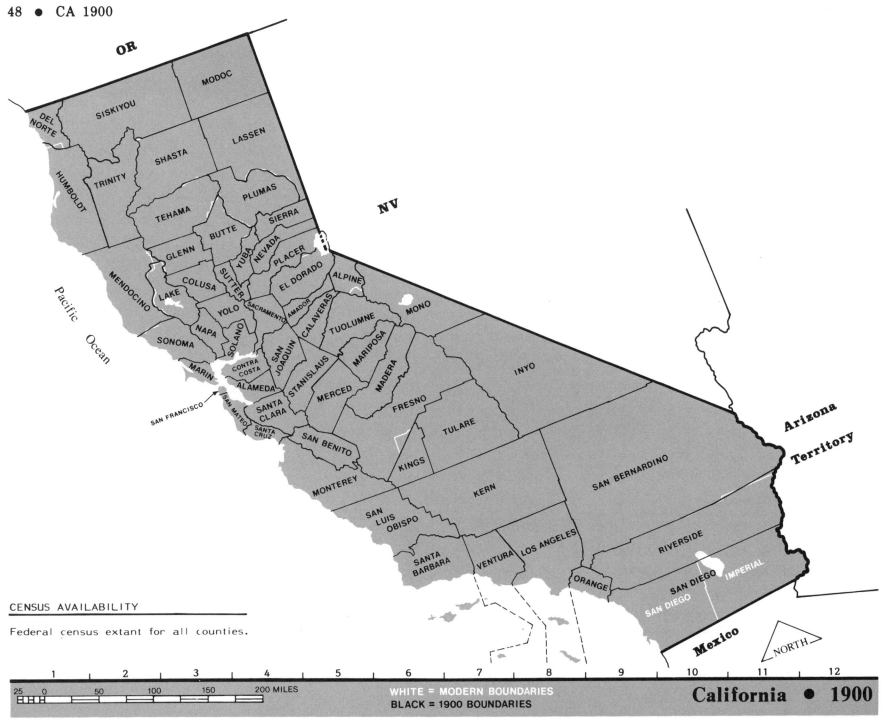

OR

MODOC

SISKIYOU

DEL
NORTE

LASSEN

SHASTA

TRINITY

HUMBOLDT

PLUMAS

NV

TEHAMA

SIERRA

BUTTE

GLENN

NEVADA

YUBA

PLACER

COLUSA

SUTTER

EL DORADO

ALPINE

MENDOCINO

LAKE

YOLO

SACRAMENTO

AMADOR

CALAVERAS

MONO

NAPA

SOLANO

TUOLUMNE

Pacific

SONOMA

CONTRA
COSTA

SAN
JOAQUIN

MARIPOSA

Ocean

MARIN

ALAMEDA

STANISLAUS

MADERA

INYO

SAN FRANCISCO

SAN MATEO

SANTA
CLARA

MERCED

SANTA
CRUZ

FRESNO

SAN BENITO

TULARE

Arizona

MONTEREY

KINGS

Territory

KERN

SAN BERNARDINO

SAN
LUIS
OBISPO

RIVERSIDE

LOS ANGELES

SANTA
BARBARA

VENTURA

ORANGE

SAN DIEGO

IMPERIAL

SAN DIEGO

Mexico

NORTH

CENSUS AVAILABILITY

Federal census extant for all counties.

| 1 | 2 | 3 | 4 | 5 | 6 | 7 | 8 | 9 | 10 | 11 | 12 |

25 0   50   100   150   200 MILES

WHITE = MODERN BOUNDARIES
BLACK = 1900 BOUNDARIES

California ● **1900**

MAP GUIDE TO THE U.S. FEDERAL CENSUSES, 1790-1920 by William Thorndale and William Dollarhide. Copyright 1987, all rights reserved.

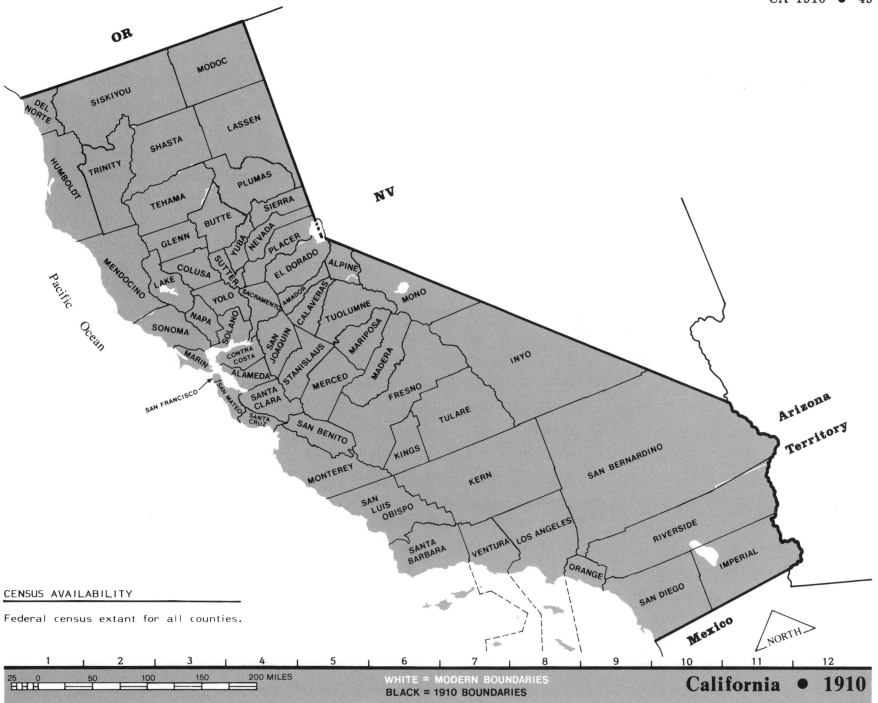

OR

MODOC

SISKIYOU

DEL
NORTE

LASSEN

HUMBOLDT

SHASTA

TRINITY

PLUMAS

NV

TEHAMA

SIERRA

BUTTE

GLENN

YUBA

NEVADA

PLACER

MENDOCINO

COLUSA

SUTTER

EL DORADO

ALPINE

LAKE

YOLO

SACRAMENTO

AMADOR

MONO

Pacific

CALAVERAS

TUOLUMNE

NAPA

SOLANO

SONOMA

Ocean

MARIN

CONTRA
COSTA

SAN
JOAQUIN

STANISLAUS

MARIPOSA

MADERA

ALAMEDA

INYO

SAN FRANCISCO

SAN MATEO

SANTA
CLARA

MERCED

FRESNO

Arizona

SANTA
CRUZ

SAN BENITO

TULARE

Territory

KINGS

MONTEREY

KERN

SAN BERNARDINO

SAN LUIS
OBISPO

RIVERSIDE

SANTA
BARBARA

VENTURA

LOS ANGELES

IMPERIAL

ORANGE

SAN DIEGO

Mexico

NORTH

CENSUS AVAILABILITY

Federal census extant for all counties.

1   2   3   4   5   6   7   8   9   10   11   12

25 0   50   100   150   200 MILES

WHITE = MODERN BOUNDARIES
BLACK = 1910 BOUNDARIES

California ● 1910

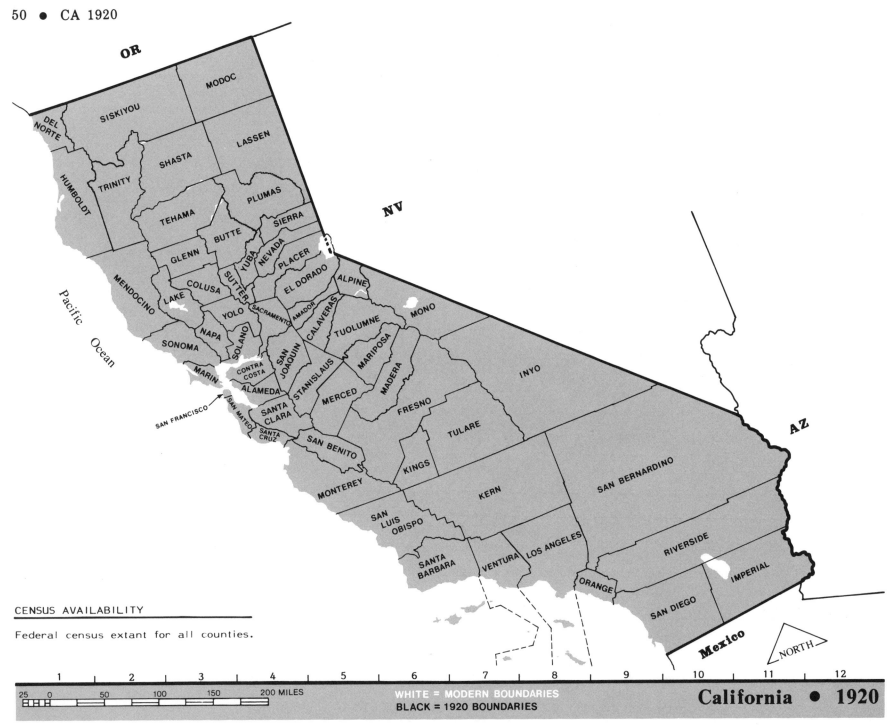

OR

MODOC

SISKIYOU

DEL NORTE

LASSEN

SHASTA

HUMBOLDT

TRINITY

PLUMAS

TEHAMA

NV

BUTTE

SIERRA

GLENN

YUBA

NEVADA

PLACER

COLUSA

SUTTER

EL DORADO

ALPINE

MENDOCINO

LAKE

SACRAMENTO

AMADOR

YOLO

CALAVERAS

MONO

NAPA

SOLANO

TUOLUMNE

SONOMA

CONTRA COSTA

SAN JOAQUIN

MARIPOSA

MARIN

ALAMEDA

STANISLAUS

MADERA

SAN FRANCISCO

SAN MATEO

SANTA CLARA

MERCED

FRESNO

INYO

SANTA CRUZ

SAN BENITO

Pacific Ocean

KINGS

TULARE

MONTEREY

KERN

SAN BERNARDINO

SAN LUIS OBISPO

SANTA BARBARA

VENTURA

LOS ANGELES

RIVERSIDE

AZ

ORANGE

IMPERIAL

SAN DIEGO

Mexico

NORTH

CENSUS AVAILABILITY

Federal census extant for all counties.

1 2 3 4 5 6 7 8 9 10 11 12

25 0 50 100 150 200 MILES

WHITE = MODERN BOUNDARIES
BLACK = 1920 BOUNDARIES

California ● 1920

MAP GUIDE TO THE U.S. FEDERAL CENSUSES, 1790-1920 by William Thorndale and William Dollarhide. Copyright 1987, all rights reserved.

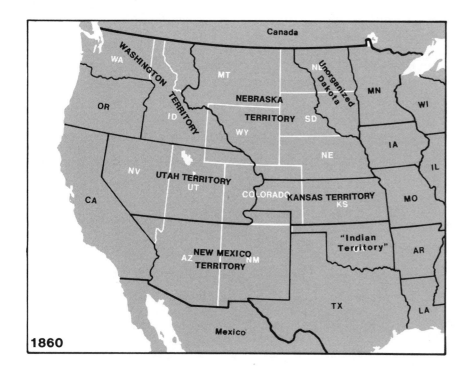

1860

CENSUS AVAILABILITY - COLORADO 1860

In 1860, what is now Colorado lay in four territorial jurisdictions, of which three had censuses taken in the area. All of these censuses are extant:

KANSAS TERRITORY

The mining camps and towns in the part of Colorado then Kansas Territory were enumerated in Arapahoe County. Five paper counties created by Kansas Territory in parts of the illustrated Arapahoe are omitted from the enlarged 1860 census map. Also not shown are the ephemeral counties legislated by the "Territory of Jefferson," the local government not recognized by Congress.

NEBRASKA TERRITORY

Boulder, Altoona, and other northeastern Colorado towns were enumerated at the end of the Nebraska census as the unorganized area west of 101°30'.

NEW MEXICO TERRITORY

The Rio Grande Valley in Colorado (also known as the San Luis Valley) was enumerated in Taos County. Whether any individuals in Mora County's 1860 schedules lived north of the present-day Colorado-New Mexico line was not determined, but it is unlikely.

UTAH TERRITORY

The dashed lines on the enlarged map for 1860 show the statutory eastern limits of five Utah counties, but this Colorado area was unsettled by whites in 1860 and not enumerated.

NORTH PARK - COLORADO 1870-1885

The valley called North Park, which is present-day Jackson County, lies east of the Continental Divide, as the enlarged 1860 map shows. The valley was not settled by whites in 1860 and 1870, but in 1870 was assumed by local officials to be part of Summit County. North Park in the 1880 and 1885 censuses was enumerated as part of Grand County, despite being claimed by Larimer. In 1886, the Colorado Supreme Court ruled that statutorily North Park had been in Larimer County since 1861.

The 1860 federal census taken on the Great Plains had some jurisdictional anomalies worth noting. Modern Oklahoma as the "Indian Territory" was enumerated for non-Indians, the name lists now found at the end of the Arkansas census. What became Colorado was part of four territories, as explained below. The Dakota remnant of Minnesota Territory -- the western part of the territory not included in the state of Minnesota in 1858 -- was enumerated in 1860 despite having no territorial government. Further, the trading posts in Nebraska Territory on the west bank of the Missouri River were enumerated with unorganized Dakota, as was one post on the Yellowstone River in what is now Montana. The last part of the microfilmed 1860 census for Nebraska Territory contains the Fort Laramie area in present-day Wyoming, some Colorado mining towns, the U.S. Army's Fort Randall in present-day extreme southern South Dakota, the Pawnee Indian Reservation in Nebraska, and 24 names in unorganized country presumably within today's Nebraska.

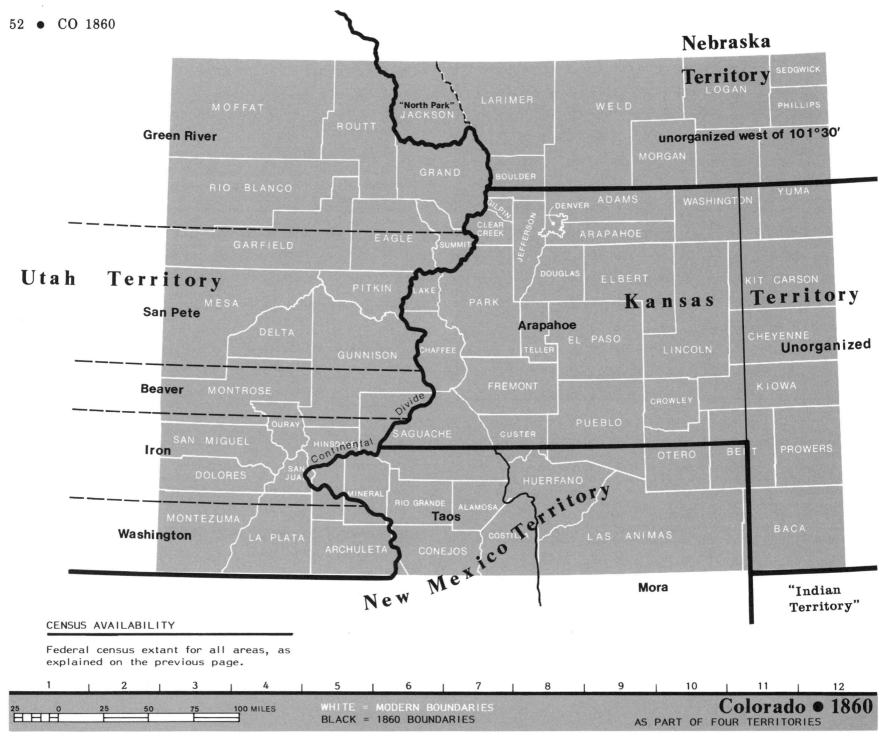

Nebraska Territory

Utah Territory

Kansas Territory

New Mexico Territory

"Indian Territory"

Green River

San Pete

Beaver

Iron

Washington

MOFFAT
ROUTT
"North Park" JACKSON
LARIMER
WELD
SEDGWICK
LOGAN
PHILLIPS

unorganized west of 101°30'

MORGAN

RIO BLANCO
GRAND
BOULDER
GILPIN
CLEAR CREEK
DENVER
ADAMS
WASHINGTON
YUMA

GARFIELD
EAGLE
SUMMIT
JEFFERSON
ARAPAHOE

MESA
PITKIN
LAKE
DOUGLAS
ELBERT
KIT CARSON

DELTA
PARK
Arapahoe
EL PASO
TELLER
LINCOLN
CHEYENNE

Unorganized

GUNNISON
CHAFFEE
FREMONT
KIOWA

MONTROSE
Divide
CROWLEY

OURAY
HINSDALE
Continental
SAGUACHE
CUSTER
PUEBLO
OTERO
BENT
PROWERS

SAN MIGUEL
SAN JUAN
HUERFANO

DOLORES
MINERAL
RIO GRANDE
ALAMOSA

MONTEZUMA
Taos
COSTILLA
LAS ANIMAS
BACA

LA PLATA
ARCHULETA
CONEJOS

Mora

CENSUS AVAILABILITY

Federal census extant for all areas, as explained on the previous page.

1 2 3 4 5 6 7 8 9 10 11 12

25 0 25 50 75 100 MILES

WHITE = MODERN BOUNDARIES
BLACK = 1860 BOUNDARIES

Colorado ● 1860
AS PART OF FOUR TERRITORIES

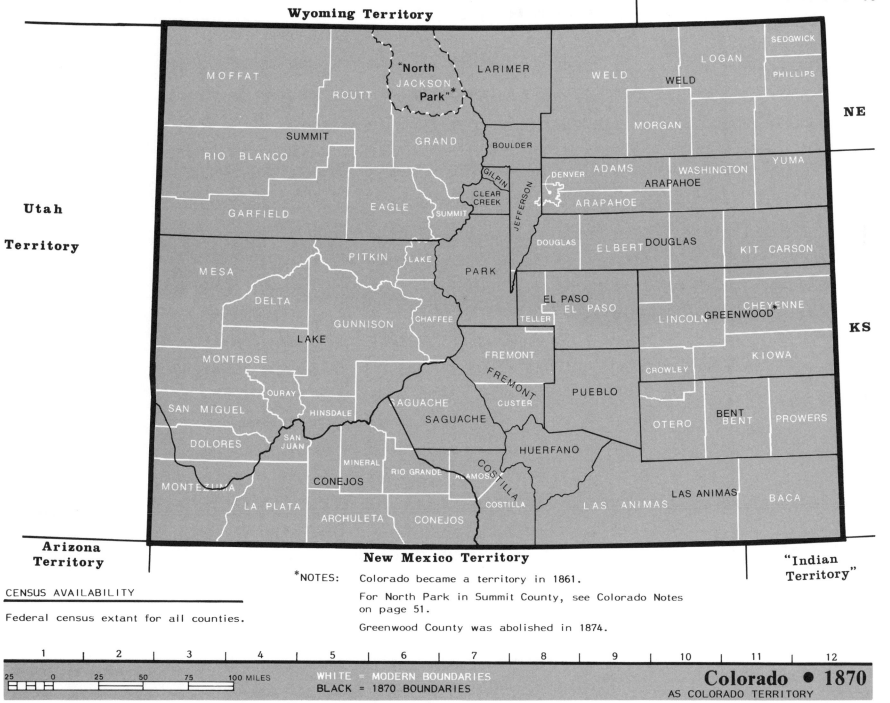

Wyoming Territory

MOFFAT

ROUTT

"North JACKSON Park"*

LARIMER

SEDGWICK

LOGAN

PHILLIPS

WELD

WELD

NE

SUMMIT

GRAND

BOULDER

MORGAN

RIO BLANCO

GILPIN

DENVER

ADAMS

WASHINGTON

YUMA

Utah

CLEAR CREEK

ARAPAHOE

Territory

GARFIELD

EAGLE

SUMMIT

JEFFERSON

ARAPAHOE

MESA

PITKIN

LAKE

DOUGLAS

ELBERT

DOUGLAS

KIT CARSON

PARK

DELTA

EL PASO

EL PASO

CHEYENNE*

MONTROSE

GUNNISON

CHAFFEE

LINCOLN

GREENWOOD

KS

LAKE

FREMONT

KIOWA

OURAY

FREMONT

CROWLEY

SAN MIGUEL

HINSDALE

SAGUACHE

CUSTER

PUEBLO

DOLORES

SAN JUAN

SAGUACHE

OTERO

BENT

BENT

PROWERS

MONTEZUMA

MINERAL

HUERFANO

COSTILLA

LAS ANIMAS

RIO GRANDE

ALAMOSA

LA PLATA

ARCHULETA

CONEJOS

CONEJOS

COSTILLA

COSTILLA

LAS ANIMAS

BACA

Arizona
Territory

New Mexico Territory

"Indian
Territory"

CENSUS AVAILABILITY

Federal census extant for all counties.

*NOTES: Colorado became a territory in 1861.

For North Park in Summit County, see Colorado Notes
on page 51.

Greenwood County was abolished in 1874.

1   2   3   4   5   6   7   8   9   10   11   12

25   0   25   50   75   100 MILES

WHITE = MODERN BOUNDARIES
BLACK = 1870 BOUNDARIES

Colorado ● 1870
AS COLORADO TERRITORY

MAP GUIDE TO THE U.S. FEDERAL CENSUSES, 1790-1920 by William Thorndale and William Dollarhide. Copyright 1987, all rights reserved.

Wyoming Territory

NE

SEDGWICK

MOFFAT

ROUTT

LARIMER

LOGAN

WELD

PHILLIPS

ROUTT

"North
JACKSON Park"*

WELD

NE

MORGAN

GRAND*

BOULDER

RIO BLANCO

GILPIN

ADAMS

WASHINGTON

YUMA

DENVER

SUMMIT

CLEAR
CREEK

ARAPAHOE

Utah

EAGLE

SUMMIT

JEFFERSON

GARFIELD

ARAPAHOE

Territory

DOUGLAS

ELBERT

KIT CARSON

MESA

PITKIN

LAKE

ELBERT

PARK

DELTA

EL PASO

GUNNISON

CHEYENNE

EL PASO

CHAFFEE

TELLER

LINCOLN

GUNNISON

MONTROSE

FREMONT

KIOWA

CROWLEY

BENT

OURAY

PUEBLO

SAN MIGUEL

SAGUACHE

CUSTER

HINSDALE

OTERO

BENT

PROWERS

OURAY

SAN
JUAN

HINSDALE

DOLORES

MINERAL

RIO GRANDE

HUERFANO

COSTILLA

RIO GRANDE

MONTEZUMA

ALAMOSA

LA PLATA

LAS ANIMAS

BACA

LA PLATA

COSTILLA

ARCHULETA

CONEJOS

LAS ANIMAS

CONEJOS

**Arizona
Territory**

New Mexico Territory

**"Indian
Territory"**

CENSUS AVAILABILITY

Federal census extant for all counties.

*NOTES:

Colorado became a state in 1876.

For North Park in Grand County, see Colorado Notes
on page 51.

1	2	3	4	5	6	7	8	9	10	11	12

25 0 25 50 75 100 MILES

WHITE = MODERN BOUNDARIES
BLACK = 1880 BOUNDARIES

Colorado ● 1880

MAP GUIDE TO THE U.S. FEDERAL CENSUSES, 1790-1920 by William Thorndale and William Dollarhide. Copyright 1987, all rights reserved.

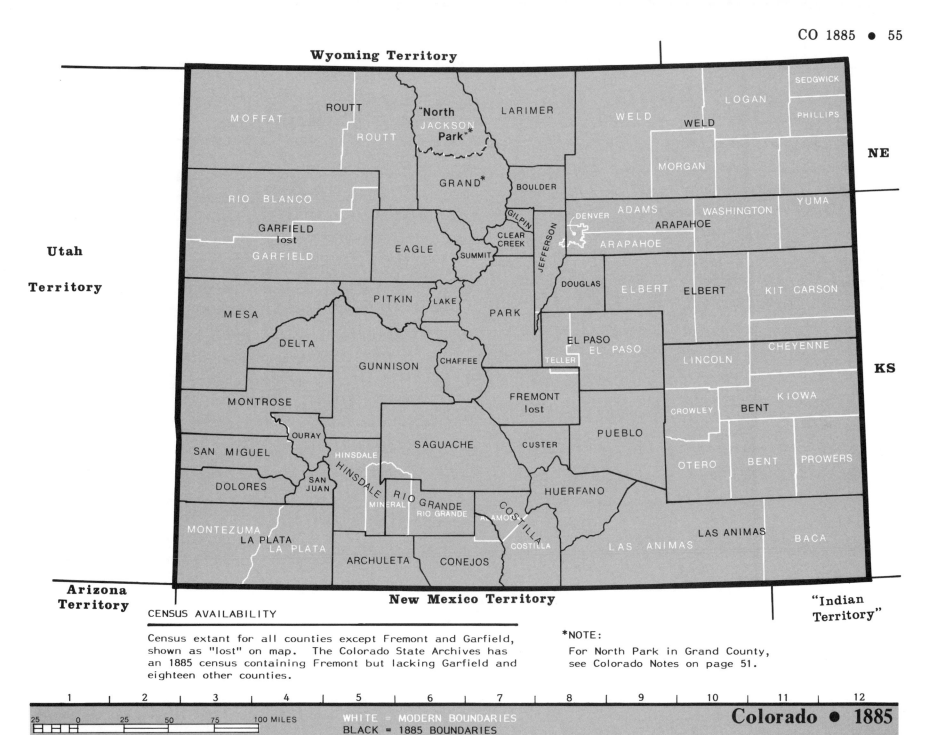

Wyoming Territory

NE

Utah

Territory

KS

Arizona
Territory

New Mexico Territory

"Indian
Territory"

CENSUS AVAILABILITY

Census extant for all counties except Fremont and Garfield,
shown as "lost" on map. The Colorado State Archives has
an 1885 census containing Fremont but lacking Garfield and
eighteen other counties.

*NOTE:

For North Park in Grand County,
see Colorado Notes on page 51.

| 1 | 2 | 3 | 4 | 5 | 6 | 7 | 8 | 9 | 10 | 11 | 12 |

25 0 25 50 75 100 MILES

WHITE = MODERN BOUNDARIES
BLACK = 1885 BOUNDARIES

Colorado ● 1885

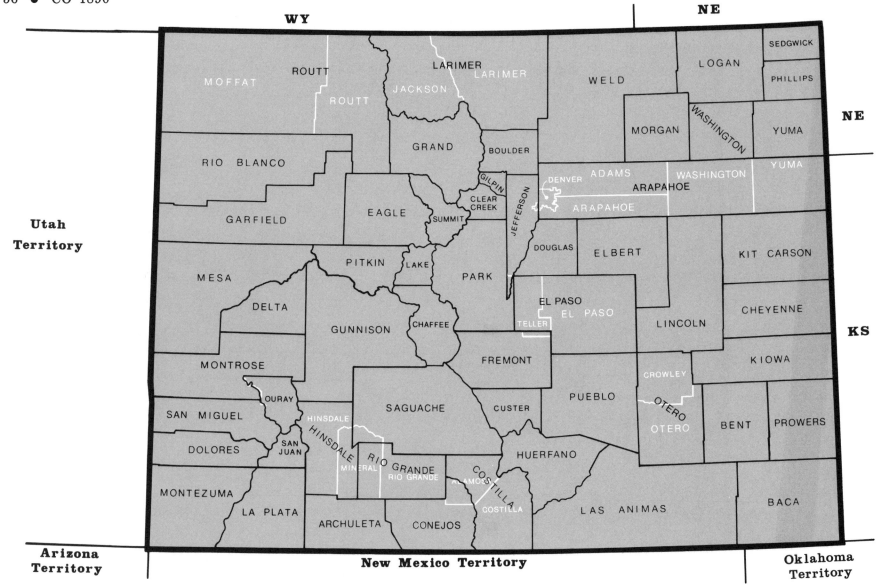

WY

NE

NE

KS

Utah
Territory

Arizona
Territory

New Mexico Territory

Oklahoma
Territory

MOFFAT
ROUTT
ROUTT
LARIMER
LARIMER
JACKSON
GRAND
BOULDER
WELD
LOGAN
SEDGWICK
PHILLIPS
MORGAN
WASHINGTON
YUMA
RIO BLANCO
GILPIN
CLEAR CREEK
DENVER
ADAMS
WASHINGTON
YUMA
GARFIELD
EAGLE
SUMMIT
JEFFERSON
ARAPAHOE
ARAPAHOE
MESA
PITKIN
LAKE
PARK
DOUGLAS
ELBERT
KIT CARSON
DELTA
GUNNISON
CHAFFEE
EL PASO
EL PASO
CHEYENNE
OURAY
TELLER
LINCOLN
MONTROSE
FREMONT
SAN MIGUEL
HINSDALE
HINSDALE
SAN JUAN
SAGUACHE
CUSTER
PUEBLO
CROWLEY
OTERO
OTERO
KIOWA
DOLORES
MINERAL
RIO GRANDE
RIO GRANDE
ALAMOSA
COSTILLA
COSTILLA
BENT
PROWERS
MONTEZUMA
LA PLATA
ARCHULETA
CONEJOS
HUERFANO
LAS ANIMAS
BACA

CENSUS AVAILABILITY

Federal census <u>lost</u> for all counties.

| 1 | 2 | 3 | 4 | 5 | 6 | 7 | 8 | 9 | 10 | 11 | 12 |

25 0 25 50 75 100 MILES

WHITE = MODERN BOUNDARIES
BLACK = 1890 BOUNDARIES

Colorado ● 1890

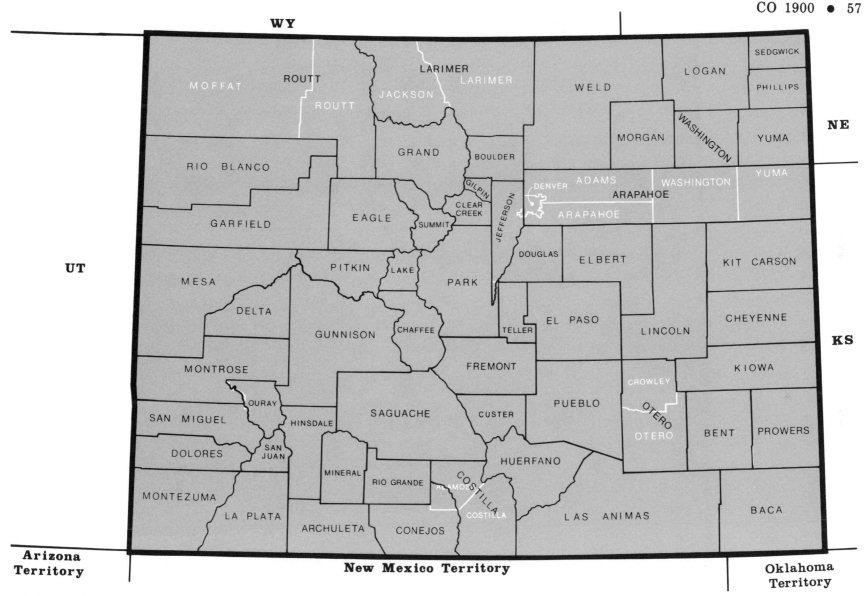

Federal census extant for all counties.

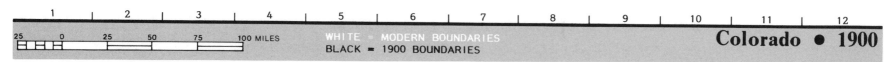

WHITE = MODERN BOUNDARIES
BLACK = 1900 BOUNDARIES

Colorado ● 1900

MAP GUIDE TO THE U.S. FEDERAL CENSUSES, 1790–1920 by William Thorndale and William Dollarhide. Copyright 1987, all rights reserved.

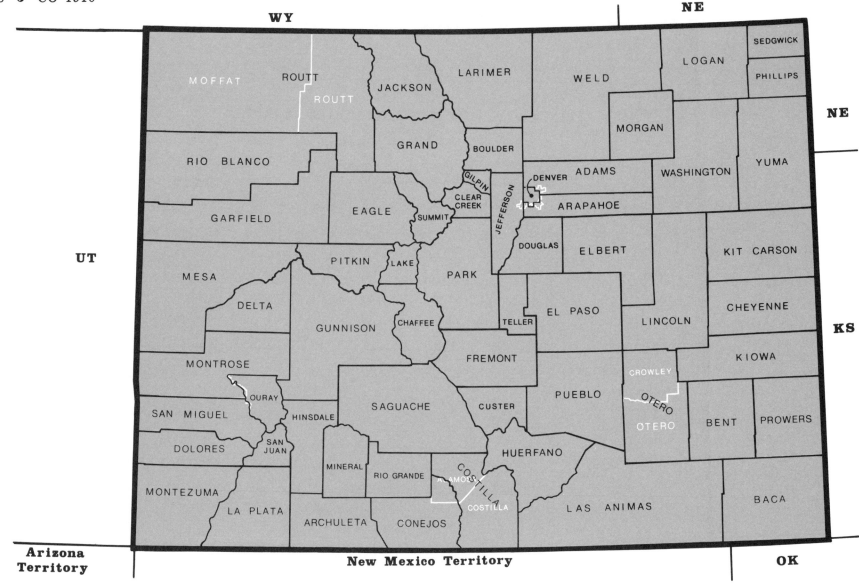

WY

NE

NE

NE

UT

KS

Arizona
Territory

New Mexico Territory

OK

SEDGWICK

LOGAN

PHILLIPS

MOFFAT

ROUTT

ROUTT

JACKSON

LARIMER

WELD

YUMA

MORGAN

RIO BLANCO

GRAND

BOULDER

ADAMS

WASHINGTON

GILPIN

DENVER

GARFIELD

EAGLE

CLEAR
CREEK

JEFFERSON

ARAPAHOE

SUMMIT

MESA

PITKIN

LAKE

PARK

DOUGLAS

ELBERT

KIT CARSON

DELTA

CHAFFEE

EL PASO

CHEYENNE

GUNNISON

LINCOLN

MONTROSE

TELLER

FREMONT

KIOWA

OURAY

CROWLEY

SAN MIGUEL

HINSDALE

SAGUACHE

CUSTER

PUEBLO

OTERO

DOLORES

SAN
JUAN

MINERAL

OTERO

BENT

PROWERS

MONTEZUMA

RIO GRANDE

ALAMOSA

COSTILLA

HUERFANO

COSTILLA

LA PLATA

COSTILLA

LAS ANIMAS

BACA

ARCHULETA

CONEJOS

CENSUS AVAILABILITY

Federal census extant for all counties.

| 1 | 2 | 3 | 4 | 5 | 6 | 7 | 8 | 9 | 10 | 11 | 12 |

25 0 25 50 75 100 MILES

WHITE = MODERN BOUNDARIES
BLACK = 1910 BOUNDARIES

Colorado ● 1910

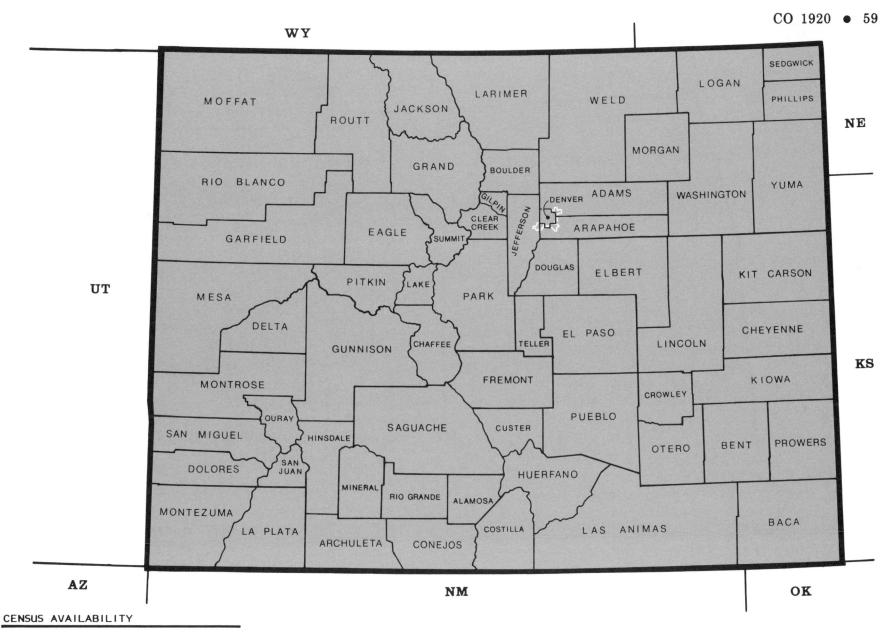

WY

NE

UT

KS

AZ

NM

OK

MOFFAT

ROUTT

JACKSON

LARIMER

WELD

LOGAN

SEDGWICK

PHILLIPS

MORGAN

RIO BLANCO

GRAND

BOULDER

ADAMS

WASHINGTON

YUMA

GILPIN

DENVER

GARFIELD

EAGLE

CLEAR CREEK

SUMMIT

JEFFERSON

ARAPAHOE

MESA

PITKIN

LAKE

PARK

DOUGLAS

ELBERT

KIT CARSON

DELTA

GUNNISON

CHAFFEE

EL PASO

LINCOLN

CHEYENNE

TELLER

MONTROSE

FREMONT

PUEBLO

CROWLEY

KIOWA

OURAY

SAGUACHE

CUSTER

SAN MIGUEL

HINSDALE

OTERO

BENT

PROWERS

SAN JUAN

DOLORES

MINERAL

RIO GRANDE

ALAMOSA

HUERFANO

MONTEZUMA

COSTILLA

LAS ANIMAS

BACA

LA PLATA

ARCHULETA

CONEJOS

CENSUS AVAILABILITY

Federal census extant for all counties.

| 1 | 2 | 3 | 4 | 5 | 6 | 7 | 8 | 9 | 10 | 11 | 12 |

25 0 25 50 75 100 MILES

WHITE = MODERN BOUNDARIES
BLACK = 1920 BOUNDARIES

Colorado ● 1920

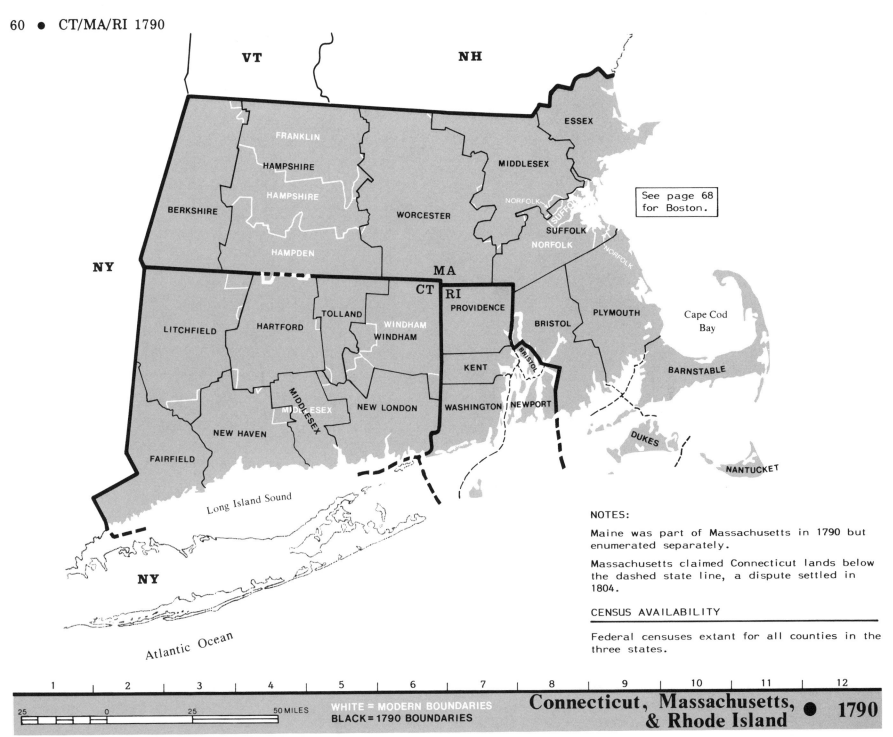

VT

NH

ESSEX

FRANKLIN

MIDDLESEX

HAMPSHIRE

HAMPSHIRE

See page 68
for Boston.

BERKSHIRE

WORCESTER

NORFOLK

SUFFOLK

SUFFOLK

NY

HAMPDEN

NORFOLK

NORFOLK

MA

CT **RI**

PROVIDENCE

Cape Cod
Bay

TOLLAND

LITCHFIELD

HARTFORD

WINDHAM

PLYMOUTH

BRISTOL

WINDHAM

KENT

BRISTOL

BARNSTABLE

MIDDLESEX

NEW LONDON

WASHINGTON

NEWPORT

NEW HAVEN

FAIRFIELD

Long Island Sound

DUKES

NANTUCKET

NY

Atlantic Ocean

NOTES:

Maine was part of Massachusetts in 1790 but
enumerated separately.

Massachusetts claimed Connecticut lands below
the dashed state line, a dispute settled in
1804.

CENSUS AVAILABILITY

Federal censuses extant for all counties in the
three states.

| 1 | 2 | 3 | 4 | 5 | 6 | 7 | 8 | 9 | 10 | 11 | 12 |

25   0   25   50 MILES

WHITE = MODERN BOUNDARIES
BLACK = 1790 BOUNDARIES

**Connecticut, Massachusetts,
& Rhode Island** ● **1790**

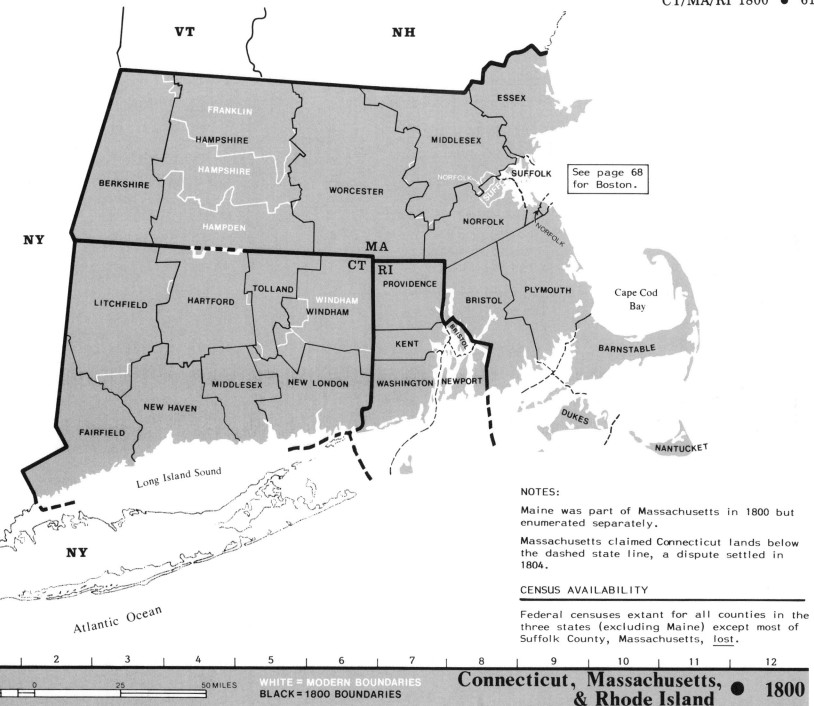

VT

NH

NY

ESSEX

FRANKLIN

HAMPSHIRE

HAMPSHIRE

MIDDLESEX

NORFOLK

SUFFOLK

See page 68 for Boston.

BERKSHIRE

WORCESTER

SUFFOLK

HAMPDEN

NORFOLK

NY

MA

CT

RI

NORFOLK

LITCHFIELD

HARTFORD

TOLLAND

WINDHAM

WINDHAM

PROVIDENCE

BRISTOL

PLYMOUTH

Cape Cod Bay

KENT

BRISTOL

MIDDLESEX

NEW LONDON

WASHINGTON NEWPORT

BARNSTABLE

NEW HAVEN

FAIRFIELD

DUKES

NANTUCKET

Long Island Sound

NY

Atlantic Ocean

NOTES:

Maine was part of Massachusetts in 1800 but enumerated separately.

Massachusetts claimed Connecticut lands below the dashed state line, a dispute settled in 1804.

CENSUS AVAILABILITY

Federal censuses extant for all counties in the three states (excluding Maine) except most of Suffolk County, Massachusetts, lost.

| 1 | 2 | 3 | 4 | 5 | 6 | 7 | 8 | 9 | 10 | 11 | 12 |

25   0   25   50 MILES   WHITE = MODERN BOUNDARIES
                                     BLACK = 1800 BOUNDARIES

Connecticut, Massachusetts, & Rhode Island ● **1800**

MAP GUIDE TO THE U.S. FEDERAL CENSUSES, 1790-1920 by William Thorndale and William Dollarhide. Copyright 1987, all rights reserved.

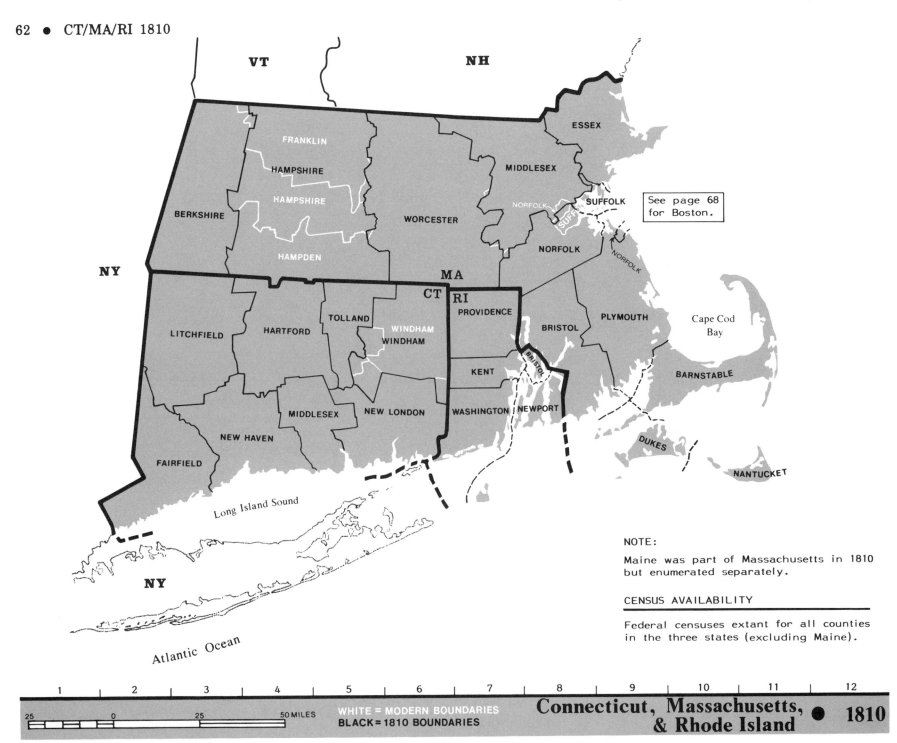

VT

NH

ESSEX

FRANKLIN

MIDDLESEX

HAMPSHIRE

HAMPSHIRE

NORFOLK

SUFFOLK

See page 68
for Boston.

BERKSHIRE

WORCESTER

SUFFOLK

NY

HAMPDEN

NORFOLK

MA

CT

NORFOLK

RI

PLYMOUTH

PROVIDENCE

Cape Cod
Bay

TOLLAND

WINDHAM

LITCHFIELD

HARTFORD

BRISTOL

WINDHAM

BRISTOL

KENT

BARNSTABLE

MIDDLESEX

NEW LONDON

WASHINGTON | NEWPORT

NEW HAVEN

DUKES

FAIRFIELD

NANTUCKET

Long Island Sound

NY

Atlantic Ocean

NOTE:

Maine was part of Massachusetts in 1810
but enumerated separately.

CENSUS AVAILABILITY

Federal censuses extant for all counties
in the three states (excluding Maine).

| 1 | 2 | 3 | 4 | 5 | 6 | 7 | 8 | 9 | 10 | 11 | 12 |

25   0   25   50 MILES

WHITE = MODERN BOUNDARIES
BLACK = 1810 BOUNDARIES

**Connecticut, Massachusetts,
& Rhode Island** ● **1810**

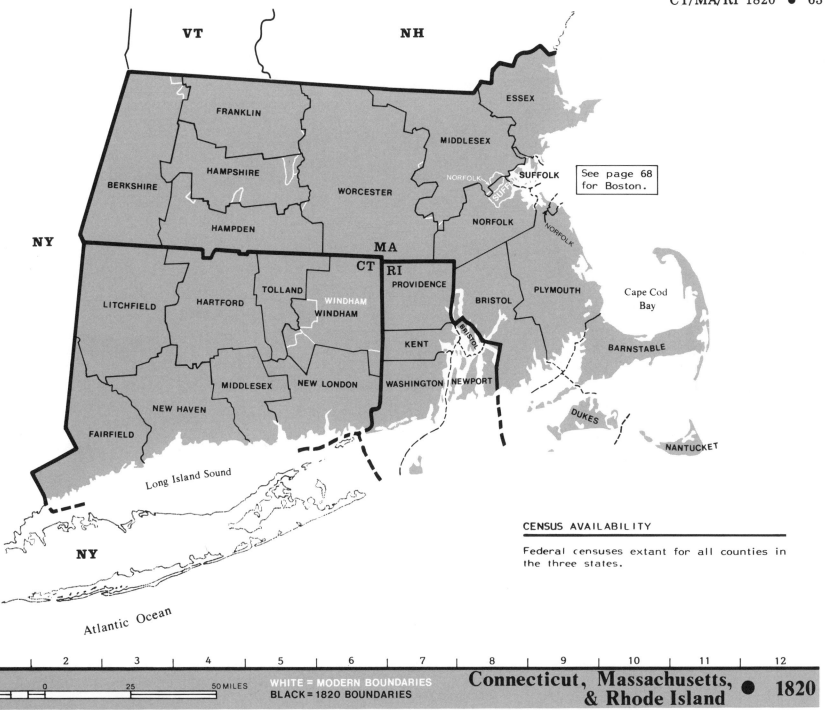

VT

NH

ESSEX

FRANKLIN

MIDDLESEX

NORFOLK SUFFOLK

HAMPSHIRE

SUFFOLK

See page 68 for Boston.

BERKSHIRE

WORCESTER

NY

HAMPDEN

NORFOLK

NORFOLK

MA

CT

RI

PLYMOUTH

Cape Cod Bay

TOLLAND

PROVIDENCE

LITCHFIELD

HARTFORD

WINDHAM

BRISTOL

WINDHAM

BRISTOL

KENT

BARNSTABLE

MIDDLESEX

NEW LONDON

WASHINGTON NEWPORT

NEW HAVEN

DUKES

FAIRFIELD

NANTUCKET

Long Island Sound

NY

CENSUS AVAILABILITY

Federal censuses extant for all counties in the three states.

Atlantic Ocean

| 1 | 2 | 3 | 4 | 5 | 6 | 7 | 8 | 9 | 10 | 11 | 12 |

25   0   25   50 MILES

WHITE = MODERN BOUNDARIES
BLACK = 1820 BOUNDARIES

Connecticut, Massachusetts, & Rhode Island ● **1820**

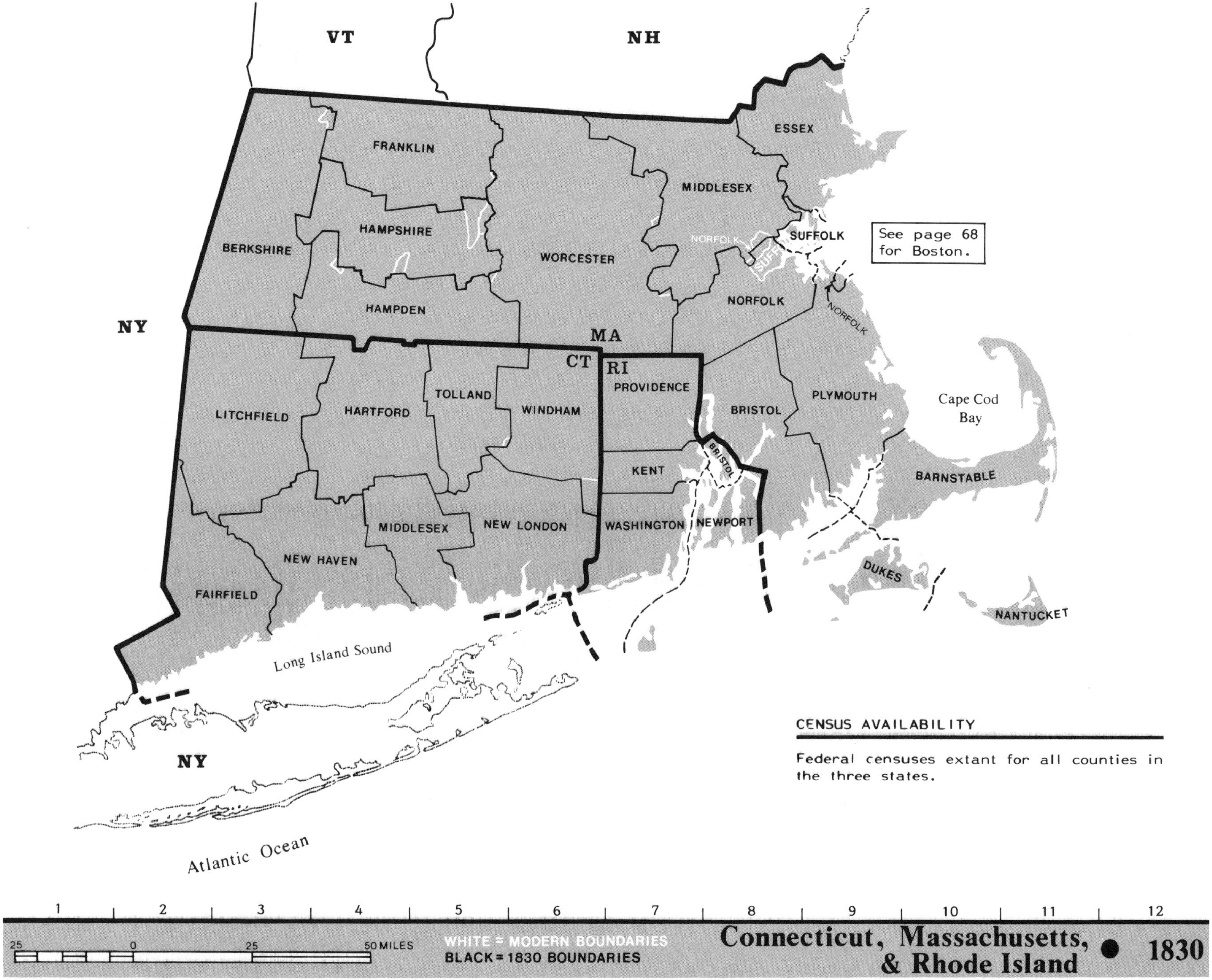

VT

NH

FRANKLIN

ESSEX

MIDDLESEX

HAMPSHIRE

BERKSHIRE

WORCESTER

SUFFOLK

NORFOLK

See page 68
for Boston.

NY

HAMPDEN

NORFOLK

NORFOLK

MA

CT RI

PROVIDENCE

PLYMOUTH

Cape Cod
Bay

LITCHFIELD

HARTFORD

TOLLAND

WINDHAM

BRISTOL

BRISTOL

KENT

MIDDLESEX

NEW LONDON

WASHINGTON NEWPORT

BARNSTABLE

NEW HAVEN

FAIRFIELD

DUKES

NANTUCKET

Long Island Sound

NY

Atlantic Ocean

CENSUS AVAILABILITY

Federal censuses extant for all counties in
the three states.

| 1 | 2 | 3 | 4 | 5 | 6 | 7 | 8 | 9 | 10 | 11 | 12 |

25 0 25 50 MILES

WHITE = MODERN BOUNDARIES
BLACK = 1830 BOUNDARIES

**Connecticut, Massachusetts, ● 1830
& Rhode Island**

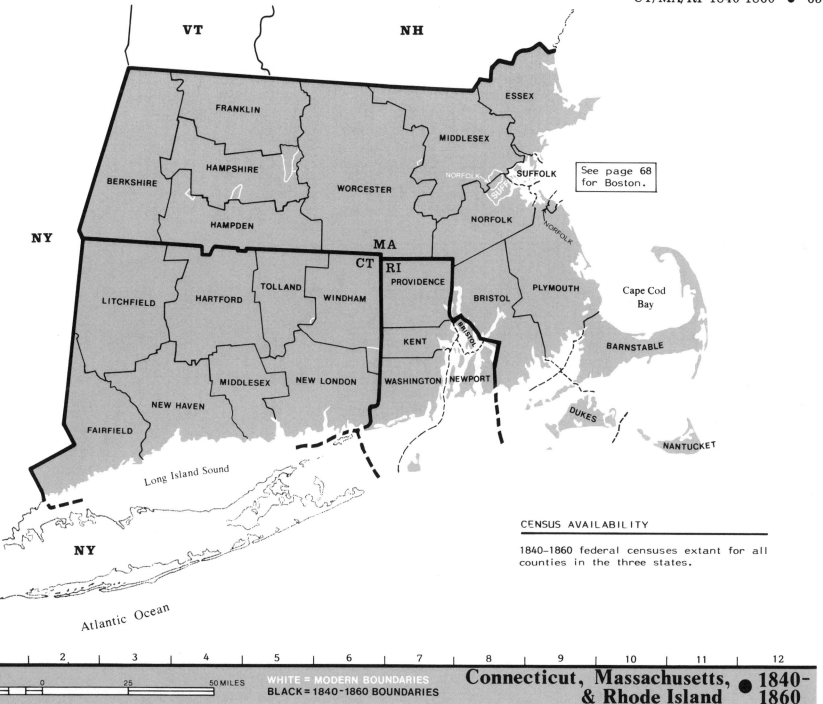

VT

NH

NY

FRANKLIN

ESSEX

HAMPSHIRE

MIDDLESEX

BERKSHIRE

WORCESTER

NORFOLK SUFFOLK

SUFF

See page 68
for Boston.

HAMPDEN

NORFOLK

NORFOLK

MA

CT RI

PROVIDENCE

PLYMOUTH

Cape Cod
Bay

LITCHFIELD HARTFORD TOLLAND

WINDHAM

BRISTOL

BRISTOL

KENT

BARNSTABLE

NEW HAVEN

MIDDLESEX NEW LONDON

WASHINGTON NEWPORT

FAIRFIELD

DUKES

NANTUCKET

Long Island Sound

NY

CENSUS AVAILABILITY

1840–1860 federal censuses extant for all
counties in the three states.

Atlantic Ocean

| 1 | 2 | 3 | 4 | 5 | 6 | 7 | 8 | 9 | 10 | 11 | 12 |

25   0   25   50 MILES

WHITE = MODERN BOUNDARIES
BLACK = 1840-1860 BOUNDARIES

**Connecticut, Massachusetts,
& Rhode Island** ● 1840-
1860

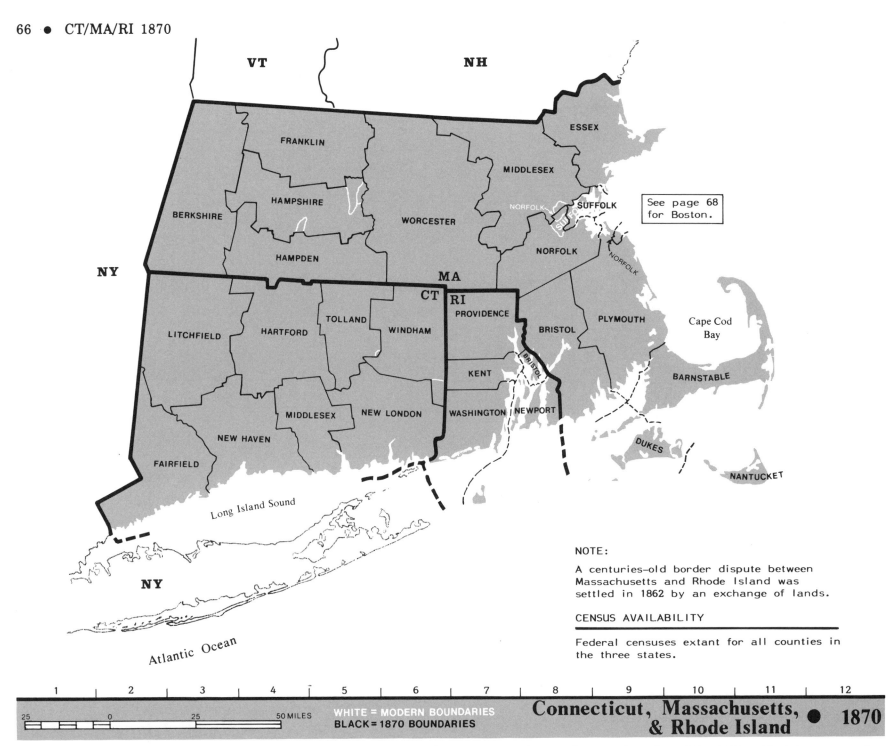

VT

NH

ESSEX

FRANKLIN

MIDDLESEX

HAMPSHIRE

BERKSHIRE

NORFOLK SUFFOLK

WORCESTER

See page 68
for Boston.

NY

NORFOLK

HAMPDEN

NORFOLK

MA

CT RI

PROVIDENCE

PLYMOUTH

Cape Cod
Bay

LITCHFIELD

HARTFORD

TOLLAND

WINDHAM

BRISTOL

BRISTOL

KENT

BARNSTABLE

MIDDLESEX

NEW LONDON

WASHINGTON NEWPORT

NEW HAVEN

DUKES

FAIRFIELD

NANTUCKET

Long Island Sound

NY

NOTE:

A centuries–old border dispute between
Massachusetts and Rhode Island was
settled in 1862 by an exchange of lands.

CENSUS AVAILABILITY

Federal censuses extant for all counties in
the three states.

Atlantic Ocean

| 1 | 2 | 3 | 4 | 5 | 6 | 7 | 8 | 9 | 10 | 11 | 12 |

25   0   25   50 MILES

WHITE = MODERN BOUNDARIES
BLACK = 1870 BOUNDARIES

**Connecticut, Massachusetts, ● 1870
& Rhode Island**

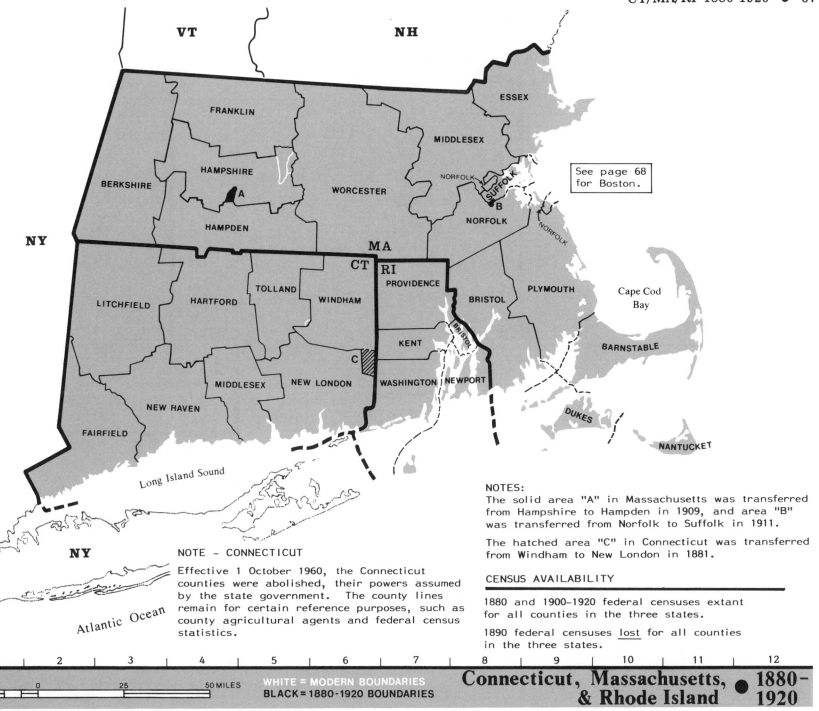

VT

NH

ESSEX

FRANKLIN

MIDDLESEX

NORFOLK SUFFOLK

HAMPSHIRE

WORCESTER

BERKSHIRE

A

NY

HAMPDEN

NORFOLK

B

NORFOLK

See page 68 for Boston.

MA

CT RI

PROVIDENCE

Cape Cod Bay

TOLLAND

LITCHFIELD

HARTFORD

WINDHAM

BRISTOL

PLYMOUTH

BRISTOL

KENT

C

BARNSTABLE

MIDDLESEX

NEW LONDON

WASHINGTON NEWPORT

NEW HAVEN

FAIRFIELD

DUKES

NANTUCKET

Long Island Sound

NY

Atlantic Ocean

NOTE – CONNECTICUT

Effective 1 October 1960, the Connecticut counties were abolished, their powers assumed by the state government. The county lines remain for certain reference purposes, such as county agricultural agents and federal census statistics.

NOTES:
The solid area "A" in Massachusetts was transferred from Hampshire to Hampden in 1909, and area "B" was transferred from Norfolk to Suffolk in 1911.

The hatched area "C" in Connecticut was transferred from Windham to New London in 1881.

CENSUS AVAILABILITY

1880 and 1900–1920 federal censuses extant for all counties in the three states.

1890 federal censuses lost for all counties in the three states.

| 1 | 2 | 3 | 4 | 5 | 6 | 7 | 8 | 9 | 10 | 11 | 12 |

25   0   25   50 MILES

WHITE = MODERN BOUNDARIES
BLACK = 1880-1920 BOUNDARIES

Connecticut, Massachusetts, & Rhode Island ● **1880–1920**

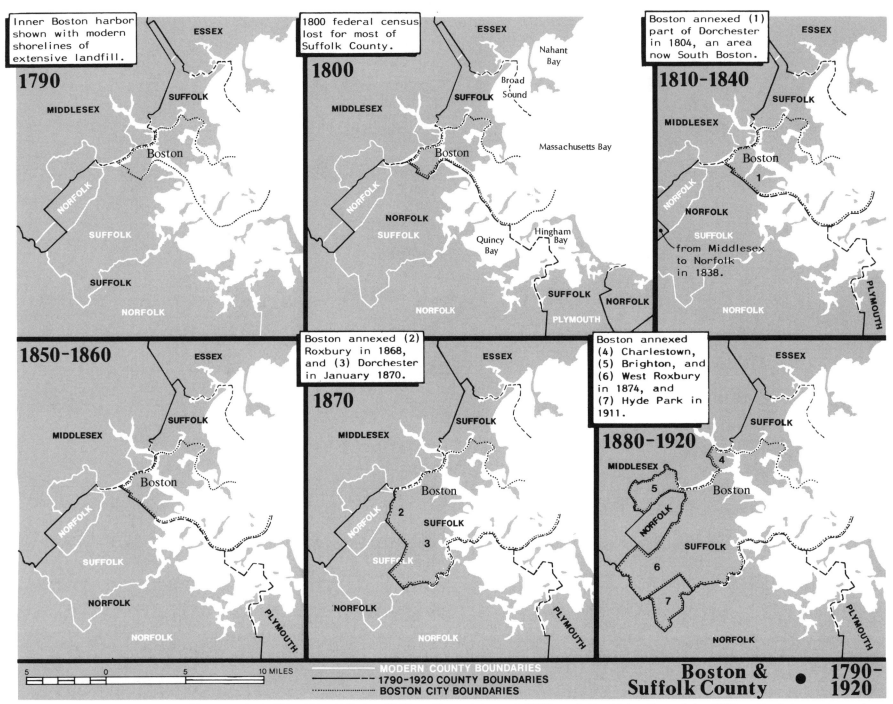

Inner Boston harbor shown with modern shorelines of extensive landfill.

1790

1800 federal census lost for most of Suffolk County.

1800

Boston annexed (1) part of Dorchester in 1804, an area now South Boston.

1810-1840

from Middlesex to Norfolk in 1838.

1850-1860

Boston annexed (2) Roxbury in 1868, and (3) Dorchester in January 1870.

1870

Boston annexed (4) Charlestown, (5) Brighton, and (6) West Roxbury in 1874, and (7) Hyde Park in 1911.

1880-1920

MODERN COUNTY BOUNDARIES
1790-1920 COUNTY BOUNDARIES
BOSTON CITY BOUNDARIES

5   0   5   10 MILES

Boston & Suffolk County ● **1790-1920**

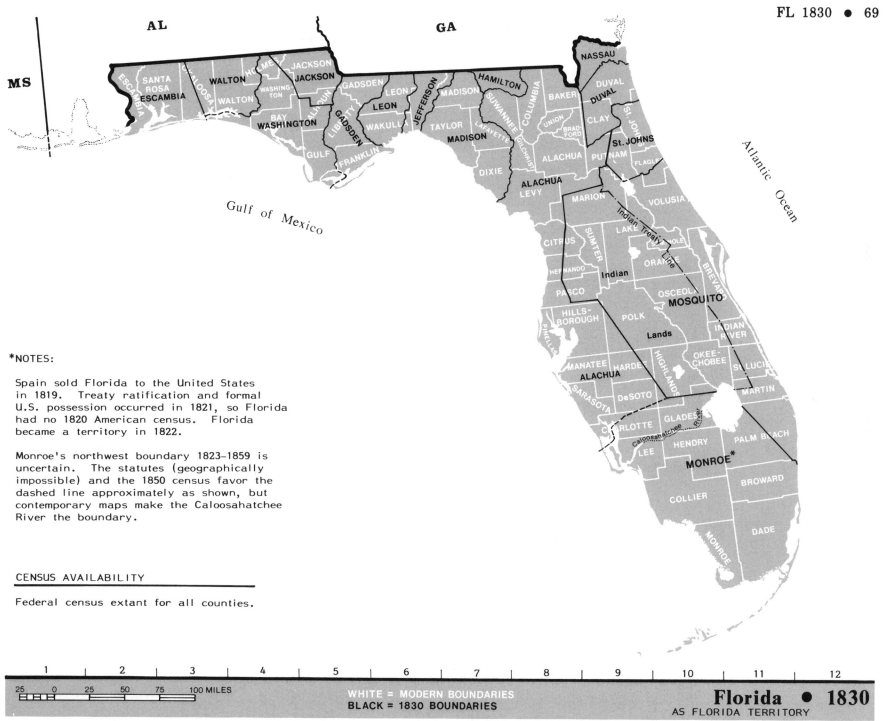

MS

AL

GA

NASSAU

ESCAMBIA
SANTA ROSA
ESCAMBIA
WALTON
WALTON
OKALOOSA
HOLMES
WASHINGTON
BAY
WASHINGTON
JACKSON
JACKSON
CALHOUN
LIBERTY
GADSDEN
GADSDEN
GULF
FRANKLIN
LEON
LEON
WAKULLA
JEFFERSON
TAYLOR
MADISON
MADISON
LAFAYETTE
SUWANNEE
DIXIE
HAMILTON
COLUMBIA
GILCHRIST
UNION
BAKER
BRADFORD
ALACHUA
ALACHUA
LEVY
DUVAL
DUVAL
CLAY
St. JOHNS
St. JOHNS
PUTNAM
FLAGLER
MARION
VOLUSIA
CITRUS
SUMTER
LAKE
SEMINOLE
Indian
ORANGE
BREVARD
HERNANDO
PASCO
OSCEOLA
MOSQUITO
INDIAN RIVER
HILLS-BOROUGH
POLK
Lands
PINELLAS
MANATEE
HARDEE
HIGHLANDS
OKEE-CHOBEE
St. LUCIE
ALACHUA
SARASOTA
DeSOTO
MARTIN
CHARLOTTE
GLADES
PALM BEACH
LEE
HENDRY
MONROE*
COLLIER
BROWARD
MONROE
DADE

Indian Treaty Line

Gulf of Mexico

Atlantic Ocean

Caloosahatchee River

*NOTES:

Spain sold Florida to the United States in 1819. Treaty ratification and formal U.S. possession occurred in 1821, so Florida had no 1820 American census. Florida became a territory in 1822.

Monroe's northwest boundary 1823–1859 is uncertain. The statutes (geographically impossible) and the 1850 census favor the dashed line approximately as shown, but contemporary maps make the Caloosahatchee River the boundary.

CENSUS AVAILABILITY

Federal census extant for all counties.

1 2 3 4 5 6 7 8 9 10 11 12

25 0 25 50 75 100 MILES

WHITE = MODERN BOUNDARIES
BLACK = 1830 BOUNDARIES

Florida ● 1830
AS FLORIDA TERRITORY

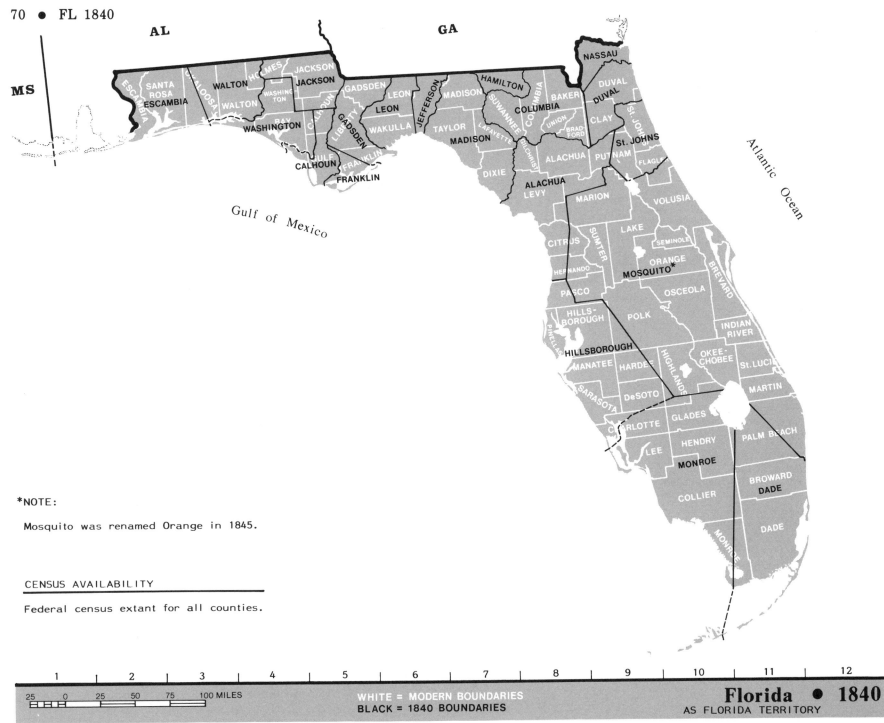

*NOTE:

Mosquito was renamed Orange in 1845.

CENSUS AVAILABILITY

Federal census extant for all counties.

Florida ● **1840**
AS FLORIDA TERRITORY

WHITE = MODERN BOUNDARIES
BLACK = 1840 BOUNDARIES

25 0 25 50 75 100 MILES

1 2 3 4 5 6 7 8 9 10 11 12

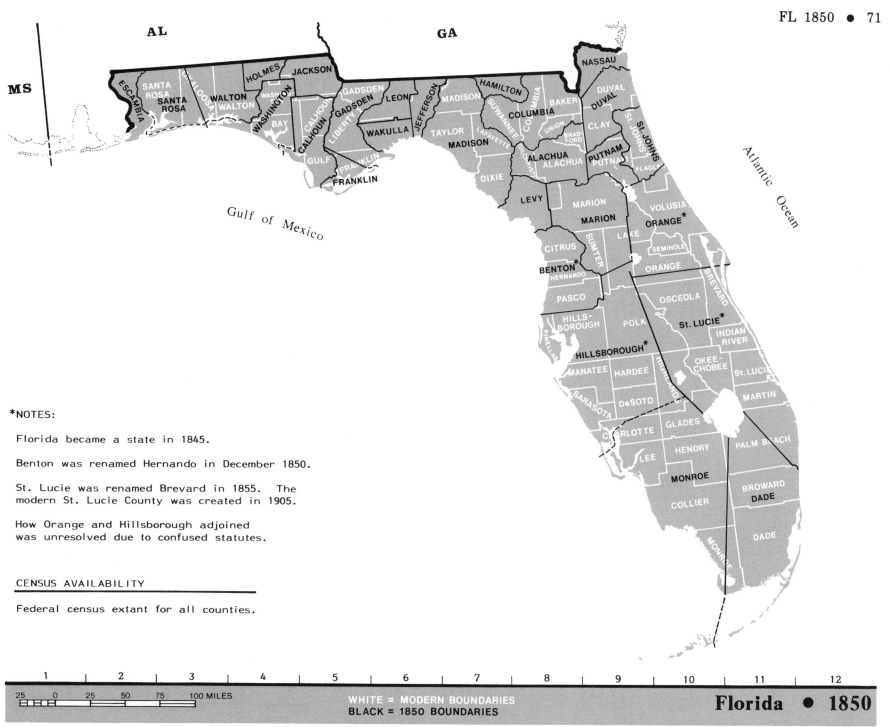

AL

GA

MS

NASSAU

ESCAMBIA
SANTA ROSA
SANTA ROSA
OKALOOSA
WALTON
WALTON
HOLMES
JACKSON
WASH'TON
WASHINGTON
BAY
CALHOUN
CALHOUN
GULF
GADSDEN
GADSDEN
LIBERTY
FRANKLIN
FRANKLIN
WAKULLA
LEON
JEFFERSON
MADISON
TAYLOR
MADISON
HAMILTON
SUWANNEE
LAFAYETTE
GILCHRIST
DIXIE
COLUMBIA
COLUMBIA
BAKER
UNION
BRADFORD
ALACHUA
ALACHUA
DUVAL
DUVAL
CLAY
ST. JOHNS
ST. JOHNS
PUTNAM
PUTNAM
FLAGLER
LEVY
MARION
MARION
VOLUSIA
ORANGE *
CITRUS
SUMTER
LAKE
SEMINOLE
ORANGE
BENTON *
HERNANDO
PASCO
OSCEOLA
BREVARD
HILLS-BOROUGH
POLK
St. LUCIE *
INDIAN RIVER
PINELLAS
HILLSBOROUGH *
OKEE-CHOBEE
ST. LUCIE
MANATEE
HARDEE
HIGHLANDS
SARASOTA
DeSOTO
MARTIN
CHARLOTTE
GLADES
PALM BEACH
LEE
HENDRY
MONROE
BROWARD
DADE
COLLIER
DADE
MONROE

Gulf of Mexico

Atlantic Ocean

*NOTES:

Florida became a state in 1845.

Benton was renamed Hernando in December 1850.

St. Lucie was renamed Brevard in 1855. The modern St. Lucie County was created in 1905.

How Orange and Hillsborough adjoined was unresolved due to confused statutes.

CENSUS AVAILABILITY

Federal census extant for all counties.

1   2   3   4   5   6   7   8   9   10   11   12

25 0 25 50 75 100 MILES

WHITE = MODERN BOUNDARIES
BLACK = 1850 BOUNDARIES

Florida ● **1850**

MAP GUIDE TO THE U.S. FEDERAL CENSUSES, 1790-1920 by William Thorndale and William Dollarhide. Copyright 1987, all rights reserved.

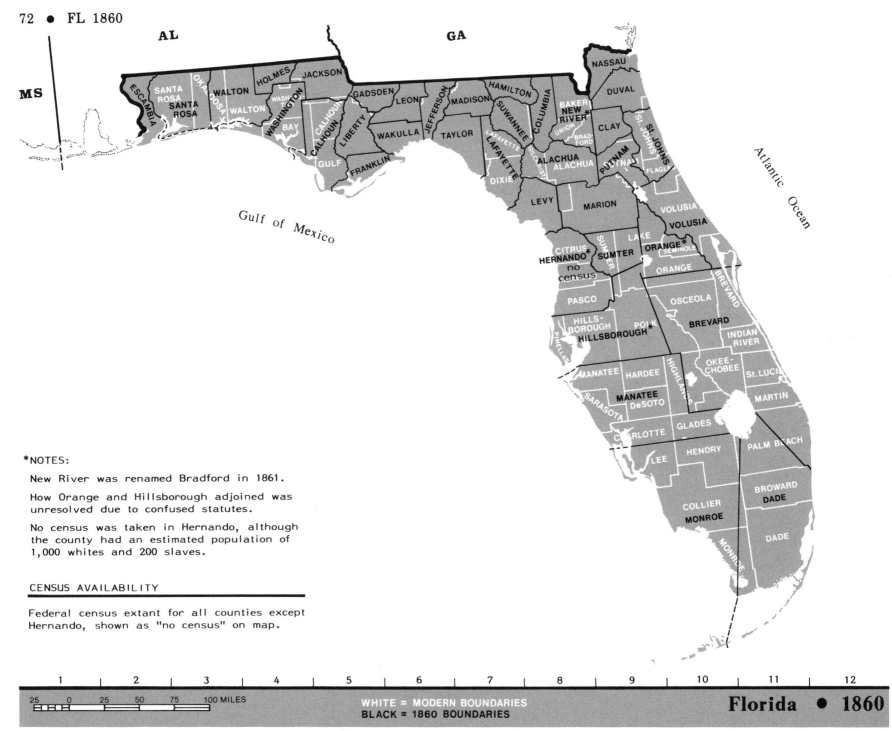

*NOTES:

New River was renamed Bradford in 1861.

How Orange and Hillsborough adjoined was unresolved due to confused statutes.

No census was taken in Hernando, although the county had an estimated population of 1,000 whites and 200 slaves.

CENSUS AVAILABILITY

Federal census extant for all counties except Hernando, shown as "no census" on map.

WHITE = MODERN BOUNDARIES
BLACK = 1860 BOUNDARIES

Florida ● 1860

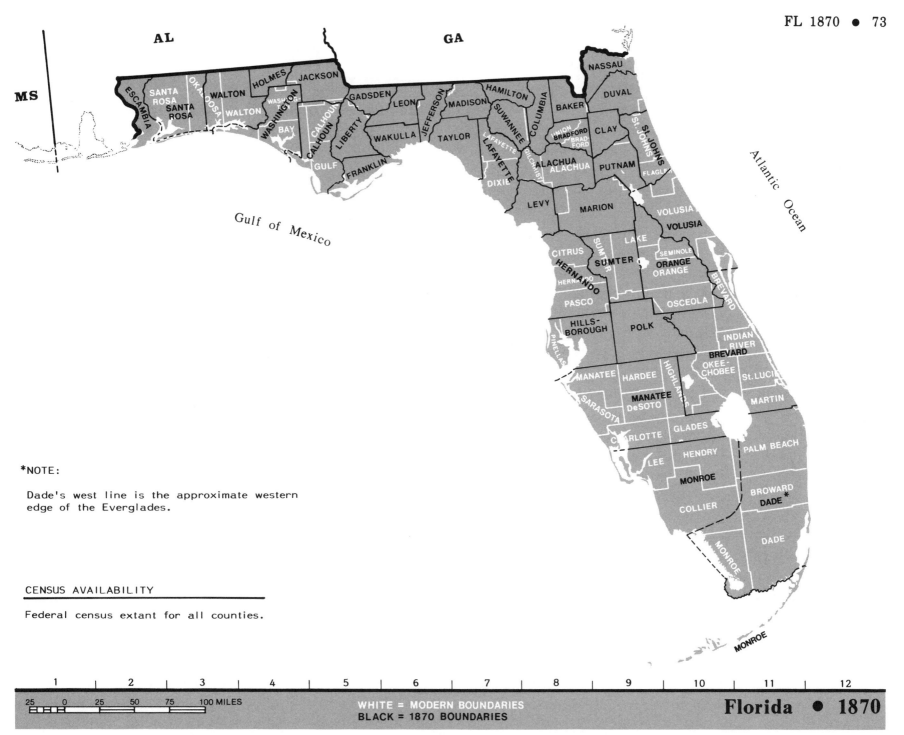

MS

AL

GA

Atlantic Ocean

Gulf of Mexico

*NOTE:

Dade's west line is the approximate western
edge of the Everglades.

CENSUS AVAILABILITY

Federal census extant for all counties.

25 0 25 50 75 100 MILES

WHITE = MODERN BOUNDARIES
BLACK = 1870 BOUNDARIES

Florida ● **1870**

MAP GUIDE TO THE U.S. FEDERAL CENSUSES, 1790-1920 by William Thorndale and William Dollarhide. Copyright 1987, all rights reserved.

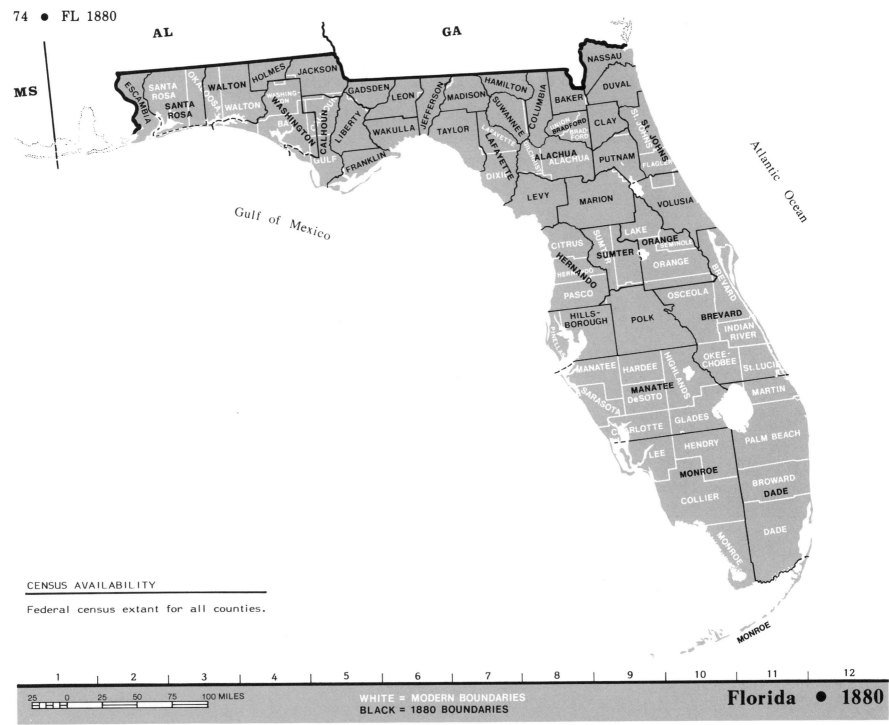

MS

AL

GA

Atlantic Ocean

Gulf of Mexico

CENSUS AVAILABILITY

Federal census extant for all counties.

| | 1 | 2 | 3 | 4 | 5 | 6 | 7 | 8 | 9 | 10 | 11 | 12 |

25   0   25   50   75   100 MILES

WHITE = MODERN BOUNDARIES
BLACK = 1880 BOUNDARIES

Florida ● 1880

MAP GUIDE TO THE U.S. FEDERAL CENSUSES, 1790-1920 by William Thorndale and William Dollarhide.   Copyright 1987, all rights reserved.

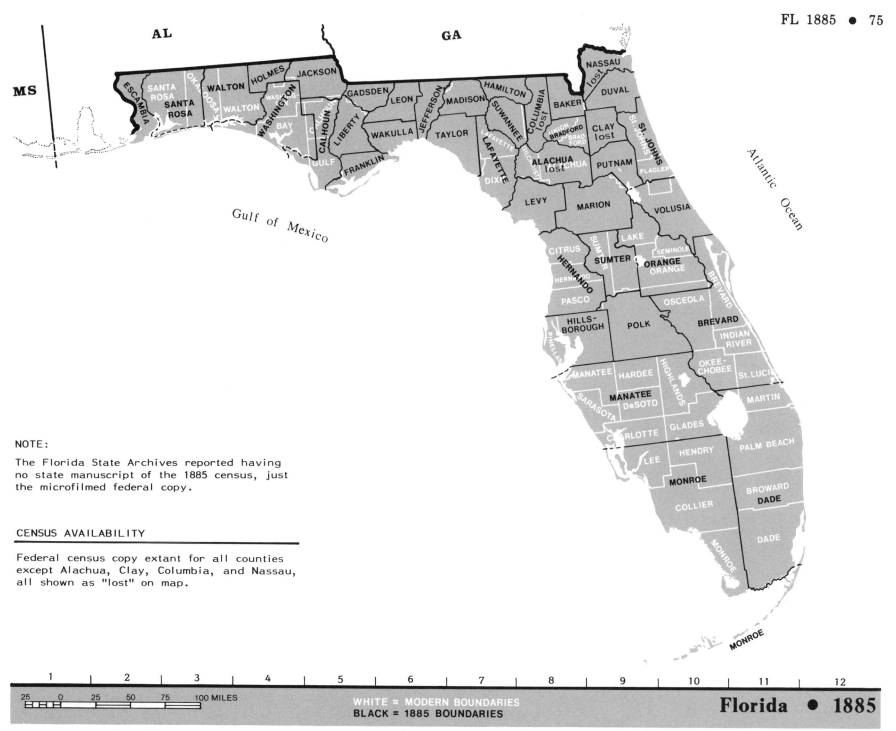

MS

AL

GA

NASSAU lost

Atlantic Ocean

Gulf of Mexico

NOTE:

The Florida State Archives reported having
no state manuscript of the 1885 census, just
the microfilmed federal copy.

CENSUS AVAILABILITY

Federal census copy extant for all counties
except Alachua, Clay, Columbia, and Nassau,
all shown as "lost" on map.

| 1 | 2 | 3 | 4 | 5 | 6 | 7 | 8 | 9 | 10 | 11 | 12 |

25 0 25 50 75 100 MILES

WHITE = MODERN BOUNDARIES
BLACK = 1885 BOUNDARIES

Florida ● 1885

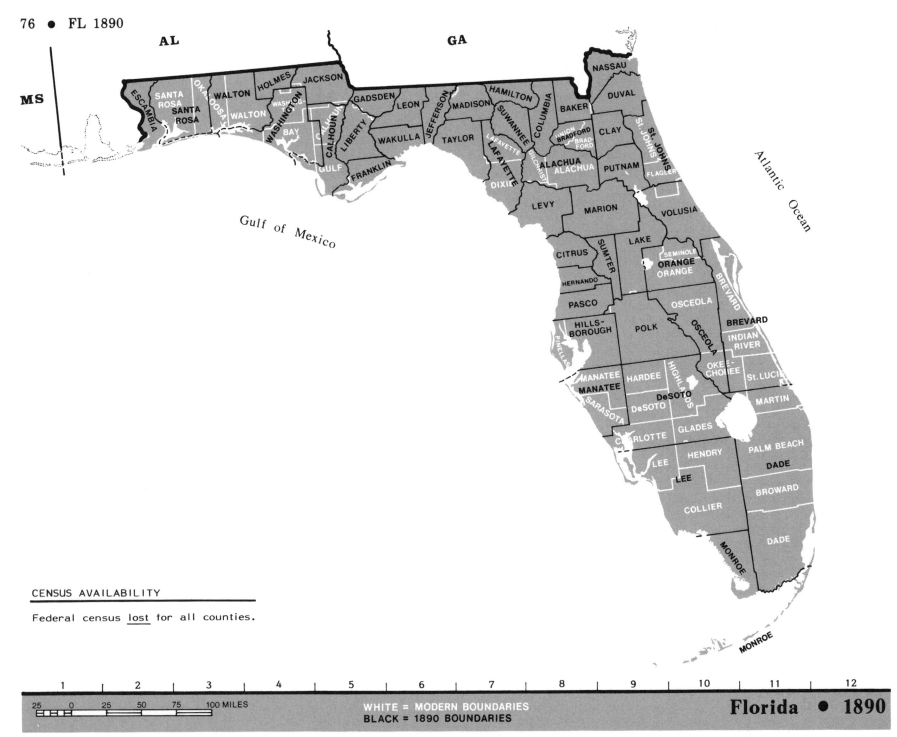

AL

GA

MS

NASSAU

ESCAMBIA

SANTA ROSA

SANTA ROSA

OKALOOSA

WALTON

WALTON

HOLMES

JACKSON

WASHINGTON

BAY

WASHINGTON

CALHOUN

CALHOUN

LIBERTY

GULF

FRANKLIN

GADSDEN

LEON

WAKULLA

JEFFERSON

MADISON

TAYLOR

HAMILTON

SUWANNEE

LAFAYETTE

LAFAYETTE

DIXIE

GILCHRIST

COLUMBIA

BAKER

UNION

BRADFORD

BRAD-FORD

ALACHUA

ALACHUA

DUVAL

CLAY

ST. JOHNS

PUTNAM

FLAGLER

St. JOHNS

LEVY

MARION

VOLUSIA

CITRUS

SUMTER

LAKE

SEMINOLE

ORANGE

ORANGE

HERNANDO

PASCO

OSCEOLA

BREVARD

BREVARD

HILLS-BOROUGH

POLK

OSCEOLA

INDIAN RIVER

PINELLAS

MANATEE

MANATEE

HARDEE

HIGHLANDS

OKEE-CHOBEE

St. LUCIE

SARASOTA

DeSOTO

DeSOTO

MARTIN

CHARLOTTE

GLADES

PALM BEACH

LEE

HENDRY

DADE

LEE

COLLIER

BROWARD

DADE

MONROE

MONROE

Atlantic Ocean

Gulf of Mexico

CENSUS AVAILABILITY

Federal census <u>lost</u> for all counties.

| 1 | 2 | 3 | 4 | 5 | 6 | 7 | 8 | 9 | 10 | 11 | 12 |

25 0 25 50 75 100 MILES

WHITE = MODERN BOUNDARIES
BLACK = 1890 BOUNDARIES

Florida ● 1890

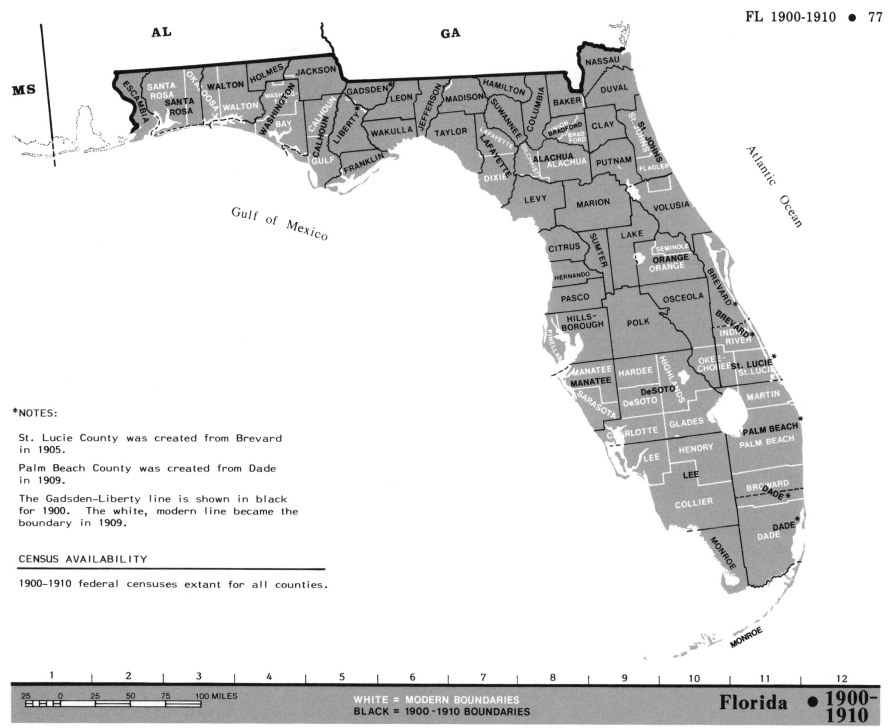

AL

GA

MS

Atlantic Ocean

Gulf of Mexico

*NOTES:

St. Lucie County was created from Brevard in 1905.

Palm Beach County was created from Dade in 1909.

The Gadsden–Liberty line is shown in black for 1900. The white, modern line became the boundary in 1909.

CENSUS AVAILABILITY

1900–1910 federal censuses extant for all counties.

WHITE = MODERN BOUNDARIES
BLACK = 1900-1910 BOUNDARIES

Florida ● **1900-1910**

25 0 25 50 75 100 MILES

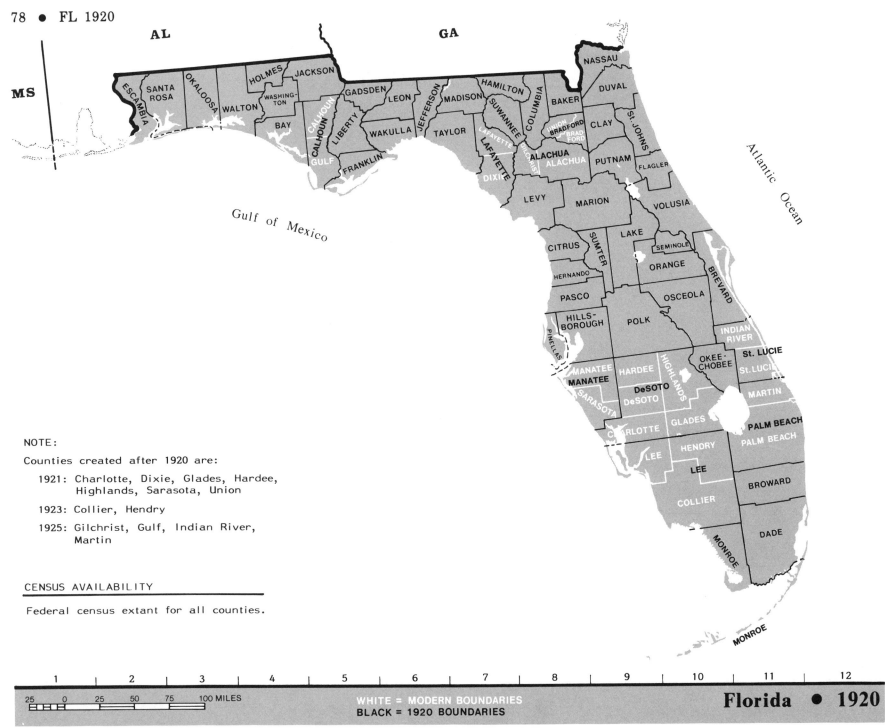

AL

GA

MS

ESCAMBIA

SANTA ROSA

OKALOOSA

WALTON

HOLMES

JACKSON

WASHING-TON

BAY

CALHOUN

GULF

LIBERTY

FRANKLIN

GADSDEN

LEON

WAKULLA

JEFFERSON

MADISON

TAYLOR

HAMILTON

SUWANNEE

LAFAYETTE

LAFAYETTE

DIXIE

COLUMBIA

BAKER

UNION

BRADFORD

BRAD FORD

ALACHUA

ALACHUA

GILCHRIST

LEVY

DUVAL

CLAY

ST. JOHNS

PUTNAM

FLAGLER

MARION

VOLUSIA

Atlantic Ocean

NASSAU

Gulf of Mexico

CITRUS

SUMTER

LAKE

SEMINOLE

ORANGE

HERNANDO

PASCO

PINELLAS

HILLS-BOROUGH

POLK

OSCEOLA

BREVARD

INDIAN RIVER

MANATEE

MANATEE

SARASOTA

HARDEE

DeSOTO

DeSOTO

HIGHLANDS

OKEE-CHOBEE

St. LUCIE

St. LUCIE

MARTIN

PALM BEACH

PALM BEACH

CHARLOTTE

LEE

GLADES

HENDRY

LEE

BROWARD

COLLIER

DADE

MONROE

MONROE

NOTE:

Counties created after 1920 are:

1921: Charlotte, Dixie, Glades, Hardee,
Highlands, Sarasota, Union

1923: Collier, Hendry

1925: Gilchrist, Gulf, Indian River,
Martin

CENSUS AVAILABILITY

Federal census extant for all counties.

| 1 | 2 | 3 | 4 | 5 | 6 | 7 | 8 | 9 | 10 | 11 | 12 |

25 0 25 50 75 100 MILES

WHITE = MODERN BOUNDARIES
BLACK = 1920 BOUNDARIES

Florida ● 1920

NC

SC

Atlantic Ocean

1790

Claimed by both the U.S. and Spain

Spanish jurisdiction

Claimed by both the U.S. and Spain

NC

Southwest Territory

Spanish Florida

Disputed Area

INDIAN LANDS

INDIAN LANDS

CENSUS AVAILABILITY

Federal census lost for all counties.

WHITE = MODERN BOUNDARIES
BLACK = 1790 BOUNDARIES

Georgia ● 1790

MAP GUIDE TO THE U.S. FEDERAL CENSUSES, 1790–1920 by William Thorndale and William Dollarhide. Copyright 1987, all rights reserved.

25 0 25 50 75 100 MILES

1 2 3 4 5 6 7 8 9 10 11 12

CHATHAM, CHATHAM, EFFINGHAM, BULLOCH, SCREVEN, BURKE, BRYAN, LIBERTY, LIBERTY, LONG, EVANS, CANDLER, TATTNALL, MCINTOSH, WAYNE, GLYNN, GLYNN, CAMDEN, CAMDEN, BRANTLEY, CHARLTON, APPLING, PIERCE, WARE, BACON, JEFF DAVIS, COFFEE, ATKINSON, CLINCH, ECHOLS, LANIER, BERRIEN, LOWNDES, COOK, BROOKS, IRWIN, TURNER, TIFT, COLQUITT, THOMAS, GRADY, DECATUR, SEMINOLE, MILLER, EARLY, CLAY, CALHOUN, BAKER, MITCHELL, TERRELL, MARION, WEBSTER, RANDOLPH, QUITMAN, STEWART, SUMTER, SCHLEY, LEE, DOUGHERTY, WORTH, COLUMBIA, RICHMOND, RICHMOND, LINCOLN, WILKES, WILKES, MCDUFFIE, JEFFERSON, GLASCOCK, WARREN, TALIAFERRO, HANCOCK, GREENE, GREENE, WASHINGTON, WASHINGTON, EMANUEL, JOHNSON, MONTGOMERY, TREUTLEN, TOOMBS, WHEELER, TELFAIR, JEFF DAVIS, BEN HILL, WILCOX, PULASKI, BLECKLEY, DODGE, LAURENS, WILKINSON, BALDWIN, PUTNAM, MORGAN, OCONEE, OGLETHORPE, CLARKE, MADISON, ELBERT, HART, FRANKLIN, BANKS, STEPHENS, FRANKLIN, JACKSON, BARROW, WALTON, NEWTON, JASPER, JONES, BIBB, TWIGGS, HOUSTON, CRAWFORD, PEACH, BLECKLEY, MACON, DOOLY, CRISP, HABERSHAM, RABUN, TOWNS, WHITE, UNION, LUMPKIN, HALL, GWINNETT, DEKALB, FORSYTH, DAWSON, PICKENS, CHEROKEE, COBB, FULTON, CLAYTON, HENRY, BUTTS, MONROE, SPALDING, LAMAR, UPSON, PIKE, FAYETTE, DOUGLAS, PAULDING, BARTOW, GORDON, GILMER, FANNIN, MURRAY, WHITFIELD, WALKER, CATOOSA, DADE, CHATTOOGA, FLOYD, POLK, HARALSON, CARROLL, HEARD, COWETA, MERIWETHER, TROUP, HARRIS, TALBOT, TAYLOR, MUSCOGEE, CHATTAHOOCHEE, STEWART, SCHLEY

NC
SC
TN
GEORGIA
AL
MS
AR
LA
FL
GEORGIA
Mississippi Territory
Spanish areas
1800

SC
Atlantic Ocean
NC
TN

EFFINGHAM
CHATHAM
SCREVEN
BRYAN
BULLOCH
BULLOCH
LIBERTY
LIBERTY
LONG
McINTOSH
McINTOSH
GLYNN
GLYNN
BURKE
BURKE
EMANUEL
EVANS
WAYNE
BRANTLEY
CAMDEN
CAMDEN
RICHMOND
CANDLER
TATTNALL
TOOMBS
PIERCE
CHARLTON
COLUMBIA
COLUMBIA
JEFFERSON
MONTGOMERY
MONTGOMERY
TREUTLEN
APPLING
BACON
WARE
LINCOLN
WARREN
GLAS-COCK
JOHNSON
WHEELER
JEFF DAVIS
COFFEE
ATKINSON
CLINCH
WARREN
HANCOCK
WASHINGTON
LAURENS
TELFAIR
IRWIN
LANIER
ECHOLS
ELBERT
ELBERT
TALIA-FERRO
GREENE
GREENE
WILKINSON
BALDWIN
DODGE
WILCOX
BEN HILL
TURNER
BERRIEN
LOWNDES
FRANKLIN
WILKES
OGLETHORPE
PUTNAM
TWIGGS
BLECKLEY
PULASKI
TIFT
COOK
BROOKS
HABERSHAM
STEPHENS
HART
MADISON
CLARKE
OCONEE
MORGAN
JASPER
JONES
BIBB
HOUSTON
DOOLY
CRISP
WORTH
COLQUITT
THOMAS
RABUN
BANKS
JACKSON
BARROW
WALTON
NEWTON
MONROE
CRAWFORD
PEACH
MACON
SUMTER
LEE
DOUGHERTY
MITCHELL
GRADY
TOWNS
WHITE
HALL
GWINNETT
ROCK-DALE
HENRY
BUTTS
LAMAR
UPSON
TALBOT
SCHLEY
TERRELL
BAKER
DECATUR
UNION
LUMPKIN
DAWSON
FORSYTH
DeKALB
CLAYTON
SPALDING
PIKE
TAYLOR
MARION
WEBSTER
RANDOLPH
CALHOUN
MILLER
SEMINOLE
FANNIN
GILMER
PICKENS
CHEROKEE
COBB
FULTON
FULTON
FAYETTE
MERIWETHER
HARRIS
MUSCO-GEE
CHATTA-HOOCHEE
STEWART
QUIT-MAN
CLAY
EARLY
MURRAY
FORSYTH
PAULDING
DOUGLAS
COWETA
TROUP
GORDON
BARTOW
POLK
HARALSON
CARROLL
HEARD
WHITFIELD
CATOOSA
WALKER
CHATTOOGA
FLOYD
PAULDING
MADISON
DADE

INDIAN LANDS
INDIAN LANDS
Spanish Florida
Mississippi Territory

NC
TN

1
2
3
4
5
6
7
8
9
10
11
12

25   0   25   50   75   100 MILES

WHITE = MODERN BOUNDARIES
BLACK = 1800 BOUNDARIES

Georgia ● 1800

MAP GUIDE TO THE U.S. FEDERAL CENSUSES, 1790–1920 by William Thorndale and William Dollarhide. Copyright 1987, all rights reserved.

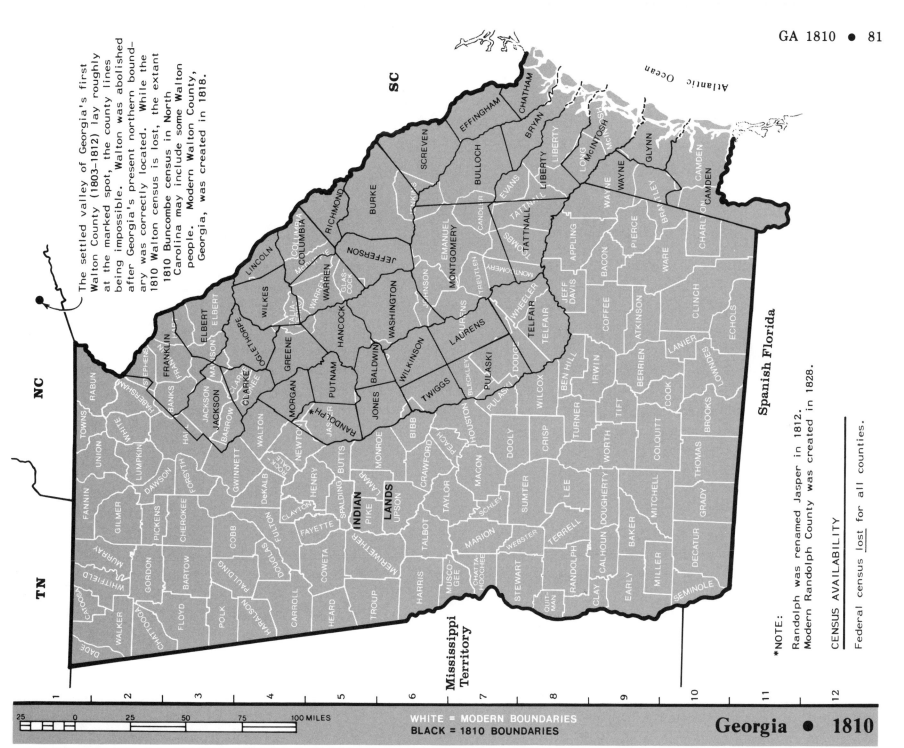

The settled valley of Georgia's first Walton County (1803–1812) lay roughly at the marked spot, the county lines being impossible. Walton was abolished after Georgia's present northern boundary was correctly located. While the 1810 Walton census is lost, the extant 1810 Buncombe census in North Carolina may include some Walton people. Modern Walton County, Georgia, was created in 1818.

*NOTE: Randolph was renamed Jasper in 1812. Modern Randolph County was created in 1828.

CENSUS AVAILABILITY

Federal census lost for all counties.

WHITE = MODERN BOUNDARIES
BLACK = 1810 BOUNDARIES

Georgia • 1810

25 0 25 50 75 100 MILES

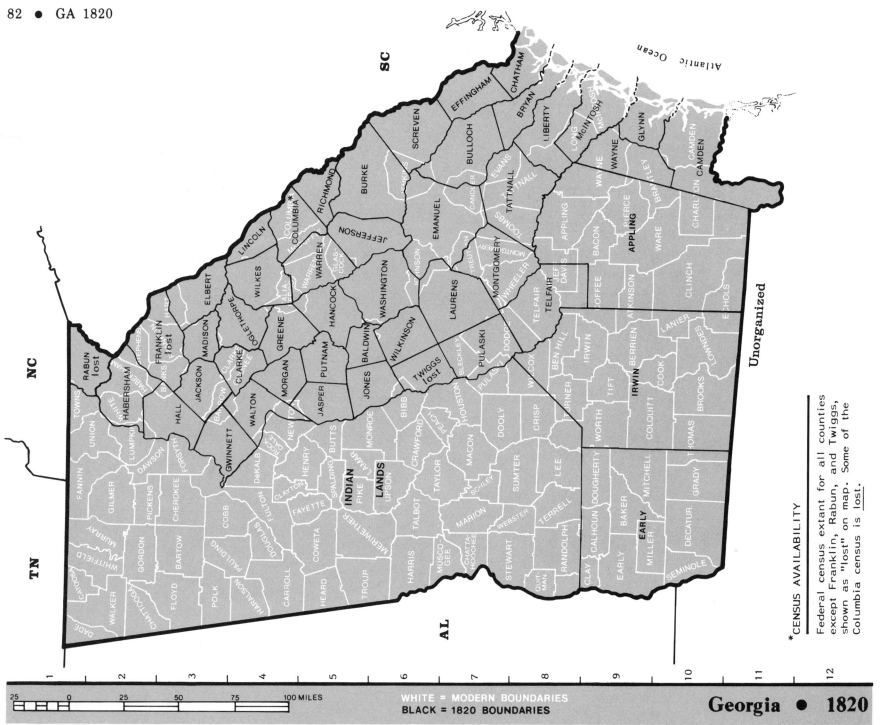

*CENSUS AVAILABILITY

Federal census extant for all counties except Franklin, Rabun, and Twiggs, shown as "lost" on map. Some of the Columbia census is lost.

WHITE = MODERN BOUNDARIES
BLACK = 1820 BOUNDARIES

Georgia ● 1820

25   0   25   50   75   100 MILES

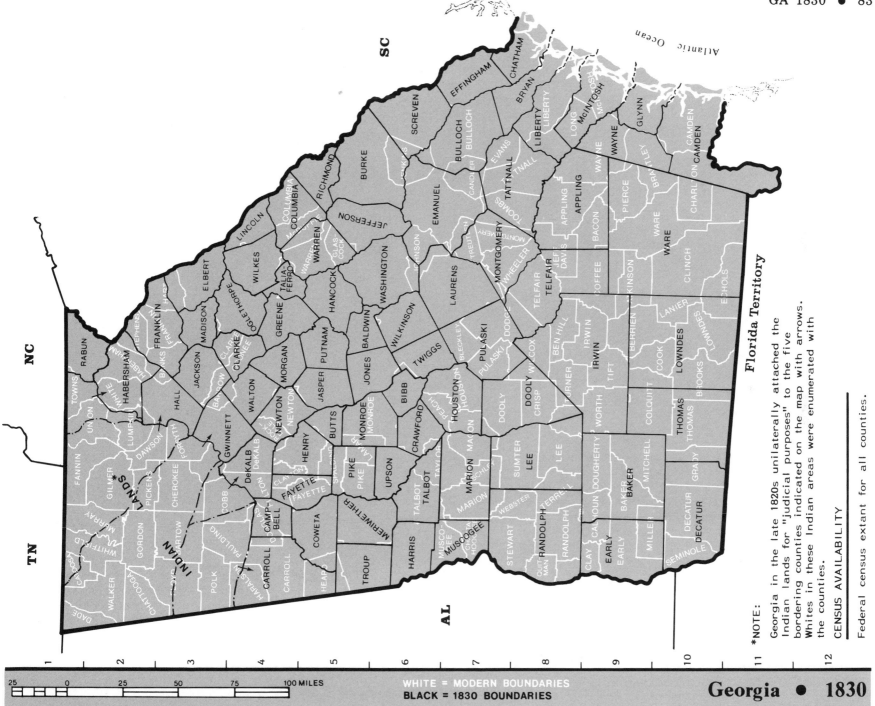

SC

NC

TN

AL

Atlantic Ocean

Florida Territory

*NOTE:

Georgia in the late 1820s unilaterally attached the Indian lands for "judicial purposes" to the five bordering counties indicated on the map with arrows. Whites in these Indian areas were enumerated with the counties.

CENSUS AVAILABILITY

Federal census extant for all counties.

WHITE = MODERN BOUNDARIES
BLACK = 1830 BOUNDARIES

Georgia ● 1830

25 0 25 50 75 100 MILES

MAP GUIDE TO THE U.S. FEDERAL CENSUSES, 1790–1920 by William Thorndale and William Dollarhide. Copyright 1987, all rights reserved.

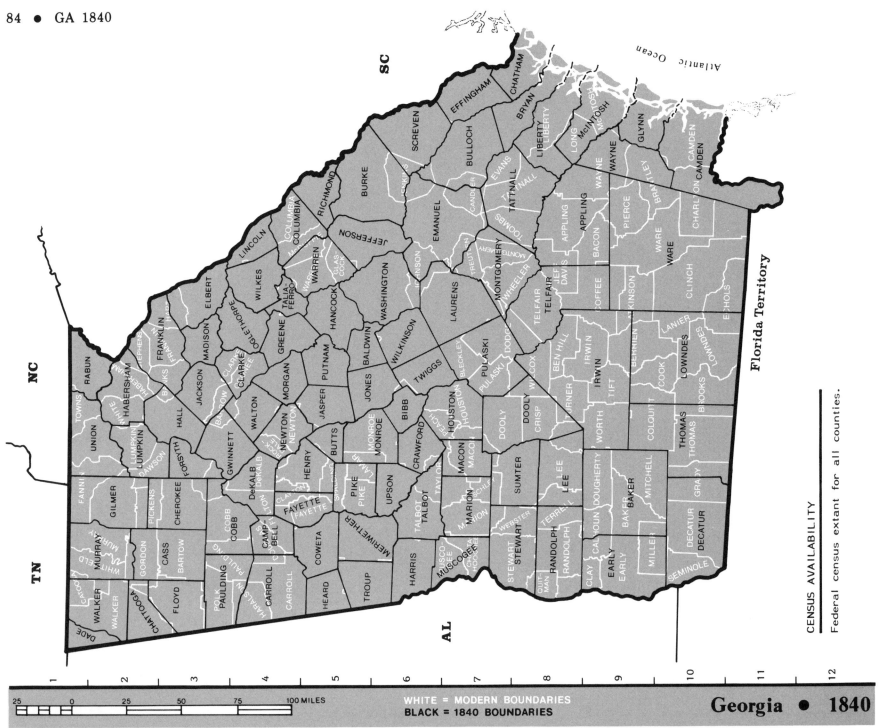

Georgia • 1840

CENSUS AVAILABILITY

Federal census extant for all counties.

SC

FL

Atlantic Ocean

NC

TN

AL

FL

CENSUS AVAILABILITY

Federal census extant for all counties.

*NOTE:
Clinch County, created in February 1850, was enumerated with its parent counties of Lowndes and Ware. The published population statistics for Clinch 1850 cover only the Lowndes portion. See Robert S. Davis, Jr., "The 1850 Federal Census of East Lanier (Clinch) County," *Georgia Genealogical Magazine* 26 (1986), 227–37.

DADE
WALKER
CATOOSA
WHITFIELD
MURRAY
GORDON
CHATTOOGA
FLOYD
CASS BARTOW
POLK
PAULDING
HARALSON
CARROLL
HEARD
TROUP
COWETA
CAMPBELL
DOUGLAS
COBB
PAULDING
FAYETTE
CLAYTON
MERIWETHER
HARRIS
MUSCOGEE
CHATTAHOOCHEE
QUITMAN
STEWART
RANDOLPH
CLAY
EARLY
MILLER
SEMINOLE
DECATUR
GRADY
THOMAS
BROOKS
LOWNDES
ECHOLS
CLINCH
CHARLTON
CAMDEN
GLYNN
WAYNE
BRANTLEY
WARE
PIERCE
BACON
APPLING
COFFEE
BERRIEN
COOK
TIFT
TURNER
WORTH
COLQUITT
MITCHELL
BAKER
DOUGHERTY
CALHOUN
TERRELL
WEBSTER
LEE
SUMTER
MARION
SCHLEY
MACON
TAYLOR
TALBOT
UPSON
PIKE
SPALDING
HENRY
BUTTS
MONROE
CRAWFORD
BIBB
JONES
TWIGGS
WILKINSON
BLECKLEY
PULASKI
DODGE
WILCOX
BEN HILL
IRWIN
JEFF DAVIS
TELFAIR
MONTGOMERY
WHEELER
LAURENS
DOOLY
CRISP
DOOLY
TREUTLEN
TOOMBS
TATTNALL
EVANS
CANDLER
EMANUEL
JOHNSON
WASHINGTON
HANCOCK
BALDWIN
PUTNAM
JASPER
MORGAN
NEWTON
WALTON
DEKALB
ROCKDALE
GWINNETT
CLARKE
OCONEE
OGLETHORPE
GREENE
TALIAFERRO
WARREN
GLASCOCK
JEFFERSON
BURKE
RICHMOND
COLUMBIA
MCDUFFIE
LINCOLN
WILKES
ELBERT
MADISON
JACKSON
BARROW
HALL
BANKS
FRANKLIN
HART
STEPHENS
HABERSHAM
WHITE
LUMPKIN
DAWSON
FORSYTH
CHEROKEE
PICKENS
GILMER
FANNIN
UNION
TOWNS
RABUN
MURRAY
SCREVEN
EFFINGHAM
CHATHAM
BRYAN
BULLOCH
LIBERTY
LONG
MCINTOSH
WORTH

MAP GUIDE TO THE U.S. FEDERAL CENSUSES, 1790–1920 by William Thorndale and William Dollarhide. Copyright 1987, all rights reserved.

25 0 25 50 75 100 MILES

WHITE = MODERN BOUNDARIES
BLACK = 1850 BOUNDARIES

Georgia ● 1850

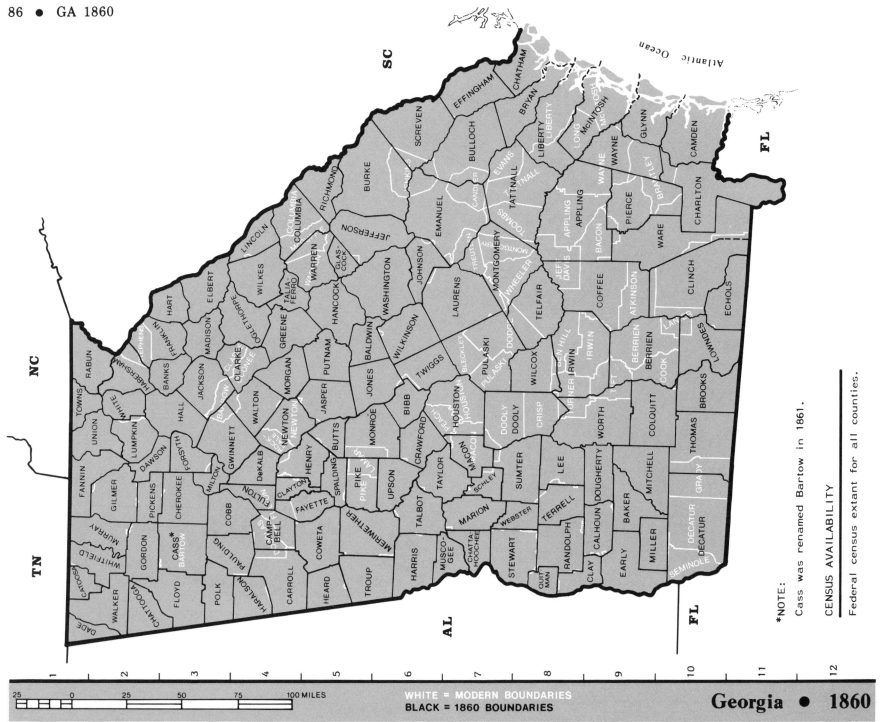

Georgia • 1860

*NOTE: Cass was renamed Bartow in 1861.

CENSUS AVAILABILITY

Federal census extant for all counties.

25 0 25 50 75 100 MILES

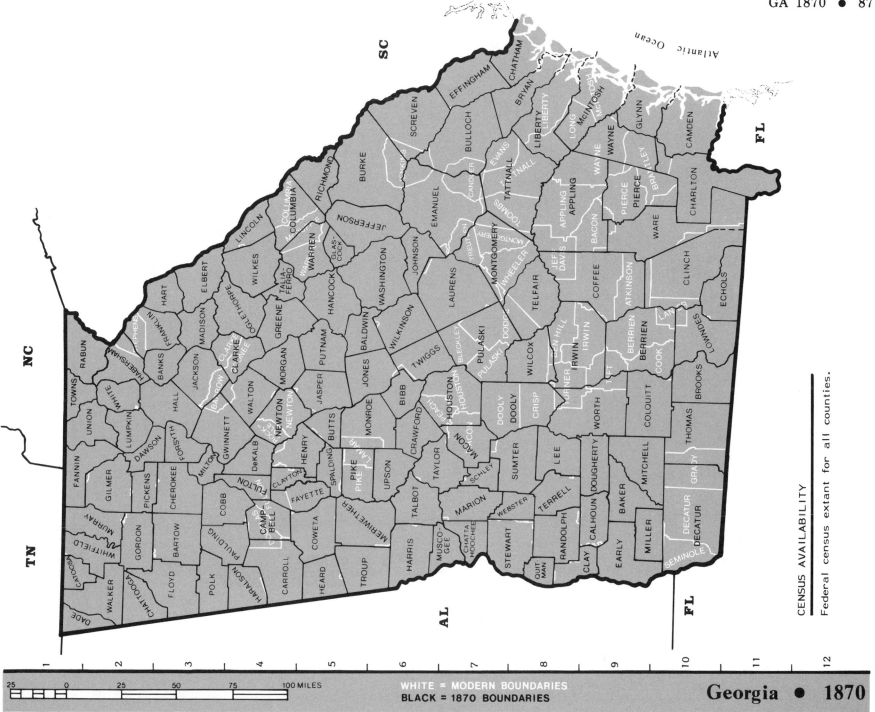

SC

Atlantic Ocean

FL

NC

TN

AL

FL

CENSUS AVAILABILITY
Federal census extant for all counties.

WHITE = MODERN BOUNDARIES
BLACK = 1870 BOUNDARIES

Georgia ● 1870

25 0 25 50 75 100 MILES

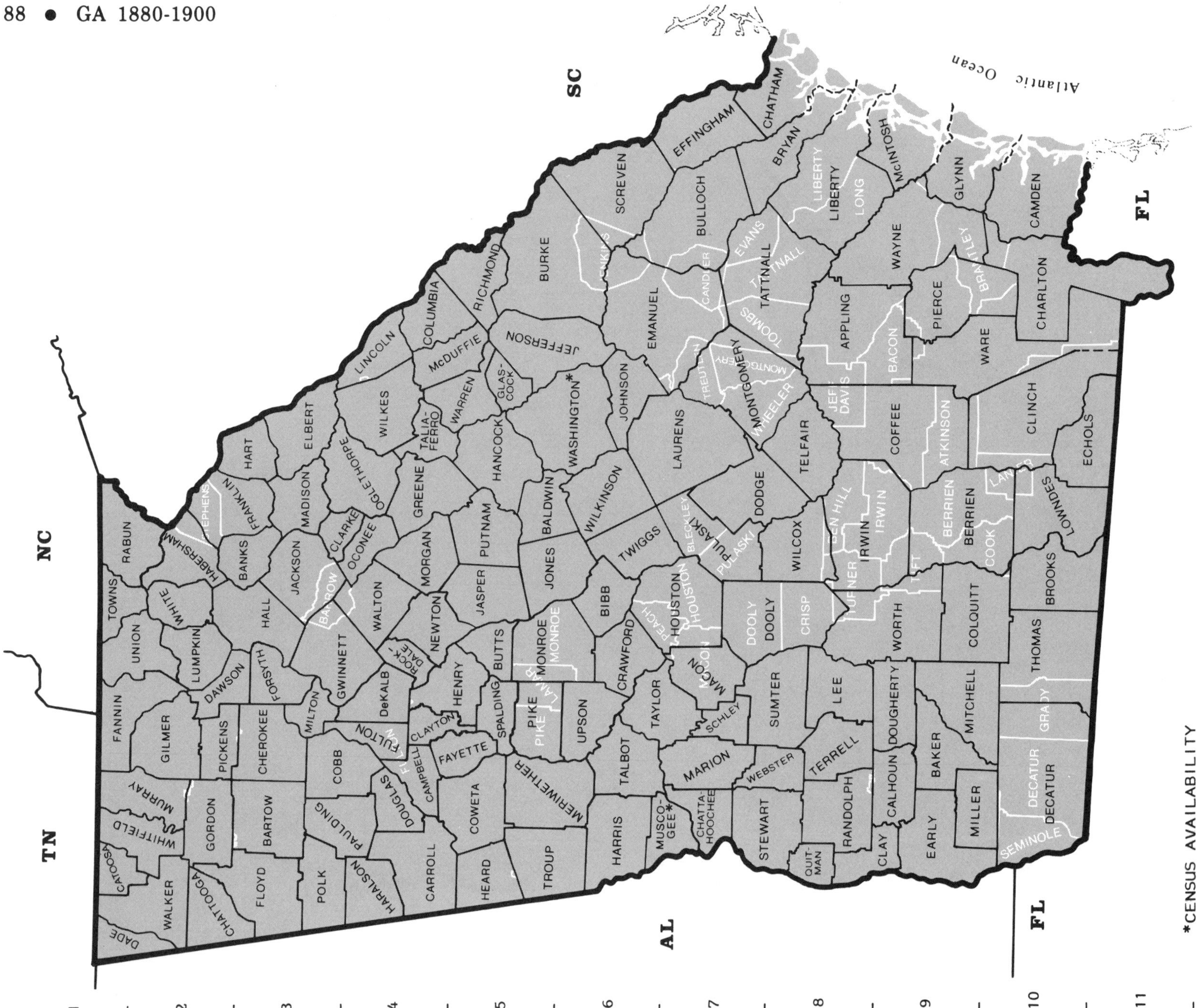

SC

TN

NC

AL

FL

Atlantic Ocean

*CENSUS AVAILABILITY

1880 and 1900 federal censuses extant for all counties.

1890 federal census lost for all counties except part of Muscogee (Columbus). But Washington 1890 survives as a list copied into the county records.

25 0 25 50 75 100 MILES

WHITE = MODERN BOUNDARIES
BLACK = 1880-1900 BOUNDARIES

Georgia ● 1880-1900

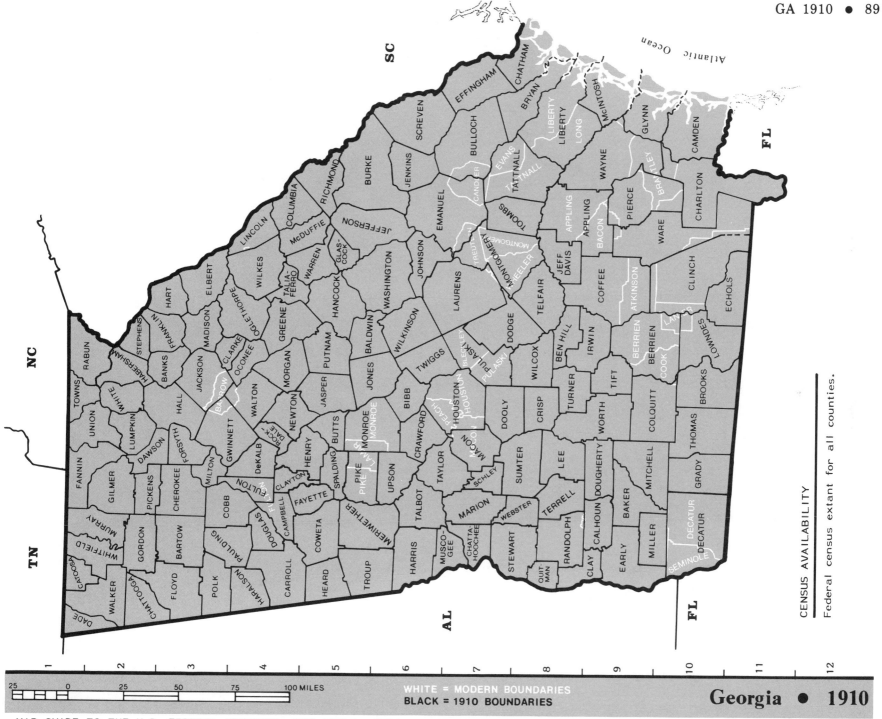

SC

NC

TN

AL

FL

FL

Atlantic Ocean

CENSUS AVAILABILITY

Federal census extant for all counties.

WHITE = MODERN BOUNDARIES
BLACK = 1910 BOUNDARIES

Georgia ● 1910

25 0 25 50 75 100 MILES

1 2 3 4 5 6 7 8 9 10 11 12

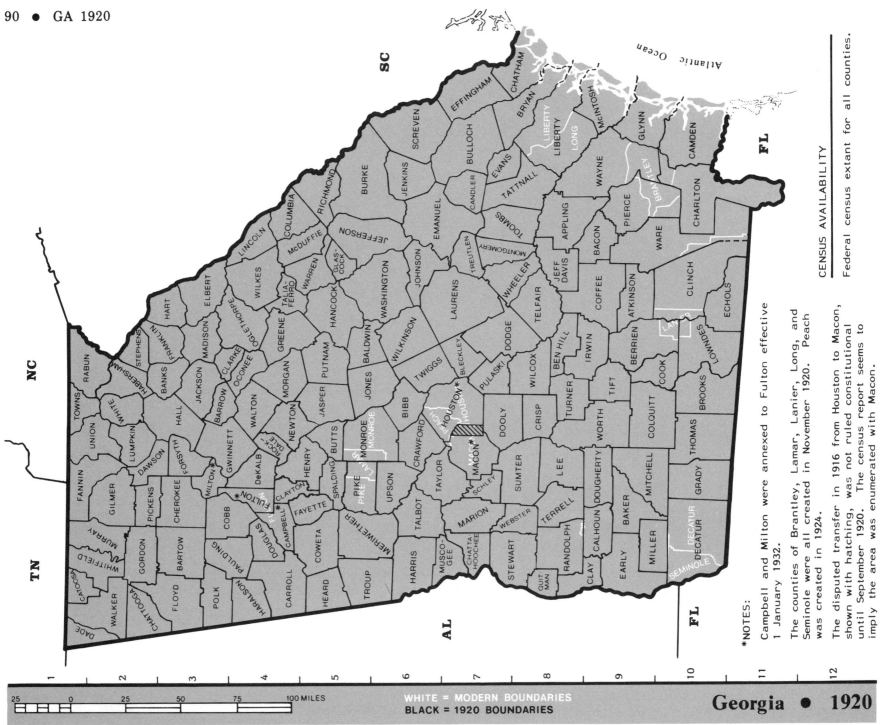

SC

NC

TN

AL

FL

FL

Atlantic Ocean

CENSUS AVAILABILITY

Federal census extant for all counties.

*NOTES:

Campbell and Milton were annexed to Fulton effective 1 January 1932.

The counties of Brantley, Lamar, Lanier, Long, and Seminole were all created in November 1920. Peach was created in 1924.

The disputed transfer in 1916 from Houston to Macon, shown with hatching, was not ruled constitutional until September 1920. The census report seems to imply the area was enumerated with Macon.

25   0   25   50   75   100 MILES

WHITE = MODERN BOUNDARIES
BLACK = 1920 BOUNDARIES

Georgia ● 1920

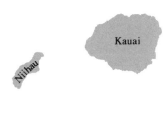

Niihau

Kauai

OCEAN

Oahu

Molokai

PACIFIC

Lanai

Maui

Kahoolawe

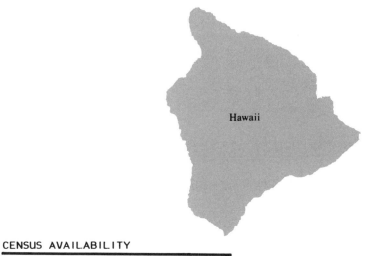

Hawaii

NOTES:

The Hawaiian Islands were annexed to the U.S. in 1898. The 1900 census day was 1 June but the federal census was still being taken when the islands became a territory effective 14 June 1900.

The census is arranged under five islands, there being no counties, with the less populated islands found in the following enumeration districts (EDs):

<u>1900</u>:

Hawaii
Kauai: Niihau ED 84.
Maui: Kahoolawe ED 107 and Lanai ED 100.
Molokai
Oahu

The first constitutional counties were organized in 1905.

Northwest of Niihau lies a string of tiny islands (such as Necker, French Frigate Shoals, and Laysan) reaching to Midway, these uninhabited islands being part of the territory and state of Hawaii if part of the Republic of Hawaii in 1898. Midway was acquired by the U.S. in 1859 and therefore remained outside Hawaii's jurisdiction.

CENSUS AVAILABILITY

Federal census extant for all islands.

1   2   3   4   5   6   7   8   9   10   11   12

25   0   25   50   75   100 MILES

Hawaii ● 1900
AS HAWAII TERRITORY

MAP GUIDE TO THE U.S. FEDERAL CENSUSES, 1790–1920 by William Thorndale and William Dollarhide. Copyright 1987, all rights reserved.

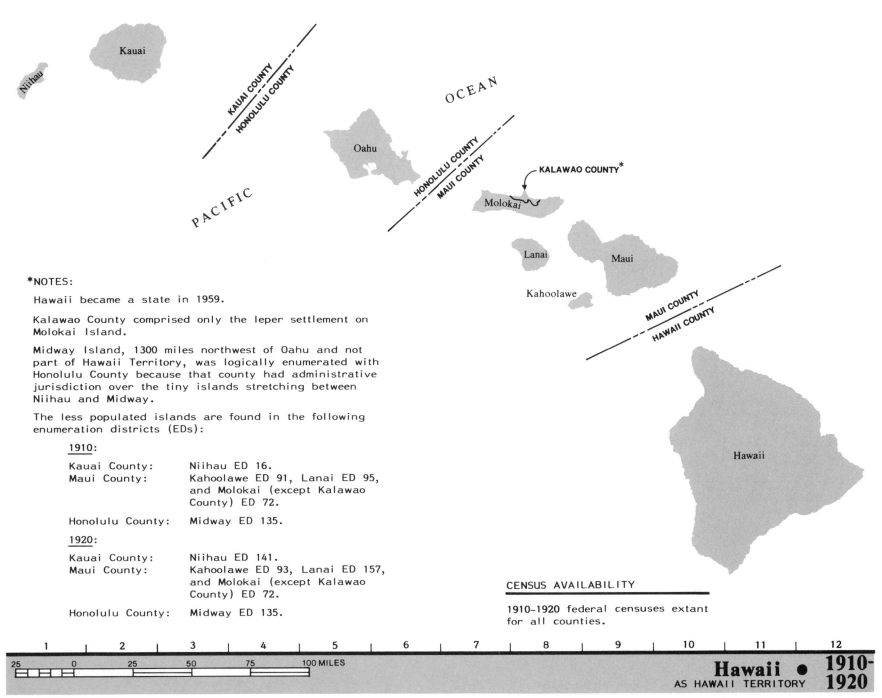

OCEAN

KAUAI COUNTY

HONOLULU COUNTY

Kauai

Niihau

Oahu

HONOLULU COUNTY

MAUI COUNTY

KALAWAO COUNTY *

Molokai

PACIFIC

Lanai

Maui

Kahoolawe

MAUI COUNTY

HAWAII COUNTY

*NOTES:

Hawaii became a state in 1959.

Kalawao County comprised only the leper settlement on Molokai Island.

Midway Island, 1300 miles northwest of Oahu and not part of Hawaii Territory, was logically enumerated with Honolulu County because that county had administrative jurisdiction over the tiny islands stretching between Niihau and Midway.

The less populated islands are found in the following enumeration districts (EDs):

1910:

Kauai County:	Niihau ED 16.
Maui County:	Kahoolawe ED 91, Lanai ED 95, and Molokai (except Kalawao County) ED 72.
Honolulu County:	Midway ED 135.

1920:

Kauai County:	Niihau ED 141.
Maui County:	Kahoolawe ED 93, Lanai ED 157, and Molokai (except Kalawao County) ED 72.
Honolulu County:	Midway ED 135.

Hawaii

CENSUS AVAILABILITY

1910–1920 federal censuses extant for all counties.

| 1 | 2 | 3 | 4 | 5 | 6 | 7 | 8 | 9 | 10 | 11 | 12 |

25 0 25 50 75 100 MILES

Hawaii ●
AS HAWAII TERRITORY
1910-1920

MAP GUIDE TO THE U.S. FEDERAL CENSUSES, 1790-1920 by William Thorndale and William Dollarhide. Copyright 1987, all rights reserved.

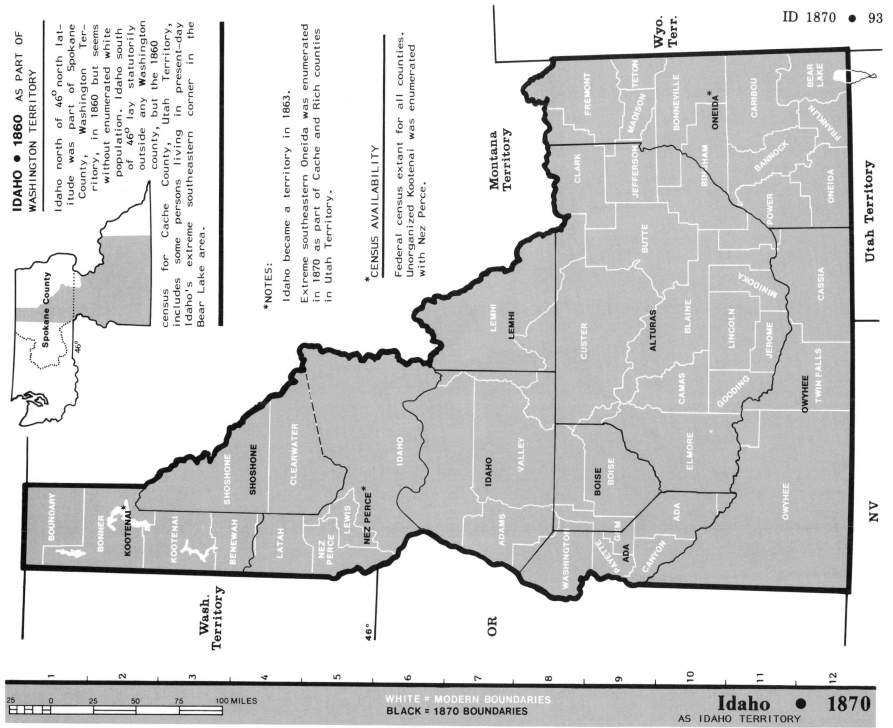

IDAHO ● 1860 AS PART OF WASHINGTON TERRITORY

Idaho north of 46° north latitude was part of Spokane County, Washington Territory, in 1860 but seems without enumerated white population. Idaho south of 46° lay statutorily outside any Washington county, but the 1860 census for Cache County, Utah Territory, includes some persons living in present-day Idaho's extreme southeastern corner in the Bear Lake area.

Spokane County

46°

*NOTES:

Idaho became a territory in 1863.

Extreme southeastern Oneida was enumerated in 1870 as part of Cache and Rich counties in Utah Territory.

*CENSUS AVAILABILITY

Federal census extant for all counties. Unorganized Kootenai was enumerated with Nez Perce.

Wyo. Terr.

Montana Territory

Wash. Territory

46°

OR

Utah Territory

NV

25 0 25 50 75 100 MILES

WHITE = MODERN BOUNDARIES
BLACK = 1870 BOUNDARIES

Idaho ● 1870
AS IDAHO TERRITORY

MAP GUIDE TO THE U.S. FEDERAL CENSUSES, 1790–1920 by William Thorndale and William Dollarhide. Copyright 1987, all rights reserved.

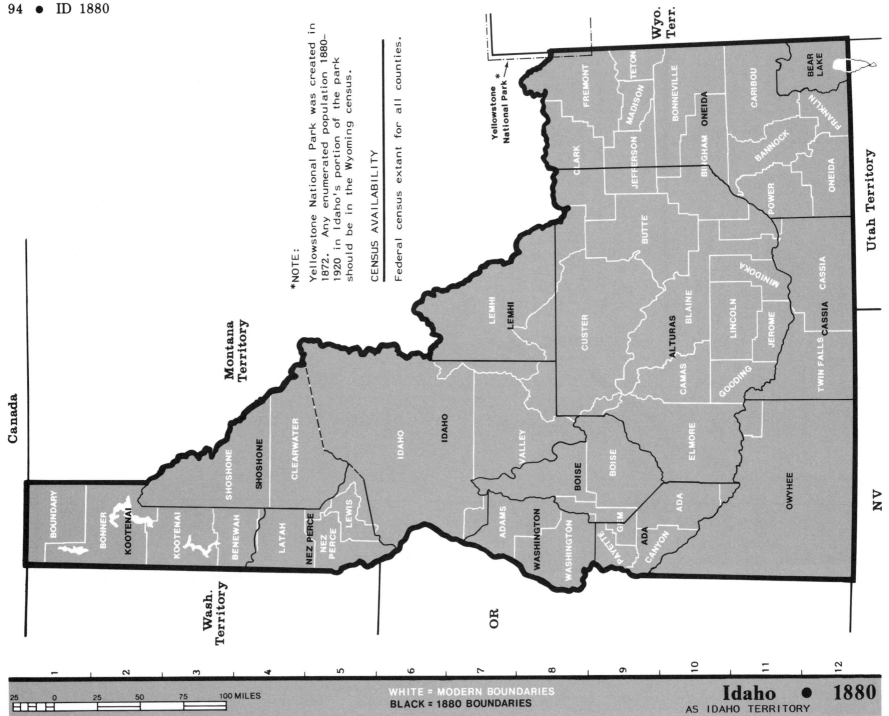

*NOTE:

Yellowstone National Park was created in 1872. Any enumerated population 1880–1920 in Idaho's portion of the park should be in the Wyoming census.

CENSUS AVAILABILITY

Federal census extant for all counties.

Yellowstone National Park *

Wyo. Terr.

Utah Territory

Montana Territory

Canada

Wash. Territory

OR

NV

WHITE = MODERN BOUNDARIES
BLACK = 1880 BOUNDARIES

Idaho ● 1880
AS IDAHO TERRITORY

25 0 25 50 75 100 MILES

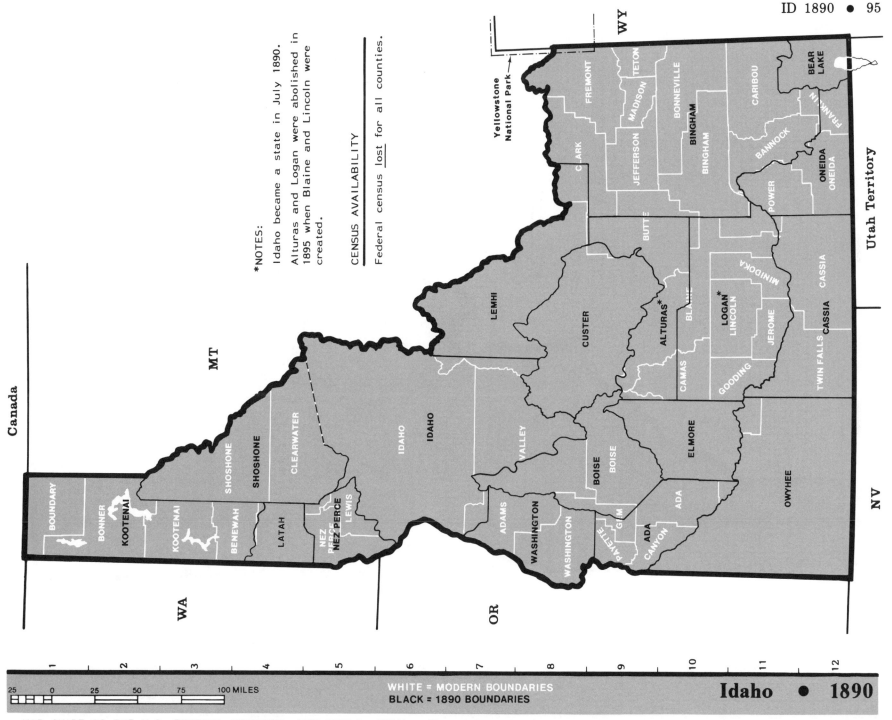

WY

Canada

MT

WA

OR

NV

Utah Territory

*NOTES:

Idaho became a state in July 1890.

Alturas and Logan were abolished in 1895 when Blaine and Lincoln were created.

CENSUS AVAILABILITY

Federal census lost for all counties.

Yellowstone National Park

BOUNDARY

BONNER

KOOTENAI

KOOTENAI

BENEWAH

LATAH

NEZ PERCE

NEZ PERCE

LEWIS

SHOSHONE

SHOSHONE

CLEARWATER

IDAHO

IDAHO

LEMHI

CUSTER

VALLEY

ADAMS

WASHINGTON

WASHINGTON

PAYETTE

GEM

CANYON

ADA

ADA

BOISE

BOISE

ELMORE

OWYHEE

ALTURAS*

BLAINE

CAMAS

GOODING

LOGAN*

LINCOLN

JEROME

MINIDOKA

CASSIA

CASSIA

CASSIA

TWIN FALLS

CLARK

BUTTE

FREMONT

TETON

MADISON

JEFFERSON

BONNEVILLE

BINGHAM

BINGHAM

BINGHAM

POWER

BANNOCK

CARIBOU

ONEIDA

ONEIDA

FRANKLIN

BEAR LAKE

1   2   3   4   5   6   7   8   9   10   11   12

25   0   25   50   75   100 MILES

WHITE = MODERN BOUNDARIES
BLACK = 1890 BOUNDARIES

Idaho ● **1890**

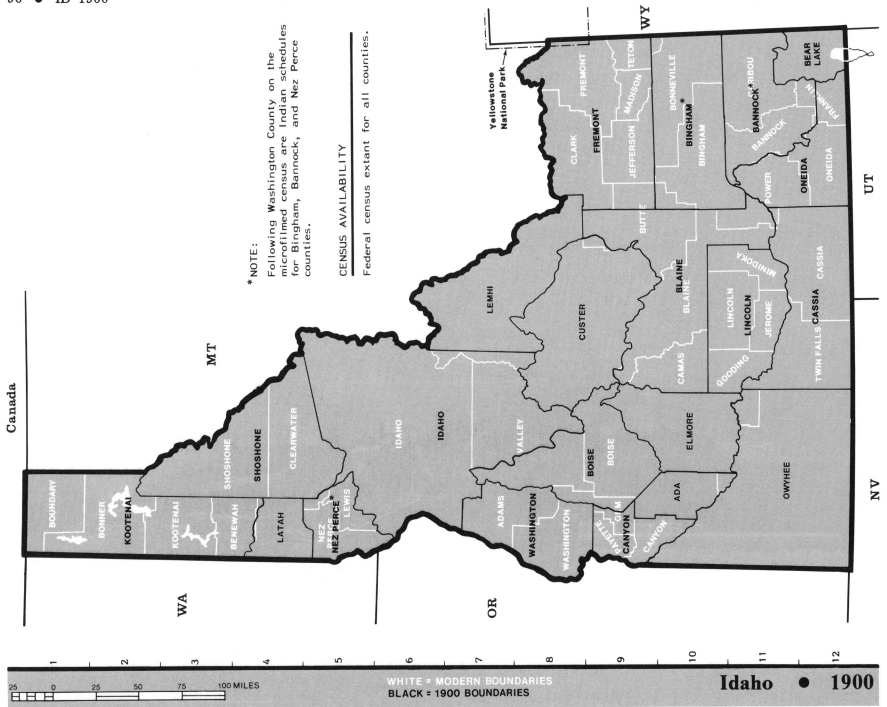

MAP GUIDE TO THE U.S. FEDERAL CENSUSES, 1790–1920 by William Thorndale and William Dollarhide. Copyright 1987, all rights reserved.

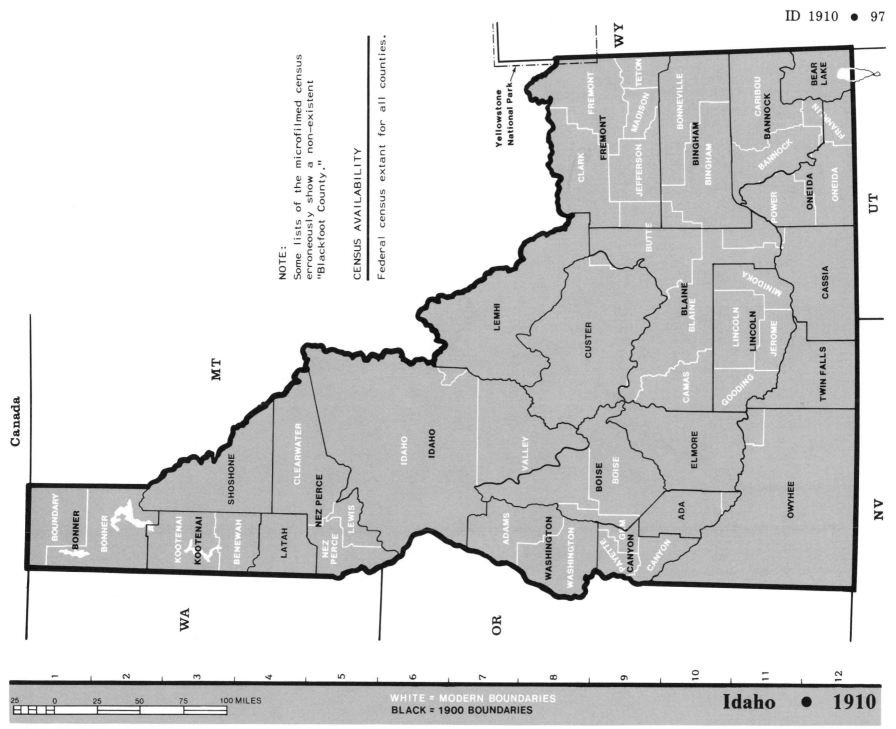

NOTE:

Some lists of the microfilmed census erroneously show a non-existent "Blackfoot County."

CENSUS AVAILABILITY

Federal census extant for all counties.

Yellowstone National Park

WY

Canada

MT

WA

OR

NV

UT

BOUNDARY

BONNER

KOOTENAI

BENEWAH

LATAH

NEZ PERCE

LEWIS

SHOSHONE

CLEARWATER

IDAHO

LEMHI

CUSTER

VALLEY

ADAMS

WASHINGTON

PAYETTE

GEM

CANYON

ADA

BOISE

ELMORE

OWYHEE

CLARK

FREMONT

JEFFERSON

MADISON

TETON

BONNEVILLE

BINGHAM

BUTTE

BLAINE

CAMAS

LINCOLN

JEROME

GOODING

MINIDOKA

CASSIA

TWIN FALLS

POWER

BANNOCK

ONEIDA

CARIBOU

FRANKLIN

BEAR LAKE

WHITE = MODERN BOUNDARIES
BLACK = 1900 BOUNDARIES

Idaho ● 1910

25   0   25   50   75   100 MILES

MAP GUIDE TO THE U.S. FEDERAL CENSUSES, 1790–1920 by William Thorndale and William Dollarhide. Copyright 1987, all rights reserved.

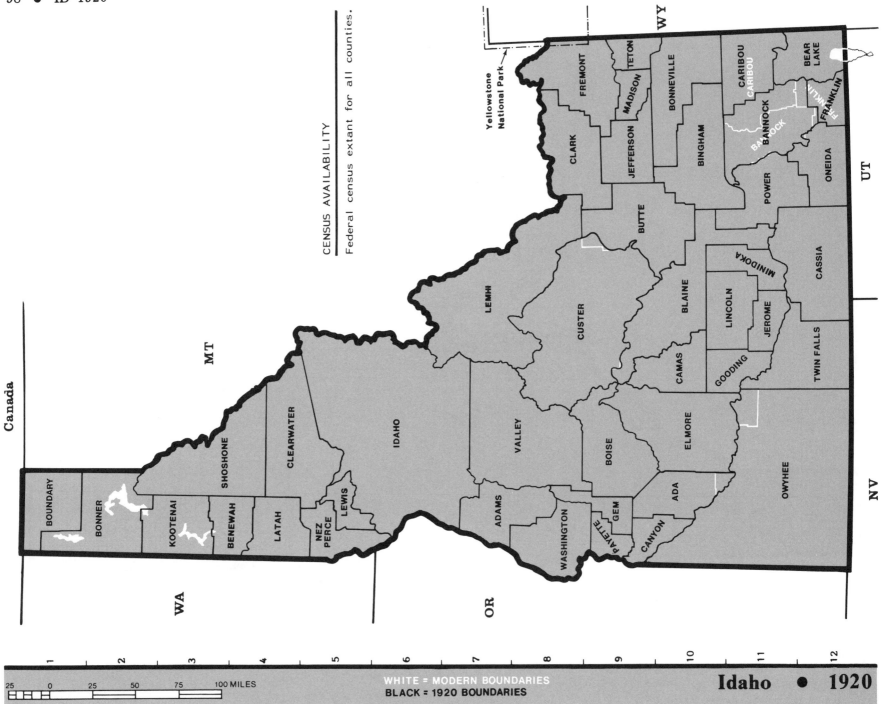

CENSUS AVAILABILITY

Federal census extant for all counties.

Yellowstone
National Park

WY

Canada

MT

WA

OR

UT

NV

BOUNDARY

BONNER

KOOTENAI

BENEWAH

LATAH

NEZ PERCE

LEWIS

SHOSHONE

CLEARWATER

IDAHO

LEMHI

CUSTER

VALLEY

ADAMS

WASHINGTON

PAYETTE

GEM

CANYON

ADA

BOISE

ELMORE

OWYHEE

CLARK

FREMONT

MADISON

TETON

JEFFERSON

BONNEVILLE

BINGHAM

BUTTE

BLAINE

CAMAS

GOODING

LINCOLN

JEROME

MINIDOKA

CASSIA

TWIN FALLS

POWER

BANNOCK

CARIBOU

CARIBOU

BEAR LAKE

FRANKLIN

FRANKLIN

ONEIDA

25   0   25   50   75   100 MILES

1 2 3 4 5 6 7 8 9 10 11 12

WHITE = MODERN BOUNDARIES
BLACK = 1920 BOUNDARIES

Idaho ● 1920

MAP GUIDE TO THE U.S. FEDERAL CENSUSES, 1790–1920 by William Thorndale and William Dollarhide. Copyright 1987, all rights reserved.

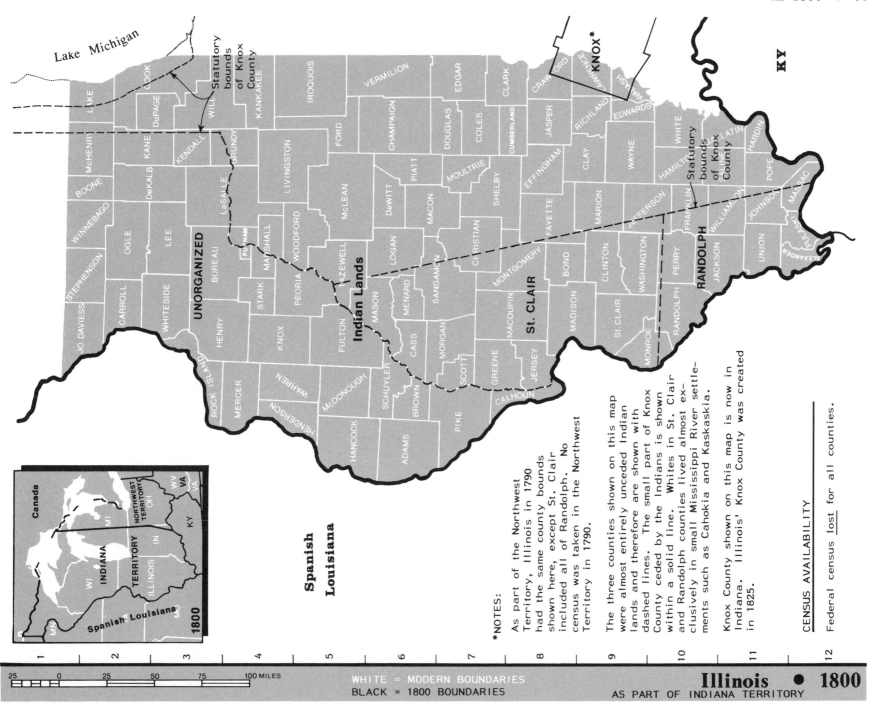

Lake Michigan

KY

Statutory bounds of Knox County

KNOX*

LAKE

COOK

DuPAGE

WILL

KANKAKEE

IROQUOIS

VERMILION

EDGAR

CLARK

CRAWFORD

LAWRENCE

WABASH

McHENRY

KANE

KENDALL

GRUNDY

FORD

CHAMPAIGN

DOUGLAS

COLES

CUMBERLAND

JASPER

RICHLAND

EDWARDS

WHITE

Statutory bounds of Knox County

BOONE

DeKALB

DuPAGE

WINNEBAGO

OGLE

LEE

LaSALLE

LIVINGSTON

McLEAN

DeWITT

PIATT

MOULTRIE

SHELBY

EFFINGHAM

FAYETTE

CLAY

WAYNE

HAMILTON

GALLATIN

SALINE

HARDIN

STEPHENSON

CARROLL

WHITESIDE

UNORGANIZED

BUREAU

PUTNAM

WOODFORD

TAZEWELL

LOGAN

MACON

CHRISTIAN

MONTGOMERY

MARION

JEFFERSON

FRANKLIN

WILLIAMSON

JOHNSON

POPE

JO DAVIESS

ROCK ISLAND

HENRY

STARK

PEORIA

KNOX

MARSHALL

MASON

MENARD

SANGAMON

BOND

CLINTON

WASHINGTON

PERRY

RANDOLPH

JACKSON

UNION

MASSAC

MERCER

WARREN

FULTON

Indian Lands

CASS

MORGAN

St. CLAIR

MADISON

St. CLAIR

MONROE

RANDOLPH

PULASKI

ALEXANDER

HENDERSON

McDONOUGH

SCHUYLER

BROWN

SCOTT

GREENE

JERSEY

MACOUPIN

PIKE

CALHOUN

HANCOCK

ADAMS

Canada

NORTHWEST TERRITORY

WV VA

VA

OH

MI

WI

INDIANA

IL

TERRITORY

KY

ILLINOIS

IN

MN

Spanish Louisiana

1800

Spanish Louisiana

*NOTES:

As part of the Northwest Territory, Illinois in 1790 had the same county bounds shown here, except St. Clair included all of Randolph. No census was taken in the Northwest Territory in 1790.

The three counties shown on this map were almost entirely unceded Indian lands and therefore are shown with dashed lines. The small part of Knox County ceded by the Indians is shown within a solid line. Whites in St. Clair and Randolph counties lived almost exclusively in small Mississippi River settlements such as Cahokia and Kaskaskia.

Knox County shown on this map is now in Indiana. Illinois' Knox County was created in 1825.

CENSUS AVAILABILITY

Federal census lost for all counties.

| 1 | 2 | 3 | 4 | 5 | 6 | 7 | 8 | 9 | 10 | 11 | 12 |

25 0 25 50 75 100 MILES

WHITE = MODERN BOUNDARIES
BLACK = 1800 BOUNDARIES

Illinois ● 1800

AS PART OF INDIANA TERRITORY

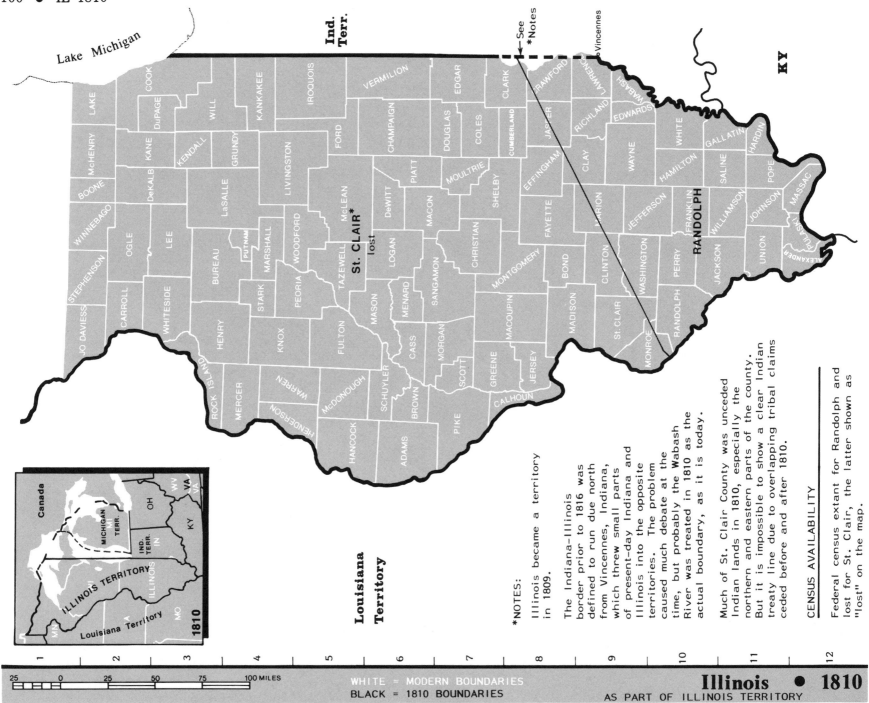

Ind. Terr.

Lake Michigan

KY

See →*Notes

Vincennes

LAKE

COOK

KANKAKEE

IROQUOIS

VERMILION

EDGAR

CLARK

CRAWFORD

LAWRENCE

WABASH

McHENRY

BOONE

DuPAGE

WILL

KANE

KENDALL

GRUNDY

FORD

CHAMPAIGN

DOUGLAS

COLES

CUMBERLAND

JASPER

RICHLAND

EDWARDS

WHITE

GALLATIN

HARDIN

WINNEBAGO

DeKALB

LaSALLE

LIVINGSTON

McLEAN

PIATT

MOULTRIE

SHELBY

EFFINGHAM

CLAY

WAYNE

HAMILTON

SALINE

POPE

OGLE

LEE

WOODFORD

DeWITT

MACON

CHRISTIAN

FAYETTE

MARION

JEFFERSON

FRANKLIN

WILLIAMSON

JOHNSON

MASSAC

STEPHENSON

BUREAU

PUTNAM

MARSHALL

STARK

PEORIA

LOGAN

SANGAMON

MONTGOMERY

BOND

CLINTON

WASHINGTON

PERRY

JACKSON

UNION

PULASKI

ALEXANDER

CARROLL

WHITESIDE

St. CLAIR*
lost

MASON

MENARD

MACOUPIN

MADISON

St. CLAIR

RANDOLPH

JO DAVIESS

ROCK ISLAND

HENRY

KNOX

FULTON

CASS

MORGAN

GREENE

JERSEY

MONROE

RANDOLPH

MERCER

WARREN

McDONOUGH

SCHUYLER

BROWN

SCOTT

CALHOUN

HENDERSON

HANCOCK

ADAMS

PIKE

Louisiana
Territory

*NOTES:

Illinois became a territory
in 1809.

The Indiana–Illinois
border prior to 1816 was
defined to run due north
from Vincennes, Indiana,
which threw small parts
of present-day Indiana and
Illinois into the opposite
territories. The problem
caused much debate at the
time, but probably the Wabash
River was treated in 1810 as the
actual boundary, as it is today.

Much of St. Clair County was unceded
Indian lands in 1810, especially the
northern and eastern parts of the county.
But it is impossible to show a clear Indian
treaty line due to overlapping tribal claims
ceded before and after 1810.

CENSUS AVAILABILITY

Federal census extant for Randolph and
lost for St. Clair, the latter shown as
"lost" on the map.

Canada

MICHIGAN TERR.

OH

WV
VA
VA

MI

IND. TERR.

IN

KY

ILLINOIS TERRITORY

ILLINOIS

MN

IA

MO

Louisiana Territory

1810

25 0 25 50 75 100 MILES

1 2 3 4 5 6 7 8 9 10 11 12

WHITE = MODERN BOUNDARIES
BLACK = 1810 BOUNDARIES

Illinois ● 1810

AS PART OF ILLINOIS TERRITORY

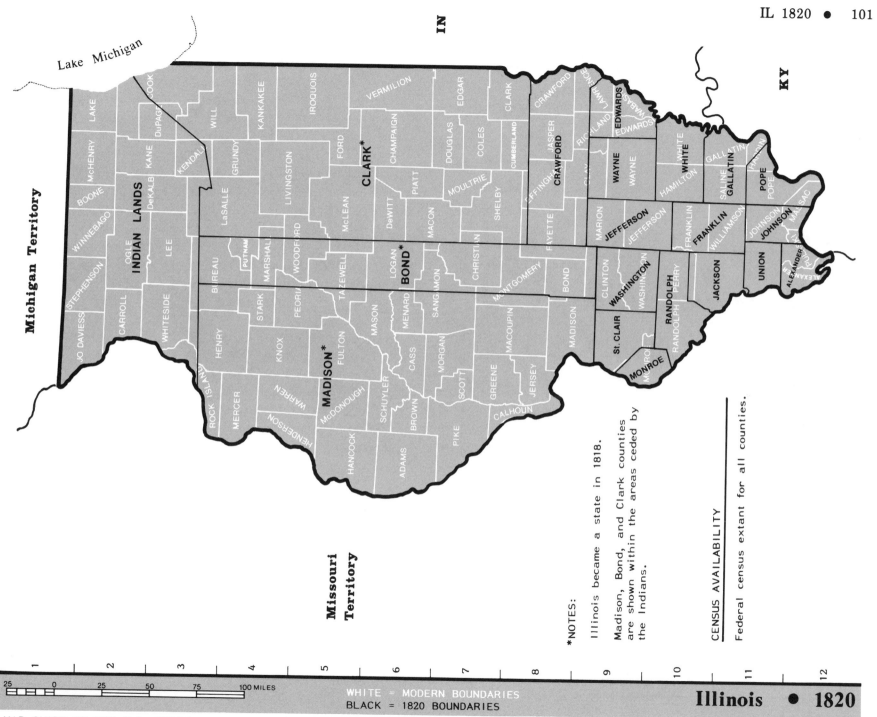

IN

KY

Lake Michigan

Michigan Territory

INDIAN LANDS

Missouri Territory

*NOTES:

Illinois became a state in 1818.

Madison, Bond, and Clark counties are shown within the areas ceded by the Indians.

CENSUS AVAILABILITY

Federal census extant for all counties.

CLARK*

BOND*

MADISON*

100 MILES

WHITE = MODERN BOUNDARIES
BLACK = 1820 BOUNDARIES

Illinois ● **1820**

MAP GUIDE TO THE U.S. FEDERAL CENSUSES, 1790–1920 by William Thorndale and William Dollarhide. Copyright 1987, all rights reserved.

IN

KY

Lake Michigan

Michigan Territory

Unorganized

MO

COOK

LAKE

McHENRY

BOONE

WINNEBAGO

STEPHENSON

JO DAVIESS

OGLE

LEE

DeKALB

KANE

DuPAGE

WILL

KENDALL

GRUNDY

IROQUOIS

KANKAKEE

VERMILION

VERMILION

FORD

CHAMPAIGN

DOUGLAS

EDGAR

EDGAR

COLES

CLARK

CLARK

CRAWFORD

JASPER

CRAWFORD

LAWRENCE

LAWRENCE

WABASH

EDWARDS

RICHLAND

CLAY

WAYNE

WHITE

HAMILTON

GALLATIN

SALINE

POPE

POPE

HARDIN

MASSAC

ALEXANDER

PULASKI

UNION

JOHNSON

JOHNSON

WILLIAMSON

FRANKLIN

FRANKLIN

JEFFERSON

MARION

CLINTON

WASHINGTON

PERRY

JACKSON

RANDOLPH

MONROE

St. CLAIR

MADISON

BOND

MONTGOMERY

MACOUPIN

GREENE

GREENE

JERSEY

CALHOUN

Detached Part of **PUTNAM**

LaSALLE

LIVINGSTON

TAZEWELL

McLEAN

TAZEWELL

WOODFORD

MARSHALL

PUTNAM

PUTNAM

STARK

PEORIA

KNOX

FULTON

MASON

DeWITT

PIATT

MACON

MACON

SHELBY

MOULTRIE

CUMBERLAND

FAYETTE

FAYETTE

EFFINGHAM

LOGAN

MENARD

SANGAMON

SANGAMON

CHRISTIAN

WINNEBAGO

CARROLL

JO DAVIESS

WHITESIDE

BUREAU

HENRY

HENRY

ROCK ISLAND

MERCER

WARREN

WARREN

HENDERSON

McDONOUGH

SCHUYLER

SCHUYLER

BROWN

CASS

MORGAN

MORGAN

SCOTT

PIKE

HANCOCK

ADAMS

25   0   25   50   75   100 MILES

WHITE = MODERN BOUNDARIES
BLACK = 1830 BOUNDARIES

Illinois   ●   **1830**

1 2 3 4 5 6 7 8 9 10 11 12

MAP GUIDE TO THE U.S. FEDERAL CENSUSES, 1790–1920 by William Thorndale and William Dollarhide.   Copyright 1987, all rights reserved.

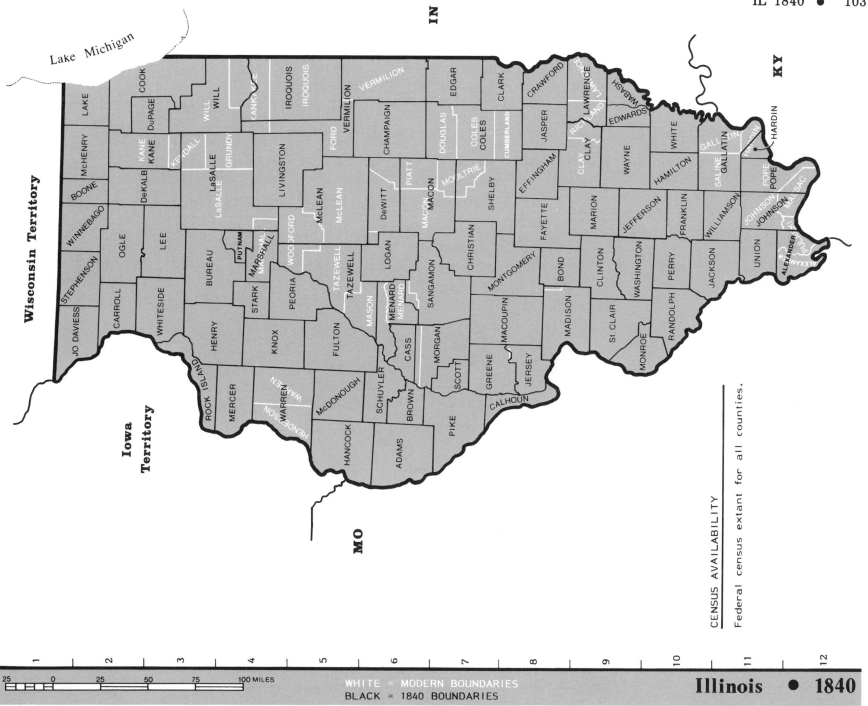

Illinois ● 1840

CENSUS AVAILABILITY
Federal census extant for all counties.

IN

KY

Lake Michigan

LAKE

COOK

DuPAGE

WILL
WILL

IROQUOIS

IROQUOIS

KANKAKEE

VERMILION

VERMILION

EDGAR

CLARK

CRAWFORD

LAWRENCE

WABASH

McHENRY

KANE

KENDALL

GRUNDY

FORD

VERMILION

CHAMPAIGN

DOUGLAS

COLES
COLES

CUMBERLAND

JASPER

RICHLAND

EDWARDS

WHITE

GALLATIN

HARDIN

BOONE

DeKALB

LaSALLE

LIVINGSTON

McLEAN

DeWITT

PIATT

MOULTRIE

SHELBY

EFFINGHAM

CLAY

WAYNE

HAMILTON

SALINE

POPE

MASSAC

WINNEBAGO

OGLE

LEE

BUREAU

PUTNAM

MARSHALL

WOODFORD

TAZEWELL

LOGAN

MACON

CHRISTIAN

FAYETTE

MARION

JEFFERSON

FRANKLIN

WILLIAMSON

JOHNSON

PULASKI

ALEXANDER

STEPHENSON

CARROLL

WHITESIDE

HENRY

STARK

PEORIA

KNOX

FULTON

MASON

MENARD

SANGAMON

MONTGOMERY

BOND

CLINTON

WASHINGTON

PERRY

JACKSON

UNION

JO DAVIESS

ROCK ISLAND

MERCER

WARREN

HENDERSON

McDONOUGH

SCHUYLER

CASS

MORGAN

MACOUPIN

MADISON

St. CLAIR

MONROE

RANDOLPH

HANCOCK

ADAMS

BROWN

SCOTT

GREENE

JERSEY

CALHOUN

PIKE

WI

IA

MO

CENSUS AVAILABILITY

Federal census extant for all counties.

1   2   3   4   5   6   7   8   9   10   11   12

25   0   25   50   75   100 MILES

WHITE = MODERN BOUNDARIES
BLACK = 1850 BOUNDARIES

Illinois ● **1850**

MAP GUIDE TO THE U.S. FEDERAL CENSUSES, 1790-1920 by William Thorndale and William Dollarhide.   Copyright 1987, all rights reserved.

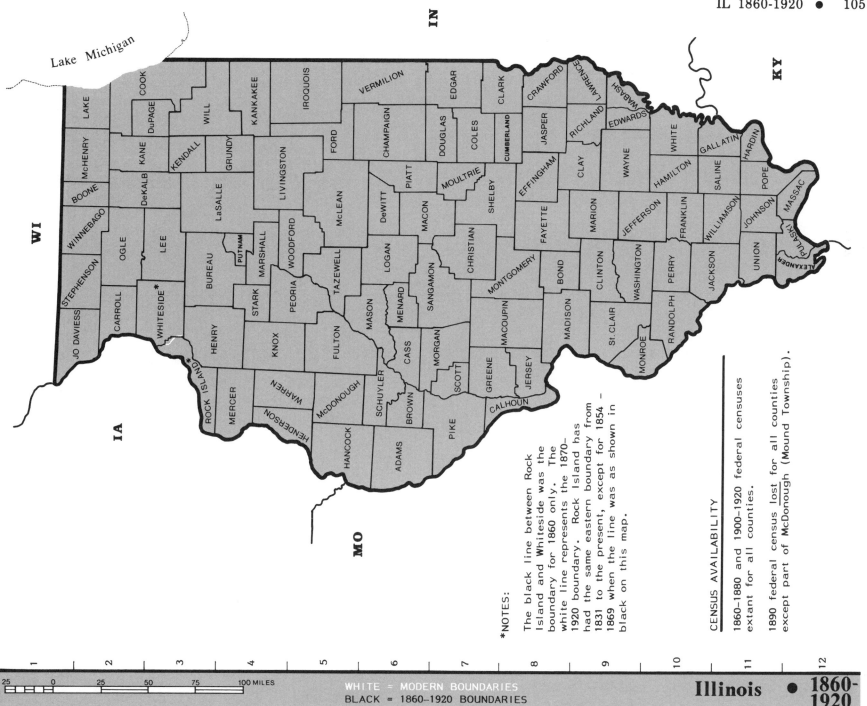

*NOTES:

The black line between Rock Island and Whiteside was the boundary for 1860 only. The white line represents the 1870–1920 boundary. Rock Island has had the same eastern boundary from 1831 to the present, except for 1854 – 1869 when the line was as shown in black on this map.

CENSUS AVAILABILITY

1860–1880 and 1900–1920 federal censuses extant for all counties.

1890 federal census lost for all counties except part of McDonough (Mound Township).

WHITE = MODERN BOUNDARIES
BLACK = 1860–1920 BOUNDARIES

Illinois ● 1860-1920

MAP GUIDE TO THE U.S. FEDERAL CENSUSES, 1790–1920 by William Thorndale and William Dollarhide. Copyright 1987, all rights reserved.

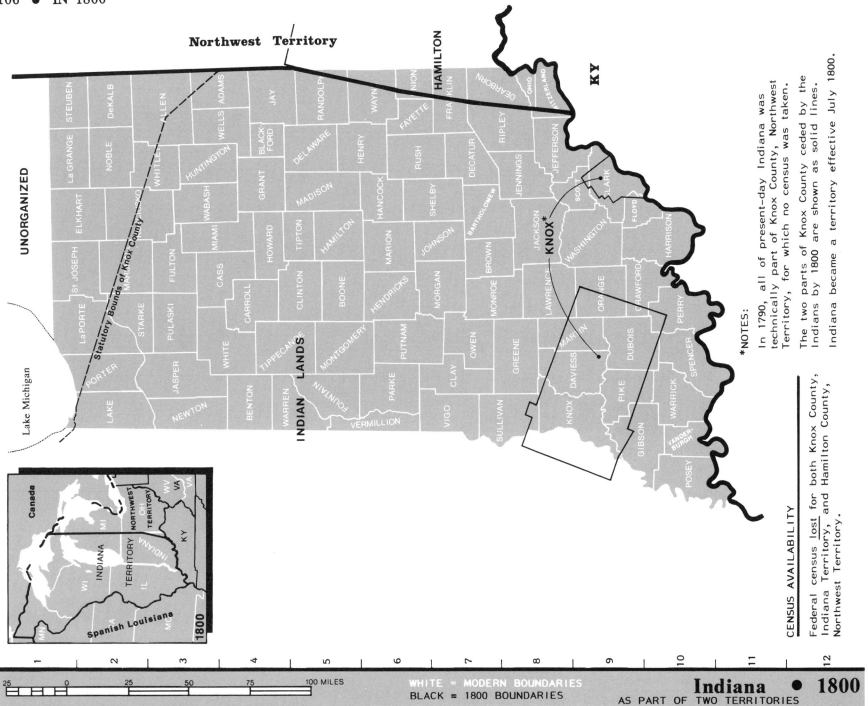

Northwest Territory

HAMILTON

KY

UNORGANIZED

Lake Michigan

*NOTES:

In 1790, all of present-day Indiana was technically part of Knox County, Northwest Territory, for which no census was taken.

The two parts of Knox County ceded by the Indians by 1800 are shown as solid lines. Indiana became a territory effective July 1800.

CENSUS AVAILABILITY

Federal census lost for both Knox County, Indiana Territory, and Hamilton County, Northwest Territory.

INDIAN LANDS

KNOX*

Statutory Bounds of Knox County

Canada

Spanish Louisiana

1800

100 MILES

WHITE = MODERN BOUNDARIES
BLACK = 1800 BOUNDARIES

Indiana ● **1800**
AS PART OF TWO TERRITORIES

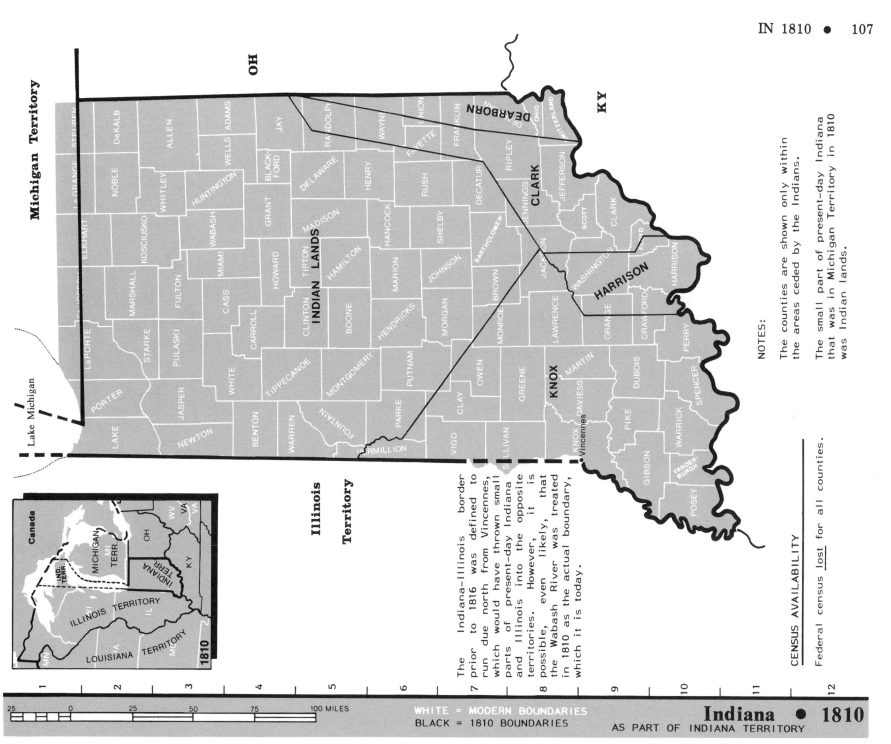

Michigan Territory

OH

KY

Illinois Territory

Lake Michigan

Canada

MICHIGAN TERR.

OH

ILLINOIS TERRITORY

IND. TERR.

KY

LOUISIANA TERRITORY

1810

MN

IA

IL

MO

WV

VA

VA

NOTES:

The counties are shown only within the areas ceded by the Indians.

The small part of present-day Indiana that was in Michigan Territory in 1810 was Indian lands.

The Indiana-Illinois border prior to 1816 was defined to run due north from Vincennes, which would have thrown small parts of present-day Indiana and Illinois into the opposite territories. However, it is possible, even likely, that the Wabash River was treated in 1810 as the actual boundary, which it is today.

CENSUS AVAILABILITY

Federal census lost for all counties.

LaGRANGE STEUBEN
DeKALB
ALLEN
NOBLE
WHITLEY
ELKHART
ST. JOSEPH
LaPORTE
PORTER
LAKE
NEWTON
JASPER
STARKE
PULASKI
MARSHALL
FULTON
KOSCIUSKO
WELLS ADAMS
HUNTINGTON
WABASH
MIAMI
CASS
WHITE
BENTON
WARREN
FOUNTAIN
TIPPECANOE
CARROLL
HOWARD
GRANT
BLACK-FORD
JAY
RANDOLPH
WAYNE
UNION
FRANKLIN
FAYETTE
DELAWARE
HENRY
RUSH
MADISON
HAMILTON
TIPTON
CLINTON
BOONE
MONTGOMERY
PARKE
VERMILLION
VIGO
CLAY
OWEN
MONROE
GREENE
SULLIVAN
KNOX
Vincennes
DAVIESS
MARTIN
LAWRENCE
ORANGE
DUBOIS
PIKE
GIBSON
VANDER-BURGH
POSEY
WARRICK
SPENCER
PERRY
CRAWFORD
HARRISON
WASHINGTON
FLOYD
CLARK
SCOTT
JEFFERSON
SWITZERLAND
OHIO
DEARBORN
RIPLEY
JENNINGS
DECATUR
BARTHOLOMEW
BROWN
JACKSON
MORGAN
JOHNSON
SHELBY
HANCOCK
MARION
HENDRICKS
PUTNAM
INDIAN LANDS
KNOX
HARRISON
CLARK

25 0 25 50 75 100 MILES

1 2 3 4 5 6 7 8 9 10 11 12

Indiana • 1810
AS PART OF INDIANA TERRITORY

Michigan Territory

Lake Michigan

OH

KY

IL

INDIAN LANDS

Steuben · DeKalb · Allen · Adams · Wells · Randolph · Jay · Wayne · Union · Franklin · Dearborn · Switzerland

LaGrange · Noble · Whitley · Huntington · Blackford · Delaware* · Henry · Fayette · Ripley · Jefferson · Ohio

Elkhart · Kosciusko · Wabash · Grant · Madison · Hancock · Rush · Decatur · Jennings · Scott · Clark · Floyd · Part of Harrison

St Joseph · Marshall · Fulton · Miami · Howard · Tipton · Hamilton · Shelby · Bartholomew · Jackson · Washington · Harrison

LaPorte · Starke · Pulaski · Cass · Clinton · Boone · Hendricks · Marion · Johnson · Brown · Monroe · Lawrence · Orange · Crawford · Perry

Porter · Jasper · White · Carroll · Tippecanoe* · Montgomery · Putnam · Morgan · Owen · Monroe · Martin · Dubois · Spencer

Lake · Newton · Benton · Warren · Fountain · Parke · Vigo · Clay · Owen · Greene · Daviess lost · Knox · Pike · Gibson · Warrick · Vanderburgh · Posey

Vermillion · Sullivan

DELAWARE*

WABASH*

*NOTES:

Ceded Indian lands were carved into the unorganized "counties" of Delaware and Wabash, which were used as census districts in 1820. The present counties of these names were formed in 1827 and 1832 respectively.

Indiana became a state in 1816.

CENSUS AVAILABILITY

Federal census extant for all counties except Daviess, shown as "lost" on map.

25 0 25 50 75 100 MILES

1 2 3 4 5 6 7 8 9 10 11 12

WHITE = MODERN BOUNDARIES
BLACK = 1820 BOUNDARIES

Indiana • 1820

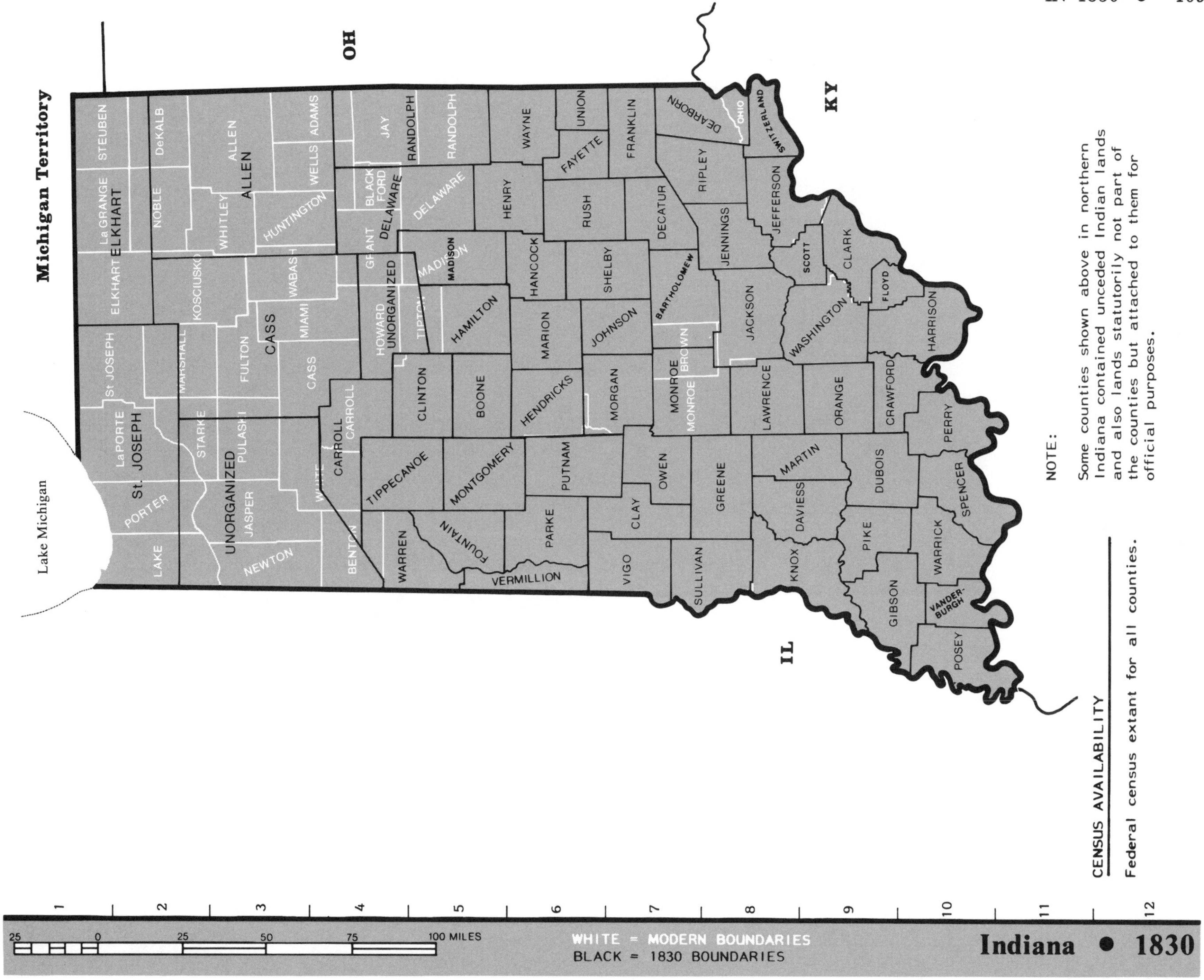

NOTE:

Some counties shown above in northern Indiana contained unceded Indian lands and also lands statutorily not part of the counties but attached to them for official purposes.

CENSUS AVAILABILITY

Federal census extant for all counties.

WHITE = MODERN BOUNDARIES
BLACK = 1830 BOUNDARIES

Indiana ● 1830

25   0   25   50   75   100 MILES

Michigan Territory

Lake Michigan

OH

KY

IL

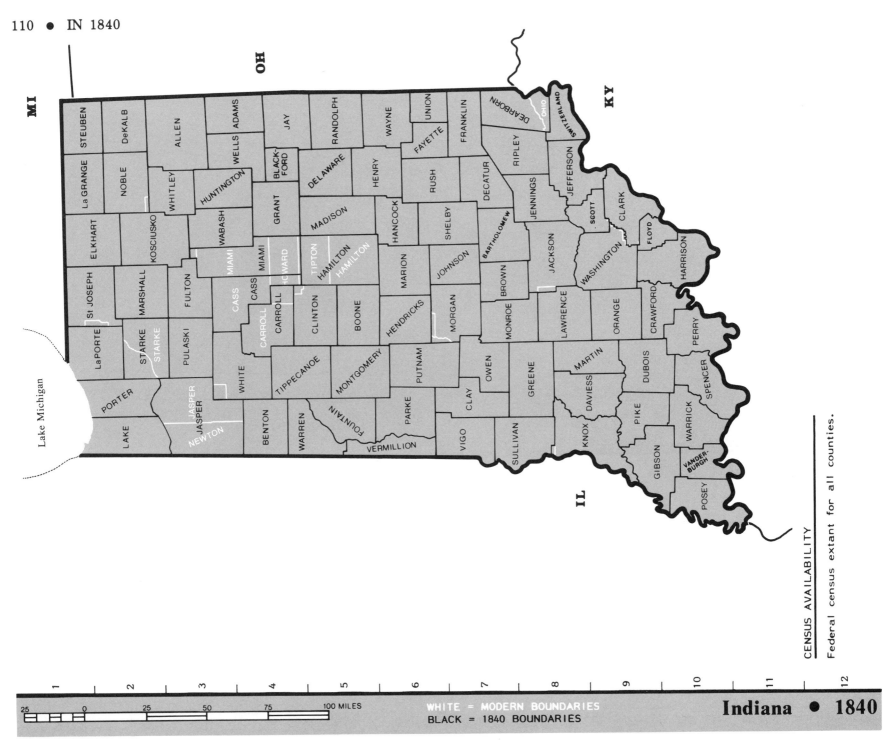

MI

OH

KY

IL

Lake Michigan

25   0   25   50   75   100 MILES

1 2 3 4 5 6 7 8 9 10 11 12

WHITE = MODERN BOUNDARIES
BLACK = 1840 BOUNDARIES

Indiana ● 1840

MAP GUIDE TO THE U.S. FEDERAL CENSUSES, 1790–1920 by William Thorndale and William Dollarhide. Copyright 1987, all rights reserved.

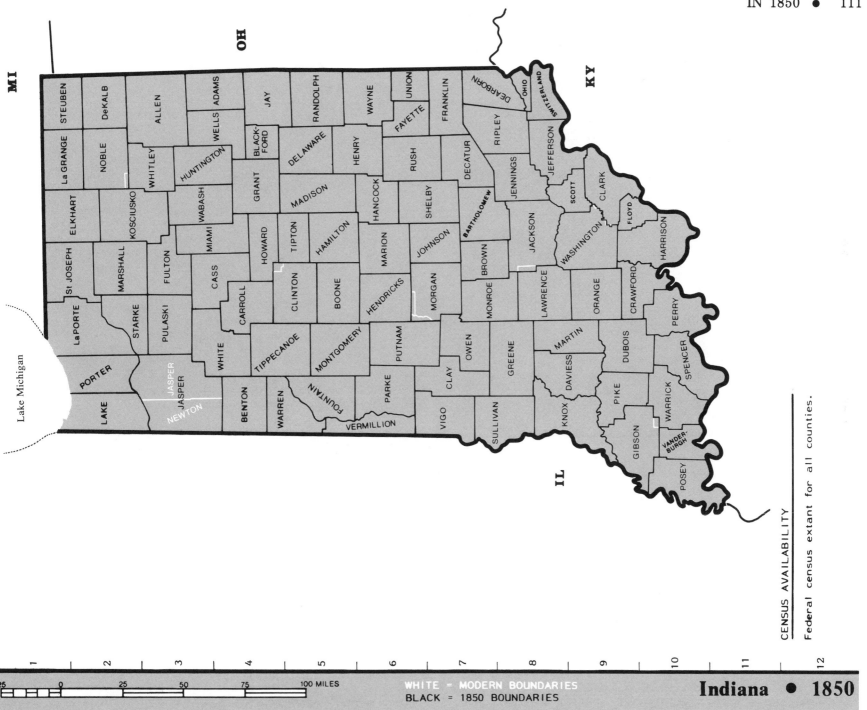

MI

OH

KY

IL

Lake Michigan

STEUBEN
DeKALB
LA GRANGE
NOBLE
ALLEN
WELLS
ADAMS
WHITLEY
HUNTINGTON
BLACK-FORD
JAY
DELAWARE
RANDOLPH
WAYNE
UNION
FAYETTE
FRANKLIN
DEARBORN
OHIO
SWITZERLAND
ELKHART
St JOSEPH
MARSHALL
KOSCIUSKO
WABASH
MIAMI
GRANT
MADISON
HENRY
HANCOCK
RUSH
SHELBY
DECATUR
RIPLEY
JENNINGS
JEFFERSON
SCOTT
CLARK
FLOYD
HARRISON
LAPORTE
STARKE
PULASKI
FULTON
CASS
HOWARD
TIPTON
HAMILTON
MARION
JOHNSON
BARTHOLOMEW
BROWN
JACKSON
WASHINGTON
CRAWFORD
PORTER
LAKE
JASPER
JASPER
NEWTON
WHITE
CARROLL
CLINTON
BOONE
HENDRICKS
MORGAN
MONROE
LAWRENCE
ORANGE
PERRY
BENTON
WARREN
FOUNTAIN
TIPPECANOE
MONTGOMERY
PARKE
PUTNAM
OWEN
GREENE
MARTIN
DUBOIS
SPENCER
VERMILLION
VIGO
CLAY
SULLIVAN
KNOX
DAVIESS
PIKE
WARRICK
GIBSON
VANDER-BURGH
POSEY

1 2 3 4 5 6 7 8 9 10 11 12

25 0 25 50 75 100 MILES

WHITE = MODERN BOUNDARIES
BLACK = 1850 BOUNDARIES

Indiana ● **1850**

MAP GUIDE TO THE U.S. FEDERAL CENSUSES, 1790–1920 by William Thorndale and William Dollarhide. Copyright 1987, all rights reserved.

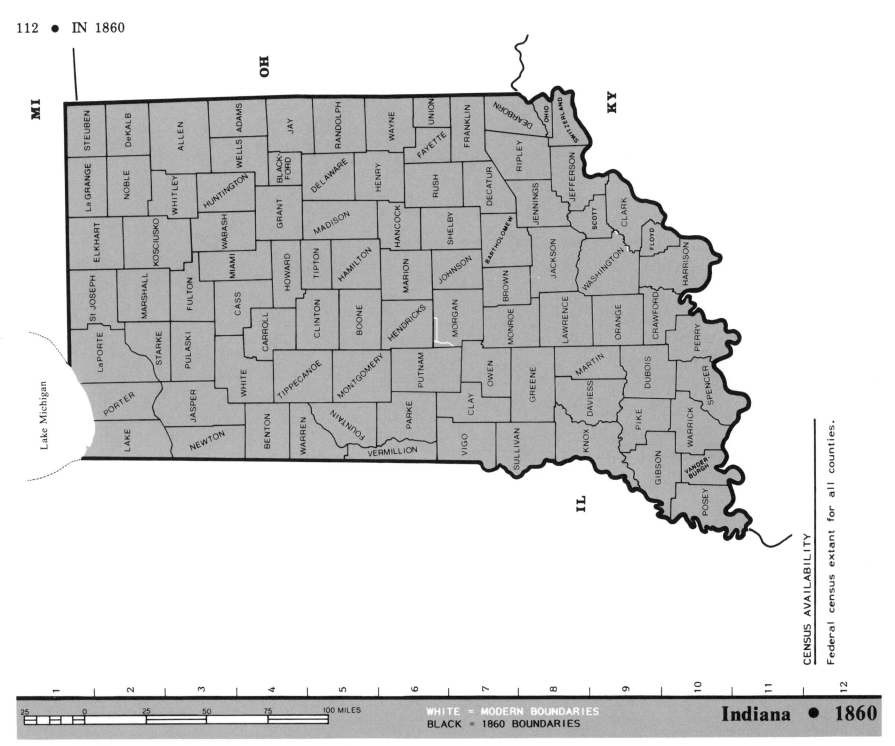

MI

OH

KY

IL

Lake Michigan

CENSUS AVAILABILITY

Federal census extant for all counties.

100 MILES

25   0   25   50   75

Indiana ● 1860

MI

OH

KY

IL

STEUBEN
DeKALB
ALLEN
ADAMS
WELLS
JAY
RANDOLPH
WAYNE
UNION
FRANKLIN
DEARBORN
OHIO
SWITZERLAND

La GRANGE
NOBLE
WHITLEY
HUNTINGTON
BLACK-FORD
DELAWARE
HENRY
FAYETTE
RIPLEY
JEFFERSON
CLARK *

ELKHART
KOSCIUSKO
WABASH
GRANT
MADISON
HANCOCK
RUSH
DECATUR
JENNINGS
SCOTT
FLOYD
HARRISON

St JOSEPH
MARSHALL
FULTON
MIAMI
HOWARD
TIPTON
HAMILTON
MARION *
SHELBY
JOHNSON
BARTHOLOMEW
JACKSON
WASHINGTON *

MARSHALL
CASS
CARROLL
CLINTON
BOONE
HENDRICKS
MORGAN
BROWN
MONROE
LAWRENCE
ORANGE
CRAWFORD
PERRY

LaPORTE
STARKE
PULASKI
WHITE
TIPPECANOE
MONTGOMERY
PUTNAM
OWEN
GREENE
MARTIN
DUBOIS
SPENCER

PORTER
JASPER
BENTON
WARREN
FOUNTAIN
PARKE
CLAY
SULLIVAN
VIGO
KNOX
DAVIESS
PIKE
WARRICK

LAKE
NEWTON
VERMILLION
GIBSON
VANDER-BURGH
POSEY

Lake Michigan

*NOTES:

The Clark-Washington boundary for 1870 varied slightly from the line shown here.

Indianapolis in Marion County was enumerated twice in 1870. The two versions of this federal census are both microfilmed.

CENSUS AVAILABILITY

1870-1880 and 1900-1920 federal censuses extant for all counties.

1890 federal census lost for all counties.

25 0 25 50 75 100 MILES

WHITE = MODERN BOUNDARIES
BLACK = 1870-1920 BOUNDARIES

Indiana • 1870-1920

MAP GUIDE TO THE U.S. FEDERAL CENSUSES, 1790-1920 by William Thorndale and William Dollarhide. Copyright 1987, all rights reserved.

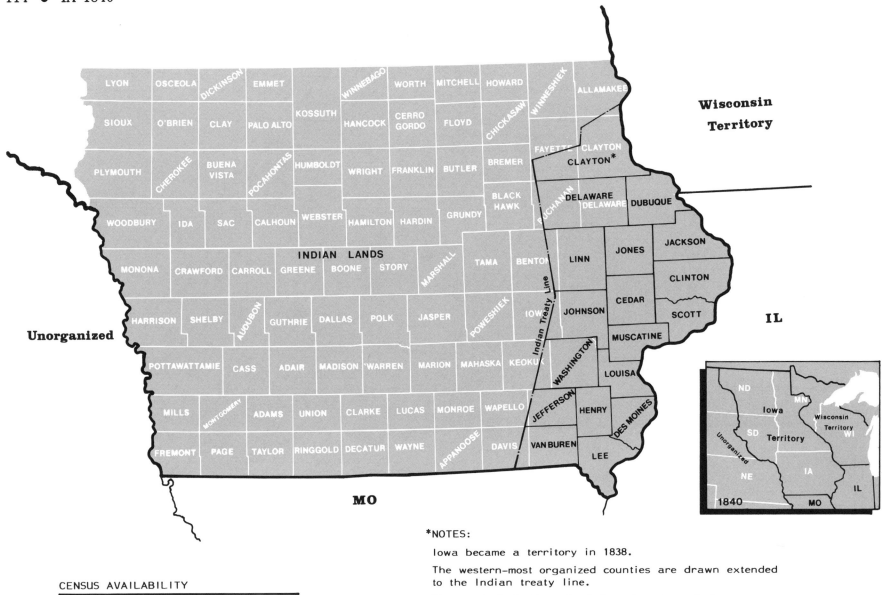

Wisconsin Territory

IL

MO

Unorganized

INDIAN LANDS

Indian Treaty Line

CENSUS AVAILABILITY

Federal census extant for all counties.

*NOTES:

Iowa became a territory in 1838.

The western-most organized counties are drawn extended to the Indian treaty line.

Clayton technically extended west and north to cover three-fourths of Iowa Territory. See Minnesota 1840 (p.170) for Clayton's precincts of Lake Pepin and St. Peter's.

| 25 | 0 | 25 | 50 | 75 | 100 MILES |

WHITE = MODERN BOUNDARIES
BLACK = 1840 BOUNDARIES

Iowa ● 1840

AS PART OF IOWA TERRITORY

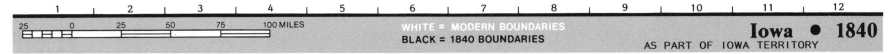

Minnesota Territory

LYON	OSCEOLA	DICKINSON	EMMET		WINNEBAGO	WORTH	MITCHELL	HOWARD	WINNESHIEK	ALLAMAKEE
SIOUX	O'BRIEN	CLAY	PALO ALTO	KOSSUTH	HANCOCK	CERRO GORDO	FLOYD	CHICKASAW		
PLYMOUTH	CHEROKEE	BUENA VISTA	POCAHONTAS	HUMBOLDT	WRIGHT	FRANKLIN	BUTLER	BREMER	FAYETTE	CLAYTON

WI

Unorganized

UNORGANIZED

WOODBURY	IDA	SAC	CALHOUN	WEBSTER	HAMILTON	HARDIN	GRUNDY	BLACK HAWK	BUCHANAN	DELAWARE	DUBUQUE

MONONA CRAWFORD CARROLL GREENE BOONE STORY MARSHALL TAMA BENTON LINN JONES JACKSON

POLK

HARRISON SHELBY AUDUBON GUTHRIE DALLAS POLK JASPER POWESHIEK IOWA JOHNSON CEDAR CLINTON

SCOTT

IL

POTTAWATTAMIE CASS ADAIR MADISON WARREN MARION MAHASKA KEOKUK WASHINGTON MUSCATINE

POTTAWATTAMIE*

WARREN

LOUISA

MILLS MONTGOMERY ADAMS UNION CLARKE LUCAS MONROE WAPELLO JEFFERSON HENRY DES MOINES

FREMONT PAGE TAYLOR RINGGOLD* DECATUR WAYNE APPANOOSE DAVIS VAN BUREN LEE

MO

*NOTES:

Iowa became a state in 1846.

Until 1849, Missouri claimed a northern border about ten miles north of the present line run in 1821. Iowa exercised jurisdiction in this disputed area.

Ringgold was unorganized and unenumerated in 1850, having little or no permanent population. By 1852, it was a township of Taylor County.

Pottawattamie's line shown here should be treated with caution.

CENSUS AVAILABILITY

Federal census extant for all counties.

| 1 | 2 | 3 | 4 | 5 | 6 | 7 | 8 | 9 | 10 | 11 | 12 |

25 0 25 50 75 100 MILES

WHITE = MODERN BOUNDARIES
BLACK = 1850 BOUNDARIES

Iowa ● 1850

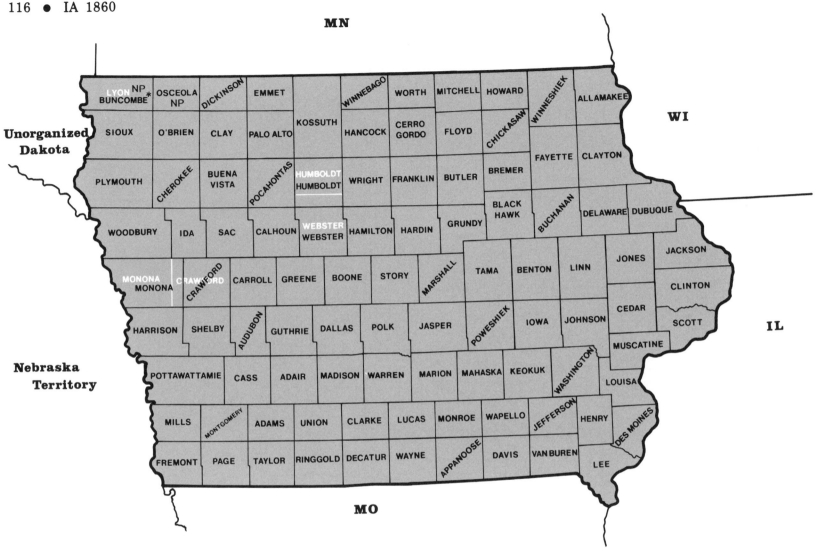

MN

Unorganized
Dakota

WI

Nebraska
Territory

MO

IL

LYON NP *
BUCANCOMBE
OSCEOLA NP
DICKINSON
EMMET
WINNEBAGO
WORTH
MITCHELL
HOWARD
WINNESHIEK
ALLAMAKEE

SIOUX
O'BRIEN
CLAY
PALO ALTO
KOSSUTH
HANCOCK
CERRO GORDO
FLOYD
CHICKASAW
FAYETTE
CLAYTON

PLYMOUTH
CHEROKEE
BUENA VISTA
POCAHONTAS
HUMBOLDT
HUMBOLDT
WRIGHT
FRANKLIN
BUTLER
BREMER
BLACK HAWK
BUCHANAN
DELAWARE
DUBUQUE

WOODBURY
IDA
SAC
CALHOUN
WEBSTER
WEBSTER
HAMILTON
HARDIN
GRUNDY

MONONA
MONONA
CRAWFORD
CRAWFORD
CARROLL
GREENE
BOONE
STORY
MARSHALL
TAMA
BENTON
LINN
JONES
JACKSON

CLINTON

HARRISON
SHELBY
AUDUBON
GUTHRIE
DALLAS
POLK
JASPER
POWESHIEK
IOWA
JOHNSON
CEDAR
SCOTT

POTTAWATTAMIE
CASS
ADAIR
MADISON
WARREN
MARION
MAHASKA
KEOKUK
WASHINGTON
MUSCATINE
LOUISA

MILLS
MONTGOMERY
ADAMS
UNION
CLARKE
LUCAS
MONROE
WAPELLO
JEFFERSON
HENRY

FREMONT
PAGE
TAYLOR
RINGGOLD
DECATUR
WAYNE
APPANOOSE
DAVIS
VAN BUREN
LEE
DES MOINES

CENSUS AVAILABILITY

Federal census extant for all counties.

*NOTES:

Buncombe and Osceola are shown as NP
(no population).

Buncombe was renamed Lyon in 1862.

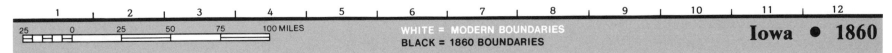

1   2   3   4   5   6   7   8   9   10   11   12

25 0   25   50   75   100 MILES   WHITE = MODERN BOUNDARIES   Iowa ● 1860
                                        BLACK = 1860 BOUNDARIES

MN

DAKOTA
TERRITORY,
1870-1880

SOUTH
DAKOTA,
1890-1920

WI

NE

IL

MO

LYON	OSCEOLA	DICKINSON	EMMET		WINNEBAGO	WORTH	MITCHELL	HOWARD	WINNESHIEK	ALLAMAKEE
SIOUX	O'BRIEN	CLAY	PALO ALTO	KOSSUTH	HANCOCK	CERRO GORDO	FLOYD	CHICKASAW	WINNESHIEK	
PLYMOUTH	CHEROKEE	BUENA VISTA	POCAHONTAS	HUMBOLDT	WRIGHT	FRANKLIN	BUTLER	BREMER	FAYETTE	CLAYTON
WOODBURY	IDA	SAC	CALHOUN	WEBSTER	HAMILTON	HARDIN	GRUNDY	BLACK HAWK	BUCHANAN	DELAWARE	DUBUQUE
MONONA	CRAWFORD	CARROLL	GREENE	BOONE	STORY	MARSHALL	TAMA	BENTON	LINN	JONES	JACKSON
HARRISON	SHELBY	AUDUBON	GUTHRIE	DALLAS	POLK	JASPER	POWESHIEK	IOWA	JOHNSON	CEDAR	CLINTON
POTTAWATTAMIE	CASS	ADAIR	MADISON	WARREN	MARION	MAHASKA	KEOKUK	WASHINGTON	MUSCATINE	SCOTT
MILLS	MONTGOMERY	ADAMS	UNION	CLARKE	LUCAS	MONROE	WAPELLO	JEFFERSON	HENRY	LOUISA
FREMONT	PAGE	TAYLOR	RINGGOLD	DECATUR	WAYNE	APPANOOSE	DAVIS	VAN BUREN	LEE	DES MOINES

CENSUS AVAILABILITY
_____

1870–1880 and 1900–1920 federal censuses extant
for all counties.

1890 federal census lost for all counties.

| 1 | 2 | 3 | 4 | 5 | 6 | 7 | 8 | 9 | 10 | 11 | 12 |

25 0 25 50 75 100 MILES

Iowa ● 1870-1920

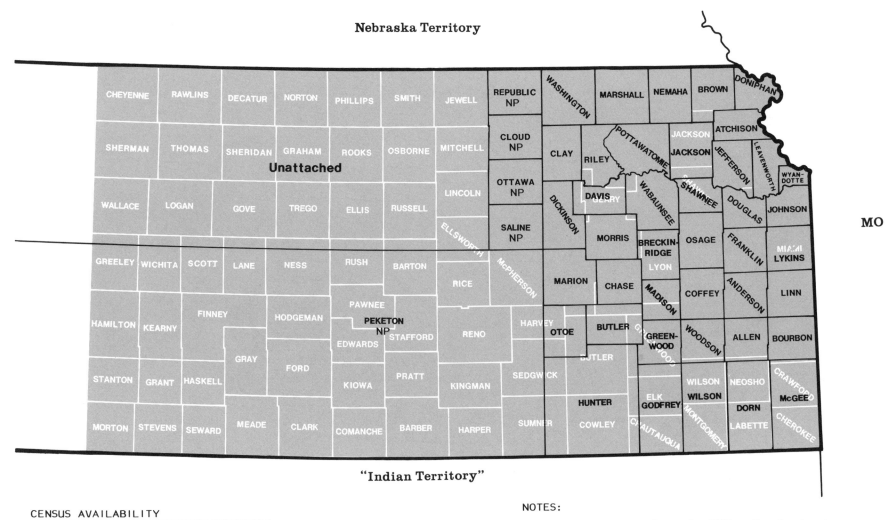

Nebraska Territory

CHEYENNE	RAWLINS	DECATUR	NORTON	PHILLIPS	SMITH	JEWELL	REPUBLIC NP	WASHINGTON	MARSHALL	NEMAHA	BROWN	DONIPHAN

Unattached

"Indian Territory"

MO

CENSUS AVAILABILITY

Federal census extant for all counties.

NOTES:

Kansas became a territory in 1854. For its borders in 1860, see Colorado Notes (p.51).

The numerous changes in county names by 1870 are not explained here.

Five counties are shown as NP (no population).

25 0 25 50 75 100 MILES

WHITE = MODERN BOUNDARIES
BLACK = 1860 BOUNDARIES

Kansas ● 1860
AS PART OF KANSAS TERRITORY

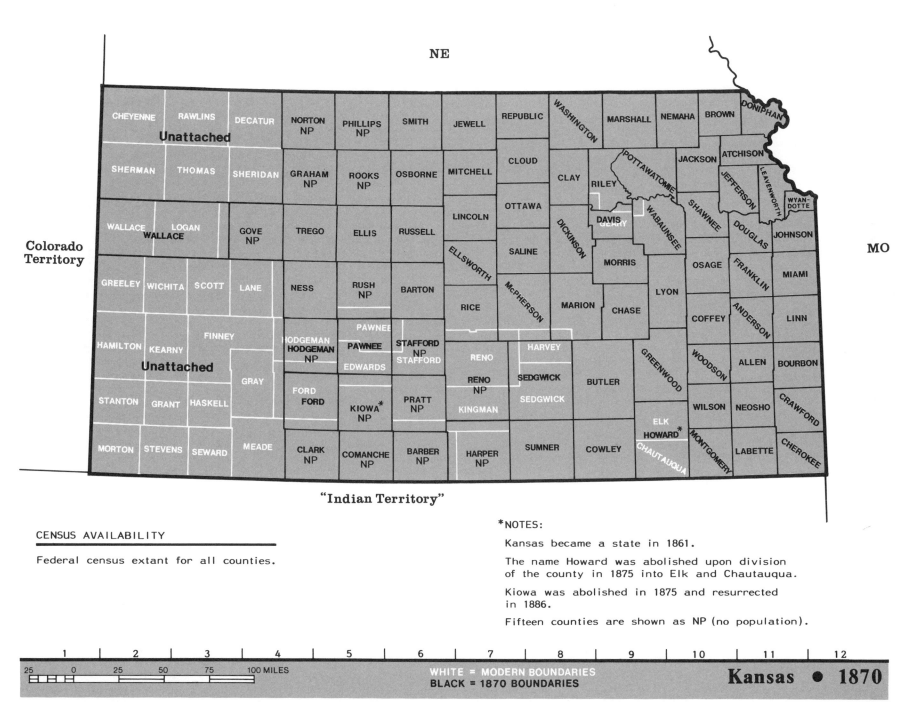

NE

Colorado
Territory

MO

"Indian Territory"

CENSUS AVAILABILITY

Federal census extant for all counties.

*NOTES:

Kansas became a state in 1861.

The name Howard was abolished upon division
of the county in 1875 into Elk and Chautauqua.

Kiowa was abolished in 1875 and resurrected
in 1886.

Fifteen counties are shown as NP (no population).

| 1 | 2 | 3 | 4 | 5 | 6 | 7 | 8 | 9 | 10 | 11 | 12 |

25 0 25 50 75 100 MILES

WHITE = MODERN BOUNDARIES
BLACK = 1870 BOUNDARIES

Kansas ● **1870**

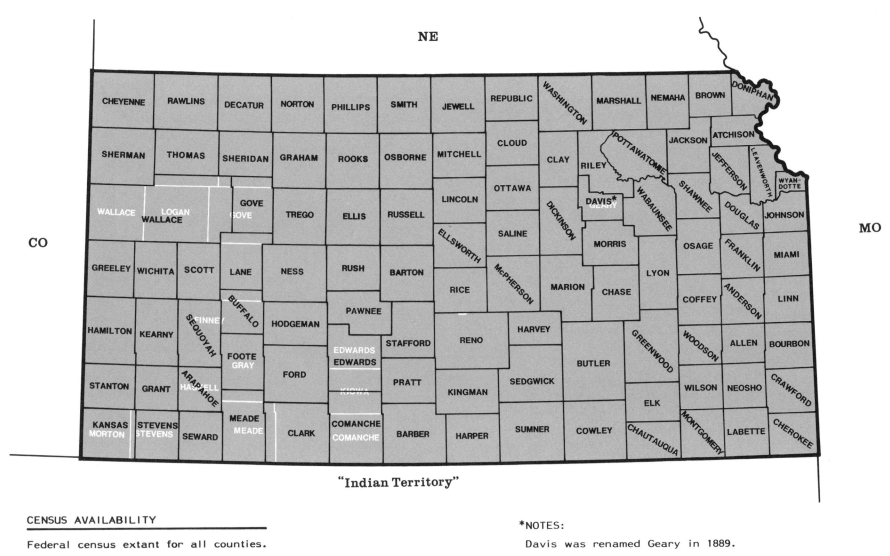

NE

CO

MO

"Indian Territory"

CENSUS AVAILABILITY

Federal census extant for all counties.

*NOTES:

Davis was renamed Geary in 1889.

Several southwestern counties were in effect renamed by creating new counties having the same or nearly identical boundaries to the old counties.

1 2 3 4 5 6 7 8 9 10 11 12

25 0 25 50 75 100 MILES

WHITE = MODERN BOUNDARIES
BLACK = 1880 BOUNDARIES

Kansas ● 1880

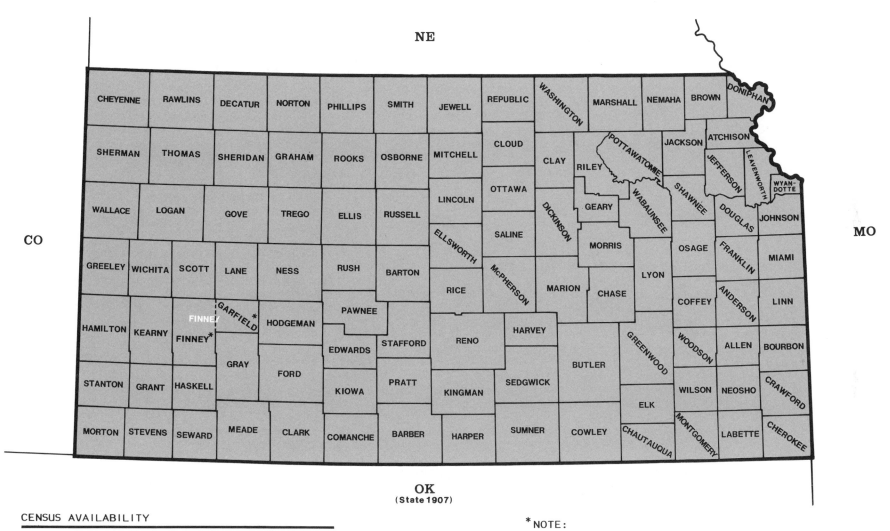

NE

CO

MO

CHEYENNE | RAWLINS | DECATUR | NORTON | PHILLIPS | SMITH | JEWELL | REPUBLIC | WASHINGTON | MARSHALL | NEMAHA | BROWN | DONIPHAN

SHERMAN | THOMAS | SHERIDAN | GRAHAM | ROOKS | OSBORNE | MITCHELL | CLOUD | CLAY | RILEY | POTTAWATOMIE | JACKSON | ATCHISON | JEFFERSON | LEAVENWORTH | WYANDOTTE

WALLACE | LOGAN | GOVE | TREGO | ELLIS | RUSSELL | LINCOLN | OTTAWA | GEARY | WABAUNSEE | SHAWNEE | DOUGLAS | JOHNSON

SALINE | DICKINSON | MORRIS

GREELEY | WICHITA | SCOTT | LANE | NESS | RUSH | BARTON | ELLSWORTH | RICE | McPHERSON | MARION | CHASE | LYON | OSAGE | FRANKLIN | MIAMI

COFFEY | ANDERSON | LINN

HAMILTON | KEARNY | FINNEY* | GARFIELD* | HODGEMAN | PAWNEE | STAFFORD | RENO | HARVEY | GREENWOOD | WOODSON | ALLEN | BOURBON

EDWARDS

GRAY | FORD | BUTLER

STANTON | GRANT | HASKELL | KIOWA | PRATT | KINGMAN | SEDGWICK | WILSON | NEOSHO | CRAWFORD

ELK

MORTON | STEVENS | SEWARD | MEADE | CLARK | COMANCHE | BARBER | HARPER | SUMNER | COWLEY | CHAUTAUQUA | MONTGOMERY | LABETTE | CHEROKEE

OK
(State 1907)

CENSUS AVAILABILITY

1890 federal census <u>lost</u> for all counties.

1900-1920 federal censuses extant for all counties.

*NOTE:

Garfield was annexed to Finney in 1893.

1 | 2 | 3 | 4 | 5 | 6 | 7 | 8 | 9 | 10 | 11 | 12

25   0   25   50   75   100 MILES

WHITE = MODERN BOUNDARIES
BLACK = 1890-1920 BOUNDARIES

Kansas ● **1890-1920**

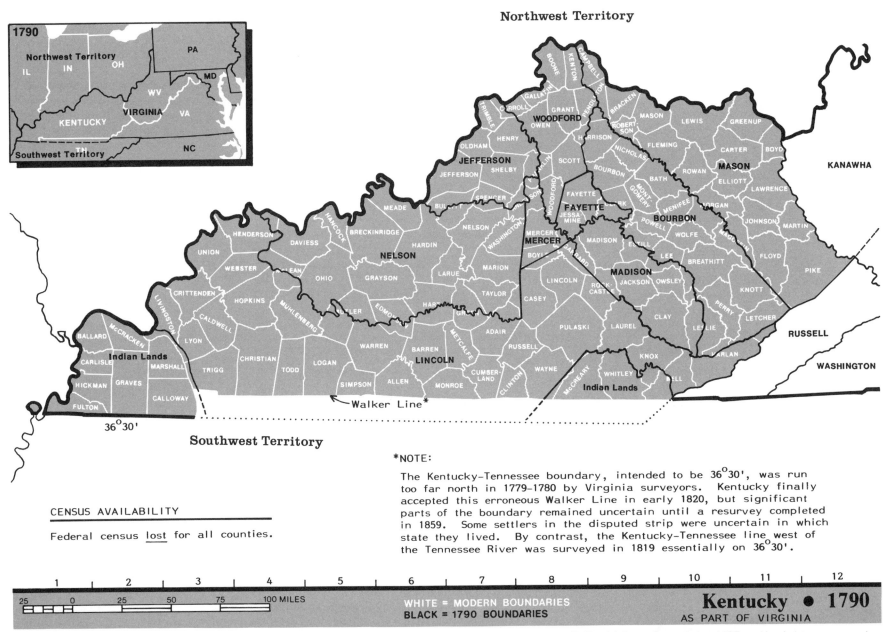

Northwest Territory

Southwest Territory

1790

Northwest Territory

IL   IN   OH   PA

WV   MD

VIRGINIA   VA

KENTUCKY

TN   NC

KANAWHA

RUSSELL

WASHINGTON

Indian Lands

Walker Line*

36°30'

*NOTE:

The Kentucky-Tennessee boundary, intended to be 36°30', was run too far north in 1779-1780 by Virginia surveyors. Kentucky finally accepted this erroneous Walker Line in early 1820, but significant parts of the boundary remained uncertain until a resurvey completed in 1859. Some settlers in the disputed strip were uncertain in which state they lived. By contrast, the Kentucky-Tennessee line west of the Tennessee River was surveyed in 1819 essentially on 36°30'.

CENSUS AVAILABILITY

Federal census lost for all counties.

1   2   3   4   5   6   7   8   9   10   11   12

25   0   25   50   75   100 MILES

WHITE = MODERN BOUNDARIES
BLACK = 1790 BOUNDARIES

Kentucky ● 1790
AS PART OF VIRGINIA

MAP GUIDE TO THE U.S. FEDERAL CENSUSES, 1790-1920 by William Thorndale and William Dollarhide. Copyright 1987, all rights reserved.

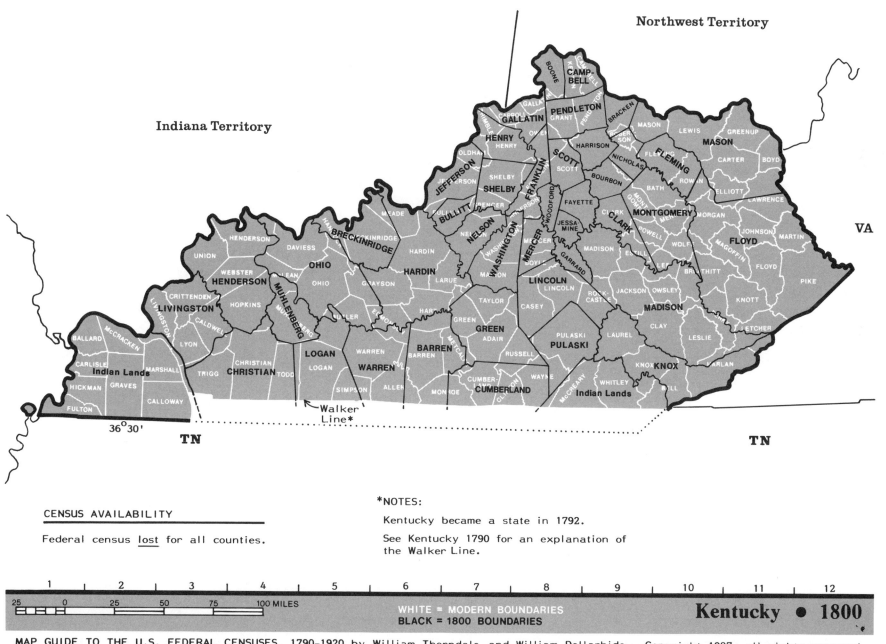

Northwest Territory

Indiana Territory

VA

Walker
Line*

36°30'

TN

TN

CENSUS AVAILABILITY

Federal census lost for all counties.

*NOTES:

Kentucky became a state in 1792.

See Kentucky 1790 for an explanation of
the Walker Line.

| 1 | 2 | 3 | 4 | 5 | 6 | 7 | 8 | 9 | 10 | 11 | 12 |

25   0   25   50   75   100 MILES

WHITE = MODERN BOUNDARIES
BLACK = 1800 BOUNDARIES

Kentucky ● 1800

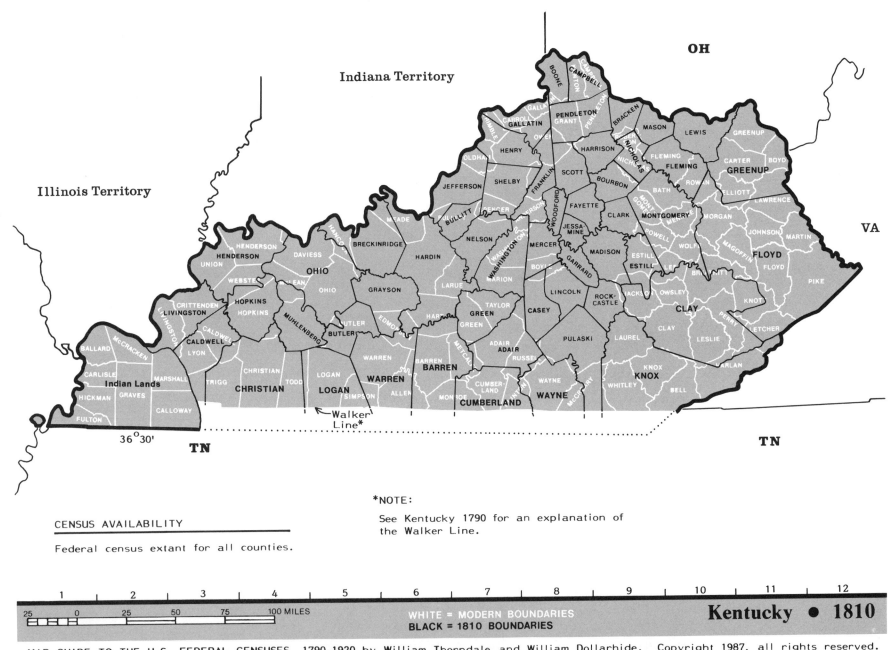

Kentucky ● 1810

CENSUS AVAILABILITY

Federal census extant for all counties.

*NOTE:

See Kentucky 1790 for an explanation of
the Walker Line.

MAP GUIDE TO THE U.S. FEDERAL CENSUSES, 1790-1920 by William Thorndale and William Dollarhide. Copyright 1987, all rights reserved.

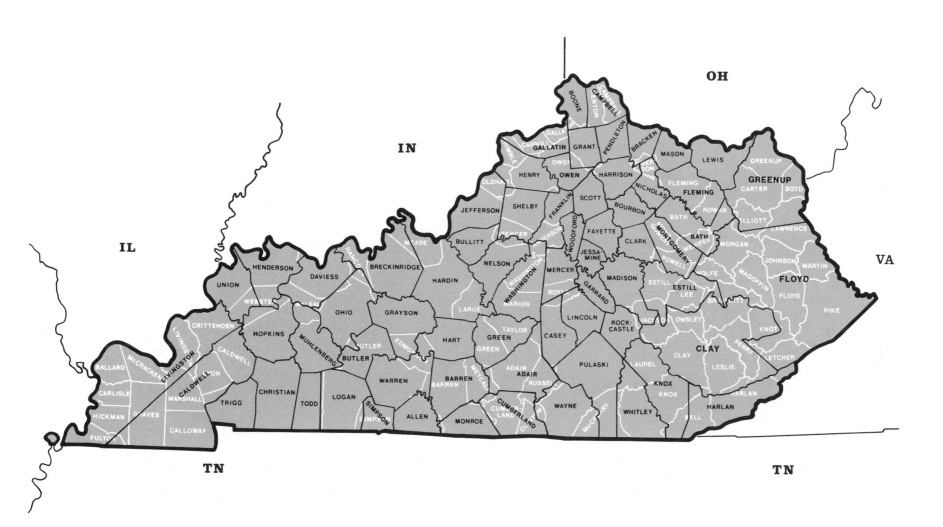

OH

IN

IL

VA

TN

TN

CENSUS AVAILABILITY

Federal census extant for all counties.

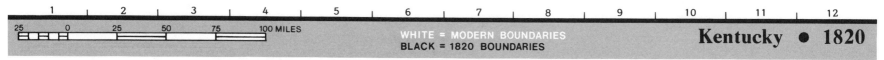

| 1 | 2 | 3 | 4 | 5 | 6 | 7 | 8 | 9 | 10 | 11 | 12 |

25   0   25   50   75   100 MILES

WHITE = MODERN BOUNDARIES
BLACK = 1820 BOUNDARIES

Kentucky ● 1820

OH

IN

IL

VA

MO

TN

TN

BOONE
CAMPBELL
CAMPBELL
KENTON
GALLATIN
GALLATIN
GRANT
PENDLETON
BRACKEN
MASON
LEWIS
GREENUP
GREENUP
OWEN
HARRISON
CARTER
BOYD
OLDHAM
HENRY
NICHOLAS
FLEMING
FLEMING
FLEMING
SCOTT
BOURBON
ROWAN
ELLIOTT
LAWRENCE
JEFFERSON
SHELBY
FRANKLIN
BATH
BATH
MONTGOMERY
MORGAN
SPENCER
ANDERSON
WOODFORD
FAYETTE
CLARK
MENIFEE
JOHNSON
MARTIN
MEADE
BULLITT
JESSA-MINE
POWELL
WOLFE
FLOYD
FLOYD
BRECKINRIDGE
NELSON
MERCER
MADISON
ESTILL
ESTILL
LEE
BREATHITT
HENDERSON
DAVIESS
HANCOCK
HARDIN
WASHINGTON
WASHINGTON
BOYLE
GARRARD
LEE
PIKE
UNION
LARUE
MARION
LINCOLN
ROCK-CASTLE
JACKSON
OWSLEY
PERRY
KNOTT
WEBSTER
OHIO
GRAYSON
HART
TAYLOR
GREEN
CASEY
LAUREL
CLAY
CLAY
LESLIE
LETCHER
CRITTENDEN
LIVINGSTON
LIVINGSTON
LEE
MUHLENBERG
BUTLER
BUTLER
EDMONSON
GREEN
ADAIR
PULASKI
HARLAN
McCRACKEN
BALLARD
HOPKINS
CALDWELL
CALDWELL
LYON
WARREN
BARREN
BARREN
RUSSELL
KNOX
HARLAN
CHRISTIAN
METCALFE
WAYNE
WHITLEY
BELL
CARLISLE
MARSHALL
TRIGG
TODD
LOGAN
SIMPSON
ALLEN
MONROE
CUMBERLAND
CUMBERLAND
CLINTON
McCREARY
HICKMAN
GRAVES
CALLOWAY
CALLOWAY
SIMPSON
FULTON

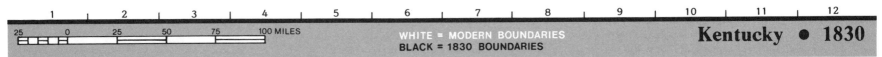

1   2   3   4   5   6   7   8   9   10   11   12

25   0   25   50   75   100 MILES

WHITE = MODERN BOUNDARIES
BLACK = 1830 BOUNDARIES

Kentucky ● 1830

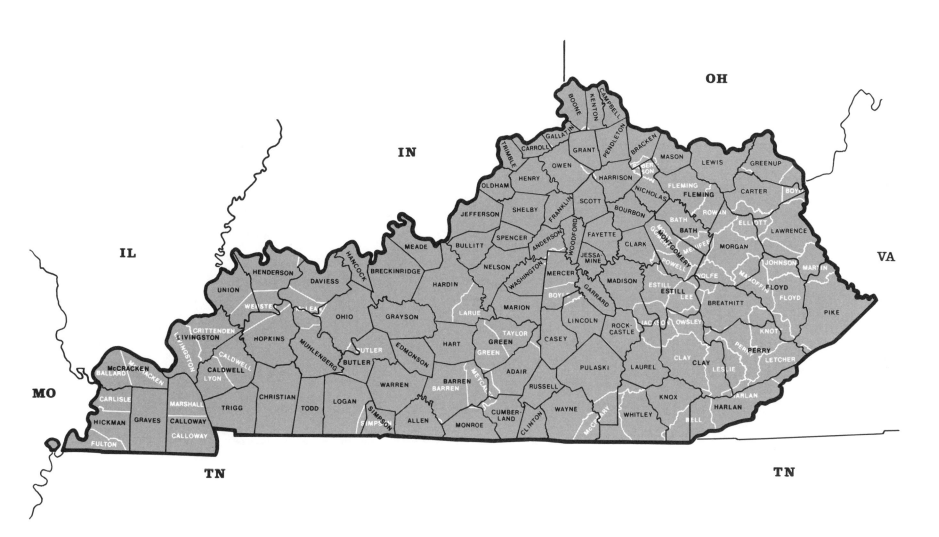

OH

IN

IL

VA

MO

TN

TN

BOONE
KENTON
CAMPBELL
GALLATIN
CARROLL
TRIMBLE
OWEN
GRANT
PENDLETON
BRACKEN
MASON
LEWIS
GREENUP
HENRY
HARRISON
ROBERTSON
NICHOLAS
FLEMING
FLEMING
CARTER
OLDHAM
BOYD
SCOTT
ROWAN
JEFFERSON
SHELBY
FRANKLIN
BOURBON
BATH
BATH
ELLIOTT
LAWRENCE
SPENCER
WOODFORD
FAYETTE
MONTGOMERY
MENIFEE
MORGAN
MEADE
BULLITT
ANDERSON
CLARK
POWELL
WOLFE
MAGOFFIN
JOHNSON
MARTIN
HENDERSON
NELSON
WASHINGTON
MERCER
JESSAMINE
MADISON
ESTILL
ESTILL
LEE
FLOYD
FLOYD
UNION
BRECKINRIDGE
HARDIN
GARRARD
BOYLE
JACKSON
OWSLEY
BREATHITT
PIKE
WEBSTER
DAVIESS
HANCOCK
GRAYSON
LARUE
MARION
LINCOLN
ROCK-CASTLE
KNOTT
CRITTENDEN
LEAD
OHIO
HART
TAYLOR
GREEN
CASEY
PERRY
PERRY
LETCHER
LIVINGSTON
HOPKINS
MUHLENBERG
GREEN
LAUREL
CLAY
CLAY
LESLIE
McCRACKEN
BALLARD
CRACKEN
CALDWELL
CALDWELL
BUTLER
BUTLER
EDMONSON
ADAIR
PULASKI
KNOX
HARLAN
LYON
WARREN
BARREN
BARREN
RUSSELL
MARSHALL
CARLISLE
CHRISTIAN
TODD
LOGAN
SIMPSON
SIMPSON
ALLEN
MONROE
METCALF
CUMBERLAND
WAYNE
CLINTON
McCREARY
WHITLEY
BELL
HARLAN
HICKMAN
GRAVES
CALLOWAY
CALLOWAY
TRIGG
FULTON

CENSUS AVAILABILITY

Federal census extant for all counties.

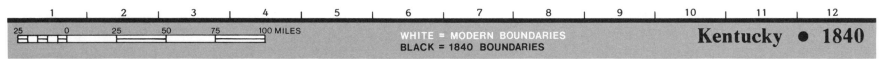

1   2   3   4   5   6   7   8   9   10   11   12

25   0   25   50   75   100 MILES

WHITE = MODERN BOUNDARIES
BLACK = 1840 BOUNDARIES

Kentucky ● 1840

MAP GUIDE TO THE U.S. FEDERAL CENSUSES, 1790–1920 by William Thorndale and William Dollarhide.   Copyright 1987, all rights reserved.

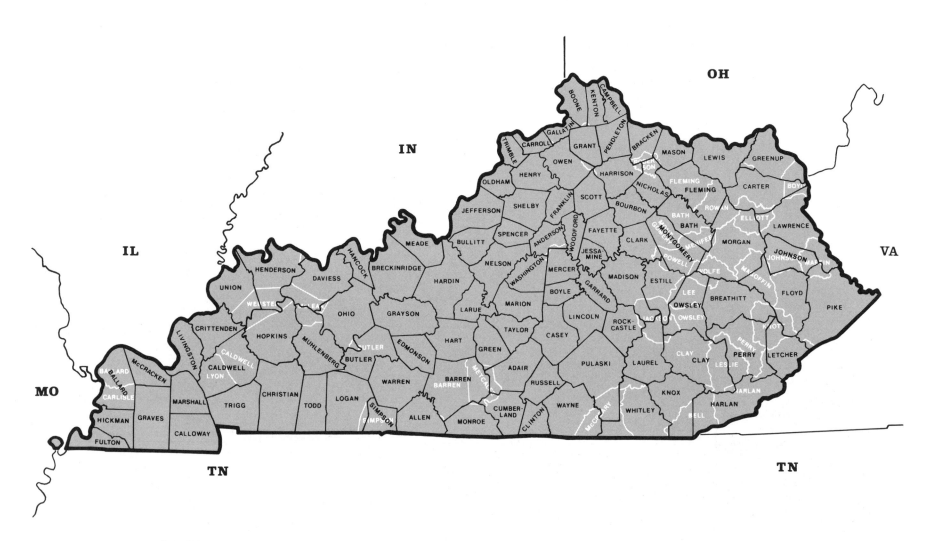

OH

IN

IL

VA

MO

TN

TN

CENSUS AVAILABILITY

Federal census extant for all counties.

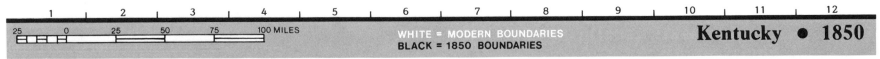

| | 1 | 2 | 3 | 4 | 5 | 6 | 7 | 8 | 9 | 10 | 11 | 12 |

25 0 25 50 75 100 MILES

WHITE = MODERN BOUNDARIES
BLACK = 1850 BOUNDARIES

Kentucky ● 1850

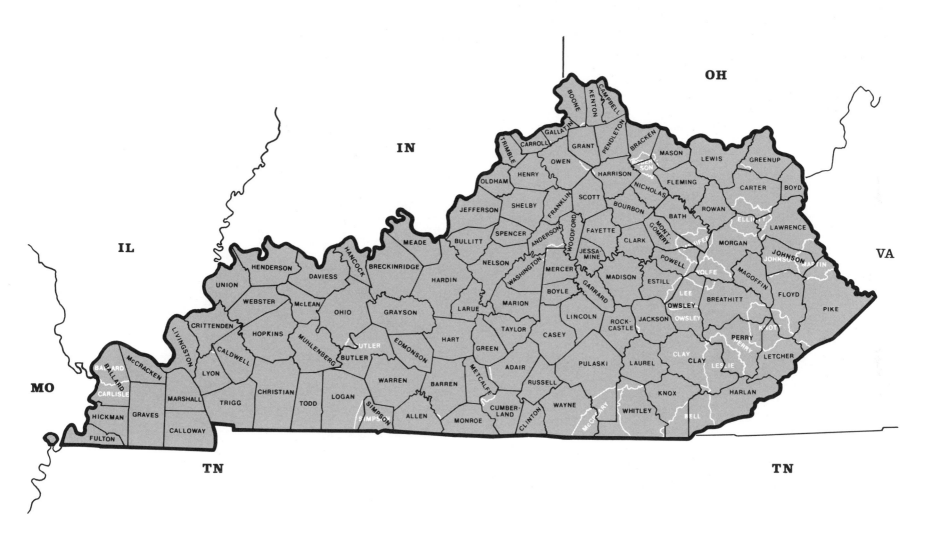

OH

IN

IL

MO

VA

TN

TN

BOONE
KENTON
CAMPBELL
GALLATIN
CARROLL
TRIMBLE
GRANT
PENDLETON
BRACKEN
OWEN
MASON
LEWIS
GREENUP
HENDERSON
HENRY
HARRISON
FLEMING
NICHOLAS
CARTER
BOYD
OLDHAM
SCOTT
ROWAN
JEFFERSON
SHELBY
FRANKLIN
BOURBON
BATH
ELLIOTT
SPENCER
WOODFORD
FAYETTE
MONT-GOMERY
LAWRENCE
MEADE
BULLITT
ANDERSON
CLARK
POWELL
MORGAN
JOHNSON
HANCOCK
BRECKINRIDGE
NELSON
MERCER
JESSA-MINE
WOLFE
MAGOFFIN
MARTIN
HENDERSON
DAVIESS
HARDIN
WASHINGTON
MADISON
ESTILL
LEE
FLOYD
UNION
BOYLE
GARRARD
BREATHITT
WEBSTER
McLEAN
OHIO
GRAYSON
LARUE
MARION
LINCOLN
OWSLEY
OWSLEY
PIKE
CRITTENDEN
HOPKINS
BUTLER
EDMONSON
HART
TAYLOR
CASEY
JACKSON
PERRY
KNOTT
LIVINGSTON
CALDWELL
MUHLENBERG
BUTLER
GREEN
ROCK-CASTLE
LAUREL
CLAY
CLAY
LESLIE
LETCHER
LYON
PULASKI
BALLARD
McCRACKEN
LYON
WARREN
BARREN
ADAIR
HARLAN
CARLISLE
MARSHALL
CHRISTIAN
METCALFE
RUSSELL
KNOX
HICKMAN
GRAVES
TRIGG
TODD
LOGAN
SIMPSON
ALLEN
CUMBER-LAND
WAYNE
McCREARY
WHITLEY
BELL
FULTON
CALLOWAY
SIMPSON
MONROE
CLINTON

CENSUS AVAILABILITY

Federal census extant for all counties.

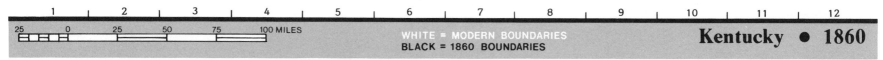

| 1 | 2 | 3 | 4 | 5 | 6 | 7 | 8 | 9 | 10 | 11 | 12 |

25   0   25   50   75   100 MILES

WHITE = MODERN BOUNDARIES
BLACK = 1860 BOUNDARIES

Kentucky ● 1860

MAP GUIDE TO THE U.S. FEDERAL CENSUSES, 1790–1920 by William Thorndale and William Dollarhide. Copyright 1987, all rights reserved.

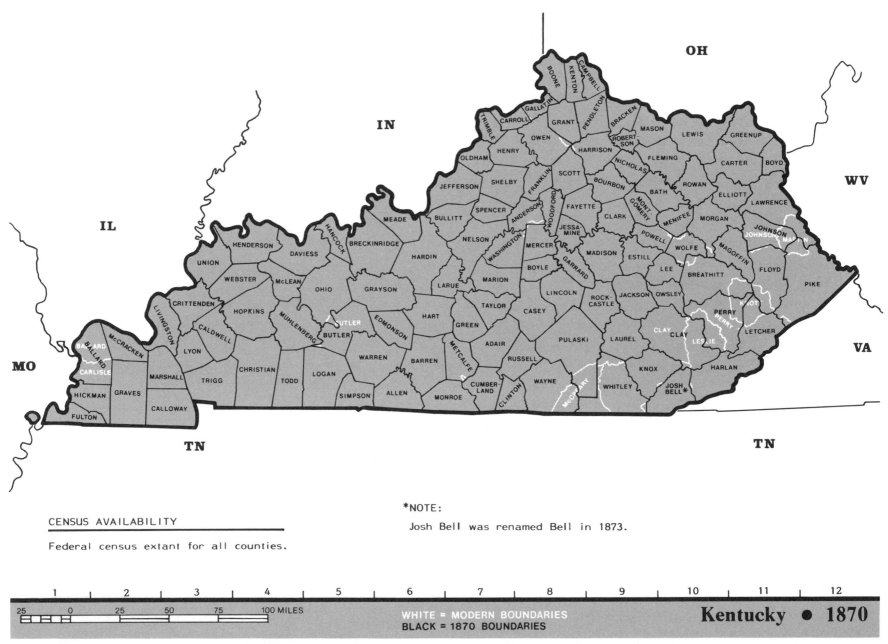

OH

IN

IL

WV

MO

VA

TN

TN

CENSUS AVAILABILITY

Federal census extant for all counties.

*NOTE:

Josh Bell was renamed Bell in 1873.

| | | | | | | | | | | | |
|1|2|3|4|5|6|7|8|9|10|11|12|

25   0   25   50   75   100 MILES

WHITE = MODERN BOUNDARIES
BLACK = 1870 BOUNDARIES

Kentucky ● 1870

MAP GUIDE TO THE U.S. FEDERAL CENSUSES, 1790–1920 by William Thorndale and William Dollarhide. Copyright 1987, all rights reserved.

OH

IN

WV

IL

MO

VA

TN

TN

CENSUS AVAILABILITY

Federal census extant for all counties.

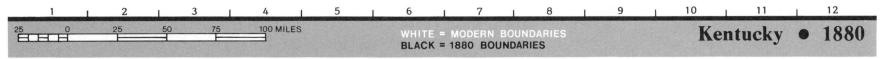

| 1 | 2 | 3 | 4 | 5 | 6 | 7 | 8 | 9 | 10 | 11 | 12 |

25   0   25   50   75   100 MILES

WHITE = MODERN BOUNDARIES
BLACK = 1880 BOUNDARIES

Kentucky ● 1880

MAP GUIDE TO THE U.S. FEDERAL CENSUSES, 1790–1920 by William Thorndale and William Dollarhide. Copyright 1987, all rights reserved.

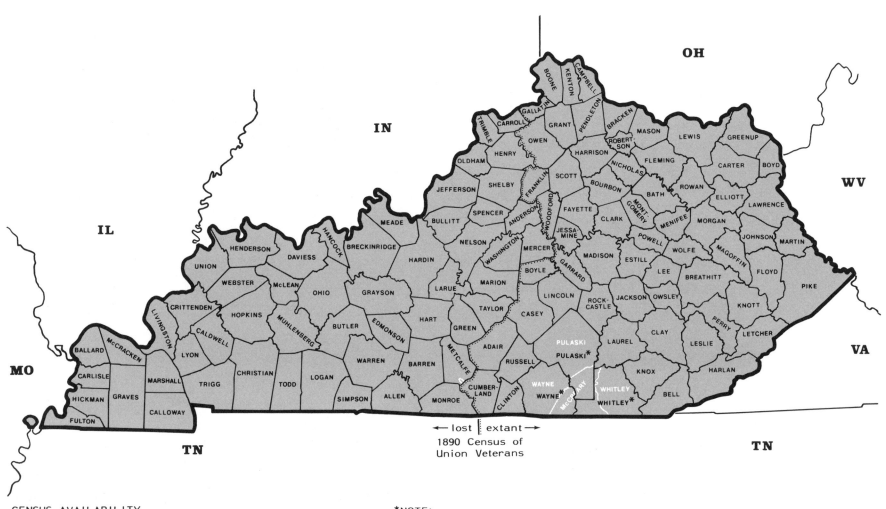

OH

IN

WV

IL

MO

TN

←— lost ┊ extant —→
1890 Census of
Union Veterans

VA

TN

CENSUS AVAILABILITY

1890 federal census <u>lost</u> for all counties. 1890 census of Union veterans <u>extant</u> for eastern Kentucky.

1900–1920 federal censuses extant for all counties.

*NOTE:

McCreary was created in 1912 from Pulaski, Wayne, and Whitley with its present, modern boundaries. The map shows the pre-1912 situation.

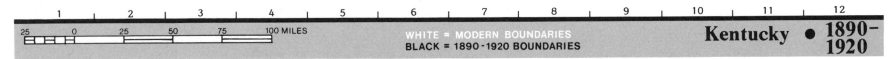

25   0   25   50   75   100 MILES

1   2   3   4   5   6   7   8   9   10   11   12

WHITE = MODERN BOUNDARIES
BLACK = 1890-1920 BOUNDARIES

Kentucky ● **1890–1920**

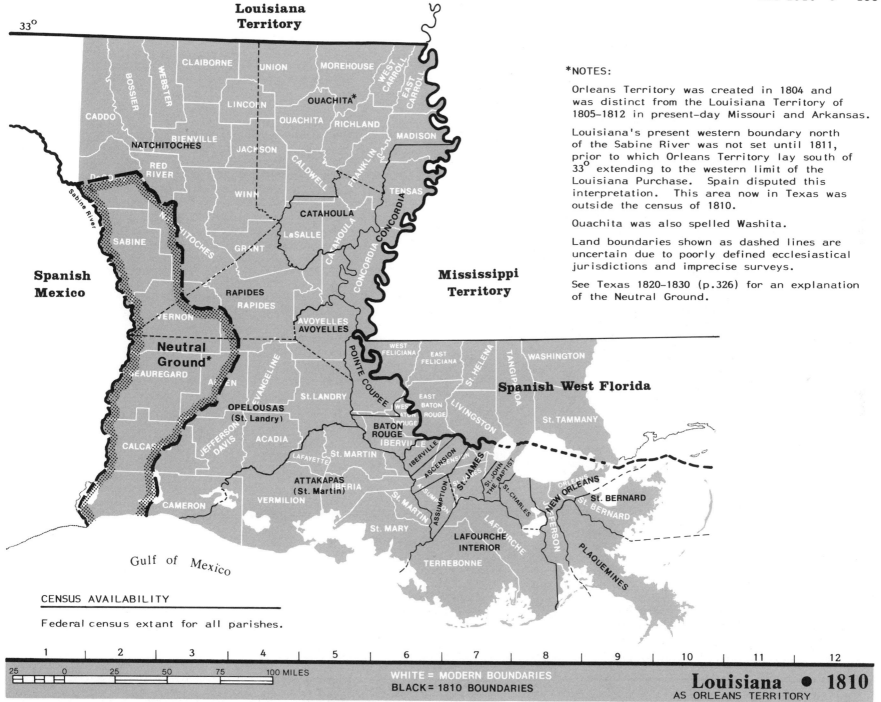

Louisiana
Territory

33°

CLAIBORNE
UNION
MOREHOUSE
WEST CARROLL
EAST CARROLL

BOSSIER
WEBSTER
CADDO
OUACHITA*

LINCOLN
OUACHITA
RICHLAND

NATCHITOCHES
BIENVILLE
JACKSON
MADISON

RED RIVER

Sabine River

WINN
CALDWELL
FRANKLIN
TENSAS

SABINE
NATCHITOCHES
CATAHOULA
LaSALLE
CATAHOULA
CONCORDIA

Spanish
Mexico

GRANT

RAPIDES
RAPIDES

VERNON
AVOYELLES
AVOYELLES

Neutral
Ground*

BEAUREGARD
ALLEN
EVANGELINE
POINTE COUPEE

OPELOUSAS
(St. Landry)
St. LANDRY

WEST FELICIANA
EAST FELICIANA
St. HELENA
TANGIPAHOA
WASHINGTON

Mississippi
Territory

CALCASIEU
JEFFERSON DAVIS
ACADIA
LAFAYETTE
St. MARTIN

EAST BATON ROUGE
WEST BATON ROUGE

LIVINGSTON
St. TAMMANY

Spanish West Florida

BATON ROUGE
IBERVILLE
IBERVILLE

ASCENSION

St. JAMES

St. JOHN THE BAPTIST

CAMERON

ATTAKAPAS
(St. Martin)
IBERIA
VERMILION

St. MARTIN
ASSUMPTION
St. CHARLES

ORLEANS
NEW ORLEANS

JEFFERSON

St. BERNARD
St. BERNARD

St. MARY

LAFOURCHE

LAFOURCHE
INTERIOR

PLAQUEMINES

TERREBONNE

Gulf of Mexico

*NOTES:

Orleans Territory was created in 1804 and
was distinct from the Louisiana Territory of
1805–1812 in present-day Missouri and Arkansas.

Louisiana's present western boundary north
of the Sabine River was not set until 1811,
prior to which Orleans Territory lay south of
33° extending to the western limit of the
Louisiana Purchase. Spain disputed this
interpretation. This area now in Texas was
outside the census of 1810.

Ouachita was also spelled Washita.

Land boundaries shown as dashed lines are
uncertain due to poorly defined ecclesiastical
jurisdictions and imprecise surveys.

See Texas 1820–1830 (p.326) for an explanation
of the Neutral Ground.

CENSUS AVAILABILITY

Federal census extant for all parishes.

1   2   3   4   5   6   7   8   9   10   11   12

25   0   25   50   75   100 MILES

WHITE = MODERN BOUNDARIES
BLACK = 1810 BOUNDARIES

Louisiana ● **1810**
AS ORLEANS TERRITORY

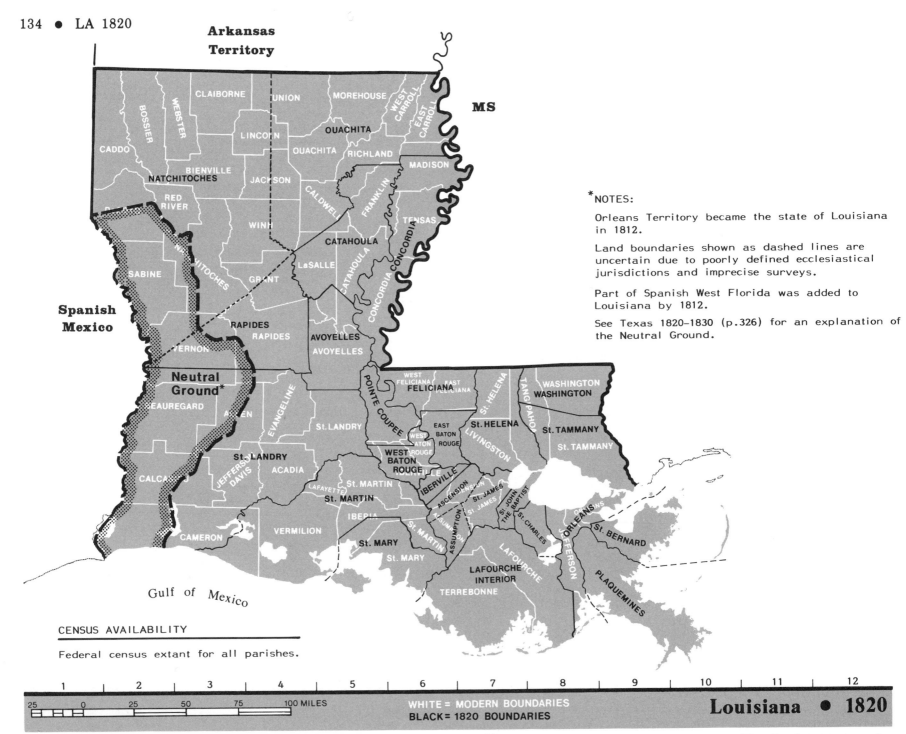

Arkansas
Territory

MS

CLAIBORNE UNION MOREHOUSE WEST CARROLL EAST CARROLL

BOSSIER WEBSTER

CADDO

OUACHITA

LINCOLN

OUACHITA RICHLAND

BIENVILLE MADISON

NATCHITOCHES JACKSON

RED RIVER CALDWELL FRANKLIN

WINN TENSAS

NATCHITOCHES CATAHOULA CONCORDIA

SABINE GRANT LaSALLE CATAHOULA CONCORDIA

Spanish
Mexico

RAPIDES RAPIDES

VERNON AVOYELLES AVOYELLES

Neutral
Ground*

BEAUREGARD POINTE COUPEE WEST FELICIANA EAST FELICIANA WASHINGTON WASHINGTON

ALLEN FELICIANA ST. HELENA TANGIPAHOA

EVANGELINE ST. LANDRY EAST BATON ROUGE ST. HELENA LIVINGSTON ST. TAMMANY

WEST BATON ROUGE ST. TAMMANY

ST. LANDRY WEST BATON ROUGE

CALCASIEU JEFFERSON DAVIS ACADIA ST. MARTIN IBERVILLE

LAFAYETTE ASCENSION ST. JAMES ST. JOHN THE BAPTIST ORLEANS ST. BERNARD

IBERIA ST. MARTIN ASSUMPTION ST. JAMES ST. CHARLES JEFFERSON

CAMERON VERMILION ST. MARY LAFOURCHE

ST. MARY LAFOURCHE INTERIOR PLAQUEMINES

TERREBONNE

Gulf of Mexico

*NOTES:

Orleans Territory became the state of Louisiana
in 1812.

Land boundaries shown as dashed lines are
uncertain due to poorly defined ecclesiastical
jurisdictions and imprecise surveys.

Part of Spanish West Florida was added to
Louisiana by 1812.

See Texas 1820–1830 (p.326) for an explanation of
the Neutral Ground.

CENSUS AVAILABILITY

Federal census extant for all parishes.

1   2   3   4   5   6   7   8   9   10   11   12

25   0   25   50   75   100 MILES

WHITE = MODERN BOUNDARIES
BLACK = 1820 BOUNDARIES

Louisiana ● 1820

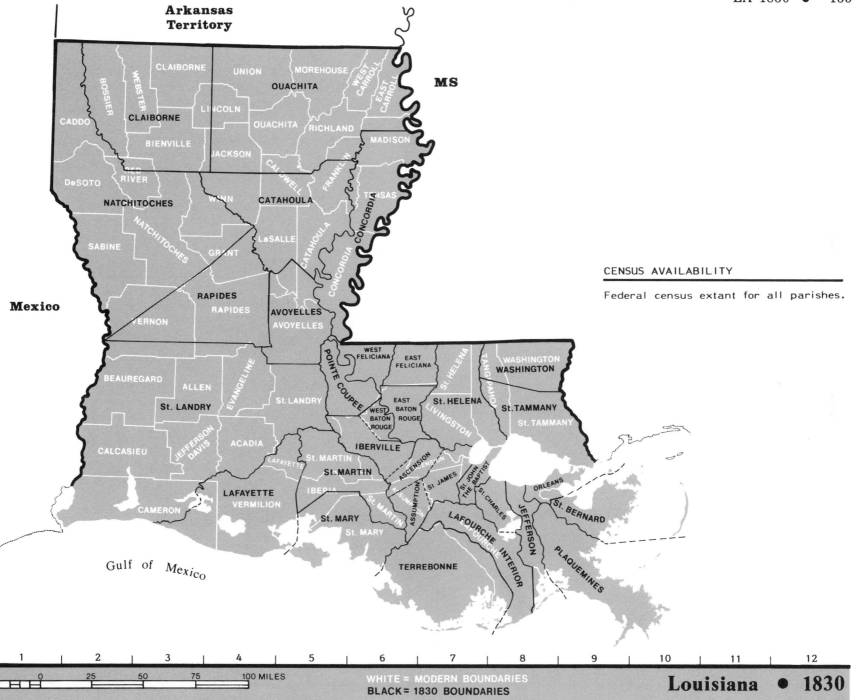

Arkansas
Territory

MS

Mexico

Gulf of Mexico

CENSUS AVAILABILITY

Federal census extant for all parishes.

CLAIBORNE
BOSSIER
WEBSTER
CADDO
CLAIBORNE
UNION
MOREHOUSE
WEST CARROLL
EAST CARROLL
OUACHITA
LINCOLN
OUACHITA
RICHLAND
MADISON
BIENVILLE
JACKSON
RED RIVER
DeSOTO
CALDWELL
FRANKLIN
NATCHITOCHES
WINN
CATAHOULA
TENSAS
CONCORDIA
NATCHITOCHES
LaSALLE
CATAHOULA
SABINE
GRANT
CONCORDIA
RAPIDES
RAPIDES
AVOYELLES
VERNON
AVOYELLES
POINTE COUPEE
WEST FELICIANA
EAST FELICIANA
ST. HELENA
TANGIPAHOA
WASHINGTON
WASHINGTON
BEAUREGARD
ALLEN
EVANGELINE
St. LANDRY
WEST BATON ROUGE
EAST BATON ROUGE
St. HELENA
LIVINGSTON
St. TAMMANY
St. TAMMANY
St. LANDRY
IBERVILLE
CALCASIEU
JEFFERSON DAVIS
ACADIA
LAFAYETTE
St. MARTIN
St. MARTIN
ASCENSION
ASCENSION
St. JAMES
St. JOHN THE BAPTIST
St. CHARLES
ORLEANS
JEFFERSON
St. BERNARD
LAFAYETTE
VERMILION
IBERIA
St. MARTIN
ASSUMPTION
LAFOURCHE INTERIOR
PLAQUEMINES
CAMERON
St. MARY
St. MARY
TERREBONNE

| 1 | 2 | 3 | 4 | 5 | 6 | 7 | 8 | 9 | 10 | 11 | 12 |

25 0 25 50 75 100 MILES

WHITE = MODERN BOUNDARIES
BLACK = 1830 BOUNDARIES

Louisiana ● 1830

MAP GUIDE TO THE U.S. FEDERAL CENSUSES, 1790-1920 by William Thorndale and William Dollarhide. Copyright 1987, all rights reserved.

AR

MS

CLAIBORNE

UNION

MOREHOUSE

WEST CARROLL

EAST CARROLL

BOSSIER

WEBSTER

UNION

CARROLL

CADDO

CLAIBORNE

LINCOLN

OUACHITA

CADDO

BIENVILLE

OUACHITA

RICHLAND

MADISON

DeSOTO

RED RIVER

JACKSON

CALDWELL

MADISON

FRANKLIN

TENSAS

NATCHITOCHES

WINN

CATAHOULA

NATCHITOCHES

LaSALLE

CONCORDIA

SABINE

GRANT

CATAHOULA

CONCORDIA

Republic
of Texas

RAPIDES

RAPIDES

VERNON

AVOYELLES

POINTE COUPEE

WEST FELICIANA

EAST FELICIANA

St. HELENA

TANGIPAHOA

WASHINGTON

WASHINGTON

BEAUREGARD

ALLEN

EVANGELINE

St. LANDRY

St. LANDRY

EAST BATON ROUGE

LIVINGSTON

St. TAMMANY

WEST BATON ROUGE

LIVINGSTON

St. TAMMANY

CALCASIEU

IBERVILLE

JEFFERSON DAVIS

ACADIA

LAFAYETTE

St. MARTIN

ASCENSION

ST. JAMES

St. JOHN THE BAPTIST

ORLEANS

CALCASIEU

St. MARTIN

ASCENSION

St. CHARLES

LAFAYETTE

IBERIA

ASSUMPTION

JEFFERSON

St. BERNARD

VERMILION

St. MARTIN

CAMERON

St. MARY

LAFOURCHE INTERIOR

PLAQUEMINES

St. MARY

TERREBONNE

Gulf of Mexico

CENSUS AVAILABILITY

Federal census extant for all parishes.

1	2	3	4	5	6	7	8	9	10	11	12

25 0 25 50 75 100 MILES

WHITE = MODERN BOUNDARIES
BLACK = 1840 BOUNDARIES

Louisiana ● 1840

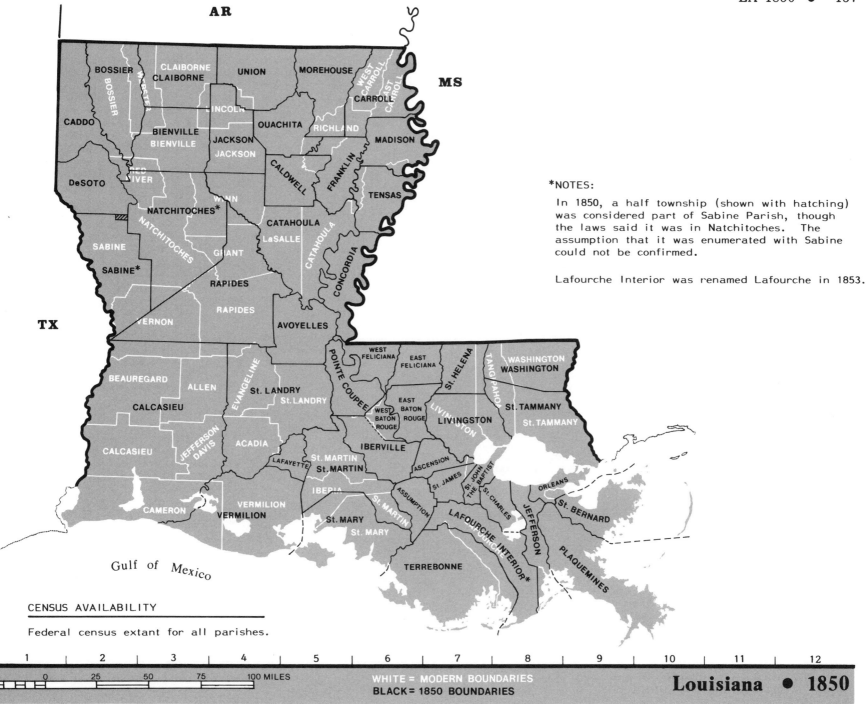

AR

MS

TX

BOSSIER
CLAIBORNE
CLAIBORNE
UNION
MOREHOUSE
WEST CARROLL
EAST CARROLL
WEBSTER
BOSSIER
LINCOLN
CARROLL
CADDO
OUACHITA
RICHLAND
BIENVILLE
BIENVILLE
JACKSON
JACKSON
MADISON
RED RIVER
CALDWELL
FRANKLIN
DeSOTO
WINN
NATCHITOCHES*
TENSAS
NATCHITOCHES
CATAHOULA
SABINE
GRANT
LaSALLE
SABINE*
RAPIDES
CATAHOULA
CONCORDIA
VERNON
RAPIDES
AVOYELLES
BEAUREGARD
EVANGELINE
ALLEN
St. LANDRY
St. LANDRY
POINTE COUPEE
WEST FELICIANA
EAST FELICIANA
St. HELENA
TANGIPAHOA
WASHINGTON
WASHINGTON
CALCASIEU
WEST BATON ROUGE
EAST BATON ROUGE
LIVINGSTON
LIVINGSTON
St. TAMMANY
St. TAMMANY
JEFFERSON DAVIS
ACADIA
LAFAYETTE
St. MARTIN
St. MARTIN
IBERVILLE
ASCENSION
St. JAMES
St. JOHN THE BAPTIST
St. CHARLES
ORLEANS
CALCASIEU
IBERIA
St. MARTIN
ASSUMPTION
JEFFERSON
St. BERNARD
CAMERON
VERMILION
VERMILION
St. MARY
St. MARY
LAFOURCHE INTERIOR*
PLAQUEMINES
TERREBONNE

Gulf of Mexico

*NOTES:

In 1850, a half township (shown with hatching) was considered part of Sabine Parish, though the laws said it was in Natchitoches. The assumption that it was enumerated with Sabine could not be confirmed.

Lafourche Interior was renamed Lafourche in 1853.

CENSUS AVAILABILITY

Federal census extant for all parishes.

1   2   3   4   5   6   7   8   9   10   11   12

25   0   25   50   75   100 MILES

WHITE = MODERN BOUNDARIES
BLACK = 1850 BOUNDARIES

Louisiana ● 1850

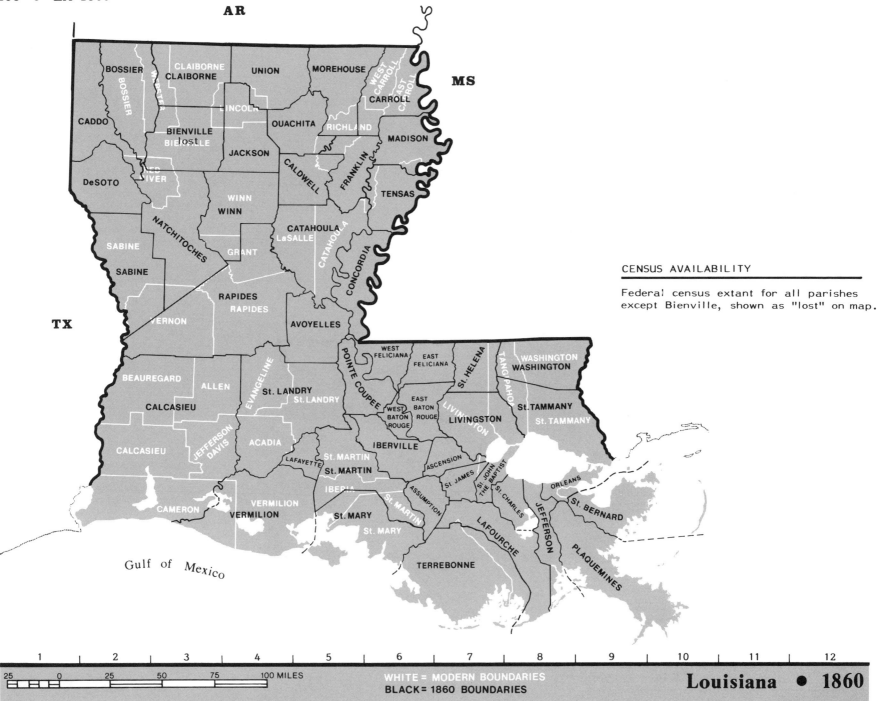

AR

MS

TX

BOSSIER

CLAIBORNE
CLAIBORNE

UNION

MOREHOUSE

WEST
CARROLL

EAST
CARROLL

BOSSIER

WEBSTER

CARROLL

CADDO

LINCOLN

OUACHITA

RICHLAND

BIENVILLE
lost
BIENVILLE

MADISON

DeSOTO

RED
RIVER

JACKSON

CALDWELL

FRANKLIN

TENSAS

WINN
WINN

NATCHITOCHES

CATAHOULA
LaSALLE

CATAHOULA

CONCORDIA

SABINE

GRANT

SABINE

NATCHITOCHES

RAPIDES
RAPIDES

VERNON

AVOYELLES

POINTE COUPEE

WEST
FELICIANA

EAST
FELICIANA

St. HELENA

WASHINGTON
WASHINGTON

TANGIPAHOA

BEAUREGARD

ALLEN

EVANGELINE

St. LANDRY
St. LANDRY

WEST
BATON
ROUGE

EAST
BATON
ROUGE

LIVINGSTON
LIVINGSTON

St. TAMMANY
St. TAMMANY

CALCASIEU

CALCASIEU

JEFFERSON
DAVIS

ACADIA

LAFAYETTE

St. MARTIN
St. MARTIN

IBERVILLE

ASCENSION

St. JAMES

St. JOHN
THE BAPTIST

ORLEANS

IBERIA

ASSUMPTION

St. CHARLES

JEFFERSON

St. BERNARD

CAMERON

VERMILION
VERMILION

St. MARY
St. MARY

St. MARTIN

LAFOURCHE

PLAQUEMINES

TERREBONNE

Gulf of Mexico

CENSUS AVAILABILITY

Federal census extant for all parishes
except Bienville, shown as "lost" on map.

1 2 3 4 5 6 7 8 9 10 11 12

25 0 25 50 75 100 MILES

WHITE = MODERN BOUNDARIES
BLACK = 1860 BOUNDARIES

Louisiana ● 1860

MAP GUIDE TO THE U.S. FEDERAL CENSUSES, 1790–1920 by William Thorndale and William Dollarhide. Copyright 1987, all rights reserved.

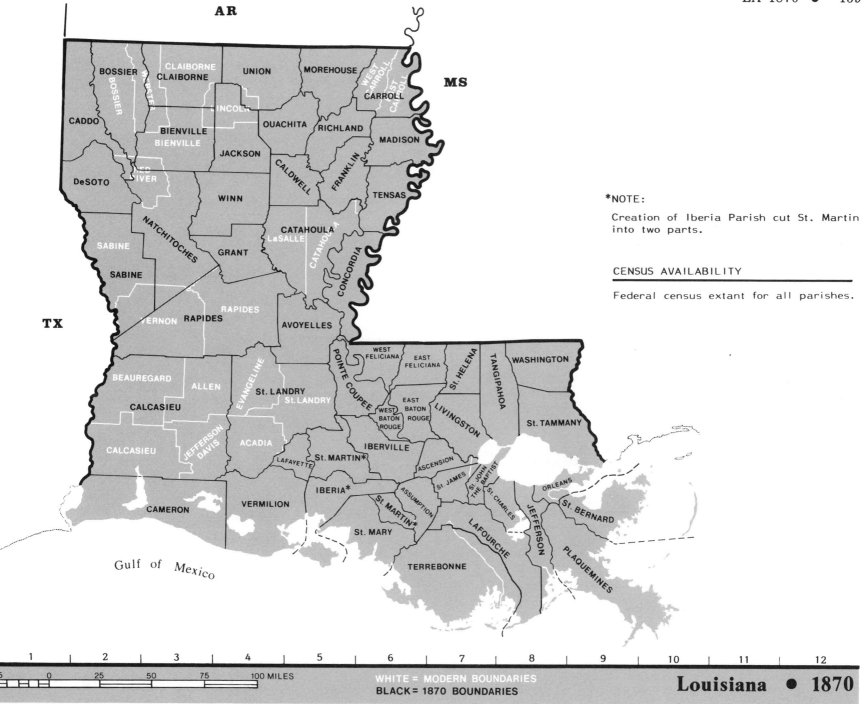

AR

MS

TX

*NOTE:

Creation of Iberia Parish cut St. Martin into two parts.

CENSUS AVAILABILITY

Federal census extant for all parishes.

Gulf of Mexico

| 1 | 2 | 3 | 4 | 5 | 6 | 7 | 8 | 9 | 10 | 11 | 12 |

25 0 25 50 75 100 MILES

WHITE = MODERN BOUNDARIES
BLACK = 1870 BOUNDARIES

Louisiana ● 1870

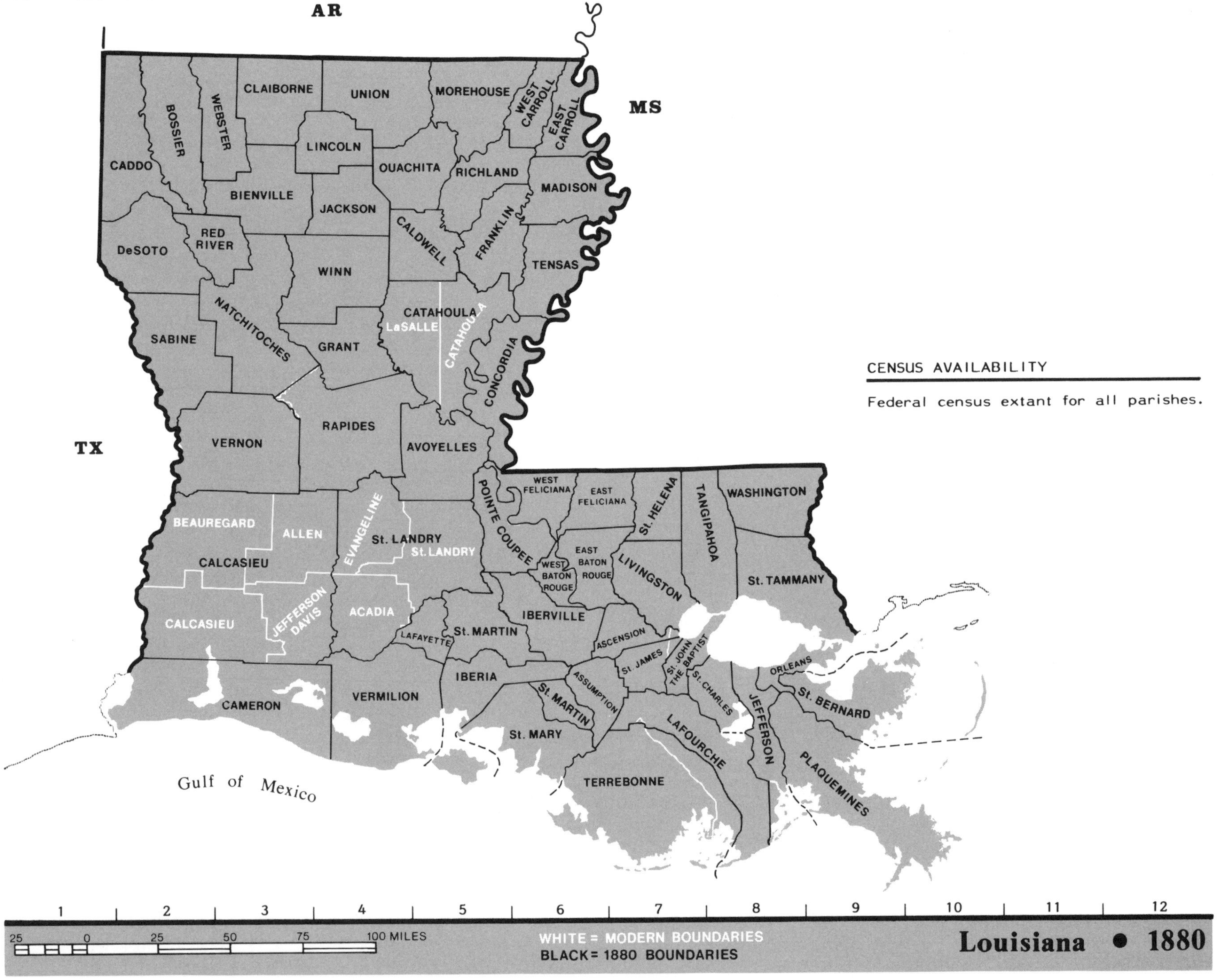

AR

MS

TX

CLAIBORNE
UNION
MOREHOUSE
WEST CARROLL
EAST CARROLL
BOSSIER
WEBSTER
CADDO
LINCOLN
OUACHITA
RICHLAND
MADISON
BIENVILLE
JACKSON
CALDWELL
FRANKLIN
DeSOTO
RED RIVER
WINN
TENSAS
NATCHITOCHES
CATAHOULA
LaSALLE
CATAHOULA
CONCORDIA
SABINE
GRANT
RAPIDES
VERNON
AVOYELLES
BEAUREGARD
ALLEN
EVANGELINE
St. LANDRY
St. LANDRY
POINTE COUPEE
WEST FELICIANA
EAST FELICIANA
St. HELENA
TANGIPAHOA
WASHINGTON
CALCASIEU
WEST BATON ROUGE
EAST BATON ROUGE
LIVINGSTON
St. TAMMANY
JEFFERSON DAVIS
ACADIA
LAFAYETTE
St. MARTIN
IBERVILLE
ASCENSION
St. JAMES
St. JOHN THE BAPTIST
St. CHARLES
ORLEANS
CALCASIEU
IBERIA
ASSUMPTION
JEFFERSON
St. BERNARD
CAMERON
VERMILION
St. MARTIN
St. MARY
LAFOURCHE
PLAQUEMINES
TERREBONNE

Gulf of Mexico

CENSUS AVAILABILITY

Federal census extant for all parishes.

| 1 | 2 | 3 | 4 | 5 | 6 | 7 | 8 | 9 | 10 | 11 | 12 |

25 0 25 50 75 100 MILES

WHITE = MODERN BOUNDARIES
BLACK = 1880 BOUNDARIES

Louisiana ● 1880

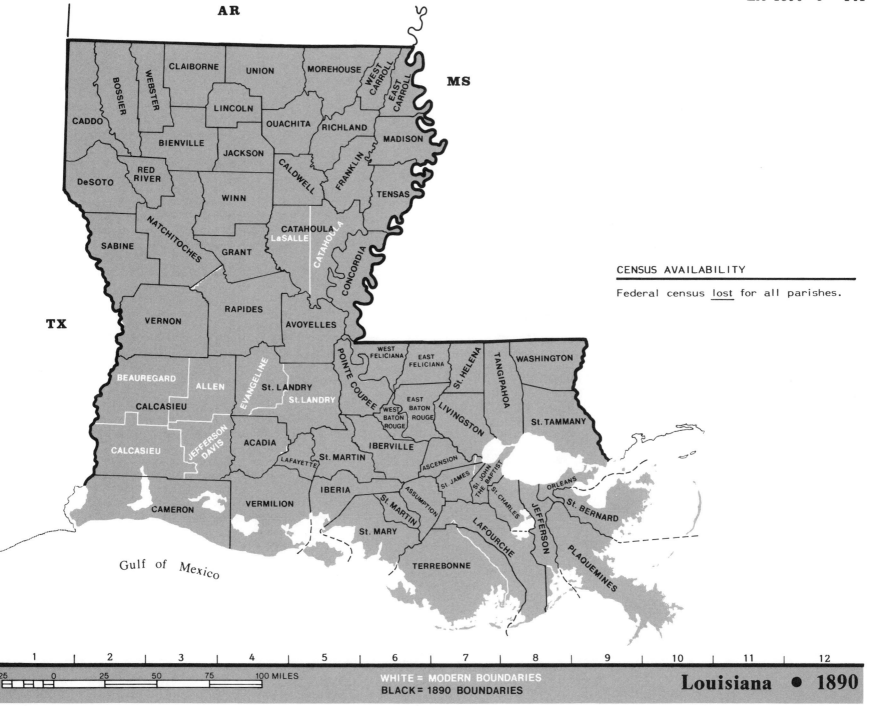

AR

MS

TX

CLAIBORNE
UNION
MOREHOUSE
WEST CARROLL
EAST CARROLL
BOSSIER
WEBSTER
CADDO
LINCOLN
OUACHITA
RICHLAND
MADISON
BIENVILLE
JACKSON
CALDWELL
FRANKLIN
DeSOTO
RED RIVER
WINN
TENSAS
NATCHITOCHES
CATAHOULA
LaSALLE
CATAHOULA
CONCORDIA
SABINE
GRANT
VERNON
RAPIDES
AVOYELLES
POINTE COUPEE
WEST FELICIANA
EAST FELICIANA
ST. HELENA
TANGIPAHOA
WASHINGTON
BEAUREGARD
ALLEN
EVANGELINE
St. LANDRY
St. LANDRY
WEST BATON ROUGE
EAST BATON ROUGE
LIVINGSTON
CALCASIEU
JEFFERSON DAVIS
ACADIA
IBERVILLE
St. TAMMANY
CALCASIEU
LAFAYETTE
St. MARTIN
ASCENSION
St. JAMES
St. JOHN THE BAPTIST
St. CHARLES
ORLEANS
CAMERON
VERMILION
IBERIA
St. MARTIN
ASSUMPTION
JEFFERSON
St. BERNARD
St. MARY
LAFOURCHE
PLAQUEMINES
TERREBONNE

Gulf of Mexico

CENSUS AVAILABILITY

Federal census lost for all parishes.

1 2 3 4 5 6 7 8 9 10 11 12

25 0 25 50 75 100 MILES

WHITE = MODERN BOUNDARIES
BLACK = 1890 BOUNDARIES

Louisiana ● 1890

MAP GUIDE TO THE U.S. FEDERAL CENSUSES, 1790–1920 by William Thorndale and William Dollarhide. Copyright 1987, all rights reserved.

AR

MS

TX

CLAIBORNE
UNION
MOREHOUSE
WEST CARROLL
EAST CARROLL

BOSSIER
WEBSTER
LINCOLN
OUACHITA
RICHLAND
MADISON

CADDO
BIENVILLE
JACKSON
FRANKLIN

DeSOTO
RED RIVER
WINN
CALDWELL
TENSAS

NATCHITOCHES
GRANT
CATAHOULA *
LaSALLE
LaSALLE *
CATAHOULA
CATAHOULA
CONCORDIA

SABINE

VERNON
RAPIDES
AVOYELLES

BEAUREGARD
ALLEN
St. LANDRY
EVANGELINE
St. LANDRY

POINTE COUPEE
WEST FELICIANA
EAST FELICIANA
St. HELENA
TANGIPAHOA
WASHINGTON

CALCASIEU

JEFFERSON DAVIS
ACADIA
WEST BATON ROUGE
EAST BATON ROUGE
LIVINGSTON
St. TAMMANY

CALCASIEU
LAFAYETTE
St. MARTIN
IBERVILLE
ASCENSION
St. JAMES
St. JOHN THE BAPTIST
St. CHARLES
ORLEANS

CAMERON
VERMILION
IBERIA
St. MARTIN
ASSUMPTION
LAFOURCHE
JEFFERSON
St. BERNARD
PLAQUEMINES

St. MARY
TERREBONNE

Gulf of Mexico

*NOTE:

The LaSalle area was in Catahoula in 1900, becoming a separate parish in 1908.

CENSUS AVAILABILITY

1900–1910 federal censuses extant for all parishes.

1 2 3 4 5 6 7 8 9 10 11 12

25 0 25 50 75 100 MILES

WHITE = MODERN BOUNDARIES
BLACK = 1900 - 1910 BOUNDARIES

Louisiana ● **1900-1910**

MAP GUIDE TO THE U.S. FEDERAL CENSUSES, 1790–1920 by William Thorndale and William Dollarhide. Copyright 1987, all rights reserved.

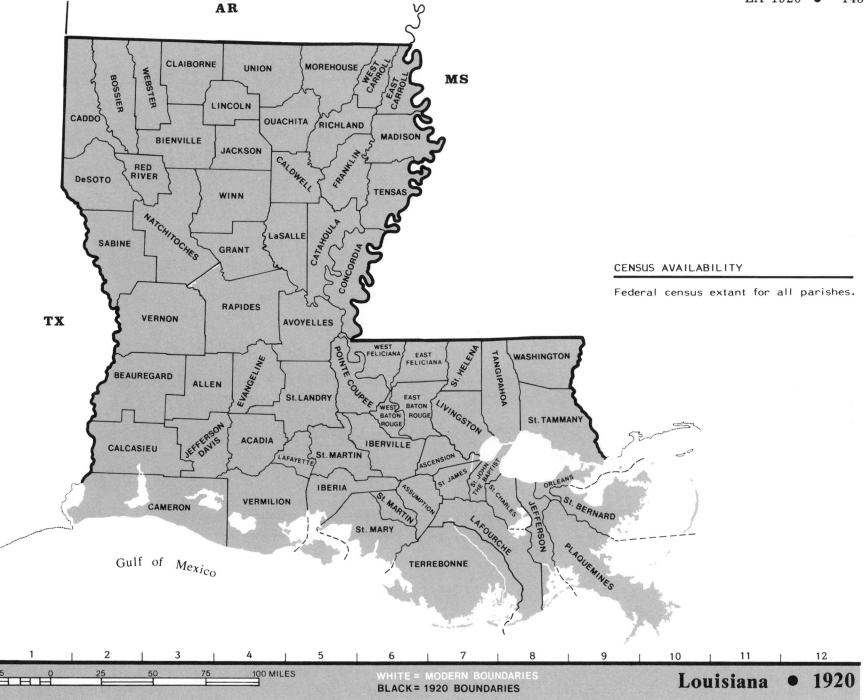

AR

MS

TX

CADDO

BOSSIER

WEBSTER

CLAIBORNE

UNION

MOREHOUSE

WEST CARROLL

EAST CARROLL

LINCOLN

OUACHITA

RICHLAND

MADISON

DeSOTO

RED RIVER

BIENVILLE

JACKSON

CALDWELL

FRANKLIN

TENSAS

SABINE

NATCHITOCHES

WINN

GRANT

LaSALLE

CATAHOULA

CONCORDIA

VERNON

RAPIDES

AVOYELLES

POINTE COUPEE

WEST FELICIANA

EAST FELICIANA

ST. HELENA

TANGIPAHOA

WASHINGTON

BEAUREGARD

ALLEN

EVANGELINE

St. LANDRY

WEST BATON ROUGE

EAST BATON ROUGE

LIVINGSTON

St. TAMMANY

CALCASIEU

JEFFERSON DAVIS

ACADIA

LAFAYETTE

St. MARTIN

IBERVILLE

ASCENSION

St. JAMES

St. JOHN THE BAPTIST

St. CHARLES

ORLEANS

St. BERNARD

CAMERON

VERMILION

IBERIA

St. MARTIN

ASSUMPTION

LAFOURCHE

JEFFERSON

PLAQUEMINES

St. MARY

TERREBONNE

Gulf of Mexico

CENSUS AVAILABILITY

Federal census extant for all parishes.

1 2 3 4 5 6 7 8 9 10 11 12

25 0 25 50 75 100 MILES

WHITE = MODERN BOUNDARIES
BLACK = 1920 BOUNDARIES

Louisiana ● 1920

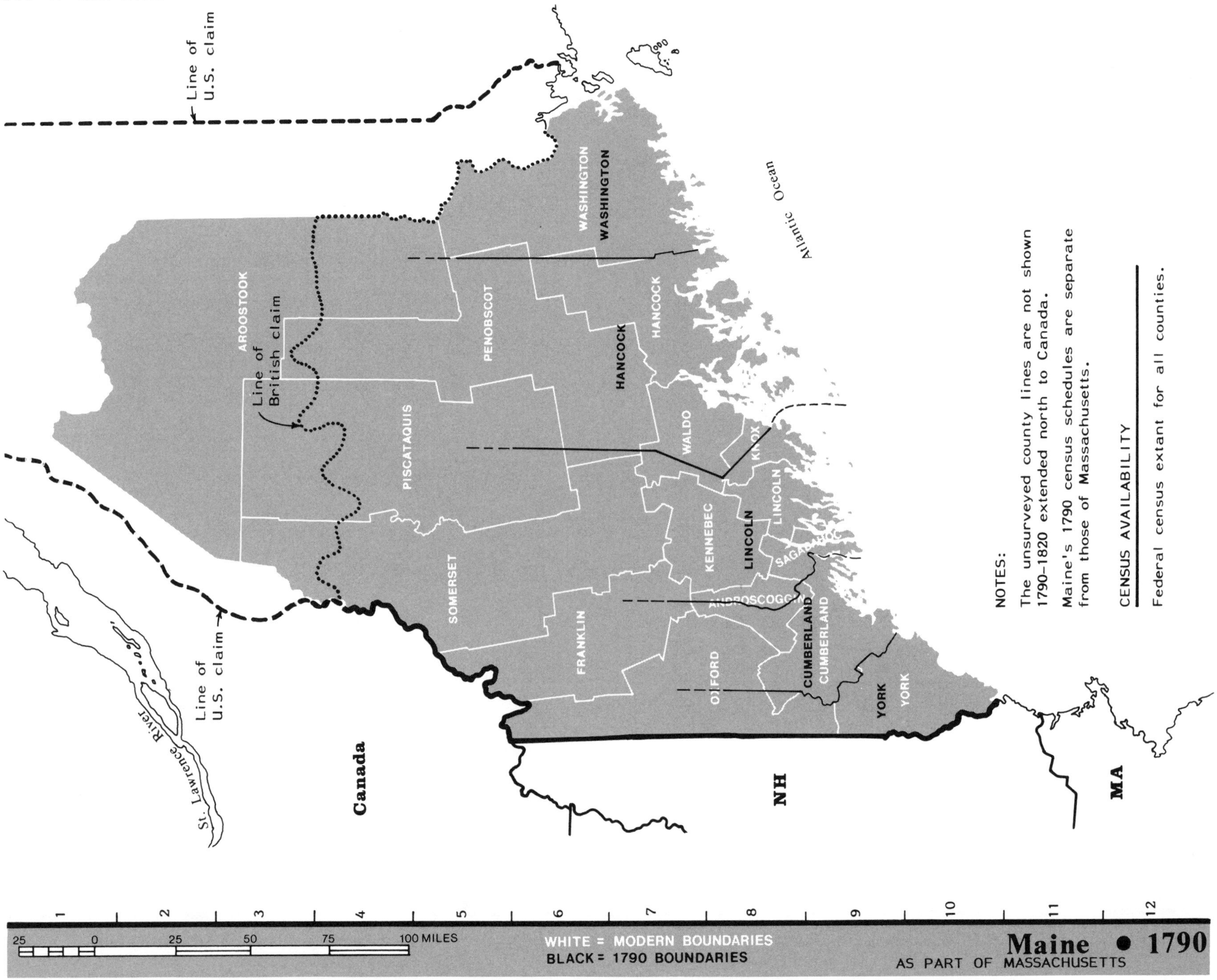

Line of
U.S. claim

Line of
U.S. claim

Line of
British claim

WASHINGTON
WASHINGTON

AROOSTOOK

Atlantic
Ocean

HANCOCK

PENOBSCOT

HANCOCK

PISCATAQUIS

WALDO

KNOX

KENNEBEC

LINCOLN

LINCOLN

SAGADAHOC

SOMERSET

ANDROSCOGGIN

FRANKLIN

CUMBERLAND

OXFORD

CUMBERLAND

YORK

YORK

St. Lawrence River

Canada

NH

MA

NOTES:

The unsurveyed county lines are not shown
1790–1820 extended north to Canada.

Maine's 1790 census schedules are separate
from those of Massachusetts.

CENSUS AVAILABILITY

Federal census extant for all counties.

| 1 | 2 | 3 | 4 | 5 | 6 | 7 | 8 | 9 | 10 | 11 | 12 |

25   0   25   50   75   100 MILES

WHITE = MODERN BOUNDARIES
BLACK = 1790 BOUNDARIES

Maine ● 1790
AS PART OF MASSACHUSETTS

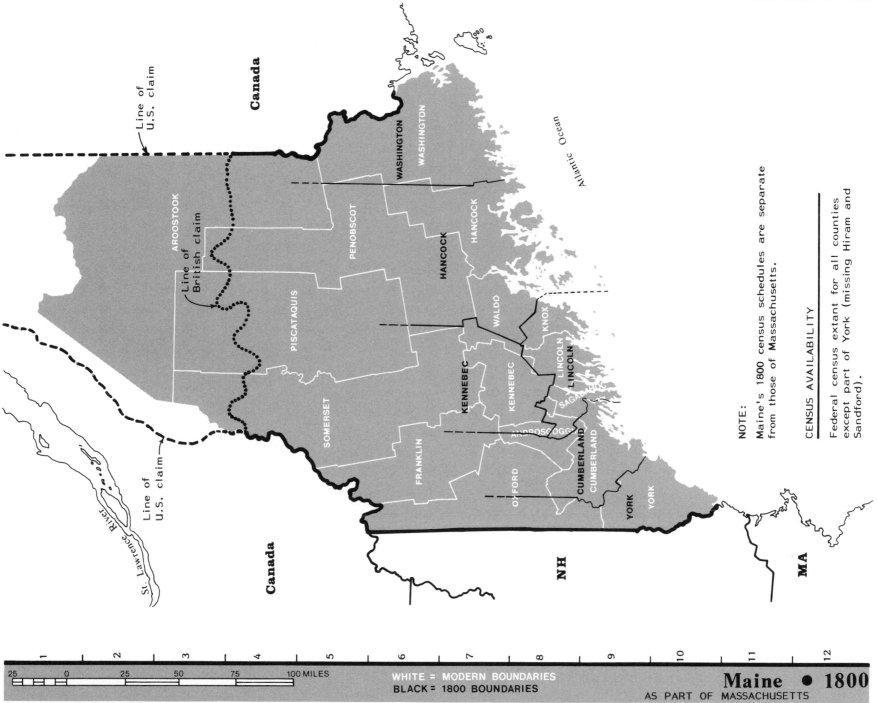

Line of
U.S. claim

Canada

Line of
British claim

AROOSTOOK

WASHINGTON
WASHINGTON

Atlantic Ocean

PENOBSCOT

HANCOCK
HANCOCK

PISCATAQUIS

WALDO

KNOX

KENNEBEC
KENNEBEC

LINCOLN
LINCOLN

SOMERSET

SAGADAHOC

FRANKLIN

ANDROSCOGGIN

OXFORD

CUMBERLAND
CUMBERLAND

YORK
YORK

St. Lawrence River

Line of
U.S. claim

Canada

NH

MA

NOTE:

Maine's 1800 census schedules are separate
from those of Massachusetts.

CENSUS AVAILABILITY

Federal census extant for all counties
except part of York (missing Hiram and
Sandford).

25 0 25 50 75 100 MILES

1 2 3 4 5 6 7 8 9 10 11 12

WHITE = MODERN BOUNDARIES
BLACK = 1800 BOUNDARIES

Maine ● 1800
AS PART OF MASSACHUSETTS

MAP GUIDE TO THE U.S. FEDERAL CENSUSES, 1790-1920 by William Thorndale and William Dollarhide. Copyright 1987, all rights reserved.

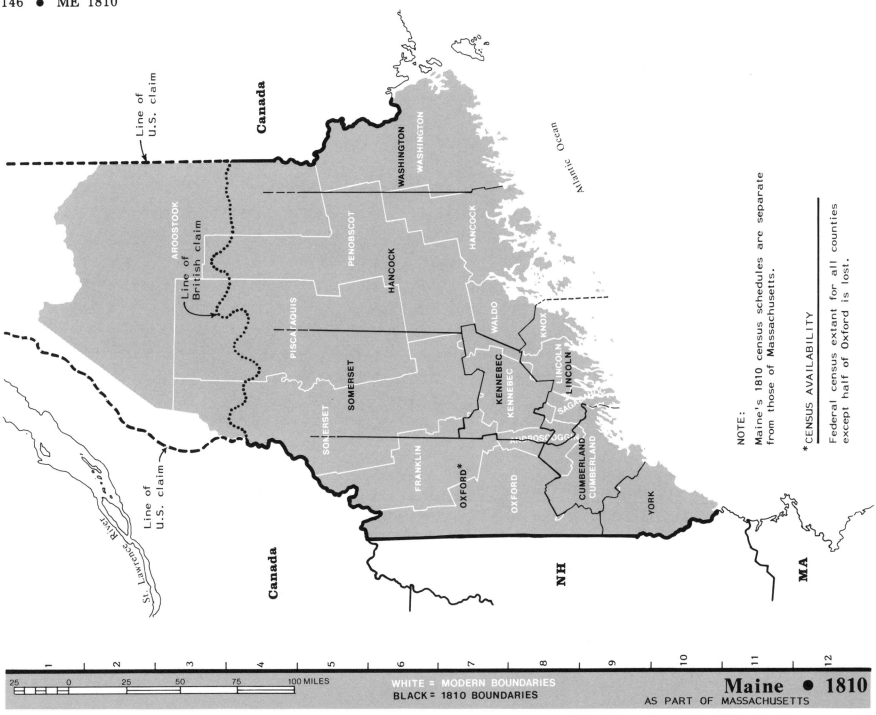

Line of
U.S. claim

Canada

Line of
British claim

Atlantic Ocean

AROOSTOOK

WASHINGTON
WASHINGTON

PENOBSCOT

HANCOCK
HANCOCK

PISCATAQUIS

SOMERSET
SOMERSET
SONERSET

WALDO

KNOX

KENNEBEC
KENNEBEC

LINCOLN
LINCOLN

SAGADAHOC

FRANKLIN

OXFORD*
OXFORD

ANDROSCOGGIN

CUMBERLAND
CUMBERLAND

YORK

Line of
U.S. claim

St. Lawrence River

Canada

NH

MA

NOTE:
Maine's 1810 census schedules are separate
from those of Massachusetts.

*CENSUS AVAILABILITY

Federal census extant for all counties
except half of Oxford is lost.

25   0   25   50   75   100 MILES

1   2   3   4   5   6   7   8   9   10   11   12

WHITE = MODERN BOUNDARIES
BLACK = 1810 BOUNDARIES

Maine ● **1810**
AS PART OF MASSACHUSETTS

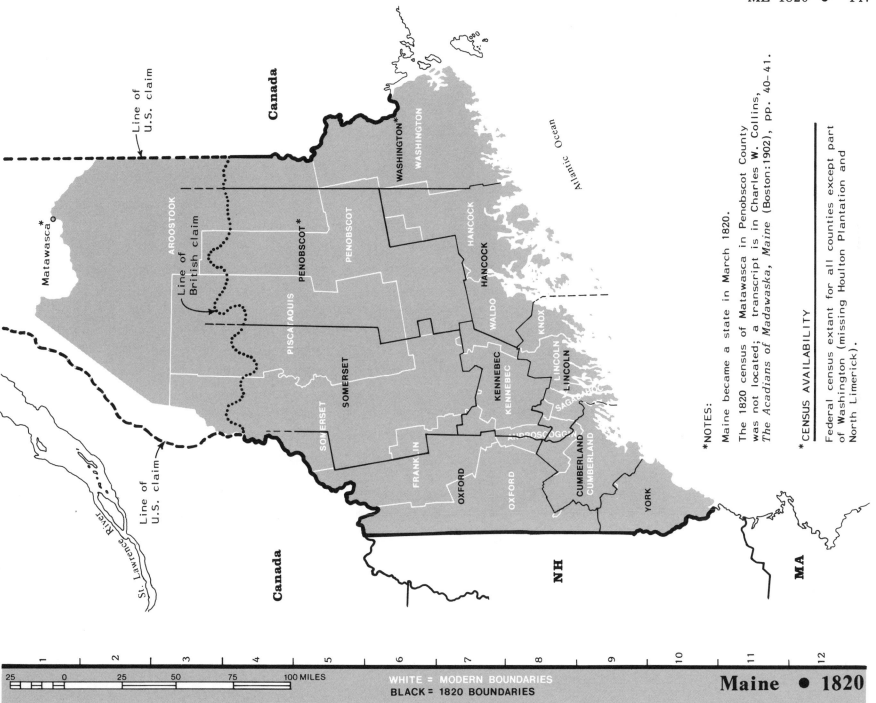

Canada

Line of
U.S. claim

Matawasca *

St. Lawrence River

Line of
U.S. claim

Canada

AROOSTOOK

Line of
British claim

PENOBSCOT *

PENOBSCOT

PISCATAQUIS

SOMERSET

SOMERSET

FRANKLIN

OXFORD

OXFORD

WASHINGTON *

WASHINGTON

HANCOCK

HANCOCK

HANCOCK

WALDO

KNOX

LINCOLN

LINCOLN

SAGADAHOC

KENNEBEC

KENNEBEC

KENNEBEC

ANDROSCOGGIN

CUMBERLAND

CUMBERLAND

YORK

Atlantic Ocean

NH

MA

*NOTES:

Maine became a state in March 1820.

The 1820 census of Matawasca in Penobscot County
was not located; a transcript is in Charles W. Collins,
The Acadians of Madawaska, Maine (Boston:1902), pp. 40–41.

*CENSUS AVAILABILITY

Federal census extant for all counties except part
of Washington (missing Houlton Plantation and
North Limerick).

25   0   25   50   75   100 MILES

WHITE = MODERN BOUNDARIES
BLACK = 1820 BOUNDARIES

Maine ● **1820**

MAP GUIDE TO THE U.S. FEDERAL CENSUSES, 1790–1920 by William Thorndale and William Dollarhide. Copyright 1987, all rights reserved.

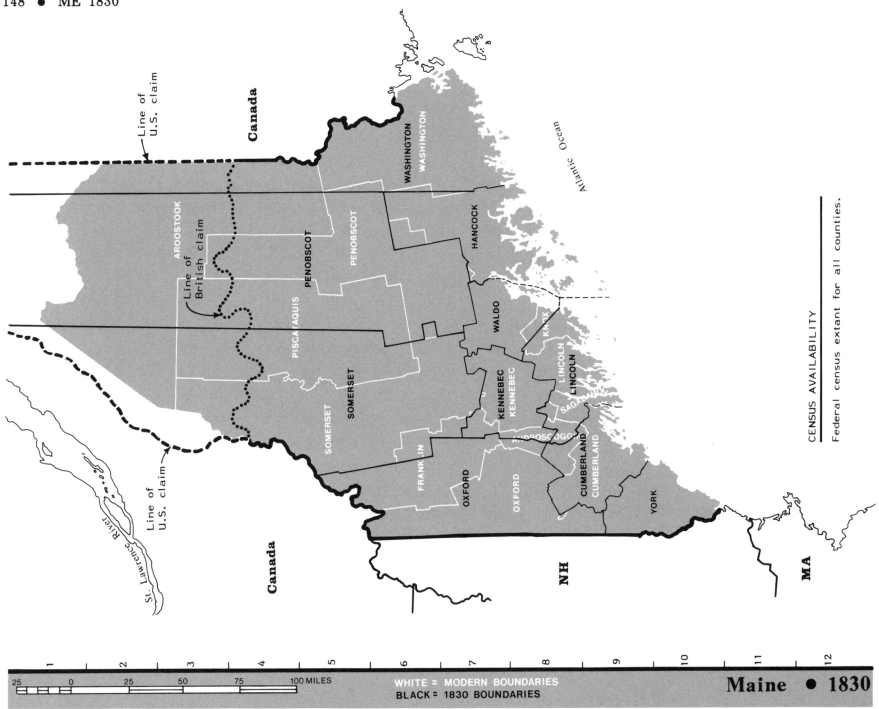

Canada

Line of
U.S. claim

Line of
British claim

Line of
U.S. claim

AROOSTOOK

WASHINGTON
WASHINGTON

PENOBSCOT

PENOBSCOT

HANCOCK

Atlantic Ocean

PISCATAQUIS

WALDO

KNOX

SOMERSET

SOMERSET

LINCOLN

LINCOLN

KENNEBEC

KENNEBEC

SAGADAHOC

FRANKLIN

ANDROSCOGGIN

OXFORD

OXFORD

CUMBERLAND

CUMBERLAND

YORK

St. Lawrence River

Canada

NH

MA

CENSUS AVAILABILITY
Federal census extant for all counties.

| 25 | 0 | 25 | 50 | 75 | 100 MILES |

WHITE = MODERN BOUNDARIES
BLACK = 1830 BOUNDARIES

Maine ● **1830**

MAP GUIDE TO THE U.S. FEDERAL CENSUSES, 1790–1920 by William Thorndale and William Dollarhide.   Copyright 1987, all rights reserved.

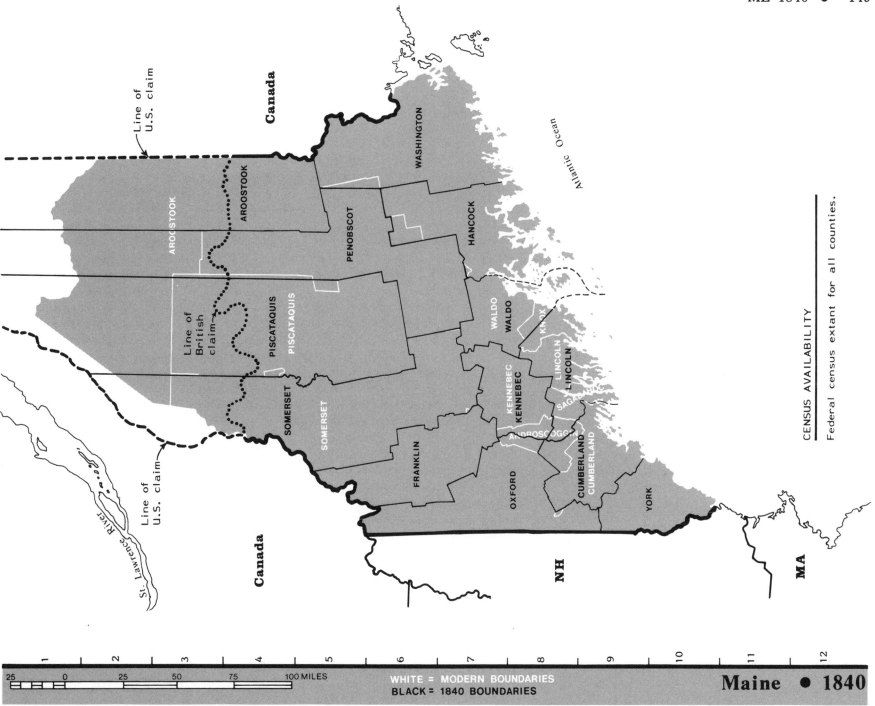

Line of U.S. claim

Canada

AROOSTOOK

AROOSTOOK

Line of British claim

PISCATAQUIS

PISCATAQUIS

Line of U.S. claim

SOMERSET

SOMERSET

St. Lawrence River

Canada

WASHINGTON

PENOBSCOT

HANCOCK

Atlantic Ocean

WALDO

WALDO

KNOX

LINCOLN

LINCOLN

KENNEBEC

KENNEBEC

SAGADAHOC

ANDROSCOGGIN

FRANKLIN

OXFORD

CUMBERLAND

CUMBERLAND

YORK

NH

MA

CENSUS AVAILABILITY

Federal census extant for all counties.

1   2   3   4   5   6   7   8   9   10   11   12

25   0   25   50   75   100 MILES

WHITE = MODERN BOUNDARIES
BLACK = 1840 BOUNDARIES

Maine ● **1840**

MAP GUIDE TO THE U.S. FEDERAL CENSUSES, 1790–1920 by William Thorndale and William Dollarhide. Copyright 1987, all rights reserved.

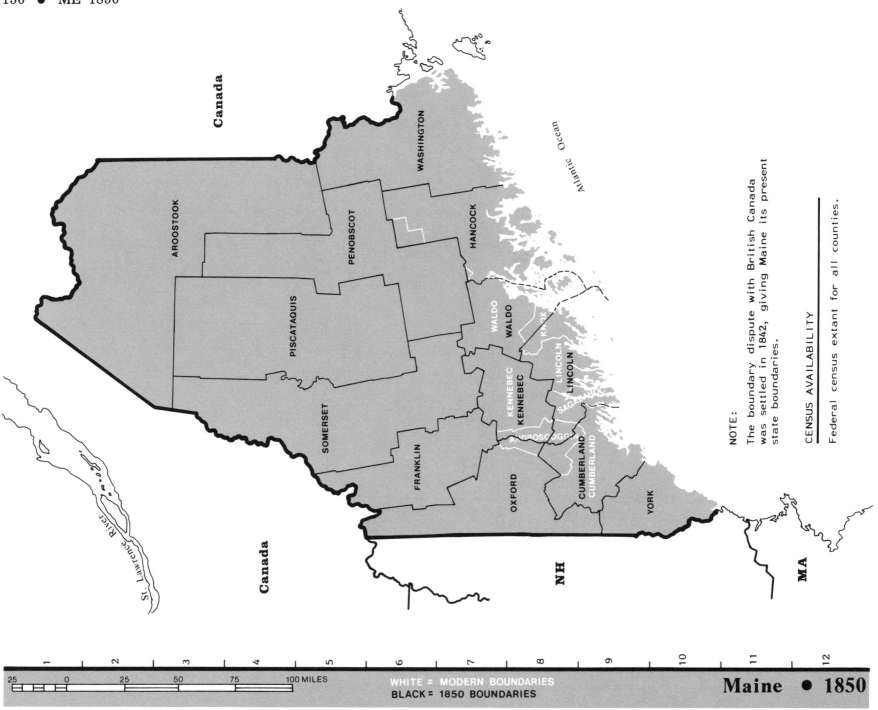

Canada

WASHINGTON

Atlantic Ocean

AROOSTOOK

PENOBSCOT

HANCOCK

PISCATAQUIS

WALDO
WALDO

KNOX

SOMERSET

KENNEBEC
KENNEBEC

LINCOLN
LINCOLN

SAGADAHOC

FRANKLIN

ANDROSCOGGIN

OXFORD

CUMBERLAND
CUMBERLAND

YORK

St. Lawrence River

Canada

NH

MA

NOTE:
The boundary dispute with British Canada was settled in 1842, giving Maine its present state boundaries.

CENSUS AVAILABILITY
Federal census extant for all counties.

25   0   25   50   75   100 MILES

WHITE = MODERN BOUNDARIES
BLACK = 1850 BOUNDARIES

Maine ● 1850

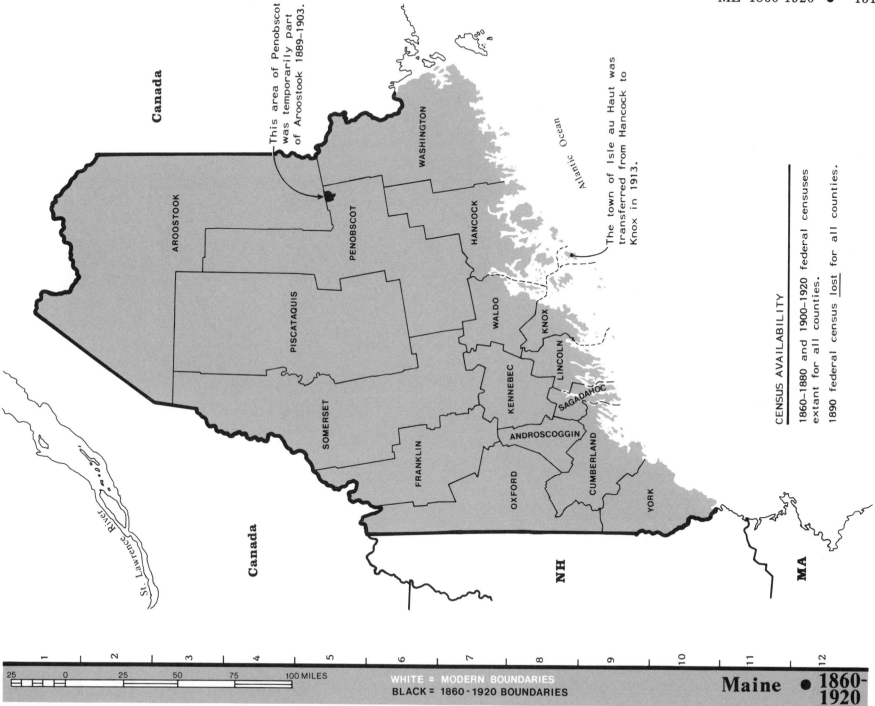

This area of Penobscot was temporarily part of Aroostook 1889-1903.

The town of Isle au Haut was transferred from Hancock to Knox in 1913.

Canada

Canada

AROOSTOOK

WASHINGTON

PENOBSCOT

HANCOCK

Atlantic Ocean

PISCATAQUIS

WALDO

KNOX

SOMERSET

KENNEBEC

LINCOLN

SAGADAHOC

FRANKLIN

ANDROSCOGGIN

OXFORD

CUMBERLAND

YORK

St. Lawrence River

NH

MA

CENSUS AVAILABILITY

1860-1880 and 1900-1920 federal censuses extant for all counties.

1890 federal census lost for all counties.

1   2   3   4   5   6   7   8   9   10   11   12

25   0   25   50   75   100 MILES

WHITE = MODERN BOUNDARIES
BLACK = 1860-1920 BOUNDARIES

Maine ● **1860-1920**

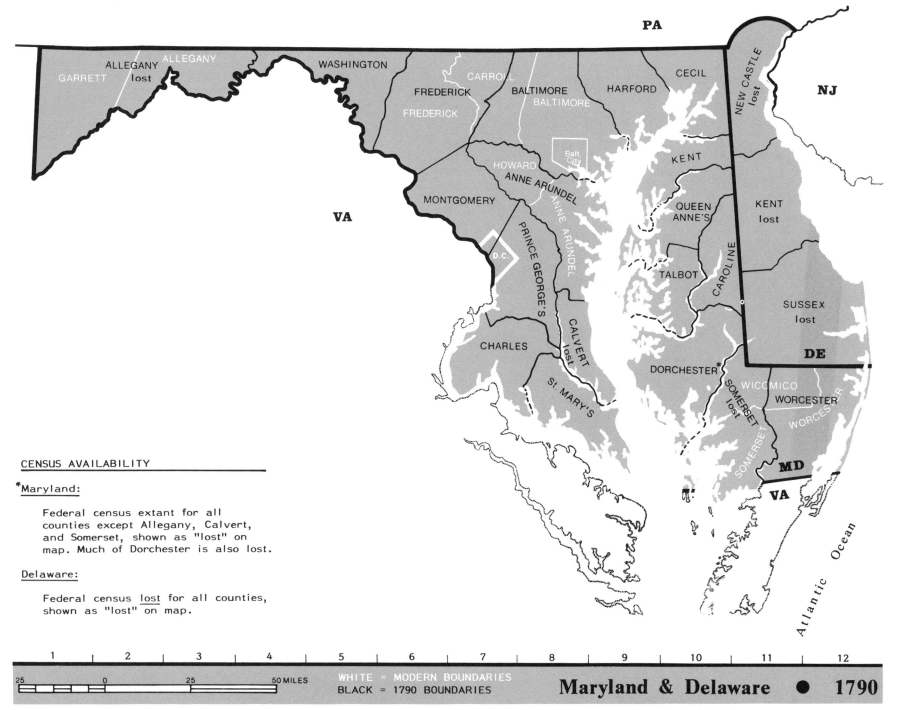

CENSUS AVAILABILITY

*Maryland:

Federal census extant for all
counties except Allegany, Calvert,
and Somerset, shown as "lost" on
map. Much of Dorchester is also lost.

Delaware:

Federal census lost for all counties,
shown as "lost" on map.

WHITE = MODERN BOUNDARIES
BLACK = 1790 BOUNDARIES

Maryland & Delaware ● **1790**

PA

ALLEGANY   ALLEGANY

GARRETT

WASHINGTON

CARROLL

CECIL

FREDERICK

HARFORD

NEW CASTLE

NJ

FREDERICK

BALTIMORE

BALTIMORE*

Balt.
City

KENT

HOWARD

ANNE ARUNDEL

MONTGOMERY

ANNE ARUNDEL

QUEEN
ANNE'S

KENT

CENSUS AVAILABILITY

D.C.

PRINCE GEORGE'S

CAROLINE

VA

TALBOT

*Maryland:

1800 federal census extant for all counties,
except Baltimore County outside of the
city of Baltimore is lost.

SUSSEX

1810–1820 federal censuses extant for all counties.

CALVERT

CHARLES

Delaware:

DE

DORCHESTER

1800–1820 federal censuses extant for all counties.

WICOMICO

WORCESTER

District of Columbia:

St. MARY'S

SOMERSET

WORCES.

1800 federal census extant for Maryland side and
lost for Virginia side.

1810 federal census lost for whole district.

MD

1820 federal census extant for whole district.

VA

NOTE:

The District of Columbia was created as a 10-mile
square in 1791, but its 1800 census was still taken
with the Maryland and Virginia schedules. In 1801,
the part from Virginia became Alexandria County and
the part from Maryland became Washington County.

Atlantic Ocean

| 1 | 2 | 3 | 4 | 5 | 6 | 7 | 8 | 9 | 10 | 11 | 12 |

25   0   25   50 MILES

WHITE = MODERN BOUNDARIES
BLACK = 1800-1820 BOUNDARIES

Maryland, Delaware, ● **1800-**
& the District of Columbia **1820**

MAP GUIDE TO THE U.S. FEDERAL CENSUSES, 1790-1920 by William Thorndale and William Dollarhide. Copyright 1987, all rights reserved.

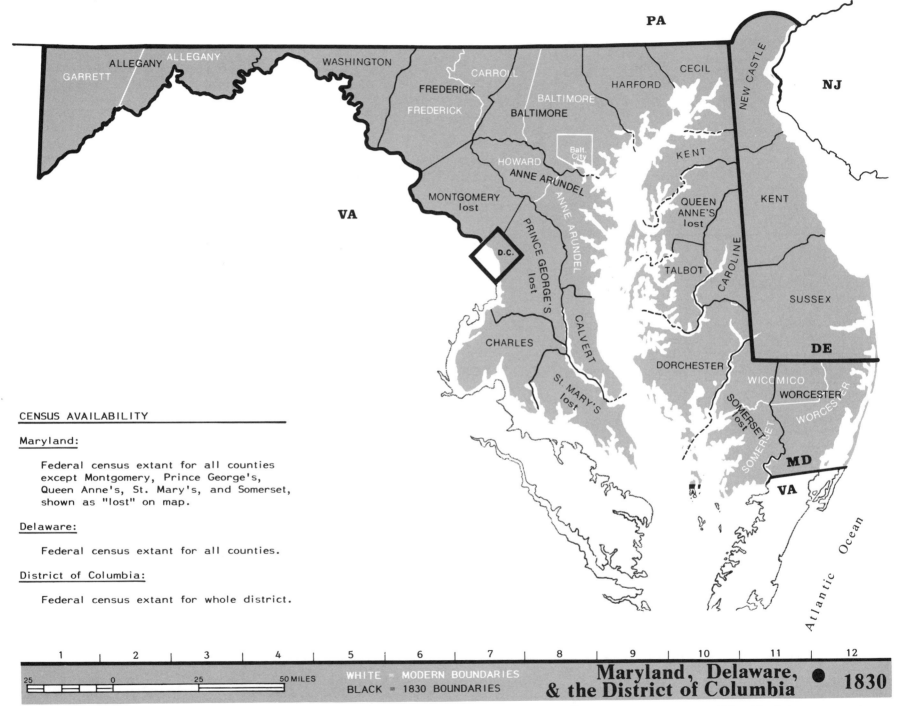

CENSUS AVAILABILITY

Maryland:

Federal census extant for all counties
except Montgomery, Prince George's,
Queen Anne's, St. Mary's, and Somerset,
shown as "lost" on map.

Delaware:

Federal census extant for all counties.

District of Columbia:

Federal census extant for whole district.

WHITE = MODERN BOUNDARIES
BLACK = 1830 BOUNDARIES

25   0   25   50 MILES

**Maryland, Delaware,
& the District of Columbia** ● 1830

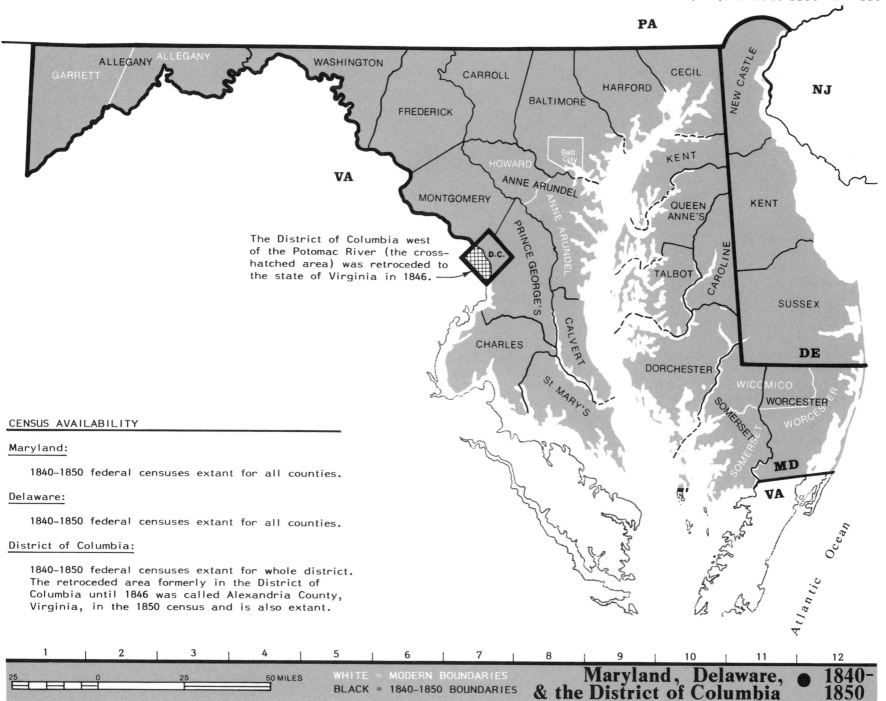

The District of Columbia west of the Potomac River (the cross-hatched area) was retroceded to the state of Virginia in 1846.

CENSUS AVAILABILITY

Maryland:

1840–1850 federal censuses extant for all counties.

Delaware:

1840–1850 federal censuses extant for all counties.

District of Columbia:

1840–1850 federal censuses extant for whole district. The retroceded area formerly in the District of Columbia until 1846 was called Alexandria County, Virginia, in the 1850 census and is also extant.

WHITE = MODERN BOUNDARIES
BLACK = 1840-1850 BOUNDARIES

Maryland, Delaware, ● **1840-**
& the District of Columbia **1850**

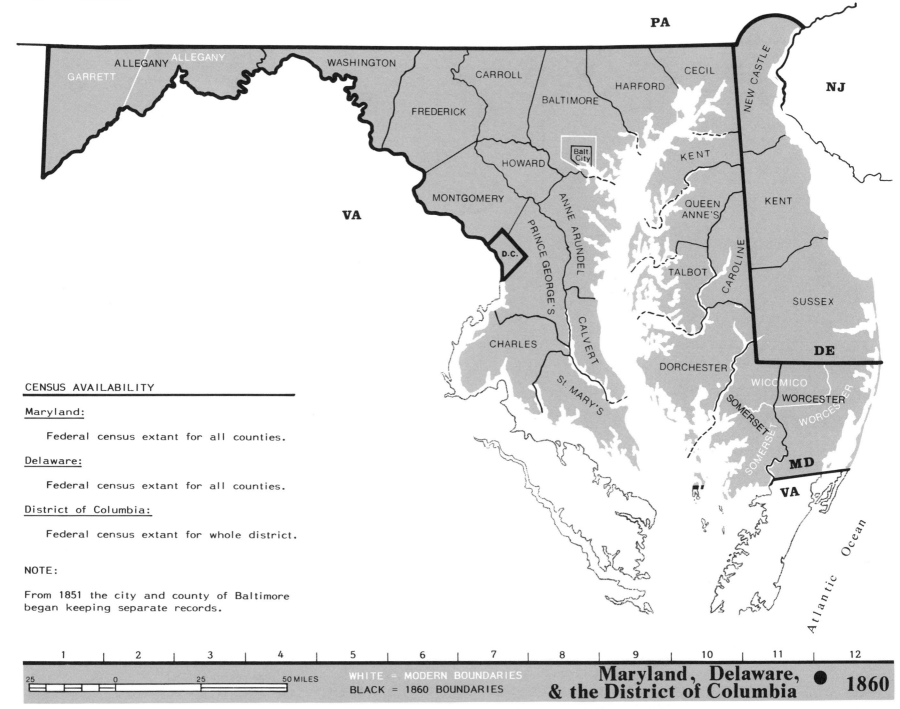

PA

NJ

GARRETT
ALLEGANY ALLEGANY
WASHINGTON
CARROLL
CECIL
HARFORD
BALTIMORE
FREDERICK
NEW CASTLE
Balt. City
HOWARD
KENT
MONTGOMERY
ANNE ARUNDEL
QUEEN ANNE'S
KENT

VA

D.C.
PRINCE GEORGE'S
TALBOT
CAROLINE
SUSSEX

CHARLES
CALVERT
DE
DORCHESTER
WICOMICO
WORCESTER
St. MARY'S
SOMERSET
WORCESTER
SOMERSET
MD
VA

Atlantic Ocean

CENSUS AVAILABILITY

Maryland:

   Federal census extant for all counties.

Delaware:

   Federal census extant for all counties.

District of Columbia:

   Federal census extant for whole district.

NOTE:

From 1851 the city and county of Baltimore
began keeping separate records.

1 2 3 4 5 6 7 8 9 10 11 12

25   0   25   50 MILES

WHITE = MODERN BOUNDARIES
BLACK = 1860 BOUNDARIES

Maryland, Delaware,
& the District of Columbia ● **1860**

MAP GUIDE TO THE U.S. FEDERAL CENSUSES, 1790–1920 by William Thorndale and William Dollarhide. Copyright 1987, all rights reserved.

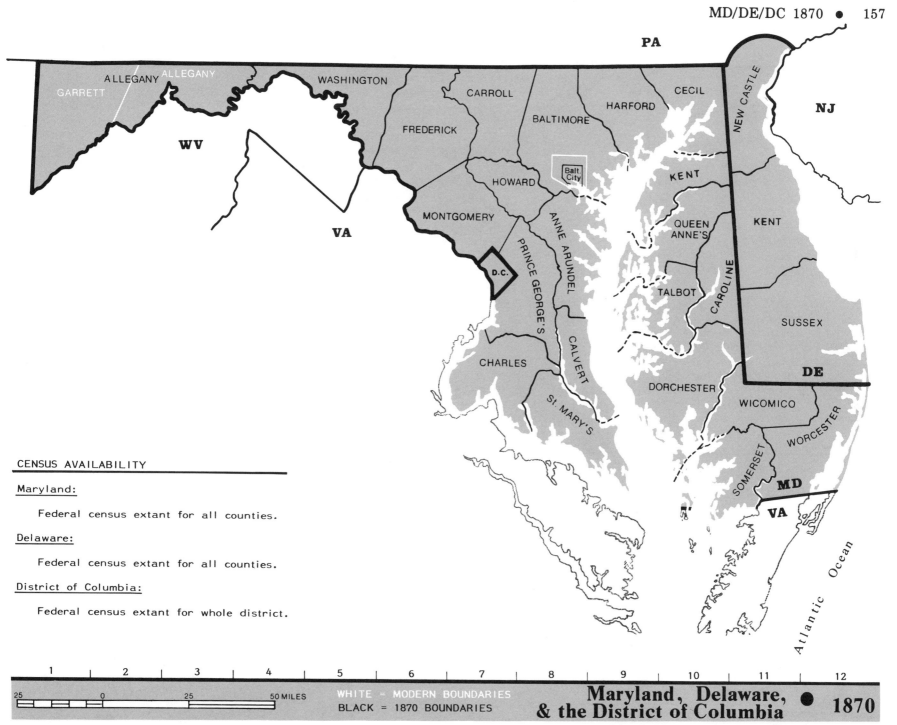

PA

ALLEGANY · ALLEGANY
GARRETT
WASHINGTON
CARROLL
CECIL
HARFORD
WV
FREDERICK
BALTIMORE
NEW CASTLE
NJ
Balt. City
HOWARD
KENT
VA
MONTGOMERY
ANNE ARUNDEL
QUEEN ANNE'S
KENT
D.C.
PRINCE GEORGE'S
CAROLINE
TALBOT
CHARLES
CALVERT
DORCHESTER
SUSSEX
St. MARY'S
WICOMICO
DE
SOMERSET
WORCESTER
MD
VA
Atlantic Ocean

CENSUS AVAILABILITY
_____

Maryland:

   Federal census extant for all counties.

Delaware:

   Federal census extant for all counties.

District of Columbia:

   Federal census extant for whole district.

| 1 | 2 | 3 | 4 | 5 | 6 | 7 | 8 | 9 | 10 | 11 | 12 |

25   0   25   50 MILES

WHITE = MODERN BOUNDARIES
BLACK = 1870 BOUNDARIES

**Maryland, Delaware, ● 1870
& the District of Columbia**

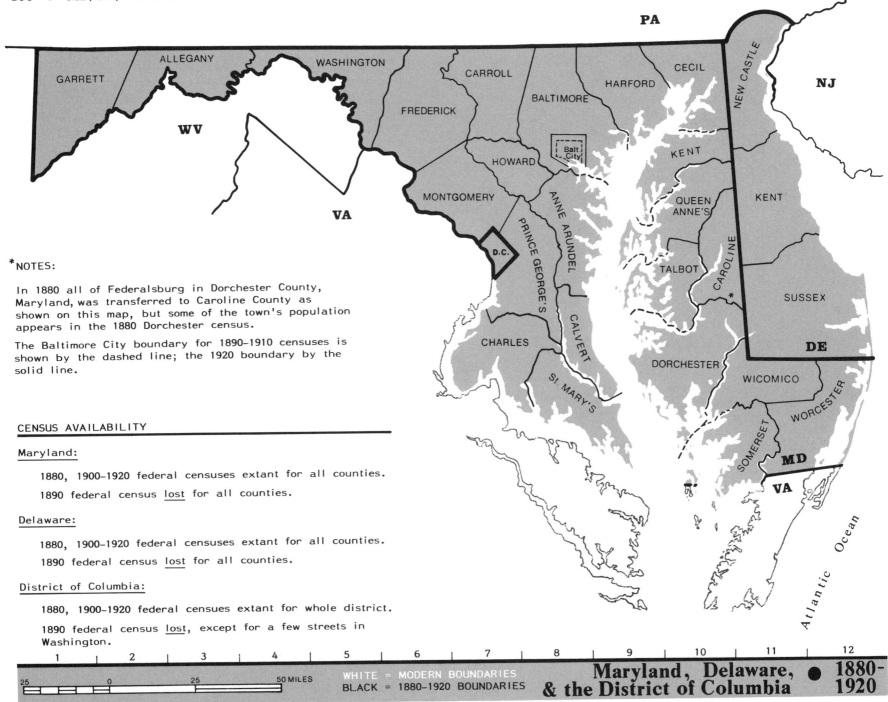

PA

ALLEGANY WASHINGTON

GARRETT CARROLL CECIL

HARFORD

WV FREDERICK BALTIMORE NEW CASTLE NJ

VA HOWARD Balt. City KENT

MONTGOMERY ANNE ARUNDEL QUEEN ANNE'S KENT

D.C. PRINCE GEORGE'S CAROLINE

*NOTES:

In 1880 all of Federalsburg in Dorchester County, Maryland, was transferred to Caroline County as shown on this map, but some of the town's population appears in the 1880 Dorchester census.

TALBOT SUSSEX

CALVERT

The Baltimore City boundary for 1890–1910 censuses is shown by the dashed line; the 1920 boundary by the solid line.

CHARLES DE

DORCHESTER

St. MARY'S WICOMICO

WORCESTER

CENSUS AVAILABILITY

SOMERSET MD

Maryland: VA

    1880, 1900–1920 federal censuses extant for all counties.

    1890 federal census lost for all counties.

Delaware:

    1880, 1900–1920 federal censuses extant for all counties.

    1890 federal census lost for all counties.

District of Columbia:

    1880, 1900–1920 federal censuses extant for whole district.

    1890 federal census lost, except for a few streets in Washington.

Atlantic Ocean

1 2 3 4 5 6 7 8 9 10 11 12

25 0 25 50 MILES

WHITE = MODERN BOUNDARIES
BLACK = 1880-1920 BOUNDARIES

Maryland, Delaware, & the District of Columbia ● 1880-1920

Lake Superior

KEWEENAW

HOUGHTON

ONTONAGON

BARAGA

Illinois Territory

GOGEBIC

IRON

MARQUETTE

DICKINSON

MENOMINEE

Indiana Territory

ALGER

SCHOOLCRAFT

LUCE

CHIPPEWA

MACKINAC

DELTA

Green Bay

Lake Michigan

CHEBOYGAN

PRESQUE ISLE

EMMET

MICHILIMACKINAC *

CHARLEVOIX

MONTMORENCY

ALPENA

ANTRIM

OTSEGO

OSCODA

ALCONA

LEELANAU

KALKASKA

CRAWFORD

IOSCO

GRAND TRAVERSE

MISSAUKEE

OGEMAW

Indian Lands

ROSCOMMON

ARENAC

BENZIE

WEXFORD

GLADWIN

Saginaw Bay

Lake Huron

HURON *

MANISTEE

OSCEOLA

CLARE

MIDLAND

BAY

TUSCOLA

SANILAC

LAKE

MASON

MECOSTA

ISABELLA

SAGINAW

LAPEER

ST. CLAIR

GENESEE

NEWAYGO

MONTCALM

GRATIOT

SHIAWASSEE

OAKLAND

MACOMB

OCEANA

CLINTON

DETROIT

Lake St. Clair

MUSKEGON

KENT

IONIA

INGHAM

LIVINGSTON

WAYNE

Indian Lands

WASHTENAW

ERIE *

OTTAWA

BARRY

EATON

Lake Erie

ALLEGAN

JACKSON

MONROE

KALAMAZOO

CALHOUN

LENAWEE

Van BUREN

BRANCH

HILLSDALE

BERRIEN

CASS

St. JOSEPH

OH

Ind. Terr.

NORTH

Canada

MN

Ind. Terr.

WI

Illinois Territory

Michigan Territory

MI

Louisiana Territory

IL

Ind. Terr. IN

OH

MO

KY

WV VA

1810

CENSUS AVAILABILITY

Federal census lost for all four civil districts except fragments extant for Detroit and Michilimackinac. Areas in Illinois and Indiana were unenumerated Indian lands.

*NOTES:

Michigan was under British occupation in 1790. The 1800 federal census taken in eastern Michigan as Wayne County, Northwest Territory, is lost, as is the Michilimackinac census in 1800 Indiana Territory.

Michigan Territory, created in 1805, was all designated Wayne County but subdivided into four civil districts. Erie and Huron are shown to the Indian treaty line. The light dashed line marks Michilimachinac's southern boundary.

See Michigan 1830 for an explanation of the Michigan-Ohio boundary.

1   2   3   4   5   6   7   8   9   10   11   12

25   0   25   50   75   100 MILES

WHITE = MODERN BOUNDARIES
BLACK = 1810 BOUNDARIES

Michigan ● 1810
AS PART OF THREE TERRITORIES

MAP GUIDE TO THE U.S. FEDERAL CENSUSES, 1790–1920 by William Thorndale and William Dollarhide. Copyright 1987, all rights reserved.

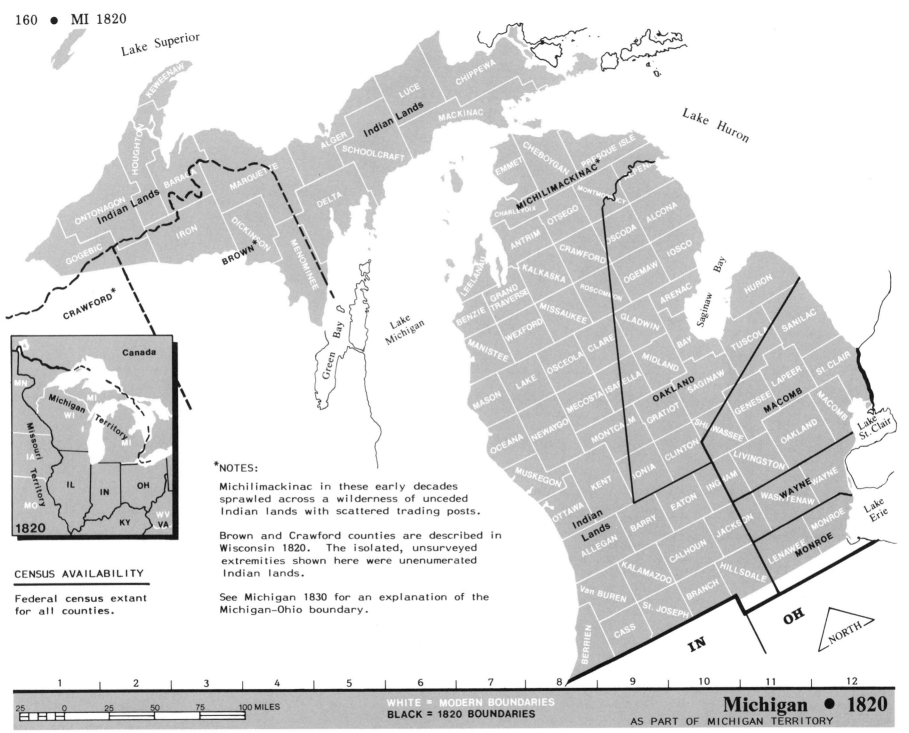

Lake Superior

KEWEENAW

HOUGHTON

ONTONAGON

Indian Lands

GOGEBIC

BARAGA

IRON

MARQUETTE

DICKINSON

BROWN *

MENOMINEE

DELTA

ALGER

SCHOOLCRAFT

Indian Lands

LUCE

MACKINAC

CHIPPEWA

Lake Huron

Green Bay

Lake Michigan

CRAWFORD *

Canada

MN
MICHIGAN
WI
Michigan Territory
MI
MI

Missouri Territory

MO

IL   IN   OH

KY   WV VA

1820

CENSUS AVAILABILITY

Federal census extant
for all counties.

*NOTES:

Michilimackinac in these early decades
sprawled across a wilderness of unceded
Indian lands with scattered trading posts.

Brown and Crawford counties are described in
Wisconsin 1820. The isolated, unsurveyed
extremities shown here were unenumerated
Indian lands.

See Michigan 1830 for an explanation of the
Michigan–Ohio boundary.

EMMET

CHARLEVOIX

LEELANAU

BENZIE

MANISTEE

GRAND TRAVERSE

ANTRIM

KALKASKA

WEXFORD

MISSAUKEE

LAKE

MASON

OSCEOLA

MECOSTA

NEWAYGO

OCEANA

MONTCALM

MUSKEGON

OTTAWA

Indian Lands

ALLEGAN

Van BUREN

BERRIEN

CASS

St. JOSEPH

KALAMAZOO

BARRY

KENT

IONIA

EATON

CALHOUN

BRANCH

HILLSDALE

JACKSON

LENAWEE

CHEBOYGAN

PRESQUE ISLE

MICHILIMACKINAC *

MONTMORENCY

ALPENA

OTSEGO

CRAWFORD

OSCODA

ALCONA

ROSCOMMON

OGEMAW

IOSCO

ARENAC

GLADWIN

CLARE

ISABELLA

MIDLAND

BAY

GRATIOT

SAGINAW

OAKLAND

SHIAWASSEE

CLINTON

INGHAM

LIVINGSTON

OAKLAND

GENESEE

LAPEER

MACOMB

MACOMB

St. CLAIR

Saginaw Bay

HURON

TUSCOLA

SANILAC

Lake St. Clair

WASHTENAW

WAYNE   WAYNE

MONROE

MONROE

Lake Erie

IN   OH

NORTH

1   2   3   4   5   6   7   8   9   10   11   12

25   0   25   50   75   100 MILES

WHITE = MODERN BOUNDARIES
BLACK = 1820 BOUNDARIES

Michigan ● 1820
AS PART OF MICHIGAN TERRITORY

MAP GUIDE TO THE U.S. FEDERAL CENSUSES, 1790–1920 by William Thorndale and William Dollarhide. Copyright 1987, all rights reserved.

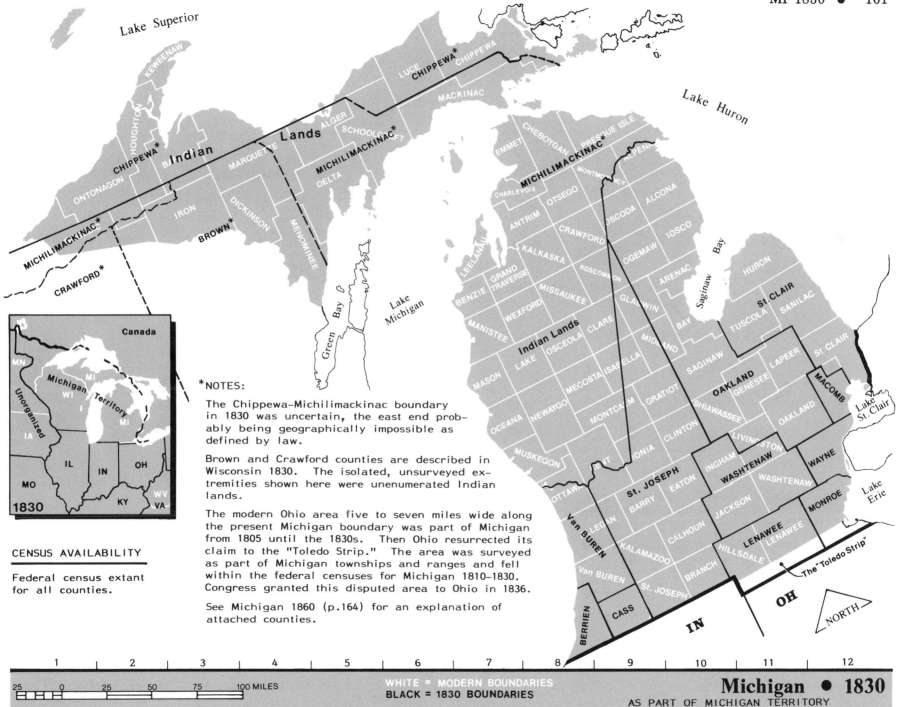

Lake Superior

CHIPPEWA

LUCE

CHIPPEWA

MACKINAC

KEWEENAW

HOUGHTON

CHIPPEWA *

Indian   Lands

ALGER

SCHOOLCRAFT

MICHILIMACKINAC *

ONTONAGON

MARQUETTE

DELTA

MICHILIMACKINAC *

IRON

DICKINSON

CRAWFORD *

BROWN *

MENOMINEE

Green Bay

Lake Michigan

EMMET

CHEBOYGAN

PRESQUE ISLE *

CHARLEVOIX

MONTMORENCY

ALPENA

ANTRIM

OTSEGO

ALCONA

LEELANAU

KALKASKA

CRAWFORD

OSCODA

IOSCO

GRAND TRAVERSE

ROSCOMMON

OGEMAW

ARENAC

BENZIE

MISSAUKEE

GLADWIN

Saginaw Bay

HURON

MANISTEE

WEXFORD

Indian Lands

CLARE

BAY

ST. CLAIR

MASON

LAKE

OSCEOLA

ISABELLA

MIDLAND

SAGINAW

TUSCOLA

SANILAC

OCEANA

NEWAYGO

MECOSTA

MONTCALM

GRATIOT

LAPEER

ST. CLAIR

MUSKEGON

IONIA

CLINTON

SHIAWASSEE

OAKLAND

GENESEE

OAKLAND

MACOMB

Lake St. Clair

KENT

OTTAWA

INGHAM

LIVINGSTON

ST. JOSEPH

BARRY

EATON

WASHTENAW

WASHTENAW

WAYNE

ALLEGAN

JACKSON

Lake Erie

VAN BUREN

KALAMAZOO

CALHOUN

LENAWEE

LENAWEE

MONROE

VAN BUREN

BRANCH

HILLSDALE

The "Toledo Strip"

BERRIEN

CASS

ST. JOSEPH

IN   OH

NORTH

MICHILIMACKINAC *

MICHILIMACKINAC *

Lake Huron

Canada

MN

MI

WI

MI

Michigan   Territory   MI

Unorganized

IA

IL   IN   OH

MO

KY   WV   VA

1830

CENSUS AVAILABILITY

Federal census extant for all counties.

*NOTES:

The Chippewa–Michilimackinac boundary in 1830 was uncertain, the east end probably being geographically impossible as defined by law.

Brown and Crawford counties are described in Wisconsin 1830. The isolated, unsurveyed extremities shown here were unenumerated Indian lands.

The modern Ohio area five to seven miles wide along the present Michigan boundary was part of Michigan from 1805 until the 1830s. Then Ohio resurrected its claim to the "Toledo Strip." The area was surveyed as part of Michigan townships and ranges and fell within the federal censuses for Michigan 1810–1830. Congress granted this disputed area to Ohio in 1836.

See Michigan 1860 (p.164) for an explanation of attached counties.

1   2   3   4   5   6   7   8   9   10   11   12

25   0   25   50   75   100 MILES

WHITE = MODERN BOUNDARIES
BLACK = 1830 BOUNDARIES

Michigan ● 1830
AS PART OF MICHIGAN TERRITORY

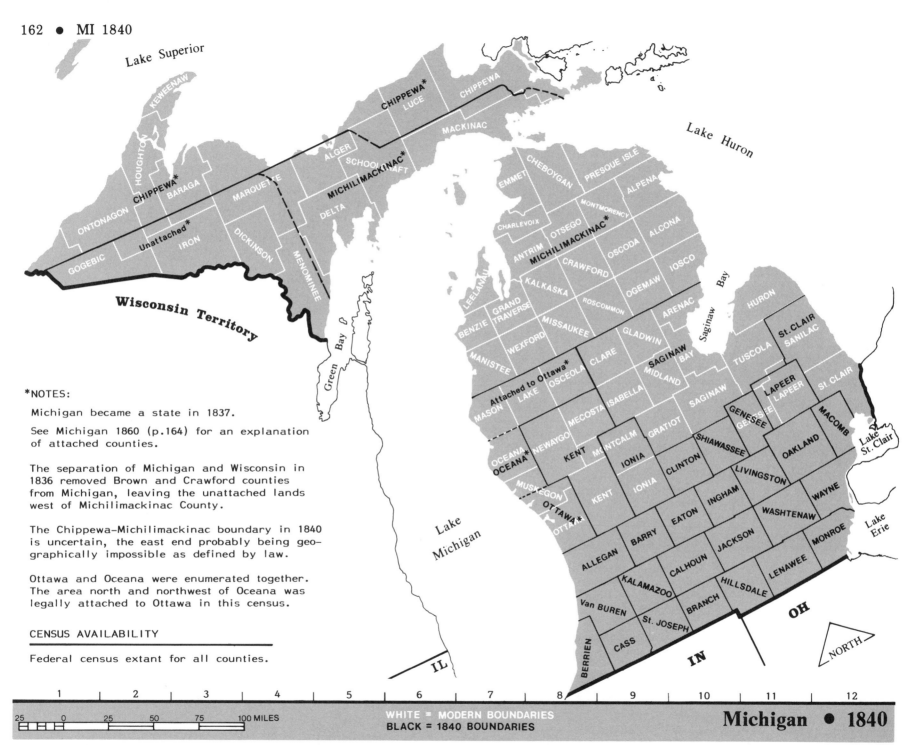

Lake Superior

KEWEENAW

CHIPPEWA *

HOUGHTON *

BARAGA

ONTONAGON

GOGEBIC

Unattached *

IRON

MARQUETTE

DICKINSON

MENOMINEE

ALGER

DELTA

SCHOOLCRAFT

CHIPPEWA *
LUCE

MICHILIMACKINAC *

MACKINAC

CHIPPEWA

Lake Huron

EMMET

CHEBOYGAN

PRESQUE ISLE

CHARLEVOIX

ANTRIM

OTSEGO

MONTMORENCY

ALPENA

ALCONA

MICHILIMACKINAC *

OSCODA

CRAWFORD

IOSCO

LEELANAU

KALKASKA

ROSCOMMON

OGEMAW

GRAND TRAVERSE

MISSAUKEE

ARENAC

BENZIE

WEXFORD

GLADWIN

SAGINAW BAY

ARENAC

Saginaw Bay

HURON

MANISTEE

Attached to Ottawa *

CLARE

SAGINAW BAY

TUSCOLA

ST. CLAIR

SANILAC

MASON

LAKE

OSCEOLA

ISABELLA

MIDLAND

SAGINAW

LAPEER
LAPEER

ST. CLAIR

MECOSTA

GENESEE

OCEANA *
OCEANA *

NEWAYGO

KENT

MONTCALM

GRATIOT

SHIAWASSEE

GENESEE

OAKLAND

MACOMB

MUSKEGON

KENT

IONIA

IONIA

CLINTON

LIVINGSTON

WAYNE

Lake St. Clair

OTTAWA *
OTTAWA *

EATON

INGHAM

WASHTENAW

Lake Erie

ALLEGAN

BARRY

JACKSON

MONROE

Lake Michigan

KALAMAZOO

CALHOUN

HILLSDALE

LENAWEE

Van BUREN

BRANCH

OH

St. JOSEPH

IN

BERRIEN

CASS

NORTH

Green Bay

Wisconsin Territory

*NOTES:

Michigan became a state in 1837.

See Michigan 1860 (p.164) for an explanation of attached counties.

The separation of Michigan and Wisconsin in 1836 removed Brown and Crawford counties from Michigan, leaving the unattached lands west of Michilimackinac County.

The Chippewa–Michilimackinac boundary in 1840 is uncertain, the east end probably being geographically impossible as defined by law.

Ottawa and Oceana were enumerated together. The area north and northwest of Oceana was legally attached to Ottawa in this census.

CENSUS AVAILABILITY

Federal census extant for all counties.

IL

| 1 | 2 | 3 | 4 | 5 | 6 | 7 | 8 | 9 | 10 | 11 | 12 |

25 0 25 50 75 100 MILES

WHITE = MODERN BOUNDARIES
BLACK = 1840 BOUNDARIES

Michigan ● 1840

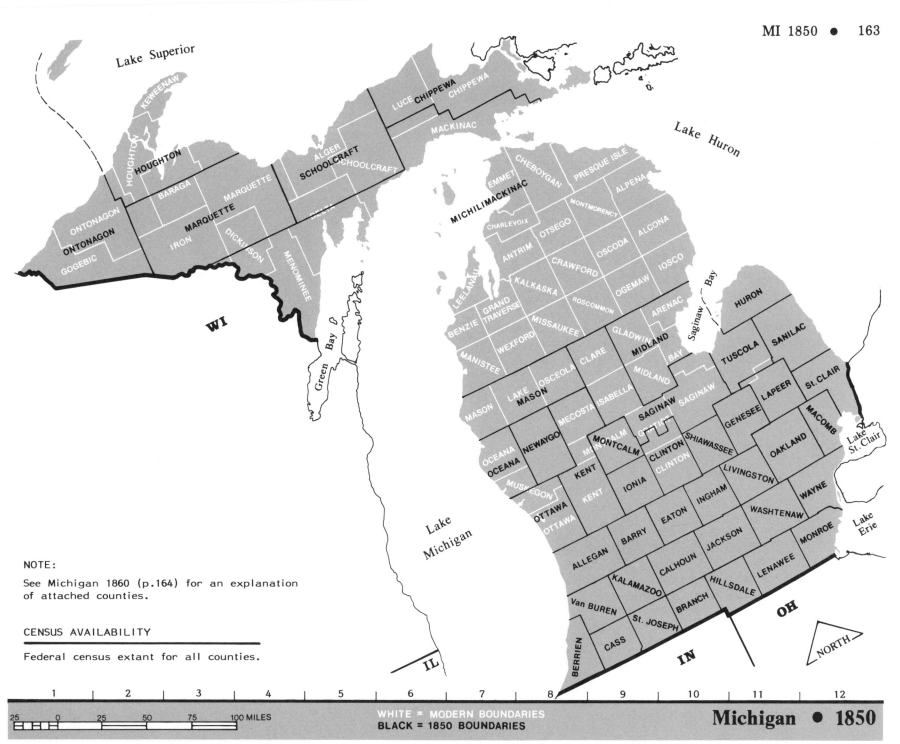

Lake Superior

KEWEENAW

HOUGHTON
HOUGHTON

ONTONAGON
ONTONAGON

GOGEBIC

BARAGA

IRON

MARQUETTE
MARQUETTE

DICKINSON

ALGER

SCHOOLCRAFT
SCHOOLCRAFT

DELTA

MENOMINEE

LUCE

CHIPPEWA

CHIPPEWA

MACKINAC

Lake Huron

WI

Green Bay

Lake Michigan

MICHILIMACKINAC

EMMET

CHEBOYGAN

PRESQUE ISLE

CHARLEVOIX

OTSEGO

MONTMORENCY

ALPENA

ANTRIM

CRAWFORD

OSCODA

ALCONA

LEELANAU

KALKASKA

ROSCOMMON

OGEMAW

IOSCO

BENZIE

GRAND TRAVERSE

MISSAUKEE

ARENAC

Saginaw Bay

HURON

MANISTEE

WEXFORD

CLARE

GLADWIN

MIDLAND
MIDLAND

BAY

TUSCOLA

SANILAC

MASON
MASON

LAKE

OSCEOLA

ISABELLA

SAGINAW
SAGINAW

LAPEER

St.CLAIR

MECOSTA

GRATIOT

GENESEE

MACOMB

OCEANA
OCEANA

NEWAYGO

MONTCALM

CLINTON
CLINTON

SHIAWASSEE

OAKLAND

Lake St. Clair

MUSKEGON

KENT

IONIA

LIVINGSTON

WAYNE

OTTAWA
OTTAWA

KENT

EATON

INGHAM

WASHTENAW

Lake Erie

ALLEGAN

BARRY

CALHOUN

JACKSON

MONROE

Van BUREN

KALAMAZOO

HILLSDALE

LENAWEE

BERRIEN

CASS

St. JOSEPH

BRANCH

OH

IN

NORTH

NOTE:

See Michigan 1860 (p.164) for an explanation of attached counties.

CENSUS AVAILABILITY

Federal census extant for all counties.

IL

1   2   3   4   5   6   7   8   9   10   11   12

25 0   25   50   75   100 MILES

WHITE = MODERN BOUNDARIES
BLACK = 1850 BOUNDARIES

Michigan ● 1850

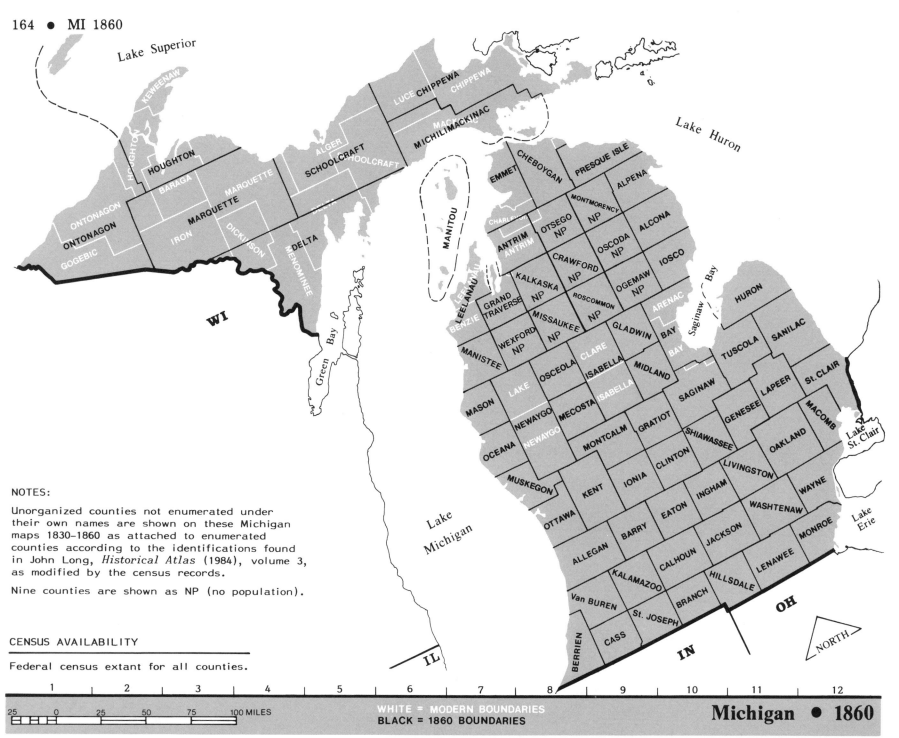

Michigan ● **1860**

NOTES:

Unorganized counties not enumerated under their own names are shown on these Michigan maps 1830–1860 as attached to enumerated counties according to the identifications found in John Long, *Historical Atlas* (1984), volume 3, as modified by the census records.

Nine counties are shown as NP (no population).

CENSUS AVAILABILITY

Federal census extant for all counties.

25   0   25   50   75   100 MILES

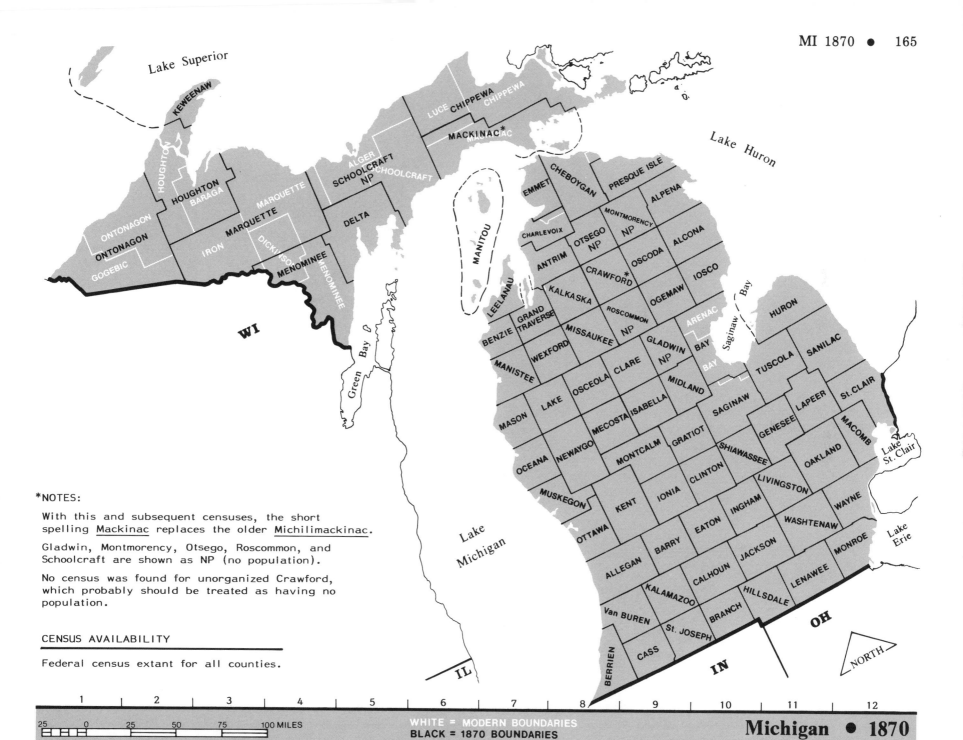

Lake Superior

KEWEENAW

HOUGHTON

HOUGHTON
BARAGA

ONTONAGON

ONTONAGON

GOGEBIC

IRON

MARQUETTE

MARQUETTE

DICKINSON

MENOMINEE

MENOMINEE

ALGER

SCHOOLCRAFT
NP

SCHOOLCRAFT

DELTA

LUCE CHIPPEWA CHIPPEWA

MACKINAC*

Lake Huron

WI

Green Bay

Lake Michigan

MANITOU

EMMET

CHARLEVOIX

ANTRIM

LEELANAU

BENZIE

MANISTEE

MASON

OCEANA

MUSKEGON

OTTAWA

ALLEGAN

Van BUREN

BERRIEN

CASS

St. JOSEPH

KALAMAZOO

BARRY

KENT

NEWAYGO

LAKE

MONTCALM

IONIA

EATON

CALHOUN

BRANCH

HILLSDALE

LENAWEE

MONROE

Lake Erie

CHEBOYGAN

PRESQUE ISLE

ALPENA

MONTMORENCY
NP

ALCONA

OTSEGO
NP

OSCODA

IOSCO

CRAWFORD
*

OGEMAW

ROSCOMMON
NP

ARENAC

KALKASKA

GRAND
TRAVERSE

MISSAUKEE

WEXFORD

OSCEOLA CLARE

GLADWIN
NP

MIDLAND

BAY

BAY

Saginaw Bay

HURON

TUSCOLA

SANILAC

SAGINAW

LAPEER

St. CLAIR

MACOMB

Lake St. Clair

MECOSTA ISABELLA

GRATIOT

GENESEE

SHIAWASSEE

OAKLAND

CLINTON

LIVINGSTON

WAYNE

INGHAM

WASHTENAW

JACKSON

OH

IN

NORTH

IL

CHARLEVOIX

*NOTES:

With this and subsequent censuses, the short
spelling Mackinac replaces the older Michilimackinac.

Gladwin, Montmorency, Otsego, Roscommon, and
Schoolcraft are shown as NP (no population).

No census was found for unorganized Crawford,
which probably should be treated as having no
population.

CENSUS AVAILABILITY

Federal census extant for all counties.

| 1 | 2 | 3 | 4 | 5 | 6 | 7 | 8 | 9 | 10 | 11 | 12 |

25   0   25   50   75   100 MILES

WHITE = MODERN BOUNDARIES
BLACK = 1870 BOUNDARIES

Michigan ● 1870

MAP GUIDE TO THE U.S. FEDERAL CENSUSES, 1790–1920 by William Thorndale and William Dollarhide.   Copyright 1987, all rights reserved.

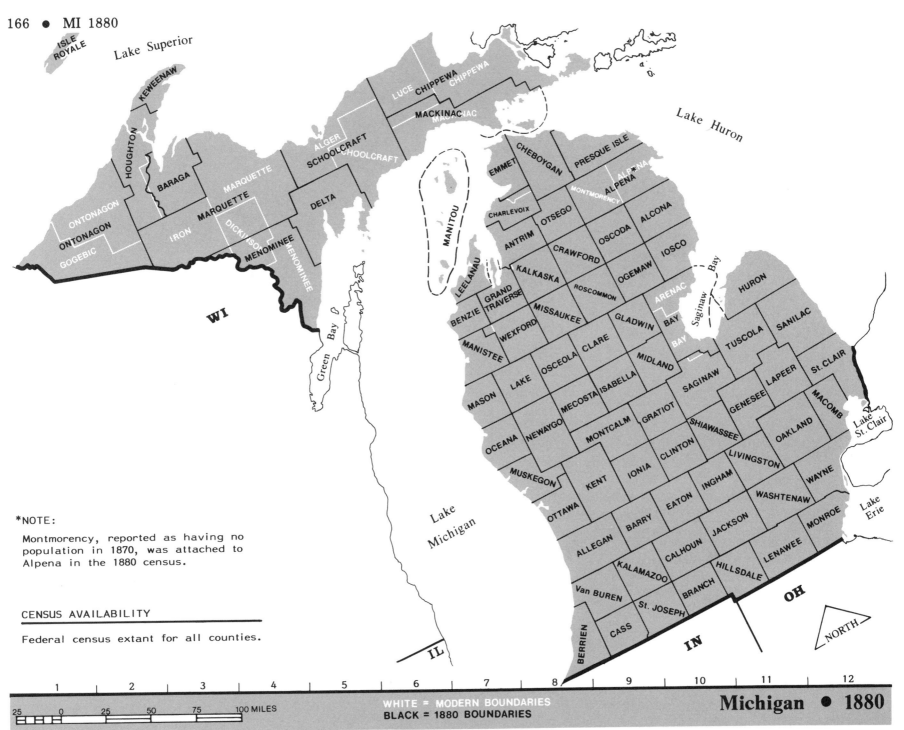

ISLE ROYALE

Lake Superior

KEWEENAW

HOUGHTON

BARAGA

ONTONAGON

GOGEBIC

IRON

MARQUETTE

MARQUETTE

DICKINSON

MENOMINEE

MENOMINEE

DELTA

ALGER

SCHOOLCRAFT

SCHOOLCRAFT

LUCE

CHIPPEWA

CHIPPEWA

MACKINAC

MACKINAC

WI

Green Bay

Lake Michigan

MANITOU

EMMET

CHEBOYGAN

PRESQUE ISLE

CHARLEVOIX

ANTRIM

OTSEGO

MONTMORENCY

ALPENA*

ALPENA

LEELANAU

GRAND TRAVERSE

KALKASKA

CRAWFORD

OSCODA

ALCONA

BENZIE

MISSAUKEE

ROSCOMMON

OGEMAW

IOSCO

WEXFORD

ARENAC

MANISTEE

LAKE

OSCEOLA

CLARE

GLADWIN

BAY

BAY

Saginaw Bay

HURON

MASON

MECOSTA

ISABELLA

MIDLAND

TUSCOLA

SANILAC

NEWAYGO

MONTCALM

GRATIOT

SAGINAW

GENESEE

LAPEER

ST. CLAIR

OCEANA

SHIAWASSEE

OAKLAND

MACOMB

Lake St. Clair

MUSKEGON

KENT

IONIA

CLINTON

LIVINGSTON

WAYNE

OTTAWA

BARRY

EATON

INGHAM

WASHTENAW

Lake Erie

ALLEGAN

CALHOUN

JACKSON

MONROE

KALAMAZOO

HILLSDALE

LENAWEE

Van BUREN

BRANCH

OH

BERRIEN

CASS

St. JOSEPH

IN

IL

Lake Huron

NORTH

*NOTE:

Montmorency, reported as having no population in 1870, was attached to Alpena in the 1880 census.

CENSUS AVAILABILITY

Federal census extant for all counties.

1 2 3 4 5 6 7 8 9 10 11 12

25 0 25 50 75 100 MILES

WHITE = MODERN BOUNDARIES
BLACK = 1880 BOUNDARIES

Michigan ● 1880

Lake Superior

ISLE
ROYALE*

KEWEENAW

HOUGHTON

ONTONAGON

BARAGA

GOGEBIC

IRON
IRON

MARQUETTE
MARQUETTE

DICKINSON

MENOMINEE
MENOMINEE

ALGER

SCHOOLCRAFT

DELTA

LUCE

MACKINAC

CHIPPEWA

Lake Huron

WI

Green Bay

Lake Michigan

MANITOU*

EMMET

CHEBOYGAN

PRESQUE ISLE

CHARLEVOIX

OTSEGO

ANTRIM

LEELANAU

GRAND
TRAVERSE

BENZIE

KALKASKA

CRAWFORD

MONTMORENCY

ALPENA

ALCONA

OSCODA

IOSCO

OGEMAW

ARENAC

Saginaw Bay

HURON

MISSAUKEE

MANISTEE

WEXFORD

OSCEOLA

CLARE

GLADWIN

ROSCOMMON

BAY

TUSCOLA

SANILAC

MASON

LAKE

MECOSTA

ISABELLA

MIDLAND

SAGINAW

GENESEE

LAPEER

ST.CLAIR

MACOMB

OCEANA

NEWAYGO

MONTCALM

GRATIOT

SHIAWASSEE

Lake
St. Clair

MUSKEGON

KENT

IONIA

CLINTON

LIVINGSTON

OAKLAND

WAYNE

OTTAWA

BARRY

EATON

INGHAM

WASHTENAW

Lake
Erie

ALLEGAN

CALHOUN

JACKSON

MONROE

KALAMAZOO

HILLSDALE

LENAWEE

Van BUREN

BRANCH

OH

St. JOSEPH

IN

BERRIEN

CASS

NORTH

*NOTES:

Manitou County was abolished in 1895.

Isle Royale County was annexed to
Keweenaw in 1897.

CENSUS AVAILABILITY

Federal census lost for all counties.

1 2 3 4 5 6 7 8 9 10 11 12

25 0 25 50 75 100 MILES

WHITE = MODERN BOUNDARIES
BLACK = 1890 BOUNDARIES

Michigan ● **1890**

MAP GUIDE TO THE U.S. FEDERAL CENSUSES, 1790-1920 by William Thorndale and William Dollarhide. Copyright 1987, all rights reserved.

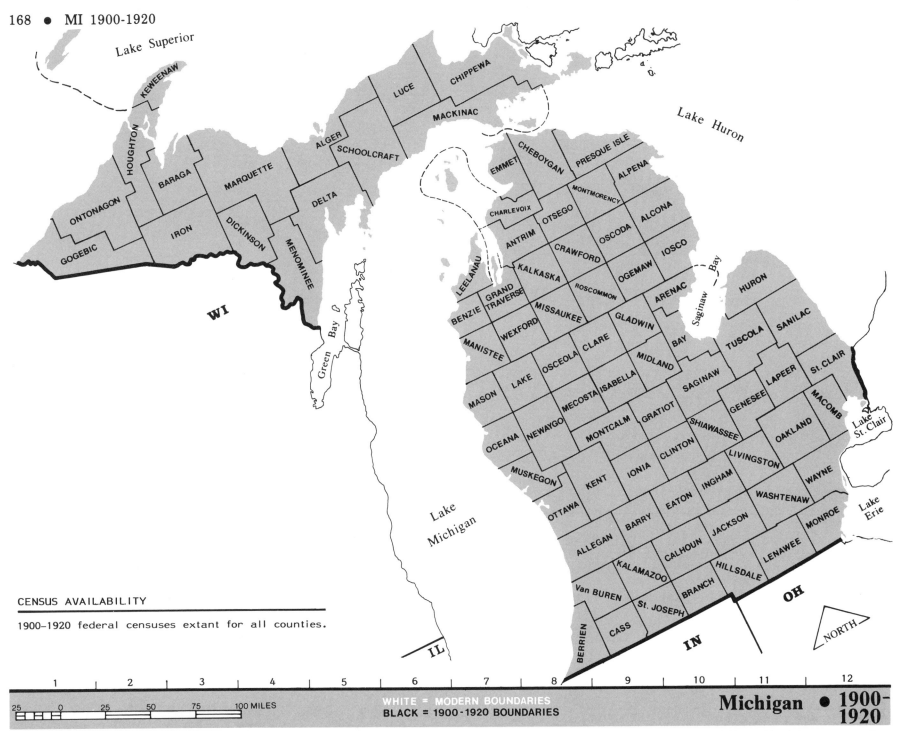

Lake Superior

KEWEENAW

HOUGHTON

ONTONAGON

BARAGA

GOGEBIC

IRON

MARQUETTE

DICKINSON

MENOMINEE

WI

LUCE

CHIPPEWA

MACKINAC

ALGER

SCHOOLCRAFT

DELTA

Lake Huron

Green Bay

EMMET

CHEBOYGAN

PRESQUE ISLE

ALPENA

CHARLEVOIX

MONTMORENCY

OTSEGO

ANTRIM

CRAWFORD

OSCODA

ALCONA

LEELANAU

KALKASKA

OGEMAW

IOSCO

GRAND TRAVERSE

ROSCOMMON

Saginaw Bay

BENZIE

MISSAUKEE

ARENAC

HURON

WEXFORD

GLADWIN

MANISTEE

CLARE

BAY

TUSCOLA

SANILAC

MASON

LAKE

OSCEOLA

MIDLAND

SAGINAW

GENESEE

LAPEER

ST. CLAIR

MECOSTA

ISABELLA

MACOMB

NEWAYGO

GRATIOT

SHIAWASSEE

OCEANA

MONTCALM

Lake St. Clair

MUSKEGON

KENT

IONIA

CLINTON

LIVINGSTON

OAKLAND

WAYNE

Lake Michigan

OTTAWA

BARRY

EATON

INGHAM

WASHTENAW

Lake Erie

ALLEGAN

CALHOUN

JACKSON

LENAWEE

MONROE

KALAMAZOO

HILLSDALE

Van Buren

BRANCH

OH

St. JOSEPH

BERRIEN

CASS

IN

IL

NORTH

CENSUS AVAILABILITY

1900–1920 federal censuses extant for all counties.

25 0 25 50 75 100 MILES

WHITE = MODERN BOUNDARIES
BLACK = 1900-1920 BOUNDARIES

Michigan ● **1900–1920**

MAP GUIDE TO THE U.S. FEDERAL CENSUSES, 1790–1920 by William Thorndale and William Dollarhide. Copyright 1987, all rights reserved.

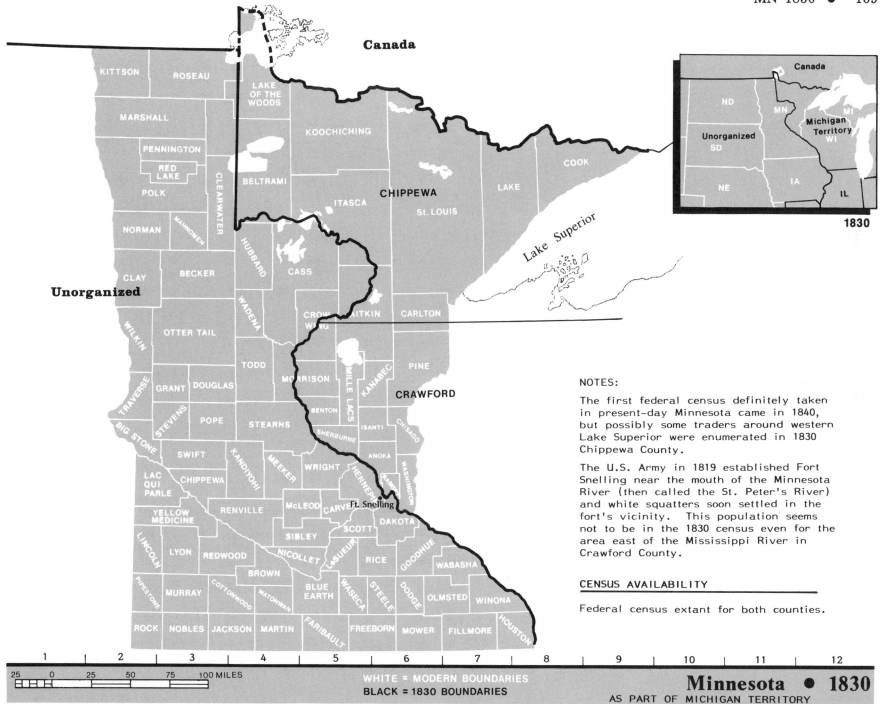

Canada

KITTSON
ROSEAU
LAKE OF THE WOODS
MARSHALL
KOOCHICHING
PENNINGTON
RED LAKE
BELTRAMI
POLK
CLEARWATER
CHIPPEWA
ITASCA
St. LOUIS
COOK
LAKE

NORMAN
MAHNOMEN
Lake Superior

Unorganized

CLAY
BECKER
HUBBARD
CASS
WADENA
CROW WING
AITKIN
CARLTON

WILKIN
OTTER TAIL
TODD
MORRISON
PINE

TRAVERSE
GRANT
DOUGLAS
MILLE LACS
KANABEC
CRAWFORD

STEVENS
POPE
STEARNS
BENTON
ISANTI
CHISAGO

BIG STONE
SWIFT
KANDIYOHI
MEEKER
SHERBURNE
ANOKA

LAC QUI PARLE
CHIPPEWA
WRIGHT
HENNEPIN
WASHINGTON

YELLOW MEDICINE
RENVILLE
McLEOD
CARVER
Ft. Snelling

LINCOLN
LYON
REDWOOD
SIBLEY
SCOTT
DAKOTA

PIPESTONE
MURRAY
COTTONWOOD
BROWN
NICOLLET
LeSUEUR
RICE
GOODHUE
WABASHA

WATONWAN
BLUE EARTH
WASECA
STEELE
DODGE
OLMSTED
WINONA

ROCK
NOBLES
JACKSON
MARTIN
FARIBAULT
FREEBORN
MOWER
FILLMORE
HOUSTON

Inset map:
Canada
ND
MN
Michigan Territory
MI
Unorganized SD
WI
NE
IA
IL
1830

NOTES:

The first federal census definitely taken in present-day Minnesota came in 1840, but possibly some traders around western Lake Superior were enumerated in 1830 Chippewa County.

The U.S. Army in 1819 established Fort Snelling near the mouth of the Minnesota River (then called the St. Peter's River) and white squatters soon settled in the fort's vicinity. This population seems not to be in the 1830 census even for the area east of the Mississippi River in Crawford County.

CENSUS AVAILABILITY

Federal census extant for both counties.

1   2   3   4   5   6   7   8   9   10   11   12

25 0 25 50 75 100 MILES

WHITE = MODERN BOUNDARIES
BLACK = 1830 BOUNDARIES

Minnesota ● 1830
AS PART OF MICHIGAN TERRITORY

KITTSON
ROSEAU
Canada
LAKE OF THE WOODS
MARSHALL
KOOCHICHING
PENNINGTON
RED LAKE
POLK
BELTRAMI
INDIAN LANDS
COOK
LAKE
St. LOUIS
Wisconsin
Lake Superior
CLEARWATER
ITASCA
NORMAN
MAHNOMEN
HUBBARD
Iowa
CLAY
BECKER
CASS
WADENA
CROW WING
AITKIN
CARLTON
Territory
TODD
MORRISON
MILLE LACS
PINE
OTTER TAIL
BENTON
Territory
TRAVERSE
GRANT
DOUGLAS
KANABEC
BIG STONE
STEVENS
POPE
STEARNS
SHERBURNE
ISANTI
CHISAGO
SWIFT
KANDIYOHI
MEEKER
WRIGHT
ANOKA
St. CROIX
LAC QUI PARLE
CHIPPEWA
CLAYTON
HENNEPIN
WASHINGTON
YELLOW MEDICINE
RENVILLE
McLEOD
CARVER
Ft. Snelling
LINCOLN
LYON
REDWOOD
SIBLEY
SCOTT
DAKOTA
NICOLLET
Le SUEUR
RICE
GOODHUE
Wabasha
WABASHA
PIPESTONE
MURRAY
COTTONWOOD
WATONWAN
BROWN
BLUE EARTH
WASECA
STEELE
DODGE
OLMSTED
WINONA
ROCK
NOBLES
JACKSON
MARTIN
FARIBAULT
FREEBORN
MOWER
FILLMORE
HOUSTON

Inset map:
Canada
ND
MN
MI
Iowa Territory
Wisconsin Territory
WI
SD
IA
Unorganized NE
IL
1840

NOTES:

St. Croix, Wisconsin Territory, is shown here within Indian cessions but its 1840 census also included the western Lake Superior region.

Clayton County, Iowa Territory, included the precincts of Lake Pepin (at present-day Wabasha) and St. Peter's (around Ft. Snelling). The fort's 96 occupants were counted but not named.

CENSUS AVAILABILITY

Federal census extant for all counties.

Scale: 1 2 3 4 5 6 7 8 9 10 11 12

25 0 25 50 75 100 MILES

WHITE = MODERN BOUNDARIES
BLACK = 1840 BOUNDARIES

Minnesota ● 1840
AS PART OF TWO TERRITORIES

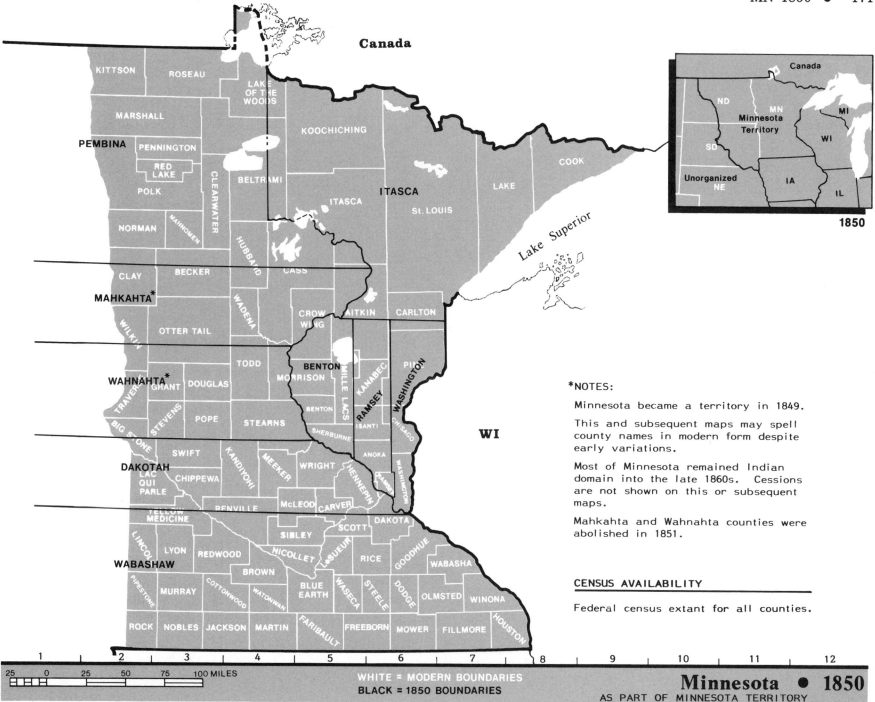

KITTSON
ROSEAU
Canada
PEMBINA
MARSHALL
LAKE OF THE WOODS
PENNINGTON
RED LAKE
KOOCHICHING
POLK
BELTRAMI
CLEARWATER
COOK
NORMAN
MAHNOMEN
ITASCA
ITASCA
LAKE
St. LOUIS
HUBBARD
CASS
CLAY
BECKER
MAHKAHTA*
Lake Superior
WADENA
CROW WING
AITKIN
CARLTON
OTTER TAIL
WILKIN
TODD
BENTON
PINE
WAHNAHTA*
GRANT
DOUGLAS
MORRISON
MILLE LACS
KANABEC
WASHINGTON
TRAVERSE
STEVENS
POPE
BENTON
RAMSEY
CHISAGO
BIG STONE
STEARNS
ISANTI
SHERBURNE
SWIFT
KANDIYOHI
MEEKER
WRIGHT
ANOKA
DAKOTAH
LAC QUI PARLE
CHIPPEWA
HENNEPIN
RAMSEY
WASHINGTON
RENVILLE
McLEOD
CARVER
WI
YELLOW MEDICINE
SCOTT
DAKOTA
LINCOLN
SIBLEY
NICOLLET
LE SUEUR
RICE
GOODHUE
LYON
REDWOOD
WABASHA
WABASHAW
BROWN
BLUE EARTH
WASECA
STEELE
DODGE
OLMSTED
WINONA
PIPESTONE
MURRAY
COTTONWOOD
WATONWAN
ROCK
NOBLES
JACKSON
MARTIN
FARIBAULT
FREEBORN
MOWER
FILLMORE
HOUSTON

Minnesota Territory (inset)
Canada
ND
MN
SD
Minnesota Territory
Unorganized NE
IA
WI
MI
IL
1850

*NOTES:

Minnesota became a territory in 1849.

This and subsequent maps may spell county names in modern form despite early variations.

Most of Minnesota remained Indian domain into the late 1860s. Cessions are not shown on this or subsequent maps.

Mahkahta and Wahnahta counties were abolished in 1851.

CENSUS AVAILABILITY

Federal census extant for all counties.

25 0 25 50 75 100 MILES

WHITE = MODERN BOUNDARIES
BLACK = 1850 BOUNDARIES

Minnesota ● 1850
AS PART OF MINNESOTA TERRITORY

MAP GUIDE TO THE U.S. FEDERAL CENSUSES, 1790-1920 by William Thorndale and William Dollarhide. Copyright 1987, all rights reserved.

Canada

KITTSON
ROSEAU
LAKE OF THE WOODS
MARSHALL
KOOCHICHING
PENNINGTON
RED LAKE
ITASCA*
POLK
BELTRAMI
LAKE
COOK
CLEARWATER
ITASCA
PEMBINA*
NORMAN
MAHNOMEN
St. LOUIS
HUBBARD
CASS
CLAY
BECKER
CASS

Lake Superior

Statutorily, supposed to meet

WADENA
CROW WING
AITKIN
CARLTON
OTTER TAIL
CROW WING
RAMSEY Detached
BUCHANAN
TODD
MORRISON
PINE
TODD
MORRISON
KANABEC
GRANT
DOUGLAS
BENTON
PINE
TRAVERSE
BENTON
STEVENS
POPE
STEARNS*
ISANTI
CHISAGO
BIG STONE
SHERBURNE
WI
SWIFT
PIERCE*
ANOKA
LAC QUI PARLE
MEEKER*
WRIGHT
HENNEPIN
WASHINGTON
MANOMIN
CHIPPEWA
RAMSEY
RENVILLE
McLEOD
CARVER
RENVILLE
BROWN
YELLOW MEDICINE
SCOTT
DAKOTA
SIBLEY
LINCOLN
LYON
REDWOOD
NICOLLET
LeSUEUR
RICE
GOODHUE
BROWN
WABASHA
ROCK ?
MURRAY ?
COTTONWOOD ?
WATONWAN
BLUE EARTH
WASECA
STEELE
DODGE
OLMSTED
WINONA
PIPESTONE
PIPESTONE
NOBLES ?
JACKSON ?
MARTIN ?
FARIBAULT
FREEBORN
MOWER
FILLMORE
HOUSTON

Indian line

1   2   3   4   5   6   7   8   9   10   11   12

25 0 25 50 75 100 MILES

*NOTES:

See North Dakota 1850-1860 (p.259) for additional information about southwestern Minnesota 1857.

Historian Robert J. Forrest says seven south-western counties had no white population in 1857 but Democrats fabricated census sched-ules to cover their ballot fraud. These seven counties are shown on the map with question marks. (See "Mythical Cities of Southwestern Minnesota," *Minnesota History* 14 (1933), 243-62.)

The Stearns-Meeker line was indefinite due to statutory imprecision. The southeastern portion of Pierce was statutorily in the unorganized county of Davis (not shown) but enumerated with Pierce.

The Pembina-Itasca line ran due south from the uncertain "middle" of the Lake of the Woods.

CENSUS AVAILABILITY

Federal census extant for all counties but see note above about fabricated schedules.

Canada
ND
MN
Minnesota Territory
MI
SD
Nebraska
WI
Territory
NE
IA
IL

1857

WHITE = MODERN BOUNDARIES
BLACK = 1857 BOUNDARIES

Minnesota ● 1857
AS PART OF MINNESOTA TERRITORY

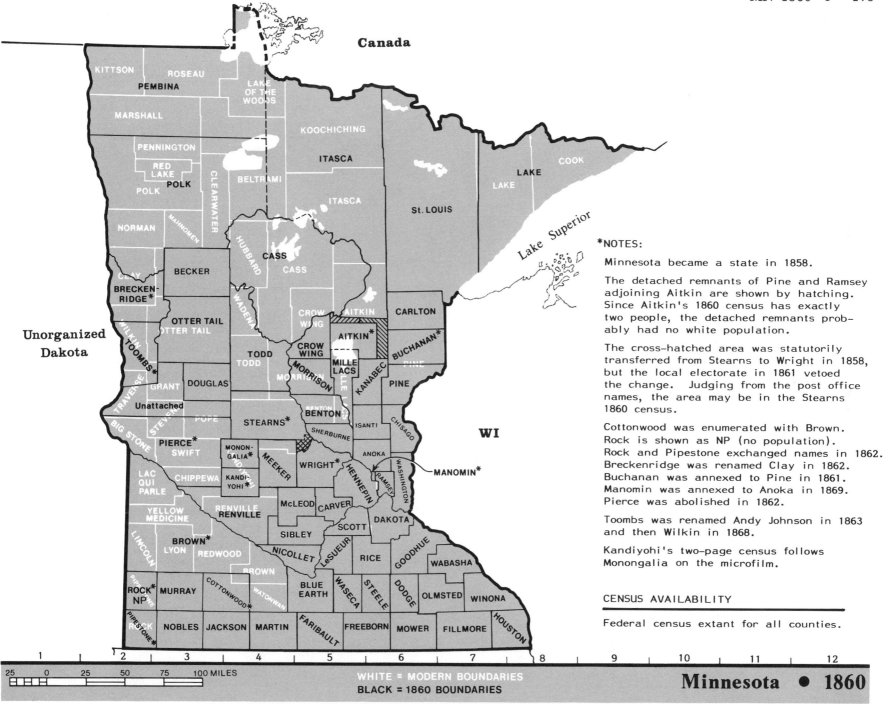

Canada

KITTSON
ROSEAU
PEMBINA
LAKE OF THE WOODS
MARSHALL
KOOCHICHING
PENNINGTON
RED LAKE
POLK
POLK
BELTRAMI
ITASCA
CLEARWATER
LAKE
LAKE
COOK
NORMAN
MAHNOMEN
ITASCA
ST. LOUIS
HUBBARD
CLAY
BECKER
CASS
CASS
BRECKEN-RIDGE*
OTTER TAIL
OTTER TAIL
WADENA
CROW WING
AITKIN
CARLTON

Lake Superior

Unorganized Dakota

WILKIN
TOOMBS*
GRANT
DOUGLAS
TODD
TODD
CROW WING
AITKIN*
BUCHANAN*
PINE
TRAVERSE
Unattached
STEVENS
POPE
MORRISON
MORRISON
MILLE LACS
MILLE LACS
KANABEC
PINE
BIG STONE
STEARNS*
BENTON
ISANTI
CHISAGO
PIERCE*
SWIFT
MONON-GALIA*
MEEKER
SHERBURNE
WRIGHT*
ANOKA
WI
LAC QUI PARLE
CHIPPEWA
KANDI-YOHI*
HENNEPIN
WASHINGTON
MANOMIN*
YELLOW MEDICINE
RENVILLE
RENVILLE
McLEOD
CARVER
RAMSEY
LINCOLN
BROWN*
LYON
SIBLEY
SCOTT
DAKOTA
REDWOOD
NICOLLET
LeSUEUR
RICE
GOODHUE
WABASHA
BROWN
PIPESTONE
COTTONWOOD
WATONWAN
BLUE EARTH
WASECA
STEELE
DODGE
OLMSTED
WINONA
ROCK* NP
MURRAY
PIPESTONE
ROCK
NOBLES
JACKSON
MARTIN
FARIBAULT
FREEBORN
MOWER
FILLMORE
HOUSTON

*NOTES:

Minnesota became a state in 1858.

The detached remnants of Pine and Ramsey adjoining Aitkin are shown by hatching. Since Aitkin's 1860 census has exactly two people, the detached remnants probably had no white population.

The cross-hatched area was statutorily transferred from Stearns to Wright in 1858, but the local electorate in 1861 vetoed the change. Judging from the post office names, the area may be in the Stearns 1860 census.

Cottonwood was enumerated with Brown. Rock is shown as NP (no population). Rock and Pipestone exchanged names in 1862. Breckenridge was renamed Clay in 1862. Buchanan was annexed to Pine in 1861. Manomin was annexed to Anoka in 1869. Pierce was abolished in 1862.

Toombs was renamed Andy Johnson in 1863 and then Wilkin in 1868.

Kandiyohi's two-page census follows Monongalia on the microfilm.

CENSUS AVAILABILITY

Federal census extant for all counties.

1 2 3 4 5 6 7 8 9 10 11 12

25 0 25 50 75 100 MILES

WHITE = MODERN BOUNDARIES
BLACK = 1860 BOUNDARIES

Minnesota ● 1860

Canada

KITTSON

ROSEAU

PEMBINA*

MARSHALL

LAKE
OF THE
WOODS

KOOCHICHING

PENNINGTON

RED
LAKE

POLK*
NP LK

ITASCA

LAKE

COOK

LAKE

Lake Superior

NORMAN

MAHNOMEN

CLEARWATER

BELTRAMI

BELTRAMI

HUBBARD

ITASCA

St. LOUIS

Dakota
Territory

CLAY

BECKER

CASS

CASS

WADENA

CROW
WING

AITKIN

CARLTON

WILKIN

OTTER TAIL

CROW
WING

AITKIN

PINE

TRAVERSE

TODD

MORRISON

MILLE LACS

KANABEC

GRANT* DOUGLAS

BENTON

STEVENS*

POPE

STEARNS

SHERBURNE

ISANTI

CHISAGO

WI

BIG STONE

LAC
QUI
PARLE*

CHIPPEWA

MONON-
GALIA*

KANDI-
YOHI

MEEKER

WRIGHT

ANOKA

HENNEPIN

RAMSEY

WASHINGTON

CHIPPEWA

LAC
QUI
PARLE

YELLOW
MEDICINE

RENVILLE

McLEOD

CARVER

SCOTT

DAKOTA

REDWOOD

LINCOLN

LYON

REDWOOD

SIBLEY

NICOLLET

LeSUEUR

RICE

GOODHUE

WABASHA

BROWN

BLUE
EARTH

WASECA

STEELE

DODGE

OLMSTED

WINONA

PIPESTONE*
NP*

MURRAY

COTTONWOOD

WATONWAN

ROCK

NOBLES

JACKSON

MARTIN

FARIBAULT

FREEBORN

MOWER

FILLMORE

HOUSTON

*NOTES:

The federal government's copy of the 1870 census is destroyed for all counties Aitkin to Sibley. Stearns to Wright survive and are microfilmed. The state's copy for all counties is filmed by the National Archives as T132. This microfilmed state copy has many county schedules divided and out of order and numerous agricultural, industrial, mortality, and vital statistics schedules intermixed with population lists.

Lac qui Parle north of the Minnesota River was disestablished in 1868 but nonetheless appears in the 1870 census. Lac qui Parle south of the river was created in 1871.

The dashed lines in Grant and Stevens may be their de facto western boundaries so far as the 1870 census is concerned.

Polk is shown as NP (no population). Pipestone is also shown as NP, being ignored by census takers for lack of population.

Monongalia was annexed to Kandiyohi in November 1870.

Pembina was renamed Kittson in 1878.

CENSUS AVAILABILITY

Federal census extant for all counties.

25 0   25   50   75   100 MILES

WHITE = MODERN BOUNDARIES
BLACK = 1870 BOUNDARIES

Minnesota ● 1870

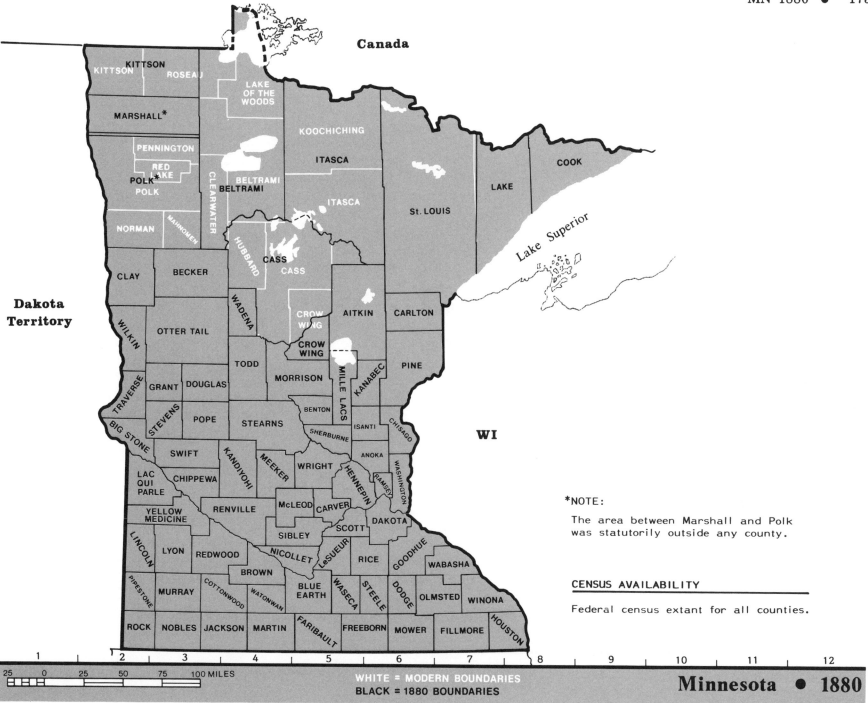

Canada

KITTSON
KITTSON
KITTSON
ROSEAU

LAKE
OF THE
WOODS

MARSHALL*

KOOCHICHING

PENNINGTON

RED
LAKE

ITASCA

COOK

POLK*
POLK

CLEARWATER

BELTRAMI
BELTRAMI

ITASCA

St. LOUIS

LAKE

NORMAN

MAHNOMEN

HUBBARD

CASS
CASS

Lake Superior

CLAY

BECKER

Dakota
Territory

WILKIN

WADENA

CROW
WING

AITKIN

CARLTON

OTTER TAIL

CROW
WING

TRAVERSE

TODD

MORRISON

MILLE LACS

KANABEC

PINE

BIG STONE

GRANT

DOUGLAS

BENTON

STEVENS

POPE

STEARNS

ISANTI

CHISAGO

WI

SHERBURNE

SWIFT

KANDIYOHI

MEEKER

WRIGHT

ANOKA

WASHINGTON

LAC
QUI
PARLE

CHIPPEWA

HENNEPIN

RAMSEY

*NOTE:

The area between Marshall and Polk
was statutorily outside any county.

YELLOW
MEDICINE

RENVILLE

McLEOD

CARVER

DAKOTA

SIBLEY

SCOTT

LINCOLN

LYON

REDWOOD

NICOLLET

LeSUEUR

RICE

GOODHUE

WABASHA

CENSUS AVAILABILITY

Federal census extant for all counties.

BROWN

PIPESTONE

MURRAY

COTTONWOOD

WATONWAN

BLUE
EARTH

WASECA

STEELE

DODGE

OLMSTED

WINONA

HOUSTON

ROCK

NOBLES

JACKSON

MARTIN

FARIBAULT

FREEBORN

MOWER

FILLMORE

1   2   3   4   5   6   7   8   9   10   11   12

25 0 25 50 75 100 MILES

WHITE = MODERN BOUNDARIES
BLACK = 1880 BOUNDARIES

Minnesota ● 1880

MAP GUIDE TO THE U.S. FEDERAL CENSUSES, 1790–1920 by William Thorndale and William Dollarhide. Copyright 1987, all rights reserved.

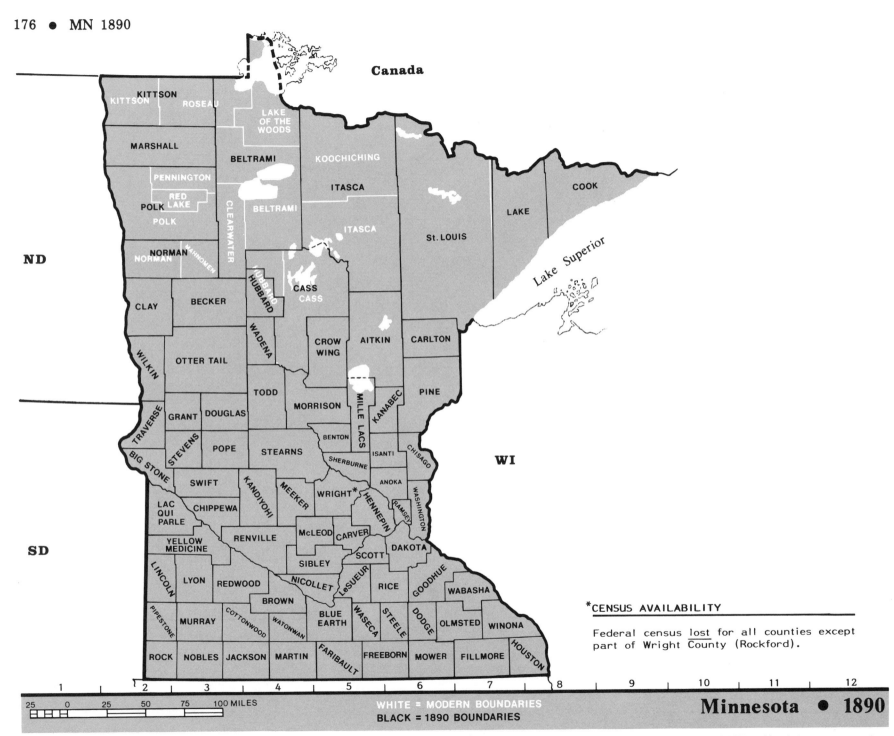

Canada

KITTSON
KITTSON
ROSEAU
LAKE OF THE WOODS
MARSHALL
BELTRAMI
KOOCHICHING
PENNINGTON
RED LAKE
POLK
ITASCA
COOK
POLK
CLEARWATER
BELTRAMI
ITASCA
LAKE
NORMAN
MAHNOMEN
NORMAN
ND
HUBBARD
HUBBARD
St. LOUIS
Lake Superior
CLAY
BECKER
CASS
CASS
WADENA
CROW WING
AITKIN
CARLTON
OTTER TAIL
WILKIN
TODD
PINE
MORRISON
MILLE LACS
KANABEC
TRAVERSE
GRANT
DOUGLAS
BENTON
STEVENS
POPE
STEARNS
ISANTI
CHISAGO
BIG STONE
SHERBURNE
WI
SWIFT
KANDIYOHI
MEEKER
WRIGHT*
ANOKA
HENNEPIN
LAC QUI PARLE
CHIPPEWA
RAMSEY
WASHINGTON
YELLOW MEDICINE
RENVILLE
McLEOD
CARVER
DAKOTA
SD
SIBLEY
SCOTT
LINCOLN
LYON
REDWOOD
NICOLLET
LeSUEUR
RICE
GOODHUE
WABASHA
BROWN
PIPESTONE
COTTONWOOD
WATONWAN
BLUE EARTH
WASECA
STEELE
DODGE
OLMSTED
WINONA
MURRAY
ROCK
NOBLES
JACKSON
MARTIN
FARIBAULT
FREEBORN
MOWER
FILLMORE
HOUSTON

*CENSUS AVAILABILITY

Federal census <u>lost</u> for all counties except part of Wright County (Rockford).

1   2   3   4   5   6   7   8   9   10   11   12

25 0   25   50   75   100 MILES

WHITE = MODERN BOUNDARIES
BLACK = 1890 BOUNDARIES

Minnesota ● 1890

MAP GUIDE TO THE U.S. FEDERAL CENSUSES, 1790–1920 by William Thorndale and William Dollarhide. Copyright 1987, all rights reserved.

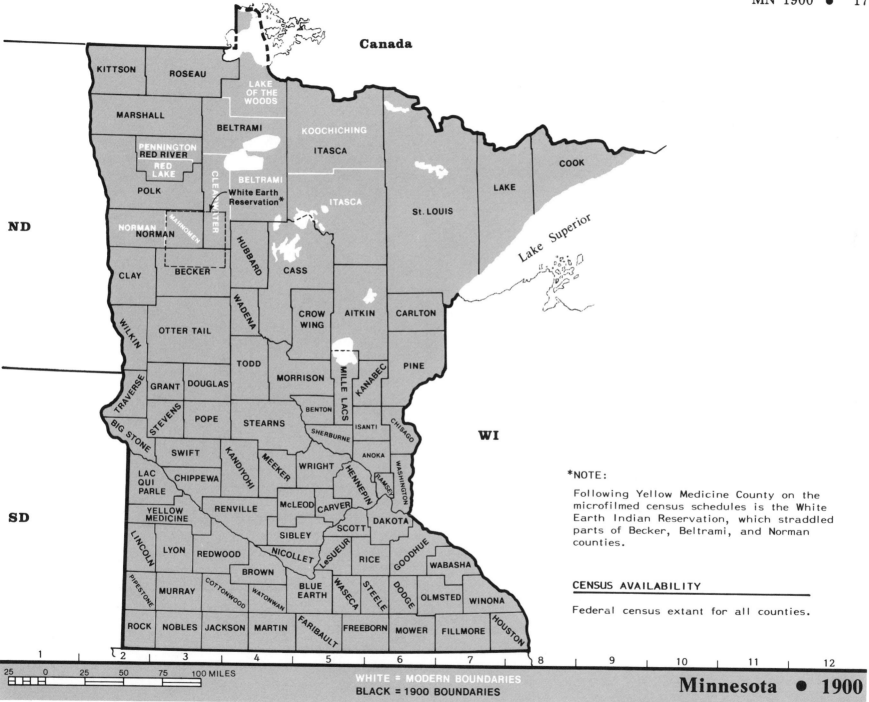

KITTSON
ROSEAU
Canada
LAKE OF THE WOODS
MARSHALL
BELTRAMI
KOOCHICHING
PENNINGTON
RED RIVER
ITASCA
RED LAKE
POLK
BELTRAMI
CLEARWATER
COOK
ND
NORMAN
White Earth Reservation*
ITASCA
LAKE
NORMAN
MAHNOMEN
St. LOUIS
Lake Superior
CLAY
BECKER
HUBBARD
CASS
WILKIN
WADENA
CROW WING
AITKIN
CARLTON
OTTER TAIL
TRAVERSE
TODD
PINE
GRANT
DOUGLAS
MORRISON
MILLE LACS
KANABEC
STEVENS
POPE
BENTON
BIG STONE
STEARNS
ISANTI
CHISAGO
SHERBURNE
WI
SWIFT
KANDIYOHI
MEEKER
WRIGHT
ANOKA
WASHINGTON
LAC QUI PARLE
CHIPPEWA
HENNEPIN
RAMSEY
YELLOW MEDICINE
RENVILLE
McLEOD
CARVER
DAKOTA
SD
SIBLEY
SCOTT
LINCOLN
LYON
REDWOOD
NICOLLET
LeSUEUR
RICE
GOODHUE
WABASHA
BROWN
PIPESTONE
MURRAY
COTTONWOOD
WATONWAN
BLUE EARTH
WASECA
STEELE
DODGE
OLMSTED
WINONA
HOUSTON
ROCK
NOBLES
JACKSON
MARTIN
FARIBAULT
FREEBORN
MOWER
FILLMORE

*NOTE:

Following Yellow Medicine County on the microfilmed census schedules is the White Earth Indian Reservation, which straddled parts of Becker, Beltrami, and Norman counties.

CENSUS AVAILABILITY

Federal census extant for all counties.

1   2   3   4   5   6   7   8   9   10   11   12

25 0 25 50 75 100 MILES

WHITE = MODERN BOUNDARIES
BLACK = 1900 BOUNDARIES

Minnesota ● 1900

Canada

KITTSON

ROSEAU

LAKE
OF THE
WOODS

MARSHALL

BELTRAMI

KOOCHICHING

PENNINGTON

RED
LAKE

CLEARWATER

BELTRAMI

COOK

POLK

ITASCA

LAKE

ND

NORMAN

MAHNOMEN

HUBBARD

St. LOUIS

Lake Superior

CLAY

BECKER

CASS

WADENA

CROW
WING

AITKIN

CARLTON

WILKIN

OTTER TAIL

TODD

MORRISON

MILLE LACS

PINE

TRAVERSE

GRANT

DOUGLAS

KANABEC

BENTON

BIG STONE

STEVENS

POPE

STEARNS

SHERBURNE

ISANTI

CHISAGO

WI

SWIFT

KANDIYOHI

MEEKER

WRIGHT

ANOKA

WASHINGTON

LAC
QUI
PARLE

CHIPPEWA

HENNEPIN

RAMSEY

NOTE:

Lake of the Woods County was created in
1922 with modern bounds.

YELLOW
MEDICINE

RENVILLE

McLEOD

CARVER

DAKOTA

SD

LINCOLN

LYON

REDWOOD

SIBLEY

SCOTT

RICE

GOODHUE

WABASHA

NICOLLET

LeSUEUR

CENSUS AVAILABILITY

1910–1920 federal censuses extant for all
counties.

PIPESTONE

MURRAY

COTTONWOOD

WATONWAN

BROWN

BLUE
EARTH

WASECA

STEELE

DODGE

OLMSTED

WINONA

ROCK

NOBLES

JACKSON

MARTIN

FARIBAULT

FREEBORN

MOWER

FILLMORE

HOUSTON

| 1 | 2 | 3 | 4 | 5 | 6 | 7 | 8 | 9 | 10 | 11 | 12 |

25 0   25   50   75   100 MILES

WHITE = MODERN BOUNDARIES
BLACK = 1910-1920 BOUNDARIES

Minnesota ● 1910-
1920

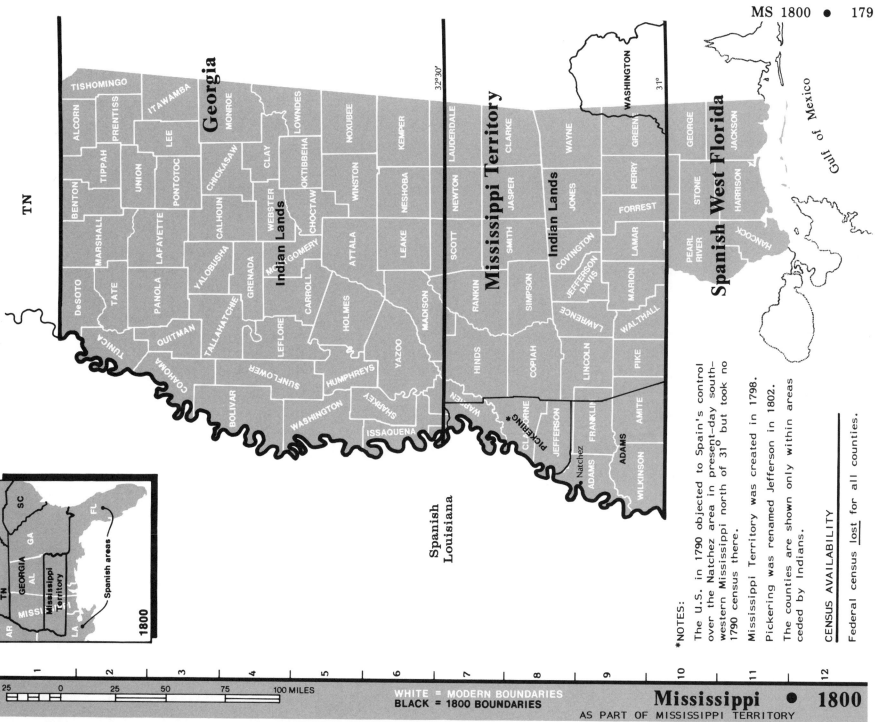

TN

Georgia

TISHOMINGO

ALCORN

PRENTISS

ITAWAMBA

MONROE

LEE

Georgia

LOWNDES

NOXUBEE

KEMPER

LAUDERDALE

Mississippi Territory

WASHINGTON

31°

Spanish West Florida

Gulf of Mexico

BENTON

TIPPAH

UNION

PONTOTOC

CHICKASAW

CLAY

OKTIBBEHA

CHOCTAW

WINSTON

NESHOBA

NEWTON

CLARKE

WAYNE

GEORGE

JACKSON

MARSHALL

LAFAYETTE

CALHOUN

WEBSTER

Indian Lands

ATTALA

LEAKE

SCOTT

JASPER

SMITH

JONES

PERRY

STONE

HARRISON

DeSOTO

TATE

PANOLA

YALOBUSHA

GRENADA

MONTGOMERY

CARROLL

HOLMES

MADISON

RANKIN

SIMPSON

COVINGTON

JEFFERSON DAVIS

MARION

LAMAR

FORREST

PEARL RIVER

HANCOCK

32°30'

TUNICA

QUITMAN

TALLAHATCHIE

LEFLORE

YAZOO

HINDS

COPIAH

LAWRENCE

LINCOLN

WALTHALL

PIKE

COAHOMA

BOLIVAR

SUNFLOWER

HUMPHREYS

SHARKEY

WARREN

CLAIBORNE

PICKERING *

JEFFERSON

FRANKLIN

AMITE

Indian Lands

Mississippi Territory

Spanish West Florida

WASHINGTON

ISSAQUENA

Natchez

ADAMS

WILKINSON

Spanish Louisiana

*NOTES:

The U.S. in 1790 objected to Spain's control over the Natchez area in present-day south-western Mississippi north of 31° but took no 1790 census there.

Mississippi Territory was created in 1798.

Pickering was renamed Jefferson in 1802.

The counties are shown only within areas ceded by Indians.

CENSUS AVAILABILITY

Federal census lost for all counties.

WHITE = MODERN BOUNDARIES
BLACK = 1800 BOUNDARIES

Mississippi ● **1800**

AS PART OF MISSISSIPPI TERRITORY

25 0 25 50 75 100 MILES

1800

SC

GA

AL

FL

TN

GEORGIA

MISSI

Mississippi Territory

AR

LA

Spanish areas

TN

TISHOMINGO

ALCORN
PRENTISS
ITAWAMBA
MONROE
LOWNDES

BENTON
TIPPAH
UNION
LEE
PONTOTOC
CHICKASAW
CLAY
OKTIBBEHA

Indian Lands

NOXUBEE
KEMPER
LAUDERDALE
CLARKE

WASHINGTON
BALDWIN

MARSHALL
LAFAYETTE
CALHOUN
WEBSTER
CHOCTAW
WINSTON
NESHOBA
NEWTON
JASPER

WAYNE
GREENE

Spanish West Florida

GEORGE
JACKSON

DeSOTO
TATE
PANOLA
YALOBUSHA
GRENADA
MONTGOMERY
ATTALA
LEAKE
SCOTT
SMITH

WAYNE
FORREST
PERRY
LAMAR

STONE
PEARL RIVER
HARRISON
HANCOCK

Gulf of Mexico

QUITMAN
TALLAHATCHIE
CARROLL
HOLMES
MADISON
RANKIN
SIMPSON
COVINGTON
JEFFERSON DAVIS
MARION
LAWRENCE
WALTHALL

TUNICA
COAHOMA
SUNFLOWER
LEFLORE
HUMPHREYS
YAZOO
HINDS
COPIAH
LINCOLN
FRANKLIN
AMITE
PIKE

BOLIVAR
WASHINGTON
SHARKEY
ISSAQUENA
WARREN
CLAIBORNE
JEFFERSON
FRANKLIN
AMITE

Louisiana Territory

Orleans Territory

ADAMS
WILKINSON

SC
GA
FL
TN
AR
MISSISSIPPI TERRITORY
Disputed area
Spanish area
1810

NOTE:

Based on its purchase of Louisiana in 1803, the U.S. claimed all of West Florida west of the Perdido River. However, that area remained under Spanish control in 1810 and was not added to Mississippi Territory until 1812.

CENSUS AVAILABILITY

Federal census lost for all counties.

1810 territorial census extant for Amite, Claiborne (including Warren), Franklin, Jefferson, and Washington.

25   1   2   3   4   5   6   7   8   9   10   11   12

25   0   25   50   75   100 MILES

WHITE = MODERN BOUNDARIES
BLACK = 1810 BOUNDARIES

Mississippi ● **1810**

AS PART OF MISSISSIPPI TERRITORY

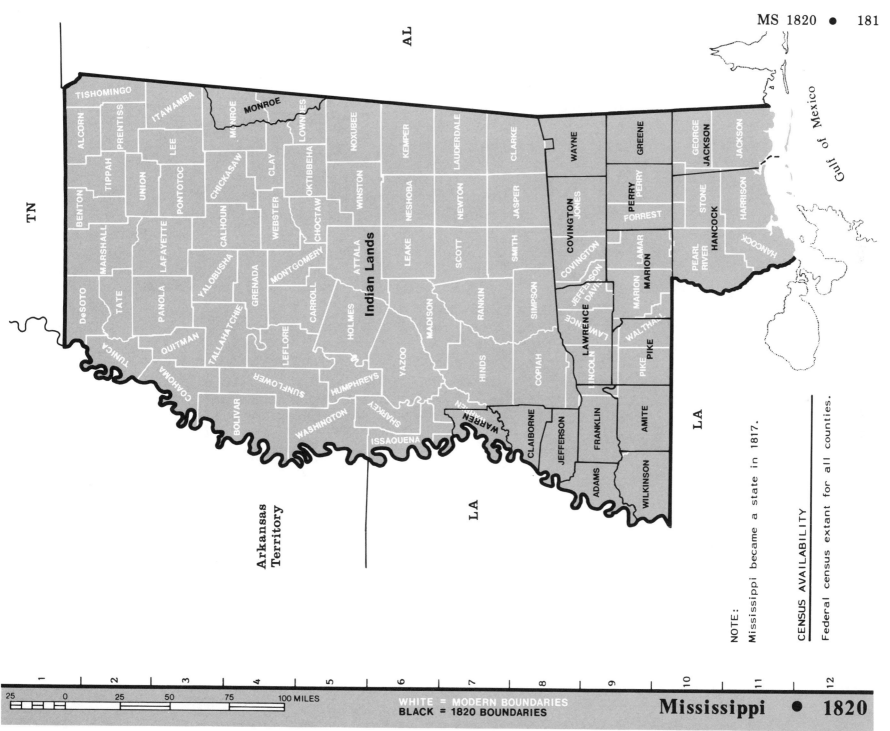

AL

TN

Gulf of Mexico

Gulf

TISHOMINGO

ALCORN

PRENTISS

ITAWAMBA

MONROE

LOWNES

NOXUBEE

KEMPER

LAUDERDALE

CLARKE

WAYNE

GREENE

GEORGE

JACKSON

JACKSON

BENTON

TIPPAH

UNION

LEE

PONTOTOC

CHICKASAW

CLAY

OKTIBBEHA

WINSTON

NESHOBA

NEWTON

JASPER

COVINGTON
JONES

PERRY

PERRY

FORREST

STONE

HANCOCK

HARRISON

MARSHALL

LAFAYETTE

CALHOUN

WEBSTER

CHOCTAW

ATTALA

LEAKE

SCOTT

SMITH

MARION

LAMAR

PEARL
RIVER

HANCOCK

DeSOTO

TATE

PANOLA

YALOBUSHA

GRENADA

MONTGOMERY

CARROLL

Indian Lands

HOLMES

MADISON

RANKIN

SIMPSON

COVINGTON

JEFFERSON
DAVIS

MARION

WALTHALL

PIKE

TUNICA

QUITMAN

TALLAHATCHIE

LEFLORE

SUNFLOWER

HUMPHREYS

YAZOO

HINDS

COPIAH

LAWRENCE

LAWRENCE

LINCOLN

PIKE

COAHOMA

BOLIVAR

WASHINGTON

SHARKEY

ISSAQUENA

WARREN

CLAIBORNE

JEFFERSON

FRANKLIN

AMITE

LA

ADAMS

WILKINSON

Arkansas
Territory

LA

LA

NOTE:
Mississippi became a state in 1817.

CENSUS AVAILABILITY
Federal census extant for all counties.

1 2 3 4 5 6 7 8 9 10 11 12

25   0   25   50   75   100 MILES

WHITE = MODERN BOUNDARIES
BLACK = 1820 BOUNDARIES

Mississippi ● **1820**

MAP GUIDE TO THE U.S. FEDERAL CENSUSES, 1790–1920 by William Thorndale and William Dollarhide. Copyright 1987, all rights reserved.

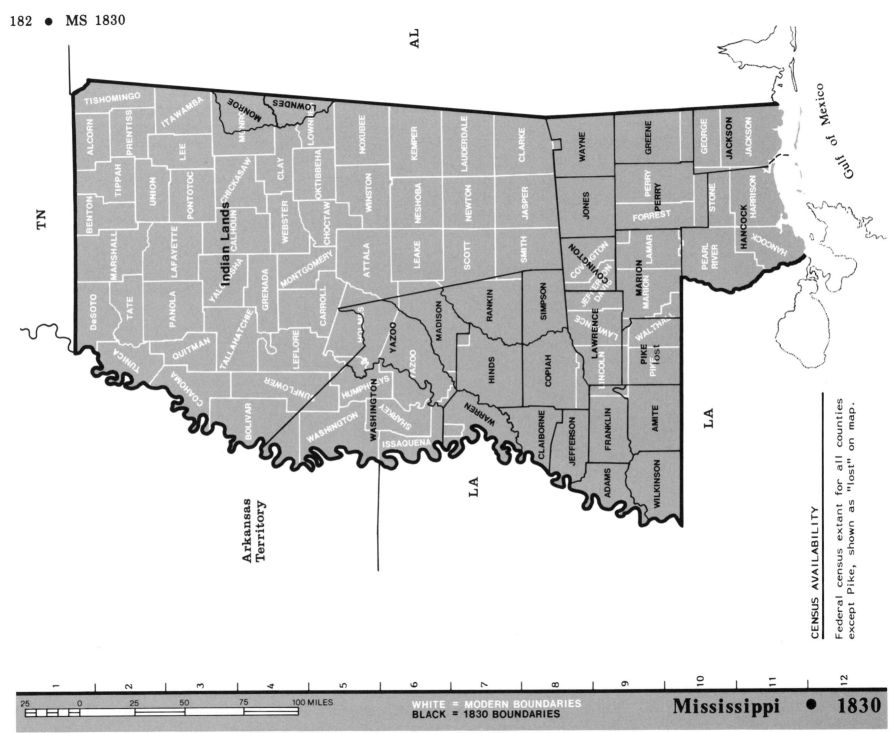

Mississippi ● **1830**

CENSUS AVAILABILITY

Federal census extant for all counties
except Pike, shown as "lost" on map.

100 MILES

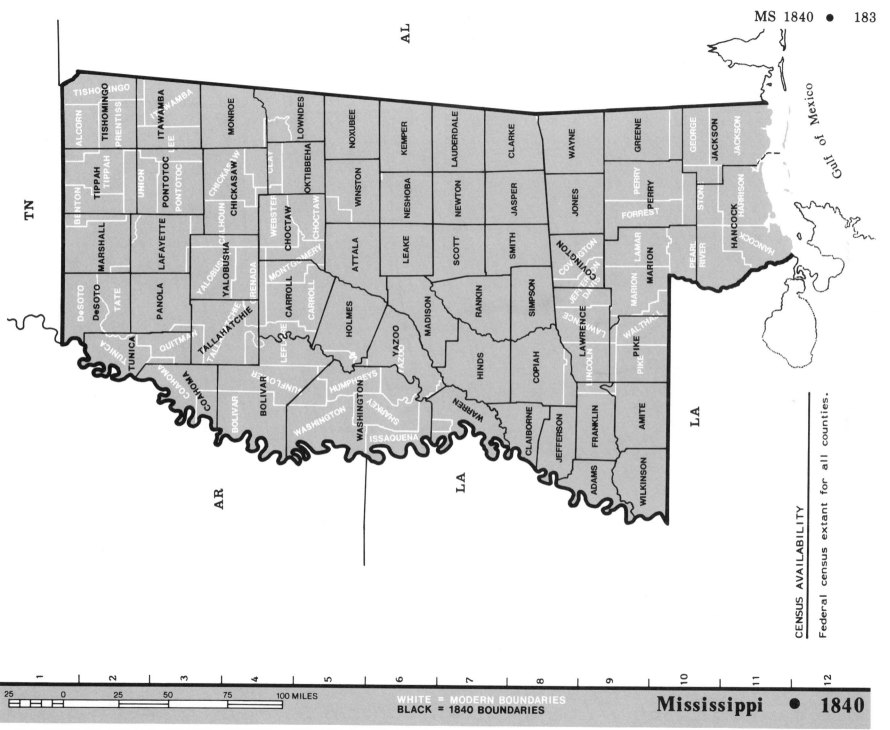

CENSUS AVAILABILITY

Federal census extant for all counties.

WHITE = MODERN BOUNDARIES
BLACK = 1840 BOUNDARIES

Mississippi ● **1840**

25 0 25 50 75 100 MILES

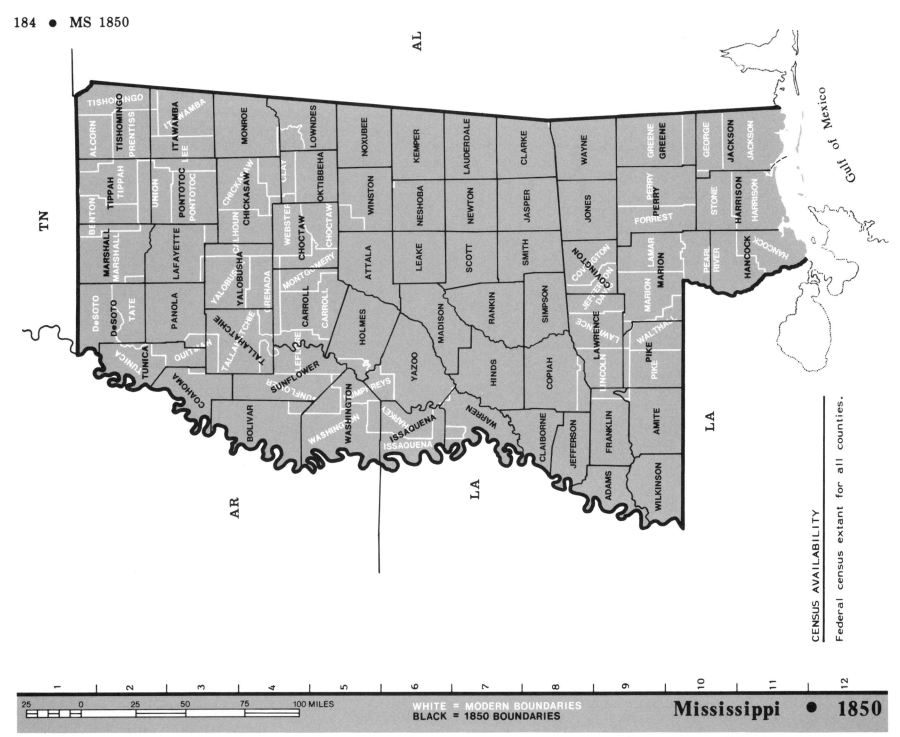

WHITE = MODERN BOUNDARIES
BLACK = 1850 BOUNDARIES

Mississippi ● **1850**

25   1   0   25   50   75   100 MILES

1   2   3   4   5   6   7   8   9   10   11   12

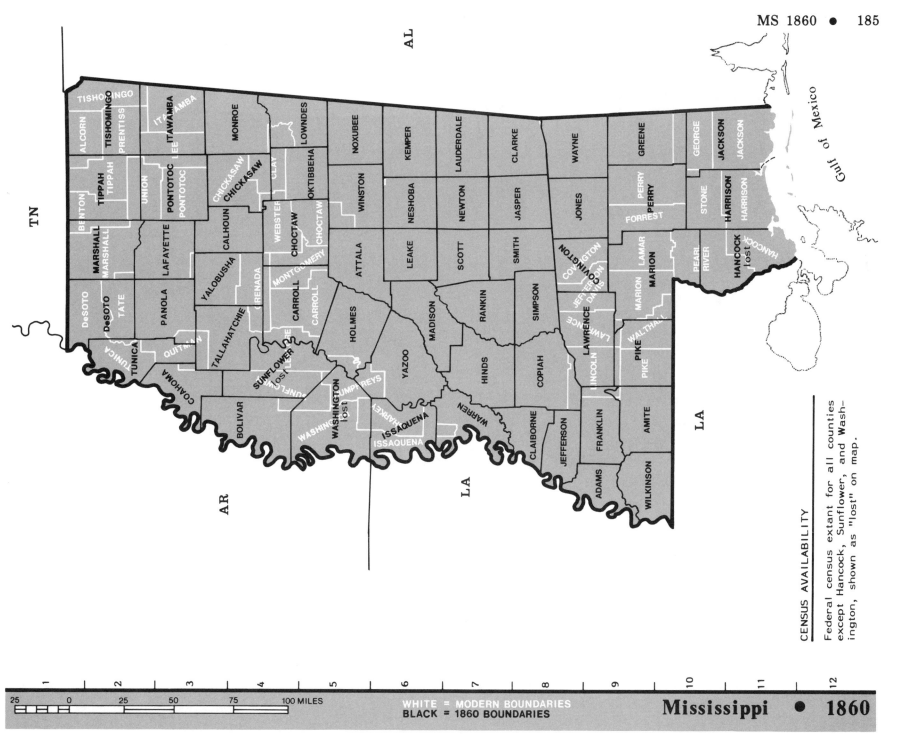

AL

TN

Gulf of Mexico

TISHOMINGO
ALCORN
TISHOMINGO
PRENTISS
ITAWAMBA
ITAWAMBA
MONROE
LOWNDES
NOXUBEE
KEMPER
LAUDERDALE
CLARKE
WAYNE
GREENE
GEORGE
JACKSON
JACKSON

BENTON
TIPPAH
TIPPAH
UNION
LEE
PONTOTOC
PONTOTOC
CHICKASAW
CHICKASAW
CLAY
OKTIBBEHA
WINSTON
NESHOBA
NEWTON
JASPER
JONES
PERRY
PERRY
FORREST
STONE
HARRISON
HARRISON

MARSHALL
MARSHALL
LAFAYETTE
CALHOUN
WEBSTER
CHOCTAW
CHOCTAW
ATTALA
LEAKE
SCOTT
SMITH
COVINGTON
COVINGTON
LAMAR
MARION
MARION
PEARL RIVER
HANCOCK
HANCOCK
lost

DeSoto
DeSOTO
TATE
PANOLA
YALOBUSHA
GRENADA
MONTGOMERY
CARROLL
CARROLL
HOLMES
MADISON
RANKIN
SIMPSON
JEFFERSON DAVIS
LAWRENCE
LAWRENCE
WALTHALL
PIKE
PIKE

TUNICA
QUITMAN
TALLAHATCHIE
SUNFLOWER
YAZOO
HINDS
COPIAH
LINCOLN
AMITE

COAHOMA
BOLIVAR
SUNFLOWER
WASHINGTON
lost
HUMPHREYS
SHARKEY
ISSAQUENA
ISSAQUENA
WARREN
CLAIBORNE
JEFFERSON
FRANKLIN
WILKINSON
ADAMS

WASHINGTON
lost

AR

LA

LA

LA

CENSUS AVAILABILITY

Federal census extant for all counties
except Hancock, Sunflower, and Washington, shown as "lost" on map.

1 2 3 4 5 6 7 8 9 10 11 12

25 0 25 50 75 100 MILES

WHITE = MODERN BOUNDARIES
BLACK = 1860 BOUNDARIES

Mississippi ● **1860**

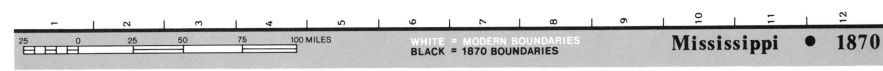

AL

TN

AR

LA

LA

Gulf of Mexico

TISHOMINGO

ALCORN PRENTISS ITAWAMBA MONROE LOWNDES NOXUBEE KEMPER LAUDERDALE CLARKE WAYNE GREENE GEORGE JACKSON

TIPPAH LEE CHICKASAW CLAY OKTIBBEHA WINSTON NESHOBA NEWTON JASPER JONES PERRY STONE HARRISON

BENTON UNION PONTOTOC CHICKASAW WEBSTER CHOCTAW ATTALA LEAKE SCOTT SMITH COVINGTON FORREST PEARL RIVER HANCOCK

MARSHALL LAFAYETTE CALHOUN CHOCTAW MADISON RANKIN SIMPSON JEFFERSON DAVIS MARION LAMAR

DeSOTO TATE PANOLA YALOBUSHA GRENADA MONTGOMERY CARROLL HOLMES LAWRENCE WALTHALL MARION

TUNICA QUITMAN TALLAHATCHIE CARROLL YAZOO HINDS COPIAH LINCOLN PIKE AMITE

COAHOMA SUNFLOWER LEFLORE HUMPHREYS MADISON WARREN CLAIBORNE FRANKLIN

BOLIVAR WASHINGTON SHARKEY ISSAQUENA JEFFERSON ADAMS WILKINSON

CENSUS AVAILABILITY

Federal census extant for all counties.

| 25 | 0 | 25 | 50 | 75 | 100 MILES |

1 2 3 4 5 6 7 8 9 10 11 12

WHITE = MODERN BOUNDARIES
BLACK = 1870 BOUNDARIES

Mississippi ● 1870

MAP GUIDE TO THE U.S. FEDERAL CENSUSES, 1790–1920 by William Thorndale and William Dollarhide. Copyright 1987, all rights reserved.

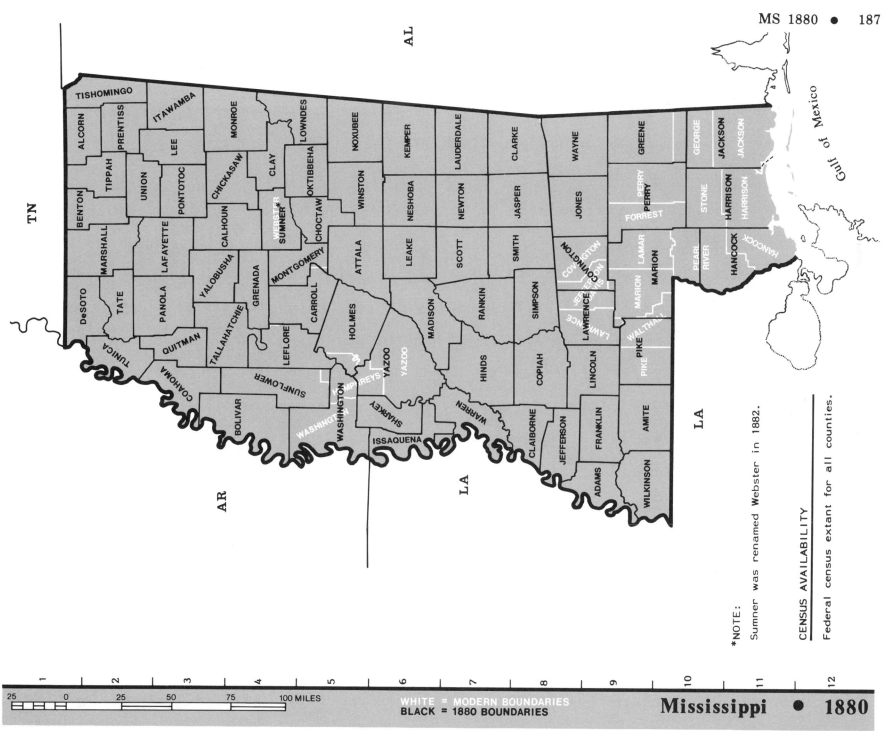

AL

TN

AR

LA

LA

LA

Gulf of Mexico

*NOTE:
Sumner was renamed Webster in 1882.

CENSUS AVAILABILITY

Federal census extant for all counties.

WHITE = MODERN BOUNDARIES
BLACK = 1880 BOUNDARIES

Mississippi ● **1880**

25 0 25 50 75 100 MILES

1 2 3 4 5 6 7 8 9 10 11 12

AL

TN

TISHOMINGO
ALCORN
PRENTISS
ITAWAMBA
TIPPAH
BENTON
UNION
LEE
PONTOTOC
MARSHALL
LAFAYETTE
MONROE
CHICKASAW
CLAY
CALHOUN
WEBSTER
OKTIBBEHA
LOWNDES
NOXUBEE
KEMPER
LAUDERDALE
CLARKE
WAYNE
GREENE
GEORGE
JACKSON

DeSoto
TATE
PANOLA
YALOBUSHA
GRENADA
MONTGOMERY
CHOCTAW
WINSTON
ATTALA
NESHOBA
LEAKE
NEWTON
SCOTT
SMITH
JASPER
JONES
PERRY
PERRY
FORREST
STONE
HARRISON
HARRISON
HANCOCK
HANCOCK

TUNICA
COAHOMA
QUITMAN
TALLAHATCHIE
PANOLA
LEFLORE
CARROLL
HOLMES
MADISON
RANKIN
SIMPSON
COVINGTON
COVINGTON
LAMAR
MARION
MARION
PEARL RIVER

SUNFLOWER
BOLIVAR
WASHINGTON
WASHINGTON
HUMPHREYS
SHARKEY
YAZOO
YAZOO
HINDS
COPIAH
LINCOLN
LAWRENCE
LAWRENCE
JEFFERSON DAVIS
PIKE
PIKE
WALTHALL

ISSAQUENA
WARREN
CLAIBORNE
JEFFERSON
FRANKLIN
AMITE
ADAMS
WILKINSON

AR

LA

LA

Gulf of Mexico

*NOTE:
The half township shown between Covington and Marion was in Covington in 1890 and in Marion in 1900.

CENSUS AVAILABILITY

1890 federal census lost for all counties.
1900 federal census extant for all counties.

25   0   25   50   75   100 MILES

WHITE = MODERN BOUNDARIES
BLACK = 1890-1900 BOUNDARIES

Mississippi ● 1890-1900

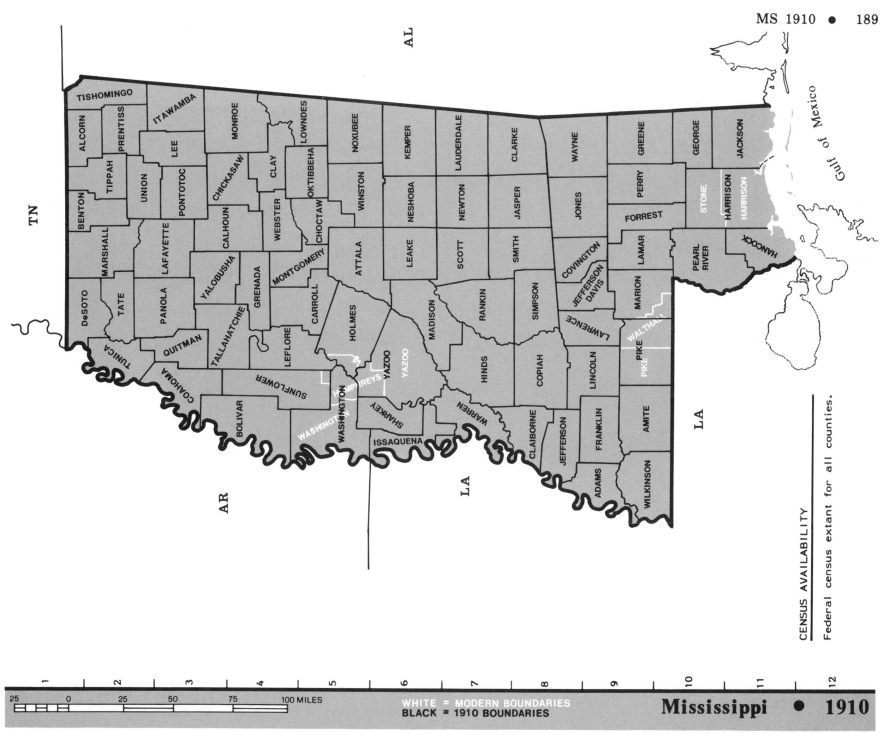

AL

TN

AR

LA

LA

Gulf of Mexico

TISHOMINGO
ALCORN
PRENTISS
ITAWAMBA
TIPPAH
BENTON
UNION
LEE
PONTOTOC
MONROE
MARSHALL
LAFAYETTE
CHICKASAW
CLAY
LOWNDES
DeSOTO
TATE
PANOLA
YALOBUSHA
CALHOUN
WEBSTER
OKTIBBEHA
CHOCTAW
TUNICA
QUITMAN
TALLAHATCHIE
GRENADA
MONTGOMERY
CARROLL
NOXUBEE
WINSTON
KEMPER
COAHOMA
BOLIVAR
SUNFLOWER
LEFLORE
HOLMES
ATTALA
LEAKE
NESHOBA
NEWTON
LAUDERDALE
CLARKE
HUMPHREYS
YAZOO
YAZOO
MADISON
SCOTT
JASPER
WAYNE
WASHINGTON
WASHINGTON
SHARKEY
ISSAQUENA
WARREN
HINDS
RANKIN
SIMPSON
SMITH
JONES
COVINGTON
JEFFERSON DAVIS
LAWRENCE
CLAIBORNE
COPIAH
LINCOLN
JEFFERSON
FRANKLIN
ADAMS
WILKINSON
AMITE
MARION
WALTHALL
PIKE
PIKE
LAMAR
FORREST
PERRY
GREENE
PEARL RIVER
STONE
HARRISON
HARRISON
HANCOCK
GEORGE
JACKSON

CENSUS AVAILABILITY

Federal census extant for all counties.

| | | 1 | | 2 | | 3 | | 4 | | 5 | | 6 | | 7 | | 8 | | 9 | | 10 | | 11 | | 12 |

25   0   25   50   75   100 MILES

WHITE = MODERN BOUNDARIES
BLACK = 1910 BOUNDARIES

Mississippi ● **1910**

AL

TN

TISHOMINGO
ALCORN
PRENTISS
ITAWAMBA
MONROE
LOWNDES
NOXUBEE
KEMPER
LAUDERDALE
CLARKE
WAYNE
GREENE
GEORGE
JACKSON
TIPPAH
UNION
LEE
CHICKASAW
CLAY
OKTIBBEHA
WINSTON
NESHOBA
NEWTON
JASPER
PERRY
STONE
HARRISON
BENTON
MARSHALL
LAFAYETTE
PONTOTOC
CALHOUN
WEBSTER
CHOCTAW
ATTALA
LEAKE
SCOTT
SMITH
JONES
FORREST
LAMAR
PEARL RIVER
HANCOCK
YALOBUSHA
GRENADA
MONTGOMERY
COVINGTON
JEFFERSON DAVIS
MARION
WALTHALL
DeSOTO
TATE
PANOLA
CARROLL
HOLMES
MADISON
RANKIN
SIMPSON
LAWRENCE
TUNICA
QUITMAN
TALLAHATCHIE
LEFLORE
YAZOO
HINDS
COPIAH
LINCOLN
PIKE
COAHOMA
SUNFLOWER
HUMPHREYS
WARREN
CLAIBORNE
FRANKLIN
AMITE
BOLIVAR
WASHINGTON
SHARKEY
JEFFERSON
ISSAQUENA
ADAMS
WILKINSON

Gulf of Mexico

AR

LA

LA

LA

CENSUS AVAILABILITY

Federal census extant for all counties.

1 2 3 4 5 6 7 8 9 10 11 12

25 0 25 50 75 100 MILES

WHITE = MODERN BOUNDARIES
BLACK = 1920 BOUNDARIES

Mississippi ● 1920

MAP GUIDE TO THE U.S. FEDERAL CENSUSES, 1790–1920 by William Thorndale and William Dollarhide. Copyright 1987, all rights reserved.

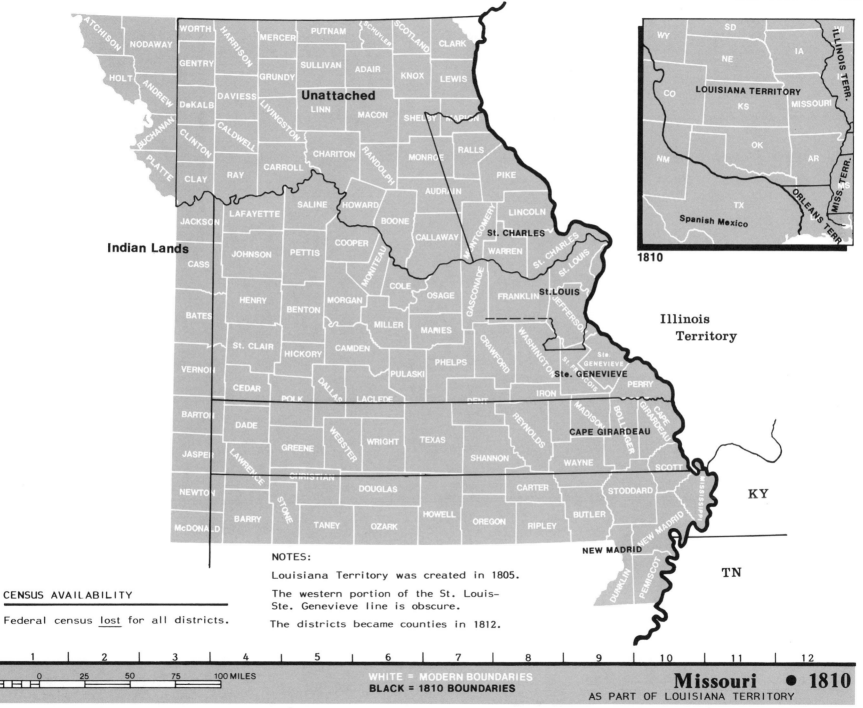

Unattached

Indian Lands

LOUISIANA TERRITORY

Spanish Mexico

Illinois Territory

St. CHARLES

St. LOUIS

Ste. GENEVIEVE

CAPE GIRARDEAU

NEW MADRID

KY

TN

1810

NOTES:

Louisiana Territory was created in 1805.

The western portion of the St. Louis–Ste. Genevieve line is obscure.

The districts became counties in 1812.

CENSUS AVAILABILITY

Federal census lost for all districts.

25   0   25   50   75   100 MILES

WHITE = MODERN BOUNDARIES
BLACK = 1810 BOUNDARIES

Missouri ● 1810
AS PART OF LOUISIANA TERRITORY

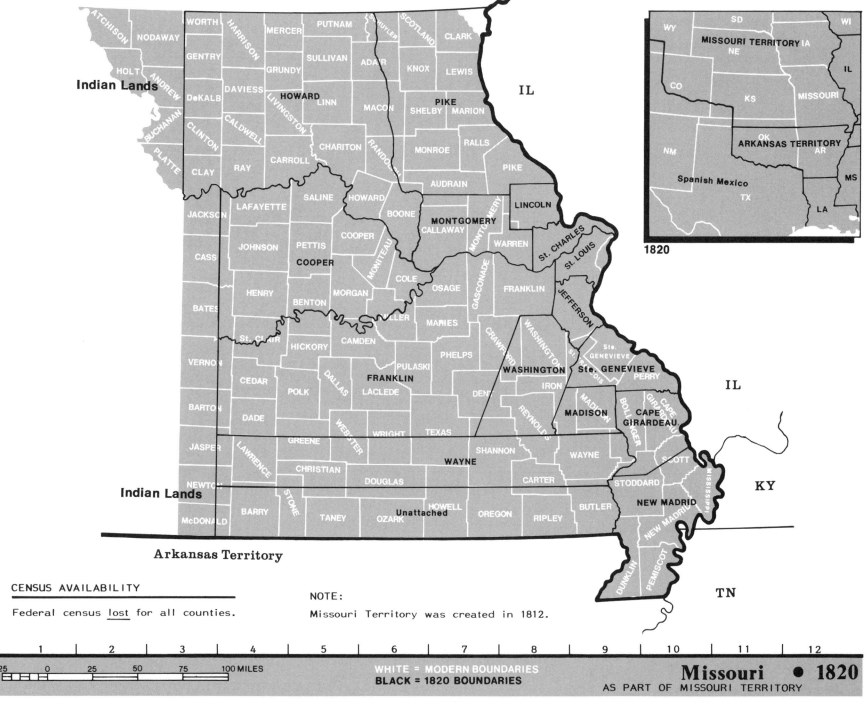

Indian Lands

IL

MISSOURI TERRITORY

ARKANSAS TERRITORY

Spanish Mexico

1820

Indian Lands

Arkansas Territory

IL

KY

TN

CENSUS AVAILABILITY

Federal census lost for all counties.

NOTE:

Missouri Territory was created in 1812.

WHITE = MODERN BOUNDARIES
BLACK = 1820 BOUNDARIES

Missouri ● **1820**
AS PART OF MISSOURI TERRITORY

25 0 25 50 75 100 MILES

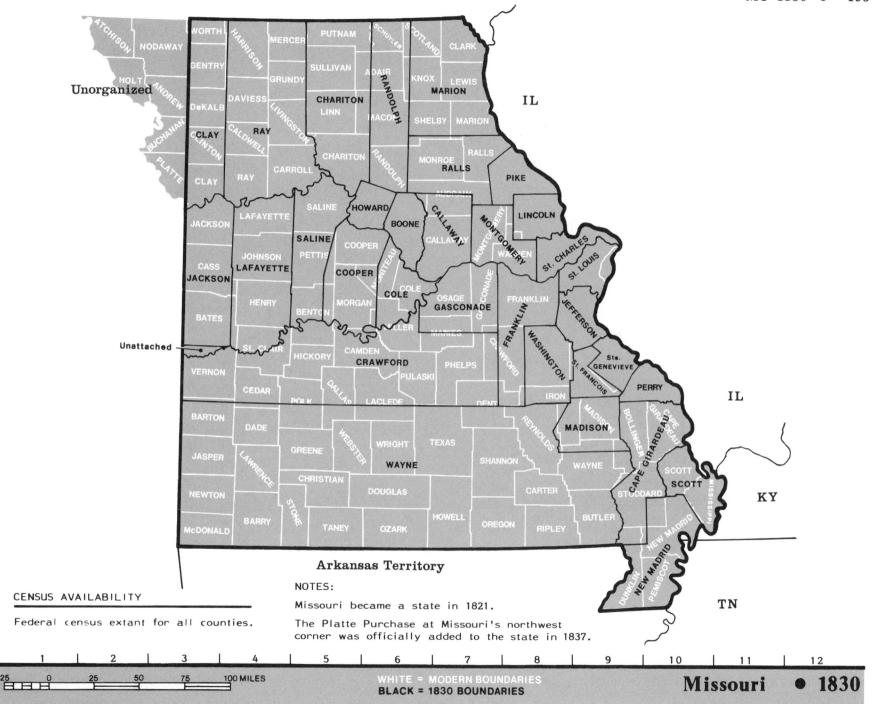

Unorganized

Unattached —

Arkansas Territory

NOTES:

Missouri became a state in 1821.

The Platte Purchase at Missouri's northwest corner was officially added to the state in 1837.

CENSUS AVAILABILITY

Federal census extant for all counties.

25 0 25 50 75 100 MILES

WHITE = MODERN BOUNDARIES
BLACK = 1830 BOUNDARIES

Missouri ● 1830

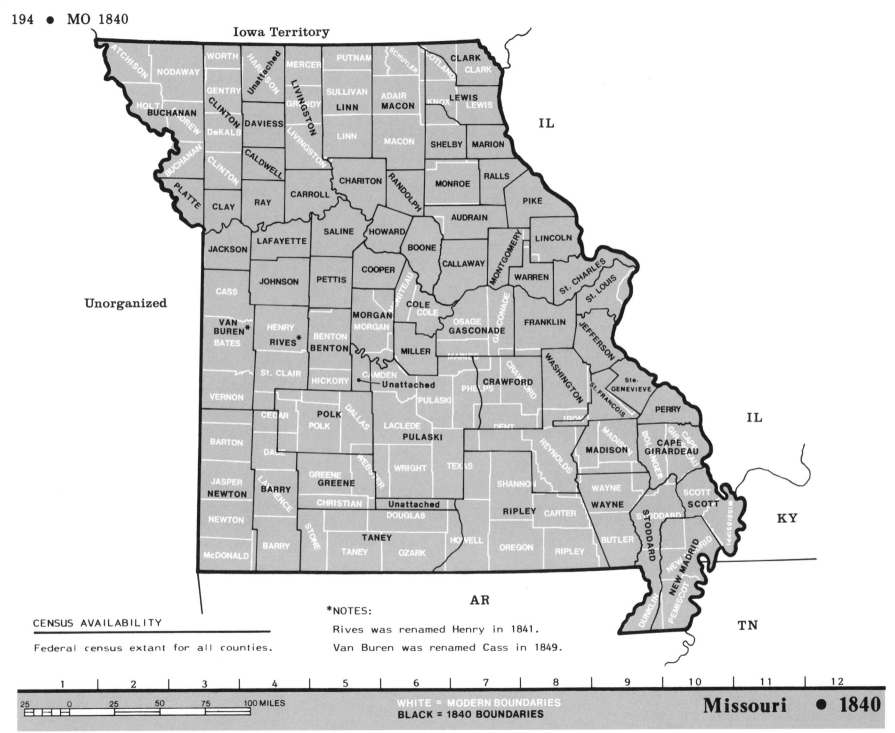

Iowa Territory

IL

IL

KY

Unorganized

AR

TN

CENSUS AVAILABILITY

Federal census extant for all counties.

*NOTES:

Rives was renamed Henry in 1841.

Van Buren was renamed Cass in 1849.

1   2   3   4   5   6   7   8   9   10   11   12

25   0   25   50   75   100 MILES

WHITE = MODERN BOUNDARIES
BLACK = 1840 BOUNDARIES

Missouri ● **1840**

MAP GUIDE TO THE U.S. FEDERAL CENSUSES, 1790–1920 by William Thorndale and William Dollarhide. Copyright 1987, all rights reserved.

IA

IL

IL

ATCHISON
NODAWAY
WORTH
GENTRY
GENTRY
HARRISON
MERCER
DODGE *
PUTNAM
SCHUYLER
SCOTLAND
CLARK
HOLT
ANDREW
DeKALB
DAVIESS
GRUNDY
SULLIVAN
ADAIR
KNOX
LEWIS
BUCHANAN
CLINTON
CALDWELL
LIVINGSTON
LINN
MACON
SHELBY
MARION
PLATTE
CLAY
RAY
CARROLL
CHARITON
RANDOLPH
MONROE
RALLS
JACKSON
LAFAYETTE
SALINE
HOWARD
BOONE
AUDRAIN
PIKE
LINCOLN
Unorganized
CASS
CASS
JOHNSON
PETTIS
COOPER
CALLAWAY
MONTGOMERY
WARREN
St. CHARLES
St. LOUIS
BATES
HENRY
BENTON
MORGAN
MONITEAU
COLE
OSAGE
OSAGE
GASCONADE
FRANKLIN
JEFFERSON
BATES
VERNON
St. CLAIR
HICKORY
CAMDEN
MILLER
MARIES
CRAWFORD
WASHINGTON
St. FRANCOIS
Ste
GENEVIEVE
PERRY
BARTON
JASPER
CEDAR
DADE
POLK
DALLAS
LACLEDE
PULASKI
PULASKI
PHELPS
DENT
IRON
MADISON
BOLINGER
CAPE
GIRARDEAU
JASPER
LAWRENCE
GREENE
GREENE
WEBSTER
WRIGHT
WRIGHT
TEXAS
SHANNON
SHANNON
REYNOLDS
MADISON
WAYNE
SCOTT
NEWTON
CHRISTIAN
DOUGLAS
CARTER
STODDARD
MISSISSIPPI
McDONALD
BARRY
STONE
TANEY
TANEY
OZARK
OZARK
HOWELL
OREGON
OREGON
RIPLEY
RIPLEY
BUTLER
DUNKLIN
NEW MADRID
NEW MADRID
PEMISCOT

KY

AR

TN

CENSUS AVAILABILITY

Federal census extant for all counties.

*NOTE:

Dodge was annexed to Putnam in 1853.

| 1 | 2 | 3 | 4 | 5 | 6 | 7 | 8 | 9 | 10 | 11 | 12 |

25 0 25 50 75 100 MILES

WHITE = MODERN BOUNDARIES
BLACK = 1850 BOUNDARIES

Missouri ● **1850**

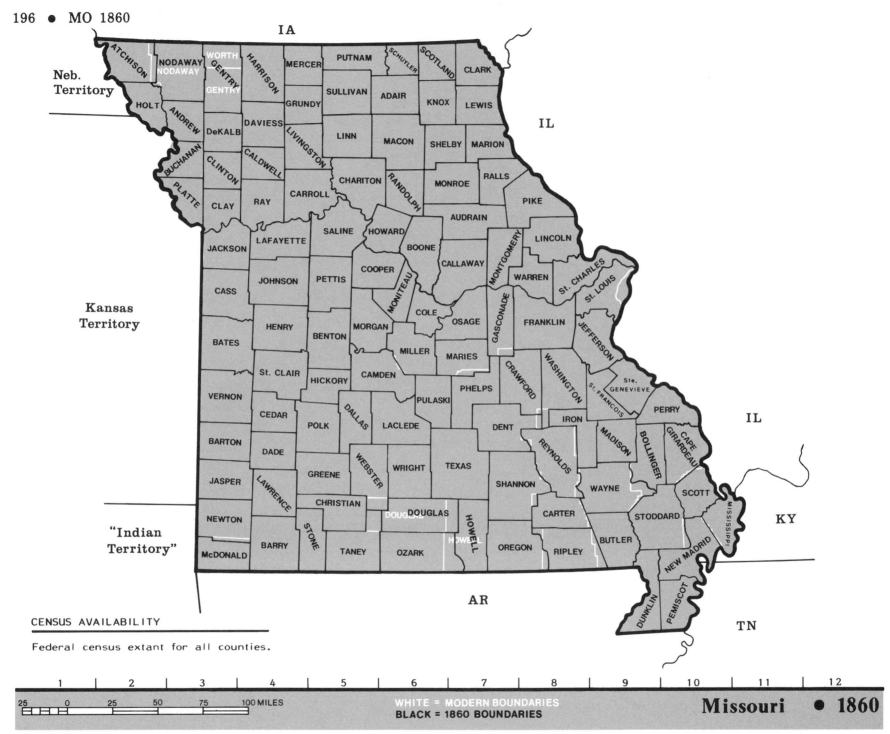

IA

Neb.
Territory

IL

ATCHISON

NODAWAY

WORTH
GENTRY

HARRISON

MERCER

PUTNAM

SCHUYLER

SCOTLAND

CLARK

HOLT

ANDREW

NODAWAY

GENTRY

SULLIVAN

ADAIR

KNOX

LEWIS

DeKALB

DAVIESS

GRUNDY

BUCHANAN

CLINTON

CALDWELL

LIVINGSTON

LINN

MACON

SHELBY

MARION

PLATTE

CLAY

RAY

CARROLL

CHARITON

RANDOLPH

MONROE

RALLS

PIKE

AUDRAIN

Kansas
Territory

JACKSON

LAFAYETTE

SALINE

HOWARD

BOONE

CALLAWAY

MONTGOMERY

WARREN

LINCOLN

St. CHARLES

St. LOUIS

CASS

JOHNSON

PETTIS

COOPER

MONITEAU

COLE

OSAGE

GASCONADE

FRANKLIN

JEFFERSON

HENRY

BENTON

MORGAN

MILLER

MARIES

WASHINGTON

St. FRANCOIS

Ste.
GENEVIEVE

PERRY

BATES

St. CLAIR

HICKORY

CAMDEN

PULASKI

PHELPS

CRAWFORD

IRON

MADISON

BOLLINGER

CAPE
GIRARDEAU

IL

VERNON

CEDAR

POLK

DALLAS

LACLEDE

DENT

REYNOLDS

SCOTT

BARTON

DADE

WEBSTER

WRIGHT

TEXAS

SHANNON

WAYNE

STODDARD

"Indian
Territory"

JASPER

LAWRENCE

GREENE

CHRISTIAN

CARTER

BUTLER

NEW MADRID

KY

MISSISSIPPI

McDONALD

BARRY

STONE

TANEY

DOUGLAS

DOUGLAS

HOWELL

HOWELL

OZARK

OREGON

RIPLEY

DUNKLIN

PEMISCOT

NEWTON

AR

TN

CENSUS AVAILABILITY

Federal census extant for all counties.

| 1 | 2 | 3 | 4 | 5 | 6 | 7 | 8 | 9 | 10 | 11 | 12 |

25 0 25 50 75 100 MILES

WHITE = MODERN BOUNDARIES
BLACK = 1860 BOUNDARIES

Missouri ● 1860

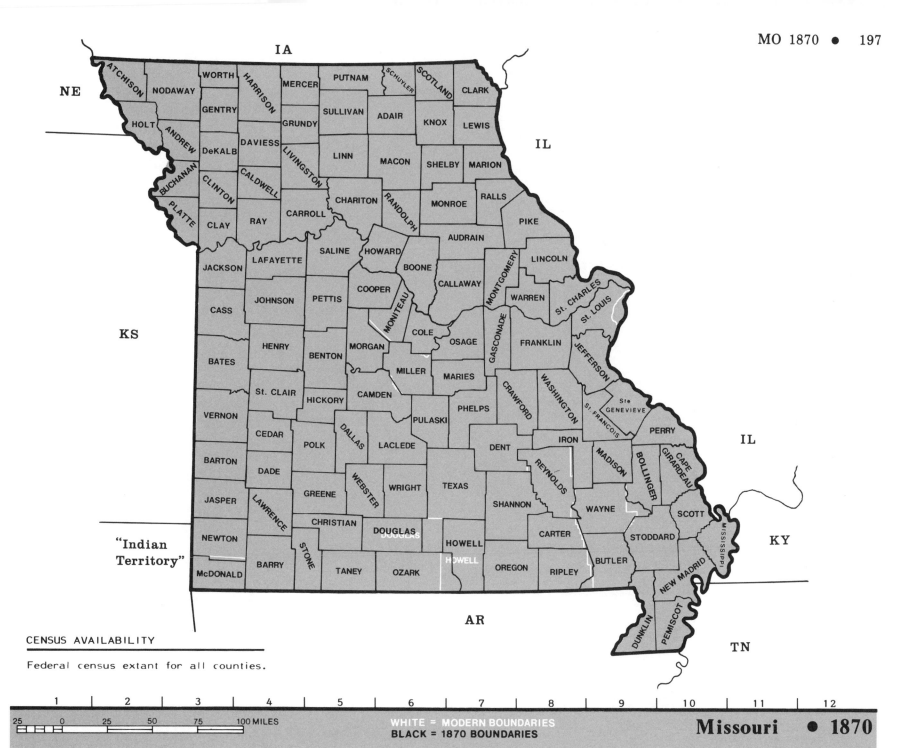

NE

IA

IL

IL

KS

"Indian
Territory"

AR

KY

TN

ATCHISON
NODAWAY
WORTH
HARRISON
MERCER
PUTNAM
SCHUYLER
SCOTLAND
CLARK
HOLT
GENTRY
SULLIVAN
ADAIR
KNOX
LEWIS
ANDREW
DeKALB
DAVIESS
GRUNDY
MACON
SHELBY
MARION
BUCHANAN
CLINTON
CALDWELL
LIVINGSTON
LINN
CHARITON
RANDOLPH
MONROE
RALLS
PLATTE
CLAY
RAY
CARROLL
PIKE
JACKSON
LAFAYETTE
SALINE
HOWARD
BOONE
AUDRAIN
LINCOLN
CASS
JOHNSON
PETTIS
COOPER
MONITEAU
CALLAWAY
MONTGOMERY
WARREN
St. CHARLES
St. LOUIS
COLE
OSAGE
GASCONADE
FRANKLIN
HENRY
BENTON
MORGAN
MILLER
MARIES
WASHINGTON
JEFFERSON
Ste
GENEVIEVE
BATES
St. CLAIR
HICKORY
CAMDEN
PHELPS
CRAWFORD
St. FRANCOIS
PERRY
VERNON
CEDAR
POLK
DALLAS
LACLEDE
PULASKI
DENT
IRON
MADISON
BOLLINGER
CAPE
GIRARDEAU
BARTON
DADE
WEBSTER
WRIGHT
TEXAS
REYNOLDS
WAYNE
SCOTT
JASPER
LAWRENCE
GREENE
SHANNON
CARTER
STODDARD
NEWTON
CHRISTIAN
DOUGLAS
HOWELL
BUTLER
NEW MADRID
McDONALD
BARRY
STONE
TANEY
OZARK
HOWELL
OREGON
RIPLEY
DUNKLIN
PEMISCOT
MISSISSIPPI

CENSUS AVAILABILITY

Federal census extant for all counties.

| 1 | 2 | 3 | 4 | 5 | 6 | 7 | 8 | 9 | 10 | 11 | 12 |

25   0   25   50   75   100 MILES

Missouri ● **1870**

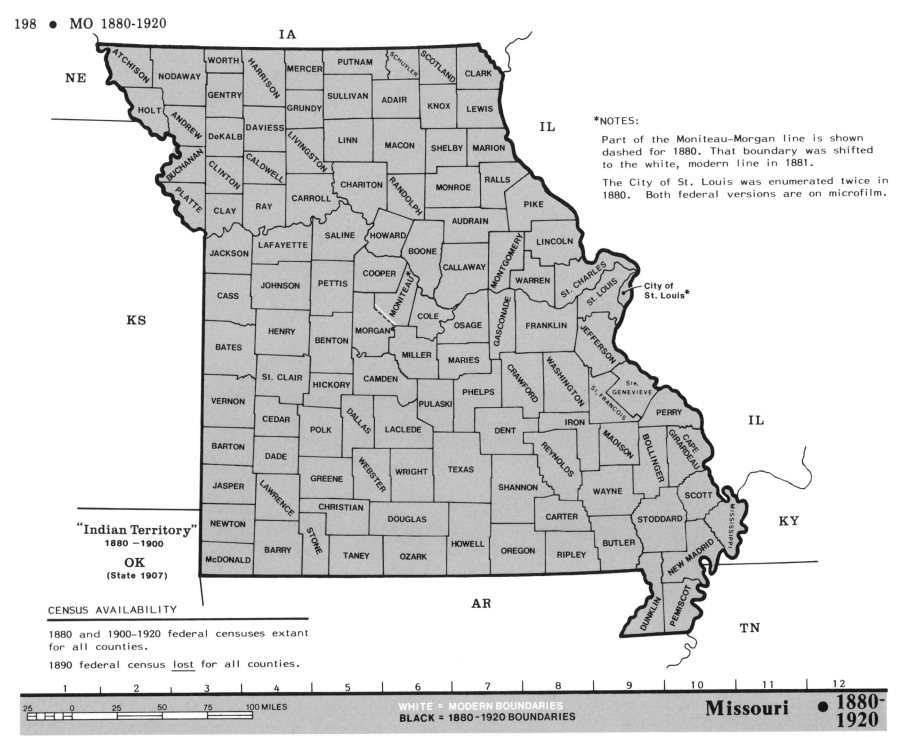

IA

NE

IL

*NOTES:

Part of the Moniteau–Morgan line is shown dashed for 1880. That boundary was shifted to the white, modern line in 1881.

The City of St. Louis was enumerated twice in 1880. Both federal versions are on microfilm.

KS

City of
St. Louis*

IL

"Indian Territory"
1880–1900

OK
(State 1907)

KY

AR

TN

CENSUS AVAILABILITY

1880 and 1900–1920 federal censuses extant for all counties.

1890 federal census lost for all counties.

| | | | | | | | | | | | |
|1|2|3|4|5|6|7|8|9|10|11|12|

25   0   25   50   75   100 MILES

WHITE = MODERN BOUNDARIES
BLACK = 1880–1920 BOUNDARIES

Missouri ● 1880–1920

MAP GUIDE TO THE U.S. FEDERAL CENSUSES, 1790–1920 by William Thorndale and William Dollarhide. Copyright 1987, all rights reserved.

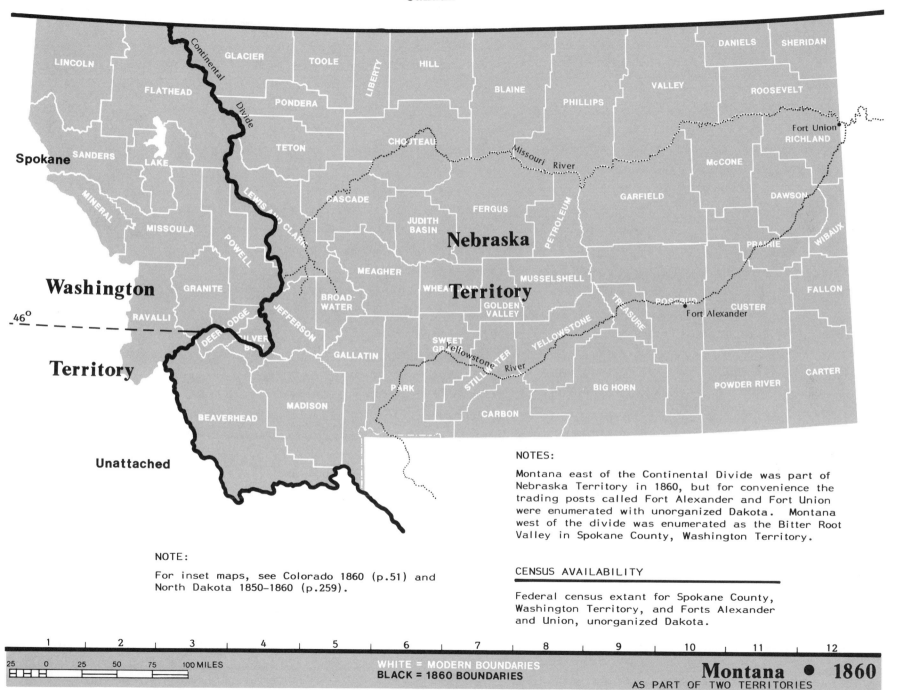

Canada

LINCOLN
GLACIER
Continental
FLATHEAD
TOOLE
LIBERTY
HILL
DANIELS
SHERIDAN
PONDERA
BLAINE
VALLEY
ROOSEVELT
Spokane
SANDERS
Divide
TETON
PHILLIPS
Fort Union
RICHLAND
LAKE
CHOUTEAU
Missouri River
McCONE
MINERAL
LEWIS AND CLARK
CASCADE
FERGUS
GARFIELD
DAWSON
MISSOULA
JUDITH BASIN
Nebraska
PRAIRIE
WIBAUX
Washington
GRANITE
POWELL
MEAGHER
WHEAT
PETROLEUM
FALLON
Territory
BROAD-WATER
GOLDEN VALLEY
Territory
MUSSELSHELL
TREASURE
ROSEBUD
CUSTER
46°
RAVALLI
DEER LODGE
SILVER
JEFFERSON
Fort Alexander
GALLATIN
YELLOWSTONE
Territory
SWEET GR.
Yellowstone
STILLWATER
River
MADISON
BEAVERHEAD
PARK
BIG HORN
POWDER RIVER
CARTER
Unattached
CARBON

NOTES:

Montana east of the Continental Divide was part of Nebraska Territory in 1860, but for convenience the trading posts called Fort Alexander and Fort Union were enumerated with unorganized Dakota. Montana west of the divide was enumerated as the Bitter Root Valley in Spokane County, Washington Territory.

NOTE:

For inset maps, see Colorado 1860 (p.51) and North Dakota 1850–1860 (p.259).

CENSUS AVAILABILITY

Federal census extant for Spokane County, Washington Territory, and Forts Alexander and Union, unorganized Dakota.

| 1 | 2 | 3 | 4 | 5 | 6 | 7 | 8 | 9 | 10 | 11 | 12 |

25 0 25 50 75 100 MILES

WHITE = MODERN BOUNDARIES
BLACK = 1860 BOUNDARIES

Montana ● **1860**
AS PART OF TWO TERRITORIES

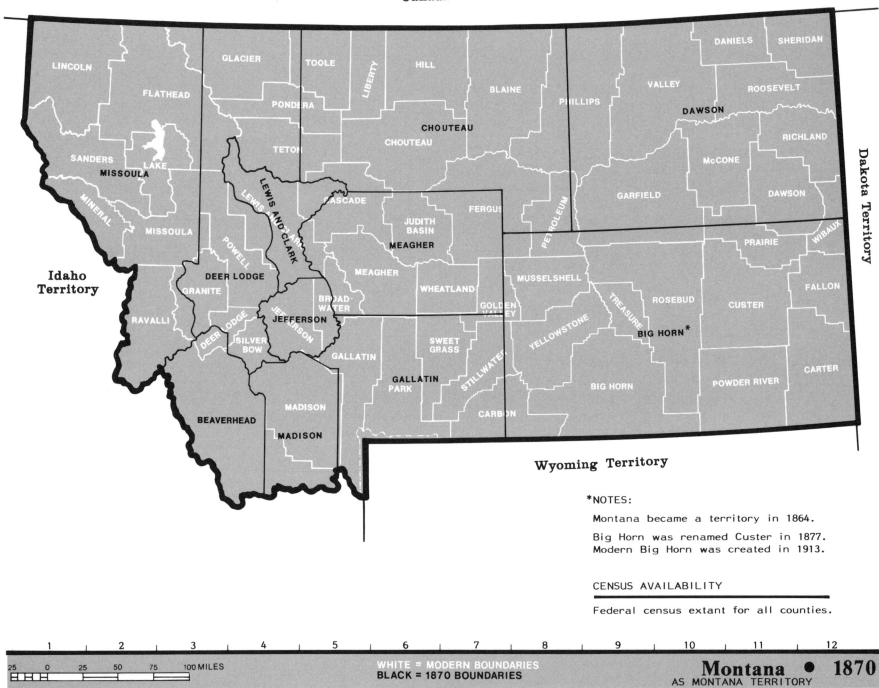

Canada

Idaho
Territory

Dakota Territory

Wyoming Territory

LINCOLN
FLATHEAD
SANDERS
LAKE
MISSOULA
MINERAL
MISSOULA
GLACIER
PONDERA
TETON
LEWIS AND CLARK
POWELL
DEER LODGE
GRANITE
RAVALLI
DEER LODGE
SILVER BOW
JEFFERSON
BEAVERHEAD
MADISON
MADISON
TOOLE
LIBERTY
HILL
CHOUTEAU
CHOUTEAU
CASCADE
JUDITH BASIN
MEAGHER
MEAGHER
BROAD-WATER
JEFFERSON
GALLATIN
GALLATIN PARK
SWEET GRASS
WHEATLAND
FERGUS
BLAINE
PHILLIPS
PETROLEUM
GARFIELD
MUSSELSHELL
GOLDEN VALLEY
STILLWATER
YELLOWSTONE
TREASURE
BIG HORN
CARBON
VALLEY
DAWSON
McCONE
DAWSON
RICHLAND
PRAIRIE
ROSEBUD
BIG HORN*
CUSTER
POWDER RIVER
DANIELS
SHERIDAN
ROOSEVELT
WIBAUX
FALLON
CARTER

*NOTES:

Montana became a territory in 1864.

Big Horn was renamed Custer in 1877.
Modern Big Horn was created in 1913.

CENSUS AVAILABILITY

Federal census extant for all counties.

1   2   3   4   5   6   7   8   9   10   11   12

25 0 25 50 75 100 MILES

WHITE = MODERN BOUNDARIES
BLACK = 1870 BOUNDARIES

Montana ● **1870**
AS MONTANA TERRITORY

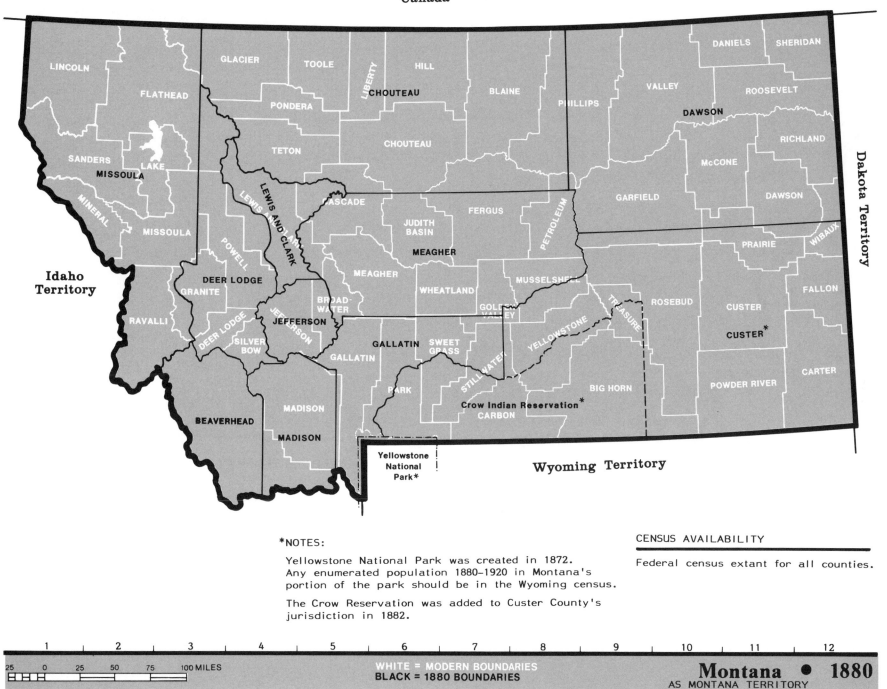

Canada

Idaho
Territory

Dakota Territory

Wyoming Territory

LINCOLN

GLACIER

TOOLE

LIBERTY

HILL

DANIELS

SHERIDAN

FLATHEAD

PONDERA

CHOUTEAU

BLAINE

VALLEY

ROOSEVELT

SANDERS

LAKE

TETON

PHILLIPS

DAWSON

MISSOULA

RICHLAND

MINERAL

CASCADE

CHOUTEAU

McCONE

LEWIS AND CLARK

FERGUS

GARFIELD

MISSOULA

DAWSON

POWELL

JUDITH
BASIN

PETROLEUM

PRAIRIE

DEER LODGE

MEAGHER

WIBAUX

GRANITE

MEAGHER

MUSSELSHELL

ROSEBUD

FALLON

RAVALLI

BROAD-
WATER

WHEATLAND

TREASURE

CUSTER

DEER LODGE

JEFFERSON

SILVER
BOW

GALLATIN

GOLDEN
VALLEY

YELLOWSTONE

CUSTER *

BEAVERHEAD

MADISON

GALLATIN

SWEET
GRASS

STILLWATER

BIG HORN

POWDER RIVER

CARTER

PARK

Crow Indian Reservation *

MADISON

CARBON

Yellowstone
National
Park*

*NOTES:

Yellowstone National Park was created in 1872.
Any enumerated population 1880–1920 in Montana's
portion of the park should be in the Wyoming census.

The Crow Reservation was added to Custer County's
jurisdiction in 1882.

CENSUS AVAILABILITY

Federal census extant for all counties.

| 1 | 2 | 3 | 4 | 5 | 6 | 7 | 8 | 9 | 10 | 11 | 12 |

25 0 25 50 75 100 MILES

WHITE = MODERN BOUNDARIES
BLACK = 1880 BOUNDARIES

Montana ● **1880**
AS MONTANA TERRITORY

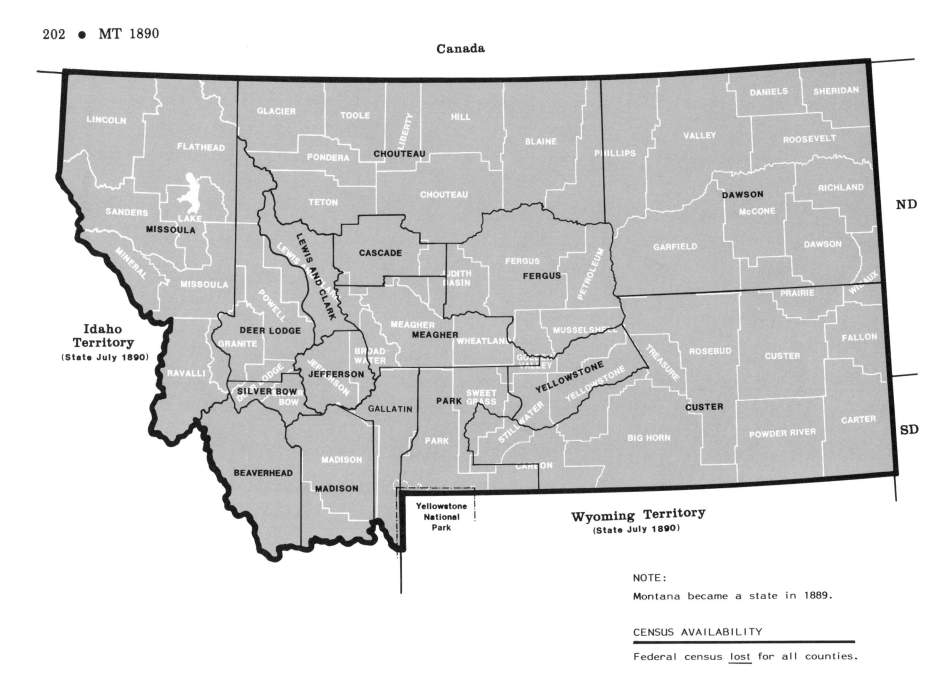

Canada

LINCOLN

GLACIER TOOLE HILL DANIELS SHERIDAN

FLATHEAD LIBERTY VALLEY ROOSEVELT

PONDERA CHOUTEAU BLAINE

SANDERS TETON PHILLIPS DAWSON RICHLAND

MINERAL CHOUTEAU McCONE

LAKE

MISSOULA CASCADE FERGUS GARFIELD DAWSON

MISSOULA LEWIS AND CLARK JUDITH FERGUS PETROLEUM

BASIN PRAIRIE WIBAUX

POWELL MEAGHER MUSSELSHELL FALLON

Idaho DEER LODGE MEAGHER WHEATLAND

Territory GRANITE BROAD- GOLDEN ROSEBUD CUSTER

(State July 1890) WATER VALLEY

RAVALLI JEFFERSON YELLOWSTONE TREASURE

DEER LODGE SILVER BOW BOW GALLATIN SWEET STILLWATER YELLOWSTONE CUSTER

SILVER BOW JEFFERSON PARK GRASS BIG HORN POWDER RIVER CARTER

MADISON PARK

BEAVERHEAD STILLWATER

MADISON CARBON

ND

SD

Yellowstone
National
Park

Wyoming Territory
(State July 1890)

NOTE:

Montana became a state in 1889.

CENSUS AVAILABILITY

Federal census lost for all counties.

| 1 | 2 | 3 | 4 | 5 | 6 | 7 | 8 | 9 | 10 | 11 | 12 |

25 0   25   50   75   100 MILES

WHITE = MODERN BOUNDARIES
BLACK = 1890 BOUNDARIES

Montana ● 1890

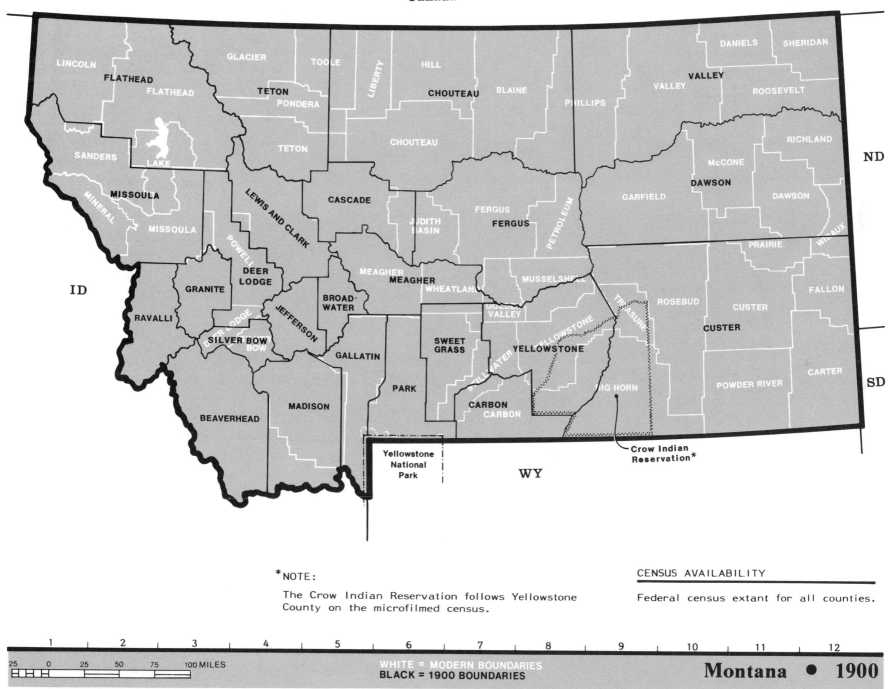

Canada

ND

ID

SD

WY

Crow Indian
Reservation*

Yellowstone
National
Park

*NOTE:

The Crow Indian Reservation follows Yellowstone
County on the microfilmed census.

CENSUS AVAILABILITY

Federal census extant for all counties.

25 0 25 50 75 100 MILES

1 2 3 4 5 6 7 8 9 10 11 12

WHITE = MODERN BOUNDARIES
BLACK = 1900 BOUNDARIES

Montana ● 1900

MAP GUIDE TO THE U.S. FEDERAL CENSUSES, 1790-1920 by William Thorndale and William Dollarhide. Copyright 1987, all rights reserved.

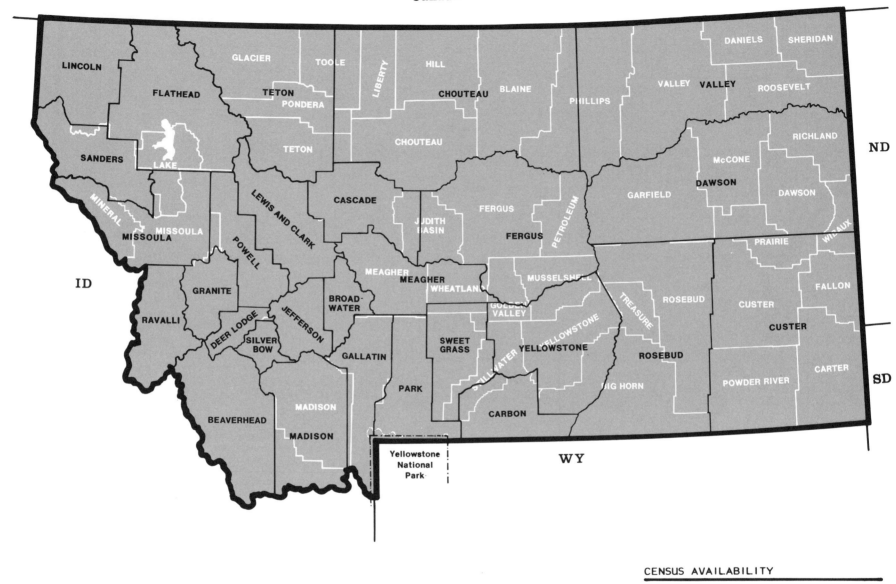

Canada

LINCOLN

FLATHEAD

GLACIER

TETON

TOOLE

LIBERTY

HILL

CHOUTEAU

BLAINE

PHILLIPS

DANIELS

SHERIDAN

VALLEY VALLEY

ROOSEVELT

SANDERS

PONDERA

TETON

CHOUTEAU

ND

RICHLAND

McCONE

DAWSON

DAWSON

MINERAL

LEWIS AND CLARK

CASCADE

JUDITH BASIN

FERGUS

FERGUS

PETROLEUM

GARFIELD

MISSOULA
MISSOULA

POWELL

PRAIRIE

WIBAUX

ID

GRANITE

MEAGHER

MEAGHER
WHEATLAND

MUSSELSHELL

TREASURE

ROSEBUD

FALLON

CUSTER

RAVALLI

DEER LODGE

JEFFERSON

BROAD-
WATER

GOLDEN
VALLEY

YELLOWSTONE

CUSTER

SILVER
BOW

GALLATIN

SWEET
GRASS

STILLWATER

YELLOWSTONE

ROSEBUD

BEAVERHEAD

MADISON

PARK

CARBON

BIG HORN

POWDER RIVER

CARTER

SD

MADISON

Yellowstone
National
Park

WY

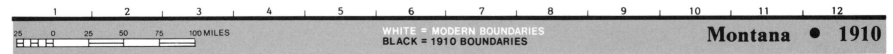

| 1 | 2 | 3 | 4 | 5 | 6 | 7 | 8 | 9 | 10 | 11 | 12 |

25 0 25 50 75 100 MILES

WHITE = MODERN BOUNDARIES
BLACK = 1910 BOUNDARIES

Montana ● 1910

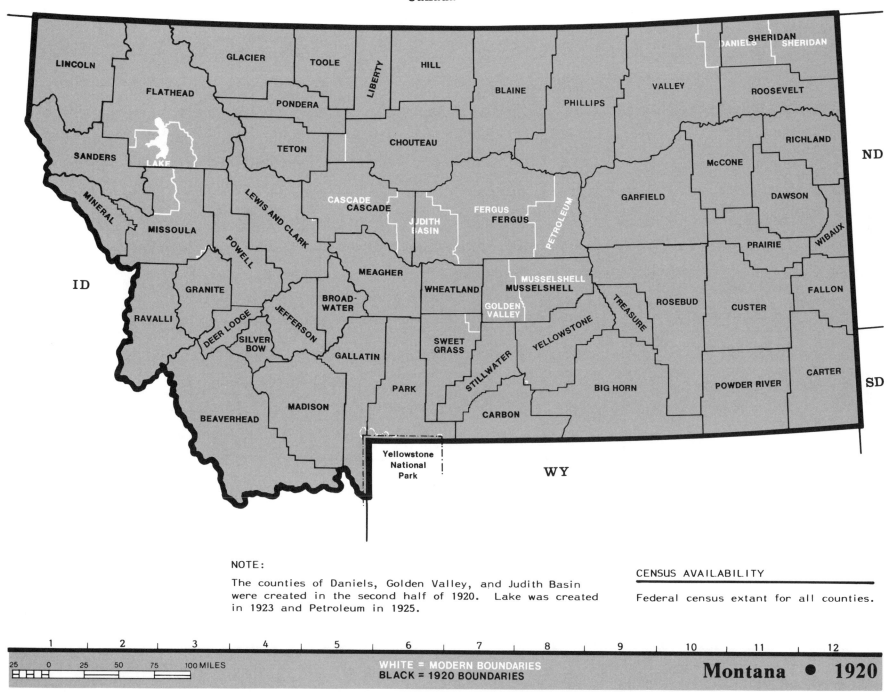

Canada

LINCOLN
GLACIER
TOOLE
HILL
SHERIDAN
DANIELS
SHERIDAN
FLATHEAD
PONDERA
LIBERTY
BLAINE
VALLEY
ROOSEVELT
SANDERS
LAKE
TETON
PHILLIPS
RICHLAND
MINERAL
MISSOULA
LEWIS AND CLARK
CHOUTEAU
McCONE
DAWSON
CASCADE
CASCADE
FERGUS
FERGUS
PETROLEUM
GARFIELD
ID
POWELL
JUDITH
BASIN
WIBAUX
GRANITE
MEAGHER
MUSSELSHELL
MUSSELSHELL
PRAIRIE
ND
RAVALLI
DEER LODGE
BROAD-
WATER
WHEATLAND
GOLDEN
VALLEY
TREASURE
ROSEBUD
CUSTER
FALLON
SILVER
BOW
JEFFERSON
SWEET
GRASS
YELLOWSTONE
BIG HORN
BEAVERHEAD
GALLATIN
STILLWATER
POWDER RIVER
CARTER
MADISON
PARK
CARBON
SD
Yellowstone
National
Park
WY

NOTE:

The counties of Daniels, Golden Valley, and Judith Basin
were created in the second half of 1920. Lake was created
in 1923 and Petroleum in 1925.

CENSUS AVAILABILITY

Federal census extant for all counties.

| 1 | 2 | 3 | 4 | 5 | 6 | 7 | 8 | 9 | 10 | 11 | 12 |

25 0 25 50 75 100 MILES

WHITE = MODERN BOUNDARIES
BLACK = 1920 BOUNDARIES

Montana ● 1920

MAP GUIDE TO THE U.S. FEDERAL CENSUSES, 1790-1920 by William Thorndale and William Dollarhide. Copyright 1987, all rights reserved.

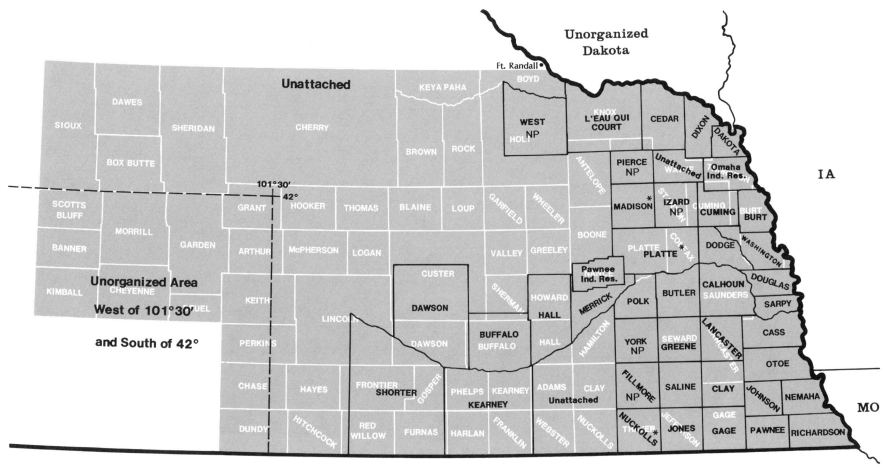

Unorganized
Dakota

Ft. Randall ●

Unattached

KEYA PAHA   BOYD

SIOUX   DAWES   SHERIDAN   CHERRY   WEST NP   KNOX L'EAU QUI COURT   CEDAR   DIXON   DAKOTA

HOLT   BROWN   ROCK   ANTELOPE   PIERCE NP   Unattached WAYNE   Omaha Ind. Res.   IA

BOX BUTTE   GRANT   HOOKER   THOMAS   BLAINE   LOUP   GARFIELD   WHEELER   MADISON *   IZARD NP   CUMING   CUMING   BURT

SCOTTS BLUFF   101°30'   42°

MORRILL   GARDEN   ARTHUR   McPHERSON   LOGAN   VALLEY   GREELEY   BOONE   PLATTE   PLATTE *   COLFAX   DODGE   WASHINGTON

BANNER   Unorganized Area   West of 101°30'   CUSTER   Pawnee Ind. Res.   DOUGLAS

KIMBALL   CHEYENNE   FUEL   KEITH   DAWSON   SHERMAN   HOWARD   MERRICK   POLK   BUTLER   CALHOUN SAUNDERS   SARPY

and South of 42°   LINCOLN   DAWSON   HALL   HAMILTON   GREENE   LANCASTER   CASS

PERKINS   BUFFALO BUFFALO   HALL   YORK NP   SEWARD   OTOE

CHASE   HAYES   FRONTIER SHORTER   GOSPER   PHELPS   KEARNEY   ADAMS   CLAY   FILLMORE NP   SALINE   CLAY   JOHNSON   NEMAHA   MO

KEARNEY   Unattached

DUNDY   HITCHCOCK   RED WILLOW   FURNAS   HARLAN   FRANKLIN   WEBSTER   NUCKOLLS   NUCKOLLS *   JEFFERSON   JONES GAGE   GAGE   PAWNEE   RICHARDSON

Kansas Territory

*NOTES:

Nebraska became a territory in 1854. For its
boundaries in 1860, see North Dakota 1850–1860
(p.259) or Colorado Notes (p.51).

Various changes in county names by 1870 are not
explained here, except note that by 1870 the
name Nuckolls had been moved west one county.

Counties without white settlers are shown
as NP (no population).

*CENSUS AVAILABILITY

Federal census extant for all counties,
Madison being enumerated with Platte.

1   2   3   4   5   6   7   8   9   10   11   12

25   0   25   50   75   100 MILES

WHITE = MODERN BOUNDARIES
BLACK = 1860 BOUNDARIES

Nebraska ● 1860
AS PART OF NEBRASKA TERRITORY

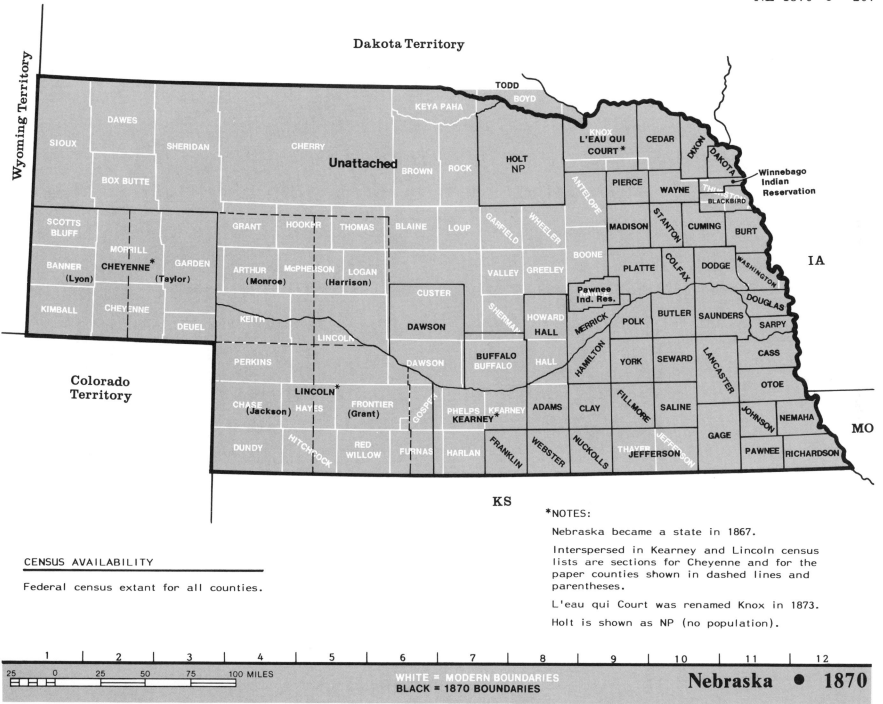

Dakota Territory

Wyoming Territory

Colorado Territory

KS

IA

MO

TODD

BOYD

KEYA PAHA

SIOUX

DAWES

SHERIDAN

CHERRY

Unattached

BROWN

ROCK

HOLT
NP

L'EAU QUI
COURT *

KNOX

CEDAR

DIXON

DAKOTA

Winnebago
Indian
Reservation

BOX BUTTE

ANTELOPE

PIERCE

WAYNE

THURSTON

BLACKBIRD

SCOTTS
BLUFF

GRANT

HOOKER

THOMAS

BLAINE

LOUP

GARFIELD

WHEELER

MADISON

STANTON

CUMING

BURT

MORRILL
CHEYENNE *
(Taylor)

GARDEN

ARTHUR
(Monroe)

McPHERSON

LOGAN
(Harrison)

VALLEY

GREELEY

BOONE

PLATTE

COLFAX

DODGE

WASHINGTON

BANNER
(Lyon)

CUSTER

SHERMAN

HOWARD

HALL

MERRICK

POLK

BUTLER

SAUNDERS

DOUGLAS

KIMBALL

CHEYENNE

KEITH

DAWSON

Pawnee
Ind. Res.

SARPY

DEUEL

LINCOLN

DAWSON

BUFFALO
Buffalo

HALL

HAMILTON

YORK

SEWARD

LANCASTER

CASS

PERKINS

LINCOLN *

OTOE

CHASE
(Jackson)

HAYES

FRONTIER
(Grant)

GOSPER

PHELPS

KEARNEY

KEARNEY *

ADAMS

CLAY

FILLMORE

SALINE

GAGE

JOHNSON

NEMAHA

DUNDY

HITCHCOCK

RED
WILLOW

FURNAS

HARLAN

FRANKLIN

WEBSTER

NUCKOLLS

THAYER

JEFFERSON

JEFFERSON

PAWNEE

RICHARDSON

CENSUS AVAILABILITY

Federal census extant for all counties.

*NOTES:

Nebraska became a state in 1867.

Interspersed in Kearney and Lincoln census
lists are sections for Cheyenne and for the
paper counties shown in dashed lines and
parentheses.

L'eau qui Court was renamed Knox in 1873.

Holt is shown as NP (no population).

1   2   3   4   5   6   7   8   9   10   11   12

25   0   25   50   75   100 MILES

WHITE = MODERN BOUNDARIES
BLACK = 1870 BOUNDARIES

Nebraska ● 1870

MAP GUIDE TO THE U.S. FEDERAL CENSUSES, 1790–1920 by William Thorndale and William Dollarhide. Copyright 1987, all rights reserved.

Dakota Territory

Wyoming Territory

IA

CO

MO

KS

*NOTES:

The tiny strip of unattached land between Nance and Greeley was added to Nance in 1881.

Burt, Cuming, and Wayne are shown extended partly into the Omaha and Winnebago Indian lands. Blackbird County covered the rest of the reservations.

CENSUS AVAILABILITY

Federal census extant for all counties.

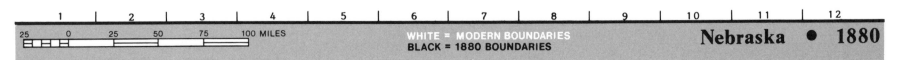

1   2   3   4   5   6   7   8   9   10   11   12

25   0   25   50   75   100 MILES   WHITE = MODERN BOUNDARIES   **Nebraska ● 1880**
                                                BLACK = 1880 BOUNDARIES

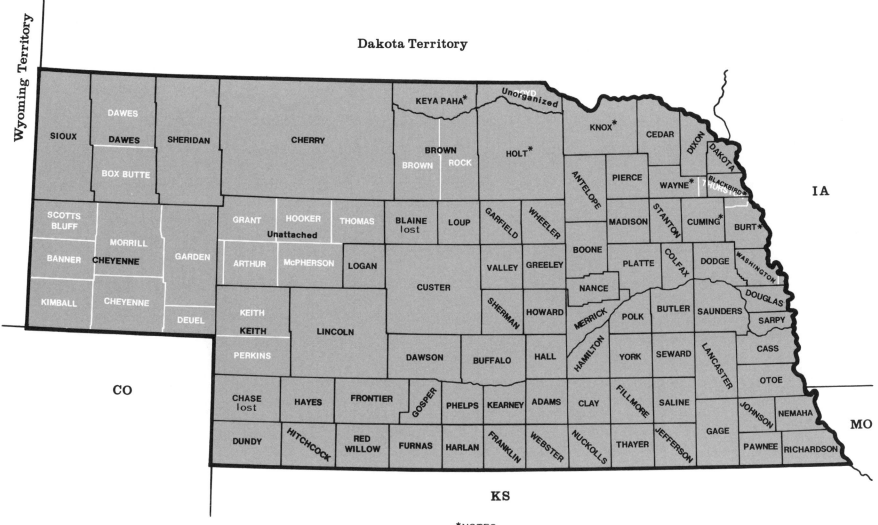

Dakota Territory

Wyoming Territory

IA

CO

MO

KS

CENSUS AVAILABILITY

Federal census extant for all counties
except Blaine and Chase, shown as
"lost" on map.

*NOTES:

Keya Paha and Knox received parts of the area transferred
in 1882 from Dakota Territory to Nebraska. But the 1883 act
adding the remainder to Holt required voter approval, which
the courts ruled was not done.

Burt, Cuming, and Wayne are shown extended partly into the
Omaha and Winnebago Indian lands. Blackbird County covered
the rest of the reservations and was renamed Thurston in 1889.

1   2   3   4   5   6   7   8   9   10   11   12

25 0 25 50 75 100 MILES

Nebraska ● 1885

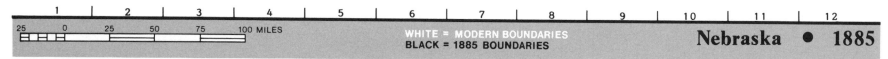

MAP GUIDE TO THE U.S. FEDERAL CENSUSES, 1790–1920 by William Thorndale and William Dollarhide. Copyright 1987, all rights reserved.

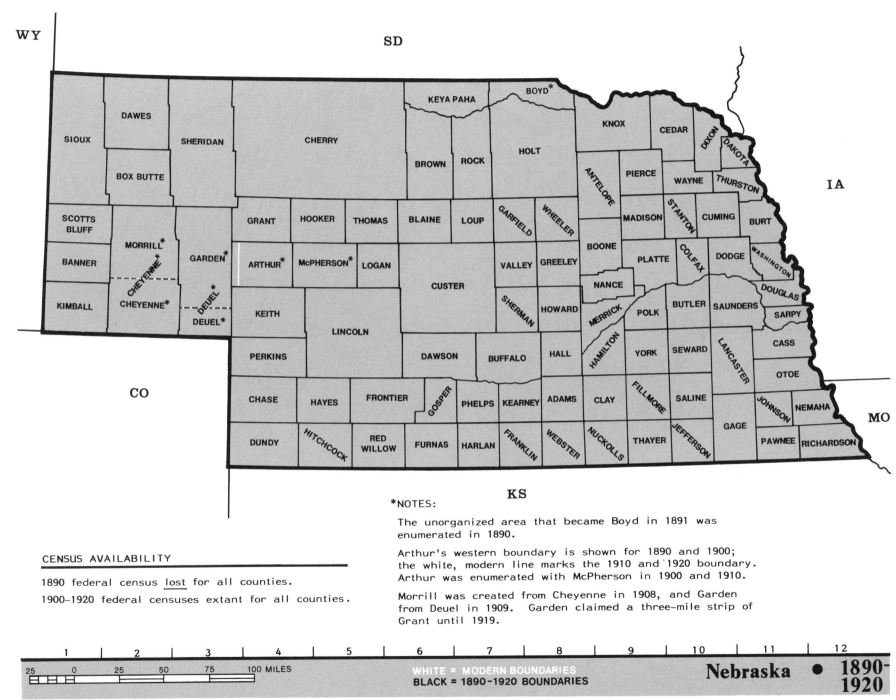

WY

SD

IA

CO

MO

KS

*NOTES:

The unorganized area that became Boyd in 1891 was enumerated in 1890.

Arthur's western boundary is shown for 1890 and 1900; the white, modern line marks the 1910 and 1920 boundary. Arthur was enumerated with McPherson in 1900 and 1910.

Morrill was created from Cheyenne in 1908, and Garden from Deuel in 1909. Garden claimed a three-mile strip of Grant until 1919.

CENSUS AVAILABILITY

1890 federal census lost for all counties.

1900-1920 federal censuses extant for all counties.

1 2 3 4 5 6 7 8 9 10 11 12

25 0 25 50 75 100 MILES

WHITE = MODERN BOUNDARIES
BLACK = 1890-1920 BOUNDARIES

Nebraska ● 1890-1920

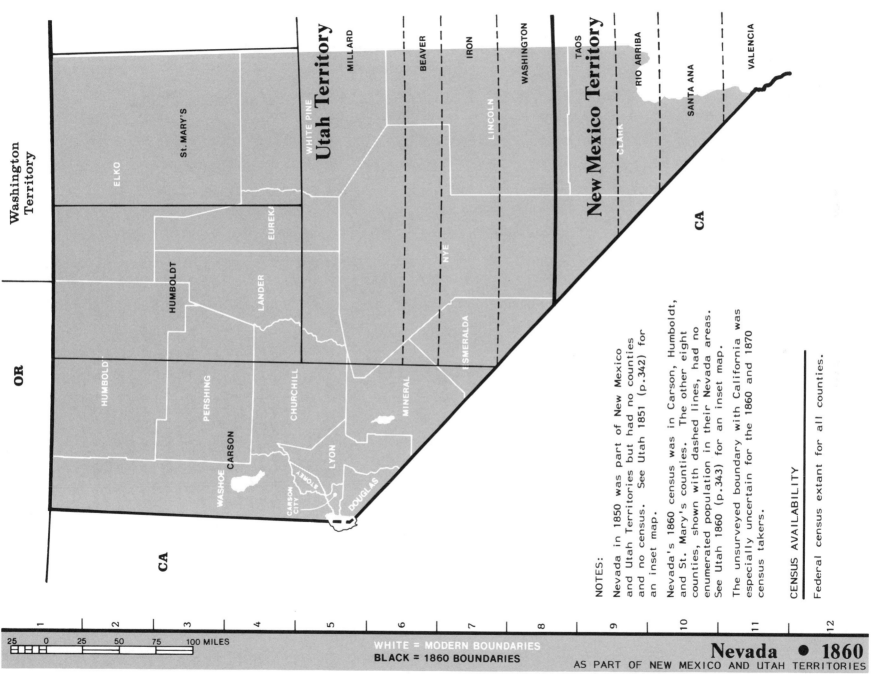

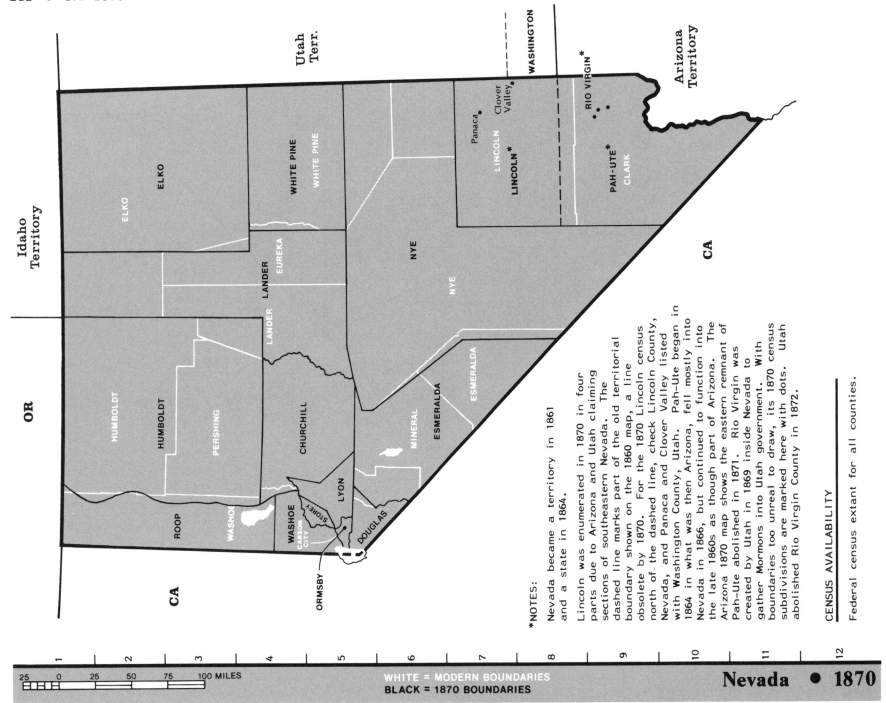

Idaho Territory

OR

CA

Utah Terr.

WASHINGTON

Arizona Territory

CA

ELKO

ELKO

WHITE PINE

WHITE PINE

RIO VIRGIN *

LINCOLN *

LINCOLN

Panaca

Clover Valley

PAH-UTE *

CLARK

LANDER

EUREKA

LANDER

NYE

NYE

HUMBOLDT

HUMBOLDT

PERSHING

CHURCHILL

ESMERALDA

ESMERALDA

MINERAL

ROOP

WASHOE

WASHOE
CARSON CITY

STOREY

LYON

DOUGLAS

ORMSBY

*NOTES:

Nevada became a territory in 1861 and a state in 1864.

Lincoln was enumerated in 1870 in four parts due to Arizona and Utah claiming sections of southeastern Nevada. The dashed line marks part of the old territorial boundary shown on the 1860 map, a line obsolete by 1870. For the 1870 Lincoln census north of the dashed line, check Lincoln County, Nevada, and Panaca and Clover Valley listed with Washington County, Utah. Pah-Ute began in 1864 in what was then Arizona, fell mostly into Nevada in 1866, but continued to function into the late 1860s as though part of Arizona. The Arizona 1870 map shows the eastern remnant of Pah-Ute abolished in 1871. Rio Virgin was created by Utah in 1869 inside Nevada to gather Mormons into Utah government. With boundaries too unreal to draw, its 1870 census subdivisions are marked here with dots. Utah abolished Rio Virgin County in 1872.

CENSUS AVAILABILITY

Federal census extant for all counties.

1   2   3   4   5   6   7   8   9   10   11   12

25 0 25 50 75 100 MILES

WHITE = MODERN BOUNDARIES
BLACK = 1870 BOUNDARIES

Nevada ● 1870

MAP GUIDE TO THE U.S. FEDERAL CENSUSES, 1790-1920 by William Thorndale and William Dollarhide. Copyright 1987, all rights reserved.

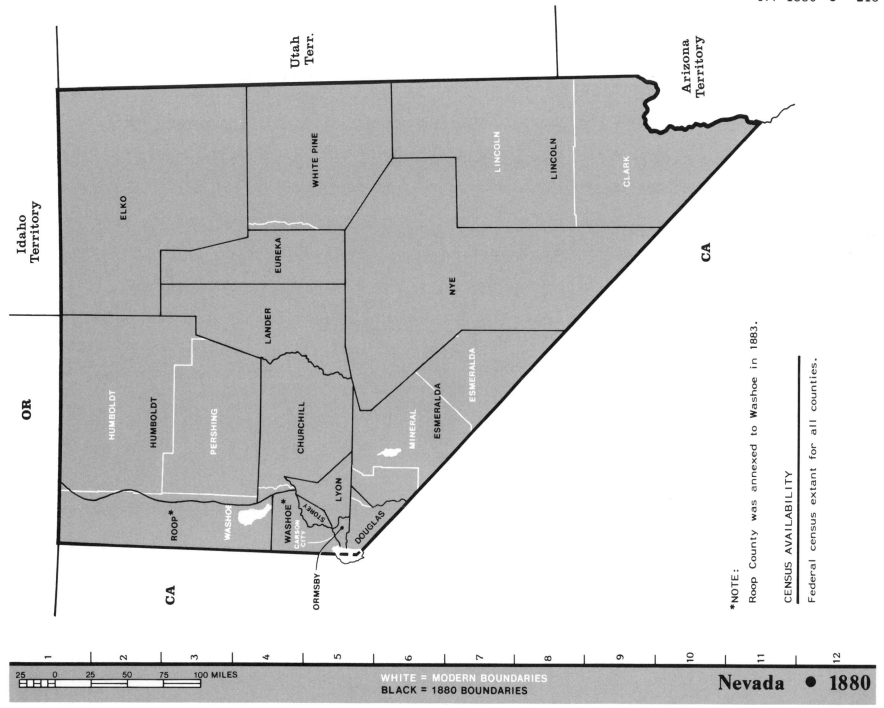

Idaho
Territory

OR

CA

Utah Terr.

Arizona
Territory

CA

ELKO

WHITE PINE

EUREKA

LINCOLN

LINCOLN

CLARK

LANDER

NYE

HUMBOLDT

HUMBOLDT

PERSHING

CHURCHILL

ESMERALDA

ESMERALDA

MINERAL

ESMERALDA

LYON

ROOP*

WASHOE

WASHOE*

STOREY

CARSON CITY

DOUGLAS

ORMSBY

*NOTE:
Roop County was annexed to Washoe in 1883.

CENSUS AVAILABILITY

Federal census extant for all counties.

25   0   25   50   75   100 MILES

WHITE = MODERN BOUNDARIES
BLACK = 1880 BOUNDARIES

Nevada ● 1880

MAP GUIDE TO THE U.S. FEDERAL CENSUSES, 1790-1920 by William Thorndale and William Dollarhide. Copyright 1987, all rights reserved.

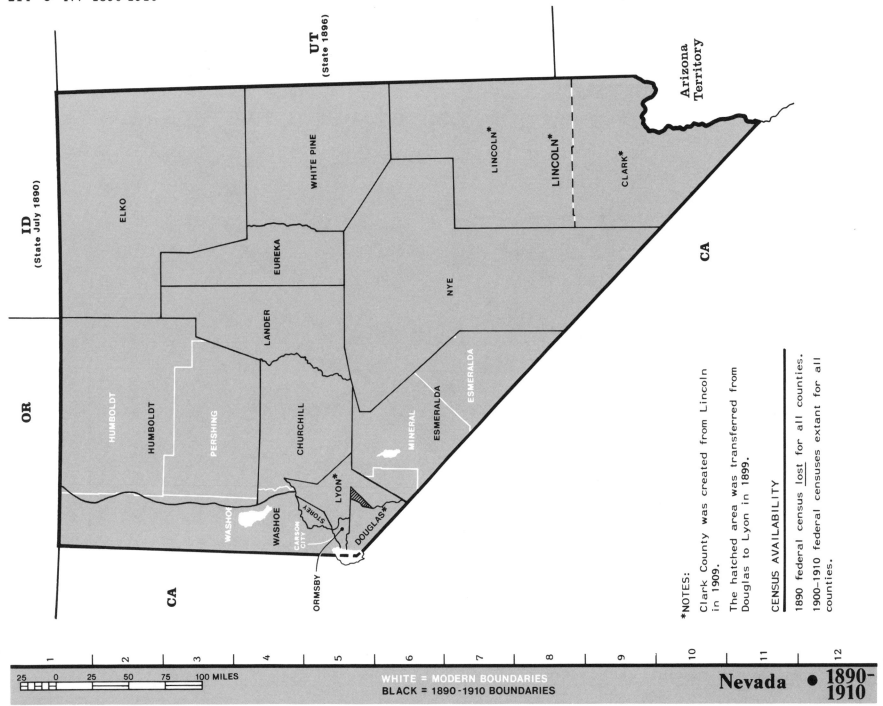

ID
(State July 1890)

OR

UT
(State 1896)

Arizona
Territory

CA

CA

ELKO

WHITE PINE

EUREKA

LINCOLN*

LINCOLN*

CLARK*

LANDER

NYE

HUMBOLDT

HUMBOLDT

PERSHING

CHURCHILL

ESMERALDA

ESMERALDA

WASHOE

WASHOE

STOREY

LYON*

MINERAL

ESMERALDA

CARSON
CITY

DOUGLAS*

ORMSBY

*NOTES:

Clark County was created from Lincoln
in 1909.

The hatched area was transferred from
Douglas to Lyon in 1899.

CENSUS AVAILABILITY

1890 federal census lost for all counties.

1900-1910 federal censuses extant for all
counties.

25   0   25   50   75   100 MILES

WHITE = MODERN BOUNDARIES
BLACK = 1890-1910 BOUNDARIES

Nevada ● **1890–1910**

MAP GUIDE TO THE U.S. FEDERAL CENSUSES, 1790-1920 by William Thorndale and William Dollarhide. Copyright 1987, all rights reserved.

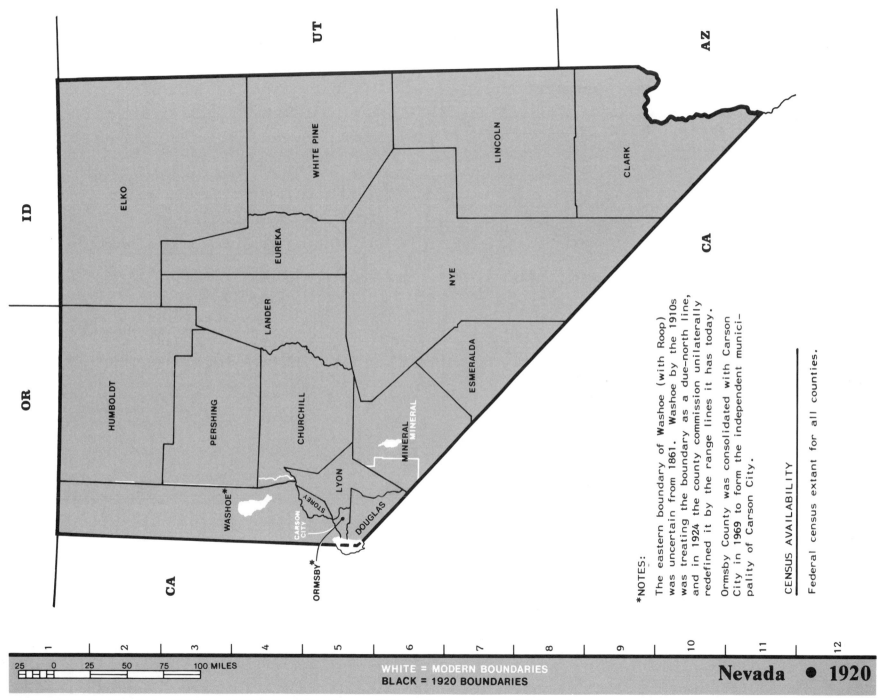

*NOTES:

The eastern boundary of Washoe (with Roop) was uncertain from 1861. Washoe by the 1910s was treating the boundary as a due-north line, and in 1924 the county commission unilaterally redefined it by the range lines it has today.

Ormsby County was consolidated with Carson City in 1969 to form the independent munici-pality of Carson City.

CENSUS AVAILABILITY

Federal census extant for all counties.

25 0 25 50 75 100 MILES

WHITE = MODERN BOUNDARIES
BLACK = 1920 BOUNDARIES

Nevada ● 1920

MAP GUIDE TO THE U.S. FEDERAL CENSUSES, 1790–1920 by William Thorndale and William Dollarhide. Copyright 1987, all rights reserved.

Canada

Line of
U.S. claim →

→ Line of
British claim

FRANKLIN

ORLEANS

ESSEX

CHITTENDEN

COOS

Maine
(in Massachusetts)

LAMOILLE

CHITTENDEN

CALEDONIA

ORANGE

GRAFTON

WASHINGTON

GRAFTON

NY

ORANGE

CARROLL

ADDISON

*

RUTLAND

WINDSOR

BELKNAP

STRAFFORD

SULLIVAN

STRAFFORD

MERRIMACK

BENNINGTON

CHESHIRE

ROCKINGHAM

WINDHAM

HILLSBOROUGH

Atlantic Ocean

ROCKINGHAM

CHESHIRE

HILLSBOROUGH

VT   NH

MA

CENSUS AVAILABILITY – VERMONT

Federal census extant for all counties.

*NOTES – VERMONT

Vermont joined the Union in March 1791. Its federal census officially began 4 April 1791, to run for five months.

Vermont county boundaries were the same for 1790 and 1791, except that the town of Hancock -- shown by dashed lines and an asterisk -- was in Windsor County in 1790 and transferred to Addison County in January 1791.

CENSUS AVAILABILITY – NEW HAMPSHIRE

Federal census extant for all counties.

| 1 | 2 | 3 | 4 | 5 | 6 | 7 | 8 | 9 | 10 | 11 | 12 |

25   0   25   50 MILES

WHITE = MODERN BOUNDARIES
BLACK = 1790 BOUNDARIES

New Hampshire & Vermont ● 1790

MAP GUIDE TO THE U.S. FEDERAL CENSUSES, 1790–1920 by William Thorndale and William Dollarhide. Copyright 1987, all rights reserved.

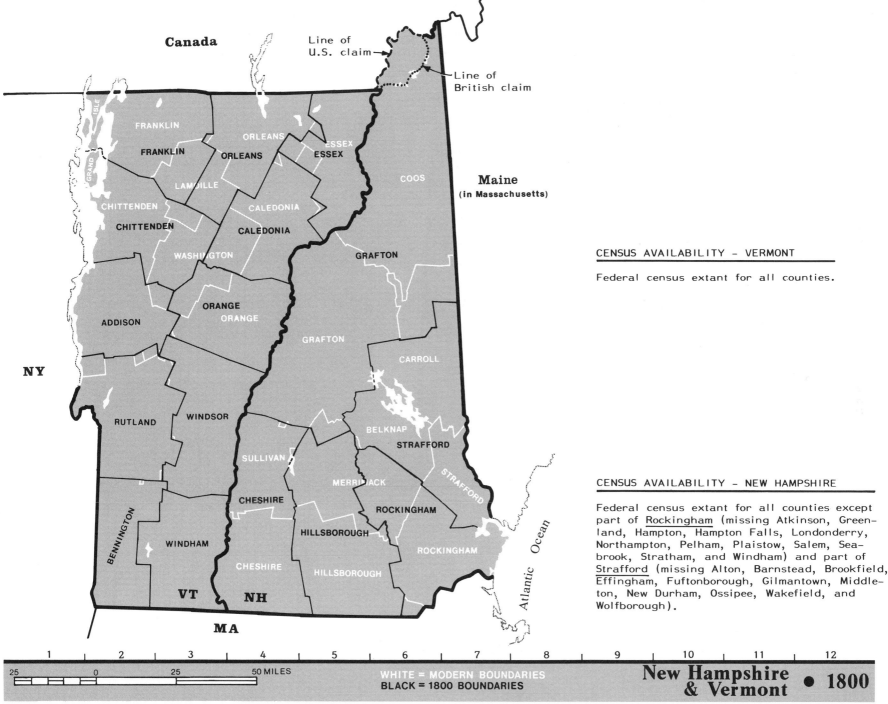

Canada

Line of
U.S. claim →

→ Line of
British claim

FRANKLIN

FRANKLIN

ORLEANS

ORLEANS

ESSEX

ESSEX

Maine
(in Massachusetts)

LAMOILLE

CHITTENDEN

CALEDONIA

CHITTENDEN

CALEDONIA

COOS

WASHINGTON

GRAFTON

NY

ADDISON

ORANGE

ORANGE

GRAFTON

CARROLL

RUTLAND

WINDSOR

BELKNAP

STRAFFORD

SULLIVAN

STRAFFORD

MERRIMACK

BENNINGTON

CHESHIRE

ROCKINGHAM

HILLSBOROUGH

WINDHAM

ROCKINGHAM

Atlantic Ocean

CHESHIRE

HILLSBOROUGH

VT   NH

MA

CENSUS AVAILABILITY – VERMONT

Federal census extant for all counties.

CENSUS AVAILABILITY – NEW HAMPSHIRE

Federal census extant for all counties except part of Rockingham (missing Atkinson, Greenland, Hampton, Hampton Falls, Londonderry, Northampton, Pelham, Plaistow, Salem, Seabrook, Stratham, and Windham) and part of Strafford (missing Alton, Barnstead, Brookfield, Effingham, Fuftonborough, Gilmantown, Middleton, New Durham, Ossipee, Wakefield, and Wolfborough).

| 1 | 2 | 3 | 4 | 5 | 6 | 7 | 8 | 9 | 10 | 11 | 12 |

25   0   25   50 MILES

WHITE = MODERN BOUNDARIES
BLACK = 1800 BOUNDARIES

**New Hampshire
& Vermont** ● **1800**

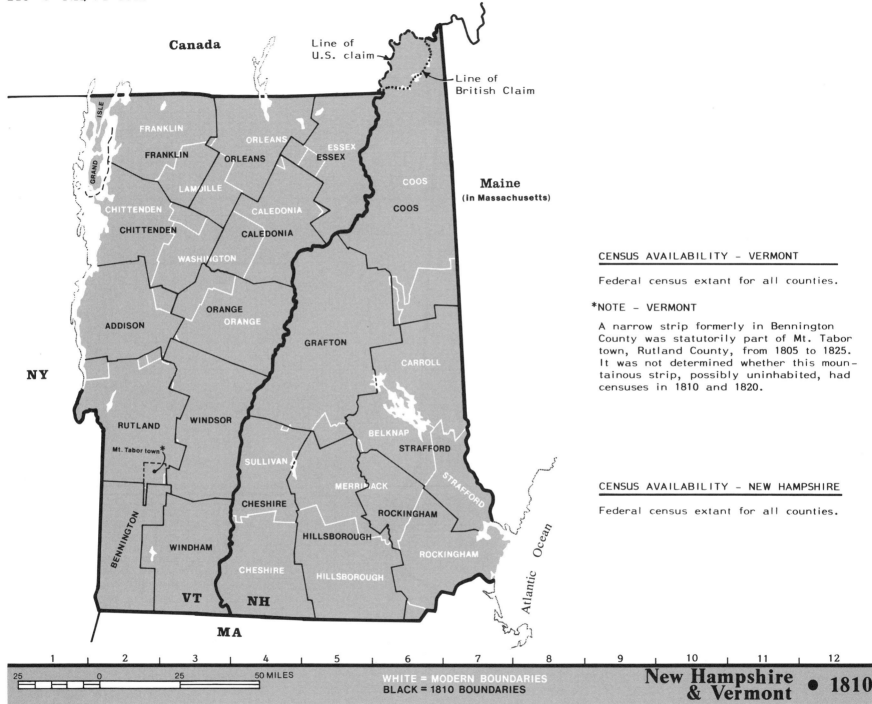

Canada

Line of
U.S. claim

Line of
British Claim

FRANKLIN

FRANKLIN

ORLEANS

ORLEANS

ESSEX

ESSEX

COOS

Maine
(in Massachusetts)

LAMOILLE

CHITTENDEN

CALEDONIA

COOS

CHITTENDEN

CALEDONIA

WASHINGTON

ORANGE

NY

ADDISON

ORANGE

GRAFTON

CARROLL

RUTLAND

WINDSOR

Mt. Tabor town *

BELKNAP

STRAFFORD

SULLIVAN

STRAFFORD

MERRIMACK

BENNINGTON

CHESHIRE

ROCKINGHAM

WINDHAM

HILLSBOROUGH

ROCKINGHAM

CHESHIRE

HILLSBOROUGH

Atlantic Ocean

VT   NH

MA

CENSUS AVAILABILITY – VERMONT

Federal census extant for all counties.

*NOTE – VERMONT

A narrow strip formerly in Bennington County was statutorily part of Mt. Tabor town, Rutland County, from 1805 to 1825. It was not determined whether this mountainous strip, possibly uninhabited, had censuses in 1810 and 1820.

CENSUS AVAILABILITY – NEW HAMPSHIRE

Federal census extant for all counties.

25 0 25 50 MILES

1 2 3 4 5 6 7 8 9 10 11 12

WHITE = MODERN BOUNDARIES
BLACK = 1810 BOUNDARIES

New Hampshire
& Vermont   ● 1810

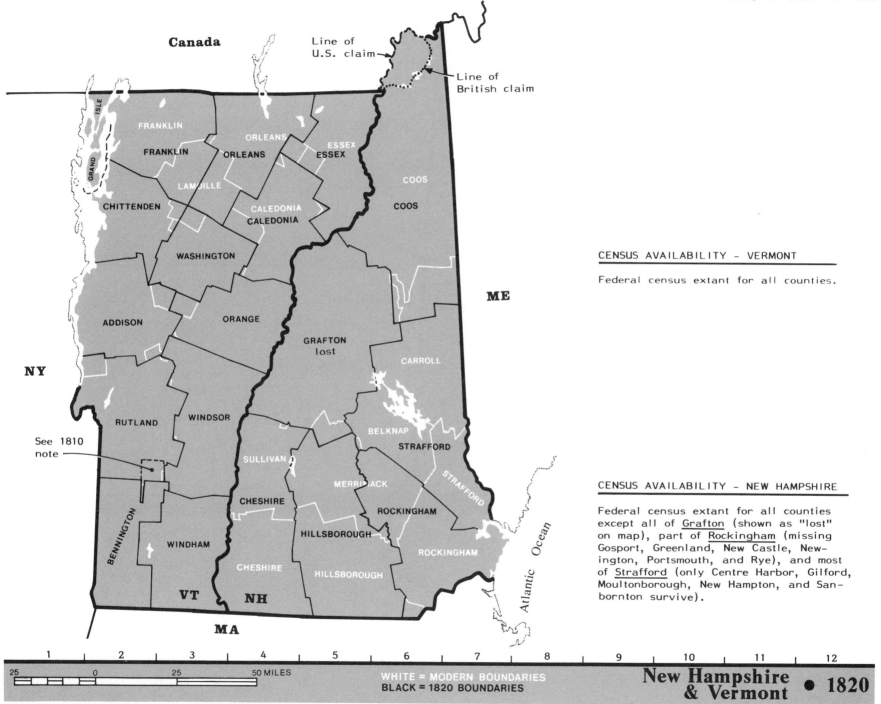

Canada

Line of
U.S. claim

Line of
British claim

FRANKLIN

FRANKLIN

ORLEANS

ORLEANS

ESSEX

ESSEX

GRAND ISLE

LAMOILLE

CHITTENDEN

CALEDONIA

CALEDONIA

COOS

COOS

WASHINGTON

ME

NY

ADDISON

ORANGE

GRAFTON
lost

CARROLL

RUTLAND

WINDSOR

See 1810
note

BELKNAP

STRAFFORD

STRAFFORD

SULLIVAN

BENNINGTON

CHESHIRE

MERRIMACK

ROCKINGHAM

WINDHAM

HILLSBOROUGH

CHESHIRE

ROCKINGHAM

HILLSBOROUGH

Atlantic Ocean

VT   NH

MA

CENSUS AVAILABILITY – VERMONT

Federal census extant for all counties.

CENSUS AVAILABILITY – NEW HAMPSHIRE

Federal census extant for all counties
except all of <u>Grafton</u> (shown as "lost"
on map), part of <u>Rockingham</u> (missing
Gosport, Greenland, New Castle, New-
ington, Portsmouth, and Rye), and most
of <u>Strafford</u> (only Centre Harbor, Gilford,
Moultonborough, New Hampton, and San-
bornton survive).

| 1 | 2 | 3 | 4 | 5 | 6 | 7 | 8 | 9 | 10 | 11 | 12 |

25   0   25   50 MILES

WHITE = MODERN BOUNDARIES
BLACK = 1820 BOUNDARIES

New Hampshire
& Vermont ● 1820

MAP GUIDE TO THE U.S. FEDERAL CENSUSES, 1790–1920 by William Thorndale and William Dollarhide. Copyright 1987, all rights reserved.

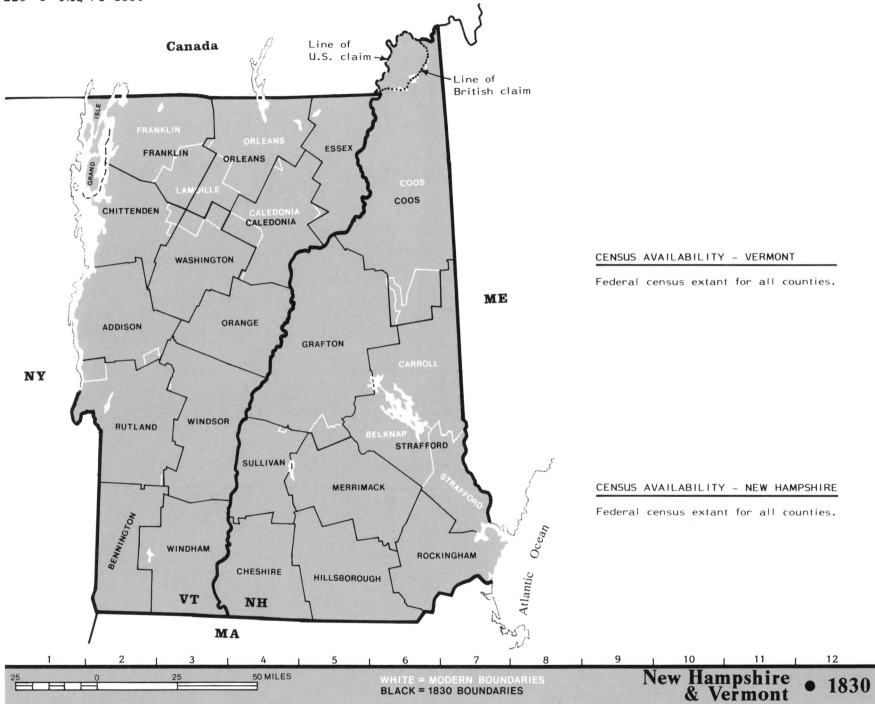

Canada

Line of
U.S. claim

Line of
British claim

FRANKLIN

ORLEANS

ESSEX

FRANKLIN

ORLEANS

GRAND ISLE

LAMOILLE

COOS

CHITTENDEN

CALEDONIA

COOS

CALEDONIA

WASHINGTON

ME

ADDISON

ORANGE

GRAFTON

NY

CARROLL

RUTLAND

WINDSOR

BELKNAP

STRAFFORD

SULLIVAN

STRAFFORD

BENNINGTON

MERRIMACK

Atlantic Ocean

WINDHAM

ROCKINGHAM

CHESHIRE

HILLSBOROUGH

VT

NH

MA

CENSUS AVAILABILITY – VERMONT

Federal census extant for all counties.

CENSUS AVAILABILITY – NEW HAMPSHIRE

Federal census extant for all counties.

1   2   3   4   5   6   7   8   9   10   11   12

25   0   25   50 MILES

WHITE = MODERN BOUNDARIES
BLACK = 1830 BOUNDARIES

**New Hampshire
& Vermont** ● **1830**

MAP GUIDE TO THE U.S. FEDERAL CENSUSES, 1790–1920 by William Thorndale and William Dollarhide. Copyright 1987, all rights reserved.

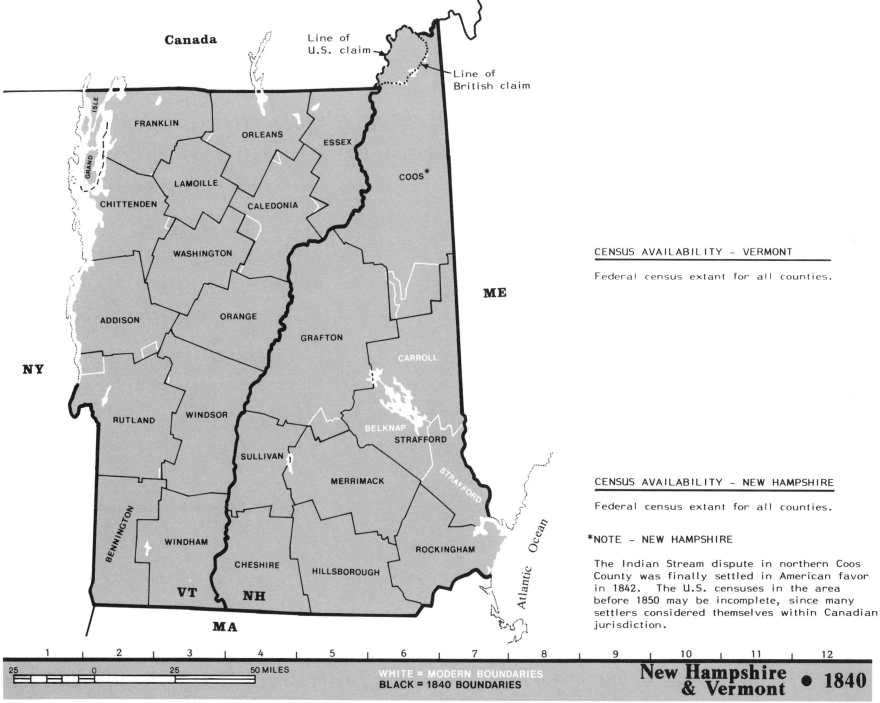

Canada

Line of
U.S. claim

Line of
British claim

FRANKLIN

ORLEANS

ESSEX

ISLE

GRAND

LAMOILLE

COOS*

CHITTENDEN

CALEDONIA

ME

WASHINGTON

CENSUS AVAILABILITY – VERMONT

Federal census extant for all counties.

NY

ADDISON

ORANGE

GRAFTON

CARROLL

RUTLAND

WINDSOR

BELKNAP

STRAFFORD

STRAFFORD

SULLIVAN

CENSUS AVAILABILITY – NEW HAMPSHIRE

Federal census extant for all counties.

MERRIMACK

*NOTE – NEW HAMPSHIRE

BENNINGTON

WINDHAM

ROCKINGHAM

Atlantic Ocean

The Indian Stream dispute in northern Coos
County was finally settled in American favor
in 1842. The U.S. censuses in the area
before 1850 may be incomplete, since many
settlers considered themselves within Canadian
jurisdiction.

CHESHIRE

HILLSBOROUGH

VT

NH

MA

| 1 | 2 | 3 | 4 | 5 | 6 | 7 | 8 | 9 | 10 | 11 | 12 |

25 0 25 50 MILES

WHITE = MODERN BOUNDARIES
BLACK = 1840 BOUNDARIES

New Hampshire
& Vermont ● 1840

MAP GUIDE TO THE U.S. FEDERAL CENSUSES, 1790–1920 by William Thorndale and William Dollarhide. Copyright 1987, all rights reserved.

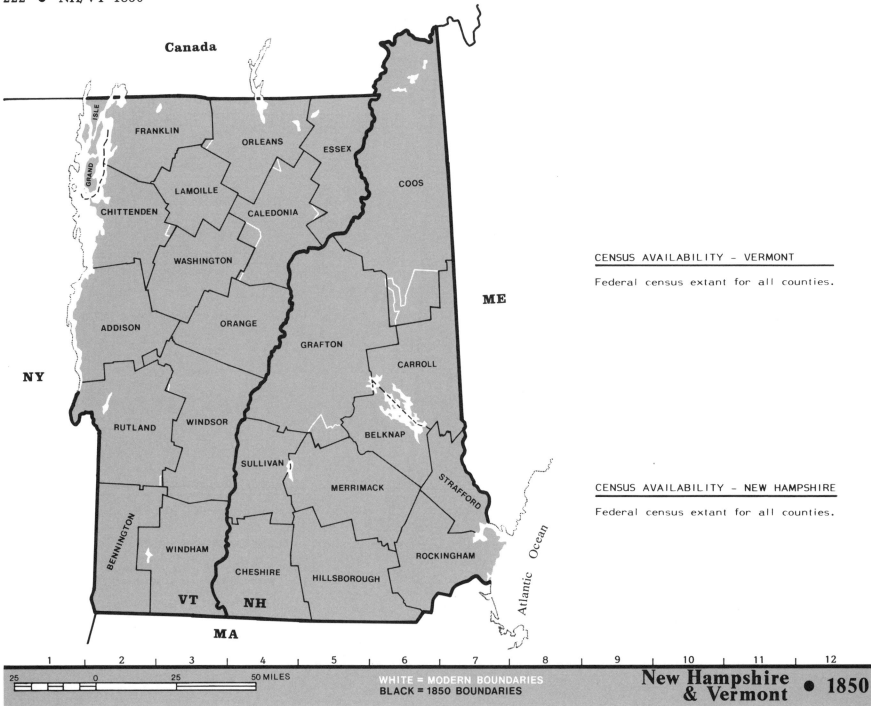

Canada

FRANKLIN

ORLEANS

ESSEX

ISLE

GRAND

LAMOILLE

COOS

CHITTENDEN

CALEDONIA

WASHINGTON

CENSUS AVAILABILITY – VERMONT

Federal census extant for all counties.

ME

ADDISON

ORANGE

GRAFTON

CARROLL

NY

RUTLAND

WINDSOR

BELKNAP

SULLIVAN

STRAFFORD

CENSUS AVAILABILITY – NEW HAMPSHIRE

Federal census extant for all counties.

BENNINGTON

MERRIMACK

WINDHAM

Atlantic Ocean

ROCKINGHAM

CHESHIRE

HILLSBOROUGH

VT   NH

MA

| 1 | 2 | 3 | 4 | 5 | 6 | 7 | 8 | 9 | 10 | 11 | 12 |

25   0   25   50 MILES

WHITE = MODERN BOUNDARIES
BLACK = 1850 BOUNDARIES

**New Hampshire
& Vermont** ● 1850

MAP GUIDE TO THE U.S. FEDERAL CENSUSES, 1790–1920 by William Thorndale and William Dollarhide. Copyright 1987, all rights reserved.

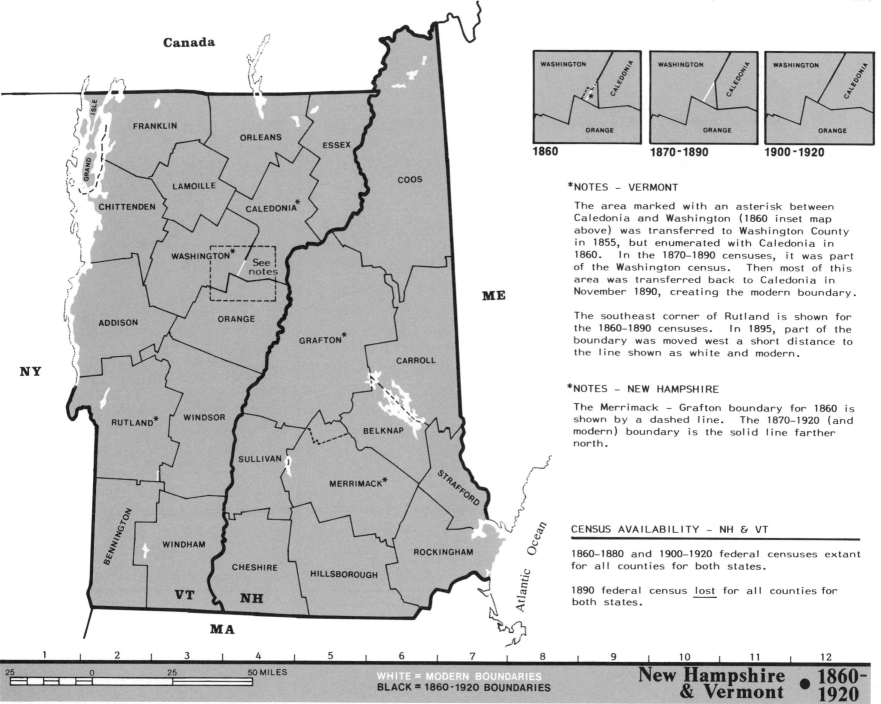

Canada

1860　**1870-1890**　**1900-1920**

WASHINGTON CALEDONIA ORANGE

FRANKLIN

ORLEANS

ESSEX

GRAND ISLE

LAMOILLE

COOS

CHITTENDEN

CALEDONIA*

WASHINGTON*

See notes

ME

ADDISON

ORANGE

GRAFTON*

CARROLL

NY

RUTLAND*

WINDSOR

BELKNAP

SULLIVAN

BENNINGTON

MERRIMACK*

STRAFFORD

WINDHAM

CHESHIRE

HILLSBOROUGH

ROCKINGHAM

Atlantic Ocean

VT　NH

MA

*NOTES – VERMONT

The area marked with an asterisk between Caledonia and Washington (1860 inset map above) was transferred to Washington County in 1855, but enumerated with Caledonia in 1860. In the 1870–1890 censuses, it was part of the Washington census. Then most of this area was transferred back to Caledonia in November 1890, creating the modern boundary.

The southeast corner of Rutland is shown for the 1860–1890 censuses. In 1895, part of the boundary was moved west a short distance to the line shown as white and modern.

*NOTES – NEW HAMPSHIRE

The Merrimack – Grafton boundary for 1860 is shown by a dashed line. The 1870–1920 (and modern) boundary is the solid line farther north.

CENSUS AVAILABILITY – NH & VT

1860–1880 and 1900–1920 federal censuses extant for all counties for both states.

1890 federal census lost for all counties for both states.

1　2　3　4　5　6　7　8　9　10　11　12

25　0　25　50 MILES

WHITE = MODERN BOUNDARIES
BLACK = 1860-1920 BOUNDARIES

New Hampshire & Vermont ● **1860-1920**

MAP GUIDE TO THE U.S. FEDERAL CENSUSES, 1790-1920 by William Thorndale and William Dollarhide. Copyright 1987, all rights reserved.

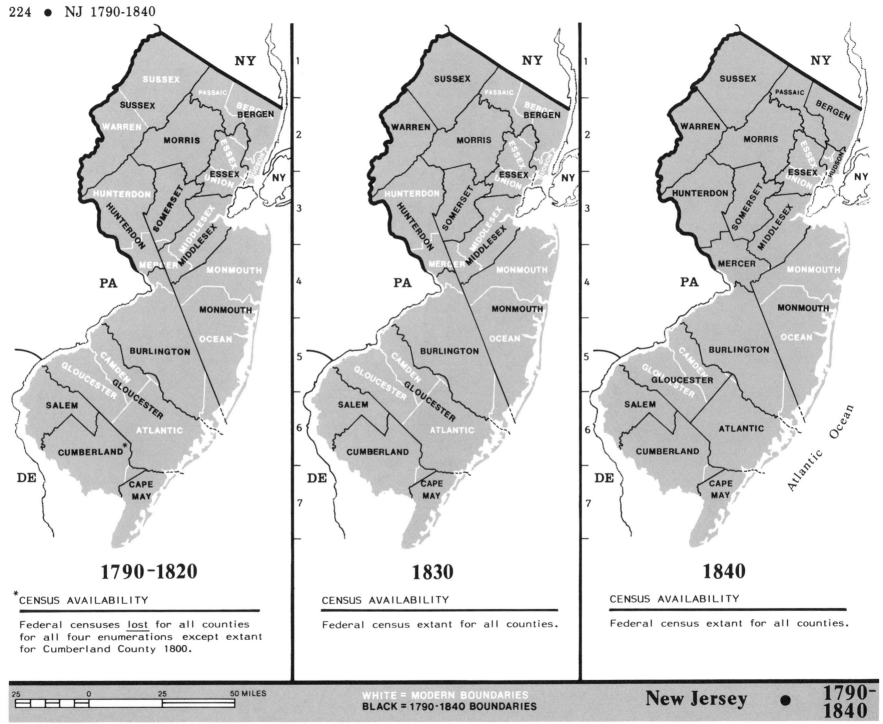

1790-1820

*CENSUS AVAILABILITY

Federal censuses lost for all counties for all four enumerations except extant for Cumberland County 1800.

1830

CENSUS AVAILABILITY

Federal census extant for all counties.

1840

CENSUS AVAILABILITY

Federal census extant for all counties.

25   0   25   50 MILES

WHITE = MODERN BOUNDARIES
BLACK = 1790-1840 BOUNDARIES

New Jersey ● **1790-1840**

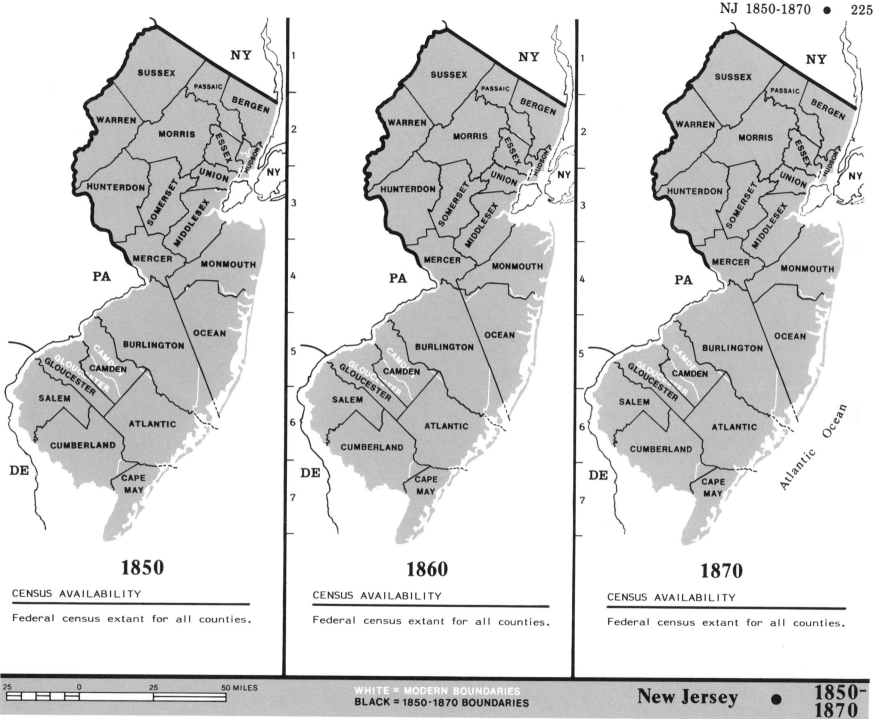

1850

CENSUS AVAILABILITY

Federal census extant for all counties.

1860

CENSUS AVAILABILITY

Federal census extant for all counties.

1870

CENSUS AVAILABILITY

Federal census extant for all counties.

25 0 25 50 MILES

WHITE = MODERN BOUNDARIES
BLACK = 1850-1870 BOUNDARIES

New Jersey ● **1850-1870**

MAP GUIDE TO THE U.S. FEDERAL CENSUSES, 1790–1920 by William Thorndale and William Dollarhide. Copyright 1987, all rights reserved.

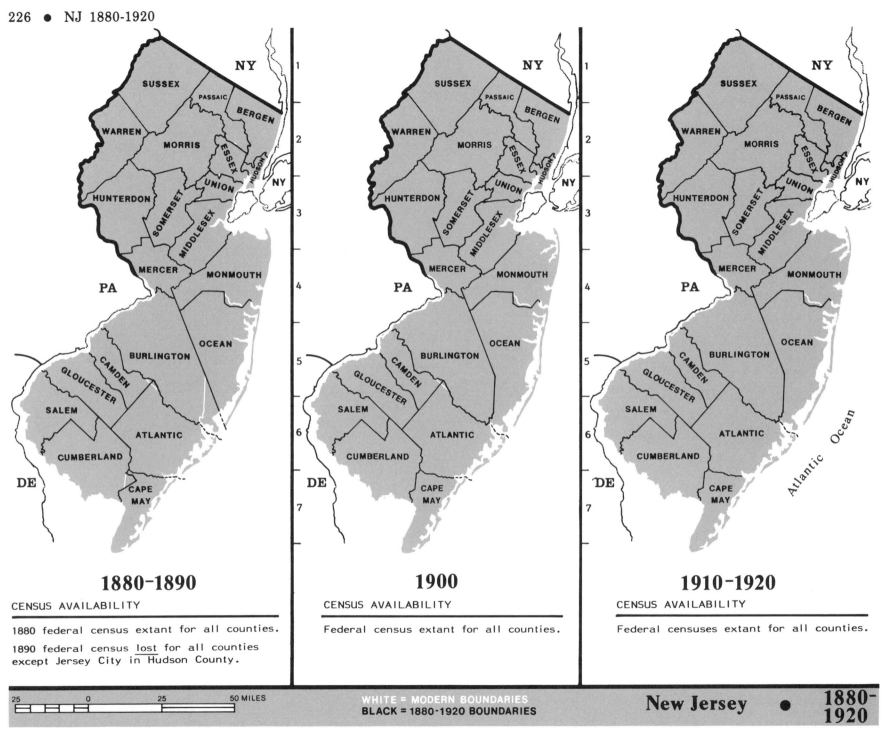

1880-1890

CENSUS AVAILABILITY

1880 federal census extant for all counties.

1890 federal census <u>lost</u> for all counties except Jersey City in Hudson County.

1900

CENSUS AVAILABILITY

Federal census extant for all counties.

1910-1920

CENSUS AVAILABILITY

Federal censuses extant for all counties.

25 0 25 50 MILES

WHITE = MODERN BOUNDARIES
BLACK = 1880-1920 BOUNDARIES

New Jersey ● **1880-1920**

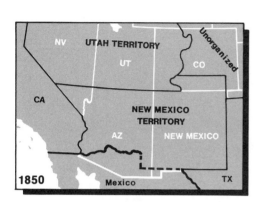

1850

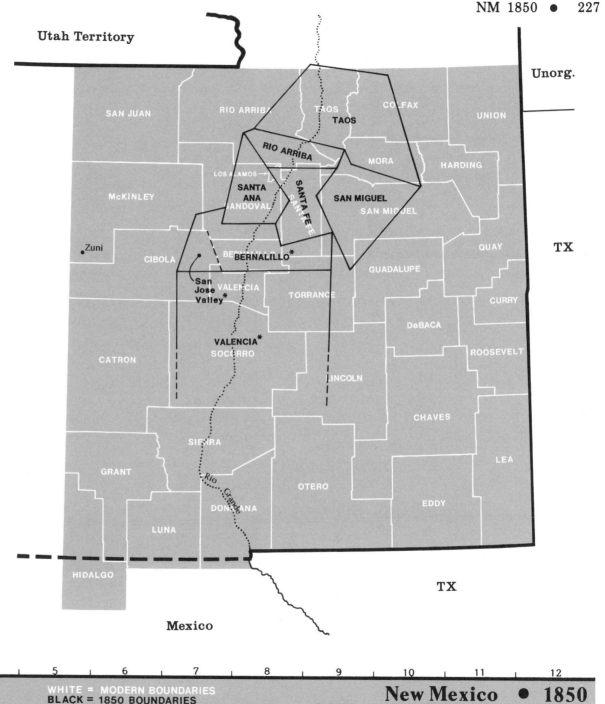

Utah Territory

Unorg.

TX

TX

Mexico

*NOTES:

The heavy dashed line represents the American boundary claim prior to the 1853 Gadsden Purchase.

The approximate county boundaries shown here are reproduced from a contemporary map.

Valencia County extended down the Rio Grande Valley to the Texas–Mexican line. Its 1850 census also included the villages of the San Jose Valley in what contemporary maps show as western Bernalillo. The first part of the 1850 Valencia schedules (to Acoma inclusive) contains these San Jose villages plus Zuni pueblo.

CENSUS AVAILABILITY

Federal census extant for all counties.

WHITE = MODERN BOUNDARIES
BLACK = 1850 BOUNDARIES

New Mexico ● 1850
AS PART OF NEW MEXICO TERRITORY

1 2 3 4 5 6 7 8 9 10 11 12

25 0 25 50 75 100 MILES

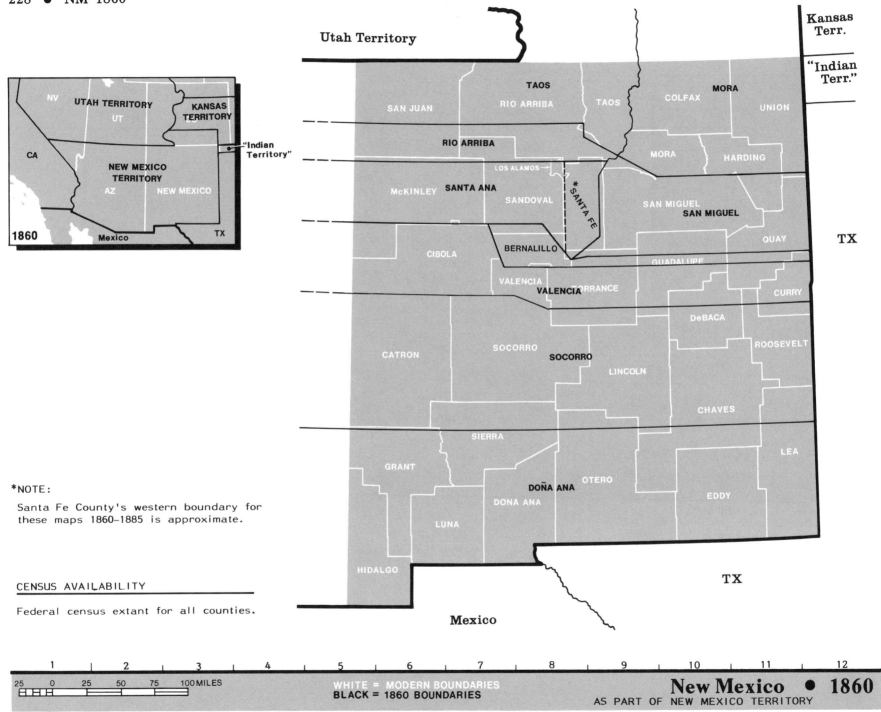

Utah Territory

Kansas Terr.

"Indian Terr."

NV
UTAH TERRITORY
UT

KANSAS TERRITORY

CA

"Indian Territory"

NEW MEXICO TERRITORY

AZ   NEW MEXICO

1860   Mexico   TX

TAOS

RIO ARRIBA   TAOS

MORA

COLFAX

UNION

SAN JUAN

RIO ARRIBA

MORA

HARDING

McKINLEY   SANTA ANA

SANDOVAL

LOS ALAMOS →

* SANTA FE

SAN MIGUEL

SAN MIGUEL

CIBOLA

BERNALILLO

QUAY

GUADALUPE

TX

VALENCIA   VALENCIA   TORRANCE

DeBACA

ROOSEVELT

CATRON   SOCORRO   SOCORRO

LINCOLN

CHAVES

CURRY

SIERRA

LEA

GRANT

OTERO

DOÑA ANA

EDDY

DONA ANA

LUNA

HIDALGO

TX

Mexico

*NOTE:

Santa Fe County's western boundary for these maps 1860–1885 is approximate.

CENSUS AVAILABILITY

Federal census extant for all counties.

1   2   3   4   5   6   7   8   9   10   11   12

25   0   25   50   75   100 MILES

WHITE = MODERN BOUNDARIES
BLACK = 1860 BOUNDARIES

New Mexico ● 1860

AS PART OF NEW MEXICO TERRITORY

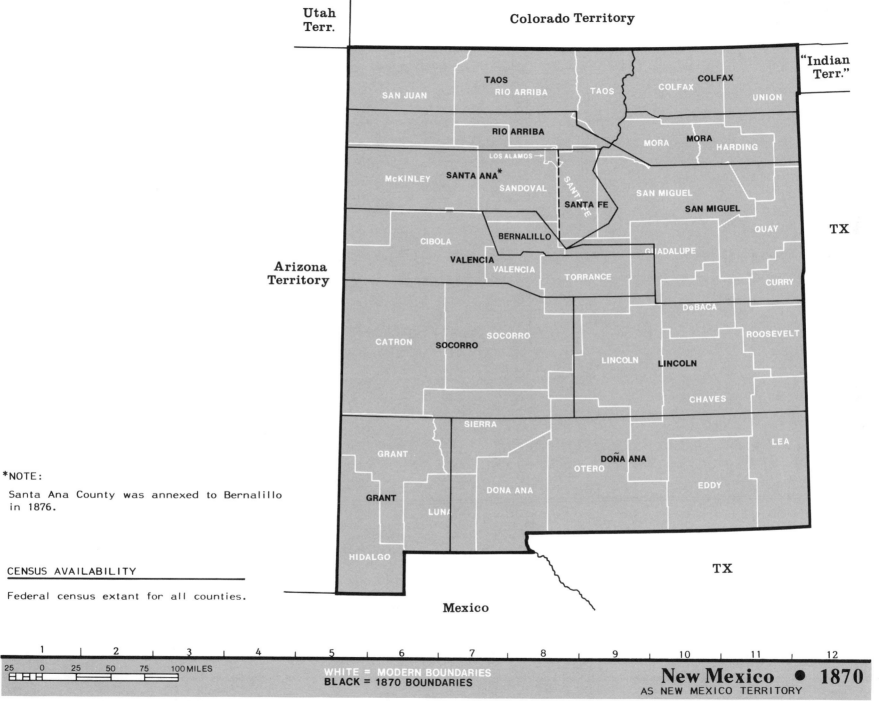

Utah Terr.

Colorado Territory

"Indian Terr."

TAOS
RIO ARRIBA
COLFAX
COLFAX
SAN JUAN
TAOS
COLFAX
UNION

RIO ARRIBA
MORA
MORA
HARDING

LOS ALAMOS →
SANTA ANA*
McKINLEY
SANDOVAL
SANTA FE
SAN MIGUEL
SANTA FE
SAN MIGUEL

BERNALILLO
CIBOLA
QUAY
VALENCIA
GUADALUPE
VALENCIA
TORRANCE
CURRY

DeBACA
CATRON
SOCORRO
SOCORRO
ROOSEVELT

Arizona Territory
LINCOLN
LINCOLN

CHAVES

SIERRA
LEA
GRANT
DOÑA ANA
OTERO
GRANT
DONA ANA
EDDY

LUNA

HIDALGO

TX

TX

Mexico

*NOTE:

Santa Ana County was annexed to Bernalillo in 1876.

CENSUS AVAILABILITY

Federal census extant for all counties.

1   2   3   4   5   6   7   8   9   10   11   12

25 0   25   50   75   100 MILES

WHITE = MODERN BOUNDARIES
BLACK = 1870 BOUNDARIES

New Mexico ● **1870**
AS NEW MEXICO TERRITORY

MAP GUIDE TO THE U.S. FEDERAL CENSUSES, 1790–1920 by William Thorndale and William Dollarhide. Copyright 1987, all rights reserved.

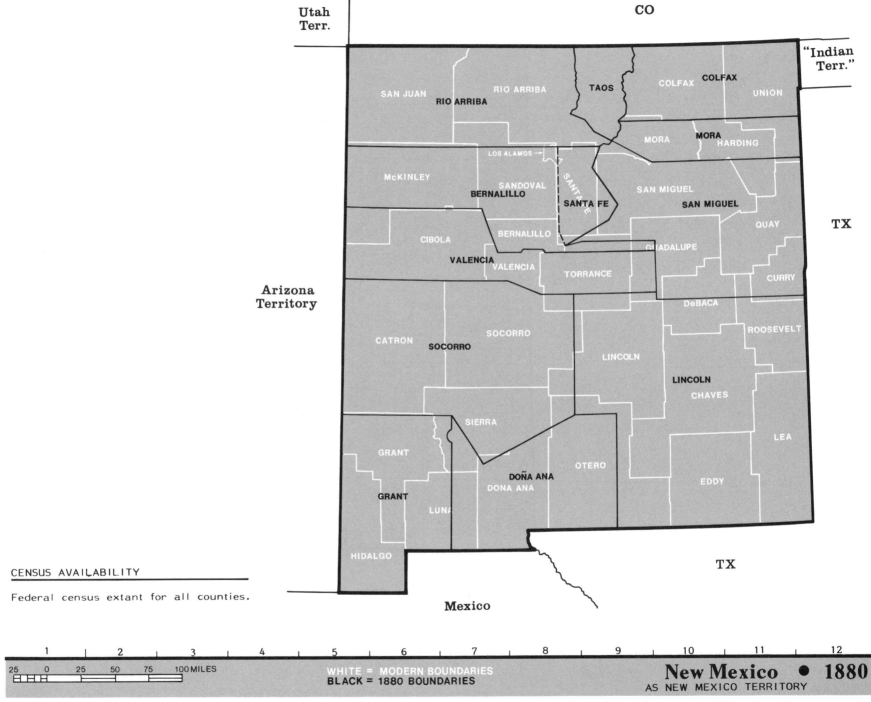

Utah
Terr.

CO

"Indian
Terr."

SAN JUAN
RIO ARRIBA
RIO ARRIBA
TAOS
COLFAX
COLFAX
UNION

MORA
MORA
HARDING

LOS ALAMOS →
McKINLEY
SANDOVAL
SANTA FE
BERNALILLO
SAN MIGUEL
SAN MIGUEL
SANTA FE

CIBOLA
BERNALILLO
QUAY
VALENCIA
VALENCIA
GUADALUPE
TORRANCE
CURRY

Arizona
Territory

DeBACA

CATRON
SOCORRO
SOCORRO
ROOSEVELT
SOCORRO
LINCOLN

LINCOLN
LINCOLN
CHAVES

SIERRA

GRANT
LEA

GRANT
OTERO
DOÑA ANA
EDDY
DONA ANA

LUNA

HIDALGO
TX

Mexico
TX

CENSUS AVAILABILITY

Federal census extant for all counties.

1   2   3   4   5   6   7   8   9   10   11   12

25 0 25 50 75 100 MILES

WHITE = MODERN BOUNDARIES
BLACK = 1880 BOUNDARIES

New Mexico ● **1880**
AS NEW MEXICO TERRITORY

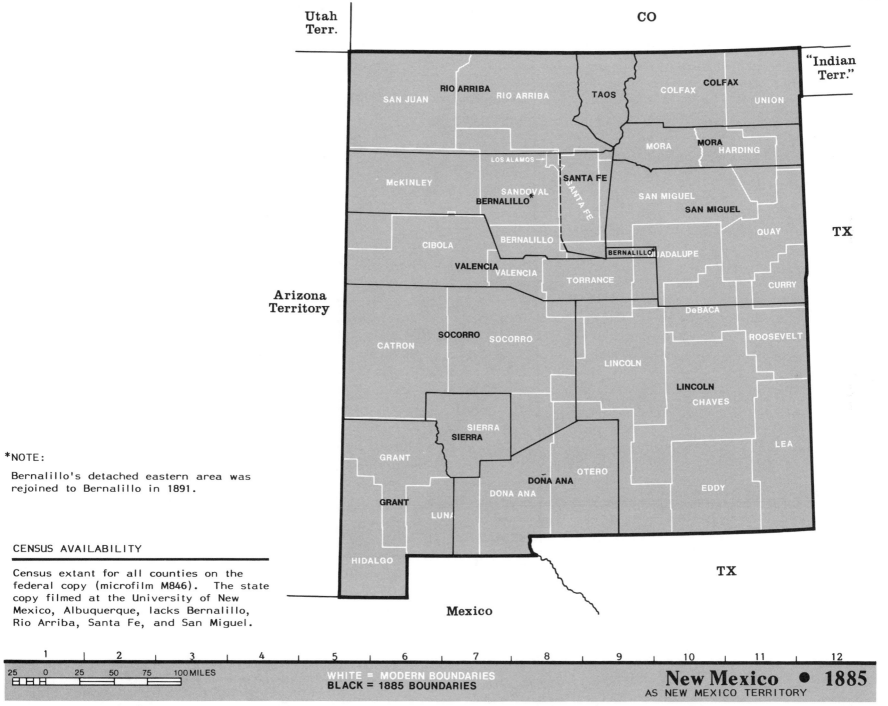

Utah Terr.

CO

"Indian Terr."

RIO ARRIBA
SAN JUAN
RIO ARRIBA
TAOS
COLFAX
COLFAX
UNION

MORA
MORA
HARDING

LOS ALAMOS →
SANTA FE
McKINLEY
SANDOVAL
BERNALILLO *
SANTA FE
SAN MIGUEL
SAN MIGUEL

CIBOLA
BERNALILLO
BERNALILLO *
GUADALUPE
QUAY

VALENCIA
VALENCIA
TORRANCE

Arizona Territory

DeBACA

CATRON
SOCORRO
SOCORRO
ROOSEVELT

LINCOLN

LINCOLN
CHAVES

SIERRA
SIERRA

GRANT

LEA

GRANT
DOÑA ANA
OTERO

DONA ANA

LUNA
EDDY

HIDALGO

TX

TX

Mexico

*NOTE:

Bernalillo's detached eastern area was rejoined to Bernalillo in 1891.

CENSUS AVAILABILITY

Census extant for all counties on the federal copy (microfilm M846). The state copy filmed at the University of New Mexico, Albuquerque, lacks Bernalillo, Rio Arriba, Santa Fe, and San Miguel.

1 2 3 4 5 6 7 8 9 10 11 12

25 0 25 50 75 100 MILES

WHITE = MODERN BOUNDARIES
BLACK = 1885 BOUNDARIES

New Mexico ● 1885
AS NEW MEXICO TERRITORY

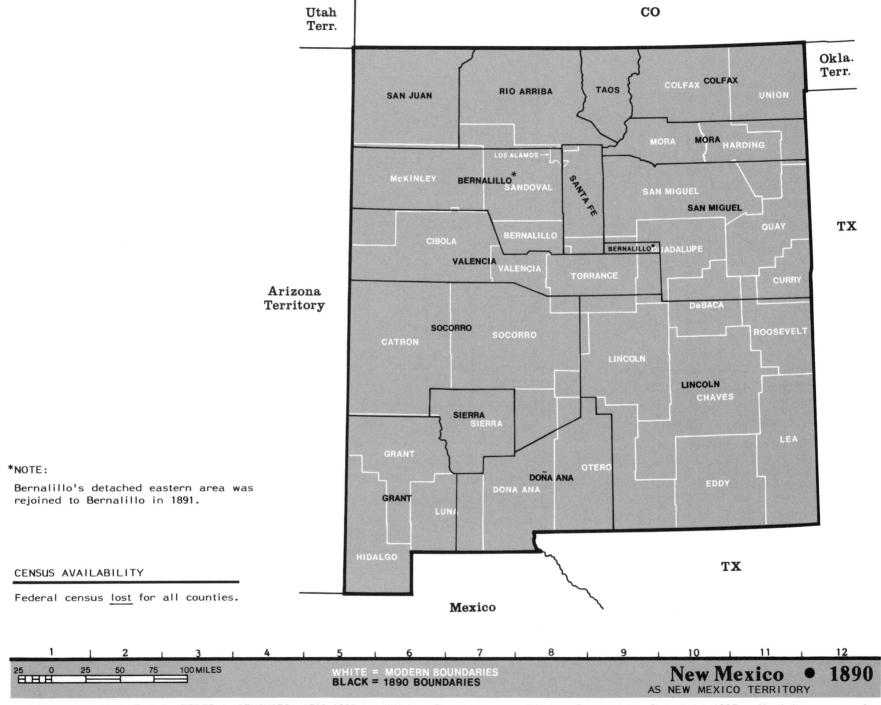

Utah
Terr.

CO

Okla.
Terr.

TX

Arizona
Territory

TX

Mexico

*NOTE:

Bernalillo's detached eastern area was
rejoined to Bernalillo in 1891.

CENSUS AVAILABILITY

Federal census lost for all counties.

SAN JUAN

RIO ARRIBA

TAOS

COLFAX COLFAX

UNION

McKINLEY

LOS ALAMOS →

BERNALILLO *
SANDOVAL

SANTA FE

MORA MORA HARDING

SAN MIGUEL

SAN MIGUEL

QUAY

CIBOLA

BERNALILLO

BERNALILLO *GUADALUPE

VALENCIA

VALENCIA

TORRANCE

CURRY

DeBACA

SOCORRO

CATRON

SOCORRO

LINCOLN

ROOSEVELT

SIERRA
SIERRA

LINCOLN
CHAVES

GRANT

LEA

GRANT

LUNA

DONA ANA
DONA ANA

OTERO

EDDY

HIDALGO

| 1 | 2 | 3 | 4 | 5 | 6 | 7 | 8 | 9 | 10 | 11 | 12 |

25 0 25 50 75 100 MILES

WHITE = MODERN BOUNDARIES
BLACK = 1890 BOUNDARIES

New Mexico ● 1890
AS NEW MEXICO TERRITORY

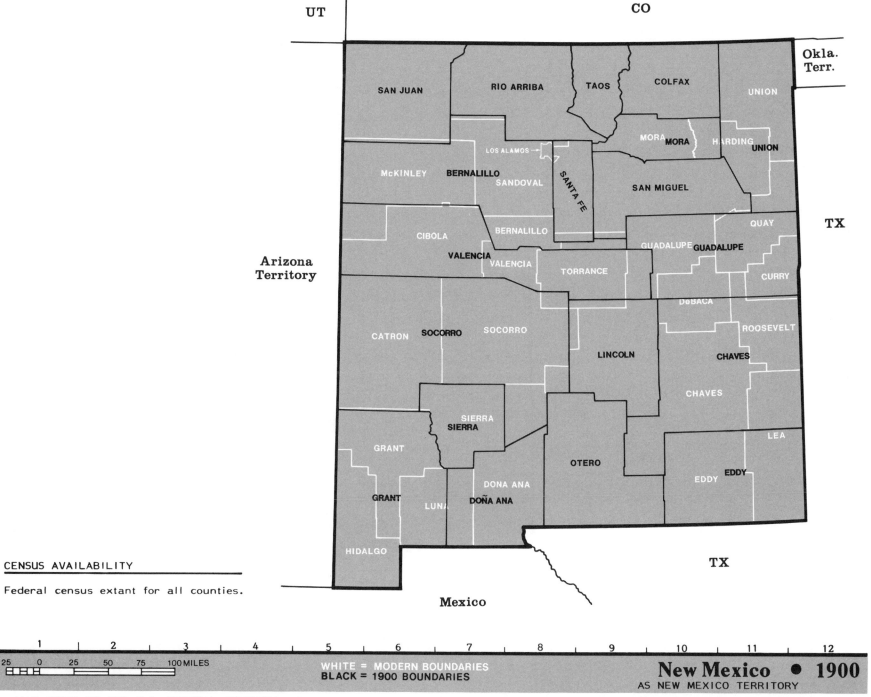

UT

CO

Okla.
Terr.

SAN JUAN

RIO ARRIBA

TAOS

COLFAX

UNION

MORA
MORA

HARDING
UNION

LOS ALAMOS →

McKINLEY

BERNALILLO
SANDOVAL

SANTA FE

SAN MIGUEL

TX

BERNALILLO

CIBOLA

QUAY

Arizona
Territory

VALENCIA
VALENCIA

GUADALUPE GUADALUPE

TORRANCE

CURRY

DeBACA

CATRON

SOCORRO
SOCORRO

ROOSEVELT

LINCOLN

CHAVES

CHAVES

SIERRA
SIERRA

LEA

GRANT

OTERO

EDDY
EDDY

EDDY

DONA ANA

GRANT
LUNA
DOÑA ANA

HIDALGO

TX

Mexico

CENSUS AVAILABILITY

Federal census extant for all counties.

1   2   3   4   5   6   7   8   9   10   11   12

25   0   25   50   75   100 MILES

New Mexico ● **1900**
AS NEW MEXICO TERRITORY

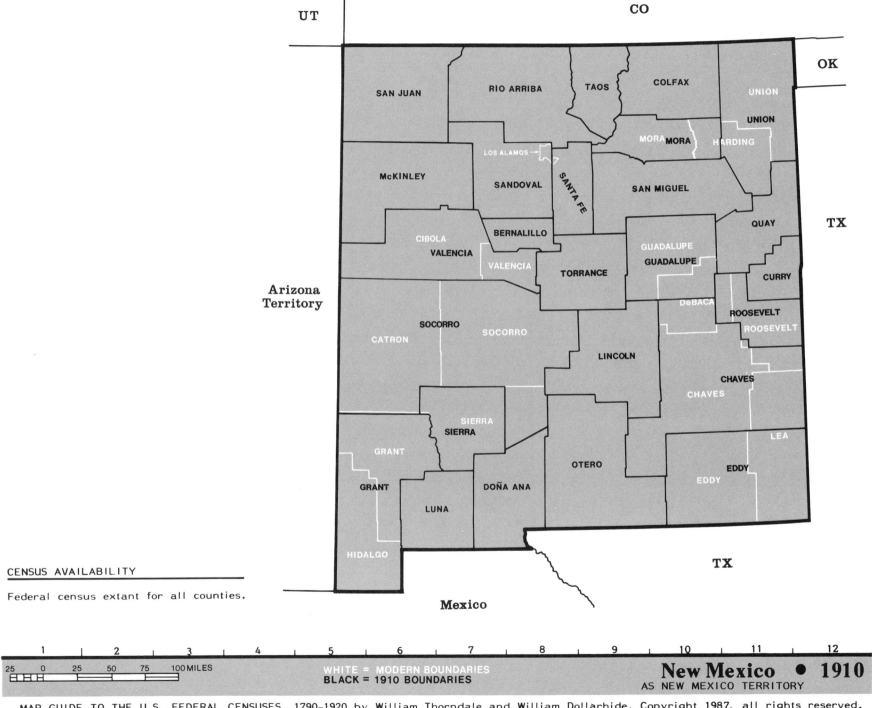

UT

CO

OK

TX

Arizona
Territory

TX

Mexico

SAN JUAN

RIO ARRIBA

TAOS

COLFAX

UNION

UNION

MORA

MORA

HARDING

McKINLEY

LOS ALAMOS →

SANDOVAL

SANTA FE

SAN MIGUEL

CIBOLA

BERNALILLO

QUAY

VALENCIA

VALENCIA

GUADALUPE

GUADALUPE

CURRY

TORRANCE

DeBACA

ROOSEVELT

ROOSEVELT

CATRON

SOCORRO

SOCORRO

LINCOLN

CHAVES

CHAVES

SIERRA

SIERRA

LEA

GRANT

OTERO

EDDY

GRANT

DOÑA ANA

EDDY

LUNA

HIDALGO

1 2 3 4 5 6 7 8 9 10 11 12

25 0 25 50 75 100 MILES

WHITE = MODERN BOUNDARIES
BLACK = 1910 BOUNDARIES

New Mexico ● 1910
AS NEW MEXICO TERRITORY

MAP GUIDE TO THE U.S. FEDERAL CENSUSES, 1790–1920 by William Thorndale and William Dollarhide. Copyright 1987, all rights reserved.

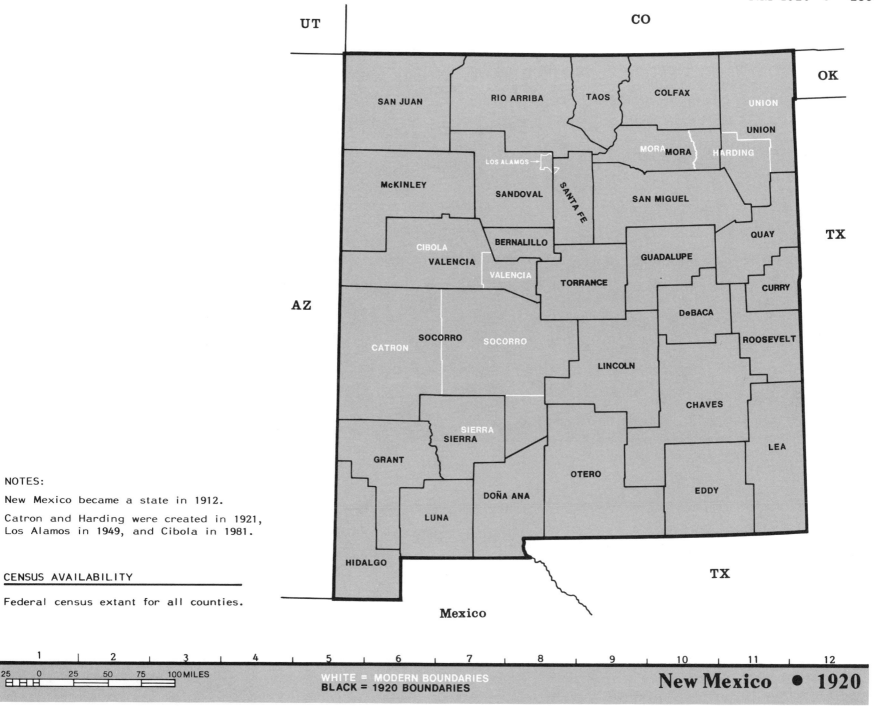

UT
CO
OK
TX

SAN JUAN
RIO ARRIBA
TAOS
COLFAX
UNION
UNION
MORA MORA
HARDING
LOS ALAMOS →
McKINLEY
SANDOVAL
SANTA FE
SAN MIGUEL
QUAY
BERNALILLO
CIBOLA
VALENCIA
GUADALUPE
VALENCIA
TORRANCE
CURRY
AZ
DeBACA
SOCORRO
CATRON
SOCORRO
ROOSEVELT
LINCOLN
CHAVES
SIERRA
SIERRA
LEA
GRANT
OTERO
DOÑA ANA
EDDY
LUNA
TX
HIDALGO
Mexico

NOTES:

New Mexico became a state in 1912.

Catron and Harding were created in 1921,
Los Alamos in 1949, and Cibola in 1981.

CENSUS AVAILABILITY

Federal census extant for all counties.

1   2   3   4   5   6   7   8   9   10   11   12

25   0   25   50   75   100 MILES

WHITE = MODERN BOUNDARIES
BLACK = 1920 BOUNDARIES

New Mexico ● 1920

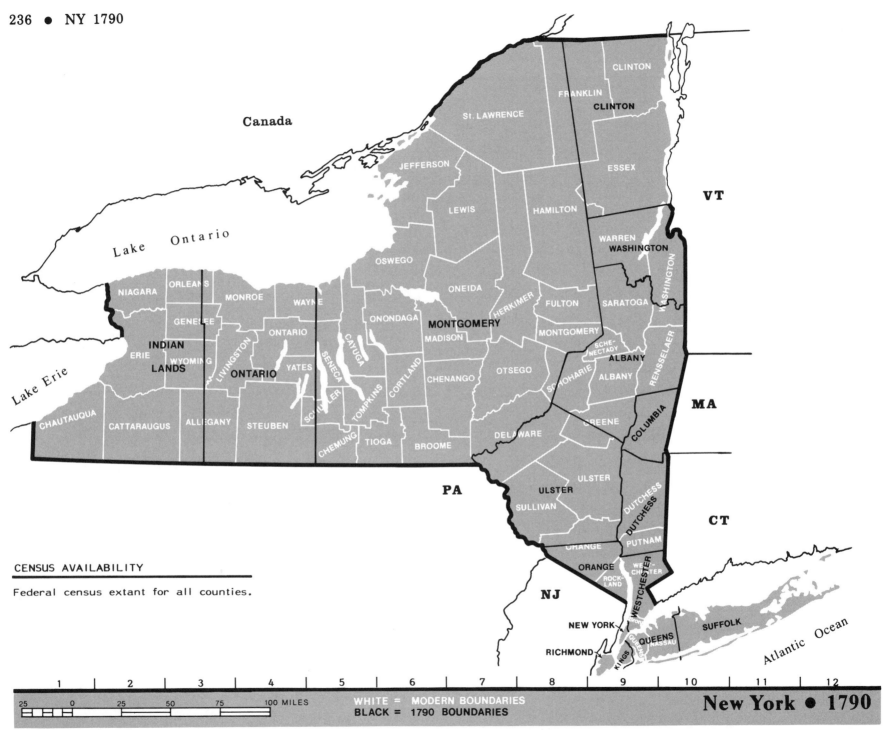

Canada

Lake Ontario

Lake Erie

CLINTON

FRANKLIN

CLINTON

St. LAWRENCE

ESSEX

JEFFERSON

LEWIS

HAMILTON

WARREN

WASHINGTON

VT

OSWEGO

ONEIDA

NIAGARA

ORLEANS

MONROE

WAYNE

FULTON

SARATOGA

WASHINGTON

GENESEE

ONTARIO

ONONDAGA

HERKIMER

MONTGOMERY

SCHE-
NECTADY

ALBANY

RENSSELAER

INDIAN
LANDS

ERIE

WYOMING

LIVINGSTON

ONTARIO

YATES

SENECA

CAYUGA

MADISON

MONTGOMERY

ALBANY

SCHOHARIE

MA

CHAUTAUQUA

CATTARAUGUS

ALLEGANY

STEUBEN

SCHUYLER

TOMPKINS

CORTLAND

CHENANGO

OTSEGO

GREENE

COLUMBIA

CHEMUNG

TIOGA

BROOME

DELAWARE

PA

ULSTER

ULSTER

SULLIVAN

DUTCHESS

DUTCHESS

PUTNAM

CT

ORANGE

ORANGE

ROCK-
LAND

WEST-
CHESTER

WESTCHESTER

NJ

NEW YORK

RICHMOND

KINGS

QUEENS

NASSAU

QUEENS

SUFFOLK

Atlantic Ocean

CENSUS AVAILABILITY

Federal census extant for all counties.

1   2   3   4   5   6   7   8   9   10   11   12

25   0   25   50   75   100 MILES

WHITE = MODERN BOUNDARIES
BLACK = 1790 BOUNDARIES

New York ● 1790

MAP GUIDE TO THE U.S. FEDERAL CENSUSES, 1790–1920 by William Thorndale and William Dollarhide.   Copyright 1987, all rights reserved.

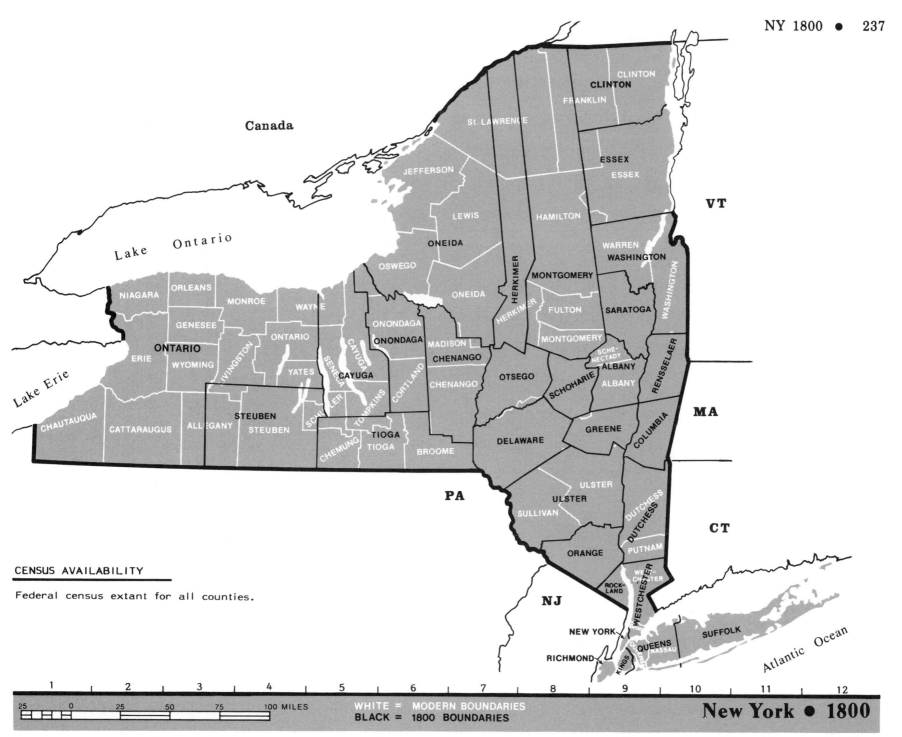

Canada

Lake Ontario

Lake Erie

VT

MA

CT

PA

NJ

Atlantic Ocean

CLINTON
CLINTON
FRANKLIN
St. LAWRENCE
JEFFERSON
ESSEX
ESSEX
LEWIS
HAMILTON
ONEIDA
WARREN
WASHINGTON
OSWEGO
NIAGARA
ORLEANS
MONROE
WAYNE
HERKIMER
MONTGOMERY
WASHINGTON
ONEIDA
HERKIMER
FULTON
SARATOGA
GENESEE
ONTARIO
ONONDAGA
ONTARIO
LIVINGSTON
ONONDAGA
MADISON
MONTGOMERY
SCHE-NECTADY
ALBANY
RENSSELAER
ERIE
WYOMING
YATES
SENECA
CAYUGA
CHENANGO
OTSEGO
ALBANY
CAYUGA
CORTLAND
CHENANGO
SCHOHARIE
STEUBEN
SCHUYLER
TOMPKINS
CHAUTAUQUA
CATTARAUGUS
ALLEGANY
STEUBEN
GREENE
COLUMBIA
CHEMUNG
TIOGA
DELAWARE
TIOGA
BROOME
ULSTER
ULSTER
DUTCHESS
SULLIVAN
DUTCHESS
PUTNAM
ORANGE
WEST-CHESTER
ROCK-LAND
WESTCHESTER
NEW YORK
QUEENS
SUFFOLK
RICHMOND
QUEENS
NASSAU
KINGS

CENSUS AVAILABILITY

Federal census extant for all counties.

| 25 | 0 | 25 | 50 | 75 | 100 MILES |

1 2 3 4 5 6 7 8 9 10 11 12

WHITE = MODERN BOUNDARIES
BLACK = 1800 BOUNDARIES

New York ● 1800

MAP GUIDE TO THE U.S. FEDERAL CENSUSES, 1790-1920 by William Thorndale and William Dollarhide. Copyright 1987, all rights reserved.

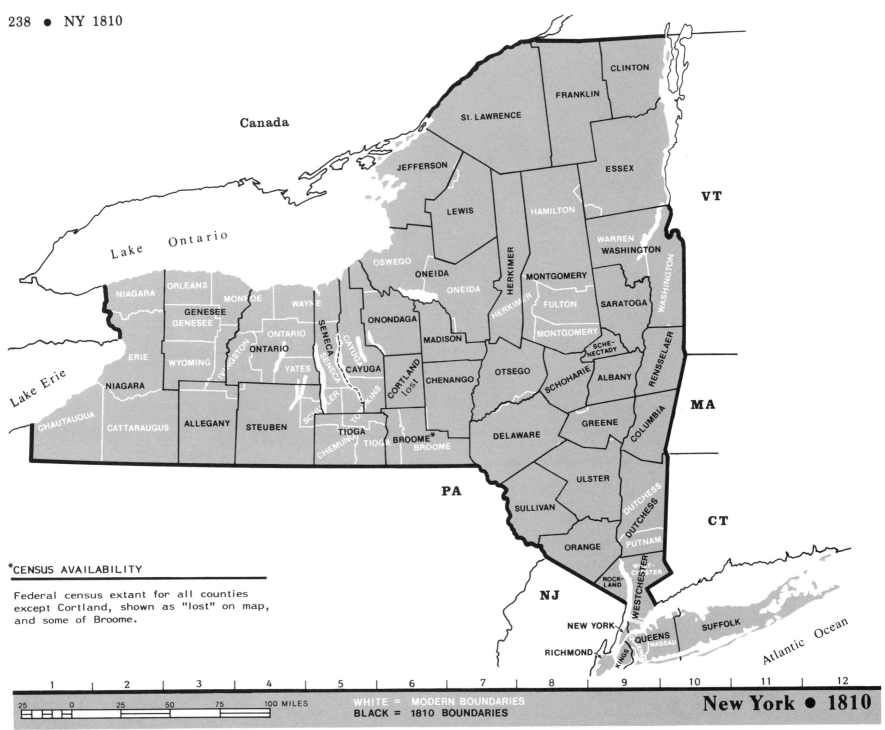

Canada

Lake Ontario

Lake Erie

CLINTON

FRANKLIN

St. LAWRENCE

JEFFERSON

ESSEX

VT

LEWIS

HAMILTON

WARREN
WASHINGTON

OSWEGO

ONEIDA

ONEIDA

HERKIMER

MONTGOMERY

WASHINGTON

NIAGARA

ORLEANS

MONROE

WAYNE

HERKIMER

FULTON

SARATOGA

GENESEE

GENESEE

ONTARIO

ONONDAGA

MONTGOMERY

ERIE

LIVINGSTON

ONTARIO

SENECA

MADISON

SCHE-
NECTADY

RENSSELAER

WYOMING

YATES

SENECA

CAYUGA

CAYUGA

CORTLAND
lost

CHENANGO

OTSEGO

SCHOHARIE

ALBANY

MA

SCHUYLER

TOMPKINS

DELAWARE

GREENE

COLUMBIA

CHAUTAUQUA

NIAGARA

CATTARAUGUS

ALLEGANY

STEUBEN

TIOGA

CHEMUNG

TIOGA

BROOME *
BROOME

ULSTER

DUTCHESS

DUTCHESS

DUTCHESS

CT

PA

SULLIVAN

PUTNAM

ORANGE

WEST-
CHESTER

NJ

ROCK-
LAND

WESTCHESTER

*CENSUS AVAILABILITY

Federal census extant for all counties
except Cortland, shown as "lost" on map,
and some of Broome.

NEW YORK

SUFFOLK

QUEENS

NASSAU

RICHMOND

KINGS

Atlantic Ocean

1   2   3   4   5   6   7   8   9   10   11   12

25   0   25   50   75   100 MILES

WHITE = MODERN BOUNDARIES
BLACK = 1810 BOUNDARIES

New York ● 1810

MAP GUIDE TO THE U.S. FEDERAL CENSUSES, 1790-1920 by William Thorndale and William Dollarhide.   Copyright 1987, all rights reserved.

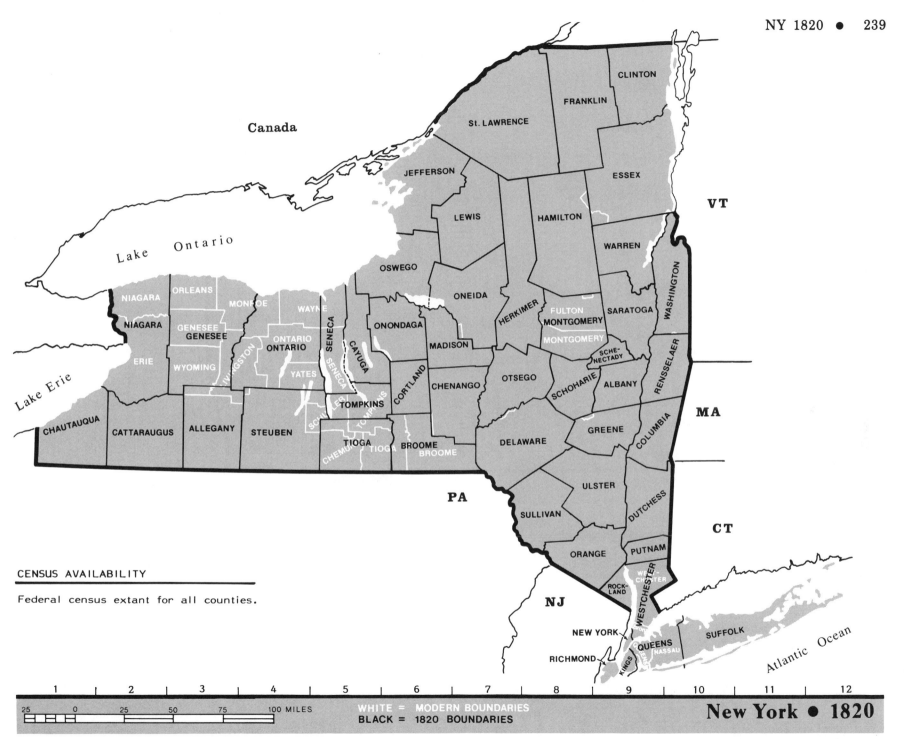

Canada

Lake Ontario

Lake Erie

St. LAWRENCE

CLINTON

FRANKLIN

JEFFERSON

ESSEX

LEWIS

HAMILTON

VT

WARREN

OSWEGO

ONEIDA

WASHINGTON

NIAGARA
ORLEANS

MONROE

WAYNE

SENECA

NIAGARA

GENESEE
GENESEE

ONTARIO
ONTARIO

SENECA

CAYUGA

ONONDAGA

HERKIMER

FULTON
MONTGOMERY

SARATOGA

MONTGOMERY

SCHE-
NECTADY

ERIE

LIVINGSTON

YATES

SENECA

MADISON

RENSSELAER

WYOMING

SCHUYLER

TOMPKINS

CORTLAND

CHENANGO

OTSEGO

SCHOHARIE

ALBANY

MA

CHAUTAUQUA

CATTARAUGUS

ALLEGANY

STEUBEN

CHEMUNG

TIOGA
TIOGA

TOMPKINS

BROOME
BROOME

DELAWARE

GREENE

COLUMBIA

ULSTER

DUTCHESS

PA

SULLIVAN

CT

ORANGE

PUTNAM

WEST-
CHESTER

ROCK-
LAND

NJ

NEW YORK

WESTCHESTER

SUFFOLK

QUEENS
NASSAU

RICHMOND

KINGS

Atlantic Ocean

CENSUS AVAILABILITY

Federal census extant for all counties.

1   2   3   4   5   6   7   8   9   10   11   12

25   0   25   50   75   100 MILES

WHITE = MODERN BOUNDARIES
BLACK = 1820 BOUNDARIES

New York ● 1820

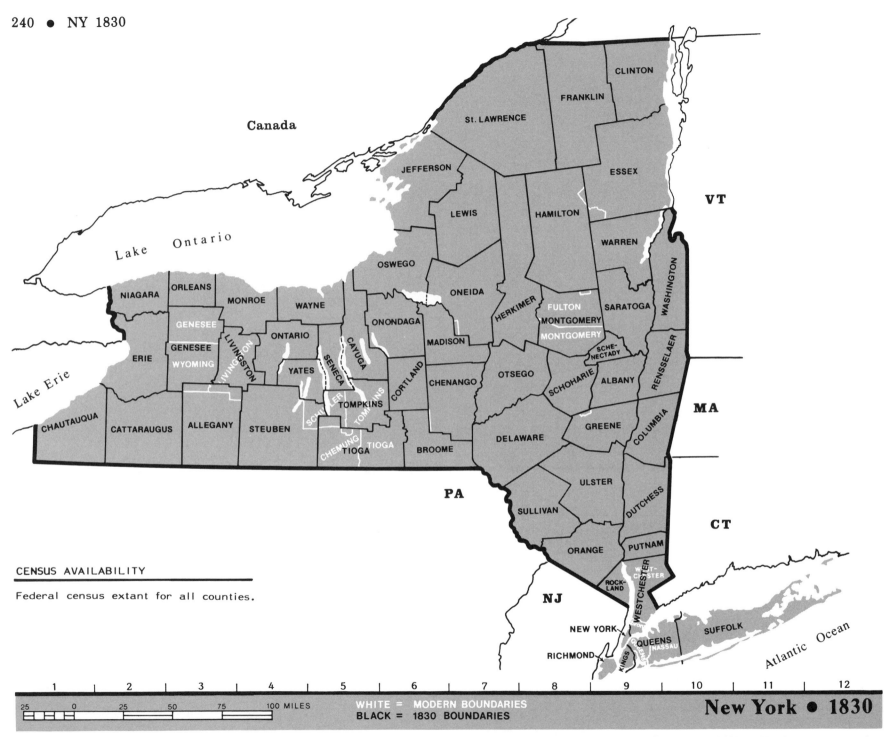

Canada

Lake Ontario

Lake Erie

CLINTON

FRANKLIN

St. LAWRENCE

JEFFERSON

ESSEX

VT

LEWIS

HAMILTON

WARREN

OSWEGO

WASHINGTON

NIAGARA

ORLEANS

MONROE

WAYNE

ONEIDA

SARATOGA

HERKIMER

FULTON

MONTGOMERY

MONTGOMERY

MA

GENESEE

GENESEE

WYOMING

LIVINGSTON

ONTARIO

ONONDAGA

SCHE-
NECTADY

RENSSELAER

ERIE

YATES

SENECA

CAYUGA

MADISON

ALBANY

CHAUTAUQUA

CATTARAUGUS

ALLEGANY

STEUBEN

SCHUYLER

TOMPKINS

CORTLAND

CHENANGO

OTSEGO

SCHOHARIE

GREENE

COLUMBIA

CHEMUNG

TIOGA

TIOGA

TOMPKINS

BROOME

DELAWARE

PA

ULSTER

DUTCHESS

CT

SULLIVAN

ORANGE

PUTNAM

WEST-
CHESTER

NJ

ROCK-
LAND

WESTCHESTER

Atlantic Ocean

NEW YORK

SUFFOLK

QUEENS

NASSAU

RICHMOND

KINGS

CENSUS AVAILABILITY

Federal census extant for all counties.

25   0   25   50   75   100 MILES

1   2   3   4   5   6   7   8   9   10   11   12

WHITE = MODERN BOUNDARIES
BLACK = 1830 BOUNDARIES

New York ● 1830

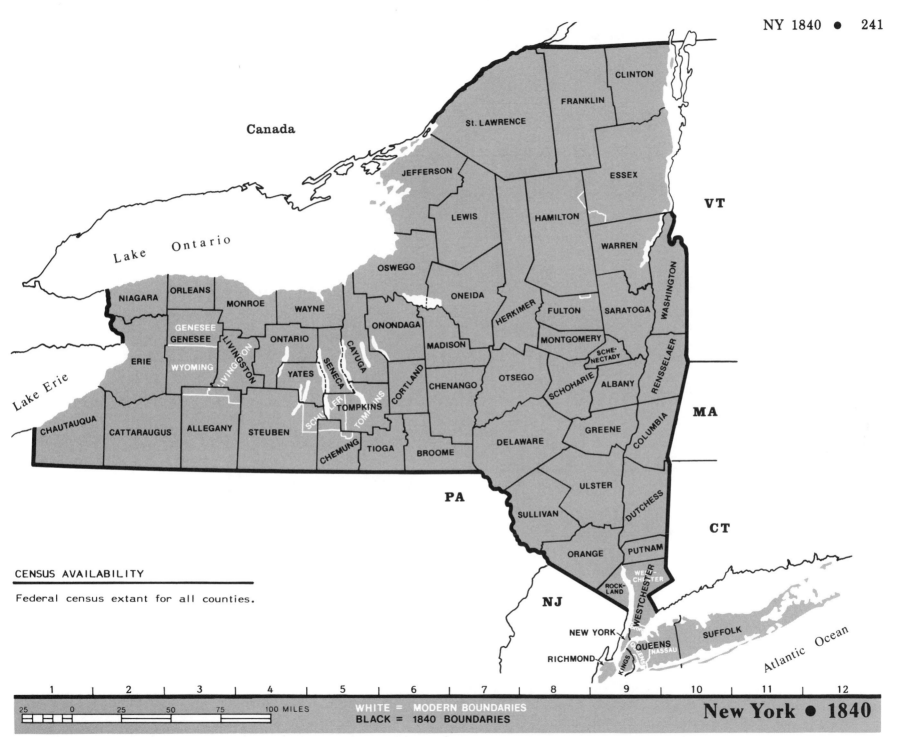

Canada

Lake Ontario

Lake Erie

CLINTON

FRANKLIN

St. LAWRENCE

JEFFERSON

ESSEX

VT

LEWIS

HAMILTON

WARREN

OSWEGO

WASHINGTON

NIAGARA

ORLEANS

MONROE

WAYNE

ONEIDA

HERKIMER

FULTON

SARATOGA

GENESEE
GENESEE

ONTARIO

ONONDAGA

MONTGOMERY

**SCHE-
NECTADY**

ERIE

WYOMING

LIVINGSTON

YATES

SENECA

CAYUGA

MADISON

CORTLAND

CHENANGO

OTSEGO

SCHOHARIE

ALBANY

RENSSELAER

MA

SCHUYLER

TOMPKINS

CHAUTAUQUA

CATTARAUGUS

ALLEGANY

STEUBEN

CHEMUNG

TIOGA

BROOME

DELAWARE

GREENE

COLUMBIA

ULSTER

DUTCHESS

CT

SULLIVAN

ORANGE

PUTNAM

PA

**WEST-
CHESTER**

**ROCK-
LAND**

NJ

NEW YORK

RICHMOND

KINGS

QUEENS

NASSAU

SUFFOLK

Atlantic Ocean

CENSUS AVAILABILITY

Federal census extant for all counties.

| 1 | 2 | 3 | 4 | 5 | 6 | 7 | 8 | 9 | 10 | 11 | 12 |

25   0   25   50   75   100 MILES

WHITE = MODERN BOUNDARIES
BLACK = 1840 BOUNDARIES

New York ● 1840

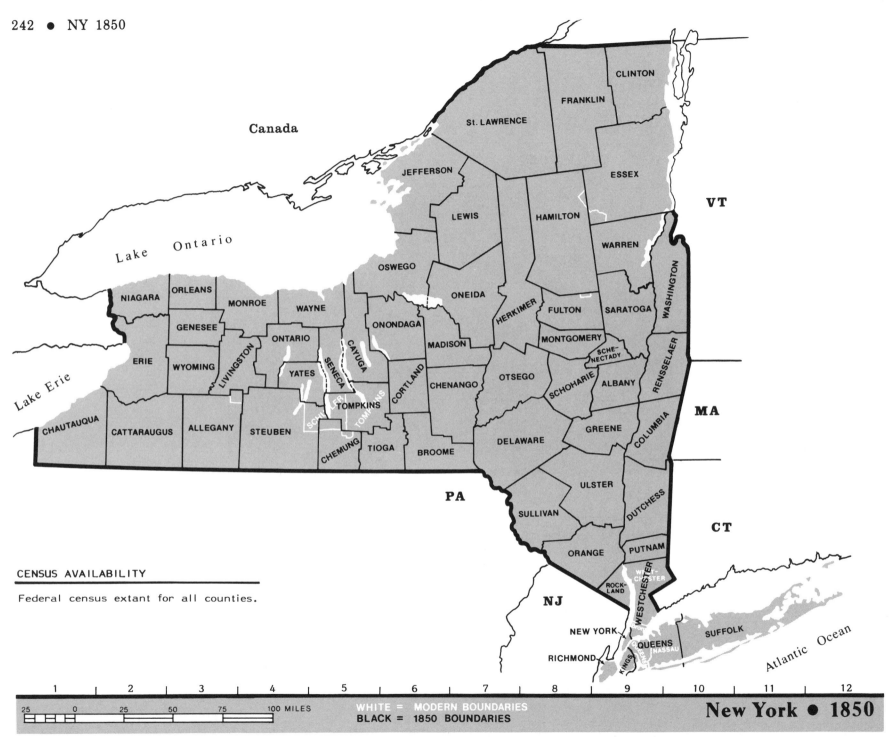

Canada

Lake Ontario

Lake Erie

CLINTON

FRANKLIN

St. LAWRENCE

JEFFERSON

ESSEX

VT

LEWIS

HAMILTON

WARREN

OSWEGO

NIAGARA

ORLEANS

MONROE

WAYNE

ONEIDA

SARATOGA

WASHINGTON

GENESEE

ONTARIO

ONONDAGA

HERKIMER

FULTON

MONTGOMERY

ERIE

WYOMING

LIVINGSTON

YATES

SENECA

CAYUGA

MADISON

SCHE-
NECTADY

ALBANY

RENSSELAER

MA

CHAUTAUQUA

CATTARAUGUS

ALLEGANY

STEUBEN

SCHUYLER

TOMPKINS

CORTLAND

CHENANGO

OTSEGO

SCHOHARIE

GREENE

COLUMBIA

CHEMUNG

TIOGA

BROOME

DELAWARE

ULSTER

DUTCHESS

CT

PA

SULLIVAN

ORANGE

PUTNAM

NJ

ROCK-
LAND

WEST-
CHESTER

NEW YORK

SUFFOLK

Atlantic Ocean

QUEENS

NASSAU

RICHMOND

KINGS

CENSUS AVAILABILITY

Federal census extant for all counties.

1   2   3   4   5   6   7   8   9   10   11   12

25   0   25   50   75   100 MILES

WHITE = MODERN BOUNDARIES
BLACK = 1850 BOUNDARIES

New York ● 1850

MAP GUIDE TO THE U.S. FEDERAL CENSUSES, 1790–1920 by William Thorndale and William Dollarhide.   Copyright 1987, all rights reserved.

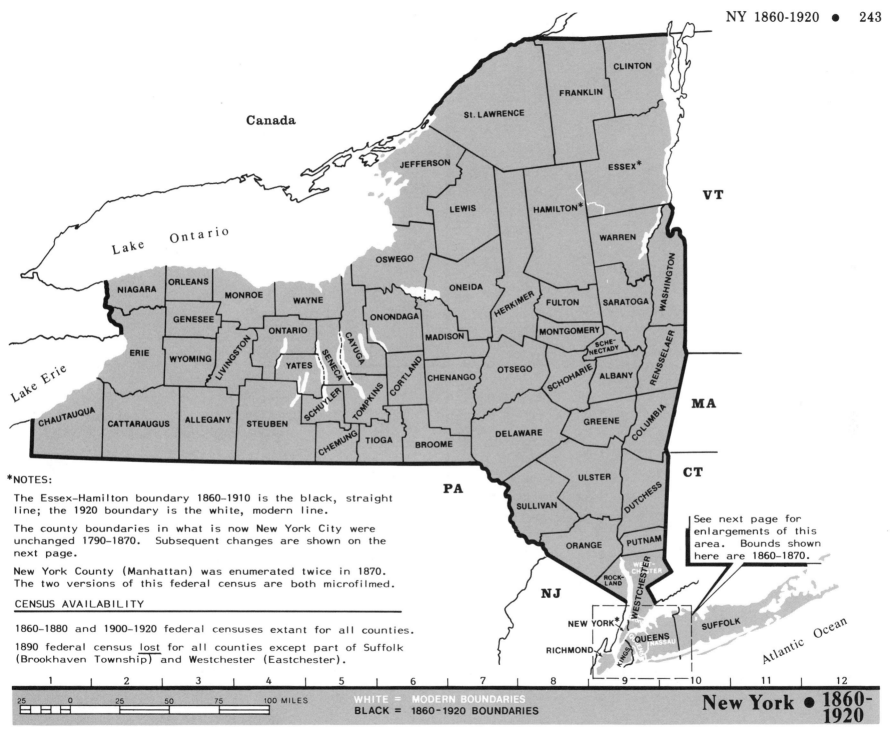

Canada

Lake Ontario

Lake Erie

VT

MA

CT

PA

NJ

Atlantic Ocean

CLINTON

FRANKLIN

St. LAWRENCE

JEFFERSON

ESSEX*

LEWIS

HAMILTON*

WARREN

OSWEGO

NIAGARA

ORLEANS

MONROE

WAYNE

ONEIDA

HERKIMER

FULTON

SARATOGA

WASHINGTON

GENESEE

ONONDAGA

ONTARIO

MADISON

MONTGOMERY

SCHE-NECTADY

RENSSELAER

ERIE

WYOMING

LIVINGSTON

YATES

SENECA

CAYUGA

CORTLAND

CHENANGO

OTSEGO

SCHOHARIE

ALBANY

SCHUYLER

TOMPKINS

COLUMBIA

CHAUTAUQUA

CATTARAUGUS

ALLEGANY

STEUBEN

CHEMUNG

TIOGA

BROOME

DELAWARE

GREENE

ULSTER

DUTCHESS

SULLIVAN

ORANGE

PUTNAM

WEST-CHESTER

ROCK-LAND

NEW YORK*

RICHMOND

KINGS

QUEENS

NASSAU

SUFFOLK

*NOTES:

The Essex–Hamilton boundary 1860–1910 is the black, straight line; the 1920 boundary is the white, modern line.

The county boundaries in what is now New York City were unchanged 1790–1870. Subsequent changes are shown on the next page.

New York County (Manhattan) was enumerated twice in 1870. The two versions of this federal census are both microfilmed.

CENSUS AVAILABILITY

1860–1880 and 1900–1920 federal censuses extant for all counties.

1890 federal census lost for all counties except part of Suffolk (Brookhaven Township) and Westchester (Eastchester).

See next page for enlargements of this area. Bounds shown here are 1860–1870.

25   0   25   50   75   100 MILES

1   2   3   4   5   6   7   8   9   10   11   12

WHITE = MODERN BOUNDARIES
BLACK = 1860-1920 BOUNDARIES

New York ● 1860-1920

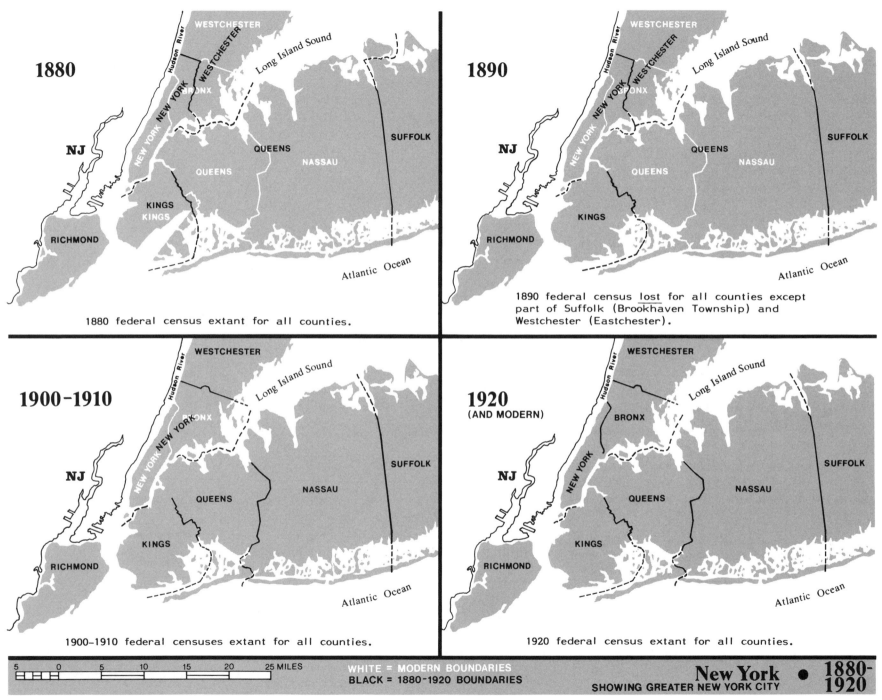

1880

1880 federal census extant for all counties.

1890

1890 federal census lost for all counties except part of Suffolk (Brookhaven Township) and Westchester (Eastchester).

1900–1910

1900–1910 federal censuses extant for all counties.

1920
(AND MODERN)

1920 federal census extant for all counties.

5   0   5   10   15   20   25 MILES

WHITE = MODERN BOUNDARIES
BLACK = 1880–1920 BOUNDARIES

New York ● **1880–1920**
SHOWING GREATER NEW YORK CITY

MAP GUIDE TO THE U.S. FEDERAL CENSUSES, 1790–1920 by William Thorndale and William Dollarhide. Copyright 1987, all rights reserved.

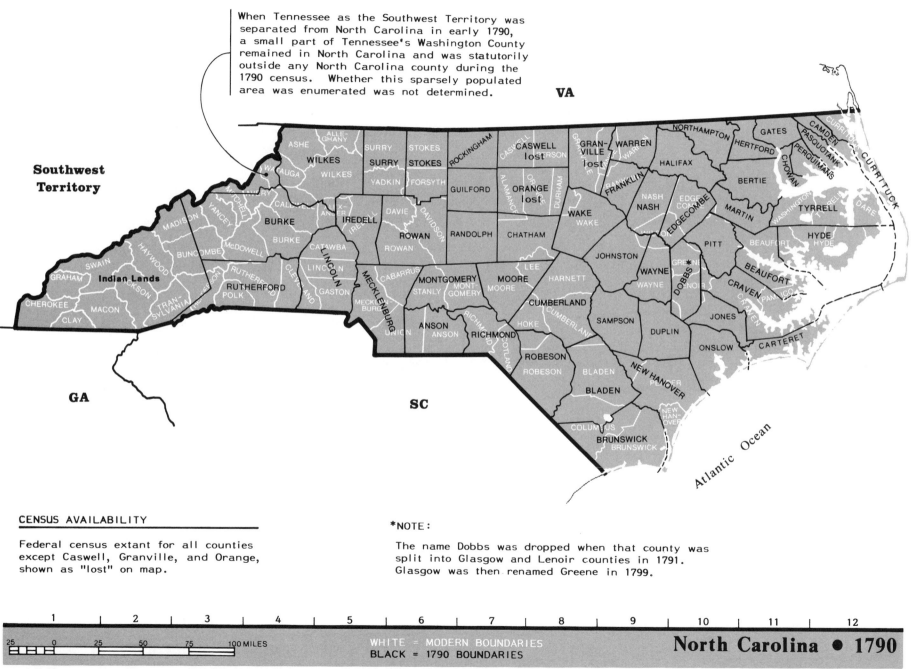

When Tennessee as the Southwest Territory was separated from North Carolina in early 1790, a small part of Tennessee's Washington County remained in North Carolina and was statutorily outside any North Carolina county during the 1790 census. Whether this sparsely populated area was enumerated was not determined.

VA

Southwest Territory

GA

SC

Atlantic Ocean

CENSUS AVAILABILITY

Federal census extant for all counties except Caswell, Granville, and Orange, shown as "lost" on map.

*NOTE:

The name Dobbs was dropped when that county was split into Glasgow and Lenoir counties in 1791. Glasgow was then renamed Greene in 1799.

1 2 3 4 5 6 7 8 9 10 11 12

25 0 25 50 75 100 MILES

WHITE = MODERN BOUNDARIES
BLACK = 1790 BOUNDARIES

North Carolina ● 1790

MAP GUIDE TO THE U.S. FEDERAL CENSUSES, 1790–1920 by William Thorndale and William Dollarhide. Copyright 1987, all rights reserved.

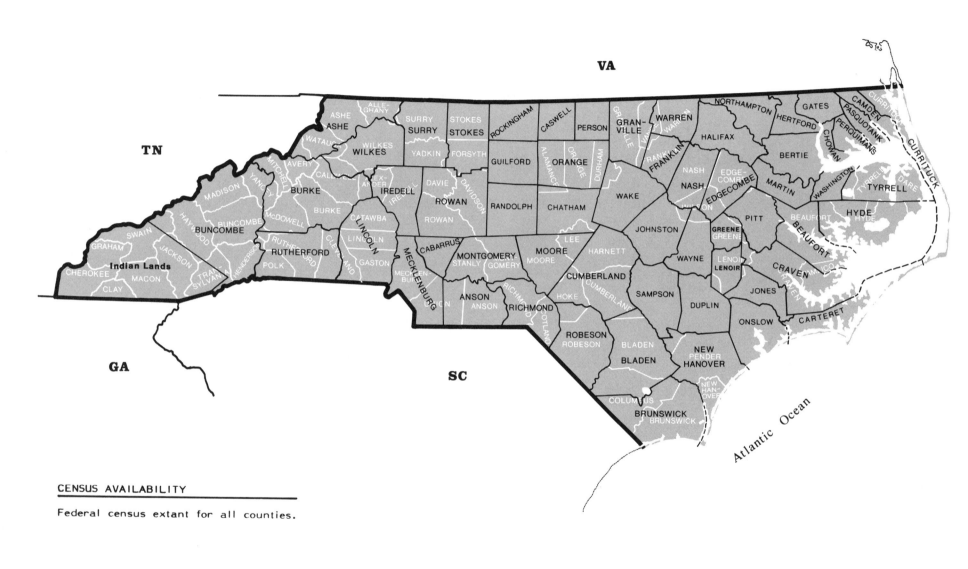

VA

TN

GA

SC

Atlantic Ocean

Indian Lands

CENSUS AVAILABILITY

Federal census extant for all counties.

25   0   25   50   75   100 MILES

North Carolina ● 1800

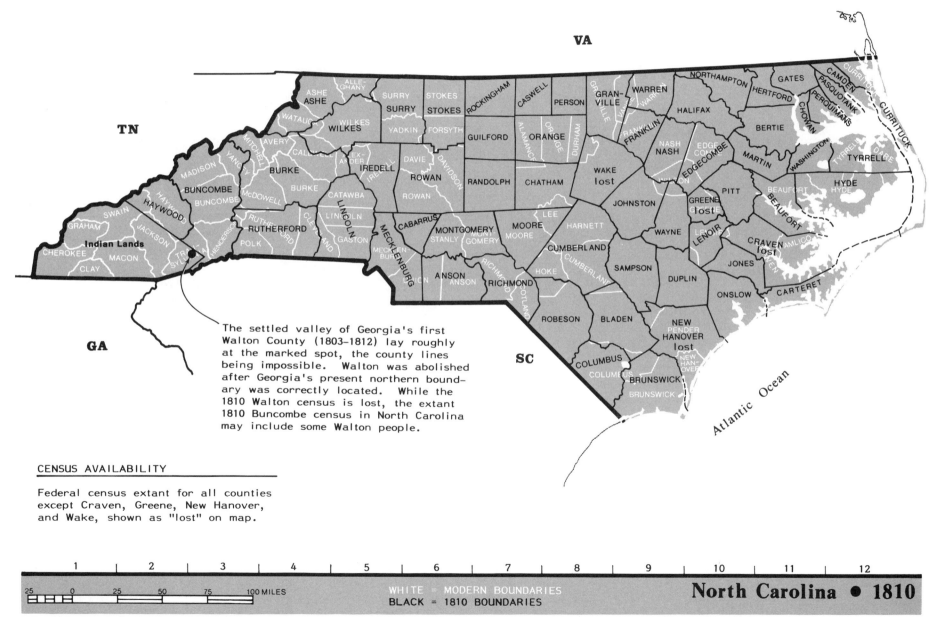

VA

TN

GA

SC

Indian Lands

The settled valley of Georgia's first
Walton County (1803–1812) lay roughly
at the marked spot, the county lines
being impossible. Walton was abolished
after Georgia's present northern boundary was correctly located. While the
1810 Walton census is lost, the extant
1810 Buncombe census in North Carolina
may include some Walton people.

Atlantic Ocean

CENSUS AVAILABILITY

Federal census extant for all counties
except Craven, Greene, New Hanover,
and Wake, shown as "lost" on map.

WHITE = MODERN BOUNDARIES
BLACK = 1810 BOUNDARIES

25   0   25   50   75   100 MILES

North Carolina ● 1810

1   2   3   4   5   6   7   8   9   10   11   12

MAP GUIDE TO THE U.S. FEDERAL CENSUSES, 1790–1920 by William Thorndale and William Dollarhide. Copyright 1987, all rights reserved.

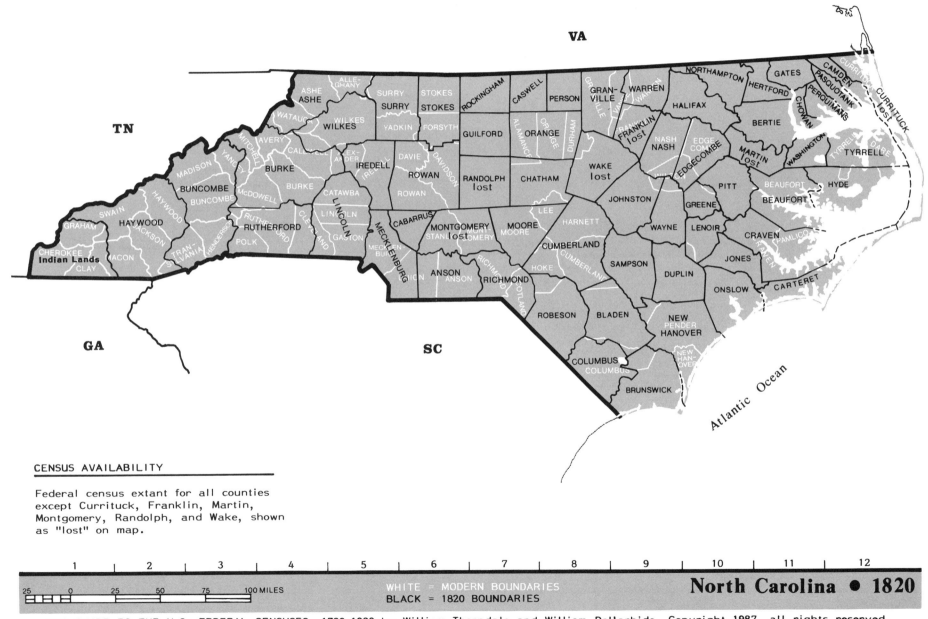

CENSUS AVAILABILITY

Federal census extant for all counties
except Currituck, Franklin, Martin,
Montgomery, Randolph, and Wake, shown
as "lost" on map.

WHITE = MODERN BOUNDARIES
BLACK = 1820 BOUNDARIES

North Carolina ● 1820

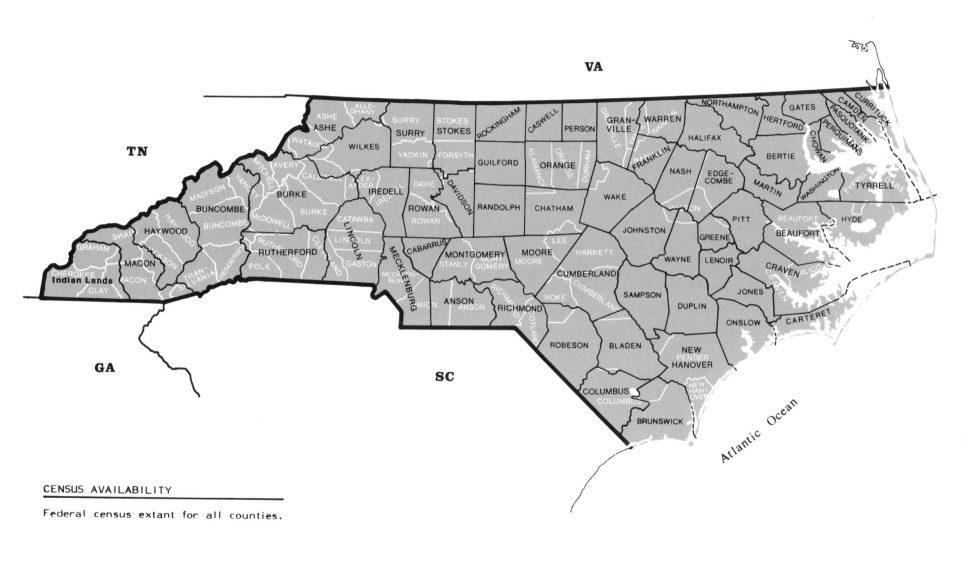

VA

TN

GRAHAM
CHEROKEE
Indian Lands
CLAY
MACON
MACON
SWAIN
JACKSON
HAYWOOD
TRANSYLVANIA
HENDERSON
POLK
RUTHERFORD
RUTHERFORD
MADISON
YANCEY
BUNCOMBE
BUNCOMBE
McDOWELL
CLEVELAND
GASTON
LINCOLN
LINCOLN
GASTON
MITCHELL
AVERY
CALDWELL
BURKE
BURKE
CATAWBA
ALEXANDER
IREDELL
IREDELL
WATAUGA
WILKES
ASHE
ASHE
ALLE-GHANY
SURRY
SURRY
YADKIN
FORSYTH
DAVIE
DAVIDSON
ROWAN
ROWAN
STOKES
STOKES
GUILFORD
RANDOLPH
CABARRUS
MECKLENBURG
MECKLEN-BURG
UNION
ANSON
ANSON
MONTGOMERY
STANLY
MONT-GOMERY
ALAMANCE
ORANGE
ORANGE
DURHAM
CHATHAM
RICHMOND
SCOTLAND
MOORE
MOORE
LEE
HARNETT
CUMBERLAND
CUMBERLAND
HOKE
ROBESON
BLADEN
COLUMBUS
COLUMBUS
BRUNSWICK
NEW HAN-OVER
NEW PENDER HANOVER
SAMPSON
DUPLIN
ONSLOW
CARTERET
ROCKINGHAM
CASWELL
PERSON
GRAN-VILLE
WARREN
WARREN
FRANKLIN
VANCE
WAKE
JOHNSTON
WAYNE
LENOIR
JONES
CRAVEN
PAMLICO
GREENE
WILSON
NASH
EDGE-COMBE
PITT
BEAUFORT
BEAUFORT
HYDE
MARTIN
WASHINGTON
TYRRELL
TYRRELL
DARE
HALIFAX
BERTIE
CHOWAN
PERQUIMANS
PASQUOTANK
CAMDEN
CURRITUCK
GATES
HERTFORD
NORTHAMPTON

GA

SC

Atlantic Ocean

CENSUS AVAILABILITY
_____

Federal census extant for all counties.

1   2   3   4   5   6   7   8   9   10   11   12

25   0   25   50   75   100 MILES

WHITE = MODERN BOUNDARIES
BLACK = 1830 BOUNDARIES

North Carolina ● 1830

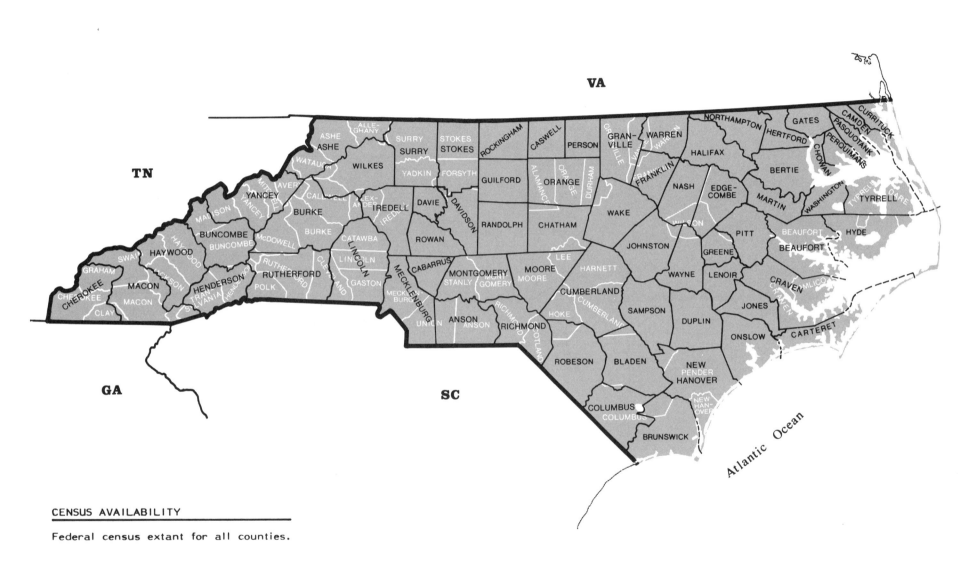

VA

TN

GA

SC

Atlantic Ocean

CENSUS AVAILABILITY

Federal census extant for all counties.

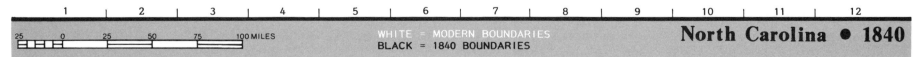

| 1 | 2 | 3 | 4 | 5 | 6 | 7 | 8 | 9 | 10 | 11 | 12 |

25 0   25   50   75   100 MILES

WHITE = MODERN BOUNDARIES
BLACK = 1840 BOUNDARIES

North Carolina ● 1840

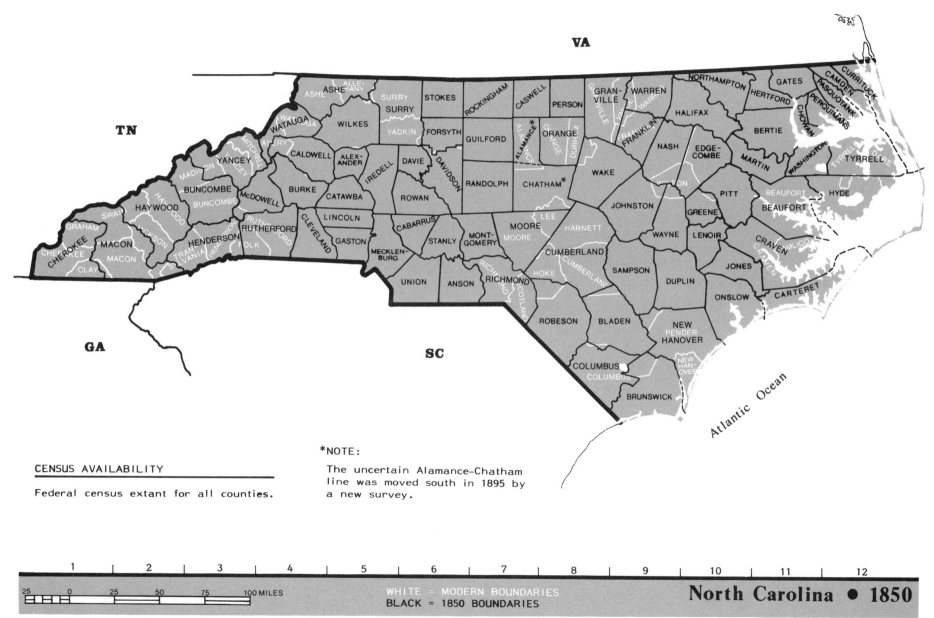

CENSUS AVAILABILITY

Federal census extant for all counties.

*NOTE:

The uncertain Alamance–Chatham line was moved south in 1895 by a new survey.

25 0   25   50   75   100 MILES

North Carolina ● 1850

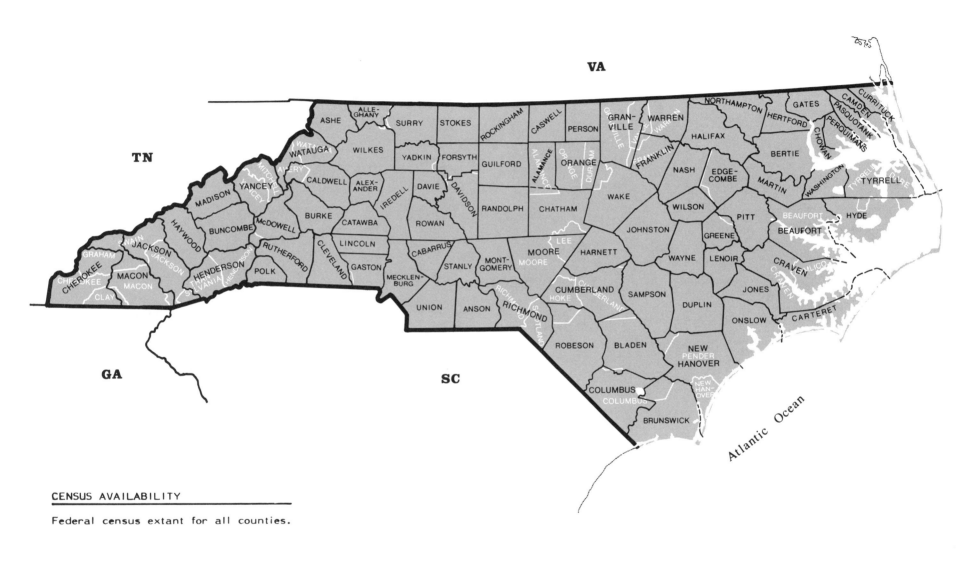

CENSUS AVAILABILITY

Federal census extant for all counties.

WHITE = MODERN BOUNDARIES
BLACK = 1860 BOUNDARIES

North Carolina ● 1860

MAP GUIDE TO THE U.S. FEDERAL CENSUSES, 1790–1920 by William Thorndale and William Dollarhide. Copyright 1987, all rights reserved.

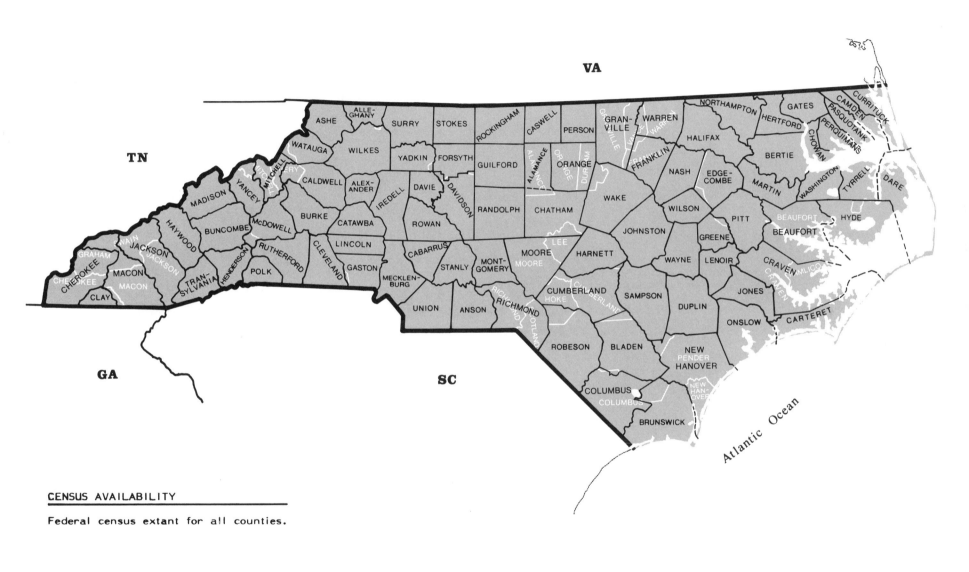

North Carolina ● 1870

CENSUS AVAILABILITY

Federal census extant for all counties.

1 2 3 4 5 6 7 8 9 10 11 12

25 0 25 50 75 100 MILES

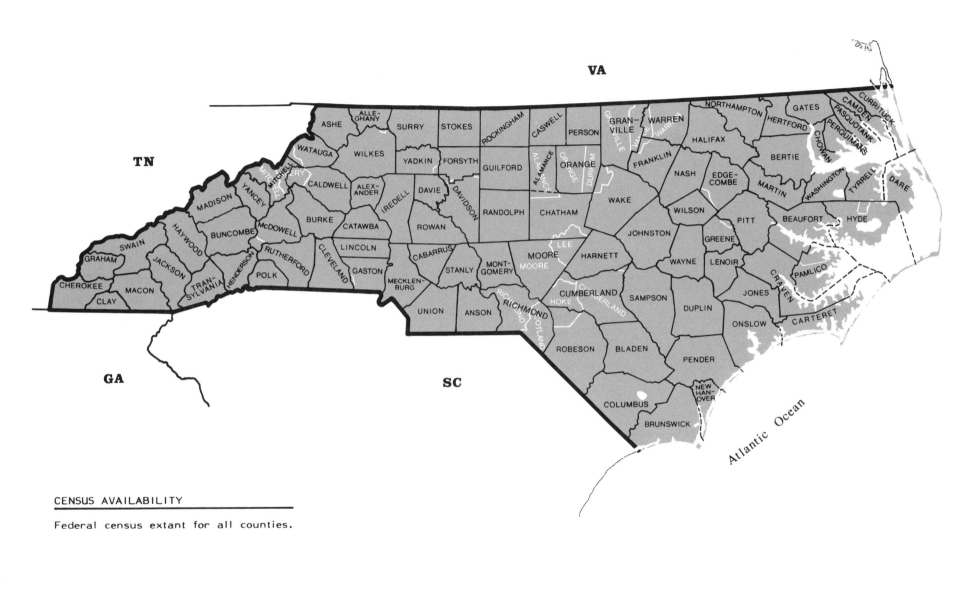

VA

TN

GA

SC

Atlantic Ocean

CENSUS AVAILABILITY

Federal census extant for all counties.

| 1 | 2 | 3 | 4 | 5 | 6 | 7 | 8 | 9 | 10 | 11 | 12 |

25 0 25 50 75 100 MILES

WHITE = MODERN BOUNDARIES
BLACK = 1880 BOUNDARIES

North Carolina ● 1880

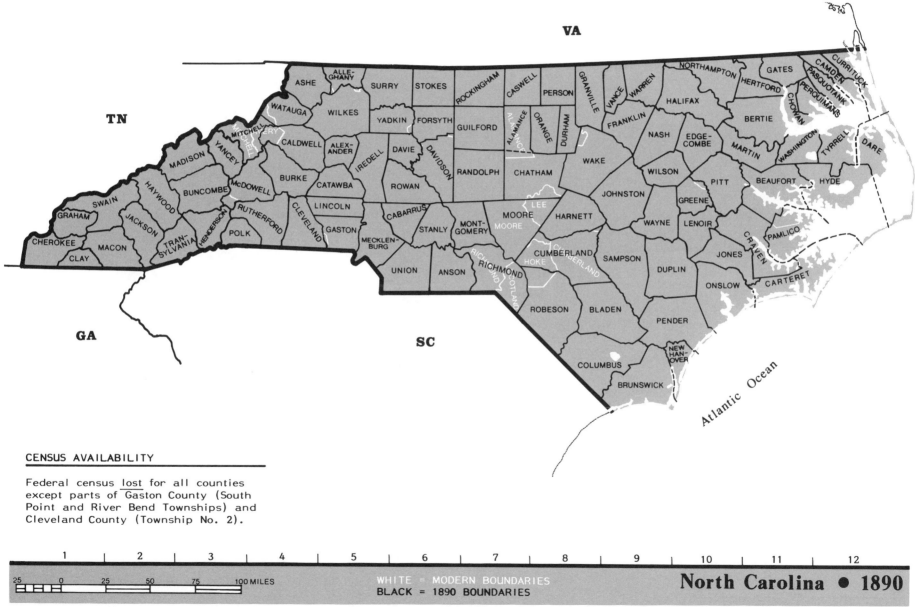

CENSUS AVAILABILITY

Federal census lost for all counties except parts of Gaston County (South Point and River Bend Townships) and Cleveland County (Township No. 2).

WHITE = MODERN BOUNDARIES
BLACK = 1890 BOUNDARIES

25   0   25   50   75   100 MILES

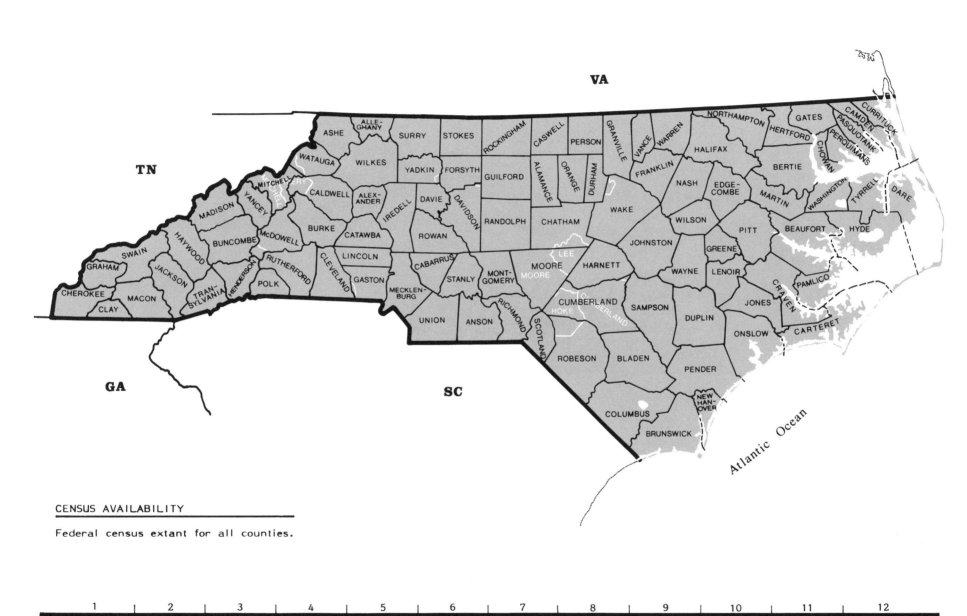

CENSUS AVAILABILITY

Federal census extant for all counties.

North Carolina ● 1900

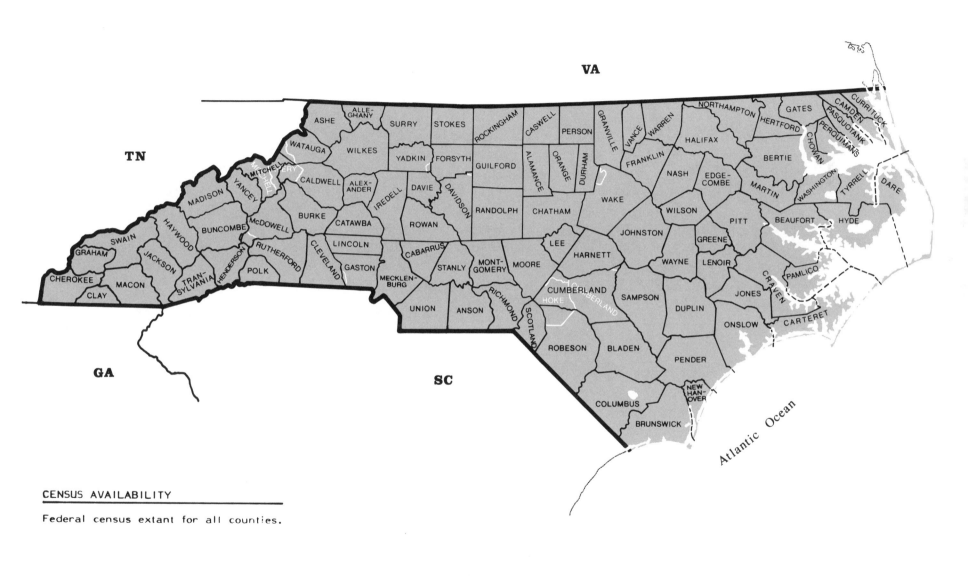

VA

TN

GA

SC

Atlantic Ocean

CURRITUCK
CAMDEN
PASQUOTANK
PERQUIMANS
CHOWAN
GATES
NORTHAMPTON
HERTFORD
ALLE-GHANY
ASHE
SURRY
STOKES
ROCKINGHAM
CASWELL
PERSON
GRANVILLE
VANCE
WARREN
HALIFAX
BERTIE
WATAUGA
WILKES
YADKIN
FORSYTH
GUILFORD
ALAMANCE
ORANGE
DURHAM
FRANKLIN
NASH
EDGE-COMBE
MARTIN
WASHINGTON
TYRRELL
DARE
MITCHELL
CALDWELL
ALEX-ANDER
DAVIE
DAVIDSON
WAKE
WILSON
PITT
BEAUFORT
HYDE
MADISON
YANCEY
BURKE
IREDELL
RANDOLPH
CHATHAM
JOHNSTON
GREENE
HAYWOOD
BUNCOMBE
McDOWELL
CATAWBA
ROWAN
LEE
HARNETT
WAYNE
LENOIR
SWAIN
LINCOLN
CABARRUS
MOORE
CRAVEN
PAMLICO
GRAHAM
JACKSON
RUTHERFORD
CLEVELAND
GASTON
STANLY
MONT-GOMERY
SAMPSON
DUPLIN
JONES
CHEROKEE
TRAN-SYLVANIA
HENDERSON
POLK
MECKLEN-BURG
RICHMOND
CUMBERLAND
ONSLOW
CARTERET
MACON
CLAY
UNION
ANSON
SCOTLAND
HOKE
ROBESON
BLADEN
PENDER
NEW HAN-OVER
COLUMBUS
BRUNSWICK

CENSUS AVAILABILITY

Federal census extant for all counties.

1   2   3   4   5   6   7   8   9   10   11   12

25 0 25 50 75 100 MILES

WHITE = MODERN BOUNDARIES
BLACK = 1910 BOUNDARIES

North Carolina ● 1910

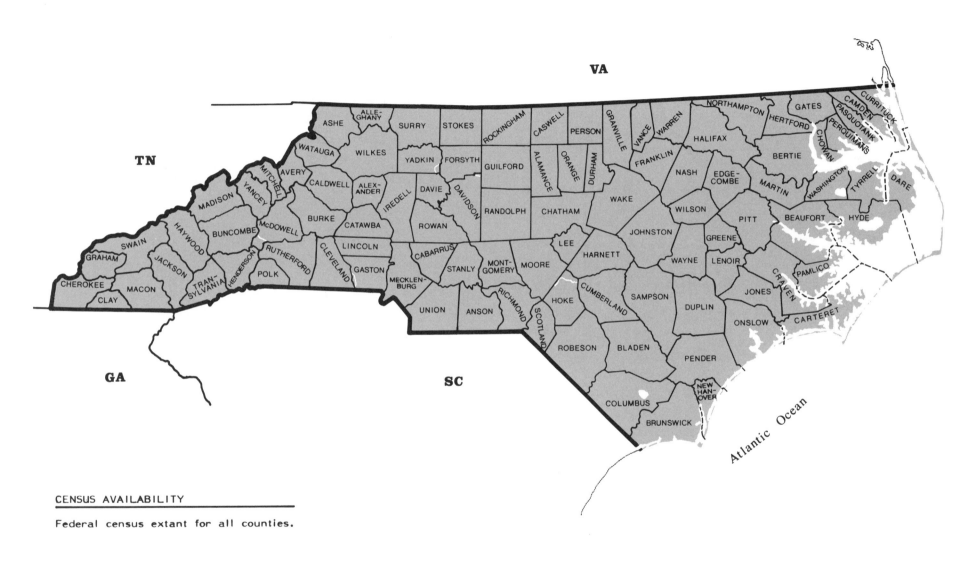

VA

TN

GA

SC

CURRITUCK

ASHE ALLE-GHANY SURRY STOKES ROCKINGHAM CASWELL PERSON GRANVILLE VANCE WARREN NORTHAMPTON HERTFORD GATES CAMDEN PASQUOTANK

WATAUGA WILKES YADKIN FORSYTH GUILFORD ALAMANCE ORANGE DURHAM FRANKLIN HALIFAX BERTIE CHOWAN PERQUIMANS

AVERY CALDWELL ALEX-ANDER DAVIE DAVIDSON NASH EDGE-COMBE MARTIN WASHINGTON TYRRELL DARE

MITCHELL MADISON YANCEY IREDELL WAKE

HAYWOOD BUNCOMBE McDOWELL BURKE CATAWBA ROWAN RANDOLPH CHATHAM WILSON PITT BEAUFORT HYDE

SWAIN LINCOLN JOHNSTON GREENE

GRAHAM JACKSON RUTHERFORD CLEVELAND GASTON CABARRUS LEE HARNETT WAYNE LENOIR CRAVEN PAMLICO

CHEROKEE MACON TRAN-SYLVANIA HENDERSON POLK MECKLEN-BURG STANLY MONT-GOMERY MOORE JONES

CLAY UNION ANSON RICHMOND HOKE CUMBERLAND SAMPSON DUPLIN ONSLOW CARTERET

SCOTLAND ROBESON BLADEN PENDER

COLUMBUS NEW HAN-OVER

BRUNSWICK

Atlantic Ocean

CENSUS AVAILABILITY

Federal census extant for all counties.

1   2   3   4   5   6   7   8   9   10   11   12

25   0   25   50   75   100 MILES

North Carolina ● 1920

MAP GUIDE TO THE U.S. FEDERAL CENSUSES, 1790–1920 by William Thorndale and William Dollarhide. Copyright 1987, all rights reserved.

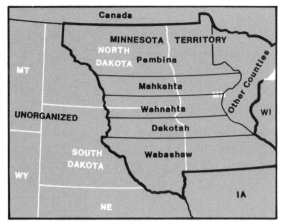

Map A • 1850

Minnesota Territory in 1850 had five western counties defined to run deep into Indian lands to the territory's west boundary of the Missouri-White Earth rivers. The only white settlers in the present-day Dakotas in 1850 were enumerated in Pembina County, Minnesota Territory, along the Red River.

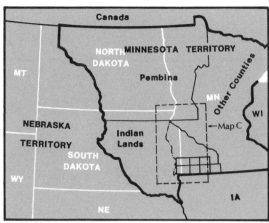

Map B • 1857

This map outlines the western-most counties for Minnesota Territory in 1857. Pembina County was nearly all unceded Indian lands, but its Red River settlers in present-day North Dakota are listed in the 1857 census for Minnesota Territory.

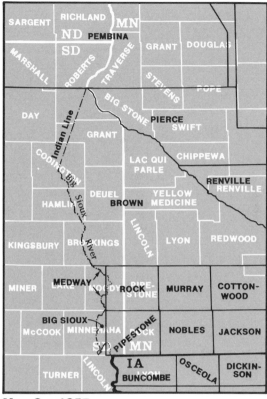

Map C • 1857

The map above shows part of eastern South Dakota and western Minnesota, including the 1851 Indian treaty line running mostly with the Big Sioux River. See Minnesota 1857 regarding Pipestone and Rock. The paper counties of Big Sioux and Medway (also called Midway) were not enumerated in 1857, though a few dozen whites had settled in Big Sioux by August 1857. Medway was defined to lie between Rock County and the Big Sioux River, but a section of the river ran east of the Rock boundary. Big Sioux and Medway lost their legal existence after the disappearance of Minnesota Territory in 1858.

Unorganized Dakota – 1860

For North Dakota 1860, see full-size map on the next page. For South Dakota 1860, see page 306.

Minnesota statehood in 1858 left the western remnant of old Minnesota Territory without territorial government until 1861. The 1860 census for "Unorganized Dakota" is extant and includes population in both present-day North and South Dakota. It also includes trading posts in Nebraska Territory on the Missouri River's west bank and upper reaches, including Fort Alexander in what is now Montana. However, the U.S. Army's Fort Randall was enumerated with Nebraska Territory. Two sites in the 1860 Dakota census were not identified: Orphan's Village (two inhabitants) presumably in North Dakota's Red River area, and the Old Trading House (23 inhabitants) north of the Niobrara River in present-day South Dakota.

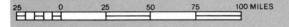

WHITE = MODERN BOUNDARIES
BLACK = 1850-1860 BOUNDARIES

North Dakota •
MISCELLANEOUS
1850-1860

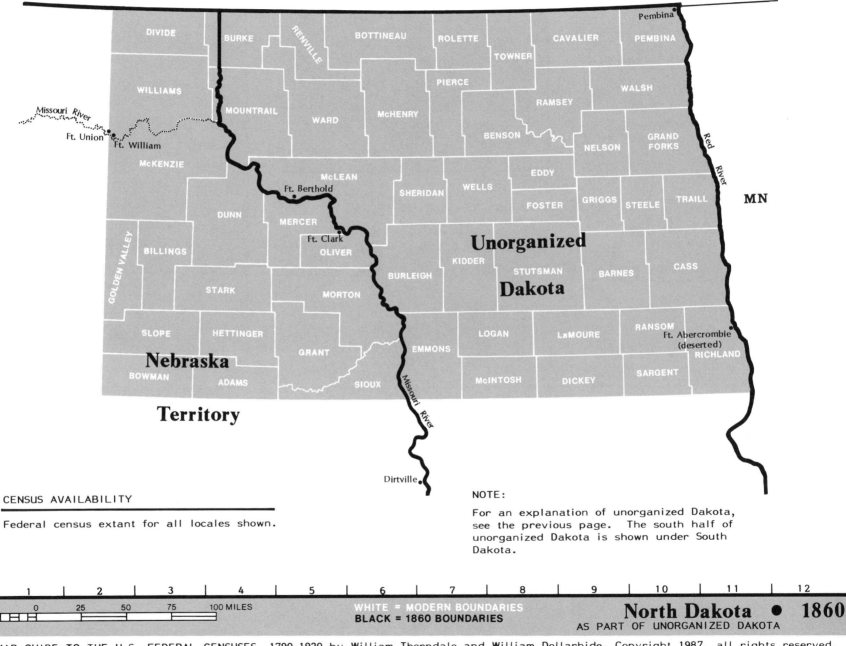

Canada

DIVIDE

BURKE

RENVILLE

BOTTINEAU

ROLETTE

CAVALIER

Pembina

PEMBINA

TOWNER

WILLIAMS

MOUNTRAIL

PIERCE

WARD

McHENRY

RAMSEY

WALSH

Missouri River

Ft. Union Ft. William

BENSON

NELSON

GRAND FORKS

Red River

MN

McKENZIE

McLEAN

Ft. Berthold

SHERIDAN

WELLS

EDDY

FOSTER

GRIGGS

STEELE

TRAILL

DUNN

MERCER

Ft. Clark

OLIVER

Unorganized

GOLDEN VALLEY

BILLINGS

KIDDER

STUTSMAN

Dakota

BARNES

CASS

BURLEIGH

STARK

MORTON

SLOPE

HETTINGER

LOGAN

LaMOURE

RANSOM

Ft. Abercrombie
(deserted)

Nebraska

GRANT

EMMONS

RICHLAND

BOWMAN

ADAMS

SIOUX

Missouri River

McINTOSH

DICKEY

SARGENT

Territory

Dirtville.

CENSUS AVAILABILITY

Federal census extant for all locales shown.

NOTE:

For an explanation of unorganized Dakota, see the previous page. The south half of unorganized Dakota is shown under South Dakota.

| 1 | 2 | 3 | 4 | 5 | 6 | 7 | 8 | 9 | 10 | 11 | 12 |

25   0   25   50   75   100 MILES

WHITE = MODERN BOUNDARIES
BLACK = 1860 BOUNDARIES

North Dakota ● **1860**
AS PART OF UNORGANIZED DAKOTA

MAP GUIDE TO THE U.S. FEDERAL CENSUSES, 1790–1920 by William Thorndale and William Dollarhide. Copyright 1987, all rights reserved.

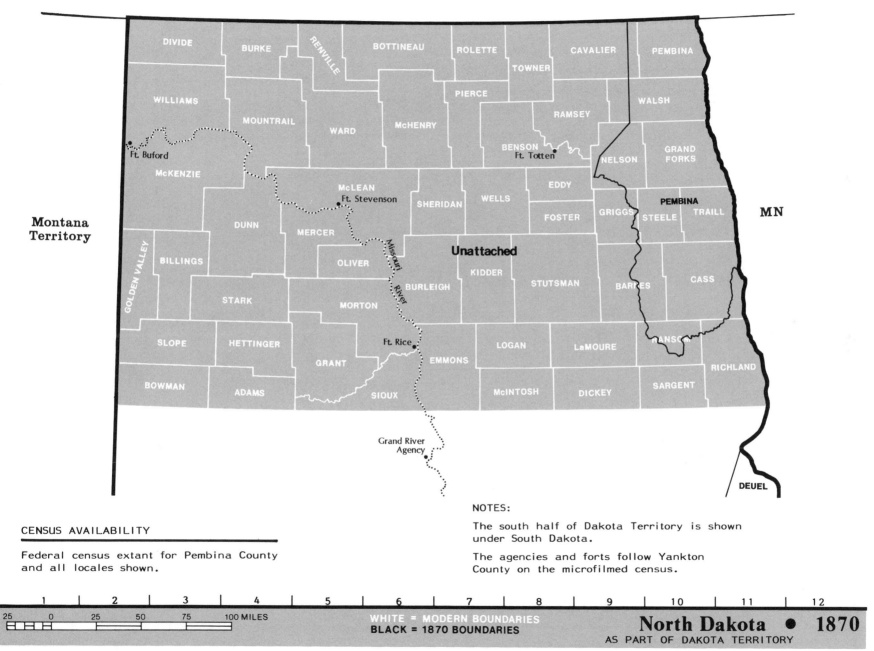

Canada

Montana
Territory

MN

DIVIDE

BURKE

RENVILLE

BOTTINEAU

ROLETTE

CAVALIER

PEMBINA

TOWNER

WILLIAMS

MOUNTRAIL

WARD

McHENRY

PIERCE

RAMSEY

WALSH

Ft. Buford

McKENZIE

BENSON

Ft. Totten

NELSON

GRAND
FORKS

McLEAN
Ft. Stevenson

SHERIDAN

WELLS

EDDY

PEMBINA

DUNN

MERCER

Missouri River

Unattached

FOSTER

GRIGGS

STEELE

TRAILL

GOLDEN VALLEY

BILLINGS

OLIVER

KIDDER

BURLEIGH

STUTSMAN

BARNES

CASS

STARK

MORTON

SLOPE

HETTINGER

Ft. Rice

LOGAN

LaMOURE

RANSOM

RICHLAND

GRANT

EMMONS

SARGENT

BOWMAN

ADAMS

SIOUX

McINTOSH

DICKEY

Grand River
Agency

DEUEL

NOTES:

The south half of Dakota Territory is shown
under South Dakota.

The agencies and forts follow Yankton
County on the microfilmed census.

CENSUS AVAILABILITY

Federal census extant for Pembina County
and all locales shown.

| 1 | 2 | 3 | 4 | 5 | 6 | 7 | 8 | 9 | 10 | 11 | 12 |

25   0   25   50   75   100 MILES

WHITE = MODERN BOUNDARIES
BLACK = 1870 BOUNDARIES

North Dakota ● **1870**
AS PART OF DAKOTA TERRITORY

MAP GUIDE TO THE U.S. FEDERAL CENSUSES, 1790-1920 by William Thorndale and William Dollarhide. Copyright 1987, all rights reserved.

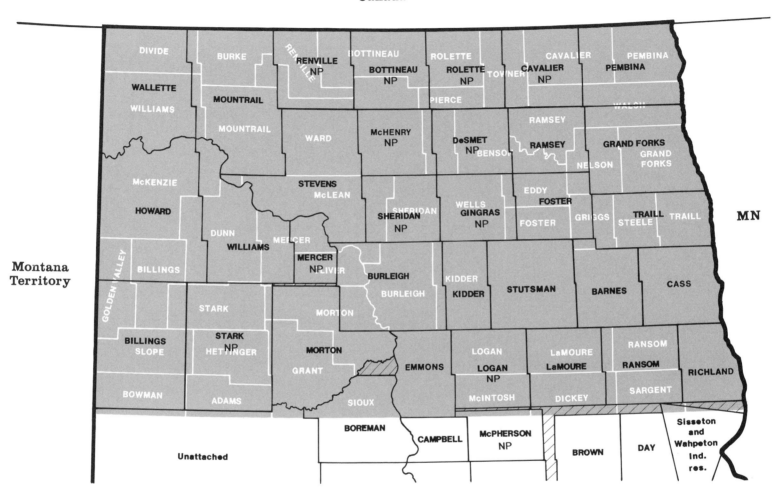

Canada

Montana
Territory

MN

CENSUS AVAILABILITY

Federal census extant for all counties.

NOTES:

The south half of Dakota Territory is shown under South Dakota.

Paper counties without white settlers are shown as NP (no population).

Unattached, non-county areas are shown with hatching.

The numerous changes in county names 1880–1910 are not noted on this or subsequent sheets.

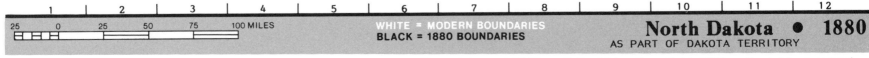

1   2   3   4   5   6   7   8   9   10   11   12

25   0   25   50   75   100 MILES

WHITE = MODERN BOUNDARIES
BLACK = 1880 BOUNDARIES

North Dakota ● 1880
AS PART OF DAKOTA TERRITORY

Canada

Montana
Territory

MN

CENSUS AVAILABILITY

Dakota census lists survive for 37 counties. The 17 counties within present-day North Dakota are shown as "extant" on map.

*NOTES:

The south half of Dakota Territory is shown under South Dakota.

Unattached, non-county areas are shown with hatching.

The legal Kidder–Stutsman boundary was the white, modern line, since voters rejected the 1885 creation of Stanton. However, Stanton appears in the census.

1 2 3 4 5 6 7 8 9 10 11 12

25   0   25   50   75   100 MILES

North Dakota ● 1885
AS PART OF DAKOTA TERRITORY

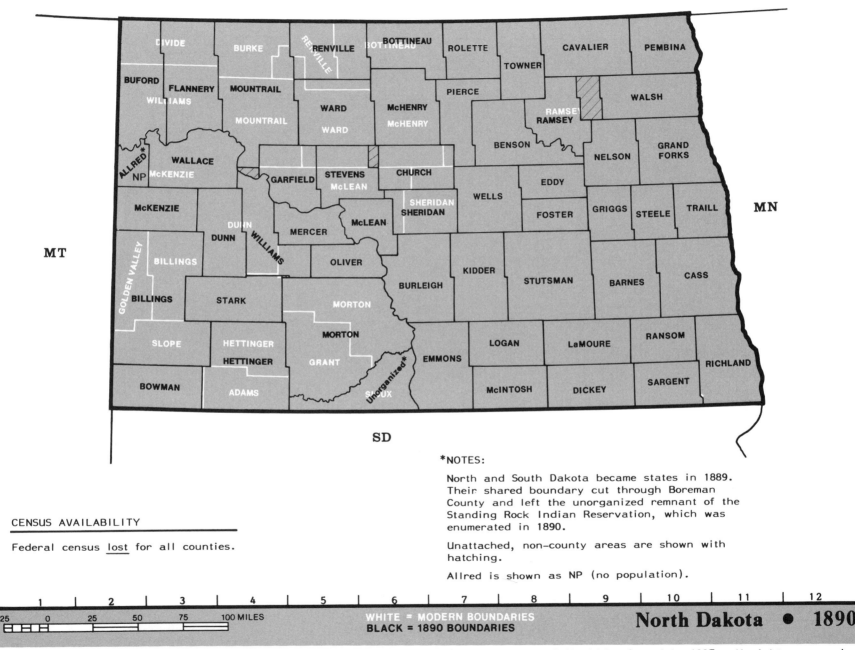

Canada

MT

MN

SD

*NOTES:

North and South Dakota became states in 1889. Their shared boundary cut through Boreman County and left the unorganized remnant of the Standing Rock Indian Reservation, which was enumerated in 1890.

Unattached, non-county areas are shown with hatching.

Allred is shown as NP (no population).

CENSUS AVAILABILITY

Federal census lost for all counties.

WHITE = MODERN BOUNDARIES
BLACK = 1890 BOUNDARIES

North Dakota ● 1890

25   0   25   50   75   100 MILES

1 2 3 4 5 6 7 8 9 10 11 12

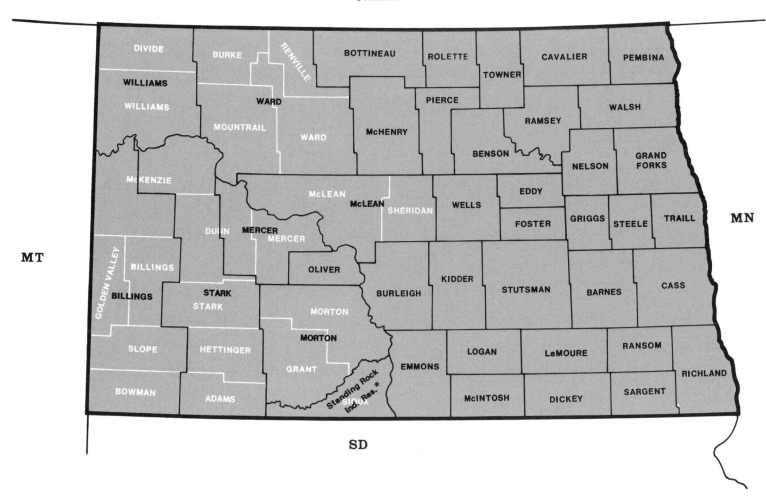

Canada

DIVIDE

BURKE

RENVILLE

BOTTINEAU

ROLETTE

CAVALIER

PEMBINA

WILLIAMS

WILLIAMS

WARD

TOWNER

PIERCE

RAMSEY

WALSH

MOUNTRAIL

WARD

McHENRY

BENSON

McKENZIE

GRAND
FORKS

NELSON

McLEAN

McLEAN

SHERIDAN

WELLS

EDDY

MT

DUNN

MERCER

MERCER

FOSTER

GRIGGS

STEELE

TRAILL

MN

GOLDEN VALLEY

BILLINGS

OLIVER

KIDDER

BILLINGS

STARK

STARK

BURLEIGH

STUTSMAN

BARNES

CASS

MORTON

SLOPE

HETTINGER

MORTON

LOGAN

LaMOURE

RANSOM

GRANT

EMMONS

RICHLAND

Standing Rock
Ind. Res. *

BOWMAN

ADAMS

SIOUX

McINTOSH

DICKEY

SARGENT

SD

CENSUS AVAILABILITY

Federal census extant for all counties.

*NOTE:

Parts of the Standing Rock census are headed
"Boreman County," an outdated reference to the
pre–1889 situation.

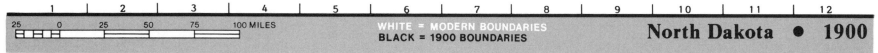

| 1 | 2 | 3 | 4 | 5 | 6 | 7 | 8 | 9 | 10 | 11 | 12 |

25 0 25 50 75 100 MILES

WHITE = MODERN BOUNDARIES
BLACK = 1900 BOUNDARIES

North Dakota ● 1900

MAP GUIDE TO THE U.S. FEDERAL CENSUSES, 1790–1920 by William Thorndale and William Dollarhide. Copyright 1987, all rights reserved.

Canada

DIVIDE BURKE RENVILLE BOTTINEAU ROLETTE TOWNER CAVALIER PEMBINA

WILLIAMS MOUNTRAIL WARD McHENRY PIERCE RAMSEY WALSH

BENSON NELSON GRAND FORKS

McKENZIE McLEAN SHERIDAN WELLS EDDY GRIGGS STEELE TRAILL

GOLDEN VALLEY* BILLINGS* DUNN MERCER OLIVER FOSTER

MT

BILLINGS* STARK MORTON* KIDDER BURLEIGH STUTSMAN BARNES CASS

SLOPE* HETTINGER MORTON* LOGAN LaMOURE RANSOM

GRANT* EMMONS RICHLAND

BOWMAN ADAMS SIOUX* McINTOSH DICKEY SARGENT

MN

SD

CENSUS AVAILABILITY

1910–1920 federal censuses extant for all counties.

*NOTES:

Golden Valley in 1912 and Slope in 1914 were created from Billings with their modern boundaries.

Morton's 1910 census included Grant (created in 1916) and the Standing Rock Indian Reservation (which became Sioux County in 1914).

1 2 3 4 5 6 7 8 9 10 11 12

25 0 25 50 75 100 MILES

WHITE = MODERN BOUNDARIES
BLACK = 1910-1920 BOUNDARIES

North Dakota ● 1910-1920

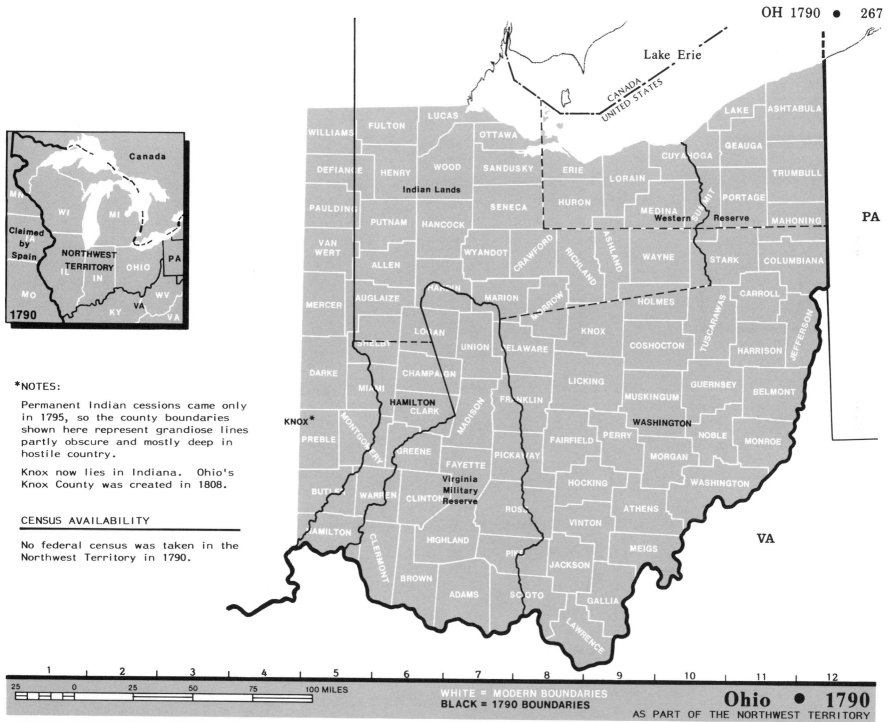

Lake Erie

CANADA
UNITED STATES

PA

Canada

Claimed
by
Spain

NORTHWEST
TERRITORY

PA

1790

Indian Lands

Western Reserve

Virginia
Military
Reserve

VA

WILLIAMS · **FULTON** · **LUCAS** · **OTTAWA** · **DEFIANCE** · **HENRY** · **WOOD** · **SANDUSKY** · **ERIE** · **LORAIN** · **CUYAHOGA** · **GEAUGA** · **LAKE** · **ASHTABULA** · **TRUMBULL** · **PORTAGE** · **MAHONING** · **PAULDING** · **PUTNAM** · **HANCOCK** · **SENECA** · **HURON** · **MEDINA** · **SUMMIT** · **VAN WERT** · **WYANDOT** · **CRAWFORD** · **RICHLAND** · **ASHLAND** · **WAYNE** · **STARK** · **COLUMBIANA** · **ALLEN** · **HARDIN** · **MARION** · **MORROW** · **HOLMES** · **CARROLL** · **MERCER** · **AUGLAIZE** · **LOGAN** · **UNION** · **DELAWARE** · **KNOX** · **COSHOCTON** · **TUSCARAWAS** · **HARRISON** · **JEFFERSON** · **DARKE** · **CHAMPAIGN** · **FRANKLIN** · **LICKING** · **MUSKINGUM** · **GUERNSEY** · **BELMONT** · **MIAMI** · **HAMILTON** · **CLARK** · **MADISON** · **FAIRFIELD** · **PERRY** · **MORGAN** · **NOBLE** · **MONROE** · **PREBLE** · **GREENE** · **FAYETTE** · **PICKAWAY** · **HOCKING** · **WASHINGTON** · **BUTLER** · **WARREN** · **CLINTON** · **ROSS** · **VINTON** · **ATHENS** · **HAMILTON** · **CLERMONT** · **HIGHLAND** · **PIKE** · **MEIGS** · **BROWN** · **ADAMS** · **SCIOTO** · **JACKSON** · **GALLIA** · **LAWRENCE** · **MONTGOMERY**

WASHINGTON

KNOX*

*NOTES:

Permanent Indian cessions came only
in 1795, so the county boundaries
shown here represent grandiose lines
partly obscure and mostly deep in
hostile country.

Knox now lies in Indiana. Ohio's
Knox County was created in 1808.

CENSUS AVAILABILITY

No federal census was taken in the
Northwest Territory in 1790.

1   2   3   4   5   6   7   8   9   10   11   12

25   0   25   50   75   100 MILES

WHITE = MODERN BOUNDARIES
BLACK = 1790 BOUNDARIES

Ohio ● **1790**
AS PART OF THE NORTHWEST TERRITORY

Lake Erie

CANADA
UNITED STATES

WAYNE

Indiana
Territory

PA

VA

KY

1800

Claimed by Spain

INDIANA TERRITORY

NORTH-WEST

OHIO TERR.

PA

Canada

MN

WI

MI

IA

IL

IN

MO

KY

WV VA

VA

*NOTES:

Hamilton, Ross, and Washington are shown north to the 1795 Indian treaty line.

The Western Reserve was ceded by Connecticut in May 1800 and became Trumbull in July, but only the eastern part of the county was free of Indian titles.

Except for the Detroit area, Wayne County was essentially Indian lands. Ohio's present Wayne County was created in 1808 and organized in 1812.

CENSUS AVAILABILITY

Federal census lost for all counties except Washington, shown as "extant" on map.

WILLIAMS
FULTON
LUCAS
OTTAWA
DEFIANCE
HENRY
WOOD
SANDUSKY
ERIE
LORAIN
CUYAHOGA
LAKE
ASHTABULA
GEAUGA
TRUMBULL*
TRUMBULL
PORTAGE
MAHONING
PAULDING
PUTNAM
HANCOCK
SENECA
HURON
MEDINA
SUMMIT
Western Reserve
Indian Lands
VAN WERT
ALLEN
WYANDOT
CRAWFORD
RICHLAND
ASHLAND
WAYNE
STARK
COLUMBIANA
MERCER
AUGLAIZE
HARDIN
MARION
MORROW
KNOX
HOLMES
COSHOCTON
TUSCARAWAS
CARROLL
HARRISON
JEFFERSON
SHELBY
LOGAN
UNION
DELAWARE
LICKING
MUSKINGUM
GUERNSEY
BELMONT
DARKE
CHAMPAIGN
MIAMI
CLARK
MADISON
FRANKLIN
FAIRFIELD
PERRY
WASHINGTON*
extant
NOBLE
MONROE
PREBLE
GREENE
FAYETTE
PICKAWAY
ROSS*
HOCKING
MORGAN
WASHINGTON
MONTGOMERY
HAMILTON*
BUTLER
WARREN
CLINTON
ROSS
VINTON
ATHENS
HAMILTON
CLERMONT
HIGHLAND
PIKE
MEIGS
BROWN
ADAMS
ADAMS
SCIOTO
JACKSON
GALLIA
LAWRENCE

Indiana Territory

PA

VA

KY

Ohio ● 1800

AS PART OF THE NORTHWEST TERRITORY

WHITE = MODERN BOUNDARIES
BLACK = 1800 BOUNDARIES

1   2   3   4   5   6   7   8   9   10   11   12

25   0   25   50   75   100 MILES

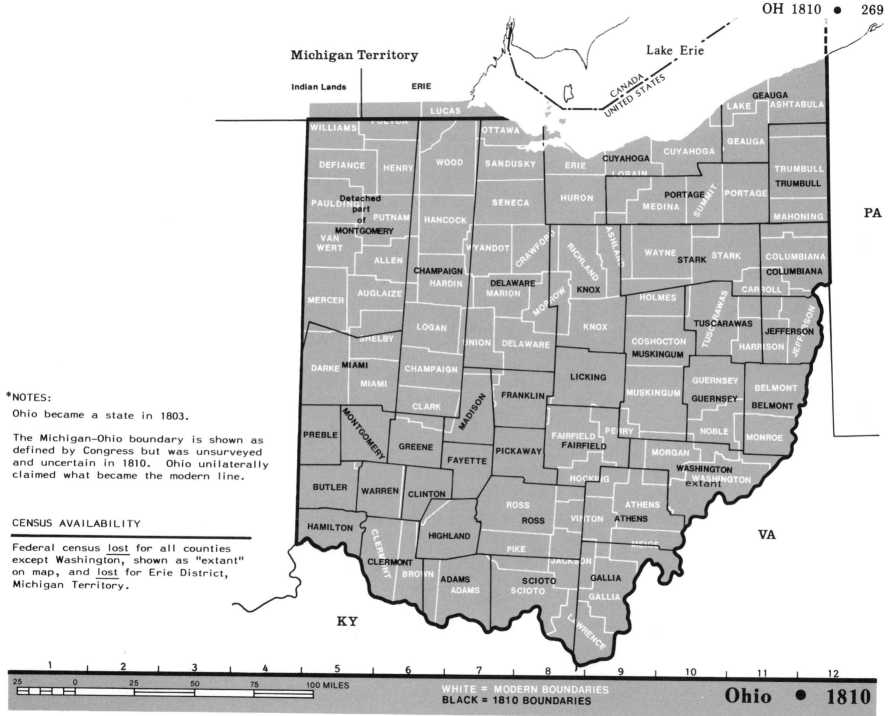

OH 1810 • 269

Michigan Territory

Lake Erie

Indian Lands   ERIE

CANADA
UNITED STATES

PA

VA

KY

*NOTES:

Ohio became a state in 1803.

The Michigan–Ohio boundary is shown as
defined by Congress but was unsurveyed
and uncertain in 1810. Ohio unilaterally
claimed what became the modern line.

CENSUS AVAILABILITY

Federal census lost for all counties
except Washington, shown as "extant"
on map, and lost for Erie District,
Michigan Territory.

WHITE = MODERN BOUNDARIES
BLACK = 1810 BOUNDARIES

Ohio   •   1810

25   0   25   50   75   100 MILES

1   2   3   4   5   6   7   8   9   10   11   12

MAP GUIDE TO THE U.S. FEDERAL CENSUSES, 1790–1920 by William Thorndale and William Dollarhide. Copyright 1987, all rights reserved.

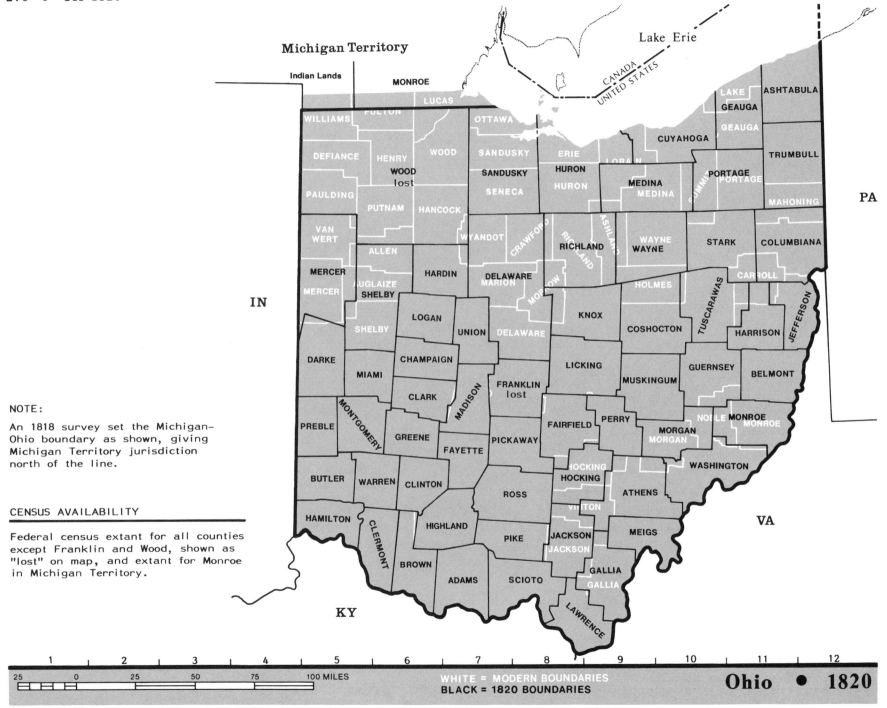

NOTE:

An 1818 survey set the Michigan-Ohio boundary as shown, giving Michigan Territory jurisdiction north of the line.

CENSUS AVAILABILITY

Federal census extant for all counties except Franklin and Wood, shown as "lost" on map, and extant for Monroe in Michigan Territory.

WHITE = MODERN BOUNDARIES
BLACK = 1820 BOUNDARIES

Ohio ● 1820

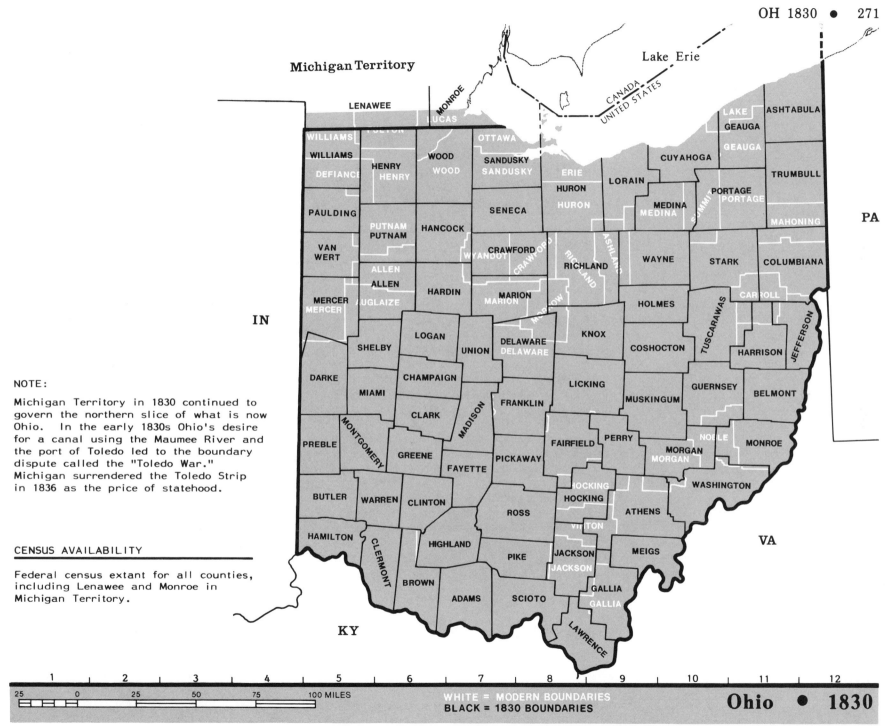

Michigan Territory

Lake Erie

CANADA
UNITED STATES

PA

IN

VA

KY

NOTE:

Michigan Territory in 1830 continued to govern the northern slice of what is now Ohio. In the early 1830s Ohio's desire for a canal using the Maumee River and the port of Toledo led to the boundary dispute called the "Toledo War." Michigan surrendered the Toledo Strip in 1836 as the price of statehood.

CENSUS AVAILABILITY

Federal census extant for all counties, including Lenawee and Monroe in Michigan Territory.

LENAWEE

MONROE
LUCAS

FULTON

WILLIAMS
WILLIAMS

HENRY
HENRY

WOOD
WOOD

OTTAWA

SANDUSKY
SANDUSKY

LAKE
GEAUGA
GEAUGA

ASHTABULA

CUYAHOGA

TRUMBULL

DEFIANCE

ERIE

HURON
HURON

LORAIN

PAULDING

SENECA

HANCOCK

MEDINA
MEDINA

PORTAGE
PORTAGE

SUMMIT

MAHONING

PUTNAM
PUTNAM

WYANDOT

CRAWFORD
CRAWFORD

RICHLAND

ASHLAND

WAYNE

STARK

COLUMBIANA

VAN
WERT

ALLEN
ALLEN

HARDIN

MARION
MARION

RICHLAND

MORROW

HOLMES

CARROLL

MERCER
MERCER

AUGLAIZE

MORROW

KNOX

COSHOCTON

TUSCARAWAS

HARRISON

JEFFERSON

LOGAN

UNION

DELAWARE
DELAWARE

SHELBY

DARKE

CHAMPAIGN

LICKING

MUSKINGUM

GUERNSEY

BELMONT

MIAMI

MADISON

FRANKLIN

CLARK

NOBLE

MONROE

MONTGOMERY

GREENE

FAYETTE

PICKAWAY

FAIRFIELD

PERRY

MORGAN
MORGAN

PREBLE

WASHINGTON

BUTLER

WARREN

CLINTON

ROSS

HOCKING
HOCKING

ATHENS

HAMILTON

HIGHLAND

VINTON

CLERMONT

PIKE

JACKSON
JACKSON

MEIGS

BROWN

ADAMS

SCIOTO

GALLIA
GALLIA

LAWRENCE

| 1 | | 2 | 3 | 4 | 5 | 6 | 7 | 8 | 9 | 10 | 11 | 12 |

25   0   25   50   75   100 MILES

WHITE = MODERN BOUNDARIES
BLACK = 1830 BOUNDARIES

Ohio ● 1830

MAP GUIDE TO THE U.S. FEDERAL CENSUSES, 1790–1920 by William Thorndale and William Dollarhide. Copyright 1987, all rights reserved.

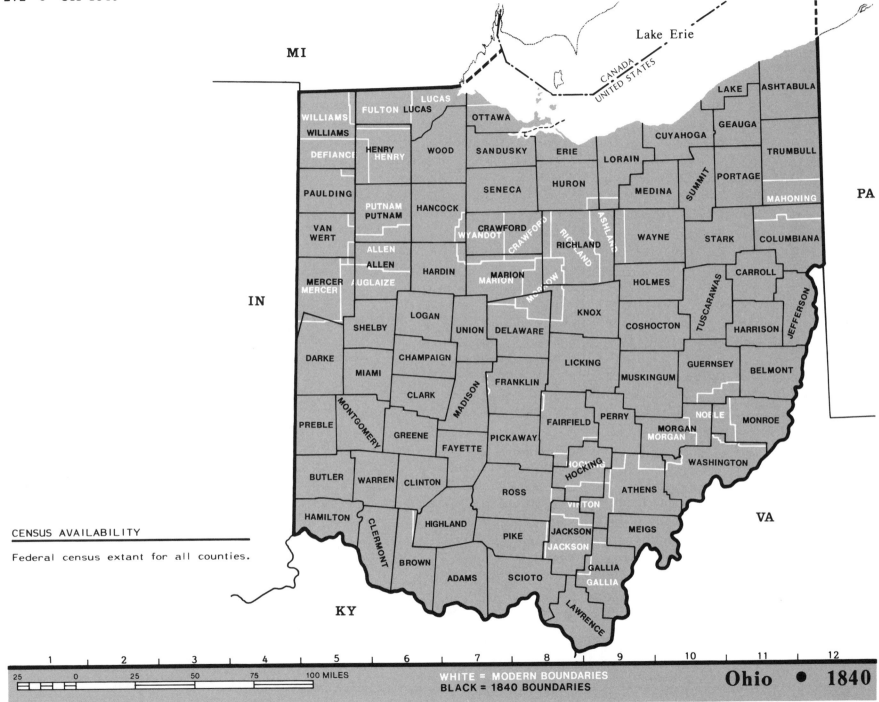

MI

Lake Erie

CANADA
UNITED STATES

IN

PA

VA

KY

| 1 | 2 | 3 | 4 | 5 | 6 | 7 | 8 | 9 | 10 | 11 | 12 |

25   0   25   50   75   100 MILES

WHITE = MODERN BOUNDARIES
BLACK = 1840 BOUNDARIES

Ohio ● 1840

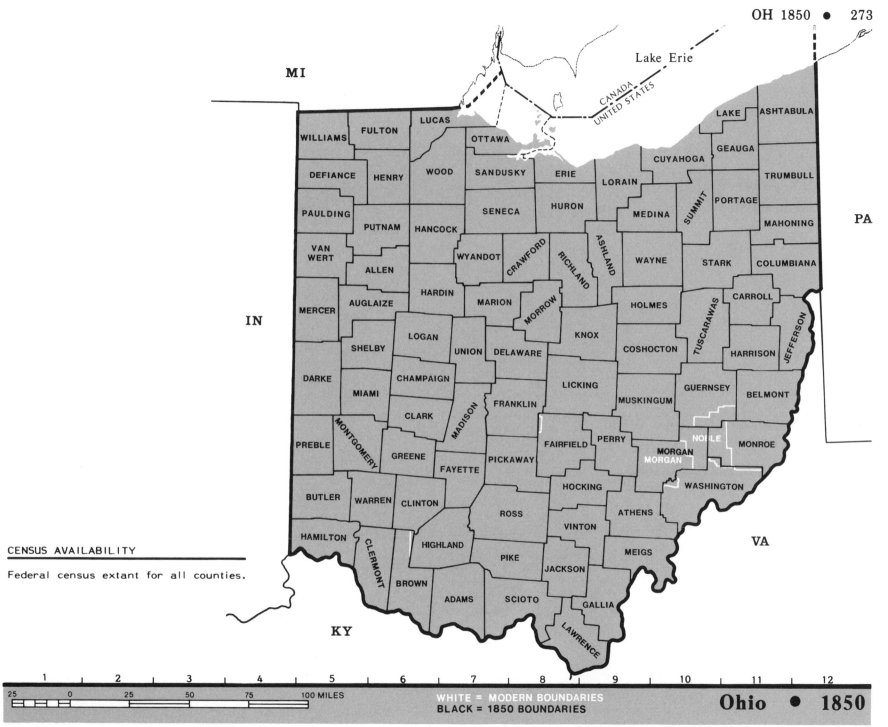

OH 1850 ● 273

MI

Lake Erie

CANADA
UNITED STATES

PA

IN

VA

KY

CENSUS AVAILABILITY

Federal census extant for all counties.

LAWRENCE

1 2 3 4 5 6 7 8 9 10 11 12

25 0 25 50 75 100 MILES

WHITE = MODERN BOUNDARIES
BLACK = 1850 BOUNDARIES

Ohio ● 1850

MAP GUIDE TO THE U.S. FEDERAL CENSUSES, 1790–1920 by William Thorndale and William Dollarhide. Copyright 1987, all rights reserved.

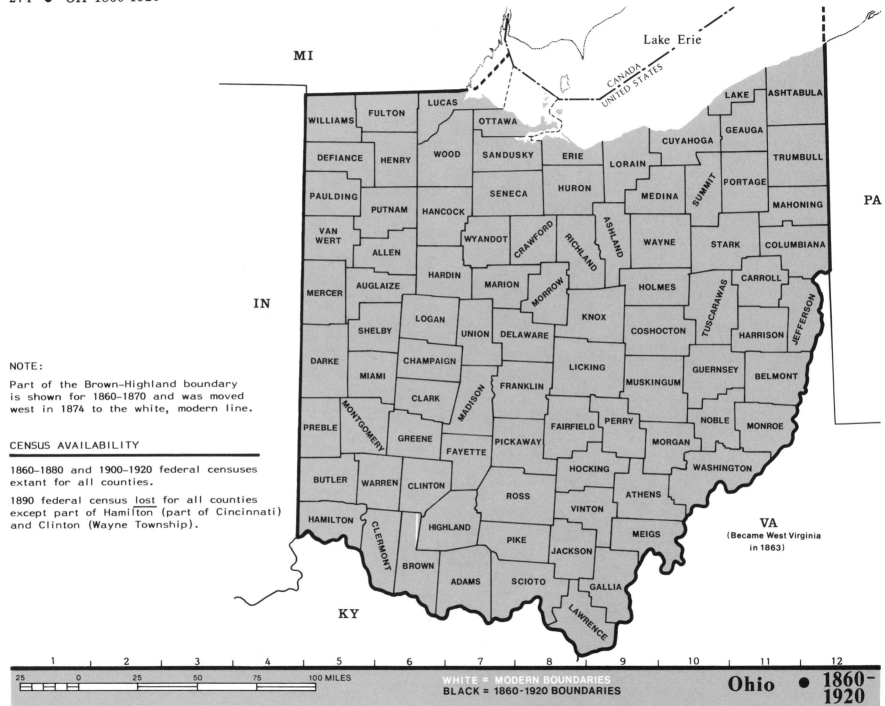

MI

Lake Erie

CANADA
UNITED STATES

PA

IN

NOTE:

Part of the Brown-Highland boundary
is shown for 1860-1870 and was moved
west in 1874 to the white, modern line.

CENSUS AVAILABILITY

1860-1880 and 1900-1920 federal censuses
extant for all counties.

1890 federal census lost for all counties
except part of Hamilton (part of Cincinnati)
and Clinton (Wayne Township).

VA
(Became West Virginia
in 1863)

KY

| WILLIAMS | FULTON | LUCAS | OTTAWA | | | | LAKE | ASHTABULA |

WILLIAMS, FULTON, LUCAS, OTTAWA, DEFIANCE, HENRY, WOOD, SANDUSKY, ERIE, LORAIN, CUYAHOGA, GEAUGA, LAKE, ASHTABULA, TRUMBULL, PAULDING, PUTNAM, HANCOCK, SENECA, HURON, MEDINA, SUMMIT, PORTAGE, MAHONING, VAN WERT, ALLEN, WYANDOT, CRAWFORD, RICHLAND, ASHLAND, WAYNE, STARK, COLUMBIANA, MERCER, AUGLAIZE, HARDIN, MARION, MORROW, HOLMES, TUSCARAWAS, CARROLL, JEFFERSON, LOGAN, KNOX, COSHOCTON, HARRISON, SHELBY, UNION, DELAWARE, DARKE, CHAMPAIGN, LICKING, MUSKINGUM, GUERNSEY, BELMONT, MIAMI, FRANKLIN, MADISON, CLARK, PERRY, NOBLE, MONROE, PREBLE, MONTGOMERY, GREENE, FAIRFIELD, MORGAN, FAYETTE, PICKAWAY, HOCKING, WASHINGTON, BUTLER, WARREN, CLINTON, ROSS, ATHENS, HAMILTON, CLERMONT, HIGHLAND, VINTON, MEIGS, BROWN, PIKE, JACKSON, GALLIA, ADAMS, SCIOTO, LAWRENCE

1   2   3   4   5   6   7   8   9   10   11   12

25   0   25   50   75   100 MILES

WHITE = MODERN BOUNDARIES
BLACK = 1860-1920 BOUNDARIES

Ohio ● 1860-1920

MAP GUIDE TO THE U.S. FEDERAL CENSUSES, 1790-1920 by William Thorndale and William Dollarhide. Copyright 1987, all rights reserved.

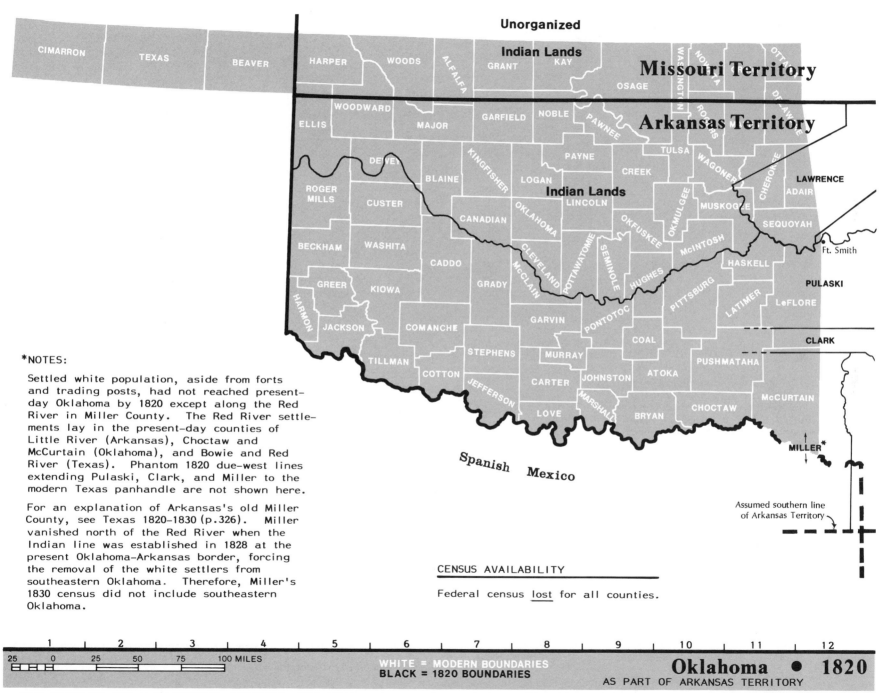

Unorganized

Indian Lands

Missouri Territory

Arkansas Territory

Indian Lands

LAWRENCE

Ft. Smith

PULASKI

CLARK

Spanish Mexico

MILLER*

Assumed southern line
of Arkansas Territory

CIMARRON · TEXAS · BEAVER · HARPER · WOODS · ALFALFA · GRANT · KAY · OSAGE · WASHINGTON · NOWATA · CRAIG · OTTAWA · DELAWARE · ELLIS · WOODWARD · MAJOR · GARFIELD · NOBLE · PAWNEE · TULSA · WAGONER · CHEROKEE · ADAIR · ROGER MILLS · CUSTER · BLAINE · KINGFISHER · LOGAN · PAYNE · CREEK · OKMULGEE · MUSKOGEE · SEQUOYAH · DEWEY · LINCOLN · OKLAHOMA · OKFUSKEE · McINTOSH · BECKHAM · WASHITA · CANADIAN · CLEVELAND · POTTAWATOMIE · SEMINOLE · HUGHES · HASKELL · GREER · KIOWA · CADDO · GRADY · McCLAIN · PONTOTOC · PITTSBURG · LATIMER · LeFLORE · HARMON · JACKSON · COMANCHE · GARVIN · COAL · PUSHMATAHA · McCURTAIN · TILLMAN · STEPHENS · MURRAY · JOHNSTON · ATOKA · COTTON · JEFFERSON · CARTER · MARSHALL · LOVE · BRYAN · CHOCTAW

*NOTES:

Settled white population, aside from forts
and trading posts, had not reached present-
day Oklahoma by 1820 except along the Red
River in Miller County. The Red River settlements lay in the present-day counties of
Little River (Arkansas), Choctaw and
McCurtain (Oklahoma), and Bowie and Red
River (Texas). Phantom 1820 due-west lines
extending Pulaski, Clark, and Miller to the
modern Texas panhandle are not shown here.

For an explanation of Arkansas's old Miller
County, see Texas 1820–1830 (p.326). Miller
vanished north of the Red River when the
Indian line was established in 1828 at the
present Oklahoma-Arkansas border, forcing
the removal of the white settlers from
southeastern Oklahoma. Therefore, Miller's
1830 census did not include southeastern
Oklahoma.

CENSUS AVAILABILITY

Federal census <u>lost</u> for all counties.

1 2 3 4 5 6 7 8 9 10 11 12

25 0 25 50 75 100 MILES

WHITE = MODERN BOUNDARIES
BLACK = 1820 BOUNDARIES

Oklahoma • **1820**
AS PART OF ARKANSAS TERRITORY

Kansas Territory

MO

CIMARRON | TEXAS | BEAVER
Unattached

TX

HARPER | WOODS | ALFALFA | GRANT | KAY | Quapaws and Senecas | NOWATA | OTTAWA | CRAIG

WASHINGTON | DELAWARE

Cherokee Outlet

OSAGE

Cherokees

WOODWARD | GARFIELD | NOBLE | PAWNEE | ROGERS | MAYES

ELLIS | MAJOR

DEWEY | BLAINE | KINGFISHER | LOGAN | PAYNE | CREEK | TULSA | WAGONER | CHEROKEE | ADAIR

ROGER MILLS | CUSTER | **Seminoles** | OKLAHOMA | LINCOLN | **Creeks** | OKMULGEE | MUSKOGEE | SEQUOYAH

Leased

WASHITA | CADDO | CLEVELAND | POTTAWATOMIE | SEMINOLE | OKFUSKEE | McINTOSH | HASKELL

BECKHAM | **District*** | GRADY | McCLAIN | HUGHES | PITTSBURG | LATIMER | LeFLORE

GREER | KIOWA | **Chickasaws** | PONTOTOC | COAL | **Choctaws**

HARMON | GREER* NP | JACKSON | COMANCHE | STEPHENS | GARVIN | MURRAY | PUSHMATAHA

TILLMAN | COTTON | CARTER | JOHNSTON | ATOKA | McCURTAIN

TX | JEFFERSON | MARSHALL | BRYAN | CHOCTAW

LOVE

AR

***NOTES:**

Defining the present western boundary of Arkansas in 1828 initiated eight decades of white encroachment on the "Indian Territory," a name popularized in the 1830s. Although the territory never had a unified government, the tribal jurisdictions established stable societies that attracted many thousands of whites and blacks. The Indian Territory was not enumerated in the decennial censuses from 1830 to 1880 except for non-Indians in 1860.

Texas in February 1860 created the paper county of Greer in the forks of the Red River, but permanent white settlement came only in the 1880s. Greer is shown as NP (no population).

The lands west of the Chickasaws (including "Greer County") were leased by them and the Choctaws to the U.S. government for a Plains Indians hunting ground.

CENSUS AVAILABILITY

Federal census extant for non-Indians, the microfilmed lists appearing after the 1860 census for Yell County, Arkansas.

1 | 2 | 3 | 4 | 5 | 6 | 7 | 8 | 9 | 10 | 11 | 12

25 | 0 | 25 | 50 | 75 | 100 MILES

WHITE = MODERN BOUNDARIES
BLACK = 1860 BOUNDARIES

Oklahoma ● 1860
AS THE INDIAN TERRITORY

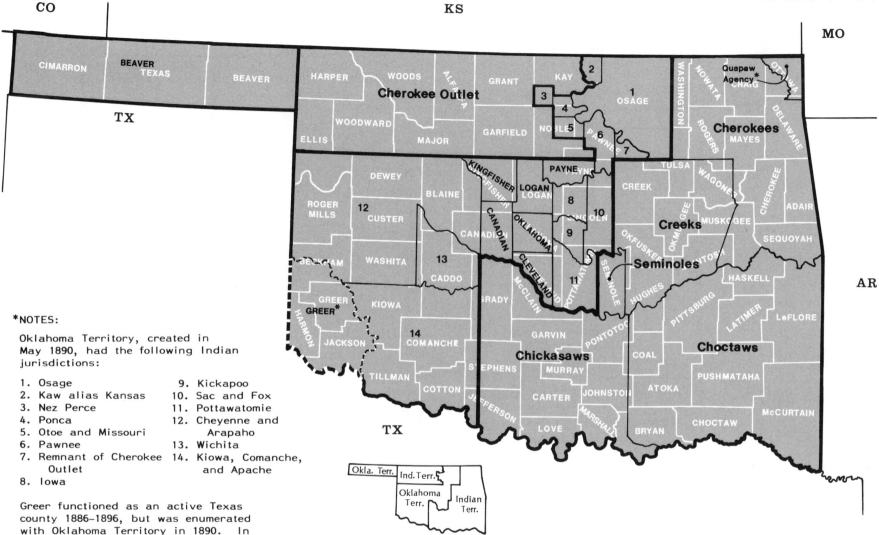

CO

KS

MO

CIMARRON

BEAVER
TEXAS

BEAVER

TX

HARPER

WOODS

ALFALFA

GRANT

KAY

2

1
OSAGE

Cherokee Outlet

WASHINGTON

NOWATA

Quapaw
Agency*

OTTAWA

CRAIG

3

4

Cherokees

MAYES

DELAWARE

WOODWARD

MAJOR

GARFIELD

NOBLE

5

6

7

ROGERS

ELLIS

PAWNEE

TULSA

CHEROKEE

ADAIR

DEWEY

KINGFISHER

PAYNE

WYN

CREEK

WAGONER

ROGER
MILLS

BLAINE

KINGFISHER

LOGAN
LOGAN

8

10

MUSKOGEE

SEQUOYAH

12
CUSTER

CANADIAN

OKLAHOMA

LINCOLN

9

OKMULGEE

Creeks

OKFUSKEE

WASHITA

CANADIAN

CLEVELAND

11

OKMULGEE

INTOSH

HASKELL

BECKHAM

13

CADDO

McCLAIN

POTTAWATOMIE

SEMINOLE

Seminoles

HUGHES

PITTSBURG

LATIMER

LeFLORE

GREER
GREER*

KIOWA

GRADY

GARVIN

PONTOTOC

Choctaws

HARMON

JACKSON

14
COMANCHE

STEPHENS

MURRAY

COAL

PUSHMATAHA

Chickasaws

TILLMAN

COTTON

JEFFERSON

CARTER

JOHNSTON

ATOKA

McCURTAIN

LOVE

BRYAN

MARSHALL

CHOCTAW

TX

AR

*NOTES:

Oklahoma Territory, created in
May 1890, had the following Indian
jurisdictions:

1. Osage   9. Kickapoo
2. Kaw alias Kansas   10. Sac and Fox
3. Nez Perce   11. Pottawatomie
4. Ponca   12. Cheyenne and
5. Otoe and Missouri   Arapaho
6. Pawnee   13. Wichita
7. Remnant of Cherokee 14. Kiowa, Comanche,
    Outlet   and Apache
8. Iowa

Greer functioned as an active Texas
county 1886–1896, but was enumerated
with Oklahoma Territory in 1890. In
1896 the U.S. Supreme Court and the
U.S. Congress reconstituted Greer as a
county in Oklahoma Territory.

The Quapaw Agency in the Indian
Territory contained reservations for
the Quapaw, Peoria, Ottawa, Shawnee,
Modoc, Wyandot, and Seneca.

Okla. Terr. Ind. Terr.

Oklahoma
Terr.   Indian
           Terr.

CENSUS AVAILABILITY – OKLAHOMA TERRITORY

Federal census lost for all Indian jurisdictions
and counties, including Greer.

Territorial census of June 1890 extant for the
seven territorial counties. Greer was not
enumerated.

CENSUS AVAILABILITY – INDIAN TERRITORY

Federal census lost for the Five Civilized
Tribes and the Quapaw Agency. Censuses
taken by the Cherokee government are
extant for both 1880 and 1890.

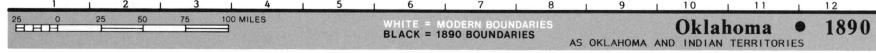

1   2   3   4   5   6   7   8   9   10   11   12

25 0 25 50 75 100 MILES

WHITE = MODERN BOUNDARIES
BLACK = 1890 BOUNDARIES

Oklahoma ● 1890
AS OKLAHOMA AND INDIAN TERRITORIES

CO

KS

MO

TX

AR

TX

CIMARRON

BEAVER
TEXAS

BEAVER

HARPER

WOODS

ALFALFA

GRANT

KAY

2

1
OSAGE

WASHINGTON

NOWATA

Quapaw
Agency*

OTTAWA

CRAIG

WOODWARD

WOODWARD

WOODS

3

NOBL
4
NOBLE

PAWNEE

ROGERS

Cherokees

DELAWARE

MAYES

ELLIS

MAJOR

GARFIELD

PAYNE

DAY*

DEWEY

BLAINE

KINGFISHER

LOGAN

CREEK

TULSA

WAGONER

CHEROKEE

ADAIR

ROGER
MILLS

ROGER
MILLS

CUSTER

CANADIAN

OKLAHOMA

LINCOLN

Creeks

OKFUSKEE

OKMULGEE

MCINTOSH

MUSKOGEE

SEQUOYAH

WASHITA

5

CADDO

CLEVELAND

POTTAWATOMIE

SEMINOLE

Seminoles

HUGHES

HASKELL

GREER

GREER

KIOWA

GRADY

McCLAIN

GARVIN

PONTOTOC

COAL

PITTSBURG

LATIMER

LeFLORE

Choctaws

HARMON

JACKSON

6
COMANCHE

Chickasaws

MURRAY

Stephens

CARTER

JOHNSTON

ATOKA

PUSHMATAHA

McCURTAIN

TILLMAN

COTTON

JEFFERSON

LOVE

MARSHALL

BRYAN

CHOCTAW

*NOTES:

Oklahoma Territory had the following
Indian jurisdictions:

1. Osage
2. Kaw alias Kansas
3. Ponca
4. Otoe and Missouri
5. Wichita
6. Kiowa, Comanche, and Apache

The Quapaw Agency in the Indian Territory
contained reservations for the Quapaw, Peoria,
Ottawa, Shawnee, Modoc, Wyandot, and Seneca.

Day County was abolished by not being
included in the 1907 constitution.

Oklahoma
Terr.

Indian
Terr.

CENSUS AVAILABILITY

Federal census extant for all counties
and Indian jurisdictions in the two
territories. The Poncas and Otoe/Missouris
were enumerated in Noble County.

1   2   3   4   5   6   7   8   9   10   11   12

25   0   25   50   75   100 MILES

WHITE = MODERN BOUNDARIES
BLACK = 1900 BOUNDARIES

Oklahoma ● 1900
AS OKLAHOMA AND INDIAN TERRITORIES

MAP GUIDE TO THE U.S. FEDERAL CENSUSES, 1790-1920 by William Thorndale and William Dollarhide. Copyright 1987, all rights reserved.

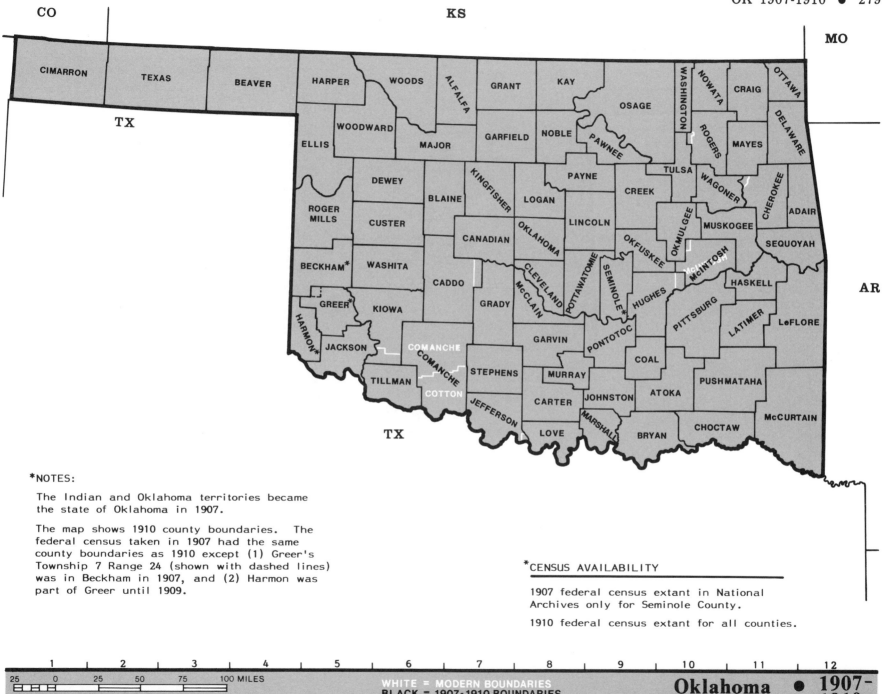

CO

KS

MO

TX

AR

CIMARRON | TEXAS | BEAVER | HARPER | WOODS | ALFALFA | GRANT | KAY

WASHINGTON | NOWATA | CRAIG | OTTAWA

WOODWARD | MAJOR | GARFIELD | NOBLE | OSAGE

ROGERS | MAYES | DELAWARE

ELLIS | PAWNEE

DEWEY | BLAINE | KINGFISHER | PAYNE | TULSA | WAGONER

ROGER MILLS | LOGAN | CREEK | CHEROKEE | ADAIR

CUSTER | CANADIAN | LINCOLN | OKMULGEE | MUSKOGEE

BECKHAM* | WASHITA | OKLAHOMA | OKFUSKEE | SEQUOYAH

McINTOSH

GREER* | KIOWA | CADDO | CLEVELAND | POTTAWATOMIE | SEMINOLE* | HUGHES | HASKELL

HARMON* | GRADY | McCLAIN | PITTSBURG | LATIMER | LeFLORE

JACKSON | COMANCHE | GARVIN | PONTOTOC

COMANCHE | STEPHENS | MURRAY | COAL | PUSHMATAHA

TILLMAN | COTTON | CARTER | JOHNSTON | ATOKA

JEFFERSON | LOVE | MARSHALL | BRYAN | CHOCTAW | McCURTAIN

*NOTES:

The Indian and Oklahoma territories became the state of Oklahoma in 1907.

The map shows 1910 county boundaries. The federal census taken in 1907 had the same county boundaries as 1910 except (1) Greer's Township 7 Range 24 (shown with dashed lines) was in Beckham in 1907, and (2) Harmon was part of Greer until 1909.

*CENSUS AVAILABILITY

1907 federal census extant in National Archives only for Seminole County.

1910 federal census extant for all counties.

1 | 2 | 3 | 4 | 5 | 6 | 7 | 8 | 9 | 10 | 11 | 12

25 | 0 | 25 | 50 | 75 | 100 MILES

WHITE = MODERN BOUNDARIES
BLACK = 1907-1910 BOUNDARIES

Oklahoma ● 1907-1910

CO
KS
MO
TX

CIMARRON | TEXAS | BEAVER | HARPER | WOODS | ALFALFA | GRANT | KAY

WASHINGTON | NOWATA | CRAIG | OTTAWA

WOODWARD | OSAGE | DELAWARE

ELLIS | GARFIELD | NOBLE | ROGERS | MAYES

MAJOR | PAWNEE

DEWEY | KINGFISHER | PAYNE | TULSA | WAGONER | CHEROKEE | ADAIR

ROGER MILLS | BLAINE | LOGAN | CREEK

CUSTER | LINCOLN | OKFUSKEE | OKMULGEE | MUSKOGEE | SEQUOYAH

CANADIAN | OKLAHOMA | OKMULGEE

BECKHAM | WASHITA | CADDO | CLEVELAND | POTTAWATOMIE | SEMINOLE | HUGHES | McINTOSH | HASKELL

GREER | KIOWA | GRADY | McCLAIN | PITTSBURG | LATIMER | LeFLORE

HARMON | JACKSON | COMANCHE | GARVIN | PONTOTOC | COAL | PUSHMATAHA

TILLMAN | STEPHENS | MURRAY | ATOKA

COTTON | JEFFERSON | CARTER | JOHNSTON | CHOCTAW | McCURTAIN

LOVE | MARSHALL | BRYAN

AR

TX

CENSUS AVAILABILITY

Federal census extant for all counties.

1 | 2 | 3 | 4 | 5 | 6 | 7 | 8 | 9 | 10 | 11 | 12

25 | 0 | 25 | 50 | 75 | 100 MILES

WHITE = MODERN BOUNDARIES
BLACK = 1920 BOUNDARIES

Oklahoma ● 1920

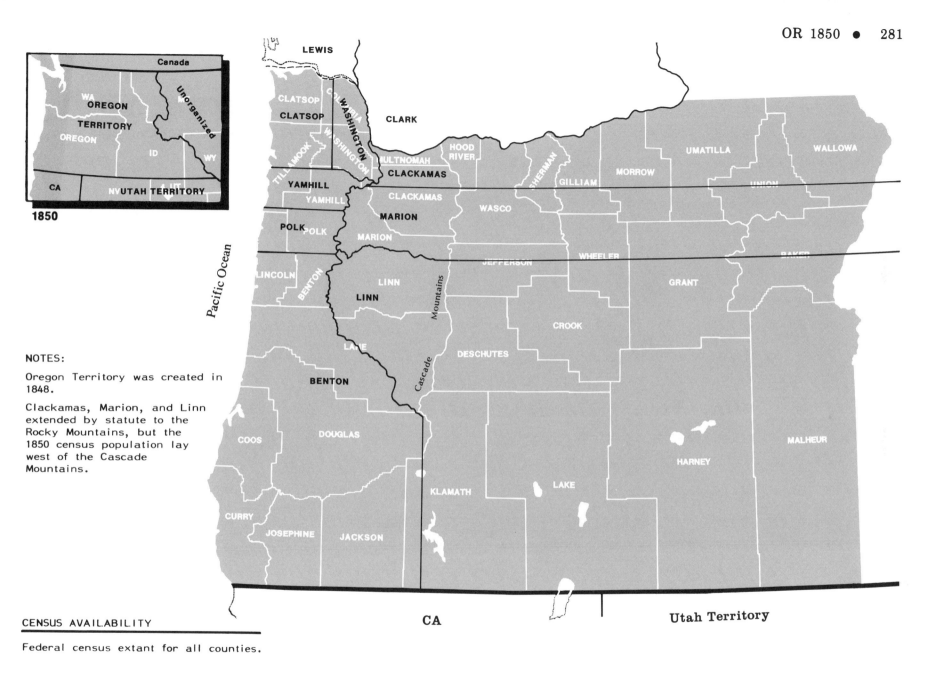

NOTES:

Oregon Territory was created in 1848.

Clackamas, Marion, and Linn extended by statute to the Rocky Mountains, but the 1850 census population lay west of the Cascade Mountains.

CENSUS AVAILABILITY

Federal census extant for all counties.

WHITE = MODERN BOUNDARIES
BLACK = 1850 BOUNDARIES

Oregon ● 1850

AS PART OF OREGON TERRITORY

25 0 25 50 75 100 MILES

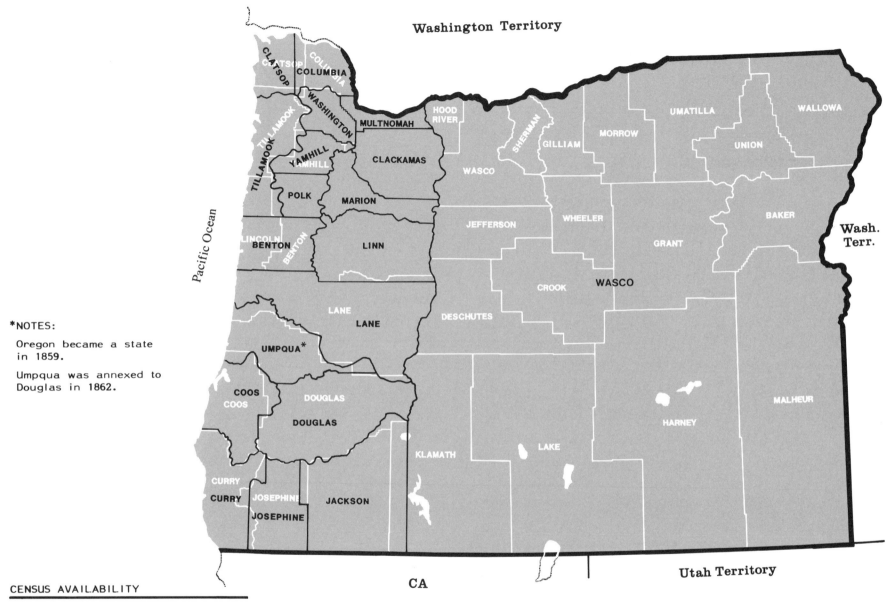

*NOTES:

Oregon became a state in 1859.

Umpqua was annexed to Douglas in 1862.

CENSUS AVAILABILITY

Federal census extant for all counties.

WHITE = MODERN BOUNDARIES
BLACK = 1860 BOUNDARIES

Oregon ● 1860

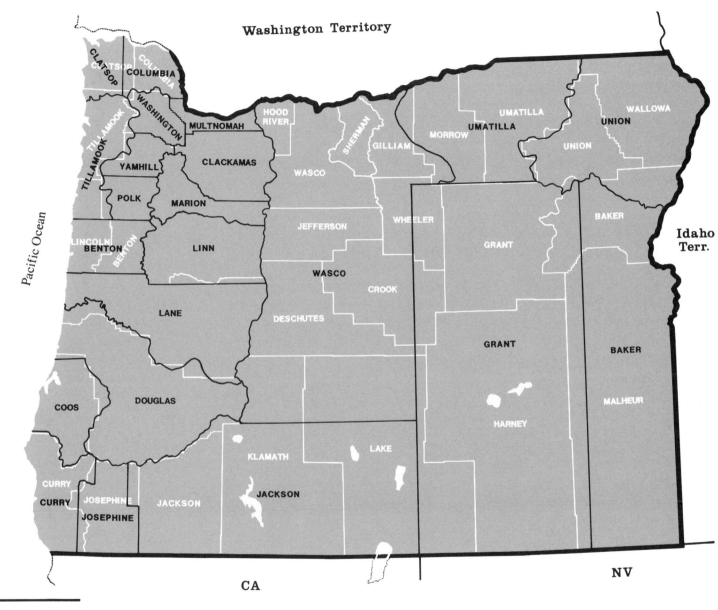

Washington Territory

Idaho
Terr.

Pacific Ocean

NV

CA

WHITE = MODERN BOUNDARIES
BLACK = 1870 BOUNDARIES

Oregon ● 1870

100 MILES

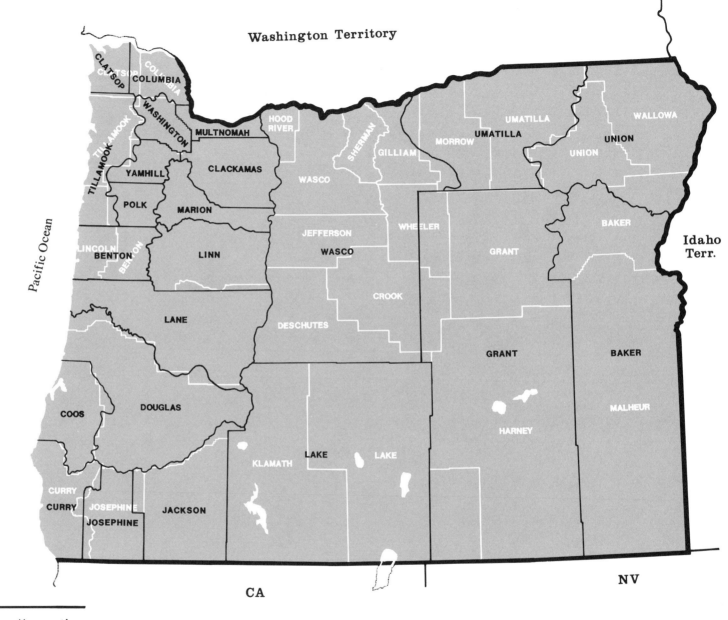

Washington Territory

CLATSOP

COLUMBIA

COLUMBIA

WASHINGTON

MULTNOMAH

HOOD RIVER

UMATILLA

UMATILLA

WALLOWA

TILLAMOOK

TILLAMOOK

CLACKAMAS

SHERMAN

GILLIAM

MORROW

UNION

UNION

YAMHILL

POLK

MARION

WASCO

Pacific Ocean

LINCOLN

BENTON

BENTON

LINN

JEFFERSON

WHEELER

BAKER

Idaho Terr.

WASCO

GRANT

LANE

CROOK

DESCHUTES

GRANT

BAKER

COOS

DOUGLAS

HARNEY

MALHEUR

CURRY

CURRY

JOSEPHINE

JOSEPHINE

JACKSON

KLAMATH

LAKE

LAKE

NV

CA

CENSUS AVAILABILITY

Federal census extant for all counties.

| 1 | 2 | 3 | 4 | 5 | 6 | 7 | 8 | 9 | 10 | 11 | 12 |

25 0 25 50 75 100 MILES

WHITE = MODERN BOUNDARIES
BLACK = 1880 BOUNDARIES

Oregon ● 1880

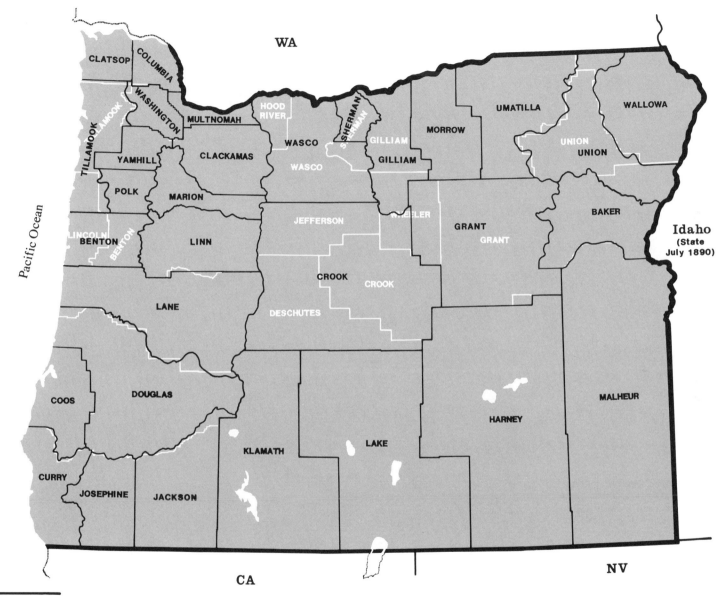

WA

CLATSOP

COLUMBIA

TILLAMOOK

WASHINGTON

MULTNOMAH

HOOD RIVER

YAMHILL

CLACKAMAS

WASCO

SHERMAN

GILLIAM

UMATILLA

MORROW

WALLOWA

POLK

MARION

WASCO

GILLIAM

UNION

UNION

Pacific Ocean

LINCOLN

BENTON

BENTON

LINN

JEFFERSON

WHEELER

GRANT

GRANT

BAKER

Idaho
(State
July 1890)

LANE

CROOK

CROOK

DESCHUTES

COOS

DOUGLAS

MALHEUR

HARNEY

CURRY

KLAMATH

LAKE

JOSEPHINE

JACKSON

CA

NV

CENSUS AVAILABILITY

Federal census <u>lost</u> for all counties.

1 2 3 4 5 6 7 8 9 10 11 12

25 0 25 50 75 100 MILES

WHITE = MODERN BOUNDARIES
BLACK = 1890 BOUNDARIES

Oregon ● 1890

MAP GUIDE TO THE U.S. FEDERAL CENSUSES, 1790–1920 by William Thorndale and William Dollarhide. Copyright 1987, all rights reserved.

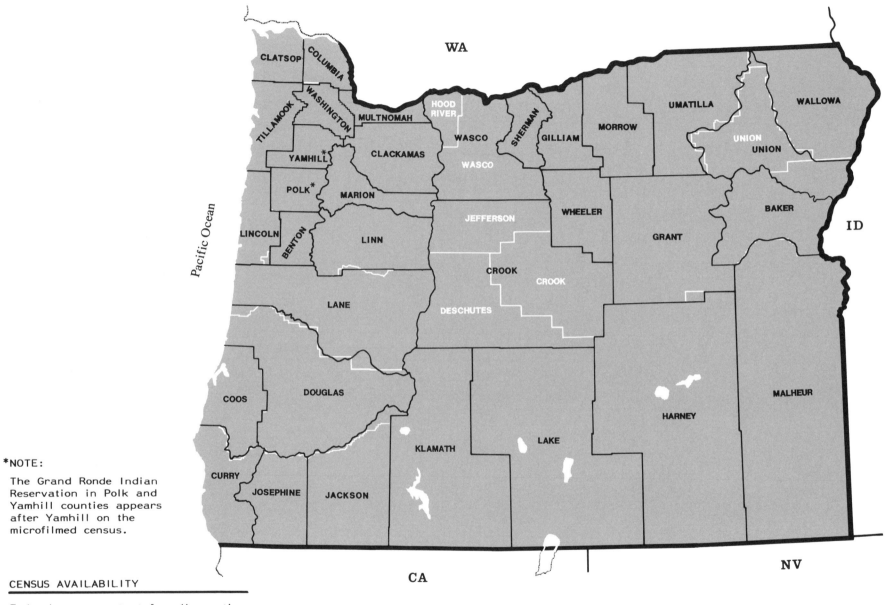

WA

CLATSOP
COLUMBIA
TILLAMOOK
WASHINGTON
MULTNOMAH
HOOD RIVER
WASCO
SHERMAN
GILLIAM
MORROW
UMATILLA
WALLOWA
YAMHILL*
CLACKAMAS
WASCO
UNION
UNION
POLK*
MARION
JEFFERSON
WHEELER
BAKER
LINCOLN
BENTON
LINN
ID
Pacific Ocean
CROOK
CROOK
GRANT
LANE
DESCHUTES
COOS
DOUGLAS
MALHEUR
HARNEY
KLAMATH
LAKE
CURRY
JOSEPHINE
JACKSON
CA
NV

*NOTE:

The Grand Ronde Indian Reservation in Polk and Yamhill counties appears after Yamhill on the microfilmed census.

CENSUS AVAILABILITY

Federal census extant for all counties.

| 1 | 2 | 3 | 4 | 5 | 6 | 7 | 8 | 9 | 10 | 11 | 12 |

25 0 25 50 75 100 MILES

WHITE = MODERN BOUNDARIES
BLACK = 1900 BOUNDARIES

Oregon ● 1900

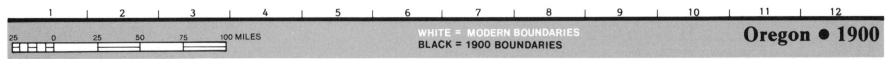

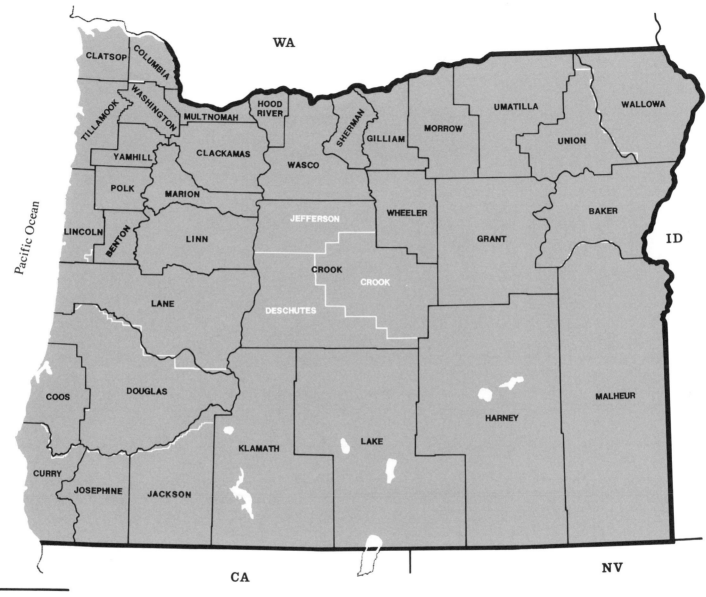

WA

CLATSOP

COLUMBIA

TILLAMOOK

WASHINGTON

MULTNOMAH

HOOD
RIVER

SHERMAN

GILLIAM

MORROW

UMATILLA

WALLOWA

UNION

YAMHILL

CLACKAMAS

WASCO

POLK

MARION

LINCOLN

BENTON

LINN

JEFFERSON

WHEELER

BAKER

Pacific Ocean

GRANT

ID

CROOK

CROOK

LANE

DESCHUTES

COOS

DOUGLAS

HARNEY

MALHEUR

CURRY

KLAMATH

LAKE

JOSEPHINE

JACKSON

CA

NV

CENSUS AVAILABILITY

Federal census extant for all counties.

| 1 | 2 | 3 | 4 | 5 | 6 | 7 | 8 | 9 | 10 | 11 | 12 |

25   0   25   50   75   100 MILES

WHITE = MODERN BOUNDARIES
BLACK = 1910 BOUNDARIES

Oregon ● 1910

MAP GUIDE TO THE U.S. FEDERAL CENSUSES, 1790–1920 by William Thorndale and William Dollarhide. Copyright 1987, all rights reserved.

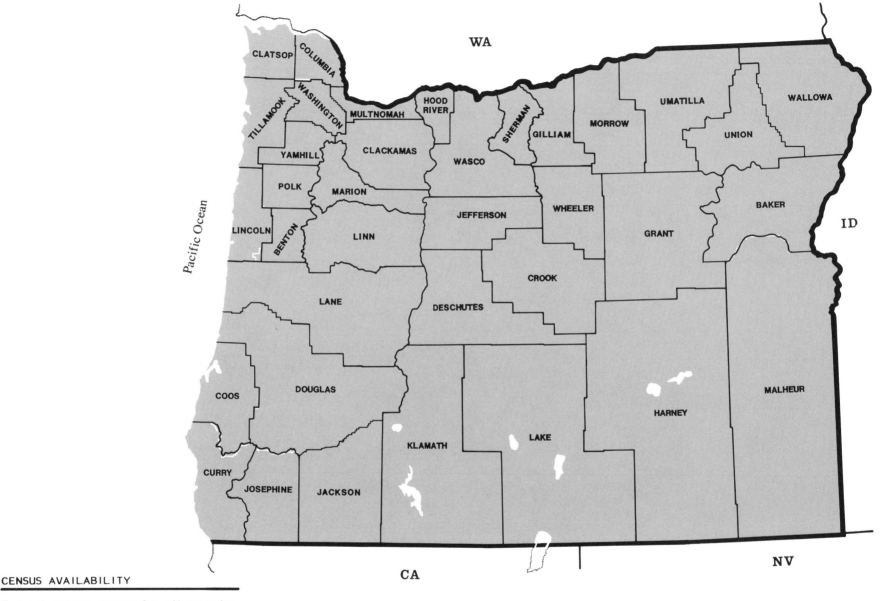

WA

CLATSOP
COLUMBIA
TILLAMOOK
WASHINGTON
MULTNOMAH
YAMHILL
CLACKAMAS
POLK
MARION
LINCOLN
BENTON
LINN
HOOD RIVER
SHERMAN
GILLIAM
MORROW
UMATILLA
WALLOWA
UNION
WASCO
JEFFERSON
WHEELER
BAKER
GRANT
CROOK
LANE
DESCHUTES
COOS
DOUGLAS
KLAMATH
LAKE
HARNEY
MALHEUR
CURRY
JOSEPHINE
JACKSON

ID

NV

CA

Pacific Ocean

CENSUS AVAILABILITY

Federal census extant for all counties.

WHITE = MODERN BOUNDARIES
BLACK = 1920 BOUNDARIES

Oregon ● 1920

25 0 25 50 75 100 MILES

1 2 3 4 5 6 7 8 9 10 11 12

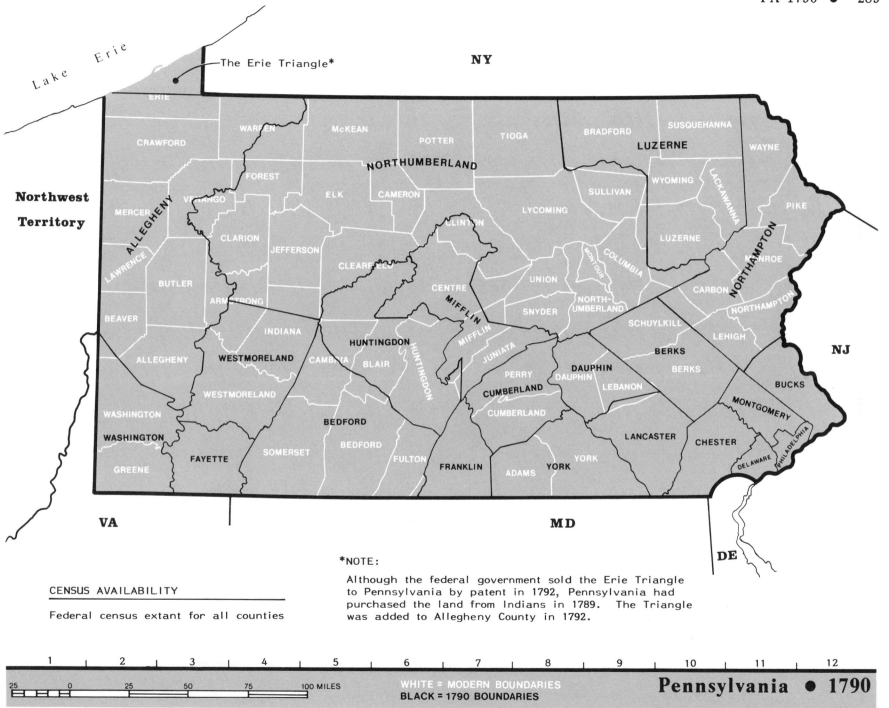

Lake Erie

The Erie Triangle*

NY

Northwest

Territory

ERIE

WARREN

McKEAN

POTTER

TIOGA

BRADFORD

SUSQUEHANNA

WAYNE

CRAWFORD

LUZERNE

NORTHUMBERLAND

FOREST

WYOMING

LACKAWANNA

PIKE

MERCER

VENANGO

ELK

CAMERON

LYCOMING

SULLIVAN

LUZERNE

ALLEGHENY

LAWRENCE

CLARION

JEFFERSON

CLINTON

MONROE

BUTLER

CLEARFIELD

UNION

COLUMBIA

CARBON

NORTHAMPTON

BEAVER

ARMSTRONG

CENTRE

MONTOUR

NORTH-
UMBERLAND

NORTHAMPTON

MIFFLIN

INDIANA

SNYDER

SCHUYLKILL

LEHIGH

ALLEGHENY

WESTMORELAND

HUNTINGDON

MIFFLIN

BERKS

NJ

CAMBRIA

BLAIR

JUNIATA

BERKS

WESTMORELAND

HUNTINGDON

PERRY

DAUPHIN

WASHINGTON

BEDFORD

CUMBERLAND

DAUPHIN

LEBANON

BUCKS

MONTGOMERY

WASHINGTON

FAYETTE

SOMERSET

BEDFORD

CUMBERLAND

LANCASTER

CHESTER

PHILADELPHIA

FULTON

DELAWARE

GREENE

FRANKLIN

ADAMS

YORK

YORK

VA

MD

DE

*NOTE:

Although the federal government sold the Erie Triangle
to Pennsylvania by patent in 1792, Pennsylvania had
purchased the land from Indians in 1789.   The Triangle
was added to Allegheny County in 1792.

CENSUS AVAILABILITY

Federal census extant for all counties

| 1 | 2 | 3 | 4 | 5 | 6 | 7 | 8 | 9 | 10 | 11 | 12 |

25   0   25   50   75   100 MILES

WHITE = MODERN BOUNDARIES
BLACK = 1790 BOUNDARIES

Pennsylvania ● 1790

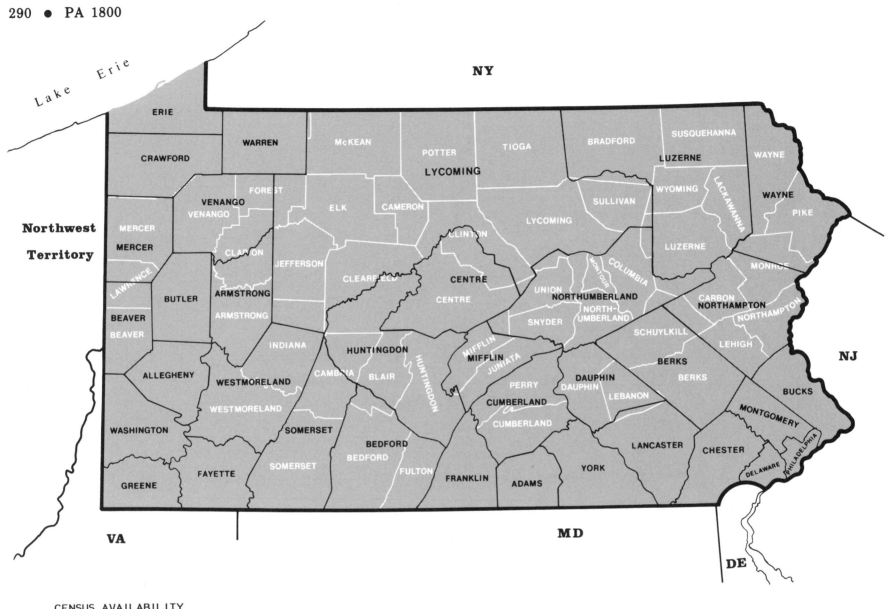

NY

Lake Erie

ERIE

WARREN

McKEAN

POTTER

TIOGA

BRADFORD

SUSQUEHANNA

WAYNE

CRAWFORD

LYCOMING

LUZERNE

WAYNE

Northwest

Territory

FOREST

VENANGO

ELK

CAMERON

LYCOMING

SULLIVAN

WYOMING

LACKAWANNA

PIKE

VENANGO

MERCER

MERCER

CLARION

JEFFERSON

CLINTON

LUZERNE

MONROE

LAWRENCE

CENTRE

UNION

NORTHUMBERLAND

COLUMBIA

MONTOUR

BUTLER

ARMSTRONG

CLEARFIELD

CENTRE

NORTH-UMBERLAND

CARBON

NORTHAMPTON

BEAVER

ARMSTRONG

SNYDER

SCHUYLKILL

NORTHAMPTON

BEAVER

INDIANA

HUNTINGDON

MIFFLIN

LEHIGH

NJ

ALLEGHENY

WESTMORELAND

CAMBRIA

BLAIR

HUNTINGDON

MIFFLIN

JUNIATA

BERKS

PERRY

DAUPHIN

BERKS

WESTMORELAND

CUMBERLAND

DAUPHIN

LEBANON

BUCKS

WASHINGTON

SOMERSET

CUMBERLAND

MONTGOMERY

BEDFORD

LANCASTER

CHESTER

SOMERSET

BEDFORD

YORK

PHILADELPHIA

FAYETTE

FULTON

FRANKLIN

ADAMS

DELAWARE

GREENE

VA

MD

DE

CENSUS AVAILABILITY

Federal census extant for all counties.

| 1 | 2 | 3 | 4 | 5 | 6 | 7 | 8 | 9 | 10 | 11 | 12 |

25　0　25　50　75　100 MILES

WHITE = MODERN BOUNDARIES
BLACK = 1800 BOUNDARIES

Pennsylvania ● 1800

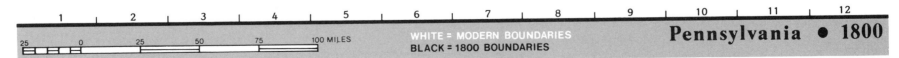

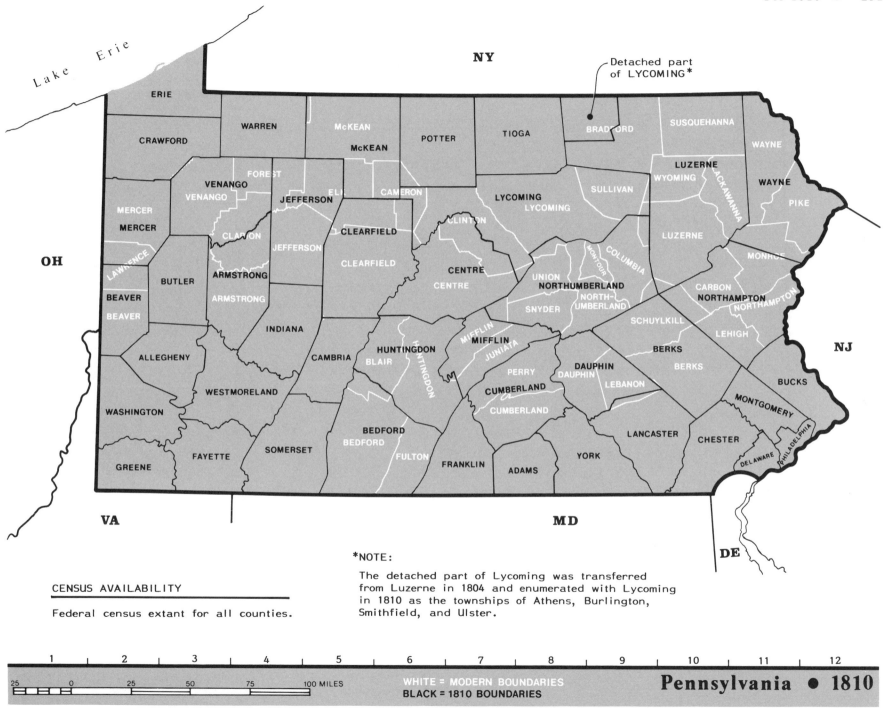

Detached part
of LYCOMING*

*NOTE:

The detached part of Lycoming was transferred
from Luzerne in 1804 and enumerated with Lycoming
in 1810 as the townships of Athens, Burlington,
Smithfield, and Ulster.

CENSUS AVAILABILITY

Federal census extant for all counties.

1   2   3   4   5   6   7   8   9   10   11   12

25   0   25   50   75   100 MILES

WHITE = MODERN BOUNDARIES
BLACK = 1810 BOUNDARIES

Pennsylvania ● 1810

MAP GUIDE TO THE U.S. FEDERAL CENSUSES, 1790–1920 by William Thorndale and William Dollarhide.   Copyright 1987, all rights reserved.

NY

Lake Erie

ERIE

WARREN

McKEAN

McKEAN

POTTER

TIOGA

BRADFORD

SUSQUEHANNA

WAYNE

CRAWFORD

OH

MERCER

MERCER

VENANGO

VENANGO

FOREST

ELK

CAMERON

LYCOMING

LYCOMING

SULLIVAN

WYOMING

LACKAWANNA

LUZERNE

PIKE

PIKE

LAWRENCE

CLARION

JEFFERSON

JEFFERSON

CLEARFIELD

CLEARFIELD

CLINTON

CENTRE

CENTRE

UNION

UNION

COLUMBIA

COLUMBIA

MONTOUR

NORTH-
UMBERLAND

MONROE

NORTHAMPTON

CARBON

NORTHAMPTON

BEAVER

BEAVER

BUTLER

ARMSTRONG

ARMSTRONG

INDIANA

SNYDER

SCHUYLKILL

LEHIGH

ALLEGHENY

CAMBRIA

HUNTINGDON

BLAIR

HUNTINGDON

MIFFLIN

MIFFLIN

JUNIATA

PERRY

DAUPHIN

DAUPHIN

BERKS

LEBANON

BUCKS

MONTGOMERY

WESTMORELAND

CUMBERLAND

WASHINGTON

BEDFORD

BEDFORD

FULTON

LANCASTER

CHESTER

PHILADELPHIA

DELAWARE

GREENE

FAYETTE

SOMERSET

FRANKLIN

ADAMS

YORK

VA

MD

DE

NJ

CENSUS AVAILABILITY

Federal census extant for all counties.

1 2 3 4 5 6 7 8 9 10 11 12

25 0 25 50 75 100 MILES

WHITE = MODERN BOUNDARIES
BLACK = 1820 BOUNDARIES

Pennsylvania ● 1820

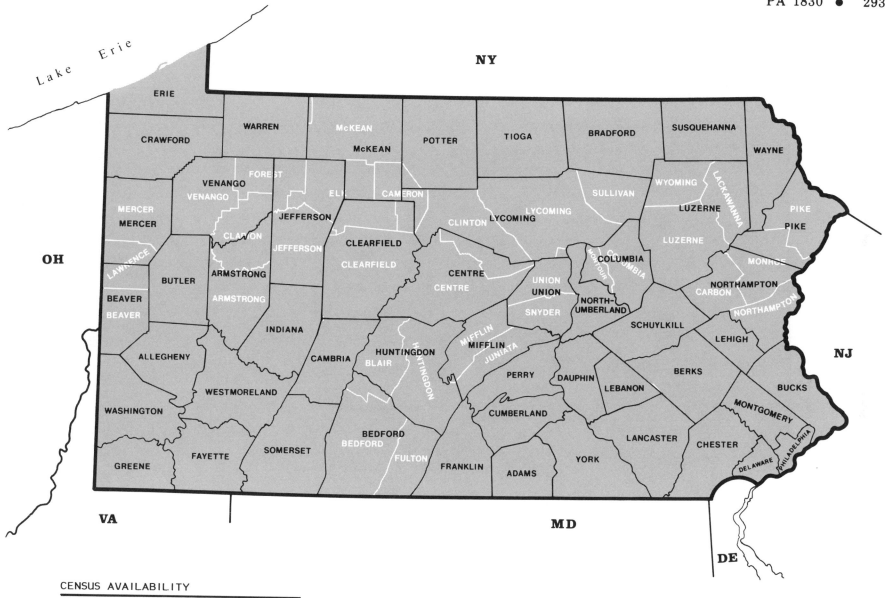

NY

Lake Erie

ERIE

WARREN

McKEAN
McKEAN

POTTER

TIOGA

BRADFORD

SUSQUEHANNA

WAYNE

CRAWFORD

OH

FOREST

VENANGO
VENANGO

ELK

CAMERON

LYCOMING
LYCOMING

SULLIVAN

WYOMING

LACKAWANNA

LUZERNE

PIKE
PIKE

MERCER
MERCER

CLARION

JEFFERSON
JEFFERSON

CLINTON

LUZERNE

LAWRENCE

BUTLER

ARMSTRONG
ARMSTRONG

CLEARFIELD
CLEARFIELD

CENTRE
CENTRE

UNION
UNION

COLUMBIA

MONTOUR

NORTH-UMBERLAND

MONROE

NORTHAMPTON
NORTHAMPTON

CARBON

BEAVER
BEAVER

SNYDER

SCHUYLKILL

LEHIGH

NJ

INDIANA

CAMBRIA

HUNTINGDON
HUNTINGDON

BLAIR

MIFFLIN
MIFFLIN

JUNIATA

ALLEGHENY

PERRY

DAUPHIN

BERKS

BUCKS

WESTMORELAND

LEBANON

MONTGOMERY

WASHINGTON

BEDFORD
BEDFORD

CUMBERLAND

LANCASTER

CHESTER

PHILADELPHIA

GREENE

FAYETTE

SOMERSET

FULTON

FRANKLIN

ADAMS

YORK

DELAWARE

VA

MD

DE

CENSUS AVAILABILITY

Federal census extant for all counties.

| 1 | 2 | 3 | 4 | 5 | 6 | 7 | 8 | 9 | 10 | 11 | 12 |

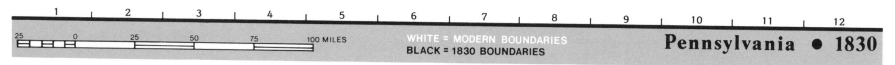

25   0   25   50   75   100 MILES

WHITE = MODERN BOUNDARIES
BLACK = 1830 BOUNDARIES

Pennsylvania ● 1830

Lake Erie

NY

ERIE

CRAWFORD

WARREN

McKEAN

McKEAN

POTTER

TIOGA

BRADFORD

SUSQUEHANNA

WAYNE

MERCER

MERCER

FOREST

VENANGO

VENANGO

ELK

CAMERON

CLINTON

CLINTON

LYCOMING

LYCOMING

SULLIVAN

WYOMING

LACKAWANNA

LUZERNE

LUZERNE

PIKE

OH

LAWRENCE

CLARION

JEFFERSON

JEFFERSON

CLEARFIELD

CLEARFIELD

COLUMBIA

MONTOUR

COLUMBIA

MONROE

MONROE

BEAVER

BEAVER

ARMSTRONG

ARMSTRONG

BUTLER

CENTRE

UNION

UNION

SNYDER

NORTH-
UMBERLAND

NORTHAMPTON

CARBON

NORTHAMPTON

SCHUYLKILL

LEHIGH

NJ

INDIANA

CAMBRIA

HUNTINGDON

BLAIR

HUNTINGDON

MIFFLIN

JUNIATA

PERRY

DAUPHIN

BERKS

BUCKS

ALLEGHENY

WESTMORELAND

LEBANON

MONTGOMERY

WASHINGTON

CUMBERLAND

LANCASTER

CHESTER

DELAWARE

PHILADELPHIA

GREENE

FAYETTE

SOMERSET

BEDFORD

BEDFORD

FULTON

FRANKLIN

ADAMS

YORK

VA

MD

DE

1 2 3 4 5 6 7 8 9 10 11 12

25 0 25 50 75 100 MILES

WHITE = MODERN BOUNDARIES
BLACK = 1840 BOUNDARIES

Pennsylvania ● 1840

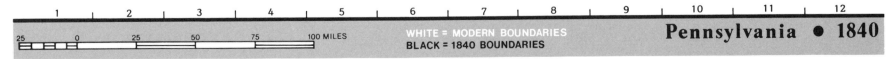

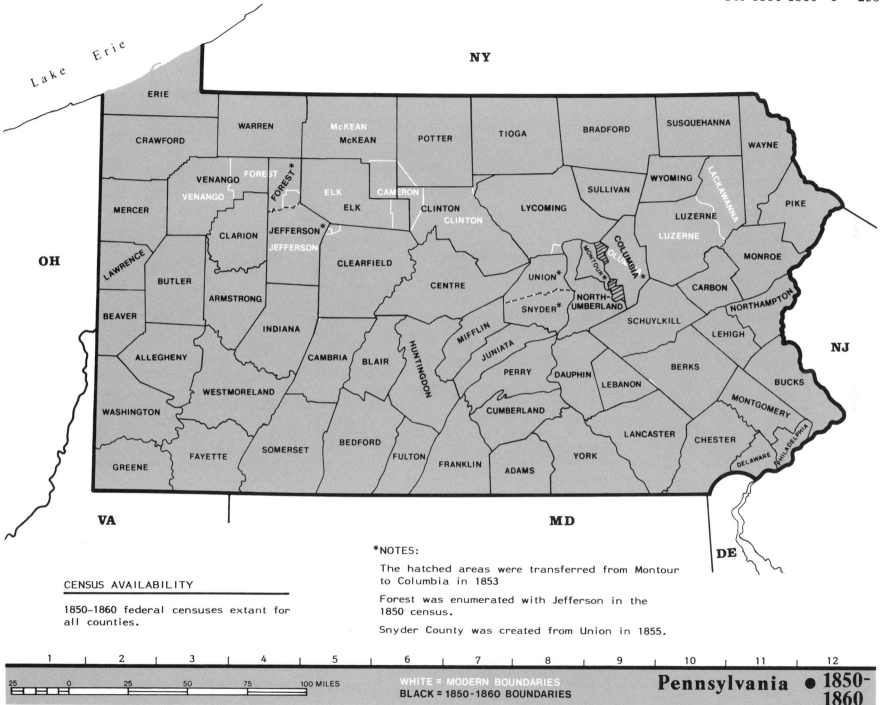

NY

Lake Erie

ERIE

WARREN

McKEAN
McKEAN

POTTER

TIOGA

BRADFORD

SUSQUEHANNA

WAYNE

CRAWFORD

OH

VENANGO
FOREST
FOREST *
VENANGO

ELK

CAMERON

CLINTON
CLINTON

LYCOMING

SULLIVAN

WYOMING

LUZERNE

LACKAWANNA

PIKE

MERCER

CLARION

JEFFERSON *
JEFFERSON

ELK

LUZERNE

MONROE

LAWRENCE

BUTLER

CLEARFIELD

CENTRE

UNION *

COLUMBIA *

CARBON

MONTOUR *

NORTH-
UMBERLAND

NORTHAMPTON

BEAVER

ARMSTRONG

SNYDER *

SCHUYLKILL

LEHIGH

NJ

INDIANA

MIFFLIN

ALLEGHENY

CAMBRIA

BLAIR

HUNTINGDON

JUNIATA

PERRY

DAUPHIN

LEBANON

BERKS

BUCKS

WESTMORELAND

CUMBERLAND

LANCASTER

MONTGOMERY

WASHINGTON

SOMERSET

BEDFORD

CHESTER

PHILADELPHIA

FULTON

FRANKLIN

ADAMS

YORK

DELAWARE

GREENE

FAYETTE

VA

MD

DE

*NOTES:

The hatched areas were transferred from Montour
to Columbia in 1853

Forest was enumerated with Jefferson in the
1850 census.

Snyder County was created from Union in 1855.

CENSUS AVAILABILITY

1850–1860 federal censuses extant for
all counties.

1 2 3 4 5 6 7 8 9 10 11 12

25   0   25   50   75   100 MILES

WHITE = MODERN BOUNDARIES
BLACK = 1850-1860 BOUNDARIES

Pennsylvania ● **1850-
1860**

MAP GUIDE TO THE U.S. FEDERAL CENSUSES, 1790-1920 by William Thorndale and William Dollarhide. Copyright 1987, all rights reserved.

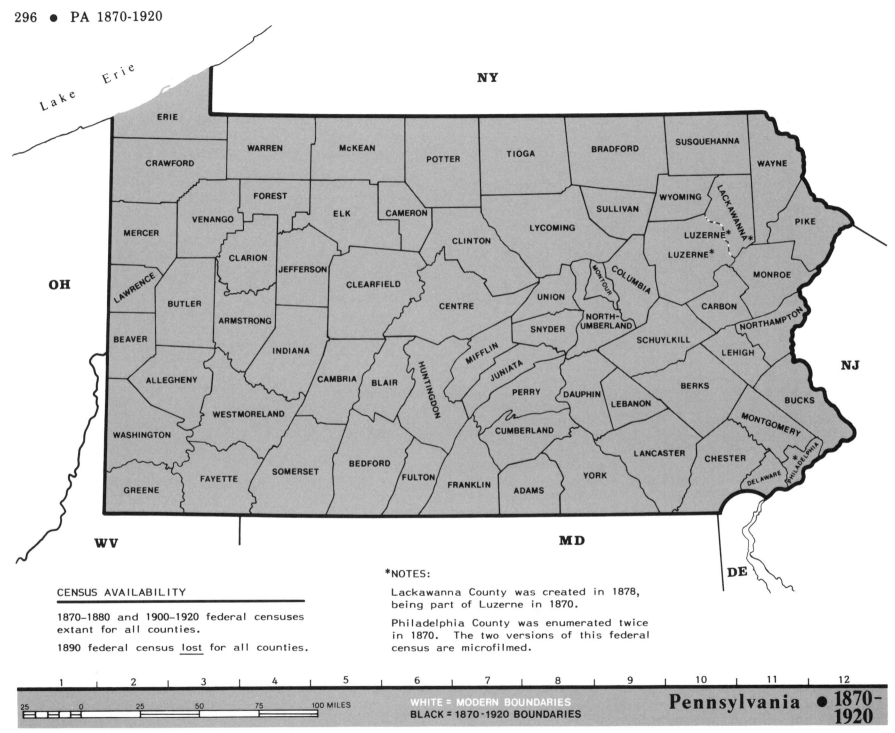

NY

Lake Erie

ERIE

CRAWFORD

WARREN

McKEAN

POTTER

TIOGA

BRADFORD

SUSQUEHANNA

WAYNE

FOREST

WYOMING

LACKAWANNA

VENANGO

ELK

CAMERON

SULLIVAN

LYCOMING

LUZERNE *

*

MERCER

CLARION

JEFFERSON

CLINTON

LUZERNE*

PIKE

OH

LAWRENCE

CENTRE

UNION

COLUMBIA

MONTOUR

NORTH-UMBERLAND

MONROE

BUTLER

ARMSTRONG

CLEARFIELD

CARBON

BEAVER

INDIANA

SNYDER

SCHUYLKILL

NORTHAMPTON

MIFFLIN

ALLEGHENY

CAMBRIA

BLAIR

HUNTINGDON

JUNIATA

LEHIGH

NJ

PERRY

DAUPHIN

BERKS

WESTMORELAND

CUMBERLAND

LEBANON

BUCKS

WASHINGTON

BEDFORD

MONTGOMERY

LANCASTER

CHESTER

PHILADELPHIA

*

SOMERSET

FULTON

YORK

DELAWARE

GREENE

FAYETTE

FRANKLIN

ADAMS

WV

MD

DE

CENSUS AVAILABILITY

1870-1880 and 1900-1920 federal censuses extant for all counties.

1890 federal census lost for all counties.

*NOTES:

Lackawanna County was created in 1878, being part of Luzerne in 1870.

Philadelphia County was enumerated twice in 1870. The two versions of this federal census are microfilmed.

1 2 3 4 5 6 7 8 9 10 11 12

25   0   25   50   75   100 MILES

WHITE = MODERN BOUNDARIES
BLACK = 1870-1920 BOUNDARIES

Pennsylvania ● 1870-1920

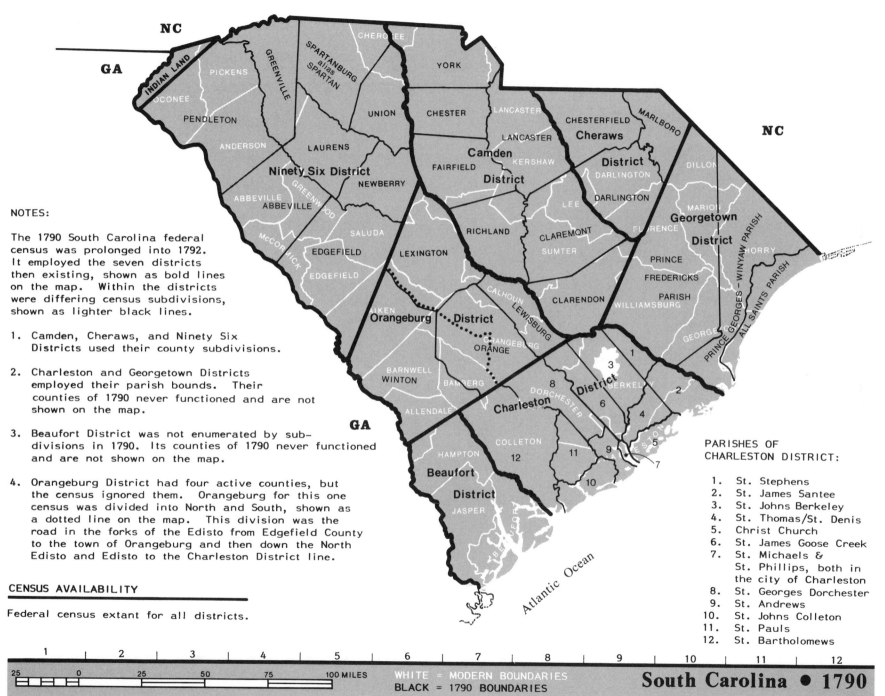

NC

GA

INDIAN LAND

OCONEE

PICKENS

PENDLETON

ANDERSON

GREENVILLE

CHEROKEE

SPARTANBURG
alias
SPARTAN

UNION

YORK

CHESTER

LANCASTER

LANCASTER

CHESTERFIELD

MARLBORO

Cheraws

District

NC

LAURENS

Ninety Six District

NEWBERRY

FAIRFIELD

Camden

District

KERSHAW

DARLINGTON

DILLON

MARION

Georgetown

District

ABBEVILLE

ABBEVILLE

GREENWOOD

SALUDA

RICHLAND

CLAREMONT

SUMTER

LEE

DARLINGTON

FLORENCE

PRINCE

FREDERICKS

PARISH

HORRY

McCORMICK

EDGEFIELD

EDGEFIELD

LEXINGTON

CALHOUN

LEWISBURG

CLARENDON

WILLIAMSBURG

GEORGETOWN

PRINCE GEORGES – WINYAW PARISH

ALL SAINTS PARISH

AIKEN

Orangeburg ● District

ORANGEBURG

ORANGE

1

St. Stephens

BARNWELL

WINTON

BAMBERG

8

DORCHESTER

District

BERKELEY

3

6

4

2

5

ALLENDALE

Charleston

7

COLLETON

HAMPTON

12

11

9

10

PARISHES OF
CHARLESTON DISTRICT:

Beaufort

District

JASPER

BEAUFORT

Atlantic Ocean

NOTES:

The 1790 South Carolina federal census was prolonged into 1792. It employed the seven districts then existing, shown as bold lines on the map. Within the districts were differing census subdivisions, shown as lighter black lines.

1. Camden, Cheraws, and Ninety Six Districts used their county subdivisions.

2. Charleston and Georgetown Districts employed their parish bounds. Their counties of 1790 never functioned and are not shown on the map.

3. Beaufort District was not enumerated by sub-divisions in 1790. Its counties of 1790 never functioned and are not shown on the map.

4. Orangeburg District had four active counties, but the census ignored them. Orangeburg for this one census was divided into North and South, shown as a dotted line on the map. This division was the road in the forks of the Edisto from Edgefield County to the town of Orangeburg and then down the North Edisto and Edisto to the Charleston District line.

CENSUS AVAILABILITY

Federal census extant for all districts.

PARISHES OF
CHARLESTON DISTRICT:

1. St. Stephens
2. St. James Santee
3. St. Johns Berkeley
4. St. Thomas/St. Denis
5. Christ Church
6. St. James Goose Creek
7. St. Michaels &
   St. Phillips, both in
   the city of Charleston
8. St. Georges Dorchester
9. St. Andrews
10. St. Johns Colleton
11. St. Pauls
12. St. Bartholomews

| 1 | 2 | 3 | 4 | 5 | 6 | 7 | 8 | 9 | 10 | 11 | 12 |

25 0 25 50 75 100 MILES

WHITE = MODERN BOUNDARIES
BLACK = 1790 BOUNDARIES

South Carolina ● 1790

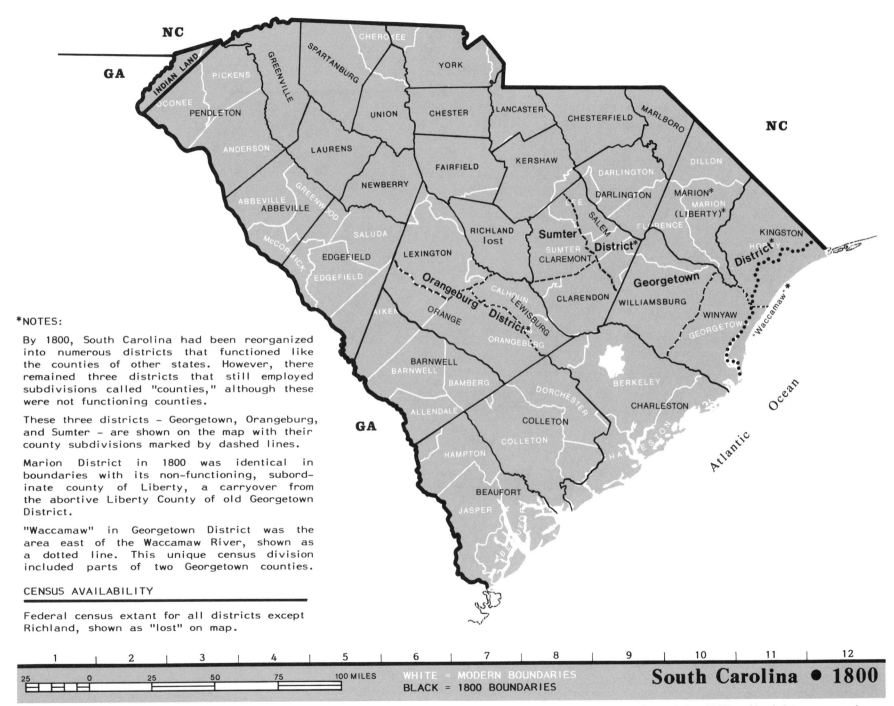

NC

GA

NC

GA

Atlantic Ocean

*NOTES:

By 1800, South Carolina had been reorganized into numerous districts that functioned like the counties of other states. However, there remained three districts that still employed subdivisions called "counties," although these were not functioning counties.

These three districts – Georgetown, Orangeburg, and Sumter – are shown on the map with their county subdivisions marked by dashed lines.

Marion District in 1800 was identical in boundaries with its non-functioning, subordinate county of Liberty, a carryover from the abortive Liberty County of old Georgetown District.

"Waccamaw" in Georgetown District was the area east of the Waccamaw River, shown as a dotted line. This unique census division included parts of two Georgetown counties.

CENSUS AVAILABILITY

Federal census extant for all districts except Richland, shown as "lost" on map.

| 25 | | 0 | 25 | 50 | 75 | 100 MILES |

WHITE = MODERN BOUNDARIES
BLACK = 1800 BOUNDARIES

South Carolina ● 1800

MAP GUIDE TO THE U.S. FEDERAL CENSUSES, 1790–1920 by William Thorndale and William Dollarhide. Copyright 1987, all rights reserved.

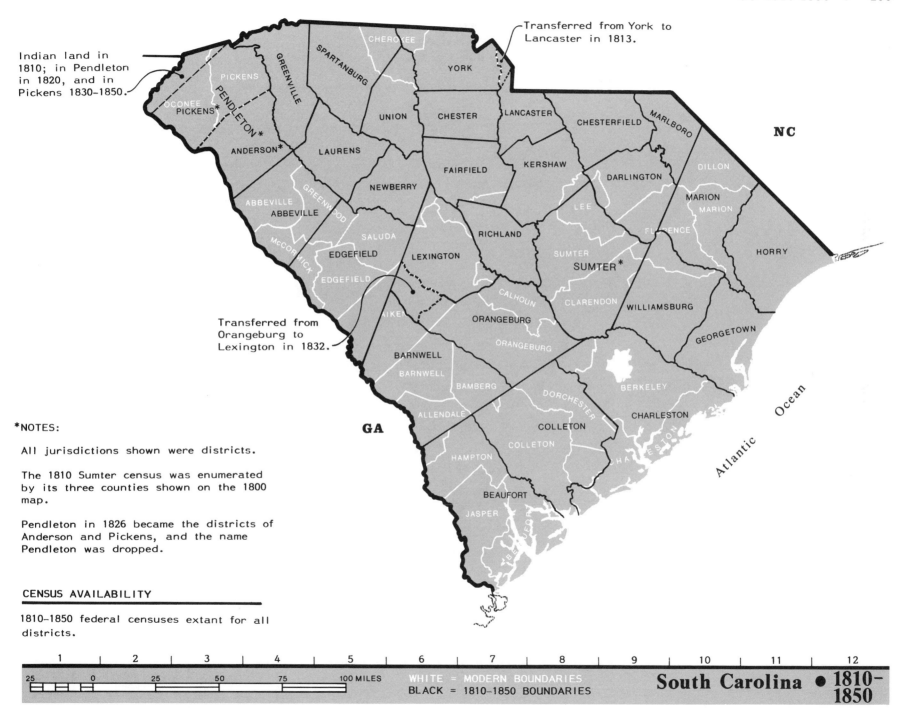

Transferred from York to
Lancaster in 1813.

Indian land in
1810; in Pendleton
in 1820, and in
Pickens 1830–1850.

NC

Transferred from
Orangeburg to
Lexington in 1832.

GA

Atlantic Ocean

*NOTES:

All jurisdictions shown were districts.

The 1810 Sumter census was enumerated
by its three counties shown on the 1800
map.

Pendleton in 1826 became the districts of
Anderson and Pickens, and the name
Pendleton was dropped.

CENSUS AVAILABILITY

1810–1850 federal censuses extant for all
districts.

| 1 | 2 | 3 | 4 | 5 | 6 | 7 | 8 | 9 | 10 | 11 | 12 |

25   0   25   50   75   100 MILES

WHITE = MODERN BOUNDARIES
BLACK = 1810–1850 BOUNDARIES

South Carolina ● **1810–1850**

MAP GUIDE TO THE U.S. FEDERAL CENSUSES, 1790–1920 by William Thorndale and William Dollarhide. Copyright 1987, all rights reserved.

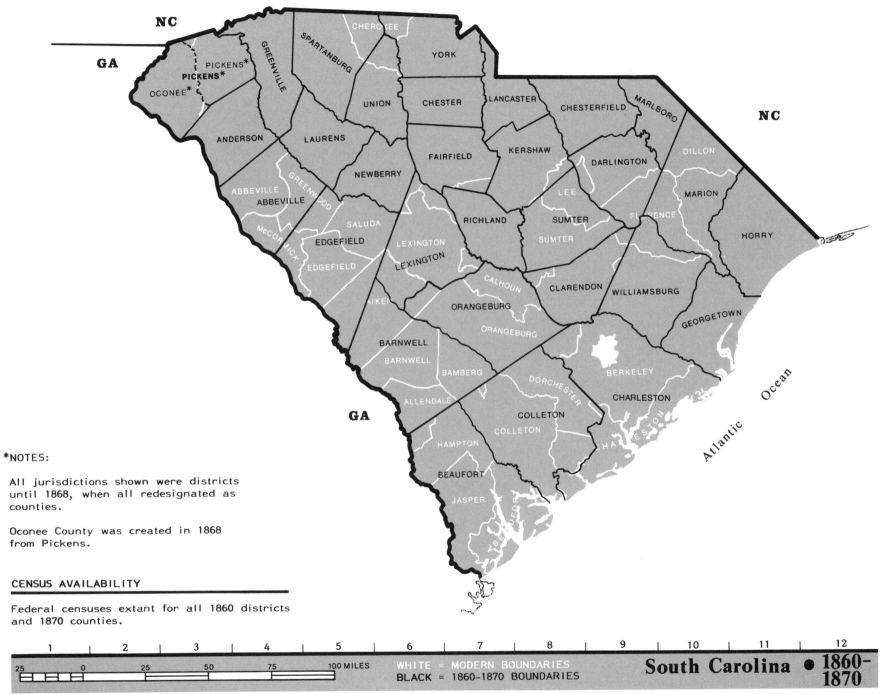

NC

GA

NC

GA

*NOTES:

All jurisdictions shown were districts until 1868, when all redesignated as counties.

Oconee County was created in 1868 from Pickens.

CENSUS AVAILABILITY

Federal censuses extant for all 1860 districts and 1870 counties.

WHITE = MODERN BOUNDARIES
BLACK = 1860-1870 BOUNDARIES

South Carolina ● 1860-1870

25   0   25   50   75   100 MILES

MAP GUIDE TO THE U.S. FEDERAL CENSUSES, 1790-1920 by William Thorndale and William Dollarhide. Copyright 1987, all rights reserved.

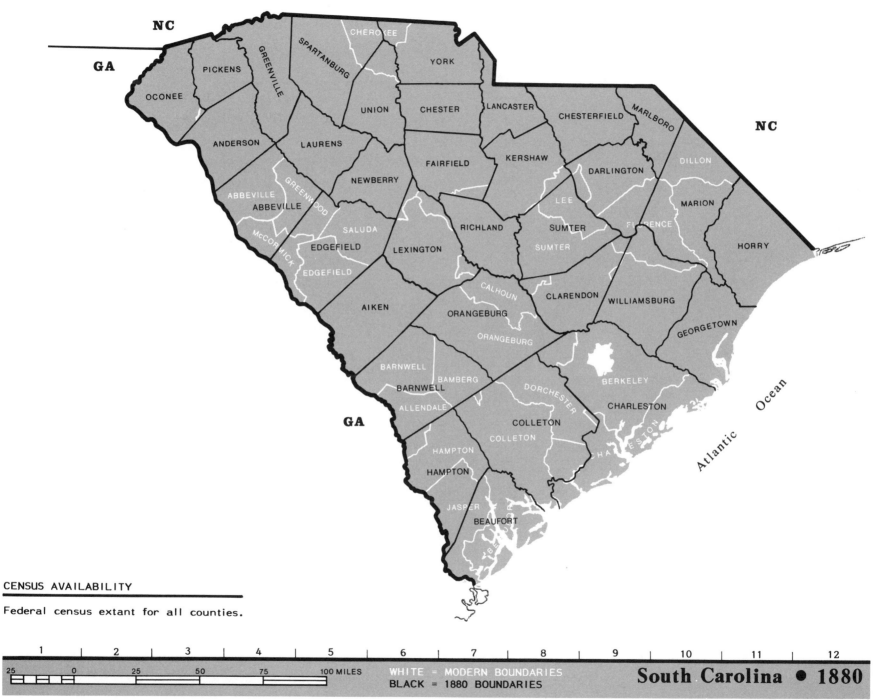

NC

GA

NC

GA

Atlantic Ocean

CHEROKEE

SPARTANBURG

YORK

PICKENS

GREENVILLE

OCONEE

UNION

CHESTER

LANCASTER

CHESTERFIELD

MARLBORO

ANDERSON

LAURENS

FAIRFIELD

KERSHAW

DARLINGTON

DILLON

NEWBERRY

GREENWOOD

ABBEVILLE

ABBEVILLE

MARION

LEE

SALUDA

RICHLAND

SUMTER

FLORENCE

McCORMICK

EDGEFIELD

LEXINGTON

SUMTER

HORRY

EDGEFIELD

CALHOUN

CLARENDON

WILLIAMSBURG

AIKEN

ORANGEBURG

GEORGETOWN

ORANGEBURG

BARNWELL

BAMBERG

DORCHESTER

BERKELEY

BARNWELL

CHARLESTON

ALLENDALE

COLLETON

CHARLESTON

COLLETON

HAMPTON

HAMPTON

JASPER

BEAUFORT

CENSUS AVAILABILITY

Federal census extant for all counties.

25   0   25   50   75   100 MILES

1 2 3 4 5 6 7 8 9 10 11 12

WHITE = MODERN BOUNDARIES
BLACK = 1880 BOUNDARIES

South Carolina ● 1880

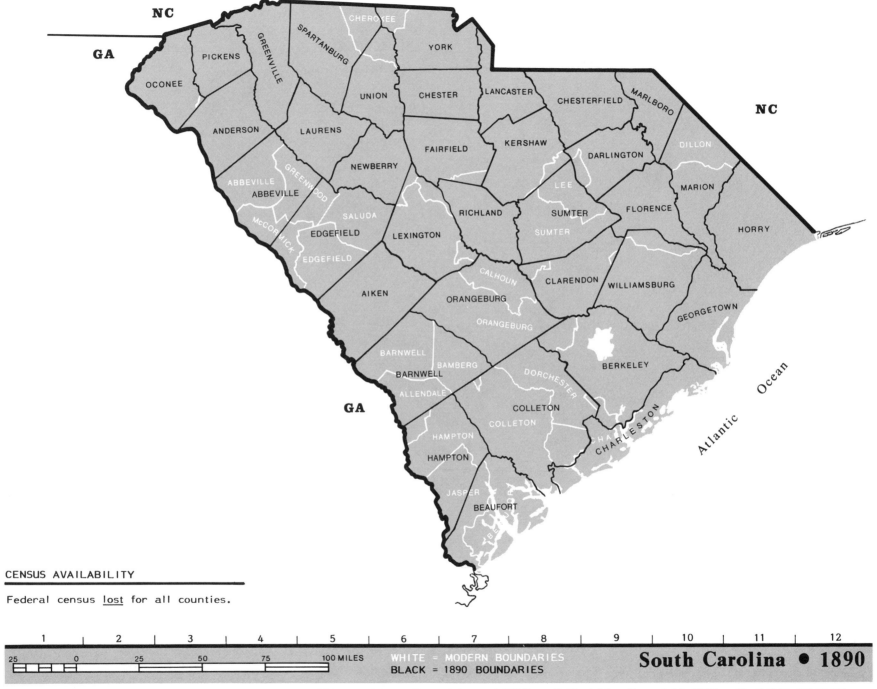

NC
GA
NC
NC
GA

OCONEE
PICKENS
GREENVILLE
SPARTANBURG
CHEROKEE
YORK
ANDERSON
LAURENS
UNION
CHESTER
LANCASTER
CHESTERFIELD
MARLBORO
ABBEVILLE
GREENWOOD
NEWBERRY
FAIRFIELD
KERSHAW
DARLINGTON
DILLON
ABBEVILLE
SALUDA
RICHLAND
LEE
SUMTER
FLORENCE
MARION
McCORMICK
EDGEFIELD
LEXINGTON
SUMTER
HORRY
EDGEFIELD
CALHOUN
CLARENDON
WILLIAMSBURG
AIKEN
ORANGEBURG
ORANGEBURG
GEORGETOWN
BARNWELL
BAMBERG
DORCHESTER
BERKELEY
BARNWELL
ALLENDALE
COLLETON
COLLETON
CHARLESTON
HAMPTON
HAMPTON
JASPER
BEAUFORT

Atlantic Ocean

CENSUS AVAILABILITY

Federal census <u>lost</u> for all counties.

| 1 | 2 | 3 | 4 | 5 | 6 | 7 | 8 | 9 | 10 | 11 | 12 |

25   0   25   50   75   100 MILES

WHITE = MODERN BOUNDARIES
BLACK = 1890 BOUNDARIES

South Carolina ● 1890

MAP GUIDE TO THE U.S. FEDERAL CENSUSES, 1790–1920 by William Thorndale and William Dollarhide. Copyright 1987, all rights reserved.

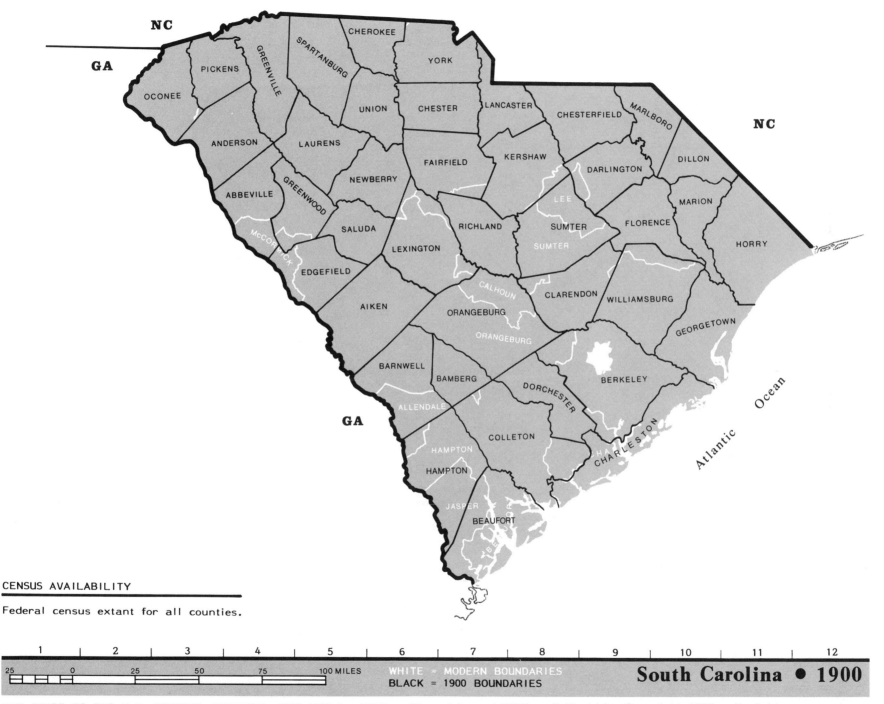

NC

GA

OCONEE

PICKENS

GREENVILLE

SPARTANBURG

CHEROKEE

YORK

NC

ANDERSON

LAURENS

UNION

CHESTER

LANCASTER

CHESTERFIELD

MARLBORO

ABBEVILLE

GREENWOOD

NEWBERRY

FAIRFIELD

KERSHAW

DARLINGTON

DILLON

McCORMICK

SALUDA

RICHLAND

LEE

SUMTER

FLORENCE

MARION

EDGEFIELD

LEXINGTON

SUMTER

HORRY

AIKEN

CALHOUN

ORANGEBURG

CLARENDON

WILLIAMSBURG

GEORGETOWN

BARNWELL

ORANGEBURG

BAMBERG

BERKELEY

ALLENDALE

DORCHESTER

GA

COLLETON

CHARLESTON

Atlantic Ocean

HAMPTON

HAMPTON

JASPER

BEAUFORT

BLUF

CENSUS AVAILABILITY

Federal census extant for all counties.

| 1 | 2 | 3 | 4 | 5 | 6 | 7 | 8 | 9 | 10 | 11 | 12 |

25 0 25 50 75 100 MILES

WHITE = MODERN BOUNDARIES
BLACK = 1900 BOUNDARIES

South Carolina ● 1900

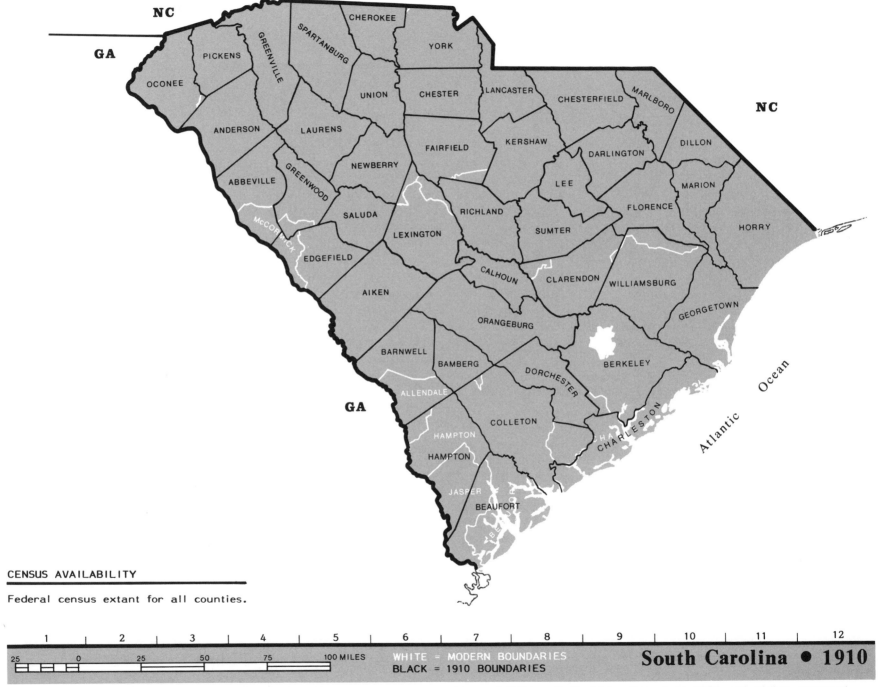

NC

GA

NC

CHEROKEE

SPARTANBURG

YORK

OCONEE

PICKENS

GREENVILLE

UNION

CHESTER

LANCASTER

CHESTERFIELD

MARLBORO

NC

ANDERSON

LAURENS

FAIRFIELD

KERSHAW

DARLINGTON

DILLON

NEWBERRY

ABBEVILLE

GREENWOOD

LEE

MARION

McCORMICK

SALUDA

RICHLAND

FLORENCE

HORRY

EDGEFIELD

LEXINGTON

SUMTER

AIKEN

CALHOUN

CLARENDON

WILLIAMSBURG

GEORGETOWN

ORANGEBURG

BARNWELL

BAMBERG

BERKELEY

GA

ALLENDALE

DORCHESTER

COLLETON

HAMPTON

CHARLESTON

HAMPTON

Atlantic Ocean

JASPER

BEAUFORT

Atlantic Ocean

CENSUS AVAILABILITY

Federal census extant for all counties.

| 1 | 2 | 3 | 4 | 5 | 6 | 7 | 8 | 9 | 10 | 11 | 12 |

25 0 25 50 75 100 MILES

WHITE = MODERN BOUNDARIES
BLACK = 1910 BOUNDARIES

South Carolina ● 1910

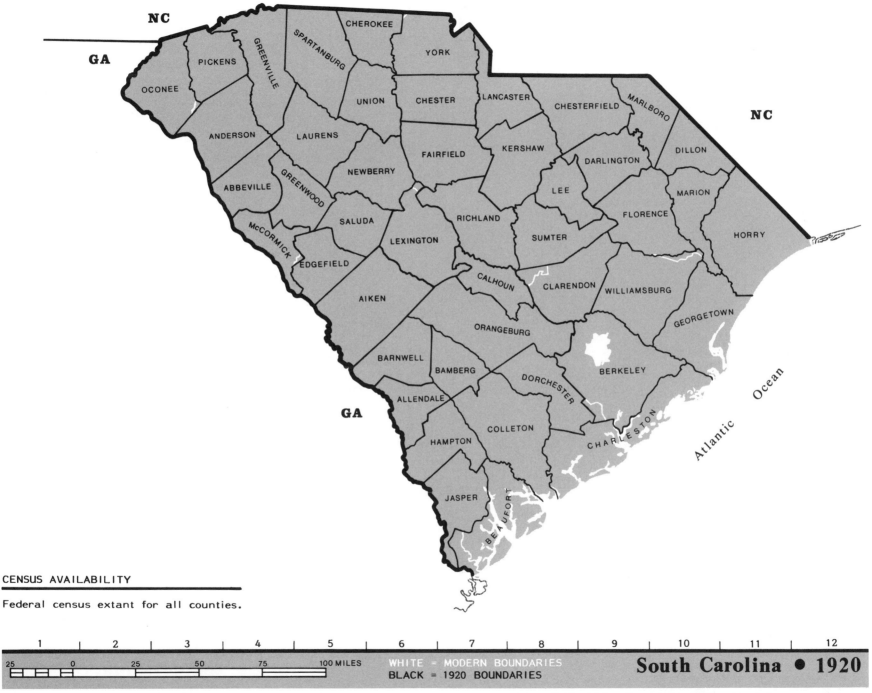

CENSUS AVAILABILITY

Federal census extant for all counties.

1	2	3	4	5	6	7	8	9	10	11	12

25   0   25   50   75   100 MILES

WHITE = MODERN BOUNDARIES
BLACK = 1920 BOUNDARIES

South Carolina ● 1920

MAP GUIDE TO THE U.S. FEDERAL CENSUSES, 1790–1920 by William Thorndale and William Dollarhide. Copyright 1987, all rights reserved.

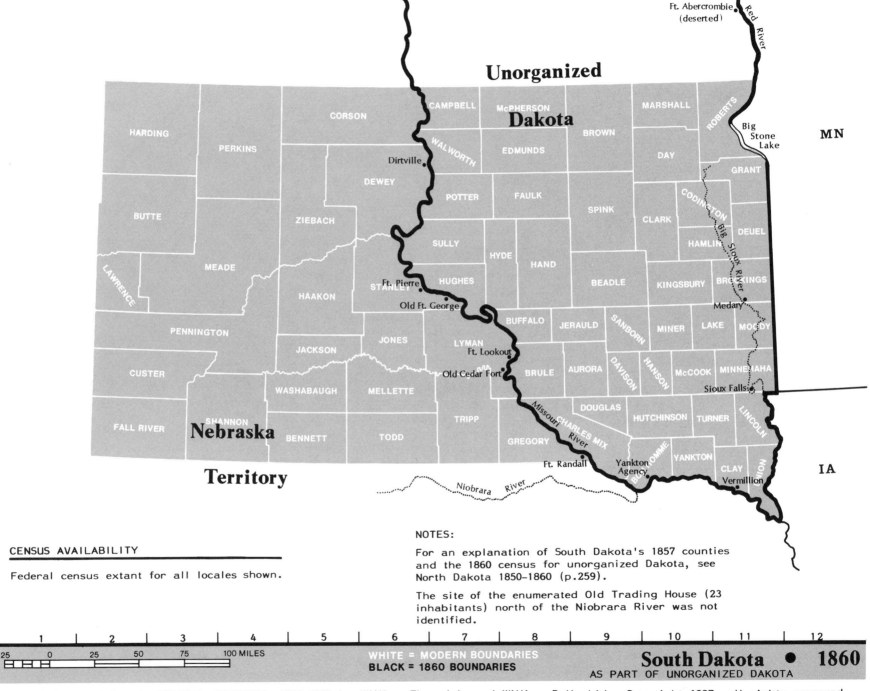

Ft. Abercrombie (deserted)

Red River

Unorganized

Dakota

MN

MARSHALL

ROBERTS

Big Stone Lake

CAMPBELL   McPHERSON

CORSON   BROWN

HARDING

DAY

GRANT

PERKINS   WALWORTH   EDMUNDS

Dirtville

CODINGTON

DEWEY   POTTER   FAULK   SPINK

BUTTE

ZIEBACH   CLARK

DEUEL

HAMLIN

MEADE   SULLY   HAND   Big Sioux River

HYDE   BROOKINGS

LAWRENCE   HAAKON   Ft. Pierre   HUGHES   BEADLE   KINGSBURY   Medary

STANLEY   Old Ft. George   BUFFALO   JERAULD   SANBORN   MINER   LAKE   MOODY

PENNINGTON   LYMAN   Ft. Lookout

JONES   MINNEHAHA

JACKSON   Old Cedar Fort   BRULE   AURORA   DAVISON   HANSON   McCOOK   Sioux Falls

CUSTER   WASHABAUGH   MELLETTE   DOUGLAS   HUTCHINSON   TURNER   LINCOLN

Nebraska

SHANNON   TRIPP   CHARLES MIX   Missouri River

FALL RIVER   BENNETT   TODD   GREGORY   Ft. Randall   Yankton Agency   YANKTON   CLAY   Vermillion

BON HOMME

Territory   Niobrara   River   IA

NOTES:

For an explanation of South Dakota's 1857 counties and the 1860 census for unorganized Dakota, see North Dakota 1850–1860 (p.259).

The site of the enumerated Old Trading House (23 inhabitants) north of the Niobrara River was not identified.

1   2   3   4   5   6   7   8   9   10   11   12

25   0   25   50   75   100 MILES

WHITE = MODERN BOUNDARIES
BLACK = 1860 BOUNDARIES

South Dakota ● **1860**
AS PART OF UNORGANIZED DAKOTA

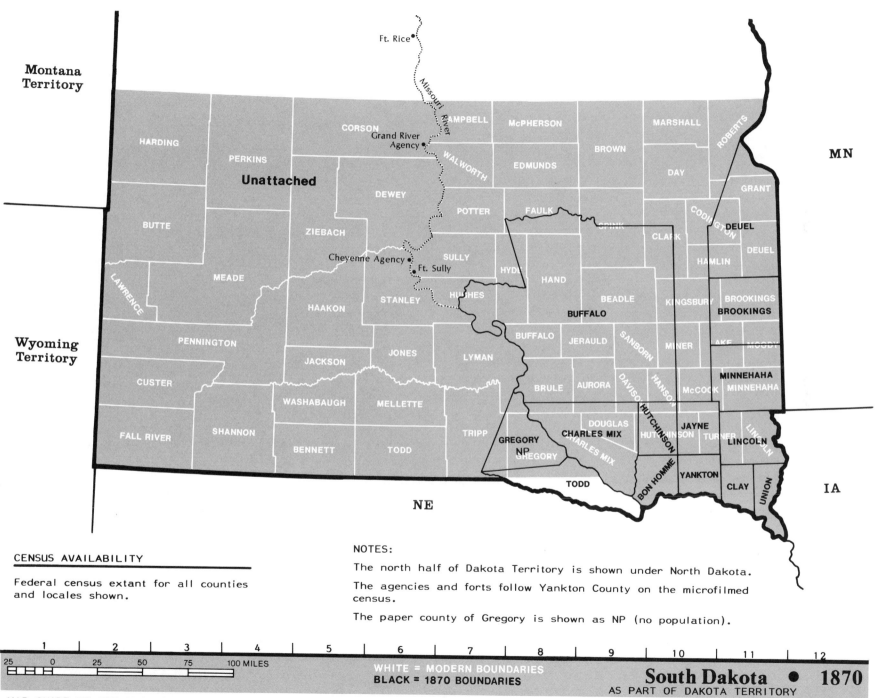

Montana
Territory

MN

Ft. Rice ●

Missouri River

HARDING

PERKINS

CORSON

Grand River
Agency ●

CAMPBELL

McPHERSON

MARSHALL

ROBERTS

Unattached

WALWORTH

BROWN

DAY

BUTTE

DEWEY

EDMUNDS

GRANT

ZIEBACH

POTTER

FAULK

CODINGTON

DEUEL

SPINK

CLARK

DEUEL

Cheyenne Agency ●
● Ft. Sully

SULLY

HAMLIN

MEADE

LAWRENCE

HYDE

HAND

BEADLE

KINGSBURY

BROOKINGS

HAAKON

STANLEY

HUGHES

BROOKINGS

Wyoming
Territory

BUFFALO

PENNINGTON

JONES

LYMAN

BUFFALO

JERAULD

SANBORN

MINER

LAKE

MOODY

CUSTER

BRULE

AURORA

DAVISON

HANSON

McCOOK

MINNEHAHA

MINNEHAHA

WASHABAUGH

MELLETTE

FALL RIVER

SHANNON

BENNETT

TODD

TRIPP

DOUGLAS

HUTCHINSON

JAYNE

TURNER

LINCOLN

**GREGORY
NP**

GREGORY

CHARLES MIX

CHARLES MIX

HUTCHINSON

LINCOLN

TODD

BON HOMME

YANKTON

CLAY

UNION

NE

IA

CENSUS AVAILABILITY

Federal census extant for all counties
and locales shown.

NOTES:

The north half of Dakota Territory is shown under North Dakota.

The agencies and forts follow Yankton County on the microfilmed
census.

The paper county of Gregory is shown as NP (no population).

1   2   3   4   5   6   7   8   9   10   11   12

25   0   25   50   75   100 MILES

WHITE = MODERN BOUNDARIES
BLACK = 1870 BOUNDARIES

South Dakota ● **1870**
AS PART OF DAKOTA TERRITORY

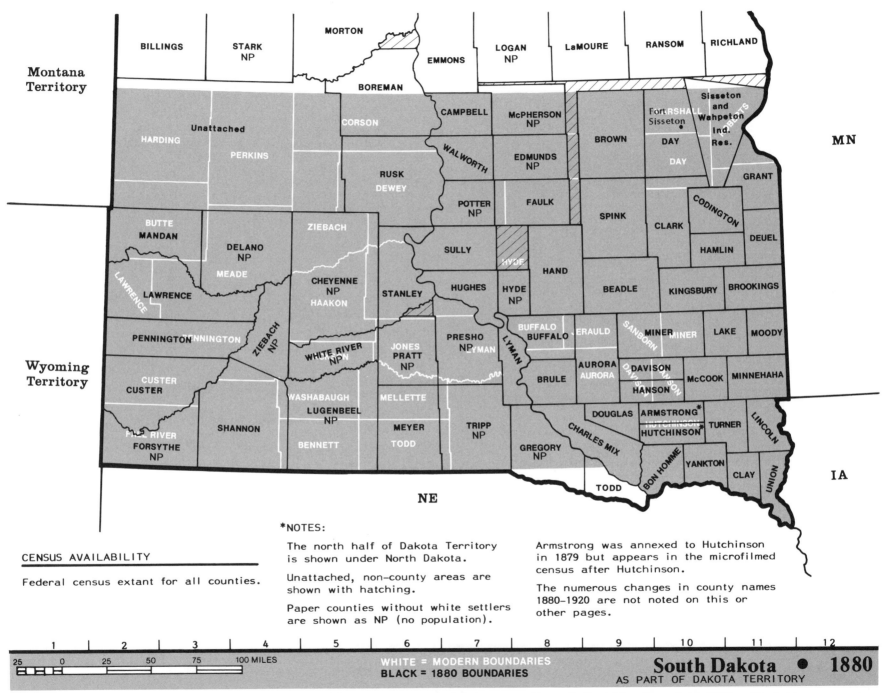

Montana
Territory

Wyoming
Territory

MN

IA

NE

*NOTES:

The north half of Dakota Territory
is shown under North Dakota.

Unattached, non-county areas are
shown with hatching.

Paper counties without white settlers
are shown as NP (no population).

Armstrong was annexed to Hutchinson
in 1879 but appears in the microfilmed
census after Hutchinson.

The numerous changes in county names
1880–1920 are not noted on this or
other pages.

CENSUS AVAILABILITY

Federal census extant for all counties.

25   0   25   50   75   100 MILES

1 2 3 4 5 6 7 8 9 10 11 12

WHITE = MODERN BOUNDARIES
BLACK = 1880 BOUNDARIES

South Dakota ● 1880
AS PART OF DAKOTA TERRITORY

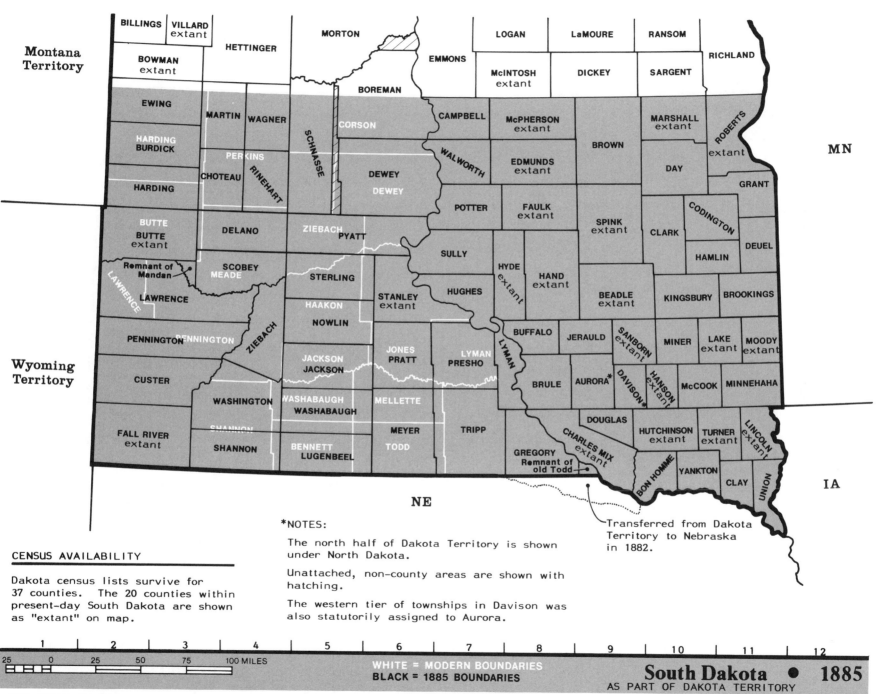

MN

NE

IA

*NOTES:

The north half of Dakota Territory is shown under North Dakota.

Unattached, non-county areas are shown with hatching.

The western tier of townships in Davison was also statutorily assigned to Aurora.

Transferred from Dakota Territory to Nebraska in 1882.

CENSUS AVAILABILITY

Dakota census lists survive for 37 counties. The 20 counties within present-day South Dakota are shown as "extant" on map.

1 2 3 4 5 6 7 8 9 10 11 12

25 0 25 50 75 100 MILES

WHITE = MODERN BOUNDARIES
BLACK = 1885 BOUNDARIES

South Dakota ● 1885
AS PART OF DAKOTA TERRITORY

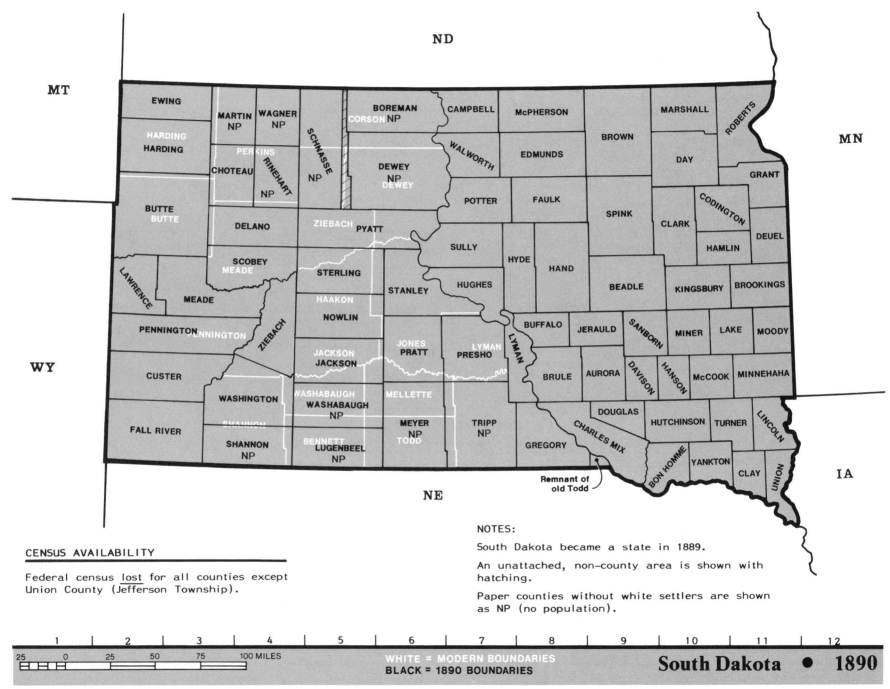

ND

MT

MN

WY

IA

NE

CENSUS AVAILABILITY

Federal census <u>lost</u> for all counties except Union County (Jefferson Township).

NOTES:

South Dakota became a state in 1889.

An unattached, non-county area is shown with hatching.

Paper counties without white settlers are shown as NP (no population).

WHITE = MODERN BOUNDARIES
BLACK = 1890 BOUNDARIES

1 2 3 4 5 6 7 8 9 10 11 12

25 0 25 50 75 100 MILES

South Dakota ● 1890

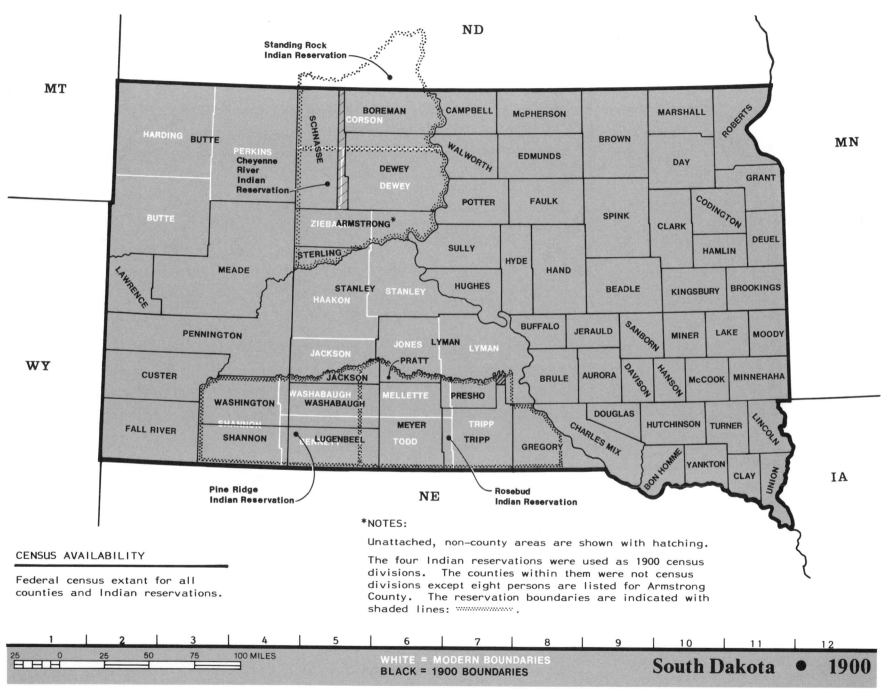

ND

MT

MN

WY

IA

NE

Standing Rock
Indian Reservation

HARDING · BUTTE

PERKINS
Cheyenne
River
Indian
Reservation

SCHNASSE

BOREMAN
CORSON

CAMPBELL

McPHERSON

MARSHALL

ROBERTS

BROWN

DEWEY
DEWEY

EDMUNDS

DAY

GRANT

BUTTE

ZIEBA ARMSTRONG*

POTTER

FAULK

SPINK

CLARK

CODINGTON

STERLING

HAMLIN

DEUEL

MEADE

LAWRENCE

SULLY

HYDE

HAND

BEADLE

KINGSBURY

BROOKINGS

STANLEY
HAAKON

STANLEY

HUGHES

PENNINGTON

JACKSON

JONES

LYMAN

LYMAN

PRATT

BUFFALO

JERAULD

SANBORN

MINER

LAKE

MOODY

HANSON

CUSTER

JACKSON

BRULE

AURORA

DAVISON

McCOOK

MINNEHAHA

WASHABAUGH
WASHABAUGH

MELLETTE

PRESHO

WASHINGTON

SHANNON

MEYER
TODD

TRIPP
TRIPP

DOUGLAS

HUTCHINSON

TURNER

LINCOLN

FALL RIVER

SHANNON

LUGENBEEL
BENNETT

GREGORY

CHARLES MIX

BON HOMME

YANKTON

CLAY

UNION

Pine Ridge
Indian Reservation

Rosebud
Indian Reservation

*NOTES:

Unattached, non-county areas are shown with hatching.

The four Indian reservations were used as 1900 census
divisions. The counties within them were not census
divisions except eight persons are listed for Armstrong
County. The reservation boundaries are indicated with
shaded lines: ▨▨▨▨▨▨ .

CENSUS AVAILABILITY

Federal census extant for all
counties and Indian reservations.

| 25 | 0 | 25 | 50 | 75 | 100 MILES |

WHITE = MODERN BOUNDARIES
BLACK = 1900 BOUNDARIES

South Dakota ● 1900

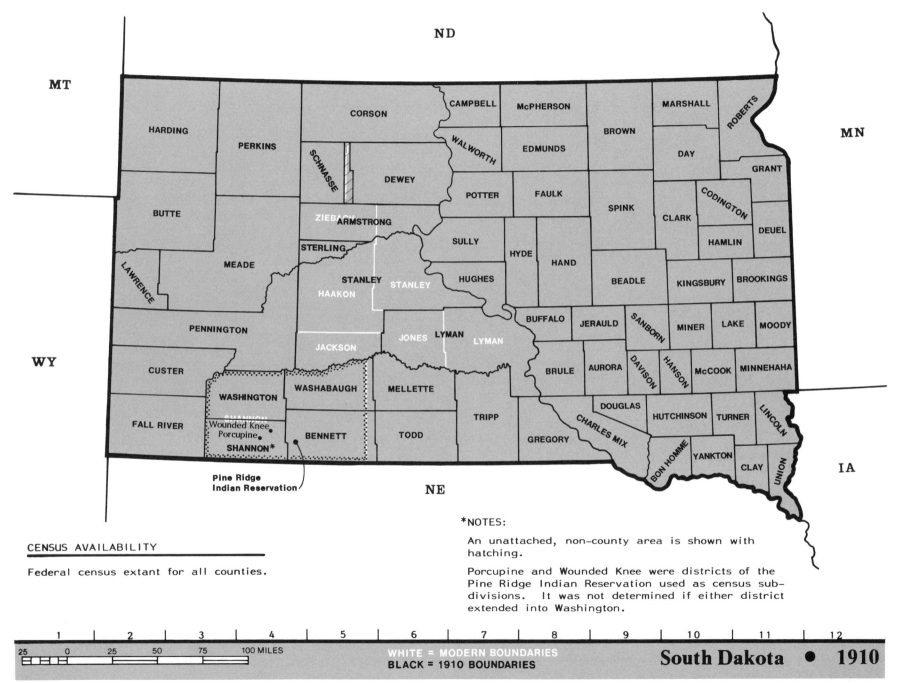

ND

MT

MN

WY

IA

NE

CENSUS AVAILABILITY

Federal census extant for all counties.

*NOTES:

An unattached, non-county area is shown with hatching.

Porcupine and Wounded Knee were districts of the Pine Ridge Indian Reservation used as census sub-divisions. It was not determined if either district extended into Washington.

1   2   3   4   5   6   7   8   9   10   11   12

25   0   25   50   75   100 MILES

WHITE = MODERN BOUNDARIES
BLACK = 1910 BOUNDARIES

South Dakota ● **1910**

MAP GUIDE TO THE U.S. FEDERAL CENSUSES, 1790–1920 by William Thorndale and William Dollarhide. Copyright 1987, all rights reserved.

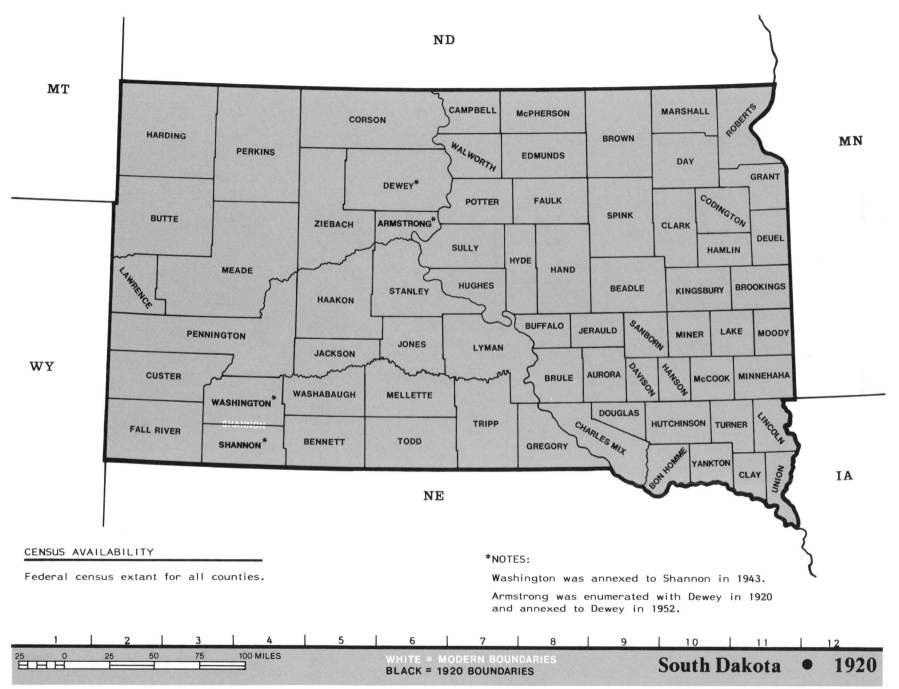

ND

MT

MN

HARDING

PERKINS

CORSON

CAMPBELL

McPHERSON

MARSHALL

ROBERTS

WALWORTH

BROWN

EDMUNDS

DAY

GRANT

BUTTE

DEWEY*

POTTER

FAULK

SPINK

CLARK

CODINGTON

DEUEL

ZIEBACH

ARMSTRONG*

SULLY

HAMLIN

MEADE

HYDE

HAND

LAWRENCE

HAAKON

STANLEY

HUGHES

BEADLE

KINGSBURY

BROOKINGS

BUFFALO

JERAULD

SANBORN

MINER

LAKE

MOODY

PENNINGTON

JONES

LYMAN

JACKSON

WY

BRULE

AURORA

DAVISON

HANSON

McCOOK

MINNEHAHA

CUSTER

WASHABAUGH

MELLETTE

WASHINGTON*

DOUGLAS

SHANNON

HUTCHINSON

TURNER

LINCOLN

FALL RIVER

SHANNON*

BENNETT

TODD

TRIPP

CHARLES MIX

GREGORY

BON HOMME

YANKTON

CLAY

UNION

IA

NE

CENSUS AVAILABILITY

Federal census extant for all counties.

*NOTES:

Washington was annexed to Shannon in 1943.

Armstrong was enumerated with Dewey in 1920
and annexed to Dewey in 1952.

1   2   3   4   5   6   7   8   9   10   11   12

25   0   25   50   75   100 MILES

WHITE = MODERN BOUNDARIES
BLACK = 1920 BOUNDARIES

South Dakota ● 1920

MAP GUIDE TO THE U.S. FEDERAL CENSUSES, 1790–1920 by William Thorndale and William Dollarhide. Copyright 1987, all rights reserved.

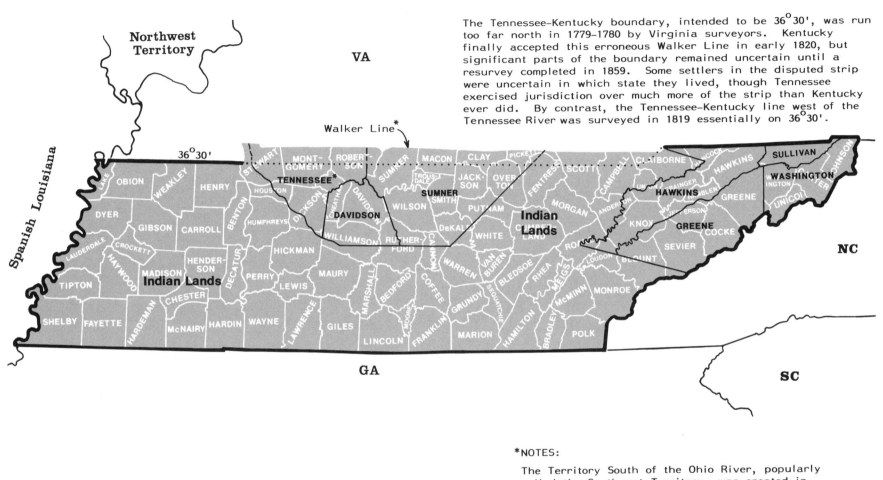

Northwest Territory

VA

The Tennessee–Kentucky boundary, intended to be 36°30', was run too far north in 1779–1780 by Virginia surveyors. Kentucky finally accepted this erroneous Walker Line in early 1820, but significant parts of the boundary remained uncertain until a resurvey completed in 1859. Some settlers in the disputed strip were uncertain in which state they lived, though Tennessee exercised jurisdiction over much more of the strip than Kentucky ever did. By contrast, the Tennessee–Kentucky line west of the Tennessee River was surveyed in 1819 essentially on 36°30'.

Walker Line*

Spanish Louisiana

36°30'

NC

GA

SC

*NOTES:

The Territory South of the Ohio River, popularly called the Southwest Territory, was created in May 1790.

By direction of the territorial governor, militia captains took a census in July 1791. The county lines were unchanged from 1790.

Tennessee County's name was dropped after its division into Montgomery and Robertson in 1796.

CENSUS AVAILABILITY

Federal census lost for all counties.

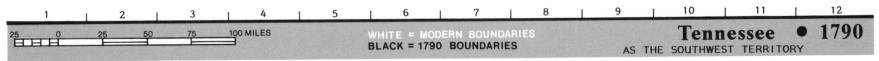

| 1 | 2 | 3 | 4 | 5 | 6 | 7 | 8 | 9 | 10 | 11 | 12 |

25 0 25 50 75 100 MILES

WHITE = MODERN BOUNDARIES
BLACK = 1790 BOUNDARIES

Tennessee ● 1790
AS THE SOUTHWEST TERRITORY

MAP GUIDE TO THE U.S. FEDERAL CENSUSES, 1790–1920 by William Thorndale and William Dollarhide. Copyright 1987, all rights reserved.

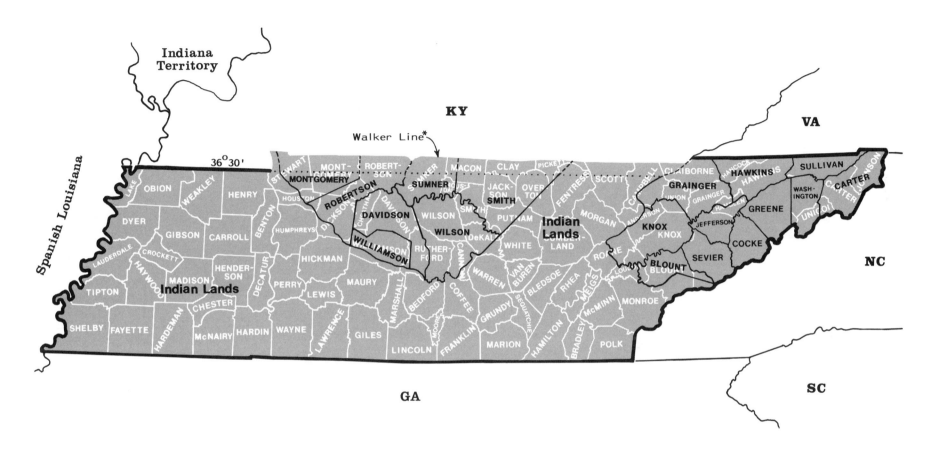

Indiana
Territory

KY

VA

Walker Line*

36°30'

Spanish Louisiana

NC

GA

SC

CENSUS AVAILABILITY

Federal census lost for all counties.

NOTES:

Tennessee became a state in 1796.

See Tennessee 1790 for an explanation of
the Walker Line.

25 0 25 50 75 100 MILES

Tennessee ● 1800

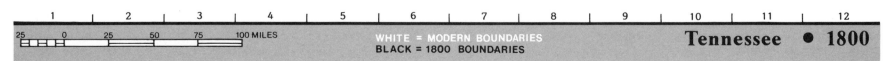

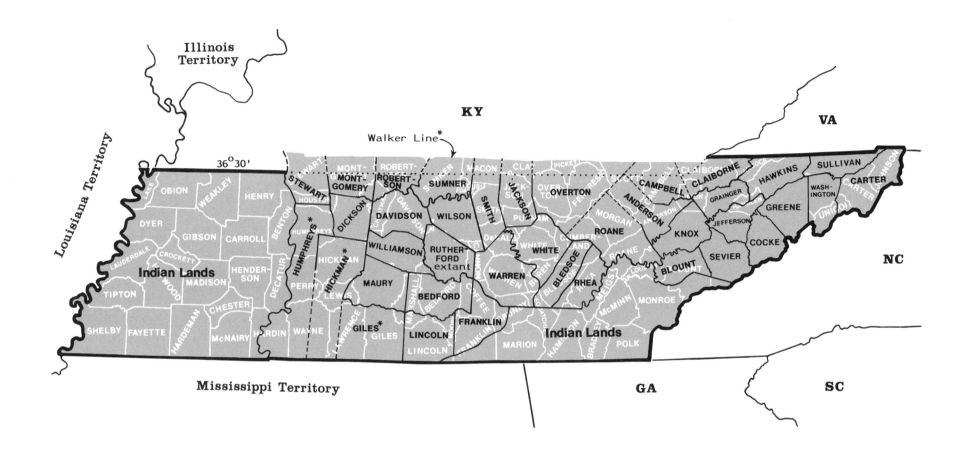

Illinois Territory

KY

VA

Walker Line*

Louisiana Territory

36°30'

STEWART
MONT-GOMERY
MONT-GOMERY
ROBERT-SON
ROBERT-SON
SUMNER
MACON
CLA
PICKE
CLAIBORNE
SULLIVAN
CARTER

OBION
WEAKLEY
HENRY
HOUST
DICKSON
DAVIDSON
WILSON
SMITH
JACKSON
OVERTON
CAMPBELL
GRAINGER
HAWKINS
WASH-INGTON

DYER
GIBSON
CARROLL
BENTON
HUMPHREYS*
DAVIDSON
WILLIAMSON
RUTHERFORD extant
DeKAL
WHITE
MORGAN
ANDERSON
JEFFERSON
GREENE
UNIC

LAUDERDALE
CROCKETT
HENDER-SON
HICKMAN*
HICKMAN
MAURY
WARREN
BLEDSOE
ROANE
ROANE
KNOX
SEVIER
COCKE

Indian Lands
MADISON
DECATUR
PERRY
LEWIS
BEDFORD
COFFEE
RHEA
McMINN
BLOUNT
MONROE

TIPTON
WOOD
CHESTER
HARDIN
WAYNE
LAWRENCE
MARSHALL
GILES*
GILES
LINCOLN
LINCOLN
FRANKLIN
MARION
HAMI
BRADLEY
POLK

SHELBY
FAYETTE
HARDEMAN
McNAIRY

NC

Indian Lands

Mississippi Territory

GA

SC

*NOTES:

Southern Hickman and Humphreys and southwestern Giles lay in the 1816 Chickasaw cession, an area previously ceded by treaties of 1805–1807.

See Tennessee 1790 for an explanation of the Walker Line.

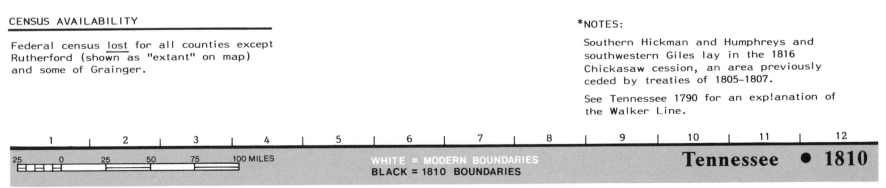

1 2 3 4 5 6 7 8 9 10 11 12

25 0 25 50 75 100 MILES

WHITE = MODERN BOUNDARIES
BLACK = 1810 BOUNDARIES

Tennessee ● 1810

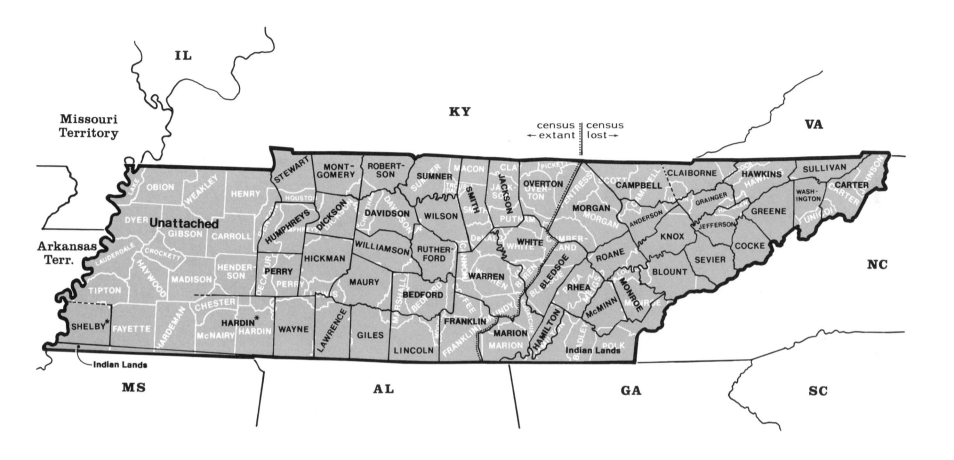

census | census
← extant | lost →

CENSUS AVAILABILITY

Federal census lost for all counties of the marshal's district of East Tennessee: Anderson, Bledsoe, Blount, Campbell, Carter, Claiborne, Cocke, Grainger, Greene, Hamilton, Hawkins, Jefferson, Knox, McMinn, Marion, Monroe, Morgan, Rhea, Roane, Sevier, Sullivan, and Washington.

*NOTE:

Hardin was created to run to the Mississippi, but eleven days later Shelby was created, its northern boundary sufficient to "include a constitutional county."

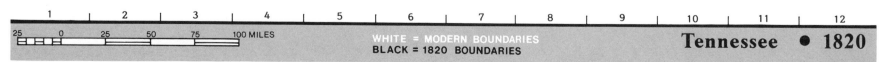

25 0 25 50 75 100 MILES

WHITE = MODERN BOUNDARIES
BLACK = 1820 BOUNDARIES

Tennessee ● 1820

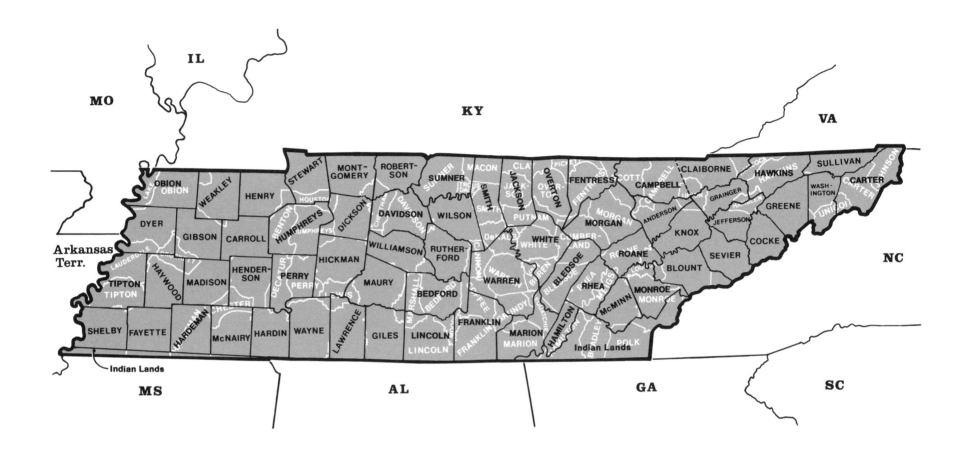

CENSUS AVAILABILITY

Federal census extant for all counties.

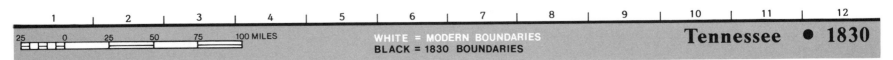

WHITE = MODERN BOUNDARIES
BLACK = 1830 BOUNDARIES

Tennessee ● 1830

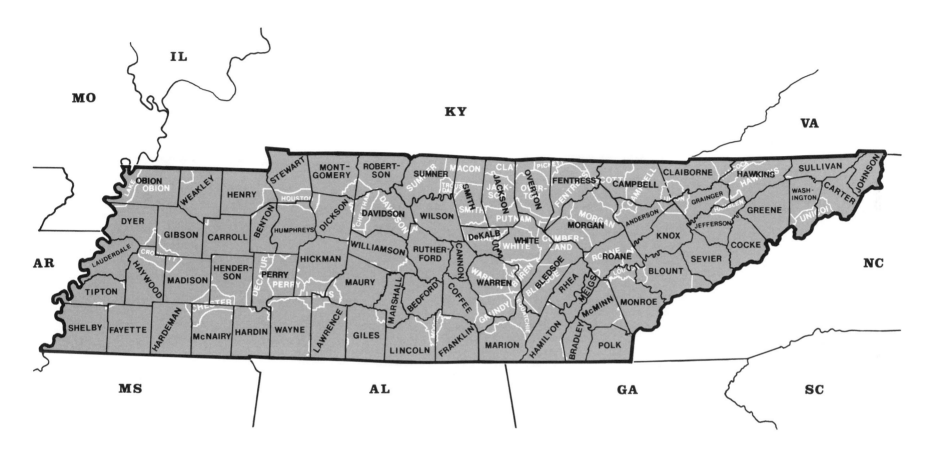

CENSUS AVAILABILITY

Federal census extant for all counties.

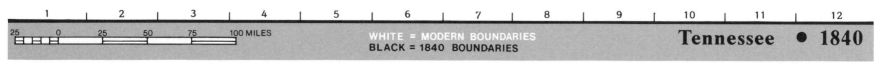

WHITE = MODERN BOUNDARIES
BLACK = 1840 BOUNDARIES

Tennessee ● 1840

25 0 25 50 75 100 MILES

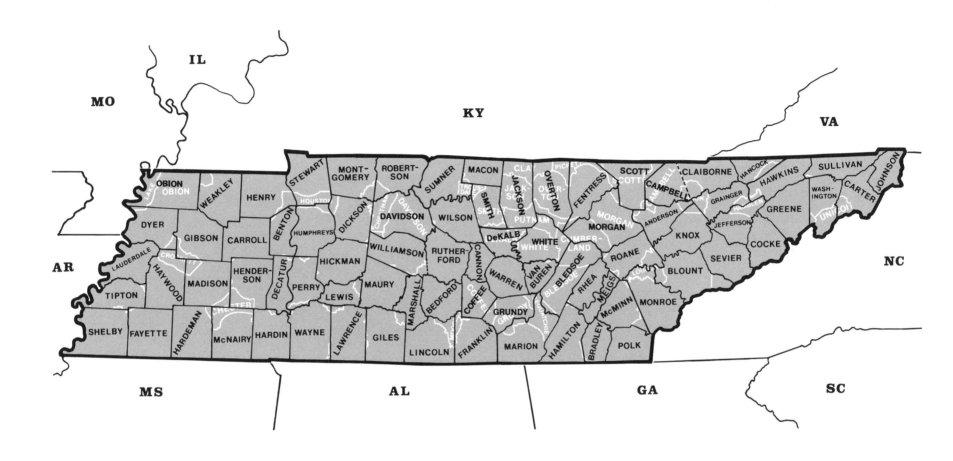

CENSUS AVAILABILITY

Federal census extant for all counties.

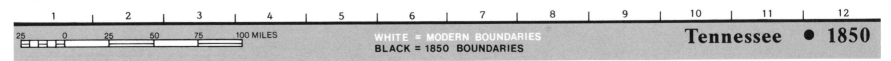

Tennessee ● 1850

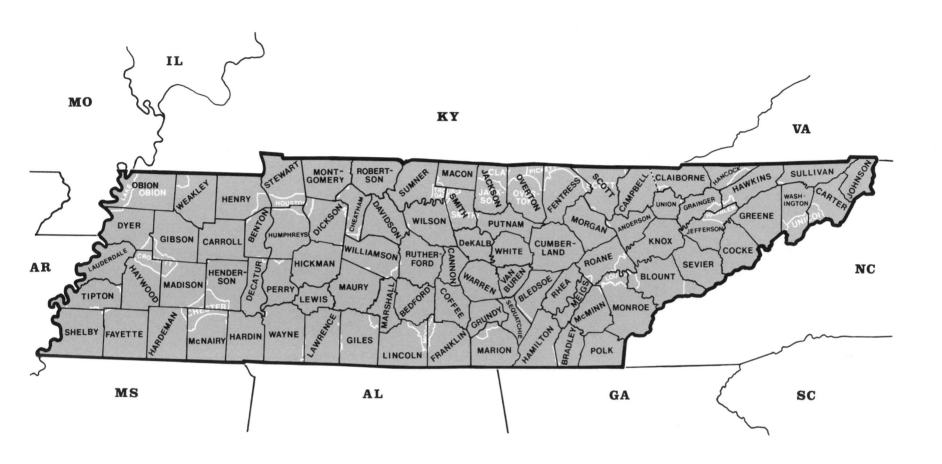

CENSUS AVAILABILITY

Federal census extant for all counties.

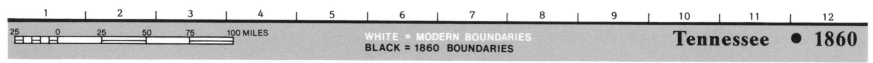

WHITE = MODERN BOUNDARIES
BLACK = 1860 BOUNDARIES

Tennessee ● 1860

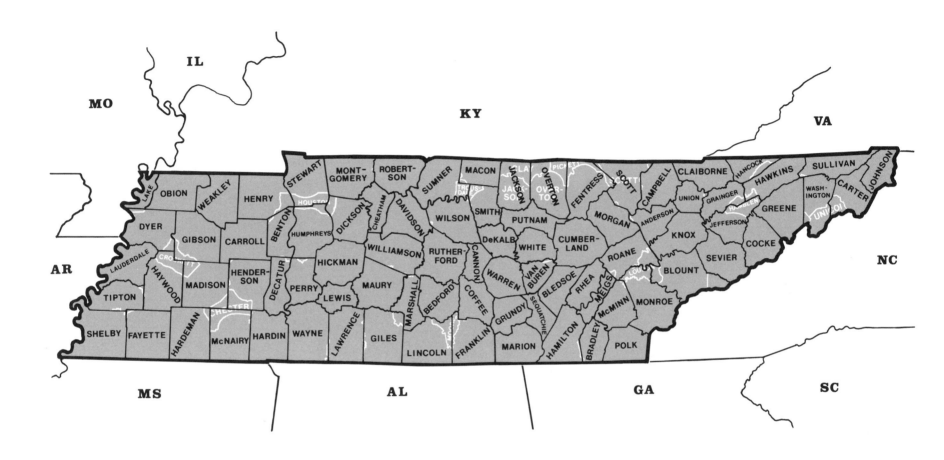

CENSUS AVAILABILITY

Federal census extant for all counties.

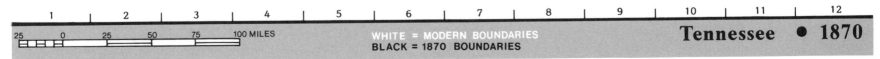

Tennessee ● 1870

25   0   25   50   75   100 MILES

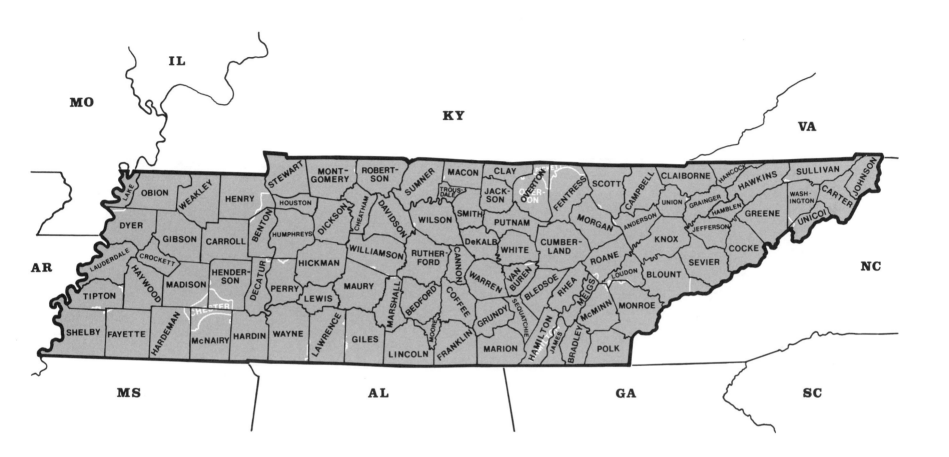

CENSUS AVAILABILITY

Federal census extant for all counties.

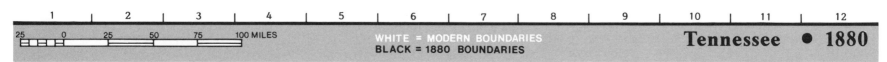

WHITE = MODERN BOUNDARIES
BLACK = 1880 BOUNDARIES

100 MILES

Tennessee ● 1880

MAP GUIDE TO THE U.S. FEDERAL CENSUSES, 1790–1920 by William Thorndale and William Dollarhide. Copyright 1987, all rights reserved.

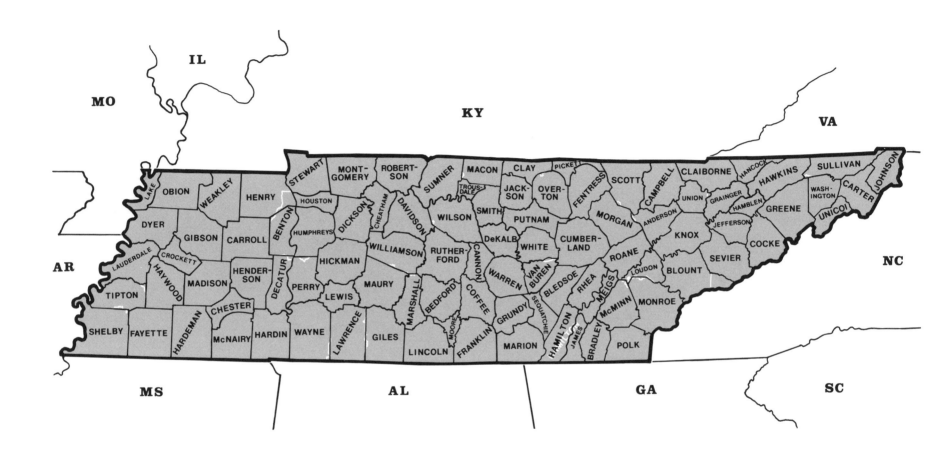

CENSUS AVAILABILITY

Federal census <u>lost</u> for all counties.

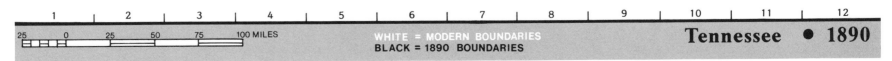

1   2   3   4   5   6   7   8   9   10   11   12

25   0   25   50   75   100 MILES

WHITE = MODERN BOUNDARIES
BLACK = 1890 BOUNDARIES

Tennessee • 1890

MAP GUIDE TO THE U.S. FEDERAL CENSUSES, 1790–1920 by William Thorndale and William Dollarhide. Copyright 1987, all rights reserved.

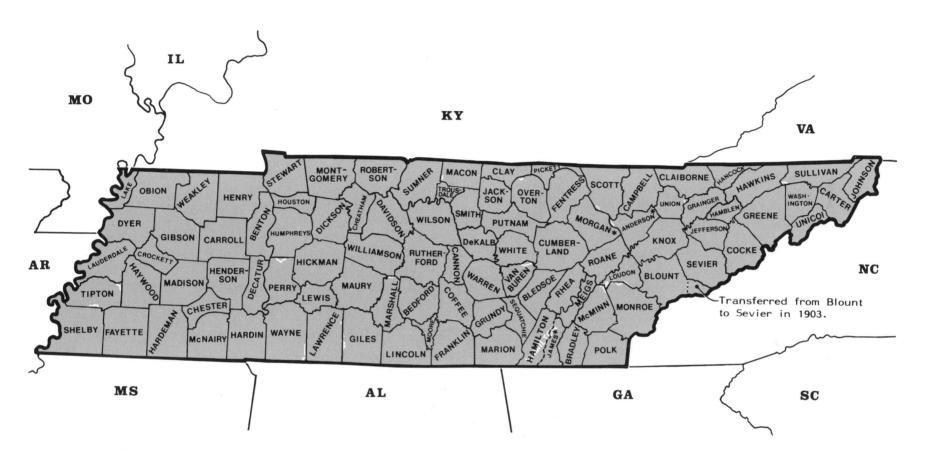

Transferred from Blount to Sevier in 1903.

CENSUS AVAILABILITY

1900–1920 federal censuses extant for all counties.

*NOTES:

Anderson is shown for 1900. The transfer of its extreme western tip to Morgan in 1903 created the modern line.

James was annexed to Hamilton effective January 1920.

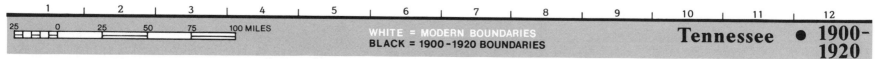

Tennessee • 1900-1920

25 0 25 50 75 100 MILES

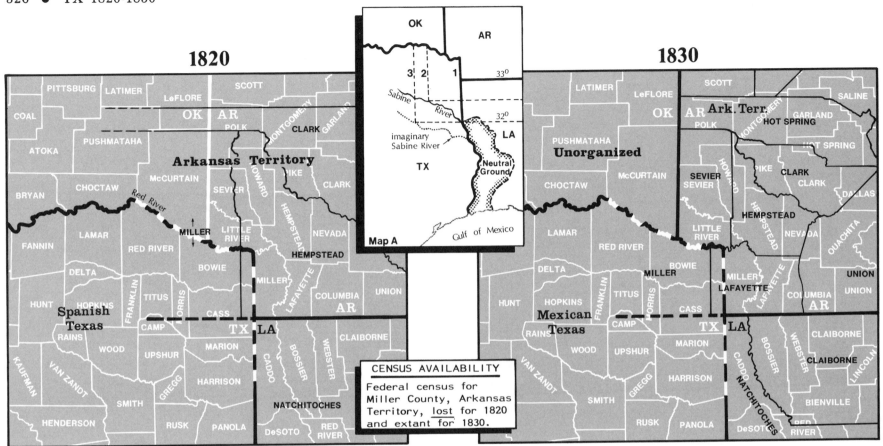

1820

1830

Map A

CENSUS AVAILABILITY

Federal census for
Miller County, Arkansas
Territory, <u>lost</u> for 1820
and extant for 1830.

The 1803 Louisiana Purchase caused a border dispute with Spain over the Louisiana-Texas boundary. Spain claimed east to the Red River; the U.S. claimed west at least to the Sabine. They made a temporary compromise in 1806 with the so-called Neutral Ground, where neither exercised jurisdiction, creating a haven for fugitives. Their 1819 treaty (ratified in 1821) finally set the permanent line to run up the Sabine River to the 32nd parallel, then due north to the Red River, which is the modern Texas line with Louisiana and Arkansas. But where the 32nd parallel crossed the Sabine was unknown, so where a line north from this imaginary point would reach the Red River was also unknown. Until the early 1830s this due-north line was so uncertain that Arkansas Territory in April 1820 inadvertently established its Miller County partly inside Texas.

Inset Map A shows how the confusion arose, with the correct, modern line labeled as line 1. Had the 32nd parallel crossed the Sabine farther north, line 2 might have resulted. Or had the Sabine turned west farther south than it does, line 3 was possible. This confusion led in 1820 to the U.S. census of Miller County enumerating the northeast corner of Spanish Texas.

In 1828 the Indian treaty line was established at the modern Oklahoma-Arkansas line, forcing white settlers to leave what is now southeastern Oklahoma. Miller's courthouse was relocated to south of Red River, and the 1830 U.S. census of Miller County, Arkansas Territory, was taken completely inside Mexican Texas. By the mid-1830s the geography was much better understood, so when the republic of Texas created its Red River County in 1836, Miller soon vanished.

25 0 25 50 75 100 MILES

Texas ● **1820-**
NORTHEAST CORNER
& ADJOINING AREAS **1830**

NOTE:

The county lines include the statutory boundary changes of January–February 1840. Texas exercised no jurisdiction over the Rio Grande Valley until the U.S. Army captured the area in 1847–1848.

AR

LA

SHELBY
SABINE
SAN AUGUSTINE
NEWTON
JASPER
NACOGDOCHES
ANGELINA
TYLER
JEFFERSON
GALVESTON

Claimed by Texas

Claimed by Texas

Mexico

Nueces River

Rio Grande

WHITE = MODERN BOUNDARIES
BLACK = 1840 BOUNDARIES

25 0 25 50 75 100 MILES

Republic of Texas

Texas ● 1840
AS THE REPUBLIC OF TEXAS

MAP GUIDE TO THE U.S. FEDERAL CENSUSES, 1790–1920 by William Thorndale and William Dollarhide. Copyright 1987, all rights reserved.

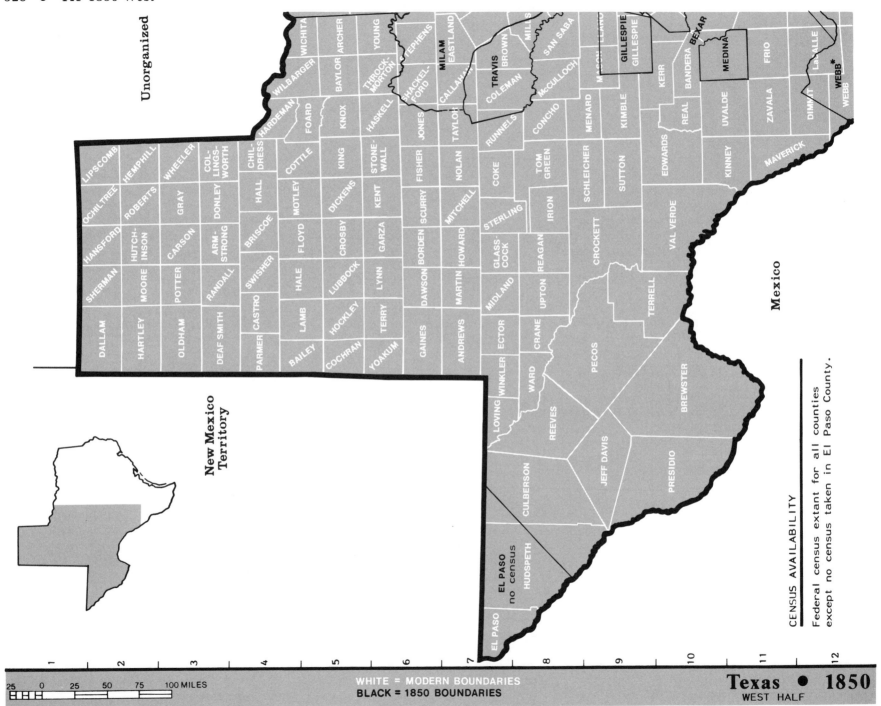

Unorganized

New Mexico Territory

Mexico

CENSUS AVAILABILITY

Federal census extant for all counties except no census taken in El Paso County.

WHITE = MODERN BOUNDARIES
BLACK = 1850 BOUNDARIES

Texas ● 1850
WEST HALF

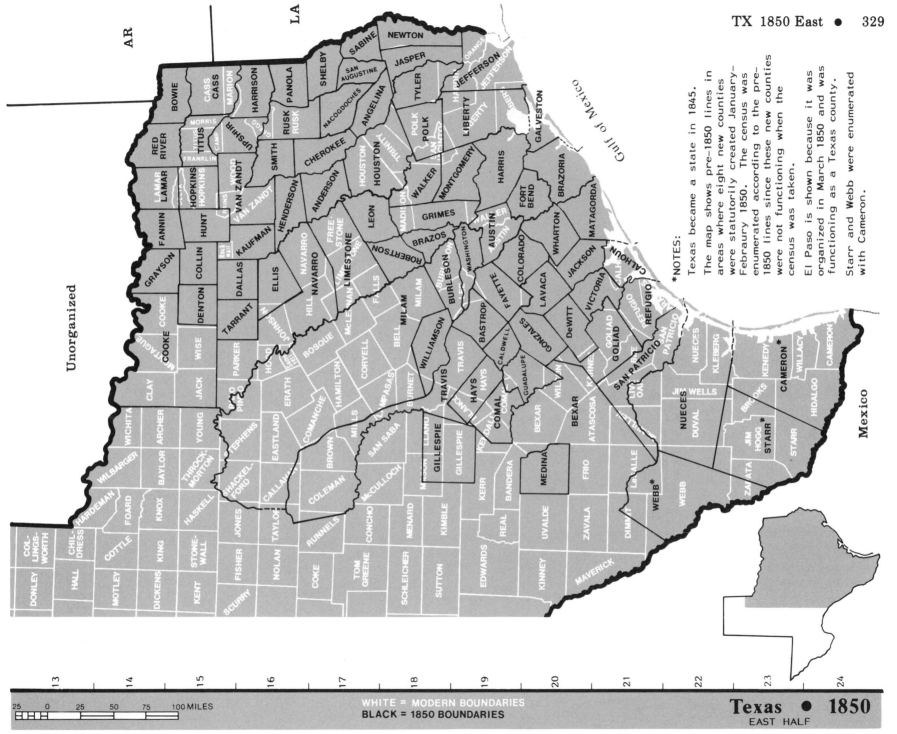

AR

LA

NEWTON

SABINE

JASPER

SHELBY

SAN AUGUSTINE

TYLER

HARRISON

PANOLA

NACOGDOCHES

ANGELINA

JEFFERSON

JEFFERSON

ORANGE

MORRIS

CASS

CASS

MARION

BOWIE

UPSHUR

UPSHUR

GREGG

RUSK

RUSK

POLK

POL
K

LIBERTY

LIBERTY

GALVESTON

Gulf of Mexico

RED RIVER

TITUS

TITUS

CAMP

CHEROKEE

SMITH

HARDIN

LAMAR

LAMAR

FRANKLIN

HOPKINS

HOPKINS

WOOD

VAN ZANDT

VAN ZANDT

HENDERSON

ANDERSON

HOUSTON

HOUSTON

TRINITY

WALKER

MONTGOMERY

HARRIS

BRAZORIA

FANNIN

HUNT

KAUFMAN

RAINS

MADISON

GRIMES

WALKER

FORT BEND

GRAYSON

COLLIN

ROCKWALL

DALLAS

ELLIS

NAVARRO

NAVARRO

FREE-
STONE

LIMESTONE

LIMESTONE

ROBERTSON

BRAZOS

LEON

WASHINGTON

AUSTIN

AUSTIN

COLORADO

WHARTON

MATAGORDA

DENTON

TARRANT

HILL

JOHNSON

McLENNAN

FALLS

BURLESON

FAYETTE

LAVACA

JACKSON

CALHOUN

COOKE

COOKE

WISE

PARKER

HOOD

SOMERVELL

BOSQUE

CORYELL

BELL

MILAM

MILAM

WILLIAMSON

BASTROP

CALDWELL

GONZALES

DEWITT

VICTORIA

GOLIAD

REFUGIO

CALHOUN

Unorganized

MONTAGUE

CLAY

JACK

WISE

ERATH

HAMILTON

MILLS

LAMPASAS

BURNET

TRAVIS

TRAVIS

HAYS

HAYS

GUADALUPE

COMAL

KARNES

SAN PATRICIO

SAN PATRICIO

LIVE OAK

NUECES

KLEBERG

KENEDY

WILLACY

CAMERON

WICHITA

ARCHER

YOUNG

STEPHENS

EASTLAND

COMANCHE

BROWN

SAN SABA

LLANO

GILLESPIE

GILLESPIE

KENDALL

BEXAR

BEXAR

ATASCOSA

JIM WELLS

BROOKS

CAMERON

WILBARGER

BAYLOR

THROCK-
MORTON

SHACKEL-
FORD

CALLAHAN

COLEMAN

McCULLOCH

MASON

MEDINA

FRIO

NUECES

DUVAL

JIM HOGG

STARR

STARR

HIDALGO

WILLACY

HARDEMAN

FOARD

KNOX

HASKELL

JONES

TAYLOR

RUNNELS

CONCHO

MENARD

KIMBLE

KERR

BANDERA

REAL

UVALDE

ZAVALA

LA SALLE

WEBB

WEBB

ZAPATA

COL-
LINGS-
WORTH

CHIL-
DRESS

COTTLE

KING

STONE-
WALL

FISHER

NOLAN

COKE

TOM GREENE

SCHLEICHER

SUTTON

EDWARDS

KINNEY

MAVERICK

DIMMIT

DONLEY

HALL

MOTLEY

DICKENS

KENT

SCURRY

Mexico

*NOTES:

Texas became a state in 1845.

The map shows pre-1850 lines in areas where eight new counties were statutorily created January-February 1850. The census was enumerated according to the pre-1850 lines since these new counties were not functioning when the census was taken.

El Paso is shown because it was organized in March 1850 and was functioning as a Texas county.

Starr and Webb were enumerated with Cameron.

| 13 | 14 | 15 | 16 | 17 | 18 | 19 | 20 | 21 | 22 | 23 | 24 |

25 0 25 50 75 100 MILES

WHITE = MODERN BOUNDARIES
BLACK = 1850 BOUNDARIES

Texas ● **1850**
EAST HALF

MAP GUIDE TO THE U.S. FEDERAL CENSUSES, 1790–1920 by William Thorndale and William Dollarhide. Copyright 1987, all rights reserved.

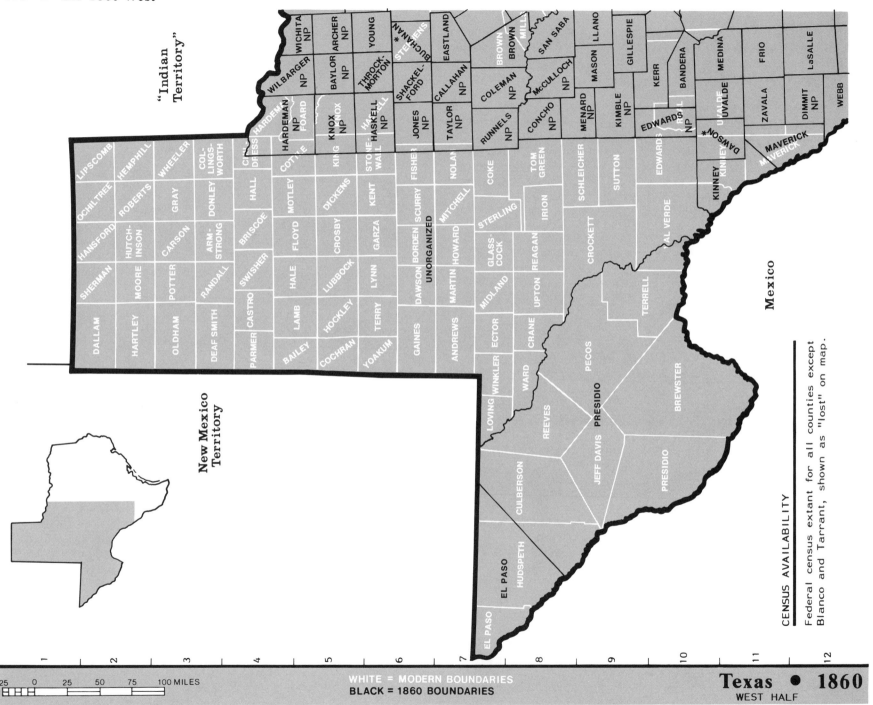

"Indian Territory"

New Mexico Territory

Mexico

LIPSCOMB
OCHILTREE
HANSFORD
SHERMAN
DALLAM
HARTLEY
MOORE
OLDHAM
HEMPHILL
ROBERTS
HUTCH-INSON
CARSON
POTTER
DEAF SMITH
WHEELER
GRAY
DONLEY
ARM-STRONG
RANDALL
COL-LINGS-WORTH
BRISCOE
SWISHER
CASTRO
PARMER
HALL
FLOYD
MOTLEY
HALE
LAMB
BAILEY
CHILD-RESS
COTTLE
DICKENS
CROSBY
HOCKLEY
COCHRAN
KING
KENT
GARZA
LYNN
TERRY
YOAKUM
STONE WALL
HASKELL NP
HARDEMAN NP
FOARD
KNOX NP
HALL
FISHER
SCURRY
BORDEN
DAWSON
GAINES
UNORGANIZED
NOLAN
MITCHELL
HOWARD
MARTIN
ANDREWS
STERLING
COKE
GLASS-COCK
MIDLAND
ECTOR
WINKLER
LOVING
WARD
CRANE
UPTON
REAGAN
IRION
TOM GREEN
SCHLEICHER
CROCKETT
PECOS
REEVES
CULBERSON
EL PASO
HUDSPETH
EL PASO
JEFF DAVIS
PRESIDIO
PRESIDIO
BREWSTER
TERRELL
SUTTON
AL VERDE
EDWARDS
EDWARDS NP
KINNEY
KINNEY
*DAWSON
MAVERICK
MAVERICK
UVALDE
ZAVALA
DIMMIT NP
WEBB
LaSALLE
FRIO
MEDINA
BANDERA
KERR
GILLESPIE
MASON
KIMBLE NP
MENARD NP
CONCHO NP
RUNNELS NP
TAYLOR NP
JONES NP
McCULLOCH NP
SAN SABA
MILL
BROWN
BROWN
COLEMAN NP
CALLAHAN NP
SHACKEL-FORD
EASTLAND
STEPHENS
BUCHANAN
*
YOUNG
ARCHER NP
WICHITA
WILBARGER
BAYLOR NP
THROCK-MORTON
LLANO

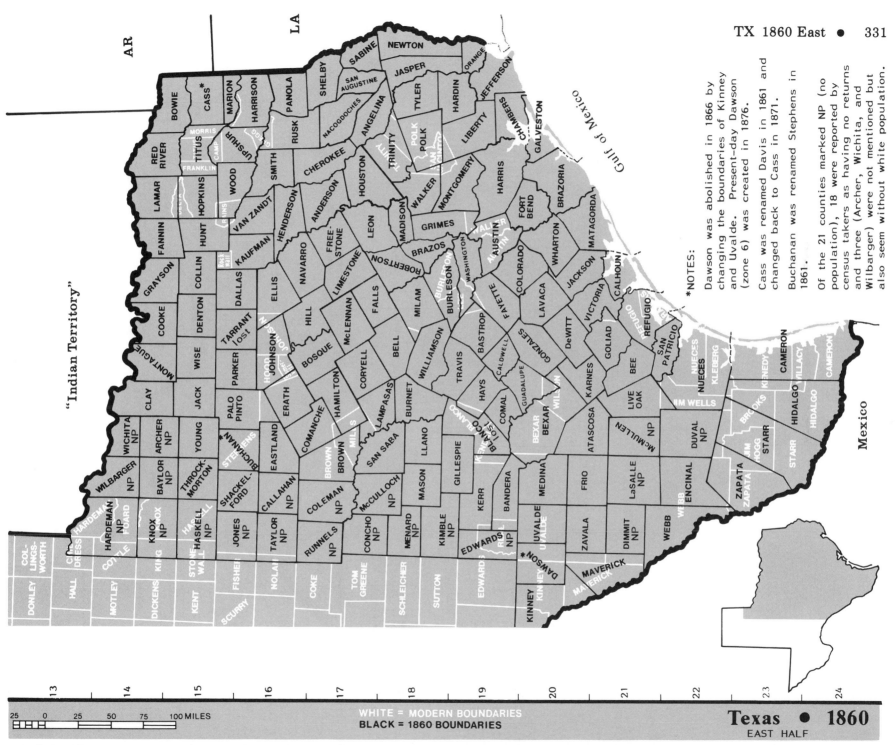

AR

LA

Gulf of Mexico

"Indian Territory"

Mexico

*NOTES:

Dawson was abolished in 1866 by changing the boundaries of Kinney and Uvalde. Present-day Dawson (zone 6) was created in 1876.

Cass was renamed Davis in 1861 and changed back to Cass in 1871.

Buchanan was renamed Stephens in 1861.

Of the 21 counties marked NP (no population), 18 were reported by census takers as having no returns and three (Archer, Wichita, and Wilbarger) were not mentioned but also seem without white population.

WHITE = MODERN BOUNDARIES
BLACK = 1860 BOUNDARIES

Texas ● **1860**
EAST HALF

25 0 25 50 75 100 MILES

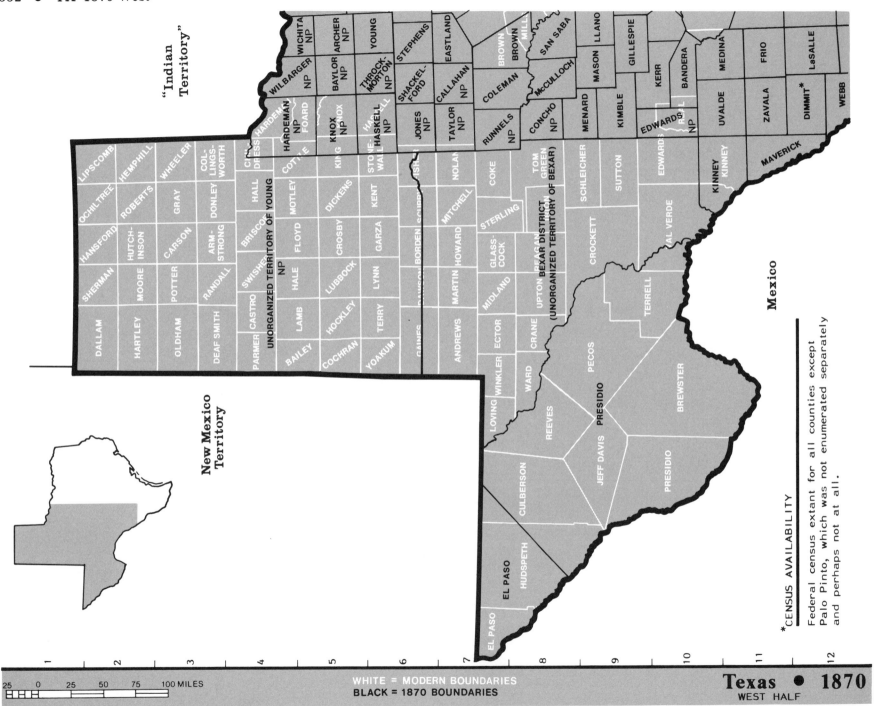

"Indian Territory"

New Mexico Territory

Mexico

WHITE = MODERN BOUNDARIES
BLACK = 1870 BOUNDARIES

25 0 25 50 75 100 MILES

Texas ● 1870
WEST HALF

MAP GUIDE TO THE U.S. FEDERAL CENSUSES, 1790-1920 by William Thorndale and William Dollarhide. Copyright 1987, all rights reserved.

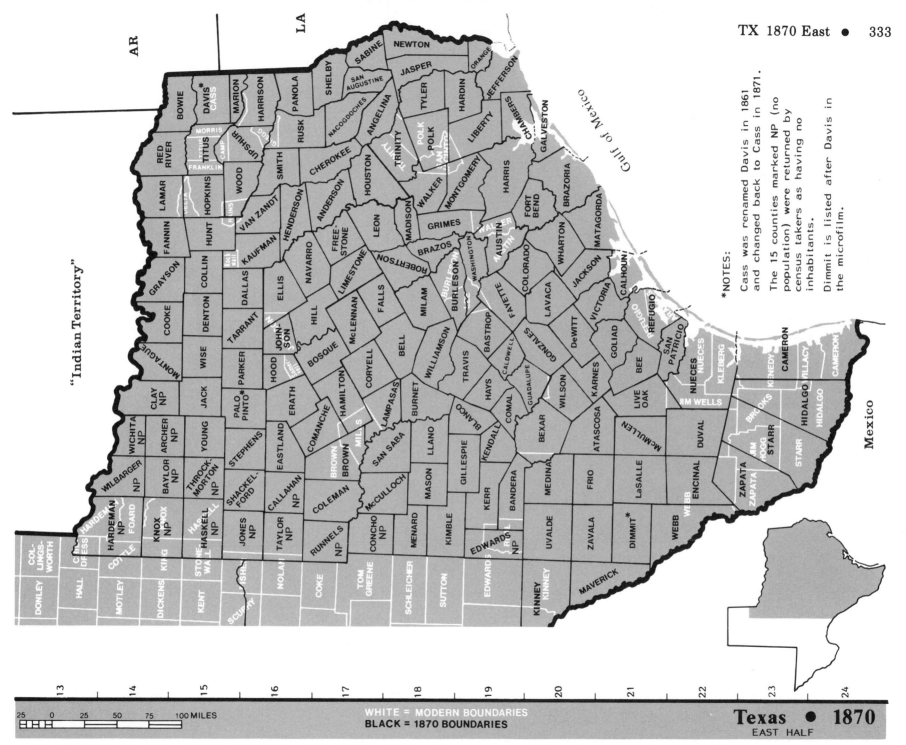

AR

LA

Gulf of Mexico

"Indian Territory"

Mexico

BOWIE
DAVIS * CASS
MARION
MORRIS
HARRISON
RED RIVER
TITUS
CAMP
FRANKLIN
UPSHUR
GREGG
PANOLA
SHELBY
SABINE
NEWTON
SAN AUGUSTINE
JASPER
NACOGDOCHES
ANGELINA
TYLER
HARDIN
JEFFERSON
ORANGE
CHAMBERS
GALVESTON
LAMAR
HOPKINS
DELTA
WOOD
RAINS
SMITH
RUSK
CHEROKEE
TRINITY
POLK
SAN JACINTO
LIBERTY
FANNIN
HUNT
ROCK WALL
VAN ZANDT
HENDERSON
ANDERSON
HOUSTON
MADISON
WALKER
MONTGOMERY
HARRIS
GRAYSON
COLLIN
DALLAS
KAUFMAN
NAVARRO
FREE-STONE
LEON
BRAZOS
GRIMES
WALLER
AUSTIN
FORT BEND
BRAZORIA
MATAGORDA
COOKE
DENTON
TARRANT
ELLIS
HILL
LIMESTONE
ROBERTSON
BURLESON
WASHINGTON
COLORADO
WHARTON
JACKSON
CALHOUN
MONTAGUE
WISE
PARKER
JOHNSON
HOOD
BOSQUE
McLENNAN
FALLS
MILAM
BELL
WILLIAMSON
BASTROP
LEE
FAYETTE
LAVACA
DEWITT
VICTORIA
REFUGIO
CLAY NP
JACK
PALO PINTO *
ERATH
COMANCHE
HAMILTON
CORYELL
TRAVIS
CALDWELL
GONZALES
GOLIAD
SAN PATRICIO
NUECES
WICHITA NP
ARCHER NP
YOUNG
STEPHENS
EASTLAND
MILLS
SAN SABA
LAMPASAS
BURNET
HAYS
COMAL
GUADALUPE
WILSON
KARNES
BEE
LIVE OAK
JIM WELLS
NUECES
KLEBERG
CAMERON
WILBARGER NP
BAYLOR NP
THROCK-MORTON NP
SHACKEL-FORD
CALLAHAN NP
COLEMAN
BROWN
LLANO
GILLESPIE
KENDALL
BLANCO
BEXAR
ATASCOSA
McMULLEN
DUVAL
BROOKS
STARR
HIDALGO
CAMERON
HARDEMAN NP
KNOX NP
HASKELL NP
JONES NP
TAYLOR NP
RUNNELS NP
CONCHO NP
McCULLOCH
MENARD
MASON
KERR
BANDERA
MEDINA
FRIO
LaSALLE
ENCINAL
WEBB
ZAPATA
JIM HOGG
STARR
COL-LINGS-WORTH
HALL
CHILD-RESS
COTTLE
FOARD
KING
STONE-WALL
HASKELL
FISHER
NOLAN
COKE
TOM GREENE
SCHLEICHER
SUTTON
EDWARDS
KINNEY
MAVERICK
ZAVALA
UVALDE
DIMMIT *
WEBB
KINNEY
DONLEY
MOTLEY
DICKENS
KENT
SCURRY
KIMBLE

25 0 25 50 75 100 MILES

WHITE = MODERN BOUNDARIES
BLACK = 1870 BOUNDARIES

Texas ● **1870**
EAST HALF

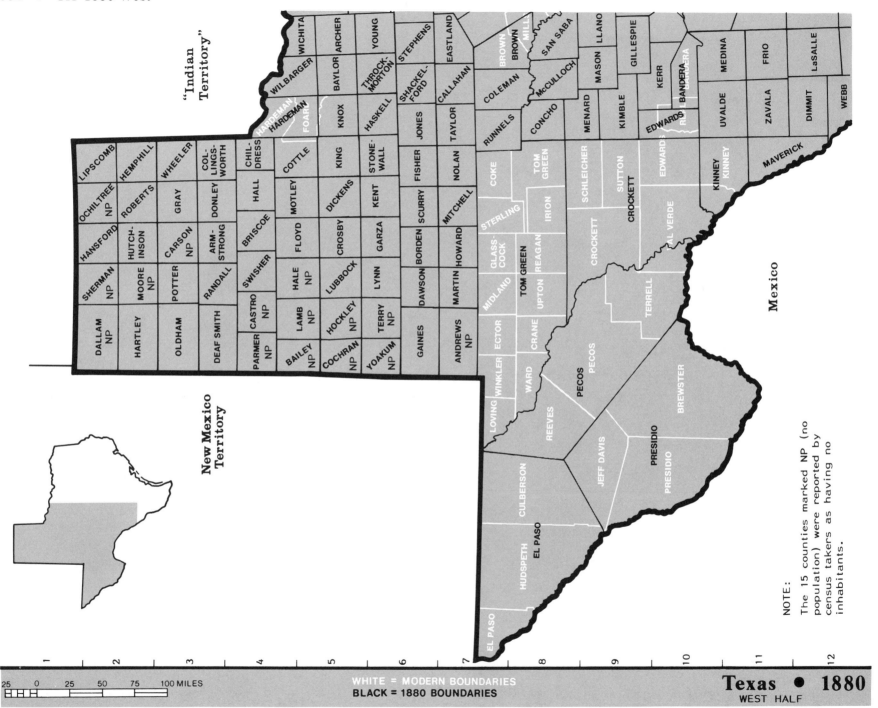

NOTE:

The 15 counties marked NP (no population) were reported by census takers as having no inhabitants.

WHITE = MODERN BOUNDARIES
BLACK = 1880 BOUNDARIES

Texas ● **1880**
WEST HALF

25 0 25 50 75 100 MILES

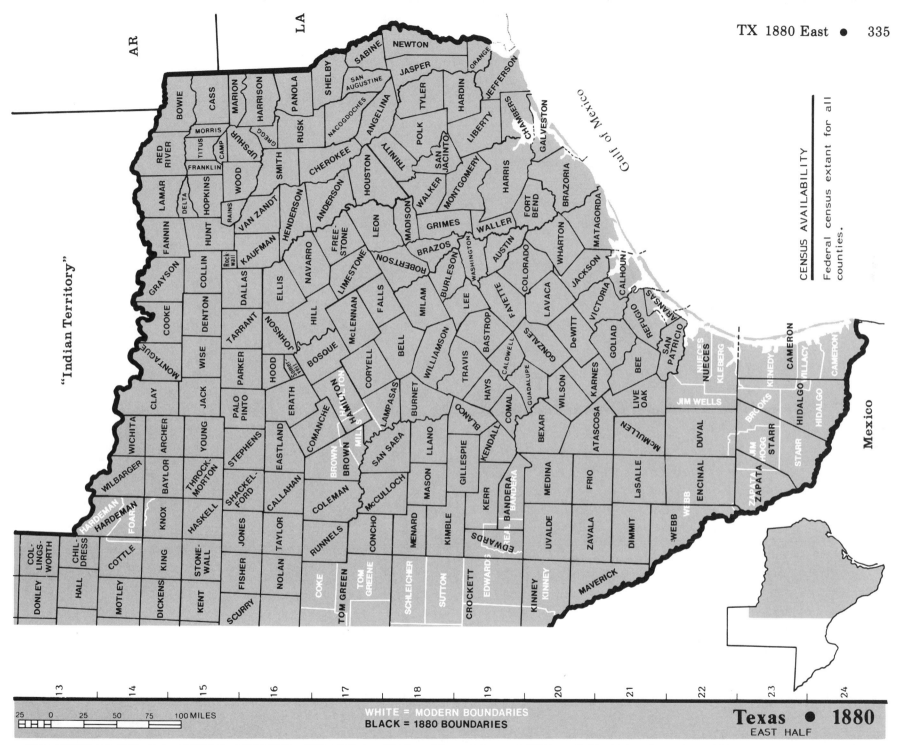

AR

LA

"Indian Territory"

Gulf of Mexico

Mexico

CENSUS AVAILABILITY

Federal census extant for all counties.

13 14 15 16 17 18 19 20 21 22 23 24

25 0 25 50 75 100 MILES

WHITE = MODERN BOUNDARIES
BLACK = 1880 BOUNDARIES

Texas ● 1880
EAST HALF

MAP GUIDE TO THE U.S. FEDERAL CENSUSES, 1790–1920 by William Thorndale and William Dollarhide. Copyright 1987, all rights reserved.

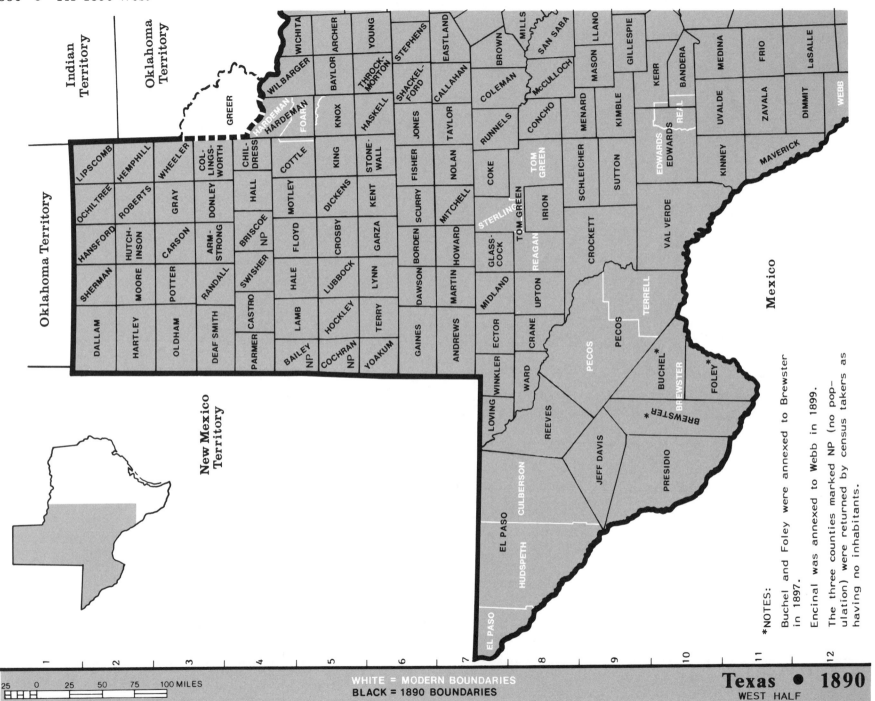

Indian Territory

Oklahoma Territory

Oklahoma Territory

New Mexico Territory

Mexico

WICHITA
ARCHER
BAYLOR
YOUNG
STEPHENS
EASTLAND
BROWN
MILLS
SAN SABA
LLANO
GILLESPIE
MASON
KERR
BANDERA
MEDINA
FRIO
LaSALLE
WEBB
WILBARGER
THROCK-MORTON
SHACKEL-FORD
CALLAHAN
COLEMAN
McCULLOCH
MENARD
KIMBLE
EDWARDS
REAL
UVALDE
ZAVALA
DIMMIT
HARDEMAN
HARDEMAN
FOARD
KNOX
HASKELL
JONES
TAYLOR
RUNNELS
CONCHO
EDWARDS
KINNEY
MAVERICK
GREER
LIPSCOMB
HEMPHILL
WHEELER
COL-LINGS-WORTH
CHIL-DRESS
COTTLE
KING
STONE-WALL
FISHER
NOLAN
COKE
TOM GREEN
SCHLEICHER
SUTTON
VAL VERDE
OCHILTREE
ROBERTS
GRAY
DONLEY
HALL
MOTLEY
DICKENS
KENT
SCURRY
MITCHELL
STERLING
TOM GREEN
IRION
REAGAN
CROCKETT
HANSFORD
HUTCH-INSON
CARSON
ARM-STRONG
BRISCOE NP
FLOYD
CROSBY
GARZA
BORDEN
GLASS-COCK
TERRELL
SHERMAN
MOORE
POTTER
RANDALL
SWISHER
HALE
LUBBOCK
LYNN
DAWSON
MARTIN
HOWARD
MIDLAND
UPTON
REAGAN
PECOS
DALLAM
HARTLEY
OLDHAM
DEAF SMITH
CASTRO
PARMER
LAMB
HOCKLEY
TERRY
YOAKUM
GAINES
ANDREWS
ECTOR
CRANE
WINKLER
WARD
PECOS
TERRELL
BUCHEL *
FOLEY *
BAILEY NP
COCHRAN NP
LOVING
REEVES
JEFF DAVIS
BREWSTER *
BREWSTER
PRESIDIO
CULBERSON
EL PASO
HUDSPETH
EL PASO

*NOTES:
Buchel and Foley were annexed to Brewster in 1897.

Encinal was annexed to Webb in 1899.

The three counties marked NP (no pop-ulation) were returned by census takers as having no inhabitants.

25 0   25   50   75   100 MILES

WHITE = MODERN BOUNDARIES
BLACK = 1890 BOUNDARIES

Texas ● 1890
WEST HALF

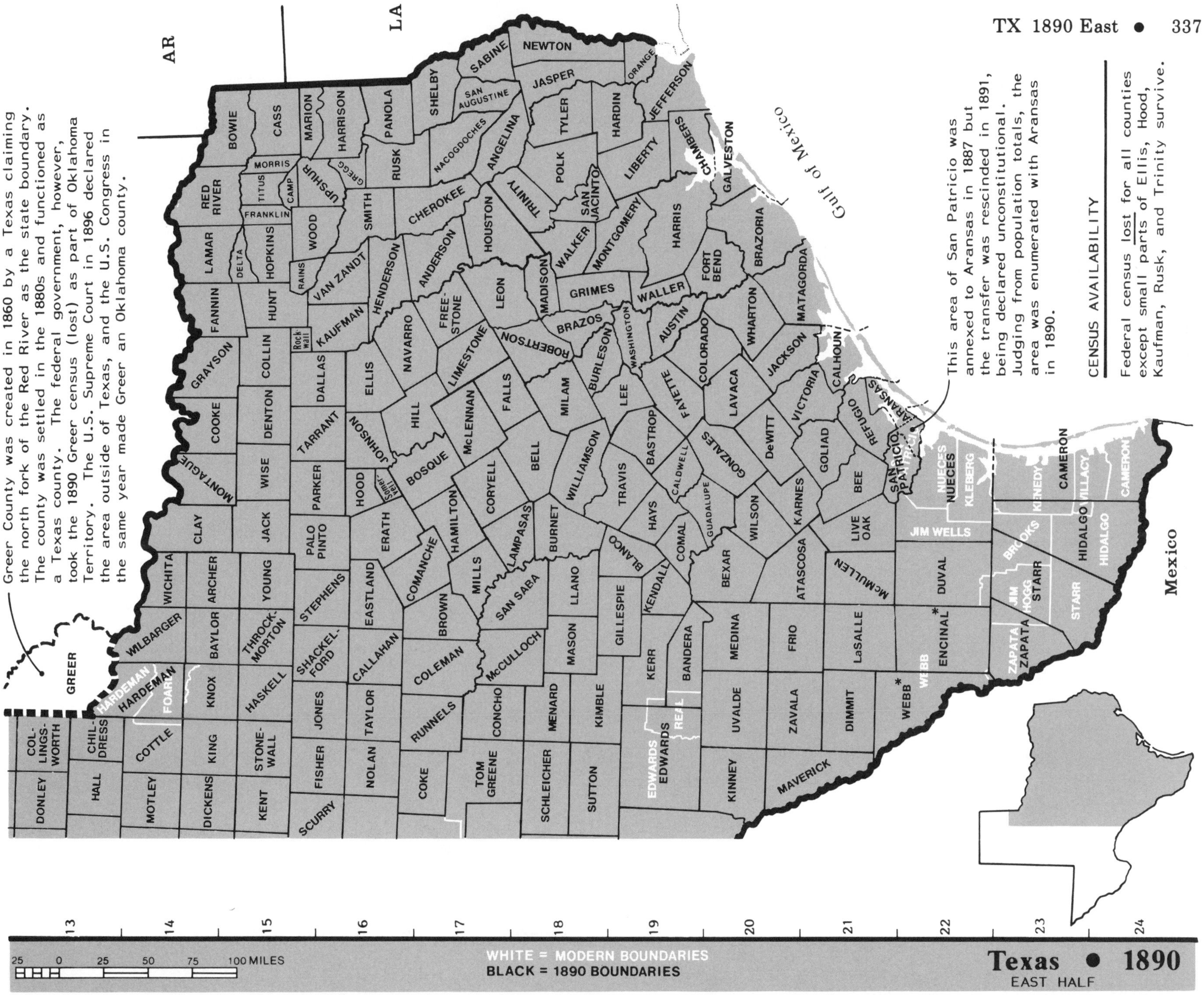

Greer County was created in 1860 by a Texas claiming the north fork of the Red River as the state boundary. The county was settled in the 1880s and functioned as a Texas county. The federal government, however, took the 1890 Greer census (lost) as part of Oklahoma Territory. The U.S. Supreme Court in 1896 declared the area outside of Texas, and the U.S. Congress in the same year made Greer an Oklahoma county.
This area of San Patricio was annexed to Aransas in 1887 but the transfer was rescinded in 1891, being declared unconstitutional. Judging from population totals, the area was enumerated with Aransas in 1890.
CENSUS AVAILABILITY
Federal census lost for all counties except small parts of Ellis, Hood, Kaufman, Rusk, and Trinity survive.
AR
LA
Gulf of Mexico
Mexico
GREER
13
14
15
16
17
18
19
20
21
22
23
24
25 0 25 50 75 100 MILES
WHITE = MODERN BOUNDARIES
BLACK = 1890 BOUNDARIES
Texas • 1890
EAST HALF

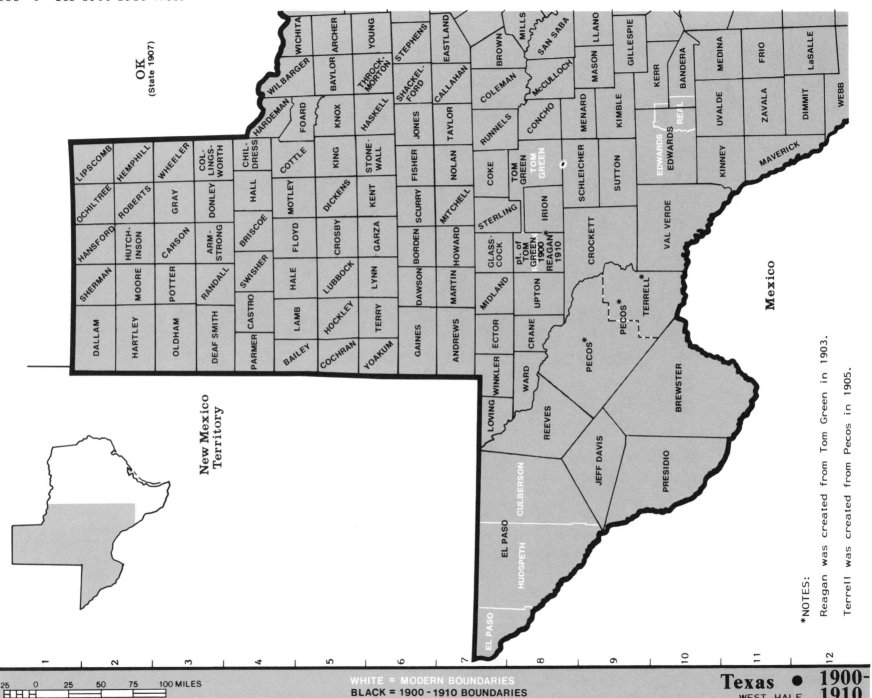

OK
(State 1907)

New Mexico
Territory

Mexico

LIPSCOMB
HEMPHILL
WHEELER
COL-LINGS-WORTH
CHIL-DRESS

OCHILTREE
ROBERTS
GRAY
DONLEY
HALL

HANSFORD
HUTCH-INSON
CARSON
ARM-STRONG
BRISCOE

SHERMAN
MOORE
POTTER
RANDALL
SWISHER

DALLAM
HARTLEY
OLDHAM
DEAF SMITH
PARMER
CASTRO

WICHITA
WILBARGER
BAYLOR
ARCHER
YOUNG
THROCK-MORTON
STEPHENS
EASTLAND

HARDEMAN
FOARD
KNOX
HASKELL
SHACKEL-FORD
CALLAHAN

COTTLE
KING
STONE-WALL
JONES
TAYLOR

MOTLEY
DICKENS
KENT
FISHER
NOLAN

FLOYD
CROSBY
GARZA
SCURRY
MITCHELL

HALE
LUBBOCK
LYNN
BORDEN

LAMB
HOCKLEY
TERRY
DAWSON
MARTIN
HOWARD

BAILEY
COCHRAN
YOAKUM
GAINES
ANDREWS

BROWN
MILLS
SAN SABA
MASON
LLANO
GILLESPIE
KERR
BANDERA
MEDINA
FRIO
LaSALLE

COLEMAN
McCULLOCH
CONCHO
MENARD
KIMBLE
EDWARDS
REAL
UVALDE
ZAVALA
DIMMIT
WEBB

RUNNELS

COKE
TOM GREEN
SCHLEICHER
SUTTON
KINNEY
MAVERICK

STERLING
IRION
VAL VERDE

GLASS-COCK
pt. of TOM GREEN 1900 REAGAN 1910
UPTON
CROCKETT

MIDLAND
ECTOR
CRANE

WINKLER
WARD
PECOS *
TERRELL *

LOVING
REEVES
PECOS *

JEFF DAVIS

CULBERSON
PRESIDIO

EL PASO
HUDSPETH
BREWSTER

EL PASO

*NOTES:

Reagan was created from Tom Green in 1903.

Terrell was created from Pecos in 1905.

1   2   3   4   5   6   7   8   9   10   11   12

25 0 25 50 75 100 MILES

WHITE = MODERN BOUNDARIES
BLACK = 1900-1910 BOUNDARIES

Texas ●
WEST HALF

1900-1910

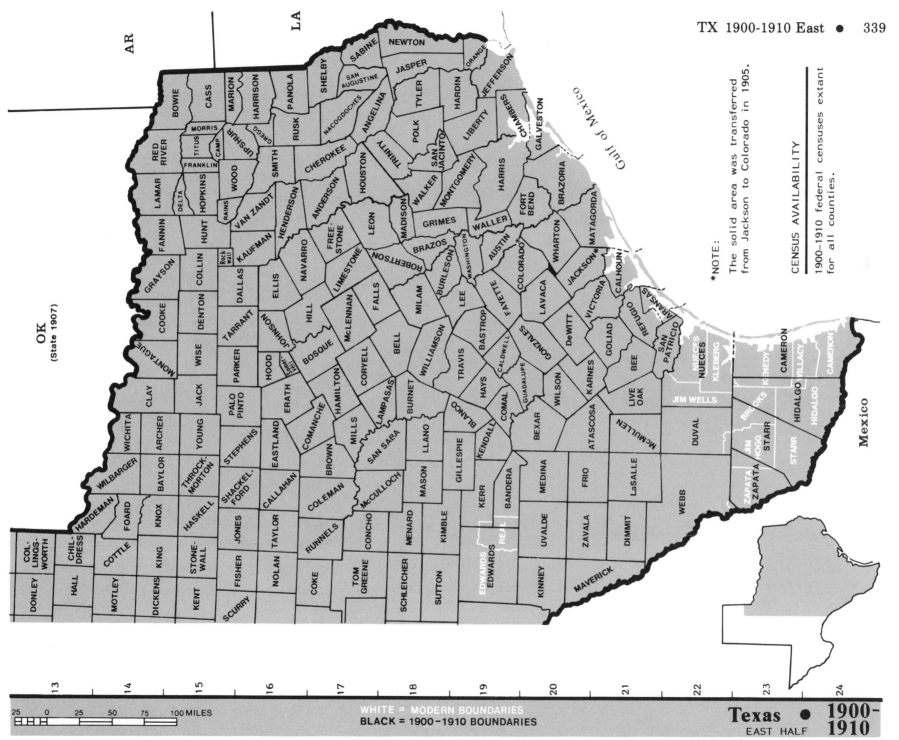

Texas ● **1900-1910**
EAST HALF

*NOTE:

The solid area was transferred
from Jackson to Colorado in 1905.

CENSUS AVAILABILITY

1900-1910 federal censuses extant
for all counties.

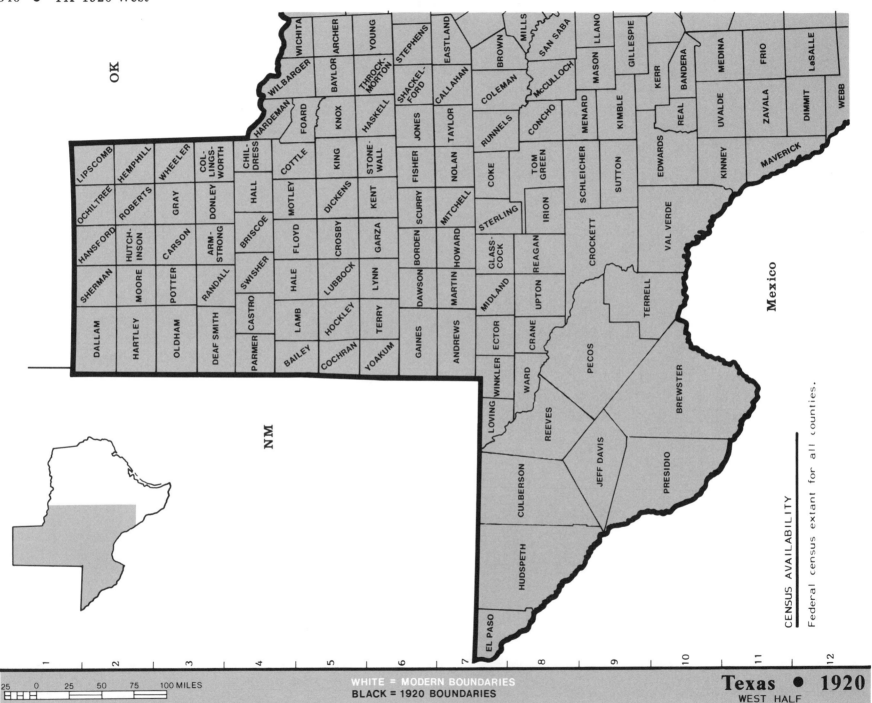

OK

NM

Mexico

LIPSCOMB
OCHILTREE
HANSFORD
SHERMAN
DALLAM

HEMPHILL
ROBERTS
HUTCH-INSON
MOORE
HARTLEY

WHEELER
GRAY
CARSON
POTTER
OLDHAM

COL-LINGS-WORTH
DONLEY
ARM-STRONG
RANDALL
DEAF SMITH

CHIL-DRESS
HALL
BRISCOE
SWISHER
CASTRO
PARMER

COTTLE
MOTLEY
FLOYD
HALE
LAMB
BAILEY

WICHITA
WILBARGER
HARDEMAN
FOARD
KNOX
KING
DICKENS
CROSBY
LUBBOCK
HOCKLEY
COCHRAN

BAYLOR ARCHER
THROCK-MORTON
HASKELL
STONE-WALL
KENT
GARZA
LYNN
TERRY
YOAKUM

YOUNG
STEPHENS
SHACKEL-FORD
JONES
FISHER
SCURRY
BORDEN
DAWSON
GAINES

EASTLAND
CALLAHAN
TAYLOR
NOLAN
MITCHELL
HOWARD
MARTIN
ANDREWS

BROWN
COLEMAN
RUNNELS
COKE
STERLING
GLASS-COCK
MIDLAND
ECTOR
WINKLER
LOVING

MILLS
SAN SABA
McCULLOCH
CONCHO
TOM GREEN
IRION
REAGAN
UPTON
CRANE
WARD
REEVES

LLANO
MASON
MENARD
SCHLEICHER
CROCKETT
PECOS

GILLESPIE
KERR
KIMBLE
SUTTON

REAL BANDERA
EDWARDS
VAL VERDE
TERRELL
BREWSTER
JEFF DAVIS
PRESIDIO
CULBERSON
HUDSPETH
EL PASO

MEDINA
UVALDE
KINNEY
MAVERICK

FRIO
ZAVALA

LaSALLE
DIMMIT
WEBB

25 0 25 50 75 100 MILES

1 2 3 4 5 6 7 8 9 10 11 12

WHITE = MODERN BOUNDARIES
BLACK = 1920 BOUNDARIES

Texas ● 1920
WEST HALF

MAP GUIDE TO THE U.S. FEDERAL CENSUSES, 1790–1920 by William Thorndale and William Dollarhide. Copyright 1987, all rights reserved.

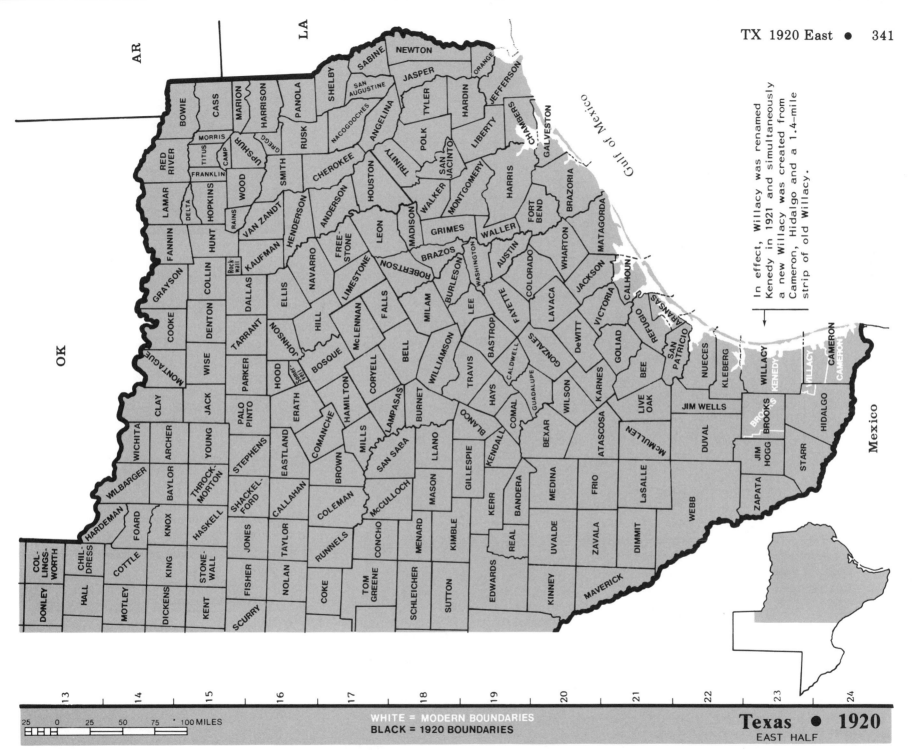

In effect, Willacy was renamed Kenedy in 1921 and simultaneously a new Willacy was created from Cameron, Hidalgo and a 1.4-mile strip of old Willacy.

Gulf of Mexico

WHITE = MODERN BOUNDARIES
BLACK = 1920 BOUNDARIES

Texas ● **1920**
EAST HALF

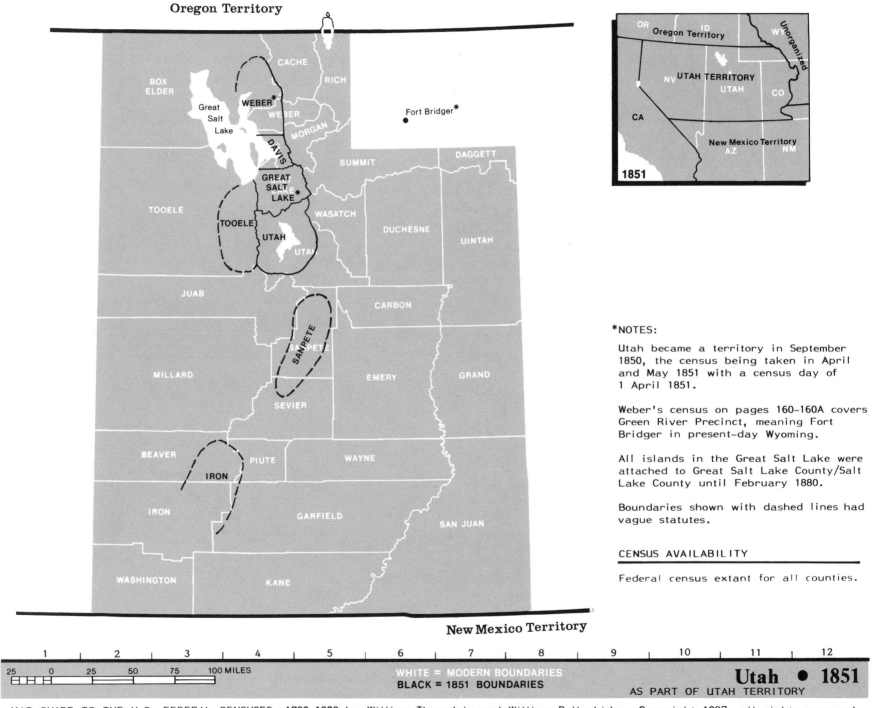

Oregon Territory

CACHE

BOX
ELDER

Great
Salt
Lake

WEBER*

RICH

WEBER

MORGAN

DAVIS

Fort Bridger*

DAGGETT

GREAT
SALT
LAKE*

SUMMIT

TOOELE

WASATCH

TOOELE

DUCHESNE

UTAH

UINTAH

UTAH

JUAB

CARBON

SANPETE

MILLARD

EMERY

GRAND

SEVIER

BEAVER

PIUTE

WAYNE

IRON

IRON

GARFIELD

SAN JUAN

WASHINGTON

KANE

New Mexico Territory

Inset map:

OR   ID   Oregon Territory   WY   Unorganized

NV   UTAH TERRITORY

CA   UTAH   CO

New Mexico Territory
AZ   NM

1851

1   2   3   4   5   6   7   8   9   10   11   12

25   0   25   50   75   100 MILES

WHITE = MODERN BOUNDARIES
BLACK = 1851 BOUNDARIES

Utah ● 1851

AS PART OF UTAH TERRITORY

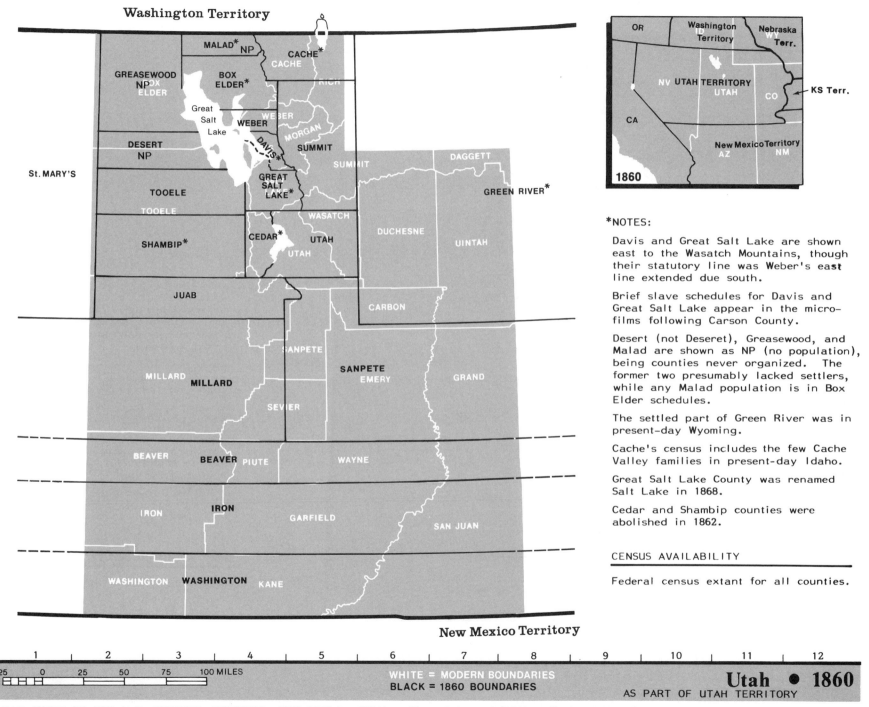

Washington Territory

MALAD* NP

CACHE*

CACHE

GREASEWOOD NP
BOX ELDER
BOX ELDER*

RICH

Great Salt Lake

WEBER
WEBER

MORGAN

DESERT NP

DAVIS*

SUMMIT

St. MARY'S

SUMMIT

DAGGETT

GREAT SALT LAKE*

GREEN RIVER*

TOOELE

WASATCH

TOOELE

CEDAR*

UTAH

SHAMBIP*

UTAH

DUCHESNE

UINTAH

JUAB

CARBON

SANPETE

SANPETE

MILLARD
MILLARD

EMERY

GRAND

SEVIER

BEAVER
BEAVER
PIUTE

WAYNE

IRON
IRON

GARFIELD

SAN JUAN

WASHINGTON
WASHINGTON
KANE

New Mexico Territory

OR
Washington Territory
ID
NV UTAH TERRITORY
UTAH
CA

Nebraska
WY
Terr.

← KS Terr.
CO

New Mexico Territory
AZ
NM

1860

*NOTES:

Davis and Great Salt Lake are shown east to the Wasatch Mountains, though their statutory line was Weber's east line extended due south.

Brief slave schedules for Davis and Great Salt Lake appear in the microfilms following Carson County.

Desert (not Deseret), Greasewood, and Malad are shown as NP (no population), being counties never organized. The former two presumably lacked settlers, while any Malad population is in Box Elder schedules.

The settled part of Green River was in present-day Wyoming.

Cache's census includes the few Cache Valley families in present-day Idaho.

Great Salt Lake County was renamed Salt Lake in 1868.

Cedar and Shambip counties were abolished in 1862.

CENSUS AVAILABILITY

Federal census extant for all counties.

1   2   3   4   5   6   7   8   9   10   11   12

25 0 25 50 75 100 MILES

WHITE = MODERN BOUNDARIES
BLACK = 1860 BOUNDARIES

Utah ● 1860
AS PART OF UTAH TERRITORY

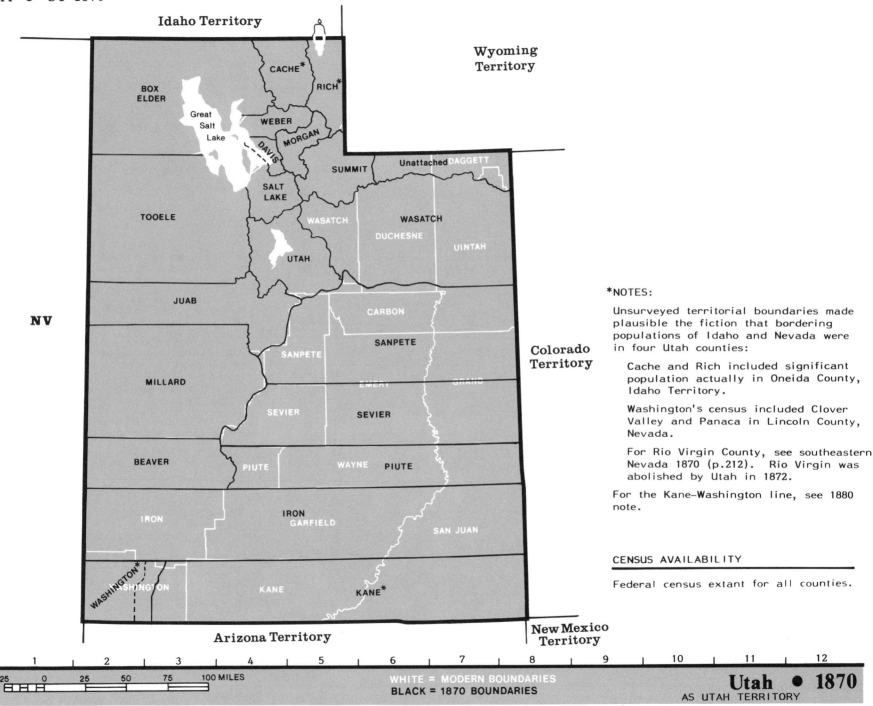

Idaho Territory

Wyoming
Territory

CACHE*

RICH*

BOX
ELDER

Great
Salt
Lake

WEBER

MORGAN

DAVIS

SUMMIT

Unattached DAGGETT

SALT
LAKE

NV

TOOELE

WASATCH

WASATCH

DUCHESNE

UINTAH

UTAH

JUAB

CARBON

Colorado
Territory

SANPETE

SANPETE

MILLARD

EMERY

GRAND

SEVIER

SEVIER

BEAVER

PIUTE

WAYNE

PIUTE

IRON

IRON
GARFIELD

SAN JUAN

WASHINGTON*

WASHINGTON

KANE

KANE*

Arizona Territory

New Mexico
Territory

*NOTES:

Unsurveyed territorial boundaries made
plausible the fiction that bordering
populations of Idaho and Nevada were
in four Utah counties:

Cache and Rich included significant
population actually in Oneida County,
Idaho Territory.

Washington's census included Clover
Valley and Panaca in Lincoln County,
Nevada.

For Rio Virgin County, see southeastern
Nevada 1870 (p.212). Rio Virgin was
abolished by Utah in 1872.

For the Kane–Washington line, see 1880
note.

CENSUS AVAILABILITY

Federal census extant for all counties.

1 2 3 4 5 6 7 8 9 10 11 12

25 0 25 50 75 100 MILES

WHITE = MODERN BOUNDARIES
BLACK = 1870 BOUNDARIES

Utah ● 1870
AS UTAH TERRITORY

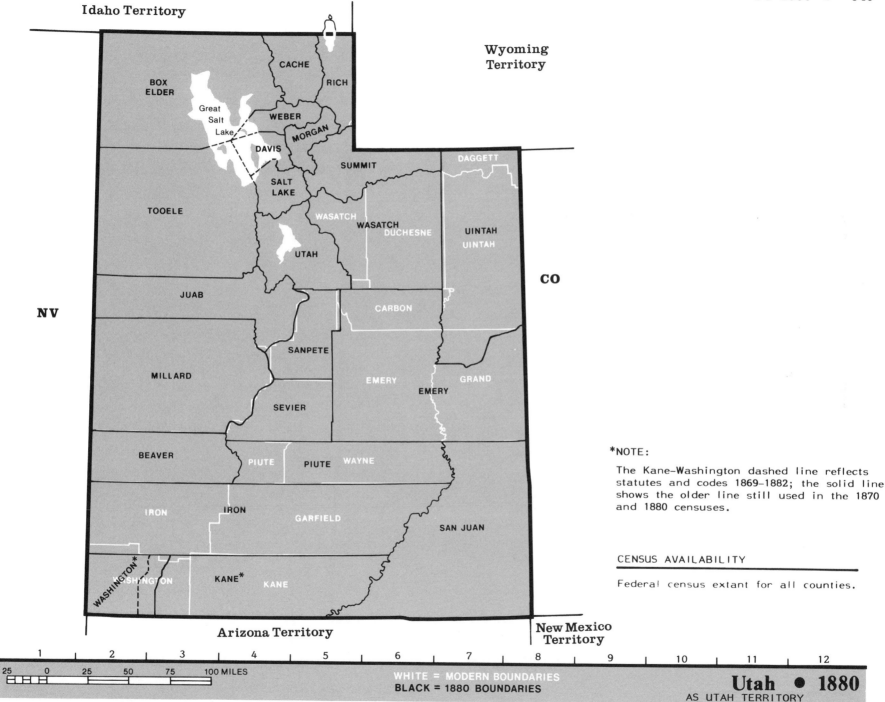

Idaho Territory

Wyoming
Territory

CACHE

BOX
ELDER

RICH

Great
Salt
Lake

WEBER

MORGAN

DAVIS

DAGGETT

SALT
LAKE

SUMMIT

NV

TOOELE

WASATCH

WASATCH
DUCHESNE

UINTAH
UINTAH

UTAH

CO

JUAB

CARBON

SANPETE

MILLARD

EMERY

GRAND

EMERY

SEVIER

*NOTE:

The Kane–Washington dashed line reflects
statutes and codes 1869–1882; the solid line
shows the older line still used in the 1870
and 1880 censuses.

BEAVER

PIUTE

PIUTE

WAYNE

IRON

IRON

GARFIELD

SAN JUAN

CENSUS AVAILABILITY

Federal census extant for all counties.

WASHINGTON*

WASHINGTON

KANE*

KANE

Arizona Territory

New Mexico
Territory

1   2   3   4   5   6   7   8   9   10   11   12

25   0   25   50   75   100 MILES

WHITE = MODERN BOUNDARIES
BLACK = 1880 BOUNDARIES

Utah ● 1880
AS UTAH TERRITORY

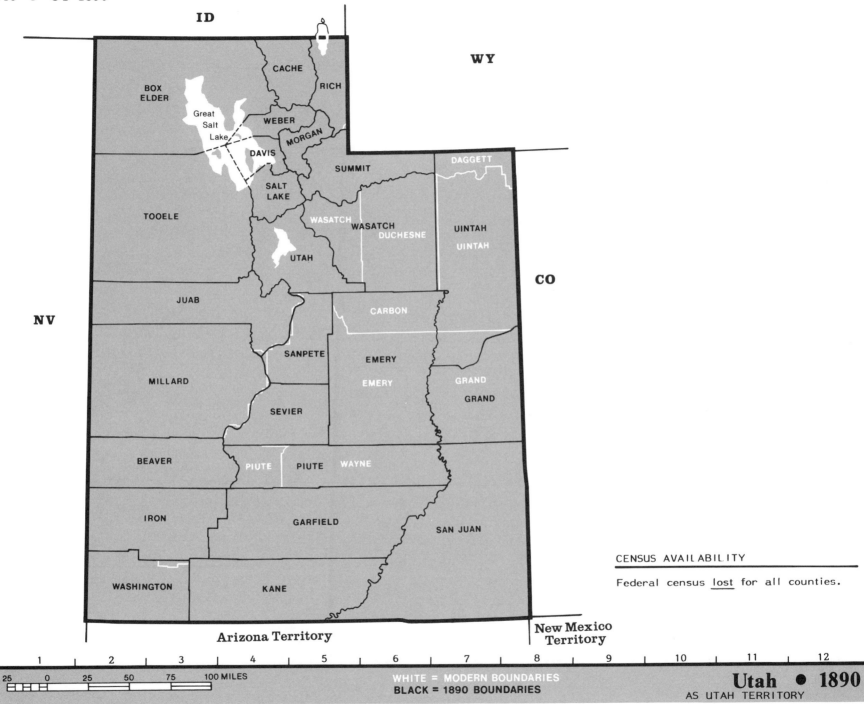

ID

WY

CACHE

RICH

BOX
ELDER

Great
Salt
Lake

WEBER

MORGAN

DAVIS

SUMMIT

DAGGETT

SALT
LAKE

WASATCH

WASATCH
DUCHESNE

UINTAH
UINTAH

TOOELE

UTAH

NV

CO

JUAB

CARBON

SANPETE

MILLARD

EMERY

EMERY

GRAND
GRAND

SEVIER

BEAVER

PIUTE
PIUTE

WAYNE

IRON

GARFIELD

SAN JUAN

WASHINGTON

KANE

CENSUS AVAILABILITY

Federal census lost for all counties.

Arizona Territory

New Mexico
Territory

1 2 3 4 5 6 7 8 9 10 11 12

25 0 25 50 75 100 MILES

WHITE = MODERN BOUNDARIES
BLACK = 1890 BOUNDARIES

Utah ● 1890
AS UTAH TERRITORY

MAP GUIDE TO THE U.S. FEDERAL CENSUSES, 1790–1920 by William Thorndale and William Dollarhide. Copyright 1987, all rights reserved.

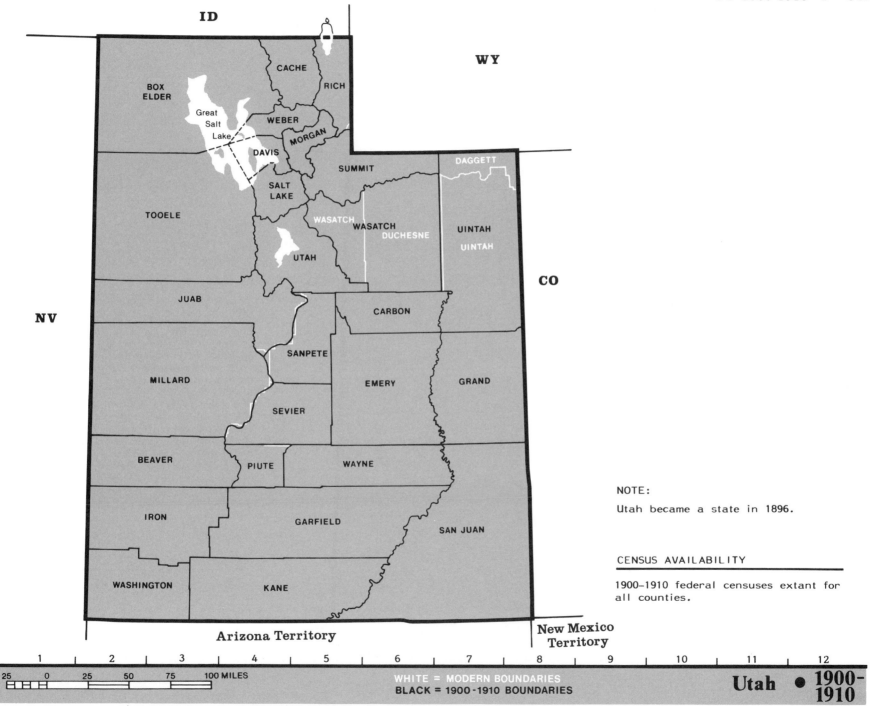

ID

WY

BOX
ELDER

CACHE

RICH

Great
Salt
Lake

WEBER

MORGAN

DAVIS

SALT
LAKE

SUMMIT

DAGGETT

NV

TOOELE

WASATCH

WASATCH
DUCHESNE

UINTAH

UINTAH

CO

UTAH

JUAB

CARBON

SANPETE

MILLARD

EMERY

GRAND

SEVIER

BEAVER

PIUTE

WAYNE

NOTE:

Utah became a state in 1896.

IRON

GARFIELD

SAN JUAN

CENSUS AVAILABILITY

1900–1910 federal censuses extant for
all counties.

WASHINGTON

KANE

Arizona Territory

New Mexico
Territory

| 1 | 2 | 3 | 4 | 5 | 6 | 7 | 8 | 9 | 10 | 11 | 12 |

25   0   25   50   75   100 MILES

WHITE = MODERN BOUNDARIES
BLACK = 1900-1910 BOUNDARIES

Utah ● 1900-
1910

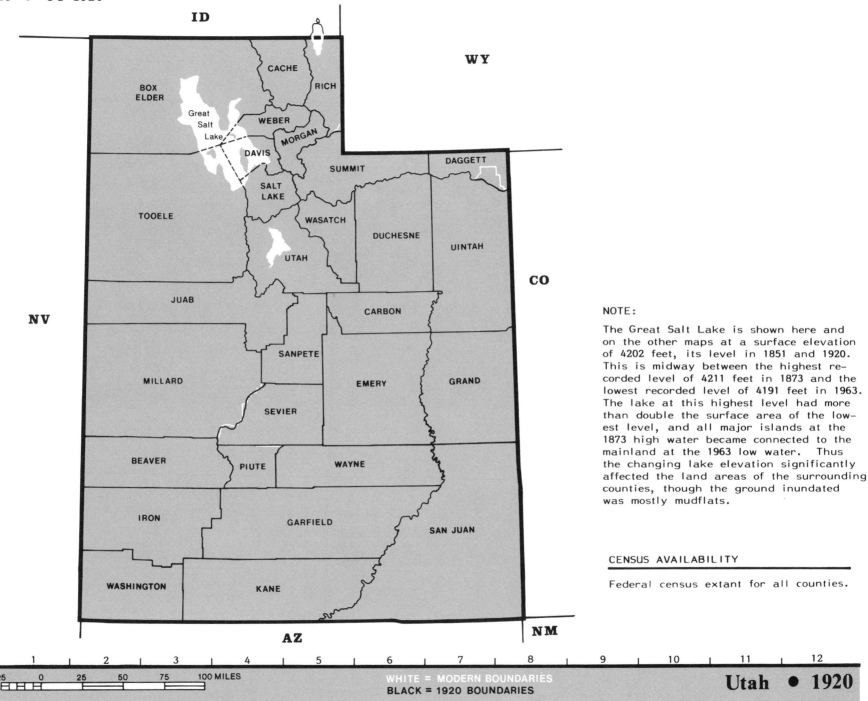

ID

WY

BOX
ELDER

CACHE

RICH

Great
Salt
Lake

WEBER

MORGAN

DAGGETT

DAVIS

SUMMIT

SALT
LAKE

TOOELE

WASATCH

DUCHESNE

UINTAH

NV

CO

JUAB

CARBON

SANPETE

MILLARD

EMERY

GRAND

SEVIER

BEAVER

PIUTE

WAYNE

IRON

GARFIELD

SAN JUAN

WASHINGTON

KANE

AZ

NM

NOTE:

The Great Salt Lake is shown here and
on the other maps at a surface elevation
of 4202 feet, its level in 1851 and 1920.
This is midway between the highest recorded level of 4211 feet in 1873 and the
lowest recorded level of 4191 feet in 1963.
The lake at this highest level had more
than double the surface area of the lowest level, and all major islands at the
1873 high water became connected to the
mainland at the 1963 low water. Thus
the changing lake elevation significantly
affected the land areas of the surrounding
counties, though the ground inundated
was mostly mudflats.

CENSUS AVAILABILITY

Federal census extant for all counties.

1   2   3   4   5   6   7   8   9   10   11   12

25   0   25   50   75   100 MILES

WHITE = MODERN BOUNDARIES
BLACK = 1920 BOUNDARIES

Utah ● 1920

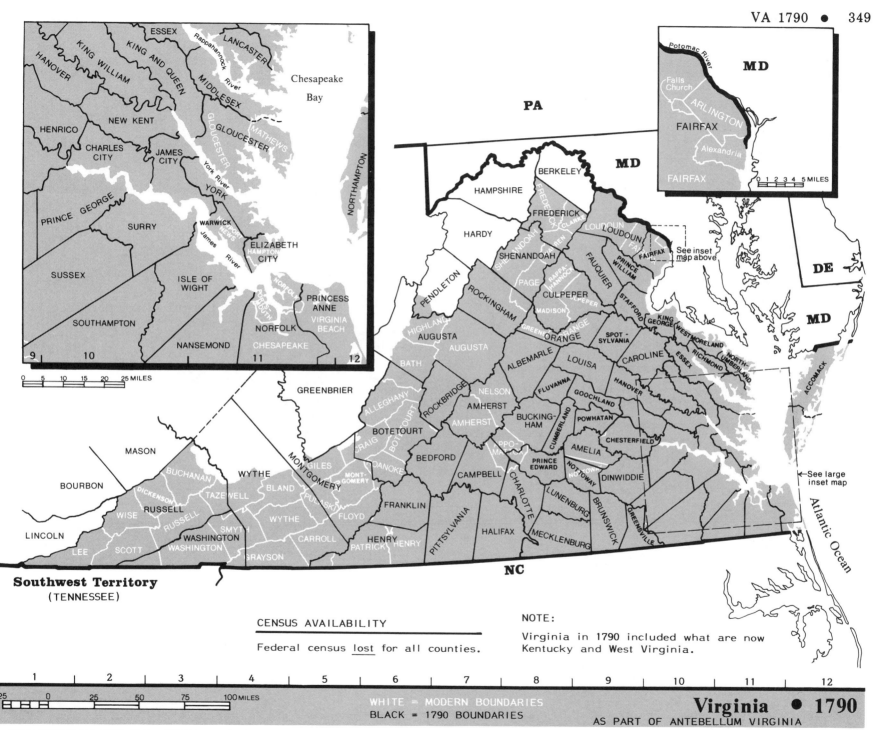

MD

Potomac River

Falls
Church

ARLINGTON

FAIRFAX

Alexandria

FAIRFAX

0 1 2 3 4 5 MILES

PA

MD

DE

MD

BERKELEY

HAMPSHIRE

FREDERICK

HARDY

FREDERICK

CLARKE

LOUDOUN

FAIRFAX

See inset
map above

SHENANDOAH

BERKELEY

PAGE

RAPPA-
HANNOCK

CULPEPER

FAUQUIER

PRINCE
WILLIAM

STAFFORD

KING
GEORGE

WESTMORELAND

PENDLETON

ROCKINGHAM

MADISON

CULPEPER

GREENE

ORANGE

SPOT-
SYLVANIA

NORTH-
UMBER-
LAND

HIGHLAND

AUGUSTA

ALBEMARLE

LOUISA

CAROLINE

ESSEX

RICHMOND

AUGUSTA

ACCOMACK

BATH

NELSON

FLUVANNA

GOOCHLAND

HANOVER

ALLEGHANY

ROCKBRIDGE

AMHERST

BUCKING-
HAM

CUMBERLAND

POWHATAN

CHESTERFIELD

BOTETOURT

AMHERST

APPO-
MATTOX

PRINCE
EDWARD

AMELIA

NOTTOWAY

DINWIDDIE

CRAIG

ROANOKE

BEDFORD

CAMPBELL

CHARLOTTE

LUNENBURG

BRUNSWICK

GREENSVILLE

MONTGOMERY

MONT-
GOMERY

PULASKI

FLOYD

FRANKLIN

PITTSYLVANIA

HALIFAX

MECKLENBURG

GILES

GREENBRIER

MASON

BOURBON

LINCOLN

BUCHANAN

DICKENSON

WYTHE

BLAND

TAZEWELL

RUSSELL

WISE

RUSSELL

SMYTH

WASHINGTON

WYTHE

CARROLL

HENRY

HENRY

PATRICK

GRAYSON

LEE

SCOTT

WASHINGTON

NC

Atlantic Ocean

←See large
inset map

Southwest Territory
(TENNESSEE)

Inset (upper left):

HANOVER

KING WILLIAM

ESSEX

KING AND QUEEN

LANCASTER

Rappahannock River

MIDDLESEX

Chesapeake
Bay

HENRICO

NEW KENT

GLOUCESTER

CHARLES
CITY

JAMES
CITY

GLOUCESTER

MATHEWS

PRINCE GEORGE

SURRY

YORK

York River

WARWICK

NEWPORT
NEWS

James River

ELIZABETH
CITY

HAMPTON

NORTHAMPTON

SUSSEX

ISLE OF
WIGHT

PORTSMOUTH

NORFOLK

PRINCESS
ANNE

SOUTHAMPTON

NANSEMOND

NORFOLK

VIRGINIA
BEACH

CHESAPEAKE

9   10   11   12

0 5 10 15 20 25 MILES

CENSUS AVAILABILITY

Federal census lost for all counties.

NOTE:

Virginia in 1790 included what are now
Kentucky and West Virginia.

1   2   3   4   5   6   7   8   9   10   11   12

25 0   25   50   75   100 MILES

WHITE = MODERN BOUNDARIES
BLACK = 1790 BOUNDARIES

Virginia ● 1790
AS PART OF ANTEBELLUM VIRGINIA

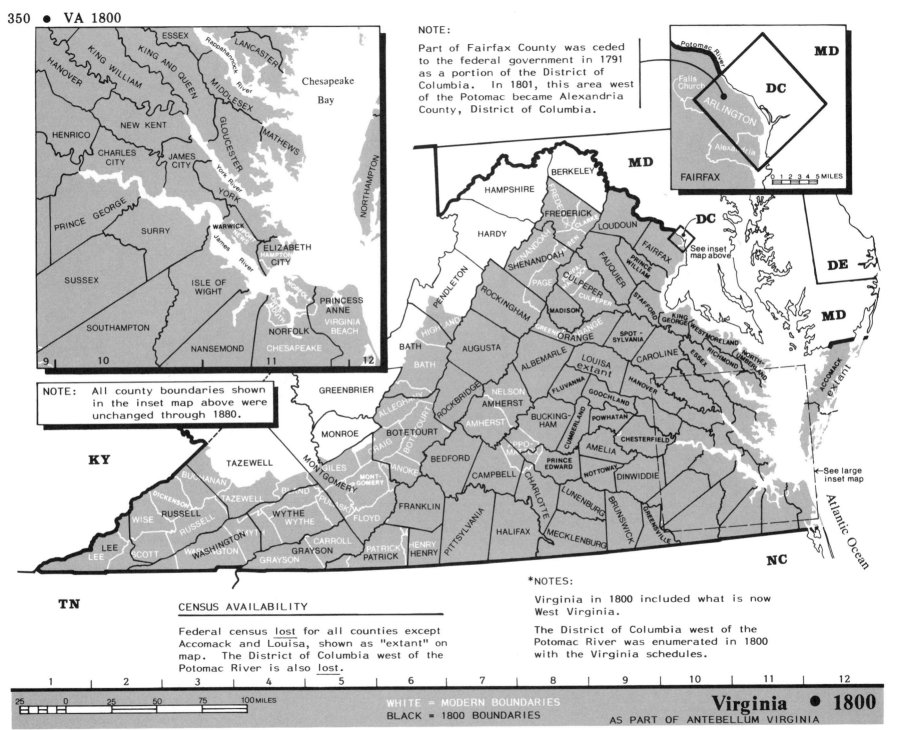

350 ● VA 1800

NOTE:

Part of Fairfax County was ceded to the federal government in 1791 as a portion of the District of Columbia. In 1801, this area west of the Potomac became Alexandria County, District of Columbia.

NOTE: All county boundaries shown in the inset map above were unchanged through 1880.

CENSUS AVAILABILITY

Federal census lost for all counties except Accomack and Louisa, shown as "extant" on map. The District of Columbia west of the Potomac River is also lost.

*NOTES:

Virginia in 1800 included what is now West Virginia.

The District of Columbia west of the Potomac River was enumerated in 1800 with the Virginia schedules.

WHITE = MODERN BOUNDARIES
BLACK = 1800 BOUNDARIES

Virginia ● 1800
AS PART OF ANTEBELLUM VIRGINIA

MAP GUIDE TO THE U.S. FEDERAL CENSUSES, 1790-1920 by William Thorndale and William Dollarhide. Copyright 1987, all rights reserved.

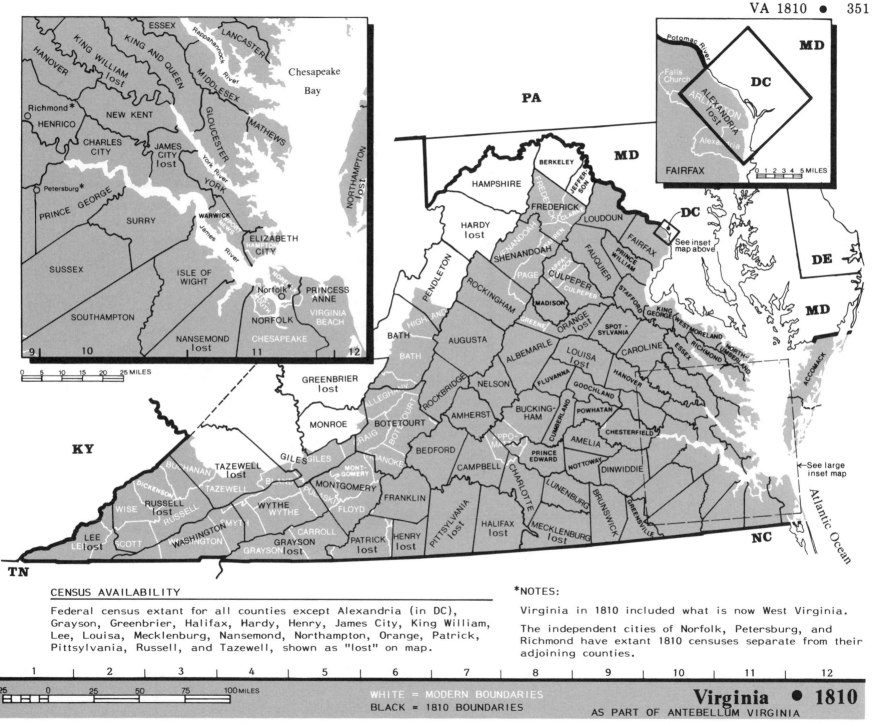

INSET MAP LABELS (upper left):

ESSEX, LANCASTER, KING WILLIAM lost, KING AND QUEEN, MIDDLESEX, Rappahannock River, HANOVER, Richmond *, HENRICO, NEW KENT, GLOUCESTER, MATHEWS, Chesapeake Bay, CHARLES CITY, JAMES CITY lost, York River, YORK, PRINCE GEORGE, Petersburg *, SURRY, WARWICK, NEWPORT NEWS, James River, ELIZABETH CITY, HAMPTON CITY, NORTHAMPTON lost, SUSSEX, ISLE OF WIGHT, Norfolk *, PRINCESS ANNE, SOUTHAMPTON, NORFOLK BOROUGH, NANSEMOND lost, CHESAPEAKE, VIRGINIA BEACH

9 10 11 12

0 5 10 15 20 25 MILES

INSET MAP (upper right):

Potomac River, MD, Falls Church, DC, ALEXANDRIA ARL lost, Alexandria, FAIRFAX

0 1 2 3 4 5 MILES

MAIN MAP LABELS:

PA, MD, DC, DE, MD, KY, TN, NC, Atlantic Ocean

BERKELEY, HAMPSHIRE, FREDERICK, JEFFERSON, CLARK, LOUDOUN, FAIRFAX, See inset map above, HARDY lost, SHENANDOAH, WARREN, PAGE, RAPPAHANNOCK, FAUQUIER, PRINCE WILLIAM, STAFFORD, KING GEORGE, WESTMORELAND, PENDLETON, ROCKINGHAM, MADISON, CULPEPER, CULPEPER, GREENE, ORANGE lost, SPOT-SYLVANIA, RICHMOND, NORTHUMBERLAND, HIGHLAND, BATH, AUGUSTA, ALBEMARLE, LOUISA lost, CAROLINE, ESSEX, ACCOMACK, BATH, NELSON, FLUVANNA, GOOCHLAND, HANOVER, GREENBRIER lost, ALLEGHANY, ROCKBRIDGE, AMHERST, BUCKING-HAM, CUMBERLAND, POWHATAN, CHESTERFIELD, MONROE, BOTETOURT, CRAIG, BEDFORD, APPOMATTOX, AMELIA, See large inset map, TAZEWELL lost, GILES, GILES, RADFORD, MONTGOMERY, FRANKLIN, CAMPBELL, PRINCE EDWARD, NOTTOWAY, DINWIDDIE, BUCHANAN, BLAND, PULASKI, CHARLOTTE, LUNENBURG, BRUNSWICK, DICKENSON, TAZEWELL, WYTHE, WYTHE, FLOYD, PITTSYLVANIA lost, HALIFAX lost, MECKLENBURG lost, GREENSVILLE, WISE, RUSSELL lost, RUSSELL, SMYTH, CARROLL, PATRICK lost, HENRY lost, LEE LEE lost, SCOTT, WASHINGTON, WASHINGTON, GRAYSON lost, GRAYSON

0 25 50 75 100 MILES 25 0

1 2 3 4 5 6 7 8 9 10 11 12

CENSUS AVAILABILITY

Federal census extant for all counties except Alexandria (in DC), Grayson, Greenbrier, Halifax, Hardy, Henry, James City, King William, Lee, Louisa, Mecklenburg, Nansemond, Northampton, Orange, Patrick, Pittsylvania, Russell, and Tazewell, shown as "lost" on map.

*NOTES:

Virginia in 1810 included what is now West Virginia.

The independent cities of Norfolk, Petersburg, and Richmond have extant 1810 censuses separate from their adjoining counties.

WHITE = MODERN BOUNDARIES
BLACK = 1810 BOUNDARIES

Virginia ● 1810
AS PART OF ANTEBELLUM VIRGINIA

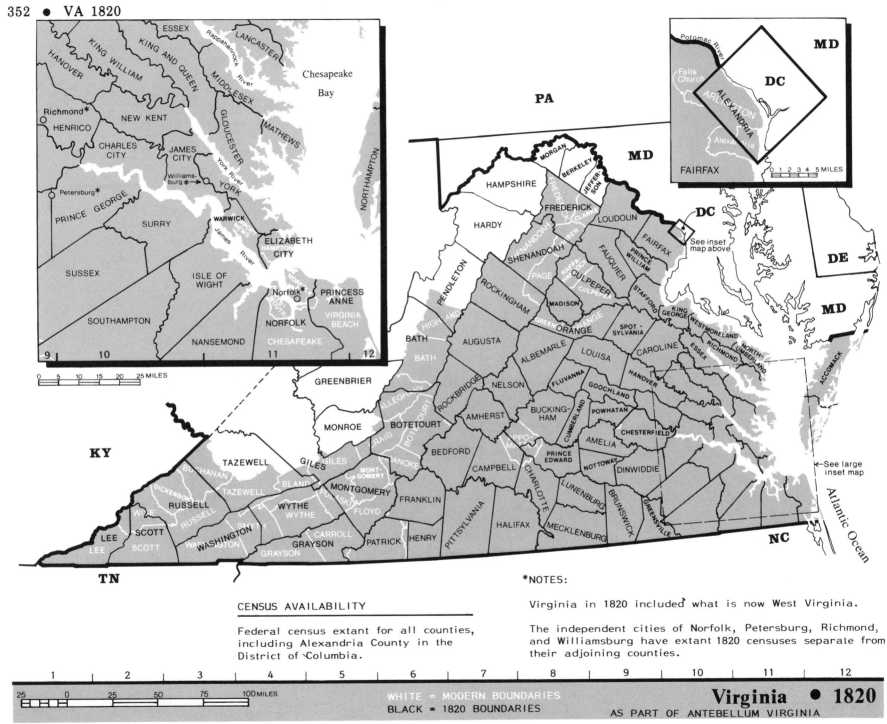

CENSUS AVAILABILITY

Federal census extant for all counties, including Alexandria County in the District of Columbia.

*NOTES:

Virginia in 1820 included what is now West Virginia.

The independent cities of Norfolk, Petersburg, Richmond, and Williamsburg have extant 1820 censuses separate from their adjoining counties.

WHITE = MODERN BOUNDARIES
BLACK = 1820 BOUNDARIES

Virginia ● 1820

AS PART OF ANTEBELLUM VIRGINIA

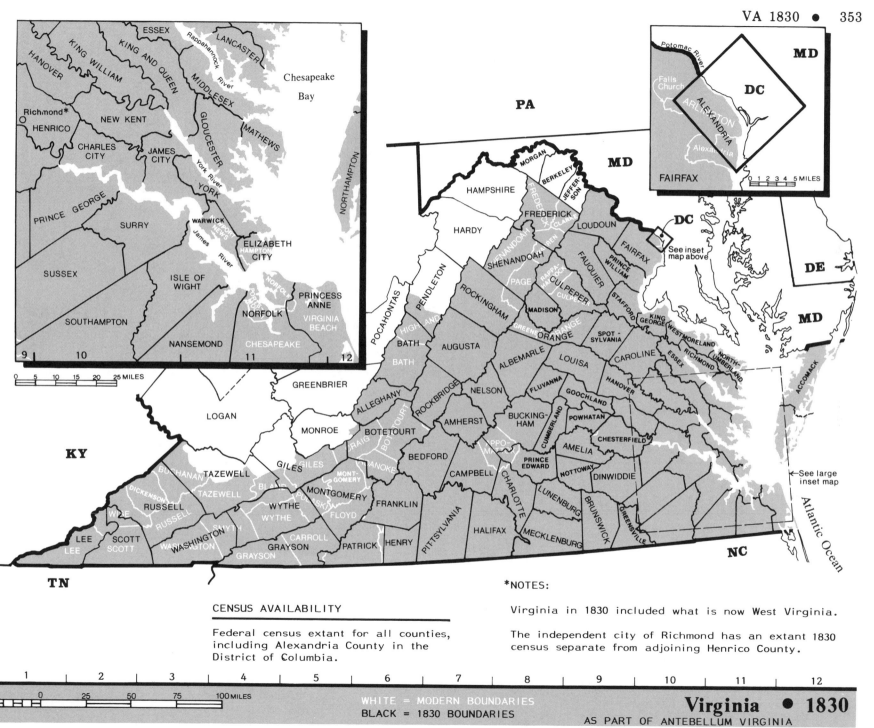

Inset map (upper left)

ESSEX
LANCASTER
KING WILLIAM
KING AND QUEEN
HANOVER
Rappahannock River
MIDDLESEX
Chesapeake Bay
Richmond*
HENRICO
NEW KENT
MATHEWS
GLOUCESTER
CHARLES CITY
JAMES CITY
York River
WARWICK
PRINCE GEORGE
SURRY
YORK
WARWICK
NEWPORT NEWS
James River
ELIZABETH CITY
SUSSEX
ISLE OF WIGHT
SOUTHAMPTON
NANSEMOND
NORFOLK
NORFOLK
PRINCESS ANNE
VIRGINIA BEACH
CHESAPEAKE
NORTHAMPTON

0 5 10 15 20 25 MILES

9   10   11   12

Inset map (upper right)

Potomac River
MD
Falls Church
DC
ALEXANDRIA
ARLINGTON
Alexandria
FAIRFAX

0 1 2 3 4 5 MILES

Main map

PA
MD
DC
DE
KY
TN
NC
Atlantic Ocean

MORGAN
BERKELEY
JEFFERSON
HAMPSHIRE
FREDERICK
HARDY
CLARKE
LOUDOUN
FAIRFAX
FREDERICK
WARREN
SHENANDOAH
PAGE
FAUQUIER
PRINCE WILLIAM
ROCKINGHAM
RAPPAHANNOCK
CULPEPER
STAFFORD
POCAHONTAS
PENDLETON
MADISON
CULPEPER
GREENE
ORANGE
KING GEORGE
WESTMORELAND
HIGHLAND
RICHMOND
NORTHUMBERLAND
BATH
AUGUSTA
ALBEMARLE
SPOT-SYLVANIA
ESSEX
BATH
LOUISA
CAROLINE
ACCOMACK
GREENBRIER
ALLEGHANY
ROCKBRIDGE
NELSON
FLUVANNA
HANOVER
LOGAN
MONROE
BOTETOURT
AMHERST
GOOCHLAND
See inset map
MONTGOMERY
CRAIG
BUCKINGHAM
POWHATAN
BEDFORD
CUMBERLAND
CHESTERFIELD
BUCHANAN
TAZEWELL
GILES
GILES
ROANOKE
APPOMATTOX
AMELIA
See large inset map
DICKENSON
TAZEWELL
BLAND
MONTGOMERY
PULASKI
CAMPBELL
PRINCE EDWARD
NOTTOWAY
DINWIDDIE
WISE
RUSSELL
WYTHE
FLOYD
FRANKLIN
CHARLOTTE
LUNENBURG
BRUNSWICK
GREENSVILLE
LEE
SCOTT
RUSSELL
WYTHE
SMYTH
WASHINGTON
CARROLL
GRAYSON
PATRICK
HENRY
PITTSYLVANIA
HALIFAX
MECKLENBURG
LEE
SCOTT
WASHINGTON
GRAYSON

*NOTES:

CENSUS AVAILABILITY

Federal census extant for all counties, including Alexandria County in the District of Columbia.

Virginia in 1830 included what is now West Virginia.

The independent city of Richmond has an extant 1830 census separate from adjoining Henrico County.

1   2   3   4   5   6   7   8   9   10   11   12

25 0 25 50 75 100 MILES

WHITE = MODERN BOUNDARIES
BLACK = 1830 BOUNDARIES

Virginia ● 1830

AS PART OF ANTEBELLUM VIRGINIA

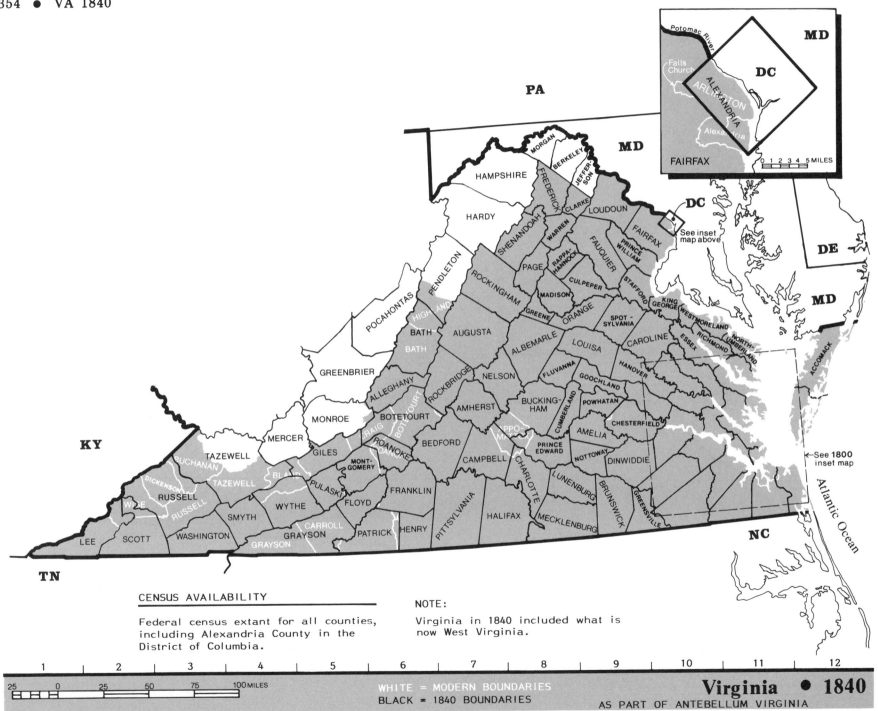

CENSUS AVAILABILITY

Federal census extant for all counties,
including Alexandria County in the
District of Columbia.

NOTE:

Virginia in 1840 included what is
now West Virginia.

WHITE = MODERN BOUNDARIES
BLACK = 1840 BOUNDARIES

Virginia ● **1840**
AS PART OF ANTEBELLUM VIRGINIA

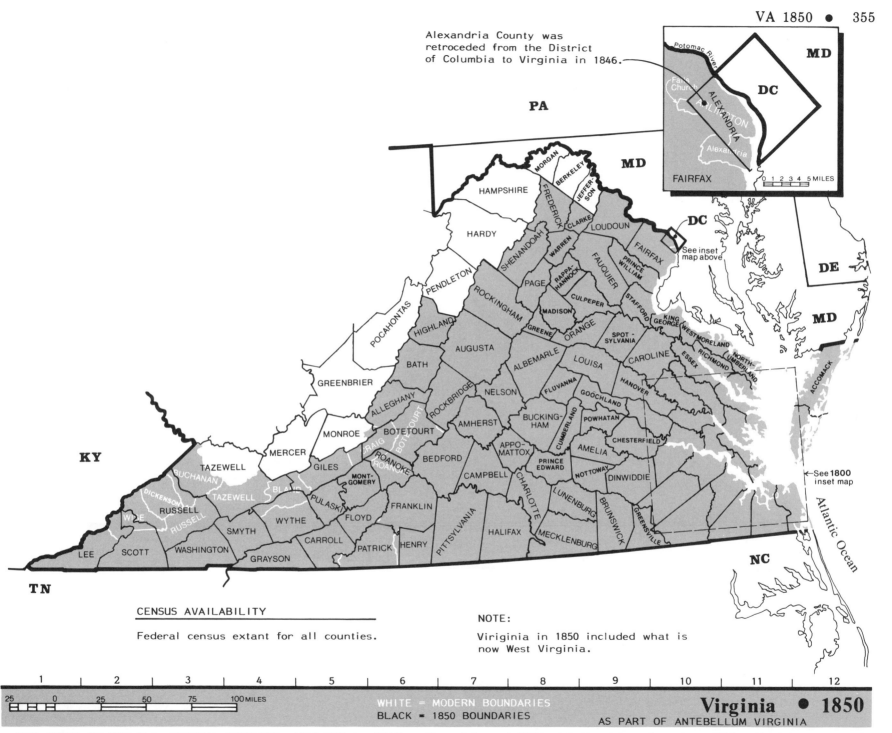

Alexandria County was
retroceded from the District
of Columbia to Virginia in 1846.

PA

MD

DC

DE

MD

FAIRFAX

0 1 2 3 4 5 MILES

See inset
map above

←See **1800**
inset map

KY

TN

NC

Atlantic Ocean

CENSUS AVAILABILITY

Federal census extant for all counties.

NOTE:

Viriginia in 1850 included what is
now West Virginia.

| 1 | 2 | 3 | 4 | 5 | 6 | 7 | 8 | 9 | 10 | 11 | 12 |

25   0   25   50   75   100 MILES

WHITE = MODERN BOUNDARIES
BLACK = 1850 BOUNDARIES

Virginia ● **1850**

AS PART OF ANTEBELLUM VIRGINIA

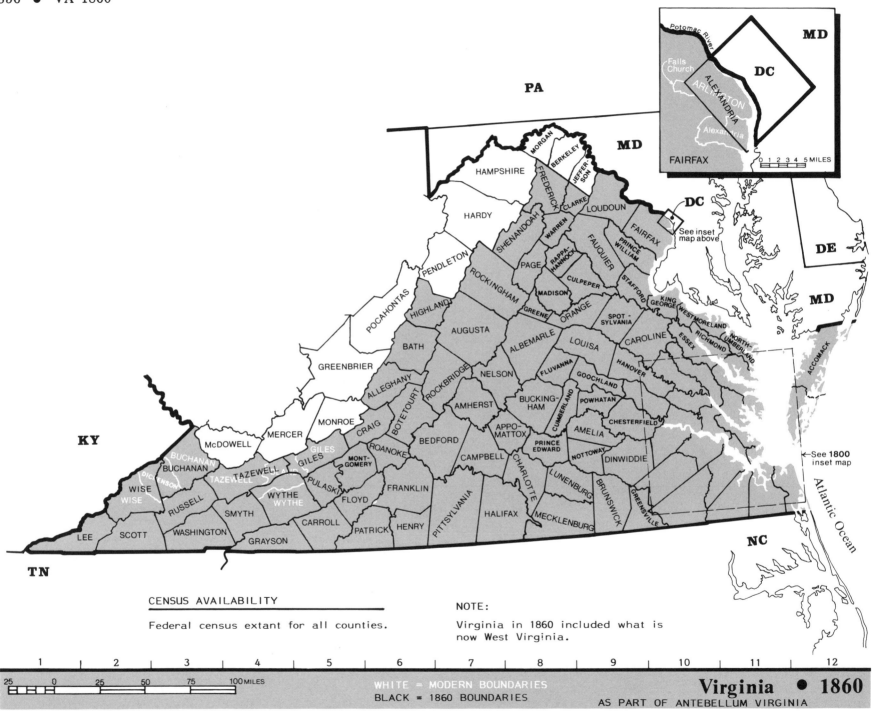

PA

MD

MORGAN

HAMPSHIRE

BERKELEY

JEFFER-SON

FREDERICK

CLARKE

LOUDOUN

Potomac River

Falls Church

ALEXANDRIA ARLINGTON

Alexandria

DC

MD

FAIRFAX

0 1 2 3 4 5 MILES

HARDY

SHENANDOAH

WARREN

FAIRFAX

DC

See inset map above

DE

MD

PENDLETON

PAGE

RAPPA-HANNOCK

FAUQUIER

PRINCE WILLIAM

STAFFORD

See inset map

ROCKINGHAM

CULPEPER

POCAHONTAS

HIGHLAND

MADISON

GREENE

ORANGE

SPOT-SYLVANIA

KING GEORGE

WESTMORELAND

RICHMOND

NORTH-UMBERLAND

AUGUSTA

ALBEMARLE

LOUISA

CAROLINE

ESSEX

BATH

GREENBRIER

NELSON

FLUVANNA

GOOCHLAND

HANOVER

ACCOMACK

ALLEGHANY

ROCKBRIDGE

AMHERST

BUCKING-HAM

CUMBERLAND

POWHATAN

CRAIG

BOTETOURT

APPO-MATTOX

CHESTERFIELD

MONROE

BEDFORD

PRINCE EDWARD

AMELIA

McDOWELL

MERCER

ROANOKE

CAMPBELL

NOTTOWAY

DINWIDDIE

KY

GILES

GILES

MONT-GOMERY

BUCHANAN

BUCHANAN

TAZEWELL

TAZEWELL

PULASKI

FLOYD

FRANKLIN

CHARLOTTE

LUNENBURG

BRUNSWICK

GREENSVILLE

DICKENSON

WYTHE

WYTHE

PITTSYLVANIA

HALIFAX

MECKLENBURG

WISE

WISE

RUSSELL

SMYTH

CARROLL

PATRICK

HENRY

LEE

SCOTT

WASHINGTON

GRAYSON

NC

TN

Atlantic Ocean

CENSUS AVAILABILITY

Federal census extant for all counties.

NOTE:

Virginia in 1860 included what is now West Virginia.

1   2   3   4   5   6   7   8   9   10   11   12

25   0   25   50   75   100 MILES

WHITE = MODERN BOUNDARIES

BLACK = 1860 BOUNDARIES

Virginia ● 1860

AS PART OF ANTEBELLUM VIRGINIA

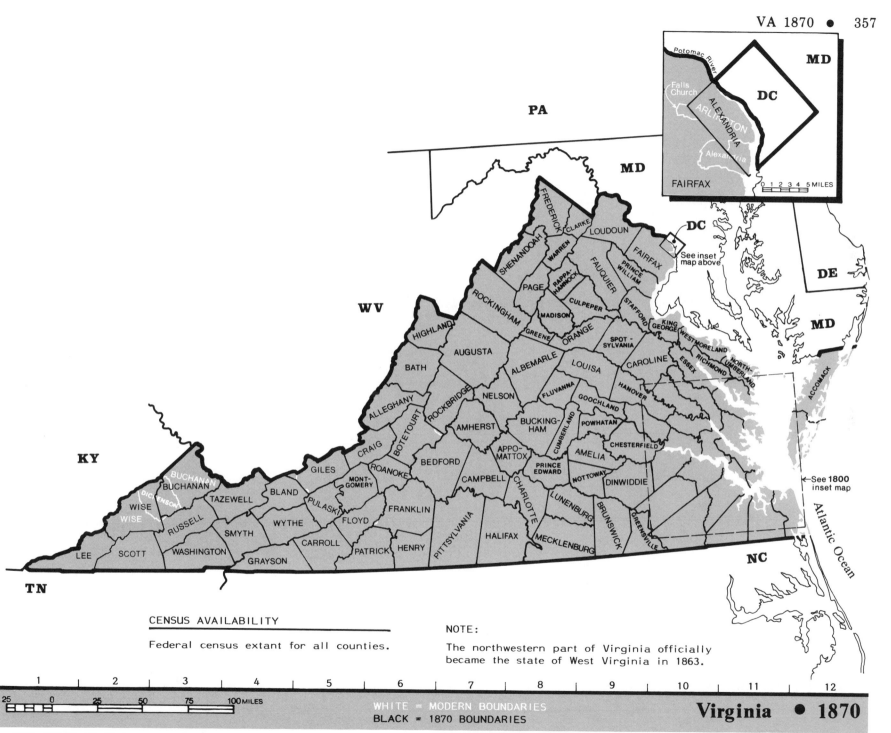

PA

MD

DC

DE

MD

FAIRFAX

Potomac River

Falls
Church

ALEXANDRIA
ARLINGTON

Alexandria

0 1 2 3 4 5 MILES

FREDERICK
CLARKE
LOUDOUN
WARREN
FAIRFAX
SHENANDOAH
FAUQUIER
PRINCE
WILLIAM
RAPPA-
HANNOCK
STAFFORD
PAGE
CULPEPER
ROCKINGHAM
MADISON
KING
GEORGE
WESTMORELAND
GREENE
ORANGE
NORTH-
UMBERLAND
HIGHLAND
SPOT-
SYLVANIA
RICHMOND
AUGUSTA
ALBEMARLE
LOUISA
CAROLINE
ESSEX
BATH
NELSON
FLUVANNA
HANOVER
ACCOMACK
ALLEGHANY
ROCKBRIDGE
GOOCHLAND
AMHERST
BUCKING-
HAM
POWHATAN
CRAIG
BOTETOURT
CUMBERLAND
CHESTERFIELD
BEDFORD
APPO-
MATTOX
AMELIA
ROANOKE
PRINCE
EDWARD
GILES
MONT-
GOMERY
CAMPBELL
NOTTOWAY
DINWIDDIE
BUCHANAN
BUCHANAN
PULASKI
CHARLOTTE
DICKENSON
TAZEWELL
BLAND
FLOYD
FRANKLIN
LUNENBURG
BRUNSWICK
GREENSVILLE
WISE
WISE
WYTHE
PITTSYLVANIA
RUSSELL
SMYTH
CARROLL
PATRICK
HENRY
HALIFAX
MECKLENBURG
LEE
SCOTT
WASHINGTON
GRAYSON

WV

KY

TN

NC

See inset
map above

See 1800
inset map

Atlantic Ocean

CENSUS AVAILABILITY

Federal census extant for all counties.

NOTE:

The northwestern part of Virginia officially
became the state of West Virginia in 1863.

1   2   3   4   5   6   7   8   9   10   11   12

25   0   25   50   75   100 MILES

WHITE = MODERN BOUNDARIES
BLACK = 1870 BOUNDARIES

Virginia ● 1870

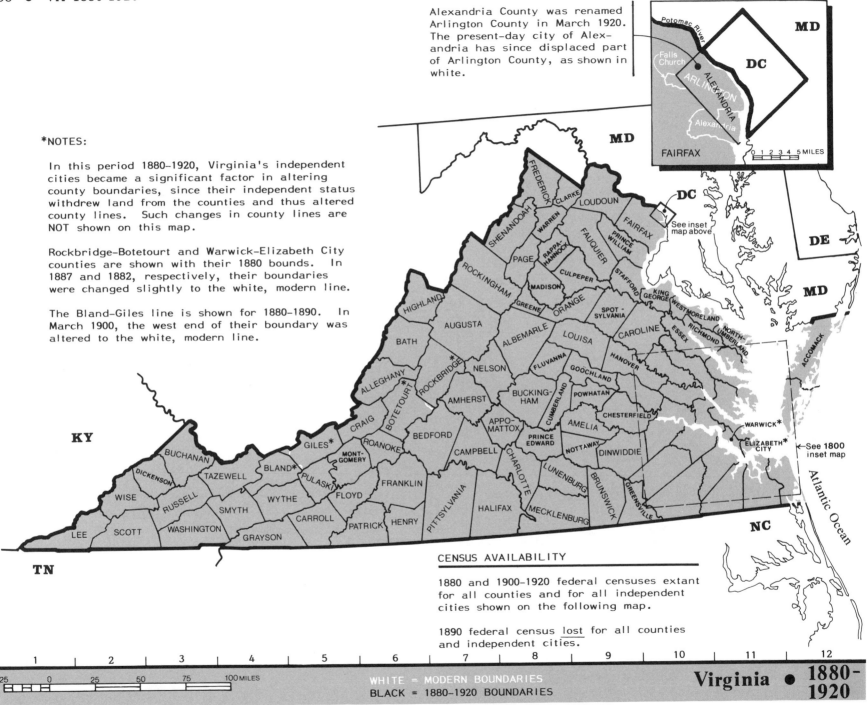

Alexandria County was renamed Arlington County in March 1920. The present-day city of Alexandria has since displaced part of Arlington County, as shown in white.

MD

DC

FAIRFAX

0 1 2 3 4 5 MILES

*NOTES:

In this period 1880–1920, Virginia's independent cities became a significant factor in altering county boundaries, since their independent status withdrew land from the counties and thus altered county lines. Such changes in county lines are NOT shown on this map.

Rockbridge–Botetourt and Warwick–Elizabeth City counties are shown with their 1880 bounds. In 1887 and 1882, respectively, their boundaries were changed slightly to the white, modern line.

The Bland–Giles line is shown for 1880–1890. In March 1900, the west end of their boundary was altered to the white, modern line.

MD

DC
See inset map above

DE

MD

See inset map above

KY

TN

NC

Atlantic Ocean

See 1800 inset map

CENSUS AVAILABILITY

1880 and 1900–1920 federal censuses extant for all counties and for all independent cities shown on the following map.

1890 federal census lost for all counties and independent cities.

1   2   3   4   5   6   7   8   9   10   11   12

25   0   25   50   75   100 MILES

WHITE = MODERN BOUNDARIES
BLACK = 1880–1920 BOUNDARIES

Virginia ● 1880-1920

Independent cities have existed in Virginia since Williamsburg was
chartered in 1722, though the degree of independence has varied.
As of 1980, forty-one independent cities are outside county boundaries
and jurisdictions. They are listed in the Rand McNally *Commercial Atlas*,
available in nearly all public libraries. In the past some cities were
enumerated separately from their adjoining counties; others with early
dates of town status have no surviving censuses prior to 1900 that
are separate from their adjoining counties.

"City" in the names of three counties -- Charles City, Elizabeth
City, and James City -- antedates counties and reflects an early
experiment in borough government.

In addition to the present 41, there have been three corporate
municipalities that are now defunct as independent cities:
(1) Manchester was incorporated in 1874 and absorbed into
Richmond in late 1910. (2) South Norfolk was incorporated
in 1921 and merged with Norfolk County in 1962 to
form the city of Chesapeake. (3) Warwick County
became the city of Warwick in 1952 and was
absorbed into the city of Newport News in
1957. These changes abolished the counties
of Norfolk and Warwick.

Also extinct are Elizabeth City County,
merged with the city of Hampton in 1952,
and Princess Anne County, consolidated
with the city of Virginia Beach in 1962.

CENSUS AVAILABILITY

Federal censuses extant for all independent
cities for dates shown.

*NOTE:

Manchester 1910-1920 censuses are with
the city of Richmond schedules.

WHITE = MODERN BOUNDARIES
BLACK = 1900-1920 CITIES

Virginia ●
INDEPENDENT CITIES CENSUSES

1900-1920

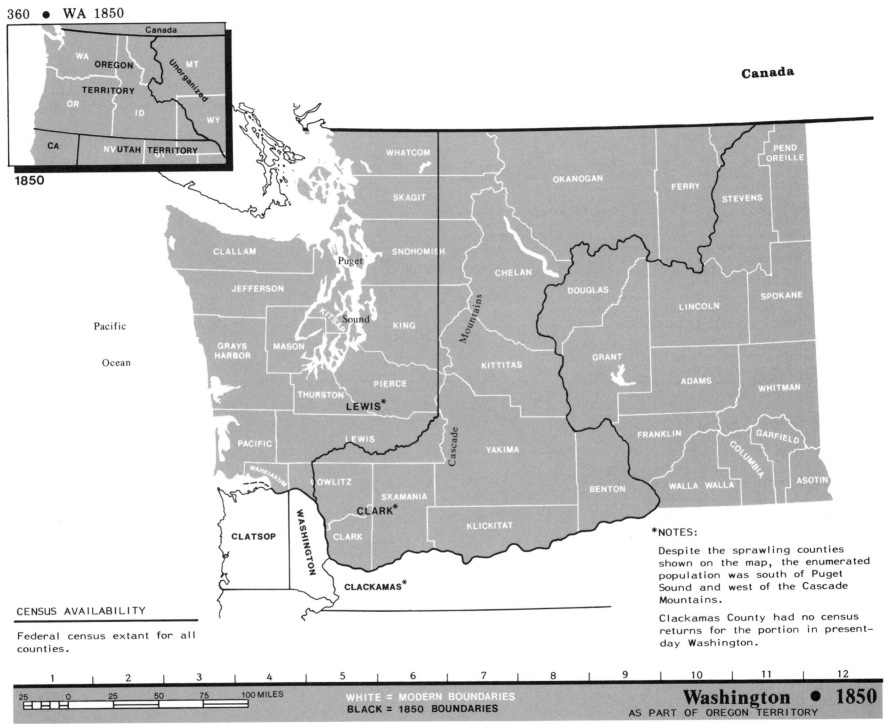

360 ● WA 1850

1850

Canada

WA OREGON MT
Unorganized
OR TERRITORY ID WY
CA NV UTAH TERRITORY UT

Canada

WHATCOM

PEND OREILLE

OKANOGAN

FERRY

STEVENS

SKAGIT

CLALLAM

SNOHOMISH

CHELAN

DOUGLAS

SPOKANE

Puget

LINCOLN

JEFFERSON

KITSAP

Sound

Pacific

KING

Mountains

Ocean

GRAYS HARBOR

MASON

GRANT

ADAMS

WHITMAN

KITTITAS

THURSTON

PIERCE

LEWIS*

FRANKLIN

GARFIELD

PACIFIC

LEWIS

YAKIMA

Cascade

COLUMBIA

BENTON

ASOTIN

WAHKIAKUM

COWLITZ

WALLA WALLA

CLARK*

SKAMANIA

WASHINGTON

CLARK

KLICKITAT

CLATSOP

*NOTES:

Despite the sprawling counties shown on the map, the enumerated population was south of Puget Sound and west of the Cascade Mountains.

CLACKAMAS*

Clackamas County had no census returns for the portion in present-day Washington.

CENSUS AVAILABILITY

Federal census extant for all counties.

1   2   3   4   5   6   7   8   9   10   11   12

25 0   25   50   75   100 MILES

WHITE = MODERN BOUNDARIES
BLACK = 1850 BOUNDARIES

Washington ● **1850**

AS PART OF OREGON TERRITORY

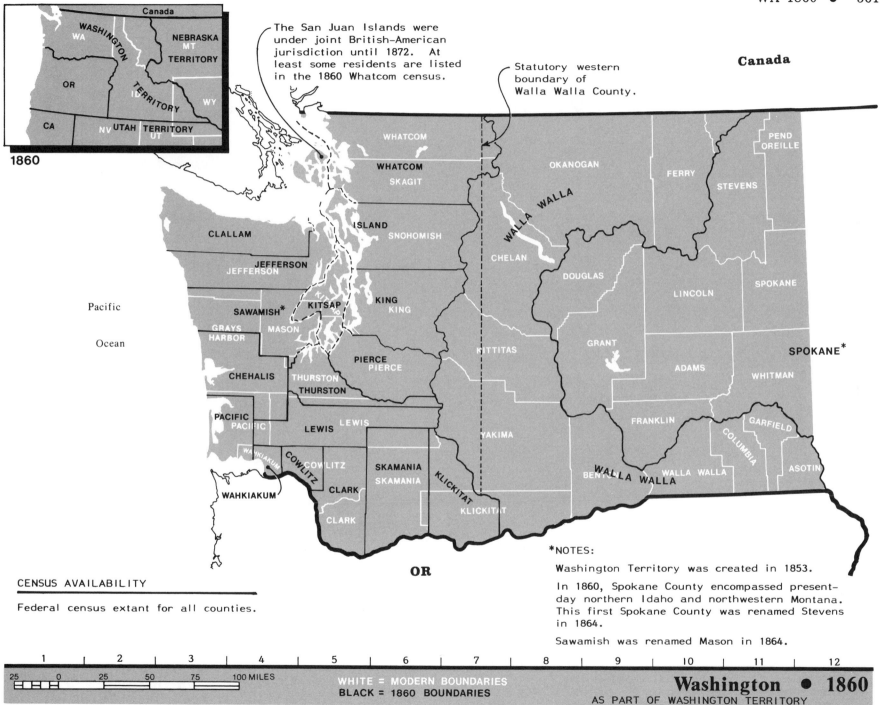

The San Juan Islands were under joint British-American jurisdiction until 1872. At least some residents are listed in the 1860 Whatcom census.

Statutory western boundary of Walla Walla County.

1860

Canada

*NOTES:

Washington Territory was created in 1853.

In 1860, Spokane County encompassed present-day northern Idaho and northwestern Montana. This first Spokane County was renamed Stevens in 1864.

Sawamish was renamed Mason in 1864.

CENSUS AVAILABILITY

Federal census extant for all counties.

WHITE = MODERN BOUNDARIES
BLACK = 1860 BOUNDARIES

Washington ● **1860**

AS PART OF WASHINGTON TERRITORY

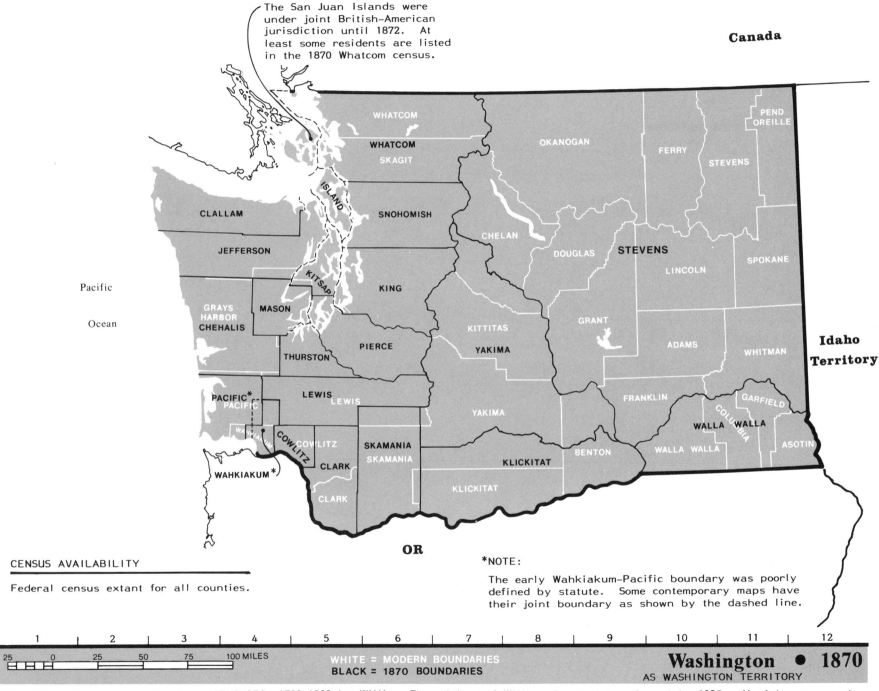

The San Juan Islands were under joint British–American jurisdiction until 1872. At least some residents are listed in the 1870 Whatcom census.

Canada

Pacific

Ocean

WHATCOM

WHATCOM

SKAGIT

ISLAND

OKANOGAN

PEND OREILLE

FERRY

STEVENS

CLALLAM

SNOHOMISH

CHELAN

DOUGLAS

STEVENS

SPOKANE

JEFFERSON

LINCOLN

KITSAP

KING

GRAYS HARBOR

MASON

CHEHALIS

GRANT

KITTITAS

YAKIMA

ADAMS

WHITMAN

Idaho Territory

THURSTON

PIERCE

PACIFIC*

PACIFIC

LEWIS

LEWIS

YAKIMA

FRANKLIN

GARFIELD

COLUMBIA

WALLA WALLA

WAHKIAKUM

COWLITZ

COWLITZ

SKAMANIA

SKAMANIA

KLICKITAT

BENTON

WALLA WALLA

ASOTIN

WAHKIAKUM*

CLARK

CLARK

KLICKITAT

OR

CENSUS AVAILABILITY

Federal census extant for all counties.

*NOTE:

The early Wahkiakum–Pacific boundary was poorly defined by statute. Some contemporary maps have their joint boundary as shown by the dashed line.

| 1 | 2 | 3 | 4 | 5 | 6 | 7 | 8 | 9 | 10 | 11 | 12 |

25 0 25 50 75 100 MILES

WHITE = MODERN BOUNDARIES
BLACK = 1870 BOUNDARIES

Washington ● 1870
AS WASHINGTON TERRITORY

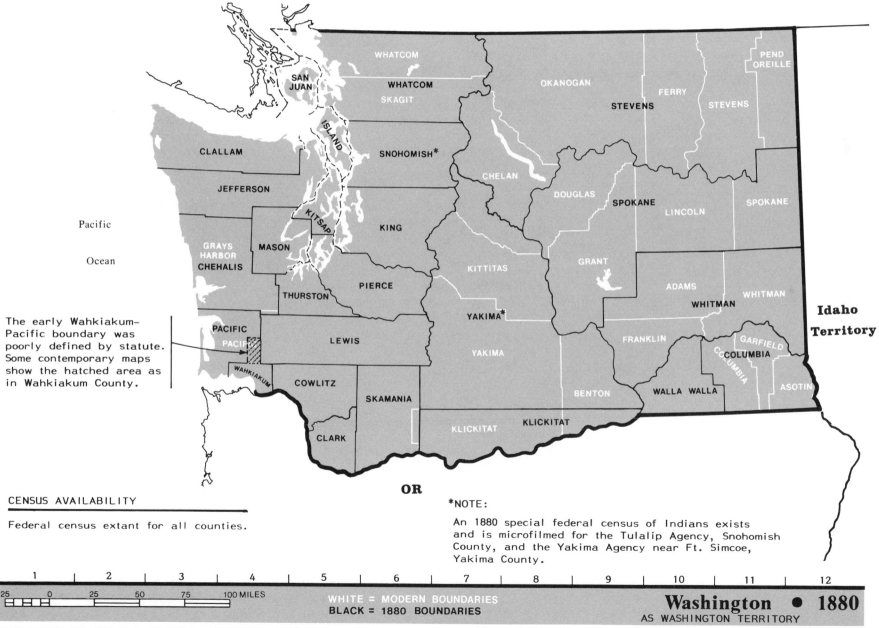

Canada

Pacific

Ocean

The early Wahkiakum–
Pacific boundary was
poorly defined by statute.
Some contemporary maps
show the hatched area as
in Wahkiakum County.

Idaho
Territory

OR

CENSUS AVAILABILITY

Federal census extant for all counties.

*NOTE:

An 1880 special federal census of Indians exists
and is microfilmed for the Tulalip Agency, Snohomish
County, and the Yakima Agency near Ft. Simcoe,
Yakima County.

WHITE = MODERN BOUNDARIES
BLACK = 1880 BOUNDARIES

25   0   25   50   75   100 MILES

1   2   3   4   5   6   7   8   9   10   11   12

Washington ● **1880**
AS WASHINGTON TERRITORY

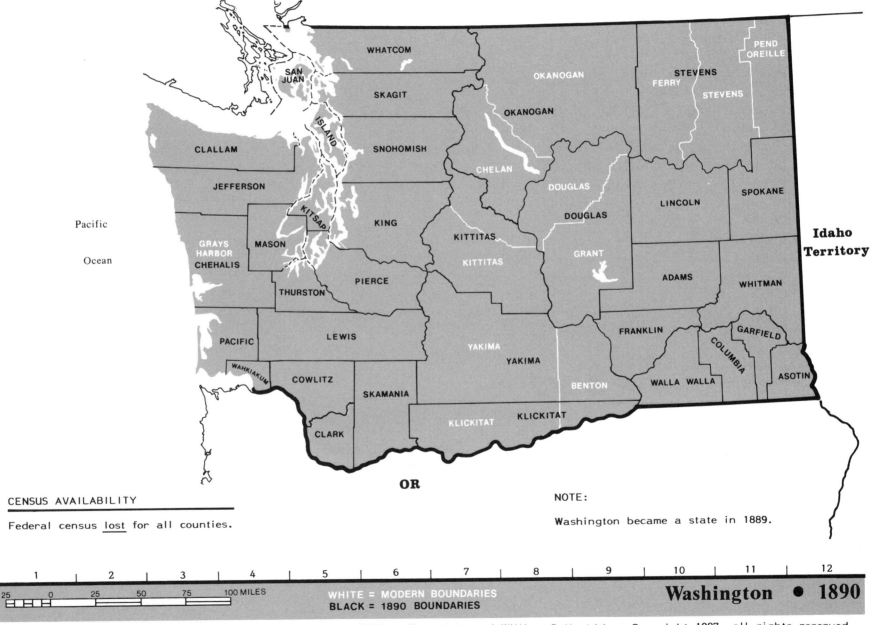

Canada

Pacific

Ocean

Idaho
Territory

OR

CENSUS AVAILABILITY

Federal census lost for all counties.

NOTE:

Washington became a state in 1889.

| 1 | 2 | 3 | 4 | 5 | 6 | 7 | 8 | 9 | 10 | 11 | 12 |

25 0 25 50 75 100 MILES

WHITE = MODERN BOUNDARIES
BLACK = 1890 BOUNDARIES

Washington ● 1890

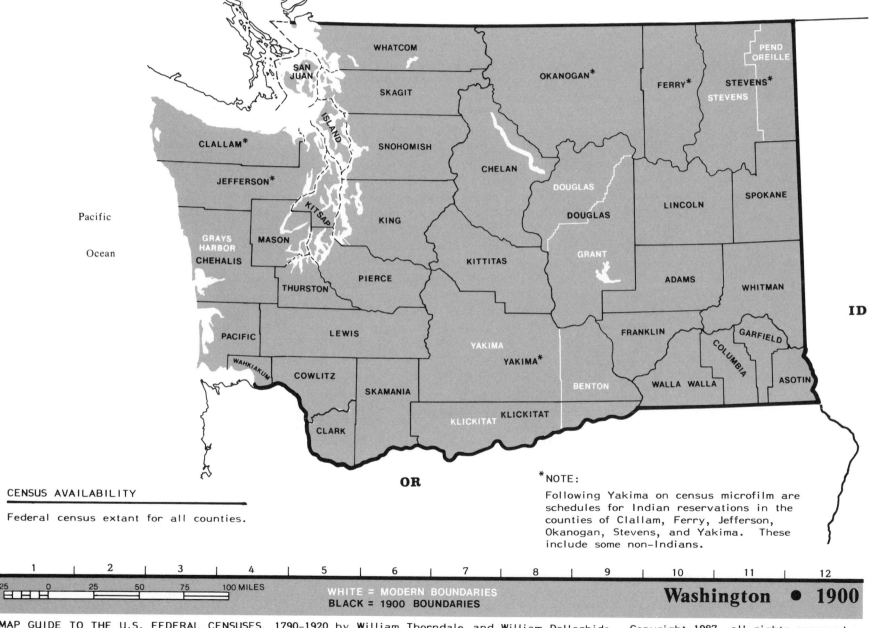

Canada

Pacific

Ocean

OR

*NOTE:

Following Yakima on census microfilm are
schedules for Indian reservations in the
counties of Clallam, Ferry, Jefferson,
Okanogan, Stevens, and Yakima. These
include some non-Indians.

ID

CENSUS AVAILABILITY

Federal census extant for all counties.

WHITE = MODERN BOUNDARIES
BLACK = 1900 BOUNDARIES

Washington ● **1900**

MAP GUIDE TO THE U.S. FEDERAL CENSUSES, 1790–1920 by William Thorndale and William Dollarhide. Copyright 1987, all rights reserved.

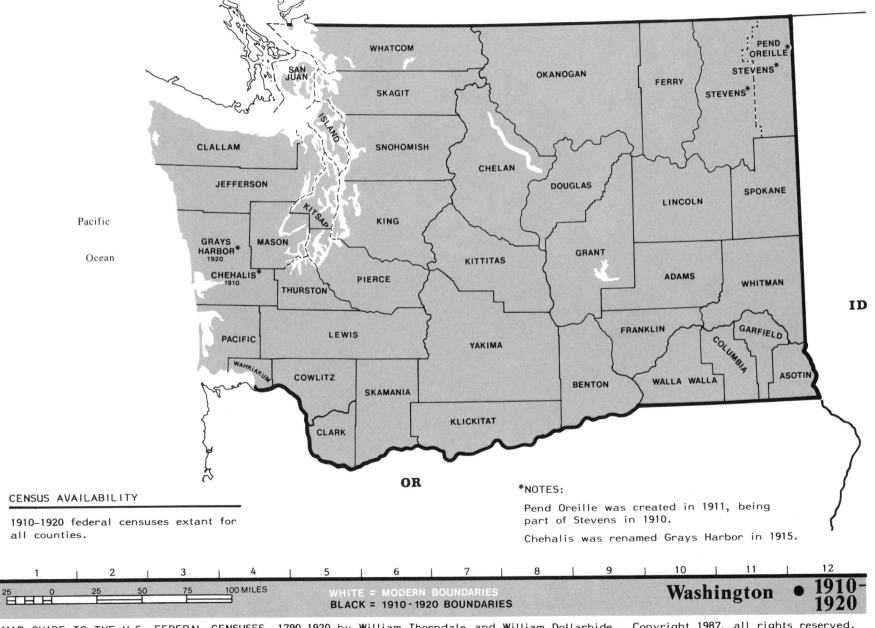

Canada

WHATCOM

SAN
JUAN

OKANOGAN

SKAGIT

FERRY

PEND
OREILLE *

STEVENS *

STEVENS *

CLALLAM

ISLAND

SNOHOMISH

JEFFERSON

CHELAN

Pacific

DOUGLAS

SPOKANE

LINCOLN

KITSAP

KING

Ocean

GRAYS
HARBOR *
1920

MASON

GRANT

CHEHALIS *
1910

KITTITAS

THURSTON

PIERCE

ADAMS

WHITMAN

PACIFIC

LEWIS

YAKIMA

FRANKLIN

GARFIELD

WAHKIAKUM

COLUMBIA

COWLITZ

ASOTIN

SKAMANIA

BENTON

WALLA WALLA

ID

KLICKITAT

CLARK

OR

*NOTES:

Pend Oreille was created in 1911, being
part of Stevens in 1910.

Chehalis was renamed Grays Harbor in 1915.

CENSUS AVAILABILITY

1910–1920 federal censuses extant for
all counties.

25   0   25   50   75   100 MILES

1   2   3   4   5   6   7   8   9   10   11   12

WHITE = MODERN BOUNDARIES
BLACK = 1910-1920 BOUNDARIES

Washington ● 1910-1920

MAP GUIDE TO THE U.S. FEDERAL CENSUSES, 1790-1920 by William Thorndale and William Dollarhide.   Copyright 1987, all rights reserved.

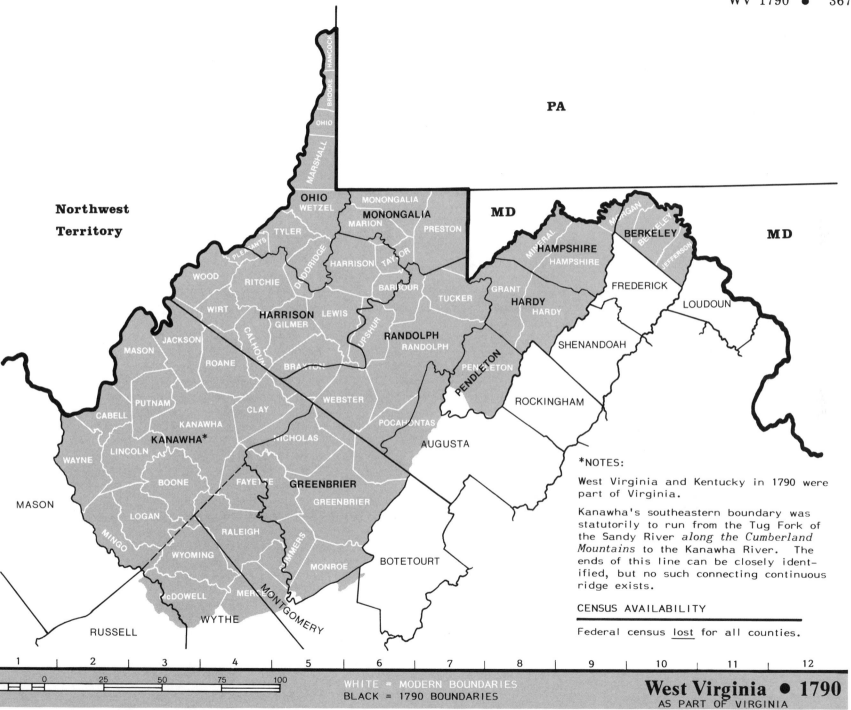

PA

Northwest
Territory

MD

MD

OHIO
WETZEL

MONONGALIA
MONONGALIA

MARION

PRESTON

BERKELEY

HAMPSHIRE

TYLER

HARRISON

TAYLOR

BARBOUR

TUCKER

GRANT

HARDY
HARDY

HAMPSHIRE

FREDERICK

JEFFERSON

WOOD

PLEASANTS

RITCHIE

DODDRIDGE

LEWIS

UPSHUR

LOUDOUN

WIRT

HARRISON
GILMER

RANDOLPH
RANDOLPH

SHENANDOAH

JACKSON

CALHOUN

BRAXTON

PENDLETON

PENDLETON

ROCKINGHAM

MASON

ROANE

WEBSTER

PUTNAM

CLAY

POCAHONTAS

CABELL

KANAWHA

AUGUSTA

KANAWHA*

NICHOLAS

WAYNE

LINCOLN

FAYETTE

MASON

BOONE

GREENBRIER

LOGAN

GREENBRIER

BOTETOURT

MINGO

RALEIGH

SUMMERS

WYOMING

MONROE

McDOWELL

MERCER

RUSSELL

MONTGOMERY

WYTHE

*NOTES:

West Virginia and Kentucky in 1790 were
part of Virginia.

Kanawha's southeastern boundary was
statutorily to run from the Tug Fork of
the Sandy River *along the Cumberland
Mountains* to the Kanawha River. The
ends of this line can be closely identified, but no such connecting continuous
ridge exists.

CENSUS AVAILABILITY

Federal census lost for all counties.

| 1 | 2 | 3 | 4 | 5 | 6 | 7 | 8 | 9 | 10 | 11 | 12 |

25   0   25   50   75   100

WHITE = MODERN BOUNDARIES
BLACK = 1790 BOUNDARIES

West Virginia ● 1790
AS PART OF VIRGINIA

PA

Northwest Territory

MD

MD

BR BROOKE HANCOCK

OHIO

MARSHALL

OHIO

WETZEL

MONONGALIA

MONONGALIA

PRESTON

MORGAN

BERKELEY

BERKELEY

TYLER

PLEASANTS

MARION

TAYLOR

MINERAL

HAMPSHIRE

JEFFERSON

WOOD

RITCHIE

DODDRIDGE

HARRISON

BARBOUR

HAMPSHIRE

WOOD

WIRT

LEWIS

TUCKER

GRANT

FREDERICK

HARRISON

GILMER

UPSHUR

HARDY

LOUDOUN

JACKSON

CALHOUN

BRAXTON

RANDOLPH

HARDY

DC

MASON

ROANE

RANDOLPH

SHENANDOAH

PUTNAM

CLAY

WEBSTER

PENDLETON

KANAWHA

PENDLETON

CABELL

KANAWHA*

POCAHONTAS

ROCKINGHAM

NICHOLAS

WAYNE

LINCOLN

BATH

BOONE

FAYETTE

GREENBRIER

LOGAN

GREENBRIER

AUGUSTA

MINGO

RALEIGH

KY

WYOMING

MONROE

MONROE

McDOWELL

MERCER

BOTETOURT

MONTGOMERY

TAZEWELL

*NOTES:

West Virginia in 1800 was part of Virginia.

See West Virginia 1790 for Kanawha's south-eastern line.

CENSUS AVAILABILITY

Federal census lost for all counties.

| 1 | 2 | 3 | 4 | 5 | 6 | 7 | 8 | 9 | 10 | 11 | 12 |

25   0   25   50   75   100

WHITE = MODERN BOUNDARIES
BLACK = 1800 BOUNDARIES

West Virginia ● 1800
AS PART OF VIRGINIA

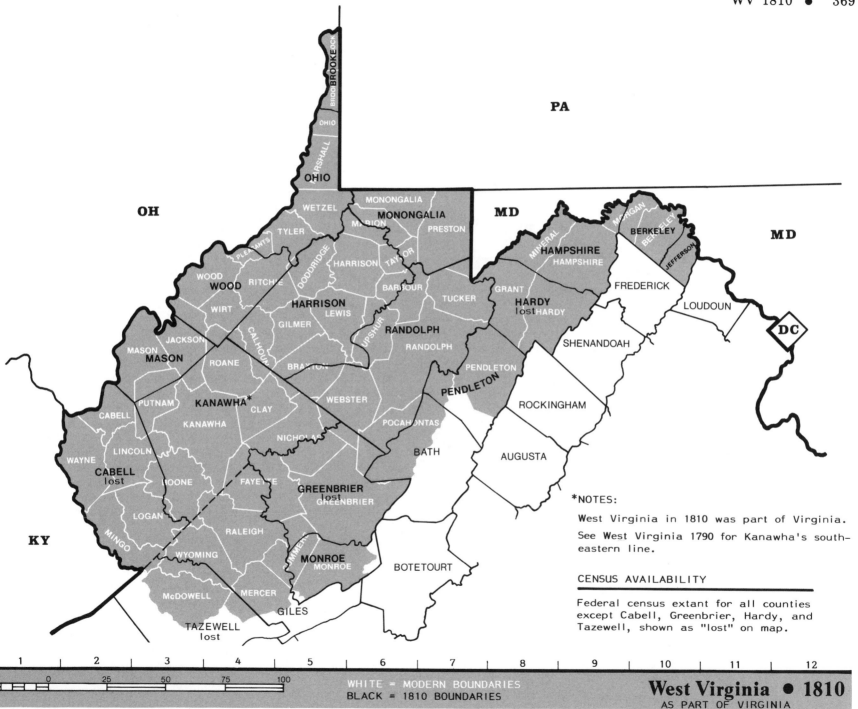

PA

OH

MD

MD

BROOKE

OHIO

MARSHALL

OHIO

WETZEL

MONONGALIA

MONONGALIA

MORGAN

BERKELEY

TYLER

MARION

PRESTON

BERKELEY

PLEASANTS

TAYLOR

MINERAL

JEFFERSON

WOOD

RITCHIE

DODDRIDGE

HARRISON

HAMPSHIRE

HAMPSHIRE

WOOD

BARBOUR

TUCKER

FREDERICK

WIRT

GILMER

LEWIS

GRANT

LOUDOUN

JACKSON

CALHOUN

UPSHUR

HARDY

DC

MASON

ROANE

BRAXTON

RANDOLPH

lost HARDY

MASON

RANDOLPH

SHENANDOAH

PUTNAM

KANAWHA *

PENDLETON

CABELL

CLAY

WEBSTER

PENDLETON

ROCKINGHAM

KANAWHA

KANAWHA

POCAHONTAS

WAYNE

LINCOLN

NICHOLAS

BATH

CABELL
lost

BOONE

FAYETTE

GREENBRIER
lost

AUGUSTA

LOGAN

GREENBRIER

*NOTES:

KY

MINGO

RALEIGH

West Virginia in 1810 was part of Virginia.

See West Virginia 1790 for Kanawha's south-eastern line.

WYOMING

SUMMERS

MONROE

MONROE

BOTETOURT

CENSUS AVAILABILITY

McDOWELL

MERCER

GILES

Federal census extant for all counties
except Cabell, Greenbrier, Hardy, and
Tazewell, shown as "lost" on map.

TAZEWELL
lost

| 1 | 2 | 3 | 4 | 5 | 6 | 7 | 8 | 9 | 10 | 11 | 12 |

25   0   25   50   75   100

WHITE = MODERN BOUNDARIES
BLACK = 1810 BOUNDARIES

West Virginia ● 1810
AS PART OF VIRGINIA

PA

OH

MD

MD

BROOKE

OHIO

OHIO

MARSHALL

WETZEL

TYLER

TYLER

MONONGALIA

MONONGALIA

MARION

PRESTON

MORGAN

BERKELEY

JEFFERSON

MINERAL

HAMPSHIRE

HAMPSHIRE

PLEASANTS

WOOD

WOOD

RITCHIE

DODDRIDGE

HARRISON

HARRISON

TAYLOR

BARBOUR

TUCKER

GRANT

HARDY

HARDY

FREDERICK

LOUDOUN

DC

WIRT

GILMER

LEWIS

LEWIS

UPSHUR

RANDOLPH

RANDOLPH

PENDLETON

SHENANDOAH

JACKSON

CALHOUN

BRAXTON

MASON

MASON

ROANE

WEBSTER

PENDLETON

ROCKINGHAM

PUTNAM

CLAY

NICHOLAS

NICHOLAS*

KANAWHA*

KANAWHA

POCAHONTAS

CABELL

LINCOLN

FAYETTE

BATH

AUGUSTA

WAYNE

CABELL

BOONE

GREENBRIER*

GREENBRIER

LOGAN

RALEIGH

SUMMERS

MINGO

WYOMING

MONROE

MONROE

BOTETOURT

McDOWELL

MERCER

GILES

TAZEWELL

KY

*NOTES:

West Virginia in 1820 was part of Virginia.

Part of the Nicholas-Greenbrier boundary is shown as a double line, the eastern (right) side being statutory and western (left) side being traditional. All subsequent maps could display this double line but only the western line, favored by map makers, is shown 1830–1920.

See West Virginia 1790 for Kanawha's southeastern line.

CENSUS AVAILABILITY

Federal census extant for all counties.

| 1 | 2 | 3 | 4 | 5 | 6 | 7 | 8 | 9 | 10 | 11 | 12 |

25 0 25 50 75 100

WHITE = MODERN BOUNDARIES
BLACK = 1820 BOUNDARIES

West Virginia ● 1820
AS PART OF VIRGINIA

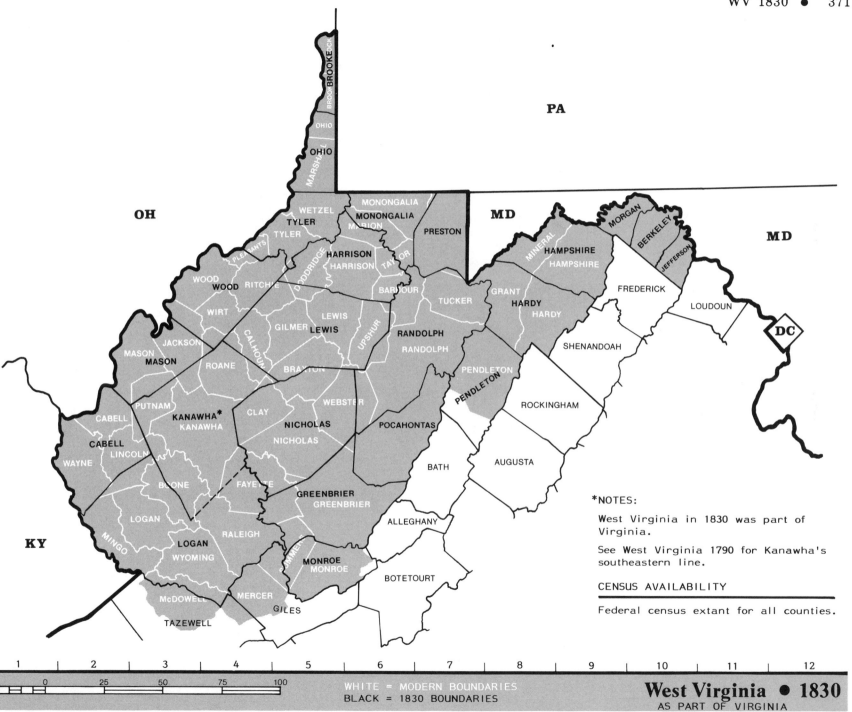

*NOTES:

West Virginia in 1830 was part of Virginia.

See West Virginia 1790 for Kanawha's southeastern line.

CENSUS AVAILABILITY

Federal census extant for all counties.

WHITE = MODERN BOUNDARIES
BLACK = 1830 BOUNDARIES

West Virginia ● 1830
AS PART OF VIRGINIA

MAP GUIDE TO THE U.S. FEDERAL CENSUSES, 1790–1920 by William Thorndale and William Dollarhide.   Copyright 1987, all rights reserved.

PA

OH

MD

MD

BROOKE

OHIO

MARSHALL

WETZEL

TYLER

TYLER

MONONGALIA

MONONGALIA

MARION

PRESTON

PLEASANTS

HARRISON

HARRISON

TAYLOR

MORGAN

BERKELEY

JEFFERSON

MINERAL

HAMPSHIRE

HAMPSHIRE

FREDERICK

CLARKE

LOUDOUN

WOOD

WOOD

RITCHIE

DODDRIDGE

BARBOUR

TUCKER

GRANT

HARDY

HARDY

DC

WIRT

LEWIS

LEWIS

GILMER

UPSHUR

RANDOLPH

SHENANDOAH

MASON

JACKSON

JACKSON

CALHOUN

ROANE

BRAXTON

BRAXTON

RANDOLPH

PENDLETON

PENDLETON

MASON

WEBSTER

ROCKINGHAM

PUTNAM

KANAWHA

KANAWHA

CLAY

NICHOLAS

NICHOLAS

POCAHONTAS

CABELL

CABELL

LINCOLN

BATH

AUGUSTA

WAYNE

BOONE

FAYETTE

FAYETTE

GREENBRIER

LOGAN

LOGAN

RALEIGH

SUMMERS

ALLEGHANY

MINGO

WYOMING

MONROE

MONROE

BOTETOURT

MERCER

MERCER

McDOWELL

GILES

TAZEWELL

KY

NOTE:

West Virginia in 1840 was part of Virginia.

CENSUS AVAILABILITY

Federal census extant for all counties.

| 1 | 2 | 3 | 4 | 5 | 6 | 7 | 8 | 9 | 10 | 11 | 12 |

25 0 25 50 75 100

WHITE = MODERN BOUNDARIES
BLACK = 1840 BOUNDARIES

West Virginia ● 1840
AS PART OF VIRGINIA

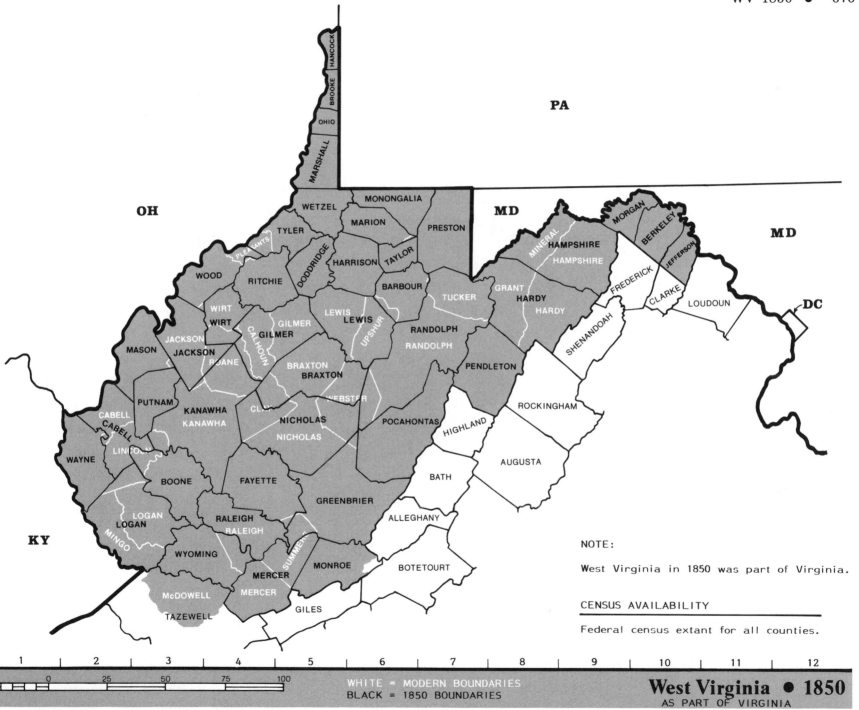

OH

PA

MD

MD

DC

KY

NOTE:

West Virginia in 1850 was part of Virginia.

CENSUS AVAILABILITY

Federal census extant for all counties.

HANCOCK
BROOKE
OHIO
MARSHALL
WETZEL
MONONGALIA
TYLER
MARION
PRESTON
PLEASANTS
WOOD
RITCHIE
DODDRIDGE
HARRISON
TAYLOR
MORGAN
BERKELEY
MINERAL
HAMPSHIRE
HAMPSHIRE
JEFFERSON
WIRT
WIRT
GILMER
LEWIS
BARBOUR
GRANT
HARDY
HARDY
FREDERICK
CLARKE
LOUDOUN
JACKSON
JACKSON
CALHOUN
GILMER
LEWIS
UPSHUR
RANDOLPH
RANDOLPH
TUCKER
SHENANDOAH
MASON
ROANE
BRAXTON
BRAXTON
PENDLETON
PUTNAM
KANAWHA
KANAWHA
CLAY
WEBSTER
POCAHONTAS
ROCKINGHAM
CABELL
CABELL
NICHOLAS
NICHOLAS
HIGHLAND
LINCOLN
WAYNE
BOONE
FAYETTE
GREENBRIER
AUGUSTA
BATH
LOGAN
LOGAN
RALEIGH
RALEIGH
ALLEGHANY
MINGO
SUMMERS
WYOMING
MERCER
MONROE
BOTETOURT
MCDOWELL
MERCER
GILES
TAZEWELL

| 1 | 2 | 3 | 4 | 5 | 6 | 7 | 8 | 9 | 10 | 11 | 12 |

25 0 25 50 75 100

WHITE = MODERN BOUNDARIES
BLACK = 1850 BOUNDARIES

West Virginia ● 1850
AS PART OF VIRGINIA

PA

OH

MD

MD

HANCOCK

BROOKE

OHIO

MARSHALL

WETZEL

MONONGALIA

TYLER

MARION

PRESTON

PLEASANTS

DODDRIDGE

HARRISON

TAYLOR

MORGAN

BERKELEY

WOOD

RITCHIE

BARBOUR

TUCKER

MINERAL

HAMPSHIRE

HAMPSHIRE

JEFFERSON

WIRT

GILMER

LEWIS

GRANT

FREDERICK

CLARKE

LOUDOUN

DC

JACKSON

CALHOUN

UPSHUR

RANDOLPH

HARDY

HARDY

MASON

ROANE

BRAXTON

PENDLETON

SHENANDOAH

PUTNAM

CLAY

WEBSTER

ROCKINGHAM

CABELL

CABELL

KANAWHA

POCAHONTAS

LINCOLN

NICHOLAS

HIGHLAND

WAYNE

BOONE

FAYETTE

BATH

AUGUSTA

LOGAN

LOGAN

RALEIGH

RALEIGH

GREENBRIER

ALLEGHANY

MINGO

WYOMING

SUMMERS

MONROE

KY

MERCER

CRAIG

McDOWELL

MERCER

GILES

BUCHANAN

TAZEWELL

NOTE:

West Virginia in 1860 was part of Virginia.

CENSUS AVAILABILITY

Federal census extant for all counties.

| 1 | 2 | 3 | 4 | 5 | 6 | 7 | 8 | 9 | 10 | 11 | 12 |

25 0 25 50 75 100

WHITE = MODERN BOUNDARIES
BLACK = 1860 BOUNDARIES

West Virginia ● 1860
AS PART OF VIRGINIA

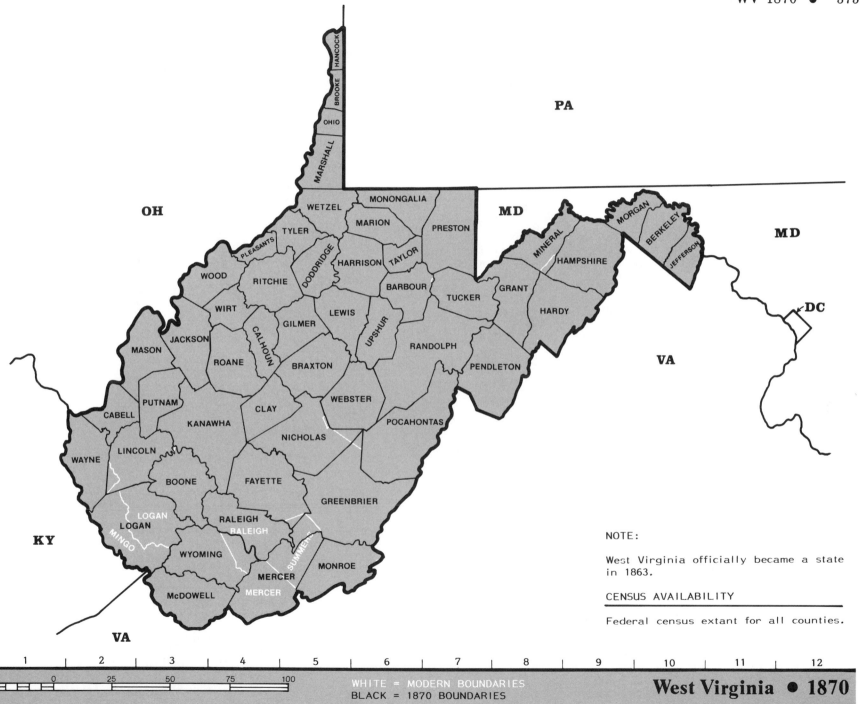

NOTE:

West Virginia officially became a state in 1863.

CENSUS AVAILABILITY

Federal census extant for all counties.

| 1 | 2 | 3 | 4 | 5 | 6 | 7 | 8 | 9 | 10 | 11 | 12 |

25   0   25   50   75   100

WHITE = MODERN BOUNDARIES
BLACK = 1870 BOUNDARIES

West Virginia ● 1870

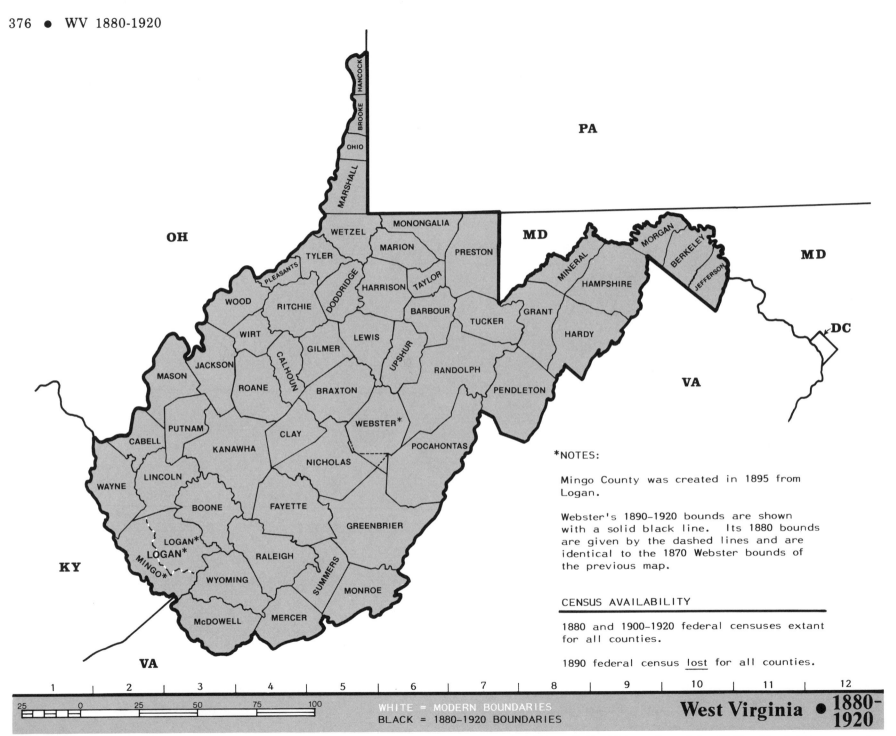

PA

OH

HANCOCK

BROOKE

OHIO

MARSHALL

WETZEL

MONONGALIA

TYLER

MARION

PRESENT

MD

PLEASANTS

DODDRIDGE

HARRISON

TAYLOR

BARBOUR

MINERAL

MORGAN

BERKELEY

JEFFERSON

MD

WOOD

RITCHIE

HAMPSHIRE

WIRT

LEWIS

TUCKER

GRANT

MD

DC

GILMER

UPSHUR

HARDY

JACKSON

CALHOUN

BRAXTON

RANDOLPH

MASON

ROANE

PENDLETON

VA

PUTNAM

CLAY

WEBSTER*

CABELL

KANAWHA

POCAHONTAS

LINCOLN

NICHOLAS

WAYNE

*NOTES:

BOONE

FAYETTE

Mingo County was created in 1895 from Logan.

LOGAN*

GREENBRIER

Webster's 1890–1920 bounds are shown with a solid black line. Its 1880 bounds are given by the dashed lines and are identical to the 1870 Webster bounds of the previous map.

LOGAN*

RALEIGH

MINGO*

WYOMING

SUMMERS

MONROE

KY

McDOWELL

MERCER

CENSUS AVAILABILITY

1880 and 1900–1920 federal censuses extant for all counties.

1890 federal census lost for all counties.

VA

1 2 3 4 5 6 7 8 9 10 11 12

25 0 25 50 75 100

West Virginia ● 1880-1920

MAP GUIDE TO THE U.S. FEDERAL CENSUSES, 1790-1920 by William Thorndale and William Dollarhide. Copyright 1987, all rights reserved.

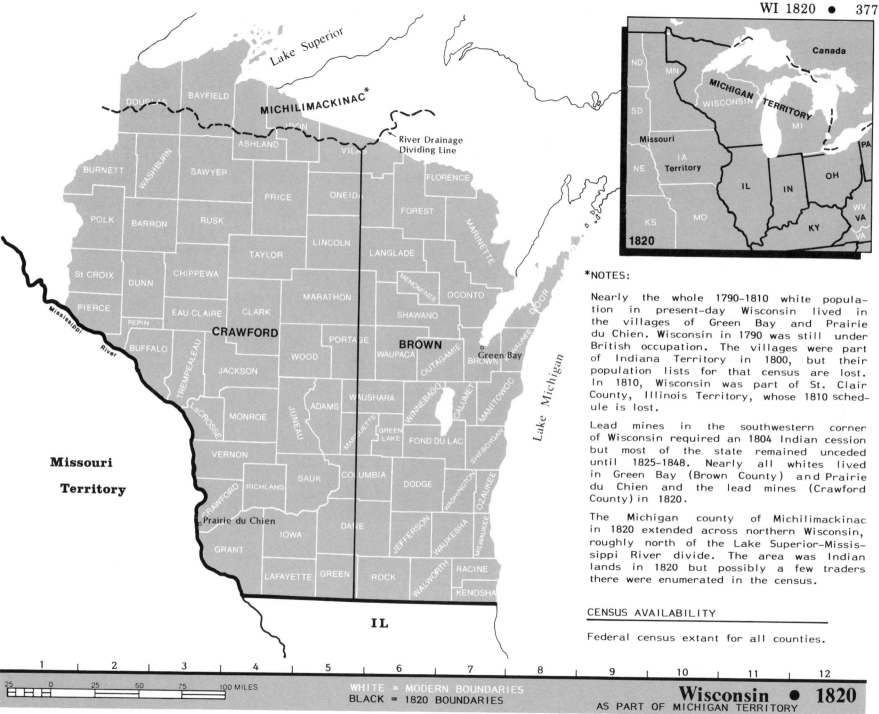

Lake Superior

MICHILIMACKINAC*

← River Drainage
Dividing Line

DOUGLAS

BAYFIELD

BURNETT

WASHBURN

SAWYER

ASHLAND

IRON

VILAS

FLORENCE

POLK

BARRON

RUSK

PRICE

ONEIDA

FOREST

MARINETTE

St CROIX

DUNN

CHIPPEWA

LINCOLN

LANGLADE

PIERCE

EAU CLAIRE

CLARK

TAYLOR

MARATHON

MENOMINEE

OCONTO

PEPIN

CRAWFORD

SHAWANO

BUFFALO

JACKSON

WOOD

PORTAGE

BROWN

WAUPACA

BROWN

Green Bay

TREMPEALEAU

WAUSHARA

OUTAGAMIE

MENOMINEE

LaCROSSE

JUNEAU

ADAMS

WINNEBAGO

CALUMET

MANITOWOC

DOOR

MONROE

MARQUETTE

GREEN
LAKE

FOND DU LAC

SHEBOYGAN

VERNON

SAUK

COLUMBIA

DODGE

OZAUKEE

RICHLAND

WASHINGTON

CRAWFORD

DANE

JEFFERSON

WAUKESHA

MILWAUKEE

IOWA

GRANT

LAFAYETTE

GREEN

ROCK

WALWORTH

RACINE

KENOSHA

Lake Michigan

Mississippi River

Missouri

Territory

Prairie du Chien

IL

Missouri Territory *(on map, left side)*

*NOTES:

Nearly the whole 1790–1810 white population in present-day Wisconsin lived in
the villages of Green Bay and Prairie
du Chien. Wisconsin in 1790 was still under
British occupation. The villages were part
of Indiana Territory in 1800, but their
population lists for that census are lost.
In 1810, Wisconsin was part of St. Clair
County, Illinois Territory, whose 1810 schedule is lost.

Lead mines in the southwestern corner
of Wisconsin required an 1804 Indian cession
but most of the state remained unceded
until 1825–1848. Nearly all whites lived
in Green Bay (Brown County) and Prairie
du Chien and the lead mines (Crawford
County) in 1820.

The Michigan county of Michilimackinac
in 1820 extended across northern Wisconsin,
roughly north of the Lake Superior-Missis-
sippi River divide. The area was Indian
lands in 1820 but possibly a few traders
there were enumerated in the census.

CENSUS AVAILABILITY

Federal census extant for all counties.

Inset map (top right):

Canada

MICHIGAN TERRITORY

ND

MN

SD

WISCONSIN

MI

Missouri

NE

IA
Territory

PA

KS

MO

IL

IN

OH

WV

VA

KY

VA

1820

1 2 3 4 5 6 7 8 9 10 11 12

25 0 25 50 75 100 MILES

WHITE = MODERN BOUNDARIES
BLACK = 1820 BOUNDARIES

Wisconsin ● 1820

AS PART OF MICHIGAN TERRITORY

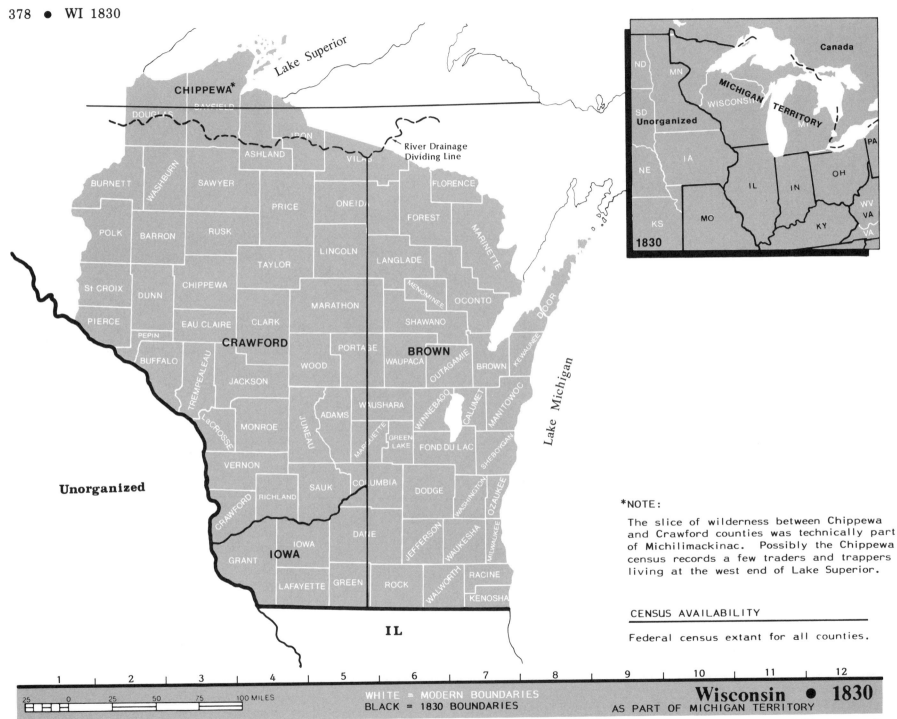

Lake Superior

CHIPPEWA*

DOUGLAS

BAYFIELD

ASHLAND

IRON

VILAS

River Drainage
Dividing Line

FLORENCE

BURNETT WASHBURN SAWYER PRICE ONEIDA

FOREST

MARINETTE

POLK BARRON RUSK LINCOLN LANGLADE

PIERCE

St CROIX DUNN CHIPPEWA TAYLOR

MENOMINEE OCONTO

MARATHON

EAU CLAIRE CLARK SHAWANO

PEPIN

CRAWFORD PORTAGE BROWN

DOOR

BUFFALO WOOD WAUPACA

TREMPEALEAU JACKSON OUTAGAMIE BROWN KEWAUNEE

LaCROSSE WAUSHARA

MARQUETTE

WINNEBAGO CALUMET MANITOWOC

Lake Michigan

MONROE JUNEAU ADAMS

GREEN
LAKE

FOND DU LAC SHEBOYGAN

Unorganized

VERNON

SAUK COLUMBIA

DODGE WASHINGTON OZAUKEE

CRAWFORD RICHLAND

DANE

JEFFERSON WAUKESHA MILWAUKEE

IOWA

GRANT IOWA

WALWORTH RACINE

LAFAYETTE GREEN ROCK KENOSHA

IL

NOTE:

The slice of wilderness between Chippewa
and Crawford counties was technically part
of Michilimackinac. Possibly the Chippewa
census records a few traders and trappers
living at the west end of Lake Superior.

CENSUS AVAILABILITY

Federal census extant for all counties.

Canada

ND MN

MICHIGAN

SD WISCONSIN TERRITORY

Unorganized MI

NE IA

PA

KS MO IL IN OH WV
VA

KY VA

1830

1 2 3 4 5 6 7 8 9 10 11 12

25 0 25 50 75 100 MILES

WHITE = MODERN BOUNDARIES
BLACK = 1830 BOUNDARIES

Wisconsin ● 1830

AS PART OF MICHIGAN TERRITORY

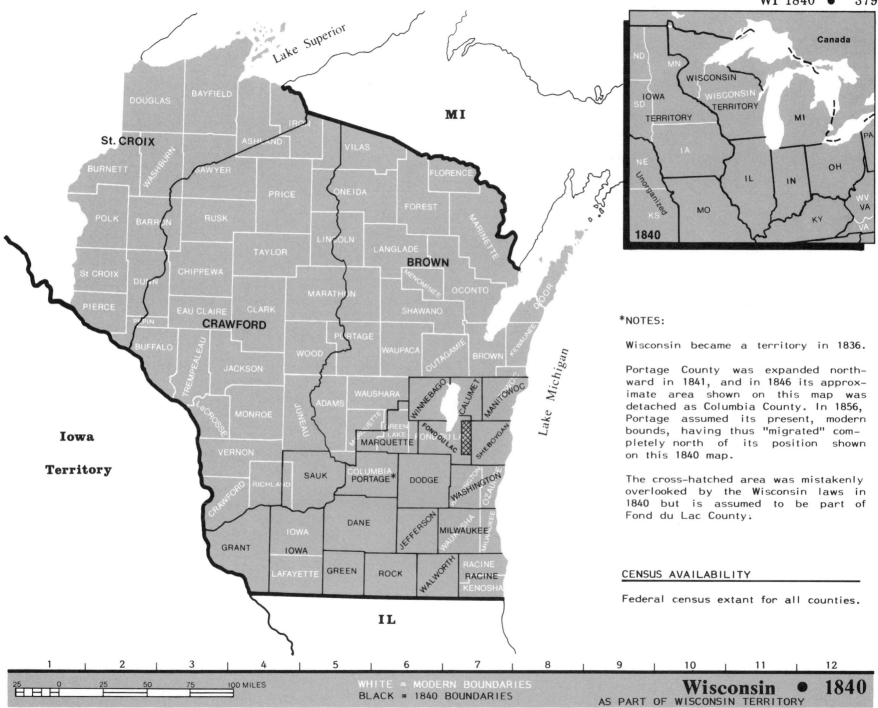

Lake Superior

MI

St. CROIX

DOUGLAS

BAYFIELD

ASHLAND

IRON

VILAS

FLORENCE

BURNETT

WASHBURN

SAWYER

PRICE

ONEIDA

FOREST

POLK

BARRON

RUSK

LINCOLN

LANGLADE

MARINETTE

St CROIX

DUNN

CHIPPEWA

TAYLOR

BROWN

MENOMINEE

OCONTO

PIERCE

EAU CLAIRE

CLARK

MARATHON

SHAWANO

DOOR

BUFFALO

CRAWFORD

PORTAGE

WOOD

WAUPACA

Lake Michigan

TREMPEALEAU

JACKSON

OUTAGAMIE

BROWN

KEWAUNEE

LaCROSSE

JUNEAU

WAUSHARA

WINNEBAGO

CALUMET

MANITOWOC

Iowa

MONROE

ADAMS

MARQUETTE

GREEN LAKE

FOND DU LAC

SHEBOYGAN

Territory

VERNON

MARQUETTE

RICHLAND

SAUK

COLUMBIA

PORTAGE*

DODGE

WASHINGTON

OZAUKEE

CRAWFORD

DANE

JEFFERSON

WAUKESHA

MILWAUKEE

IOWA

MILWAUKEE

GRANT

IOWA

LAFAYETTE

GREEN

ROCK

WALWORTH

RACINE

RACINE

KENOSHA

IL

*NOTES:

Wisconsin became a territory in 1836.

Portage County was expanded north-ward in 1841, and in 1846 its approx-imate area shown on this map was detached as Columbia County. In 1856, Portage assumed its present, modern bounds, having thus "migrated" com-pletely north of its position shown on this 1840 map.

The cross-hatched area was mistakenly overlooked by the Wisconsin laws in 1840 but is assumed to be part of Fond du Lac County.

CENSUS AVAILABILITY

Federal census extant for all counties.

Inset map: WISCONSIN, WISCONSIN TERRITORY, Canada, ND, MN, IOWA TERRITORY, SD, IA, NE, Unorganized KS, MO, IL, IN, MI, OH, PA, WV VA, KY, VA — 1840

1 2 3 4 5 6 7 8 9 10 11 12

25 0 25 50 75 100 MILES

WHITE = MODERN BOUNDARIES
BLACK = 1840 BOUNDARIES

Wisconsin ● 1840
AS PART OF WISCONSIN TERRITORY

MAP GUIDE TO THE U.S. FEDERAL CENSUSES, 1790-1920 by William Thorndale and William Dollarhide.   Copyright 1987, all rights reserved.

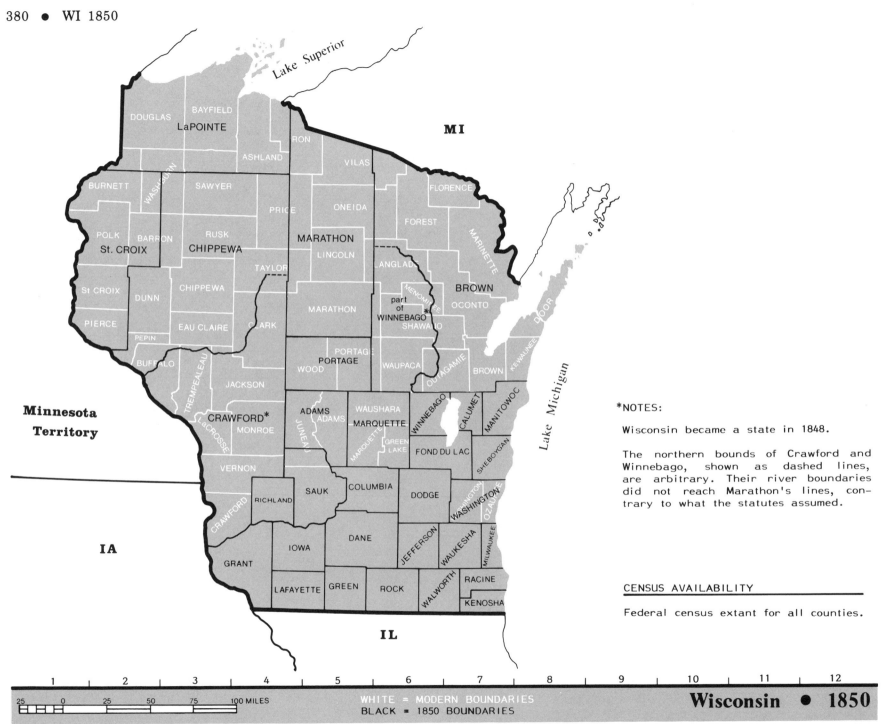

Lake Superior

MI

DOUGLAS

BAYFIELD

LaPOINTE

ASHLAND

RON

VILAS

BURNETT

WASHBURN

SAWYER

FLORENCE

POLK

BARRON

PRICE

ONEIDA

FOREST

St. CROIX

RUSK

CHIPPEWA

MARATHON

MARINETTE

LINCOLN

St CROIX

DUNN

CHIPPEWA

TAYLOR

LANGLADE

BROWN

PIERCE

EAU CLAIRE

CLARK

MARATHON

MENOMINEE

part of WINNEBAGO *

OCONTO

SHAWANO

PEPIN

PORTAGE

DOOR

BUFFALO

TREMPEALEAU

WOOD

PORTAGE

WAUPACA

OUTAGAMIE

BROWN

KEWAUNEE

JACKSON

LaCROSSE

Minnesota Territory

CRAWFORD *

MONROE

ADAMS

ADAMS

WAUSHARA

MARQUETTE

WINNEBAGO

CALUMET

MANITOWOC

Lake Michigan

JUNEAU

MARQUETTE

GREEN LAKE

FOND DU LAC

SHEBOYGAN

VERNON

IA

CRAWFORD

RICHLAND

SAUK

COLUMBIA

DODGE

WASHINGTON

OZAUKEE

MILWAUKEE

GRANT

IOWA

DANE

JEFFERSON

WAUKESHA

LAFAYETTE

GREEN

ROCK

WALWORTH

RACINE

KENOSHA

IL

*NOTES:

Wisconsin became a state in 1848.

The northern bounds of Crawford and Winnebago, shown as dashed lines, are arbitrary. Their river boundaries did not reach Marathon's lines, contrary to what the statutes assumed.

CENSUS AVAILABILITY

Federal census extant for all counties.

1 2 3 4 5 6 7 8 9 10 11 12

25 0 25 50 75 100 MILES

WHITE = MODERN BOUNDARIES
BLACK = 1850 BOUNDARIES

Wisconsin ● 1850

MAP GUIDE TO THE U.S. FEDERAL CENSUSES, 1790–1920 by William Thorndale and William Dollarhide.   Copyright 1987, all rights reserved.

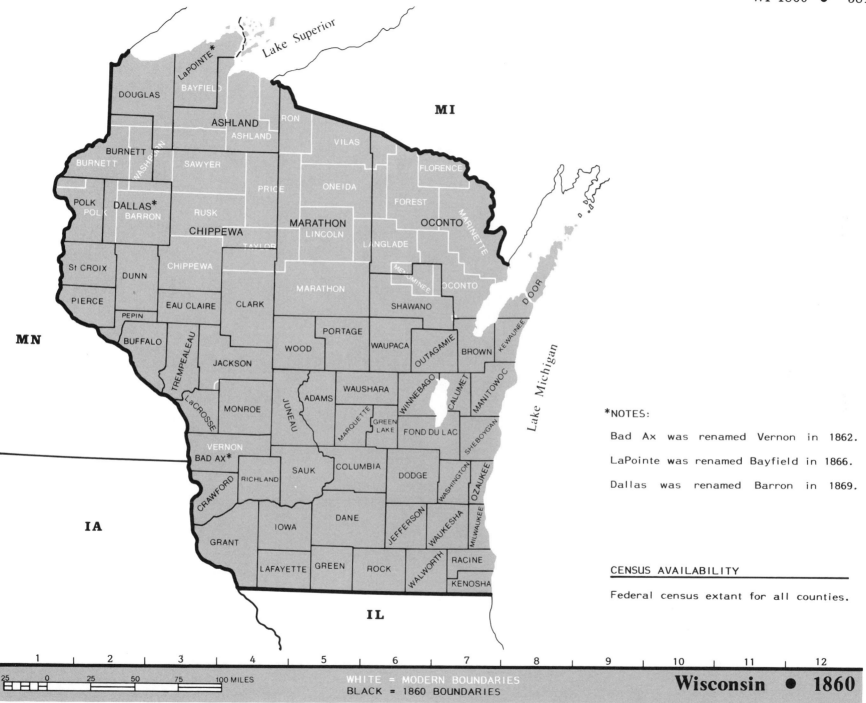

MI

MN

IA

IL

Lake Superior

Lake Michigan

DOUGLAS
LaPOINTE*
BAYFIELD
ASHLAND
ASHLAND
RON
VILAS
FLORENCE
BURNETT
BURNETT
WASHBURN
SAWYER
PRICE
ONEIDA
FOREST
MARINETTE
POLK
POLK
DALLAS*
BARRON
RUSK
MARATHON
LINCOLN
OCONTO
St CROIX
CHIPPEWA
TAYLOR
LANGLADE
DUNN
CHIPPEWA
MENOMINEE
OCONTO
PIERCE
EAU CLAIRE
CLARK
MARATHON
SHAWANO
DOOR
PEPIN
BUFFALO
TREMPEALEAU
JACKSON
WOOD
PORTAGE
WAUPACA
OUTAGAMIE
BROWN
KEWAUNEE
LaCROSSE
MONROE
JUNEAU
ADAMS
WAUSHARA
WINNEBAGO
CALUMET
MANITOWOC
MARQUETTE
GREEN LAKE
FOND DU LAC
SHEBOYGAN
VERNON
BAD AX*
SAUK
COLUMBIA
DODGE
WASHINGTON
OZAUKEE
CRAWFORD
RICHLAND
JEFFERSON
WAUKESHA
MILWAUKEE
IOWA
DANE
GRANT
LAFAYETTE
GREEN
ROCK
WALWORTH
RACINE
KENOSHA

*NOTES:

Bad Ax was renamed Vernon in 1862.

LaPointe was renamed Bayfield in 1866.

Dallas was renamed Barron in 1869.

CENSUS AVAILABILITY

Federal census extant for all counties.

1   2   3   4   5   6   7   8   9   10   11   12

25   0   25   50   75   100 MILES

WHITE = MODERN BOUNDARIES
BLACK = 1860 BOUNDARIES

Wisconsin ● **1860**

MAP GUIDE TO THE U.S FEDERAL CENSUSES, 1790–1920 by William Thorndale and William Dollarhide.   Copyright 1987, all rights reserved.

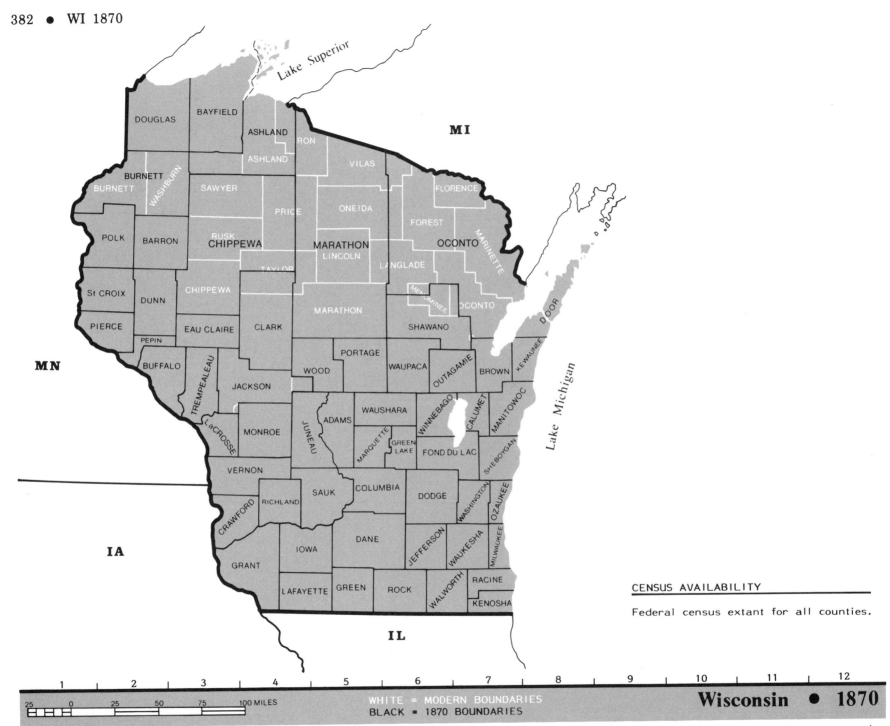

Lake Superior

MI

MN

IA

IL

Lake Michigan

DOUGLAS
BAYFIELD
ASHLAND
RON
ASHLAND
VILAS
BURNETT
BURNETT
WASHBURN
SAWYER
FLORENCE
POLK
BARRON
RUSK
PRICE
ONEIDA
FOREST
CHIPPEWA
MARATHON
OCONTO
MARINETTE
LINCOLN
St CROIX
DUNN
CHIPPEWA
TAYLOR
LANGLADE
MENOMINEE
OCONTO
PIERCE
EAU CLAIRE
CLARK
MARATHON
SHAWANO
DOOR
PEPIN
BUFFALO
TREMPEALEAU
JACKSON
WOOD
PORTAGE
WAUPACA
OUTAGAMIE
BROWN
KEWAUNEE
LaCROSSE
MONROE
JUNEAU
ADAMS
WAUSHARA
WINNEBAGO
CALUMET
MANITOWOC
MARQUETTE
GREEN LAKE
SHEBOYGAN
VERNON
SAUK
COLUMBIA
FOND DU LAC
DODGE
WASHINGTON
OZAUKEE
CRAWFORD
RICHLAND
JEFFERSON
WAUKESHA
MILWAUKEE
IOWA
DANE
GRANT
LAFAYETTE
GREEN
ROCK
WALWORTH
RACINE
KENOSHA

CENSUS AVAILABILITY

Federal census extant for all counties.

1   2   3   4   5   6   7   8   9   10   11   12

25   0   25   50   75   100 MILES

WHITE = MODERN BOUNDARIES
BLACK = 1870 BOUNDARIES

Wisconsin ● 1870

MAP GUIDE TO THE U.S. FEDERAL CENSUSES, 1790-1920 by William Thorndale and William Dollarhide. Copyright 1987, all rights reserved.

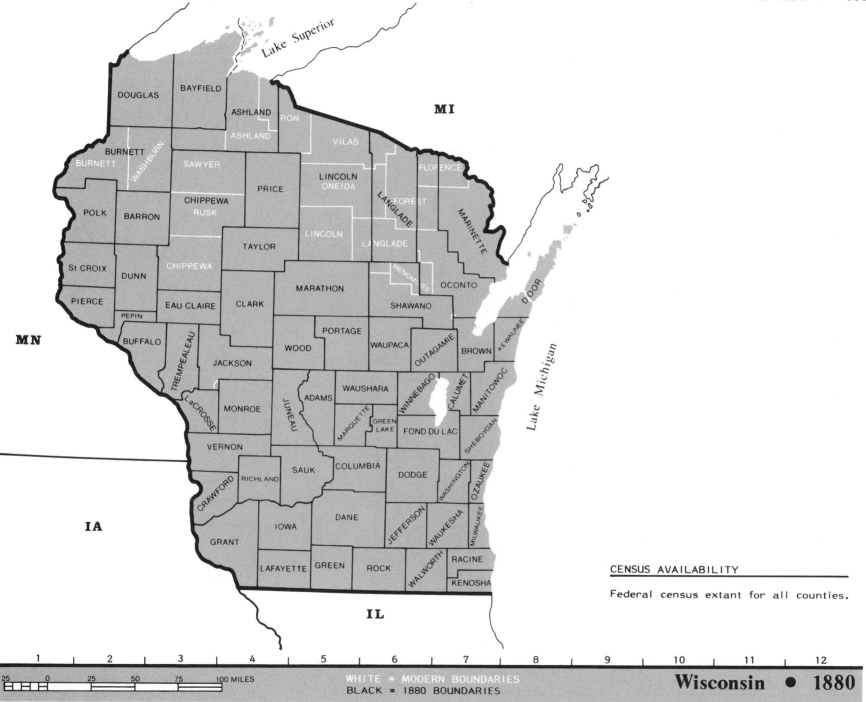

CENSUS AVAILABILITY

Federal census extant for all counties.

WHITE = MODERN BOUNDARIES
BLACK = 1880 BOUNDARIES

Wisconsin ● **1880**

MAP GUIDE TO THE U.S. FEDERAL CENSUSES, 1790–1920 by William Thorndale and William Dollarhide. Copyright 1987, all rights reserved.

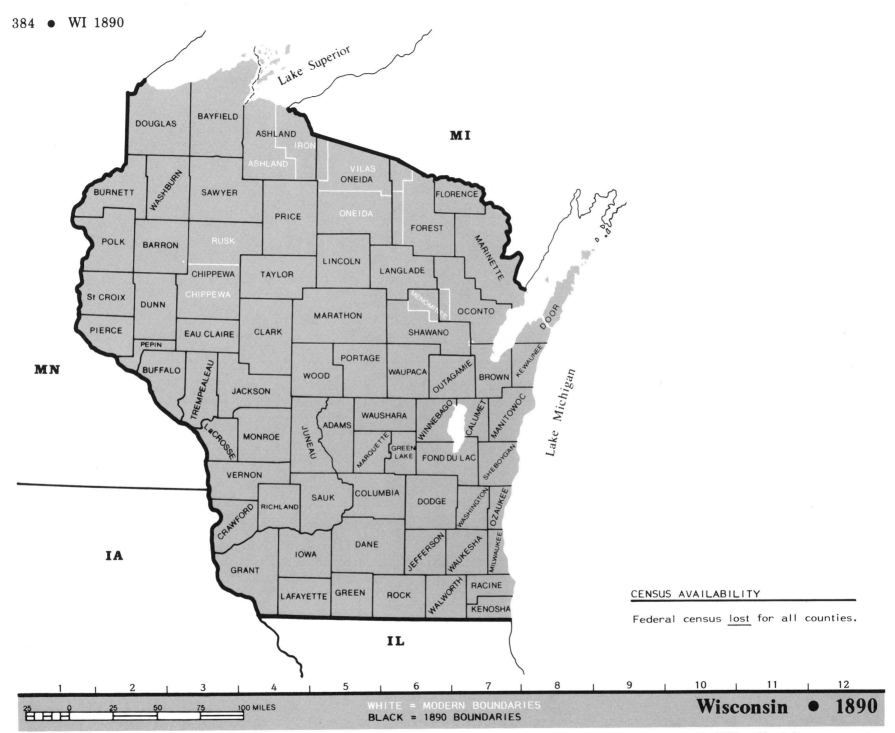

Lake Superior

MI

MN

IA

IL

Lake Michigan

DOUGLAS
BAYFIELD
ASHLAND
IRON
ASHLAND
VILAS
ONEIDA
BURNETT
WASHBURN
SAWYER
FLORENCE
ONEIDA
POLK
BARRON
PRICE
FOREST
MARINETTE
RUSK
LINCOLN
LANGLADE
St CROIX
DUNN
CHIPPEWA
TAYLOR
CHIPPEWA
MENOMINEE
OCONTO
PIERCE
EAU CLAIRE
CLARK
MARATHON
SHAWANO
PEPIN
DOOR
BUFFALO
TREMPEALEAU
JACKSON
PORTAGE
WOOD
WAUPACA
OUTAGAMIE
BROWN
KEWAUNEE
LaCROSSE
MONROE
JUNEAU
ADAMS
WAUSHARA
WINNEBAGO
CALUMET
MANITOWOC
MARQUETTE
GREEN
LAKE
FOND DU LAC
SHEBOYGAN
VERNON
CRAWFORD
RICHLAND
SAUK
COLUMBIA
DODGE
WASHINGTON
OZAUKEE
JEFFERSON
WAUKESHA
MILWAUKEE
IOWA
DANE
GRANT
WALWORTH
RACINE
LAFAYETTE
GREEN
ROCK
KENOSHA

CENSUS AVAILABILITY

Federal census lost for all counties.

1 2 3 4 5 6 7 8 9 10 11 12

25 0 25 50 75 100 MILES

WHITE = MODERN BOUNDARIES
BLACK = 1890 BOUNDARIES

Wisconsin ● **1890**

MAP GUIDE TO THE U.S. FEDERAL CENSUSES, 1790–1920 by William Thorndale and William Dollarhide. Copyright 1987, all rights reserved.

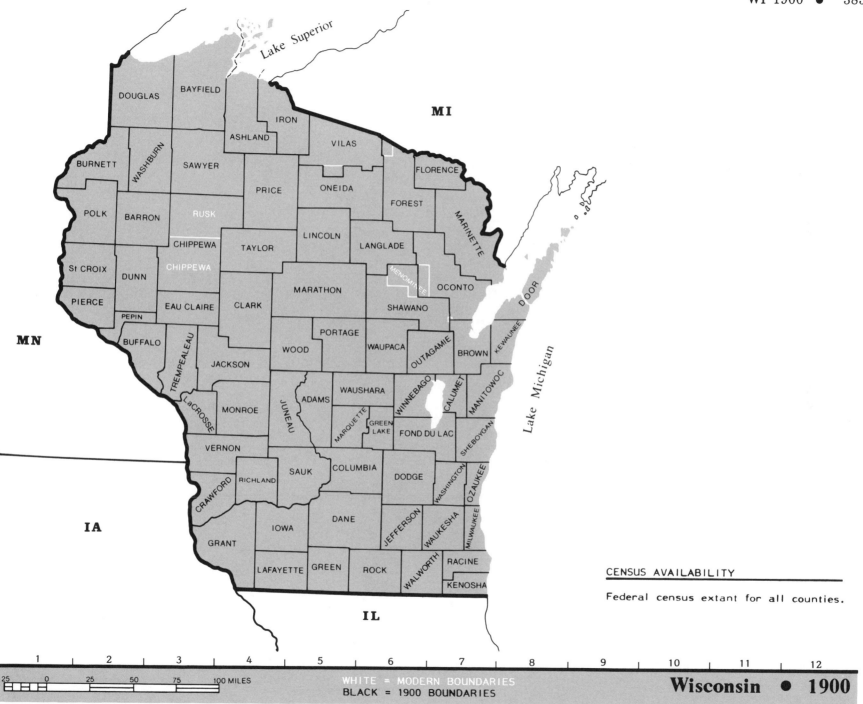

MN

MI

IA

IL

Lake Superior

Lake Michigan

DOUGLAS
BAYFIELD
IRON
ASHLAND
VILAS
FLORENCE
BURNETT
WASHBURN
SAWYER
PRICE
ONEIDA
FOREST
POLK
BARRON
RUSK
LINCOLN
LANGLADE
MARINETTE
St CROIX
DUNN
CHIPPEWA
CHIPPEWA
TAYLOR
MENOMINEE
OCONTO
PIERCE
EAU CLAIRE
CLARK
MARATHON
SHAWANO
PEPIN
BUFFALO
TREMPEALEAU
WOOD
PORTAGE
WAUPACA
OUTAGAMIE
BROWN
KEWAUNEE
DOOR
JACKSON
LaCROSSE
MONROE
JUNEAU
ADAMS
WAUSHARA
WINNEBAGO
CALUMET
MANITOWOC
MARQUETTE
GREEN LAKE
VERNON
FOND DU LAC
SHEBOYGAN
SAUK
COLUMBIA
DODGE
WASHINGTON
OZAUKEE
CRAWFORD
RICHLAND
IOWA
DANE
JEFFERSON
WAUKESHA
MILWAUKEE
GRANT
LAFAYETTE
GREEN
ROCK
WALWORTH
RACINE
KENOSHA

CENSUS AVAILABILITY

Federal census extant for all counties.

1 2 3 4 5 6 7 8 9 10 11 12

25 0 25 50 75 100 MILES

WHITE = MODERN BOUNDARIES
BLACK = 1900 BOUNDARIES

Wisconsin ● 1900

MAP GUIDE TO THE U.S. FEDERAL CENSUSES, 1790–1920 by William Thorndale and William Dollarhide. Copyright 1987, all rights reserved.

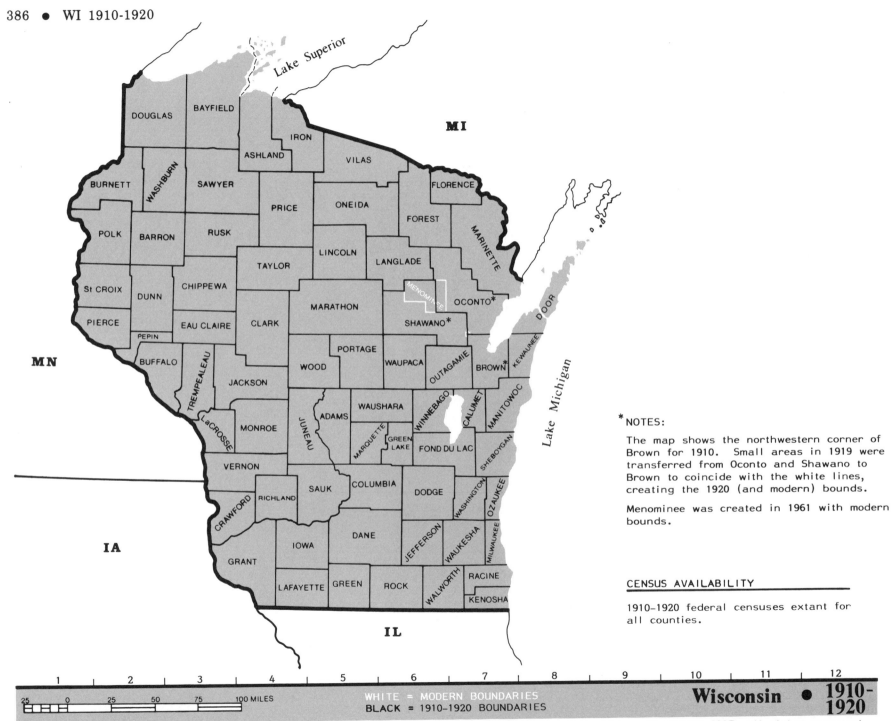

Lake Superior

MI

DOUGLAS

BAYFIELD

IRON

ASHLAND

VILAS

BURNETT

WASHBURN

SAWYER

FLORENCE

PRICE

ONEIDA

FOREST

POLK

BARRON

RUSK

MARINETTE

LINCOLN

LANGLADE

TAYLOR

St CROIX

DUNN

CHIPPEWA

MENOMINEE

OCONTO*

MARATHON

SHAWANO*

DOOR

PIERCE

EAU CLAIRE

CLARK

PEPIN

PORTAGE

MN

BUFFALO

TREMPEALEAU

JACKSON

WOOD

WAUPACA

OUTAGAMIE

BROWN*

KEWAUNEE

Lake Michigan

LaCROSSE

MONROE

JUNEAU

ADAMS

WAUSHARA

WINNEBAGO

CALUMET

MANITOWOC

MARQUETTE

GREEN LAKE

VERNON

FOND DU LAC

SHEBOYGAN

CRAWFORD

RICHLAND

SAUK

COLUMBIA

DODGE

WASHINGTON

OZAUKEE

IA

DANE

JEFFERSON

WAUKESHA

MILWAUKEE

GRANT

IOWA

LAFAYETTE

GREEN

ROCK

WALWORTH

RACINE

KENOSHA

IL

*NOTES:

The map shows the northwestern corner of Brown for 1910. Small areas in 1919 were transferred from Oconto and Shawano to Brown to coincide with the white lines, creating the 1920 (and modern) bounds.

Menominee was created in 1961 with modern bounds.

CENSUS AVAILABILITY

1910-1920 federal censuses extant for all counties.

25 0 25 50 75 100 MILES

1 2 3 4 5 6 7 8 9 10 11 12

WHITE = MODERN BOUNDARIES
BLACK = 1910-1920 BOUNDARIES

Wisconsin ● **1910-1920**

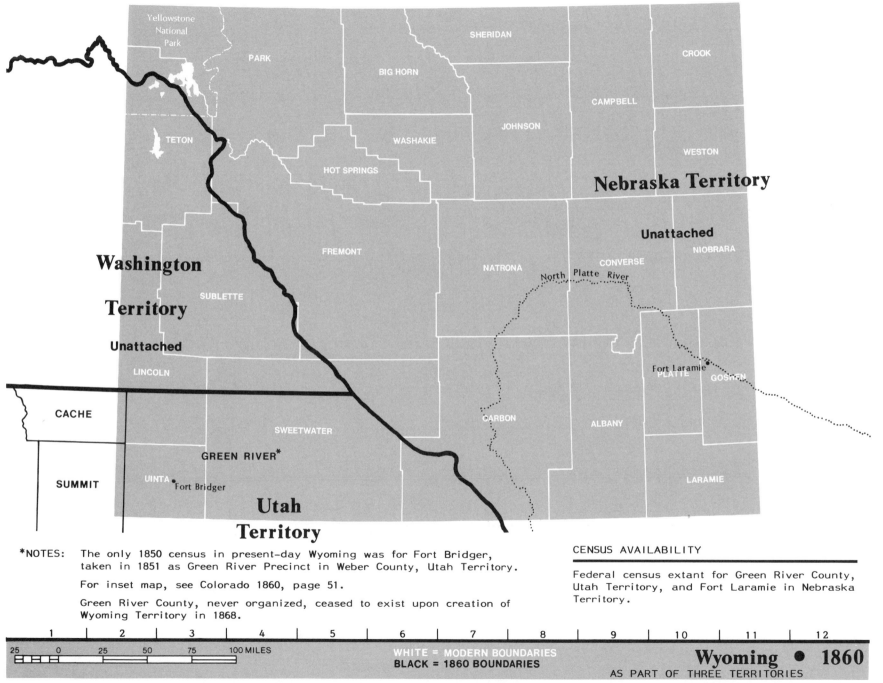

Yellowstone
National
Park

PARK

SHERIDAN

CROOK

TETON

BIG HORN

CAMPBELL

JOHNSON

WASHAKIE

WESTON

HOT SPRINGS

Nebraska Territory

Washington

FREMONT

Unattached

NIOBRARA

NATRONA

CONVERSE

Territory

North Platte River

SUBLETTE

Unattached

LINCOLN

Fort Laramie

PLATTE

GOSHEN

CACHE

SWEETWATER

CARBON

ALBANY

GREEN RIVER*

SUMMIT

UINTA ● Fort Bridger

LARAMIE

Utah

Territory

*NOTES: The only 1850 census in present–day Wyoming was for Fort Bridger,
taken in 1851 as Green River Precinct in Weber County, Utah Territory.

For inset map, see Colorado 1860, page 51.

Green River County, never organized, ceased to exist upon creation of
Wyoming Territory in 1868.

CENSUS AVAILABILITY

Federal census extant for Green River County,
Utah Territory, and Fort Laramie in Nebraska
Territory.

| 1 | 2 | 3 | 4 | 5 | 6 | 7 | 8 | 9 | 10 | 11 | 12 |

25 0   25   50   75   100 MILES

WHITE = MODERN BOUNDARIES
BLACK = 1860 BOUNDARIES

Wyoming ● 1860
AS PART OF THREE TERRITORIES

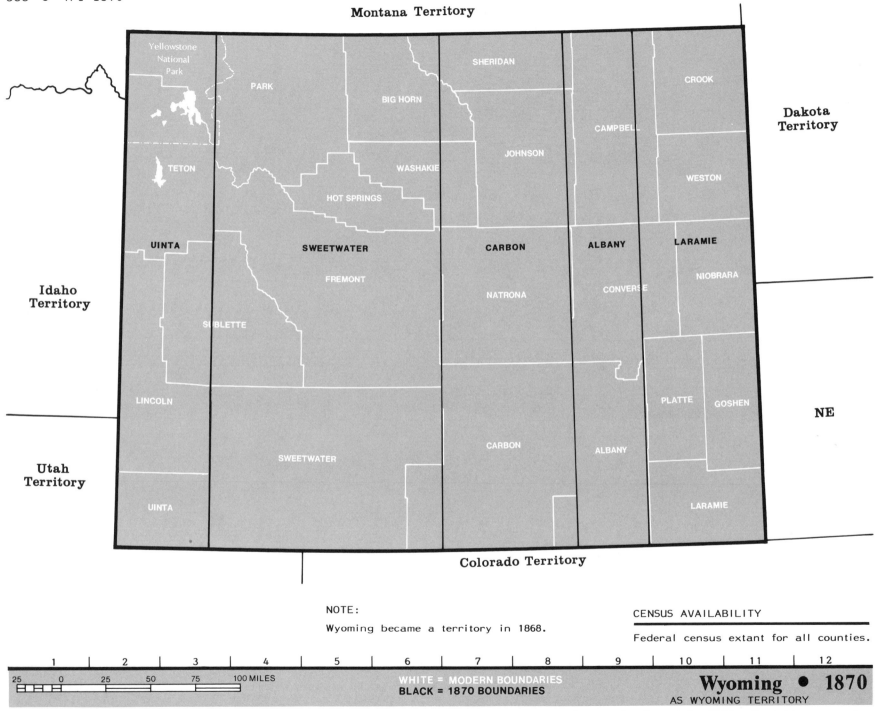

Montana Territory

Yellowstone National Park

PARK

SHERIDAN

CROOK

BIG HORN

CAMPBELL

Dakota Territory

TETON

WASHAKIE

JOHNSON

WESTON

HOT SPRINGS

UINTA

SWEETWATER

CARBON

ALBANY

LARAMIE

Idaho Territory

FREMONT

NIOBRARA

CONVERSE

NATRONA

SUBLETTE

LINCOLN

PLATTE

GOSHEN

NE

Utah Territory

SWEETWATER

CARBON

ALBANY

UINTA

LARAMIE

Colorado Territory

NOTE:

Wyoming became a territory in 1868.

CENSUS AVAILABILITY

Federal census extant for all counties.

| 1 | 2 | 3 | 4 | 5 | 6 | 7 | 8 | 9 | 10 | 11 | 12 |

25 0 25 50 75 100 MILES

WHITE = MODERN BOUNDARIES
BLACK = 1870 BOUNDARIES

Wyoming ● 1870

AS WYOMING TERRITORY

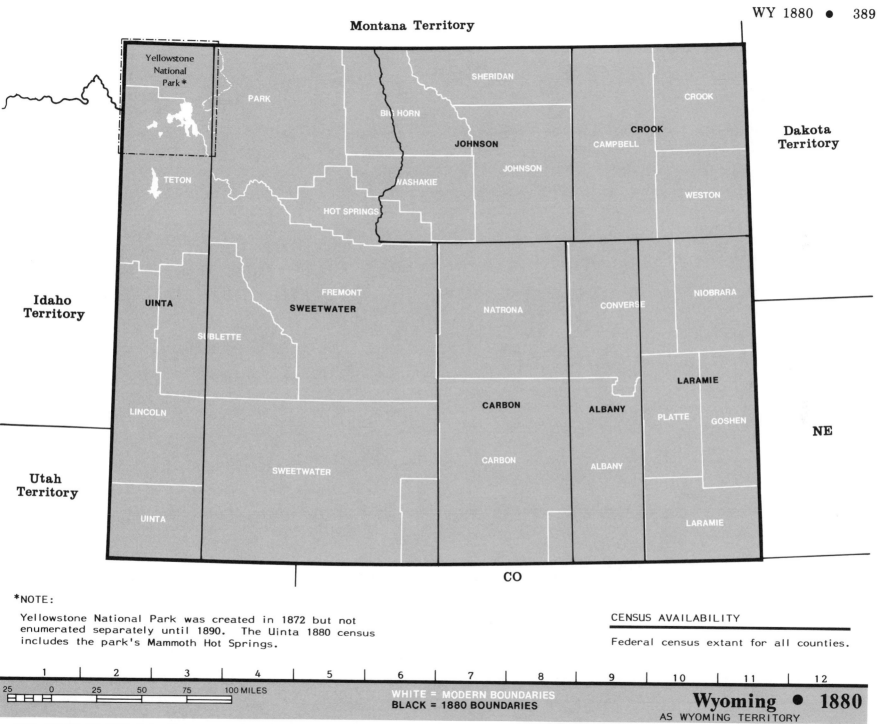

Montana Territory

Yellowstone
National
Park *

PARK

SHERIDAN

CROOK

Dakota
Territory

BIG HORN

JOHNSON

CROOK

CAMPBELL

TETON

WASHAKIE

JOHNSON

WESTON

HOT SPRINGS

Idaho
Territory

UINTA

FREMONT

NIOBRARA

SWEETWATER

NATRONA

CONVERSE

SUBLETTE

LARAMIE

CARBON

ALBANY

PLATTE

GOSHEN

NE

LINCOLN

Utah
Territory

SWEETWATER

CARBON

ALBANY

UINTA

LARAMIE

CO

*NOTE:

Yellowstone National Park was created in 1872 but not
enumerated separately until 1890. The Uinta 1880 census
includes the park's Mammoth Hot Springs.

CENSUS AVAILABILITY

Federal census extant for all counties.

| 1 | 2 | 3 | 4 | 5 | 6 | 7 | 8 | 9 | 10 | 11 | 12 |

25   0   25   50   75   100 MILES

WHITE = MODERN BOUNDARIES
BLACK = 1880 BOUNDARIES

Wyoming ● 1880
AS WYOMING TERRITORY

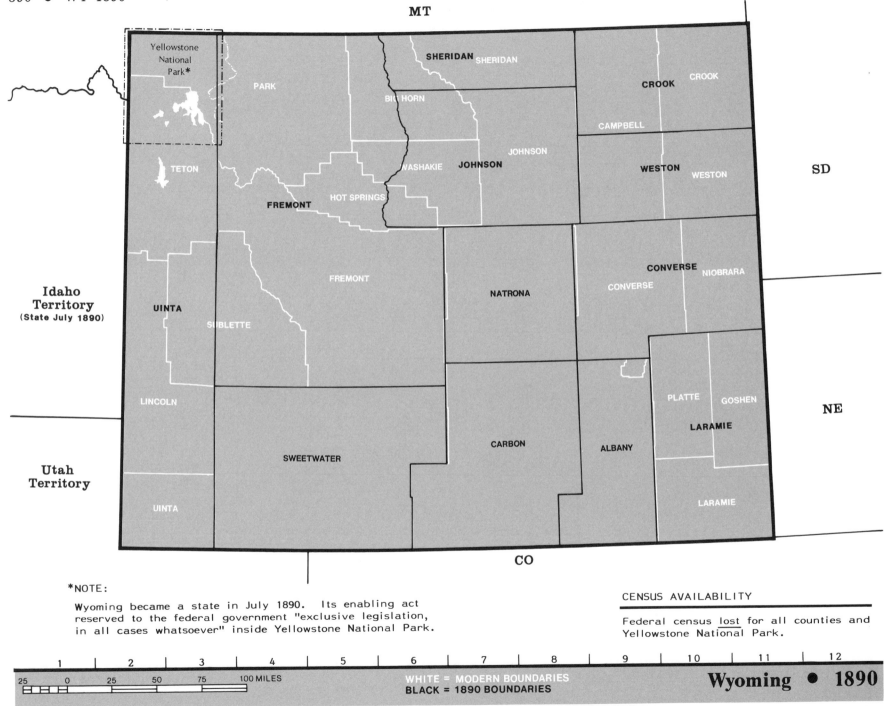

MT

Yellowstone
National
Park*

PARK

SHERIDAN SHERIDAN

CROOK CROOK

CAMPBELL

BIG HORN

TETON

WASHAKIE JOHNSON JOHNSON

WESTON WESTON

SD

FREMONT HOT SPRINGS

Idaho
Territory
(State July 1890)

FREMONT

CONVERSE NIOBRARA

CONVERSE

UINTA

SUBLETTE

NATRONA

LINCOLN

PLATTE GOSHEN

NE

LARAMIE

Utah
Territory

SWEETWATER

CARBON

ALBANY

UINTA

LARAMIE

CO

*NOTE:

Wyoming became a state in July 1890. Its enabling act
reserved to the federal government "exclusive legislation,
in all cases whatsoever" inside Yellowstone National Park.

CENSUS AVAILABILITY

Federal census lost for all counties and
Yellowstone National Park.

| 1 | 2 | 3 | 4 | 5 | 6 | 7 | 8 | 9 | 10 | 11 | 12 |

25 0 25 50 75 100 MILES

WHITE = MODERN BOUNDARIES
BLACK = 1890 BOUNDARIES

Wyoming ● 1890

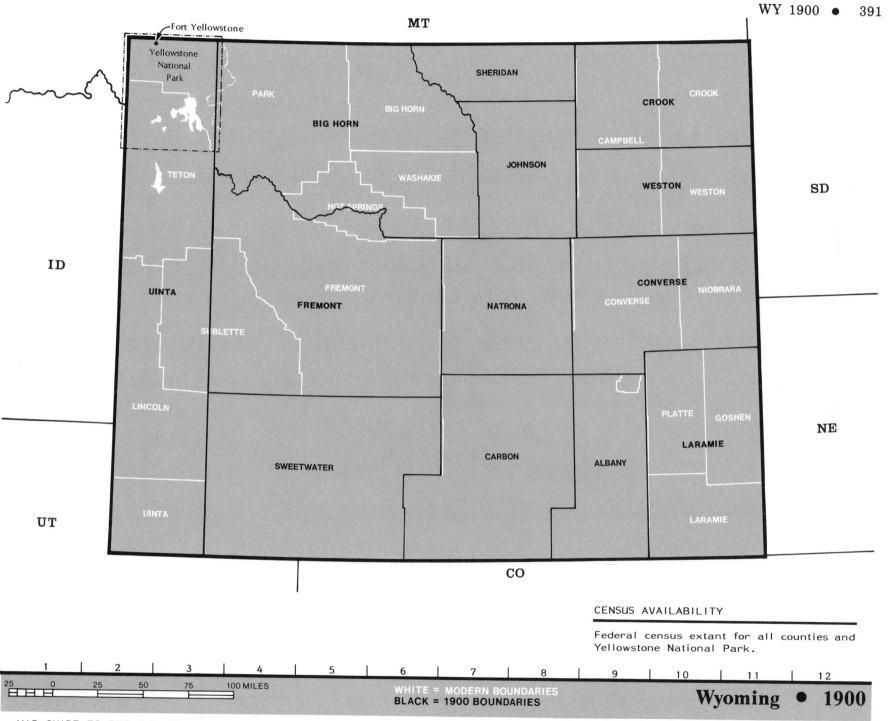

MT

Fort Yellowstone

Yellowstone
National
Park

SHERIDAN

CROOK

CROOK

PARK

BIG HORN

BIG HORN

CAMPBELL

BIG HORN

TETON

JOHNSON

WASHAKIE

WESTON

WESTON

ID

HOT SPRINGS

SD

UINTA

FREMONT

CONVERSE

NIOBRARA

FREMONT

NATRONA

CONVERSE

SUBLETTE

LINCOLN

PLATTE

GOSHEN

NE

LARAMIE

UINTA

SWEETWATER

CARBON

ALBANY

UT

UINTA

LARAMIE

CO

CENSUS AVAILABILITY

Federal census extant for all counties and
Yellowstone National Park.

| 1 | 2 | 3 | 4 | 5 | 6 | 7 | 8 | 9 | 10 | 11 | 12 |

25 0 25 50 75 100 MILES

WHITE = MODERN BOUNDARIES
BLACK = 1900 BOUNDARIES

Wyoming ● 1900

MAP GUIDE TO THE U.S. FEDERAL CENSUSES, 1790–1920 by William Thorndale and William Dollarhide. Copyright 1987, all rights reserved.

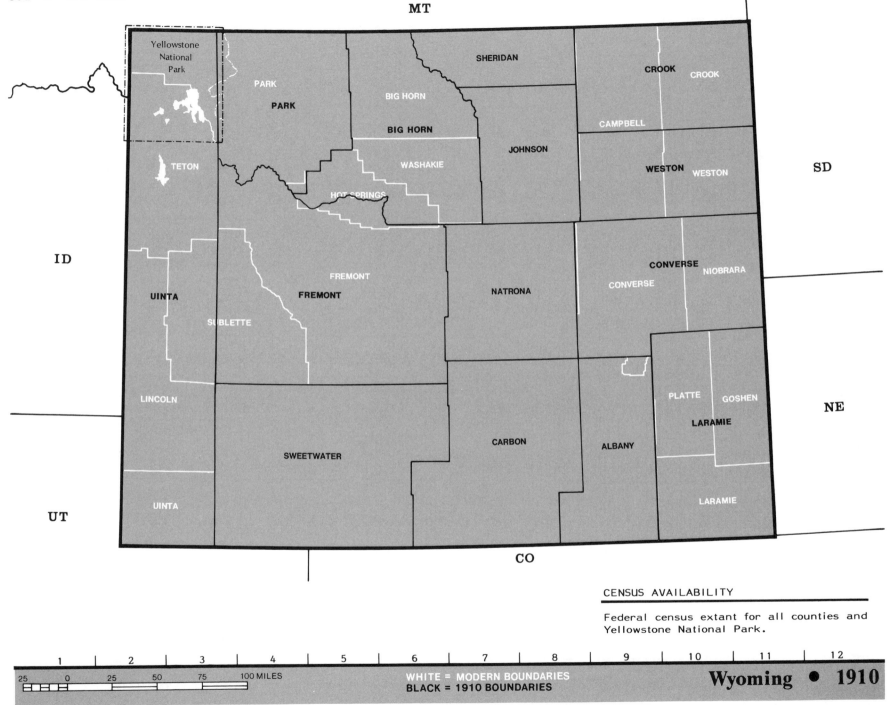

MT

Yellowstone National Park

PARK

PARK

SHERIDAN

BIG HORN

BIG HORN

WASHAKIE

HOT SPRINGS

JOHNSON

CROOK

CROOK

CAMPBELL

WESTON

WESTON

SD

TETON

ID

UINTA

FREMONT

FREMONT

SUBLETTE

NATRONA

CONVERSE

CONVERSE

NIOBRARA

LINCOLN

NE

SWEETWATER

CARBON

ALBANY

PLATTE

GOSHEN

LARAMIE

UINTA

LARAMIE

UT

CO

CENSUS AVAILABILITY

Federal census extant for all counties and Yellowstone National Park.

1   2   3   4   5   6   7   8   9   10   11   12

25   0   25   50   75   100 MILES

WHITE = MODERN BOUNDARIES
BLACK = 1910 BOUNDARIES

Wyoming ● 1910

MAP GUIDE TO THE U.S. FEDERAL CENSUSES, 1790–1920 by William Thorndale and William Dollarhide. Copyright 1987, all rights reserved.

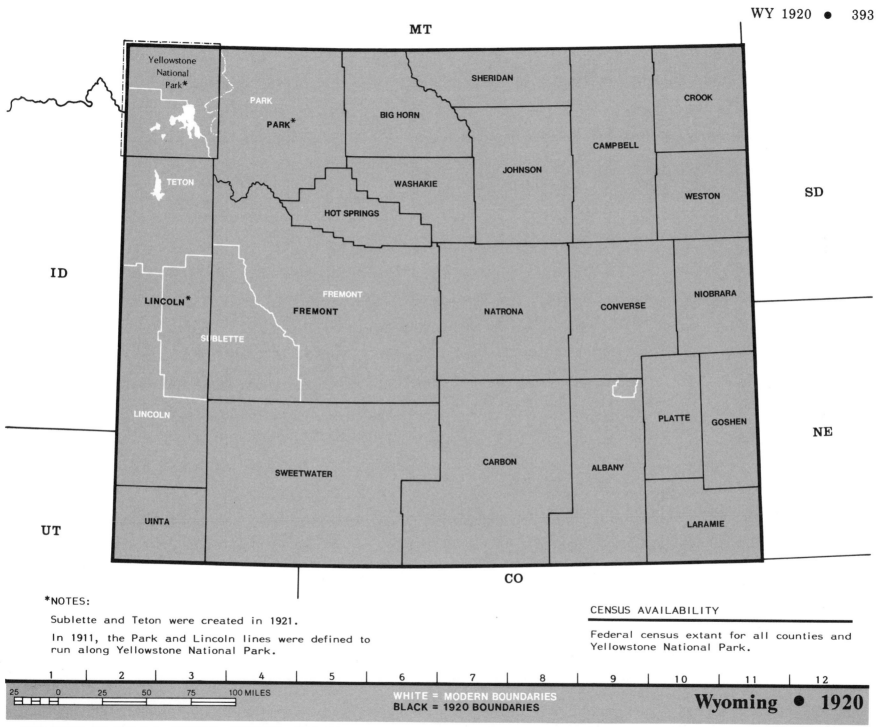

MT

Yellowstone National Park*

PARK

PARK*

SHERIDAN

CROOK

BIG HORN

CAMPBELL

TETON

JOHNSON

WASHAKIE

WESTON

SD

HOT SPRINGS

ID

FREMONT

FREMONT

NATRONA

CONVERSE

NIOBRARA

LINCOLN*

SUBLETTE

LINCOLN

PLATTE

GOSHEN

NE

SWEETWATER

CARBON

ALBANY

UINTA

LARAMIE

UT

CO

*NOTES:

Sublette and Teton were created in 1921.

In 1911, the Park and Lincoln lines were defined to run along Yellowstone National Park.

CENSUS AVAILABILITY

Federal census extant for all counties and Yellowstone National Park.

| 1 | 2 | 3 | 4 | 5 | 6 | 7 | 8 | 9 | 10 | 11 | 12 |

25 0 25 50 75 100 MILES

WHITE = MODERN BOUNDARIES
BLACK = 1920 BOUNDARIES

Wyoming ● 1920

MAP GUIDE TO THE U.S. FEDERAL CENSUSES, 1790–1920 by William Thorndale and William Dollarhide. Copyright 1987, all rights reserved.

Appendix

PITFALLS IN MAPPING BOUNDARIES

Over the 130 years covered by the *Map Guide,* there occurred many thousands of county boundary changes. Where to find descriptions of these boundaries is told in the bibliography. How to map the changes is mostly obvious, in theory: identify the boundary points on old and modern maps, and consult local histories and land ownership maps where necessary.

Nearly all county boundary changes were authorized by legislative acts. Legislatures being imperfect bodies, the wording and implementation of session laws can present difficulties, such as the following. Many of these potential pitfalls apply to state and territorial lines as well as county boundaries.

1. Boundary changes are not always clearly identified in the law's title, causing historians to miss some acts. The Desha-Drew county line was altered by section 16 of an act creating Lincoln County, Arkansas.[1] Prior to the reform constitution of 1874, a Pennsylvania law in its hodgepodge of unrelated subjects might hide boundary changes deep in the legislation.

2. A county's boundary may have been changed incidental to changing some other jurisdiction. A New England county could be defined merely by listing its component towns, so the county line would shift if a town line was altered along an adjoining county.

3. Some county changes were contingent on voter approval at a local election. Learning the results of such votes can be very difficult. Adjoining county governments sometimes had the authority to adjust their common boundary by mutual consent without notifying any state agency.

4. County boundary acts straddle the distinction between public and private/special acts, so both such sections in published session laws should be checked.

5. Indexes for pre-Civil War session laws may not be comprehensive and cannot be trusted. Short of examining every act, the researcher should at least read the title of each act and check all indexes.

6. Laws may contain typographical and publishing errors, especially in the early years when typesetters worked from longhand manuscripts. An 1829 Alabama boundary description refers to "Bigby" County when Sipsy was clearly intended.[2] An 1831 law for Midland County, Michigan, had ranges 2 and 3 *east* when west was meant, an error corrected statutorily only in 1873.[3] The modern line for Rosebud County, Montana, is range XLIV-XLV east, yet the 1907 Montana code had 14-15 east, an error in translating roman numerals.[4] Nebraska in 1881 passed a law legalizing Gosper County because the county had been functioning about eight years without a recorded creation act.[5]

7. Some defined boundaries were obscure, erroneous, or geographically impossible. A river might not run as far in a direction

as a law assumed, or legal boundaries might conflict. This latter problem sometimes caused compilers of state codes to abandon attempts to reconcile various boundary definitions. Another obscurity came from stipulating that a line should enclose some stated amount of area or population, with the surveying crew being directed to enclose "enough" area. [6]

8. The date of a boundary change may be obscure. The line may not have been surveyed, as when an act of 1845 was passed requiring the line be run between Franklin and Jefferson counties in Missouri pursuant to an 1835 act. [7] Some counties remained unorganized for many years and attached to organized counties. The census takers were inconsistent with such unorganized "paper" counties, sometimes treating them as parts of organized counties and sometimes enumerating them separately. In some early censuses on the Great Plains, the unorganized paper counties may be reported as having no population. Boundary changes just before the official day of the census raise the question of whether such changes were implemented before or after the census was taken. Through to 1900 the census day came in June or August, while legislatures in agrarian America avoided summer sessions and usually convened within months after the fall election. Therefore the *Map Guide* assumes the new boundaries passed by acts early in the year were in place by the summer censuses. Yet this could be wrong, as shown by McGee County, Kansas, which was renamed Cherokee by act of 18 February 1860 but appears as McGee in the 1860 census. [8] In 1870, the Tennessee legislature created Christiana County on 27 May—renamed Loudon almost immediately—five days before the census officially began, while Lake County was established two weeks later on 9 June. [9] Yet Lake appears in the census and Christiana/Loudon does not. The explanation may be that Christiana/Loudon required a survey to carve it from three East Tennessee counties, while Lake had the obvious bounds of all of Obion County west of Reelfoot Lake. In some states the local people simply failed to organize a new county, which had the effect of canceling the law. Crockett County, Tennessee, was created by law in 1845 but not organized until after another enabling act in 1871. This explains why Kane and Everton both erroneously show 1845 as the creation date for Crockett. [10]

9. A boundary act repealed after a few years, perhaps under pressure from irate constituents, requires answering or guessing whether the change was ever implemented. Sometimes more than twenty years passed before a change was repealed.

10. Surveyors may not have run the line as defined, as when magnetic north threw a survey line off the due-north direction. Southern Ohio counties still tilt east of true north due to a drifting compass. Yet in 1874 the Highland-Brown line was resurveyed to erase that old five-degree error. [11]

11. The location of some lines may be obvious to modern researchers but not to surveyors of a hundred years ago. Florida's town of Bowling Green lies just south of township 32 south and therefore outside Polk County. Yet maps and censuses around 1900 treated the area as inside Polk despite the county line and the town site not having moved, the county line being unchanged since 1861. [12] By contrast, a local road or mill would have been an obvious boundary point to residents a hundred years ago but possibly a mystery to the modern researcher. The tangled Appalachian terrain from Pennsylvania to Alabama confused legislators, who often opted for early county lines running from one settler's cabin to another's mill, forge, or other local improvement. Such ephemeral sites can now be very difficult to locate on a modern map.

12. In the middle decades of the nineteenth century the longitude of Washington, D.C., was thought to lie exactly seventy-seven degrees west of Greenwich. Boundary laws—especially for the Western states—might use the two longitudes interchangeably despite an actual difference of three miles, with Washington lines lying west of Greenwich lines. This caused inhabitants of a three-mile strip on the western slope of the Tetons to wonder if they lived in Idaho or Wyoming. [13]

13. A defined location may have had a meaning different from modern usage. Did the "head" of a river mean the fountainhead, the head of navigation, or the confluence of prominent forks on the upper river? In North Dakota the modern 14th Guide Meridian used to be the 13th G.M., and the present 13th G.M. was then the

13th Auxiliary G.M.

These boundary ambiguities do not affect all states equally. The most difficult state by a wide margin for the *Map Guide* was Tennessee, where cumulative obscurities and endless boundary adjustments combined to create hundreds of lines that still remain imprecisely located. The metes and bounds surveys of Middle and East Tennessee led legislators to define parts of many county lines in terms of farm boundaries. So numerous were transfers of farms and whole blocks of farms between counties that legislators coined the term "liners" for such farms. [14] By contrast, West Tennessee was surveyed early into districts and ranges, allowing simple definitions of county lines that were rarely altered.

Compounding the obscurity of Middle and East Tennessee lines were the complex Appalachian topography and the primitive level of Tennessee cartography. The 1916 edition of the Tennessee map of 1:1,000,000 made by the U.S. Geological Survey has some creek systems five and ten miles out of place, which greatly impedes reliance on that map's county lines. The absence of an accessible map collection at the Tennessee State Library and Archives also stymied research, so that finally the early state maps had to be consulted at the Library of Congress. Unfortunately, Tennessee has few early county maps and few county histories that discuss boundary changes. These abnormally imprecise sources make the *Map Guide* for Tennessee east of the Tennessee River less reliable than for the rest of the nation.

The difference between Tennessee east and west of the Tennessee River typifies a general principle of mapping old county lines: there is no standard approach to working out the boundary changes. Mississippi's county lines for the *Map Guide* were drawn over one long weekend starting with the earliest boundary law of 1799 and proceeding chronologically up to 1920. All modern lines were obtained, except for one township being out of place. For some states it was easier to work backwards from modern bounds. For others the state was divided into sections along old county lines that still survive, each section being unraveled separately working forwards, backwards, or both ways from the middle years.

Photocopies of old maps are essential. The collections at the LDS Genealogical Library and the University of Utah Marriott Library were used for most states for the *Map Guide,* though nearly three months were spent in map collections in Georgia, Kentucky, and Texas. Reconstructing old county boundaries is thus an eclectic procedure of experimenting with various ploys until a workable method is found for each individual state.

NOTES

1. Arkansas Laws 1871, 18th sess., no. 68, p. 331.

2. Alabama Laws 1829, 11th sess., p. 38.

3. Michigan Laws 1831, 4th leg., 2nd sess., p. 14, and 1873 sess., vol. 3, p. 85.

4. Montana Laws 1901, 7th sess., p. 97; E.C. Day, *Revised Codes of Montana of 1907* (Helena: State Publishing Co., 1908), p. 830.

5. Nebraska Laws 1881, 16th sess., ch. 36, p. 215.

6. Tennessee Laws 1819, 13th sess., ch. 146, p. 172; Arkansas Laws 1844, 5th sess., p. 77.

7. Missouri Laws 1844, 13th ass., 1st sess., p. 28.

8. Kansas Laws 1860, 6th sess., ch. 30, p. 68.

9. Tennessee Laws 1870, 36th ass., 2nd sess., ch. 2, p. 4; ch. 30, p. 56; ch. 77, p. 123.

10. Joseph Nathan Kane, *The American Counties,* 4th ed. (Metuchen, NJ: Scarecrow Press, 1983) p. 99; George B. Everton, Sr., *The Handy Book for Genealogists,* 7th ed. (Logan, UT: Everton Publishers, 1981), p. 270.

11. Randolph Chandler Downes, "Evolution of Ohio County Boundaries," *Ohio Archaeological and Historical Publications* 26 (1927), 446-49.

12. Our thanks to Hazel L. Bowman, Mulberry, Florida, for this example.

13. D. Brooks Green, "The Idaho-Wyoming Boundary: A Problem in Location," *Idaho Yesterdays* 23 (1979), 10-14.

14. Tennessee Laws 1871, 37th ass., ch. 14, p. 13, and 1873, 38th ass., ch. 70, p. 104.

Bibliography

NATIONAL PROJECTS

Three national projects have attempted a mapping of historical county boundaries. For an atlas never published, the Department of Agriculture created a set of U.S. maps showing all American counties at decennial intervals from 1840 to 1910, although the small scale negates much of their value.[1] For many years these maps existed only in photostatic copies. They are now available, with additional maps, in Thomas D. Rabenhorst et al., *Historical U.S. County Outline Map Collection, 1840-1980* (Baltimore: University of Maryland Baltimore County, Dept. of Geography, 1984).

The Historical Records Survey (Works Progress Administration), beginning in the late 1930s, mapped some county boundary evolutions which can be found in its published county inventories or among unpublished HRS papers. As an example of what may exist, there are twenty-four published volumes of Texas county inventories 1939-41, and they contain important maps working out boundary changes. Four additional counties have unpublished maps in the Texas HRS papers, but these maps are very preliminary in development.[2] For the location of HRS archives in the states, see Loretta L. Hefner, *The WPA Historical Records Survey: A Guide to the Unpublished Inventories, Indexes, and Transcripts* (Chicago: Society of American Archivists, 1980).

The national Historical Records Survey also attempted a mapping of county boundaries in its study of all roll-call votes in Congress, 1789-1941, a project said to have employed 350 persons at its height.[3] The HRS had to collect and map the state laws defining county lines, because congressional district boundaries usually ran along county lines. (Territories had no vote in Congress and therefore no part in the project.) Many of these county boundaries were sketched in small scale on tracing paper. The war stopped the project, so states vary greatly in the number of such working maps, with one map for Maryland, 140 for Kentucky, and none for most Western states. These crude maps are now in the Lord Collection, Record Group 69, in the National Archives' Cartographic Center, Alexandria, Virginia. The Lord Collection's collected session laws have significant gaps and must not be considered complete.

The third national undertaking was a series of three two-year projects funded by the National Endowment for the Humanities, 1975-82, and directed by John Long for the Newberry Library of Chicago.[4] The goal was to test the feasibility of creating a computerized database able to draw a county boundary for any particular day, a goal completed for fourteen states from Delaware west to the Dakotas. This covered nearly a third of the nation's counties. Based on statute laws, supplemented by old maps and local histories, the Newberry project is a model of precision in displaying former county lines. It also proved the prohibitive scope and cost of mapping former county boundaries. The project found that a computerized database was not conveniently accessible to most researchers, so maps were published in five volumes: John H. Long, ed., *Historical Atlas and Chronology of County*

Boundaries, 1788-1980 (Boston: G.K. Hall, 1984), vol. 1, Delaware, Maryland, New Jersey, Pennsylvania; vol. 2, Illinois, Indiana, Ohio; vol. 3, Michigan, Wisconsin; vol. 4, Iowa, Missouri; vol. 5, Minnesota, North Dakota, South Dakota.

A technical problem impairs some of the Newberry maps. The various boundaries are described by their statutory dates via letter codes, but inadequate editorial supervision led to misprinting some letter codes. As one example among many, a law of 11 January 1875 transferred area A out of Pratt County, South Dakota, yet the *Historical Atlas,* by incorrect coding, continues to show area A in the county until 1883. By contrast, the small-scale regional map for 1880 at the front of the volume gets the matter right. Allowing for this caveat, the Newberry/Long volumes are indispensable for the fourteen states they cover, not least for their boundary act citations and their extensive bibliographies.

GENERAL SOURCES

Mapping historical county lines must start with the boundary definitions in the session laws passed by legislatures. Maps of the early days cannot be trusted. Early map makers were often ignorant about topography and confused by the frequent changes in boundary laws. Unless the session laws are used, modern cartographic historians will make errors in reconstituting former county lines. Such pitfalls are seen in Stephen S. Birdsall and John W. Florin, *A Series of County Outline Maps of the Southeastern United States for the Period 1790-1860* (Chapel Hill: University of North Carolina, Dept. of Geography, 1973). These outline maps have the look of freehand compromises between modern boundaries and old maps. As an example, the nonexistent counties of Madison and Washington appear on the 1810 map for western Mississippi Territory, an error that the session laws would have exposed. By contrast, primary sources make highly credible the U.S. county boundary map of 1790 drawn for Lester J. Cappon et al., *Atlas of Early American History: The Revolutionary Era, 1760-1790* (Princeton: Princeton University Press, 1976), pp. 72-73, 134-35.

Nearly all state and territorial laws from 1775 are available on microfiche as *Session Laws in American States and Territories, 1775-1899* (Westport, CT: Redgrave Information Resources, n.d.). Similar microfiche reprints by Xerox and others continue the series from 1900 to the present. These RIR and Xerox collections omit session laws published only in compiled code books and not found in the usual separate session series. Researchers should therefore consult compiled statutory codes. Also, the codes sometimes collect and reconcile all county boundary descriptions and occasionally alter the lines without a new session law, though some states never put county boundary descriptions in their compiled codes. At present there is no microform collection of such codes for the fifty states. The standard listing of compiled session collections and statutory codes is Meira G. Pimsleur, *Checklists of Basic American Legal Publications* (South Hackensack, NJ: American Association of Law Libraries, 1962), with insert updates. Some session laws and codes are reprinted by Readex Microprint in the *Early American Imprints* series to 1820. Researchers of early session laws may find it more convenient to consult the microfilms by the Library of Congress of early state records, which are described in William Sumner Jenkins, ed., *A Guide to the Microfilm Collection of Early State Records* (Washington: Library of Congress, 1950, with 1951 supplement).

A few county lines were set by authority other than the legislatures of the states and territories. Federal session laws obviously established most state and territorial lines, as summarized in Franklin K. Van Zandt, *Boundaries of the United States and the Several States,* Geological Survey Professional Paper No. 909 (Washington: GPO, 1976). Also, five counties were the subject of federal acts.[5] Governors in early territorial years established or changed some county lines. Their proclamations may remain unpublished, but some are in Clarence E. Carter and John Porter Bloom, *Territorial Papers of the United States,* 28 vols. (Washington: GPO, 1934-75). A state or territorial constitution occasionally mandated the creation of a county. The constitutions appear in William F. Swindler, ed., *Sources and Documents of United States Constitutions,* 14 vols. to date (Dobbs Ferry, NY: Oceana Publications, 1973—in progress). Researchers doing a monographic study of a state's county boundary changes should also investigate court suits, however elusive. Cases ruling on the constitutionality of county enabling acts should be readily available in court reports and digests.

Some county boundaries were defined by survey grids and Indian treaty lines. For surveys, see C. Albert White, *A History of the Rectangular Survey System* (Washington: GPO, 1983?). The Indian treaty lines are listed and mapped in Charles C. Royce, *Indian Land Cessions in the United States* (Washington: GPO, 1900; reprint, New York: Arno Press, 1971). The maps in the original edition are in color and easier to understand. It might be noted that the federal censuses were instruments of the white government and assume the validity of the "cessions," irrespective of the Indian viewpoint. Part of the British proclamation line of 1763 (as later elaborated) continued into the 1800's to confine Southern counties and is traced in Louis DeVorsey, Jr., *The Indian Boundary in the Southern Colonies, 1763-1775* (Chapel Hill: University of North Carolina Press, 1961).

With their special interest in counties, federal census officials created some relevant records and maps, but these do little to clarify old county lines.[6] A local enumerator was far better placed than Washington officials to know or determine the county bounds around his district. So the Washington office maps of enumeration districts—the EDs being subdivisions first created during the 1880 reforms—were meant to divide a county so enumerators could be appointed to districts of convenient size. These ED maps do not show authoritative county lines. The surviving sketch maps—few for 1880 and 1890 but numerous thereafter—are listed in James Berton Rhoads and Charlotte M. Ashby, *Cartographic Records of the Bureau of the Census,* National Archives Preliminary Inventories No. 103 (Washington: NARS, 1958). The descriptions of ED lines are filmed in National Archives, "Descriptions of Census Enumeration Districts, 1830-1890 and 1910-1950," microfilm T1224, 146 rolls, and "Census Enumeration District Description Volumes for 1900," microfilm T1210, ten rolls. While incomplete for early decades, these listings of counties and enumeration districts show which counties the census officials thought existed.

Various studies and catalogs are available on aspects of U.S. censuses. Aside from references given in note 1 on page xxiii, additional published works on the censuses are listed in Ronald E. Grim, *Historical Geography of the United States: A Guide to Information Sources* (Detroit: Gale Research, 1982), pp. 95-100. Federal census publications are detailed in Henry J. Dubester, *Catalog of United States Census Publications 1790-1945* (New York: Greenwood Press, 1950). These publications are reprinted as National Archives, "Publications of the Bureau of the Census, 1790-1916," microfilm T825, forty-two rolls. Publications can also be located through *Bibliography and Reel Index: A Guide to the Microfilm Edition of U.S. Decennial Census Publications, 1790-1970* (Woodbridge, CT: Research Publications, 1978).

The extant microfilmed censuses are listed in three National Archives catalogs: *Federal Population Censuses, 1790-1890* (Washington: National Archives Trust Fund Board, 1979); *1900 Federal Population Census* (1978), and *The 1910 Federal Population Census* (1982). The *Map Guide* occasionally notes a territorial or state census taken in a decennial year where the federal name lists are lost. The standard though incomplete list of such nonfederal censuses is Henry J. Dubester, *State Censuses: An Annotated Bibliography of Censuses of Population Taken after the Year 1790 by States and Territories of the United States* (Washington: GPO, 1948; reprint, New York, Burt Franklin, 1967, with supplement). The published census data, but not the name lists, for Dubester's entries are collected on microfiche as listed in *Guide to State Censuses Microfiche Collection* (Millwood, NY: KTO Microform, n.d.). Many of these censuses were merely statistical and never had name lists.

STATE SOURCES

County lines for the *Map Guide* are drawn directly from original legislation for all states introduced below by the phrase "The session laws were read for..." and for states whose collected boundary acts have been published. The maps for the other states were adapted from cited available studies. Mostly not cited are county histories, compiled codes, county inventories of the Historical Records Survey, old maps, and studies on state boundary disputes. Outline maps exist for many states showing county evolutions, but their small scale and doubtful accuracy make them dubious sources. Copies of such maps were collected but rarely consulted. Exceptions are acknowledged below.

This disavowal does not include the authoritative Newberry project, cited below as Long, *Historical Atlas*. Published after most of the analogous *Map Guide* maps were done, the Newberry project provided an independent check on accuracy and inspired some corrections. But the *Map Guide* and the Newberry maps can legitimately differ because of the inconsistent way census takers recognized or ignored unorganized paper counties. Also, the *Map Guide*, with its census orientation, often excludes unceded Indian lands from frontier counties, and this despite legislation grandly extending frontier counties over vast areas controlled by Indians.

Alabama

The session laws were read for 1798-1816 Mississippi and 1816-1920 Alabama. Outline maps exist in Donald B. Dodd, *Historical Atlas of Alabama* (University, AL: University of Alabama Press, 1974). Jefferson and Marion counties are not in the federal 1820 population statistics.[7]

Alaska

The census takers, in the absence of counties in Alaska, had to create or make do with other lines. The 1880 enumeration areas can be identified by the village lists in Census Office, *Statistics of the Population of the United States at the Tenth Census (June 1, 1880)* (Washington: GPO, 1883) I:695-99. The 1890 census boundaries are described in Census Office, *Compendium of the Eleventh Census: 1890*, pt. 1, Population (Washington: GPO, 1892), p. cxxvi. Alaska enumerators first used schedule forms in the 1890 census. The two large districts of 1900 and some brief notes on earlier Alaska censuses are given in Census Office, *Twelfth Census of the United States*, vol. 2, Population, pt. 2 (Washington: GPO, 1902), pp. ccxiv-ccxv. The Alaska federal judicial divisions from March 1909 to March 1921 are defined in 35 Stat. 838, ch. 269, sec. 2. The 1870 and 1880 census name lists for Sitka are respectively in U.S. Congress, *House Executive*

Documents no. 5, 42nd Cong., 1st sess., pp. 13-26, serial 1470, and *Senate Executive Documents* no. 71, 47th Cong., 1st sess., pp. 34-37, serial 1989.

Arizona

The session laws were read for 1851-64 New Mexico and 1864-99 Arizona and compared with the Arizona codes of 1901, 1913, and 1928. Ten county boundary maps 1864-1909 are in George H. Kelly, *Legislative History. Arizona, 1864-1912* (Phoenix: The Manufacturing Stationers, 1926). See also, Henry P. Walker and Don Bufkin, *Historical Atlas of Arizona* (Norman: University of Oklahoma Press, 1979), maps 29-32. The 1864 census was taken pursuant to 9 Stat. 448, 9 September 1850, and 12 Stat. 665, 24 February 1863.

Arkansas

The session laws were read for 1806-18 Missouri and 1818-1920 Arkansas. Some notes on counties, without maps, are in John Hugh Reynolds, "County Offices," *Publications of the Arkansas Historical Association* 1 (1906), 127-39. Old Miller County is described in Rex W. Strickland, "Miller County, Arkansas Territory, the Frontier That Men Forgot," *Chronicles of Oklahoma* 18 (1940), 12-34, 154-70; 19 (1941), 37-54.

California

The California Historical Survey Commission authoritatively mapped the county line changes in Owen C. Coy, *California County Boundaries: A Study of the Division of the State into Counties and the Subsequent Changes in Their Boundaries* (Berkeley: California Historical Survey Commission, 1923). Outline maps are in Warren A. Beck and Ynez D. Haase, *Historical Atlas of California* (Norman: University of Oklahoma Press, 1974), maps 61-64.

Colorado

The county lines are analyzed and mapped in Frederic L. Paxson, "The County Boundaries of Colorado," *Colorado University Studies* 3 no. 4 (1905), 197-216. The session laws were read for 1903-19. There are good outline maps by decades for 1880-1930 in Colorado Water Conservation Board, Engineering Department, "Basic Maps of Colorado and History of Changes in County Boundaries" (unpublished, 15 May 1939), 16 pages. For notes on the Colorado portion of the Kansas 1860 census, see Clara Hamlett Robertson, *Kansas Territorial Settlers of 1860 Who Were Born in Tennessee, Virginia, North Carolina and South Carolina* (Baltimore: Genealogical Publishing Co., 1976). The court decision regarding North Park appears in 11 *Pacific Reporter* 193.

Connecticut

The session laws were read for 1776-1920. Useful for a Connecticut-Massachusetts boundary dispute in 1804 is Roland Mather Hooker, *Boundaries of Connecticut* (New Haven: Yale University Press, for the Tercentenary Commission, 1933).

Delaware

The Delaware codes of 1797, 1874, 1915, and 1974 reveal how constant the state's county lines have been. The only boundary change found 1790-1920 concerns an 1841 jog around Bombay Hook Island in the Kent-New Castle line, a change too small to map here.[8] The *Map Guide* has been collated with Long, *Historical Atlas.*

District of Columbia

The simple bounds of the district required no notable research. Those interested in details can consult Fred E. Woodward, "A Ramble Along the Boundary Stones of the District of Columbia with a Camera," *Records of the Columbia Historical Society* 10 (1907), 63-87, and Amos B. Casselman, "The Virginia Portion of the District of Columbia," ibid., 12 (1909), 115-41.

Florida

The session laws were read for 1822-1920. Outline maps are in Florida Works Progress Administration, "Development of Counties in Florida, 1820 to 1936" (unpublished single sheet, n.d.); Edward A. Fernald, *Atlas of Florida* (Tallahassee: Florida State University Foundation, 1981), pp. 130-31; and T. Stanton Dietrich, *The Urbanization of Florida's Population: An Historical Perspective of County Growth, 1830-1970* (Gainsville: University of Florida, Bureau of Economic and Business Research, 1978), pp. 13-22.

Georgia

Act citations for county boundaries are collected in Pat Bryant with Ingrid Shields, *Georgia Counties: Their Changing Boundaries,* 2nd ed. (Atlanta: State Printing Office, 1983). This work contains decennial outline maps 1790-1940, but the *Map Guide* follows the session laws. For old Walton County, see North Carolina below.

Hawaii

Hawaii's first constitutional counties date from July 1905. The natural boundaries of the islands make the counties easy to identify. Kalawao, created to help quarantine leprosy, continues as a valid county in the state's constitution.

Idaho

The session laws were read for 1854-63 Washington and 1863-1920 Idaho. An outline map for 1870 accompanies *Idaho Territory Federal Population Schedules and Mortality Schedules 1870* (Boise: Idaho Genealogical Society, 1973). See also, "Missing 1870 Census of Franklin and Bear Lake Counties, Idaho, Found in 1870 Census of Utah," *Idaho Genealogical Society Quarterly* 23 (July 1980), 10-page insert.

Illinois

Successive secretaries of state of Illinois have reissued a booklet abstracting the boundary laws and showing the line changes against modern maps. The reprint used here is Jim Edgar, *Origin and Evolution of Illinois Counties* (Springfield: State of Illinois, 1982). Because this booklet is less informative for changes after 1840, the cited laws were checked 1841-57 and the complete session laws were read for 1859-73, by which year the modern lines were in place. The *Map Guide* has been collated with Long, *Historical Atlas.*

Indiana

The county evolutions are mapped in George Pence and Nellie C. Armstrong, *Indiana Boundaries: Territory, State and County*, Indiana Historical Collections, vol. 19 (Indianapolis: Indiana Historical Bureau, 1933; reprinted, ibid., 1967). The *Map Guide* has been collated with Long, *Historical Atlas*.

Iowa

Frank Harmon Garver explained the county evolutions in "History of the Establishment of Counties in Iowa," *Iowa Journal of History and Politics* 6 (1908), 375-456, and "Boundary History of the Counties of Iowa," ibid., 7 (1909), 3-131. He also assessed the creation process in "A Critical Study of the Definition and Alteration of County Boundaries in Iowa and of the Laws by Which They Were Established," ibid., 7 (1909), 402-43. See also, Jacob A. Swisher, "History of the Organization of Counties in Iowa," ibid., 20 (1922), 483-576; John Ely Briggs, "County Evolution in 1839," *Palimpsest* 20 (1939), 93-104, and his "New Counties in 1843," ibid., 24 (1943), 365-76; and Jacob A Swisher, "Seven New Counties," ibid., 19 (1938), 22-30. The *Map Guide* has been collated with Long, *Historical Atlas*.

Kansas

The session laws were read for 1855-87, after which boundary changes were taken from Helen G. Gill, "The Establishment of Counties in Kansas," *Transactions of the Kansas State Historical Society* 8 (1903-4), 449-72. Outline maps are in Homer E. Socolofsky and Huber Self, *Historical Atlas of Kansas* (Norman: University of Oklahoma Press, 1972), maps 26, 38-41.

Kentucky

The session laws were read for 1775-92 Virginia and 1792-1920 Kentucky. A valuable set of twenty large-scale maps 1780-1912 for county lines was drawn about 1912 by the Agricultural and Industrial Development Board of Kentucky and the Department of Geography of the University of Kentucky. A blueprint set is available in the map library of the Kentucky Historical Society, Frankfort. Outline maps are in Wendell H. Rone, Sr., *An Histori-*

cal Atlas of Kentucky and Her Counties (Owensboro, KY: Progress Printing Co., 1965). Laws and maps are collected in Laura Brown Logan, "The Origin of the Counties of Kentucky" (M.A. thesis, University of Kentucky, 1951), but numerous acts are omitted without warning the reader.

Louisiana

The laws for parish boundaries are transcribed in Historical Records Survey, *County-Parish Boundaries in Louisiana* (New Orleans: Department of Archives, Louisiana State University, 1939), accompanied by untrustworthy maps. Few exact legal descriptions are known for the county and parish boundaries created in 1805 and 1807, as documented in Robert Dabney Calhoun, "The Origin and Early Development of County-Parish Government in Louisiana (1805-1845)," *Louisiana Historical Quarterly* 18 (1935), 56-160. Such early lines, especially for parishes down river from Pointe Coupee, were inferred from early maps as correlated with topography and later boundaries. For the American-Spanish dispute over southwestern Louisiana, see J. Villasana Haggard, "The Neutral Ground Between Louisiana and Texas," ibid., 28 (1945), 1001-1128.

Maine

The boundary laws are summarized without maps in Historical Records Survey, *Counties, Cities, Towns and Plantations of Maine: A Handbook of Incorporations, Dissolutions and Boundary Changes* (Augusta: Maine State Archives, 1982), printed from the 1940 typescript.

Maryland

The county evolutions are described and mapped in Edward B. Mathews, "The Counties of Maryland: Their Origin, Boundaries, and Election Districts," *Maryland Geological Survey* 6 (1906), 418-572. The counties had reached their modern boundaries by 1906, except for the annexations to Baltimore City, shown in Mary Ross Brown, *An Illustrated Genealogy of the Counties of Maryland and the District of Columbia as a Guide to Locating Records* (n.p.: the author, 1967), p. 64. The *Map Guide* has been collated with Long, *Historical Atlas*.

Massachusetts

Secretaries of the commonwealth have issued booklets listing dates for town and county boundary changes. The edition used here is Frederic W. Cook, *Historical Data Relating to Counties, Cities and Towns in Massachusetts* (Boston: Commonwealth of Massachusetts, 1948). Over the years 1898-1916 several commonwealth agencies published sixty-eight volumes of Massachusetts town atlases. These proved surprisingly unhelpful for the *Map Guide* but might aid a monographic study of Massachusetts local boundaries.

Michigan

County boundary acts are cited and most described in "Reports of Counties, Towns, and Districts," *Pioneer Collections. Report of the Pioneer Society of the State of Michigan* 1 (1877), 94-520; and William H. Hathaway, "County Organization in Michigan," *Michigan History Magazine* 2 (1918), 573-629, the latter with maps. The civil districts for 1810 are given in "Boundaries of Judicial Districts," in William Wirt Blume, *Transactions of the Supreme Court of the Territory of Michigan, 1805-1814* (Ann Arbor: University of Michigan Press, 1935), 1:3-4, with map. Richard W. Welch, *County Evolution in Michigan 1790-1897* (Lansing: Michigan Department of Education, State Library Services, 1972), is much less comprehensive for the texts of boundaries but adds information and corrects some errors in Hathaway's maps. The creation of each county is briefly sketched by William L. Jenks, "History and Meaning of the County Names of Michigan," *Michigan Pioneer and Historical Collections* 38 (1912), 439-78. Two volumes also useful are Joseph Druse, Mrs. H. E. Kappahahn, and Mrs. Melvin M. Ross, *Evolution of Michigan Townships* (Lansing: Mid-Michigan Genealogical Society, 1972); and Donna Valley Russell, *Michigan Censuses 1710-1830 under the French, British, and Americans* (Detroit: Detroit Society for Genealogical Research, 1982). The numbers from the 1 August 1800 census at Michilimackinac (Mackinac Island) have the look of estimates rather than actual counts. [9] The *Map Guide* has been collated with Long, *Historical Atlas.*

Minnesota

County evolutions are mapped in Mary Ellen Lewis, "The Establishment of County Boundaries in Minnesota" (M.A. thesis, University of Minnesota, 1946). Robert J. Forrest in his "Mythical Cities of Southwestern Minnesota," *Minnesota History* 14 (1933), 243-62, says part of the 1857 census is fraudulent, a charge seconded by Arthur Louis Finnell, "Southwest Minnesota's 1857 State Census: Notes on a Forgery," *Minnesota Genealogist* 17 (1986), 76-78. The 1857 census was taken pursuant to section 4, 11 Stat. 167, 26 February 1857. The *Map Guide* has been collated with Long, *Historical Atlas.*

Mississippi

County boundary laws are transcribed in Historical Records Survey, *State and County Boundaries of Mississippi* (Jackson: Mississippi Historical Records Survey, 1942).

Missouri

The session laws were read for 1813-1920. For the earlier territory of Louisiana, see Clarence E. Carter, *Territorial Papers of the United States,* vols. 13-14, Louisiana-Missouri Territory, 1803-1814 (Washington: GPO, 1948-49). Outline maps for early Missouri are in Marian M. Ohman, "Missouri County Organization, 1812-1876," *Missouri Historical Review* 76 (1981-82), 253-81. The *Map Guide* has been collated with Long, *Historical Atlas.*

Montana

The session laws were read for 1864-1921. Outline maps by Andy Spranger with E.L. Waldon appear in W.B. Clarke, *The Montana Title Association in Its Fiftieth Year* (Helena: Montana Title Association, 1958).

Nebraska

The session laws were read for 1855-1919. Credible outline maps are in Sylvia Nimmo, *Maps Showing the County Boundaries of Nebraska, 1854-1925* (Papillion, NE: the author, 1978). See also, Norma Kidd Green, "Ghost Counties of Nebraska," *Nebraska History* 43 (1962), 253-63.

Nevada

The session laws were read for 1851-61 Utah and 1861-1920 Nevada. Boundary changes are mapped in Stan Mottaz, "County Evolution in Nevada," *Nevada Historical Society Quarterly* 21 (1978), 25-50. Less systematic but worth consulting is Hugh A. Shamberger, "The Evolution of Nevada by Boundaries, with Name Places," in *Nevada, the Silver State* (Carson City, NV: Western States Historical Publishers, 1970), 1:145-49. See also, Donald Bufkin, "The Lost County of Pah-Ute." *Arizoniana: The Journal of Arizona History* 5 no. 2 (Summer 1964), 1-11.

New Hampshire

The session laws were read for 1783-1847 and compared with the compiled codes of 1867, 1891, and 1970.

New Jersey

The county lines are mapped in detail in John P. Snyder, *The Story of New Jersey's Civil Boundaries, 1606-1968*, Bulletin 67 (Trenton: Bureau of Geology and Topography, 1969). The *Map Guide* has been collated with Long, *Historical Atlas.*

New Mexico

The session laws were read for 1851-1920. The laws are also cited and mapped in Charles F. Coan, "The County Boundaries of New Mexico," *Southwestern Political Science Quarterly* 3 (1922), 252-86. The *Map Guide* interprets some of these boundary laws differently from Coan, as to a lesser extent do Warren A. Beck and Ynez D. Haase, *Historical Atlas of New Mexico* (Norman: University of Oklahoma Press, 1969), maps 41-51. The 1850 county boundaries are adapted from "Map of New Mexico, with Pueblos as Noted by Calhoun, 1850" in Annie Heloise Abel, ed., *The Official Correspondence of James S. Calhoun* (Washington: GPO, 1915), map pocket.

New York

The revised statutes of 1829 contain the last statutory consolidation of New York county boundary laws. The compilers of the 1918 code collected for each county the 1829 description and all subsequent statutes effecting changes: Robert C. Cumming and Frank B. Gilbert, eds., *Annotated Consolidation Laws of the State of New York as Amended to January 1, 1918,* 2nd ed. (New York: Banks Law Publishing Co., 1918), 7:8124-49. The session laws were read for 1788-1829 in conjunction with three laws consolidating county lines: *Laws of New York,* 1788, ch. 63, pp. 744-48; William P. Van Ness and John Woodworth, *Laws of the State of New York, Revised* (Albany: H.C. Southwick, 1813), ch. 39, 1:31-44; and B.F. Butler and John C. Spencer, *Revised Statutes of the State of New York* (Albany: Packard and Van Benthuysen, 1829), 3:1-19.

North Carolina

County boundary statutes are in David Leroy Corbitt, *The Formation of North Carolina Counties, 1663-1943* (Raleigh: State Department of Archives and History, 1950; reprint, ibid., 1975, with "Supplementary Data and Corrections"). Large-scale maps for all North Carolina counties have been published by Garland P. Stout, "Historical Research Maps: North Carolina Counties" (Greensboro, NC: G.P. Stout, 1972-80), 100 loose sheets. These were less helpful than the title might suggest, since Stout's interest lay in identifying early towns and roads rather than former boundary points. Outline maps are in Worth S. Ray, *Old Albemarle and Its Absentee Landlords,* Part IV of *Lost Tribes of North Carolina* (Austin, TX: the author, 1947; reprint, Baltimore: Genealogical Publishing Co., 1960); and Wallace R. Draughon and William Perry Johnson, *North Carolina Genealogical Reference,* 2nd ed. (Durham: Wallace R. Draughon, 1966), pp. 179-93. Georgia's old Walton County inside North Carolina is described in Robert Scott Davis, Jr., "The Settlement at the Head of the French Broad or the Bizarre Story of the First Walton County, Georgia," *North Carolina Genealogical Society Journal* 7 (1981), 62-74.

North Dakota

The session laws were read for 1862-89 Dakota Territory and 1889-99 North Dakota. The boundary changes are carefully traced in Luella J. Hall, "History of the Formation of Counties in North Dakota," *Collections of the State Historical Society [of North*

Dakota] 5 (1923), 169-250. The extant 1885 name lists appear in "The Dakota Territorial Census of 1885," *Collections of the State Historical Society of North Dakota* 4 (1913), 338-448. The *Map Guide* has been collated with Long, *Historical Atlas.*

Ohio

The laws on county lines are collected and mapped in Randolph Chandler Downes, "Evolution of Ohio County Boundaries," *Ohio Archaeological and Historical Quarterly* 36 (1927), 340-477. A discussion confined to pre-1803 counties is in J.F. Laning, "The Evolution of Ohio Counties," *Ohio Archaeological and Historical Publications* 5 (1898), 326-50. The *Map Guide* has been collated with Long, *Historical Atlas.*

Oklahoma

County boundaries in the territory and state of Oklahoma were set by the executive branch, not the legislative, and are not described in session laws and compiled codes. The county descriptions 1890-1906 should be in the papers of the territorial governors and the U.S. Interior secretaries, collections not searched for the *Map Guide.* A commission for each of the Twin Territories established the bounds for the new state's seventy-five counties, the lines being described in the 1907 state constitution. New counties and land transfers between counties since statehood are made by petition from the voters, the standard of permissible changes being severely restricted. The governor proclaims all changes approved by the voters of all counties affected. Only two new counties have been created since 1907—in 1909 and 1912—and less than a dozen minor boundary alterations have been adopted. Thus the absence of the usual session acts and codified laws for county boundary research is offset by the few lines changed.

The Oklahoma maps of the *Map Guide* are based mostly on secondary sources. The 1890 county lines are given in John W. Morris, ed., *Boundaries of Oklahoma* (Oklahoma City: Oklahoma Historical Society, 1980), pp. 118-19. Also used were John W. Morris, Charles R. Goins, and Edwin C. Reynolds, *Historical Atlas of Oklahoma,* 2nd ed. (Norman: University of Oklahoma Press, 1976); an 1890 map of Oklahoma in Census Bureau, *Report on*

Indians Taxed and Indians Not Taxed in the United States (Except Alaska) at the Eleventh Census: 1890 (Washington: GPO, 1894), following p. 242; and "Notes Regarding Changes in County Boundaries," in Bureau of the Census, *Fourteenth Census of the United States Taken in the Year 1920*, vol. 1, Population (Washington: GPO, 1921), p. 145.

The political districts and/or counties of the Five Civilized Tribes, excepting the Seminoles, were used as census subdivisions. Such boundaries are shown in the atlas by Morris et al. and on the Census Bureau's 1890 map, but these differ significantly between each other and with the subdivisions in the censuses. This imprecision and the lack of access to tribal records, including acts of tribal legislatures, explains the omission from the *Map Guide* of political subdivisions in the Indian Territory below the level of tribal nations.

Oregon

The session laws were read for 1843-1920. Background discussion and outline maps are in Frederick V. Holman, "Oregon Counties: Their Creations and the Origins of Their Names," *Quarterly of the Oregon Historical Society* 11 (1910), 1-81, 227; William G. Loy et al., *Atlas of Oregon* (Eugene: University of Oregon Press, 1976); and Erma Skyles Brown, *Oregon County Boundary Change Maps, 1843-1916* (Lebanon, OR: End of Trail Researchers, 1970). Something of the one defunct county is discussed in Verne Bright, "The Lost County, Umpqua, Oregon, and It's [sic] Early Settlements," *Oregon Historical Quarterly* 51 (1950), 111-26.

Pennsylvania

The session laws were read for 1776-1876. The reform constitution of 1874 says in Article 3, section 7: "The General Assembly shall not pass any local or special law ... locating or changing county seats, erecting new counties or changing county lines...." The only change in county boundaries found after this date was the creation of Lackawanna by court decree in 1878. Outline maps are in [William L. Iscrupe], *Pennsylvania Line: A Research Guide to Pennsylvania Genealogy and Local History,* 3rd ed. (Laughlintown, PA: Southwest Pennsylvania Genealogical Services, 1983), pp. 126-42; and Land Office Bureau, *Maps Showing the Development of Pennsylvania* (Harrisburg?: Department of Internal Affairs, 1920; reprint, Pittsburgh: Jean Morris, 1976). Not much help for line changes were the maps for twenty-eight counties in L.E. Wilt, *County Historical Maps of Pennsylvania* (Harrisburg: Archives Publishing Company of Pennsylvania, 1941-46). The *Map Guide* has been collated with Long, *Historical Atlas*.

Rhode Island

The county lines are mapped in detail in John Hutchins Cady, *Rhode Island Boundaries, 1636-1936* (Providence?: Rhode Island Tercentenary Commission, 1936).

South Carolina

The session laws were read for 1776-1921. Early laws are also found in Thomas Cooper and David L. McCord, *Statutes at Large of South Carolina,* 8 vols. (Columbia: By Authority of the Legislature, 1836-40). Essential for early place-names and district lines is Robert Mills, *Atlas of the State of South Carolina* (Baltimore: F. Lucas, Jr., 1825; reprint, Easley, SC: Southern Historical Press, 1980).

South Dakota

The session laws were read for 1862-89 Dakota Territory and 1890-1920 South Dakota. Outline maps are in "Dakota's Counties," *The Wi-Iyohi: Monthly Bulletin of the South Dakota Historical Society* 13 no. 3 (1 June 1959), 1-15. The *Map Guide* has been collated with Long, *Historical Atlas*.

Tennessee

The session laws 1777-1891 for county boundaries are transcribed in Henry D. Whitney, *Land Laws of Tennessee* (Chattanooga: J.M. Deardorff & Sons, 1891). The session laws were read for 1891-1919. Boundary act citations are also collected in Robert T. Shannon, *A Compilation of the Tennessee Statutes* (Nashville: Tennessee Law Book Publishing Co., 1917), 1:68-85, a very valuable source. Defunct counties are discussed in Robert M. McBride, "Lost Counties of Tennessee," *East Tennessee Historical Society's Publications* 38 (1966), 3-15. The surveyed districts of East Tennessee are little-known but discussed briefly in E.D. Heppert, Jr., "Tennessee Valley Surveying 1745 to 1780," *Surveying and Mapping* 35 (1975), 347-54. Indispensable is Mathew Rhea's 1832 map of Tennessee, reprinted for Robert M. McBride and Owen Meredith, *Eastin Morris' Tennessee Gazetteer 1834* (Nashville: The Gazetteer Press, 1971). The Walker Line dispute is thoroughly mapped in James W. Sames III, *Four Steps West* (Versailles, KY: the author, 1971).

Texas

The session laws were read for 1846-1921 and compared with H.P.N. Gammel, *The Laws of Texas,* 20 vols. (Austin: Gammel Book Co., 1898-1920), as cited in *Index to Gammel's Laws of Texas 1822-1905* (Austin: H.P.N. Gammel, 1906). The last official reconciliation of all Texas county boundaries is the *Revised Statutes of Texas* (Austin: State Printing Office, 1887), pp. 116-55, which can be supplemented by John Sayles and Henry Sayles, *Early Laws of Texas* (St. Louis: Gilbert Book Co., 1888), 1:575-623; and R.L. Batts, *Batts' Annotated Revised Civil Statutes of Texas, 1895* (Austin: Eugene von Boeckman Publishing Co., 1897-99), 1:362-431. Sources for the traditional western border inherited by the republic are given in I.J. Cox, "The Southwest Boundary of Texas," *Southwestern Historical Quarterly* (then the *Quarterly of the Texas State Historical Association)* 6 (1902-03), 81-102. Outline maps for early counties are in Seymour V. Connor, "The Evolution of County Government in the Republic of Texas," ibid., 55 (1951-52), 163-200; and Imogene Kennedy and J. Leon Kennedy, *Genealogical Records in Texas* (Baltimore: Genealogical Publishing Co., 1987). For a piece of Texas that got away, see Berlin B. Chapman, "The Claim of Texas to Greer County," *Southwestern Historical Quarterly*, 53 (1949-50), 19-34, 164-79, 404-21.

Utah

The session laws were read for 1851-1920. Outline maps are in James B. Allen, "The Evolution of County Boundaries in Utah,"

Utah Historical Quarterly 23 (1955), 261-78; and Deon C. Greer et al., *Atlas of Utah* (Provo: Weber State College and Brigham Young University Press, 1981), pp. 162-65. The latter on page 45 shows the fluctuating levels of the Great Salt Lake.

Vermont

The session laws were read for 1779-1861 and mapped with the aid of J. Kevin Graffagnino, *The Shaping of Vermont from the Wilderness to the Centennial 1749-1877* (Rutland: Vermont Heritage Press, with the Bennington Museum, 1983). A detailed study of county lines was done by Virgil L. McCarty, "Evolution of Vermont Counties" (unpublished, Historical Records Survey, 1942), copy at the Vermont Historical Society.

Virginia

The law citations are listed in Morgan Poitiaux Robinson, "Virginia Counties: Those Resulting from Virginia Legislation," *Bulletin of the Virginia State Library* 9 (1916), 5-283. The session laws were read for 1915-20. Netti Schreiner-Yantis includes maps in her several books on tax and census lists for southwestern Virginia counties, these being especially helpful for a difficult area. Martha W. Hiden, *How Justice Grew. Virginia Counties: An Abstract of Their Formation* (Williamsburg: Virginia 350th Anniversary Celebration Corporation, 1957), is a brief, popularized account, but not useful for boundary locations. The information on independent cities is from (1) the National Archives' lists of microfilms for the 1900 and 1910 censuses; (2) an unpublished 1920 list by its cartographic division; (3) a list compiled by the office of the Virginia secretary of state; (4) J.R.V. Daniel, *A Hornbook of Virginia History* (Richmond: Division of History, Virginia Department of Conservation and Development, 1949), pp. 27-32; and (5) David G. Temple, *Merger Politics: Local Government Consolidation in Tidewater Virginia* (Charlottesville: University Press of Virginia, 1972).

Washington

The session laws were read for 1843-53 Oregon and 1853-1920 Washington. The boundary statutes are transcribed in Newton

Carl Abbott and Fred E. Carver, *The Evolution of Washington Counties* (Yakima: Yakima Valley Genealogical Society and Klickitat County Historical Society, 1979). This is Abbott's unpublished master's thesis from the University of Washington, 1927, with additional maps supplied by Carver. The maps were not followed for the *Map Guide*.

West Virginia

Decennial maps were adapted from Edgar B. Sims, *Making a State: Formation of West Virginia, Including Maps, Illustrations, Plats, Grants and the Acts of the Virginia Assembly and the Legislature of West Virginia Creating the Counties* (Charleston: State of West Virginia, 1956). Drawing early Virginia lines for the *Map Guide* produced some minor differences with Sims' maps, but anyone reconstructing county lines in the jumbled Appalachian watersheds will appreciate the magnitude of Sims' work. The boundary statutes are also available in Historical Records Survey, *West Virginia County Formations and Boundary Changes* (Charleston: Historical Records Survey, 1939), which lacks maps.

Wisconsin

The statutes are transcribed and mapped in Historical Records Survey, *Origin and Legislative History of County Boundaries in Wisconsin* (Madison: Wisconsin Historical Records Survey, 1942). The boundary evolutions for each county (without maps) are given in Louise Phelps Kellogg, "Organization, Boundaries, and Names of Wisconsin Counties," *Proceedings of the State Historical Society of Wisconsin* 57 (1909), 184-231. The *Map Guide* has been collated with Long, *Historical Atlas*.

Wyoming

The session laws were read for 1869-1920. There are two outline maps in Thomas S. Chamblin, ed., *The Historical Encyclopedia of Wyoming* (Cheyenne: Wyoming Historical Institute, 1970), 1:7.

NOTES

1. For early *published* statistical atlases, see Lester J. Cappon, "The Historical Map in American Atlases," *Annals of the Association of American Geographers* 69 (1979), 623-26.

2. Texas Historical Records Survey Collection, Boxes 4G304-305, Barker Texas History Center, University of Texas-Austin.

3. Kenneth C. Martis, *The Historical Atlas of the United States Congressional Districts, 1784-1983* (New York: Free Press, Macmillan, 1982), p. 31.

4. John H. Long, "Historical Boundary File," *Mapline,* special no. 3 (April 1979), 6 pp. Our thanks to the National Endowment for the Humanities for copies of the several project reports, and to John Long for transcripts of conference talks. The project funding exceeded $380,000.

5. Latah Co., Idaho, 25 Stat. 147, 14 May 1888; San Juan Co., New Mexico, 25 Stat. 336, 19 July 1888; Greer Co., Oklahoma, 29 Stat. 155, 4 May 1896; Osage Co., Oklahoma, 34 Stat. 267, 16 June 1906; and Sierra Co., New Mexico, 36 Stat. 879, 10 May 1909. The two 1888 acts reflect a misinterpretation of an 1886 act of Congress, for which see 24 Stat. 170, 30 July 1886, and 25 Stat. 336, 19 July 1888.

6. Something of the geography division of the Census Bureau is given in Katherine H. Davidson and Charlotte M. Ashby, *Records of the Bureau of the Census* (Washington: NARS, 1964), pp. 52-53; and A.W. von Struve, "Geography in the Census Bureau," *Economic Geography* 16 (1940), 275-80.

7. The governor of Alabama by letter of 17 November 1821 relayed to the U.S. Secretary of State some late census returns for two (unnamed) counties but added, "I am informed that several other counties have been omitted." The state of Alabama also took a census in 1820, and on 1 December 1820 the Huntsville *Alabama Republican* published the compiled statistics. Its county list agrees with the federal list except for adding Jefferson (population 4114) and Marion (no returns received). This background now makes sense of the federal census report. The totals for twenty-two Alabama counties are printed in the 1820 federal report with the federal marshal's certification date of 31 August 1821. A separate page follows listing two more counties as certified by the marshal on 7 November 1821, these presumably being the two counties whose late returns the governor relayed. A third page in the federal report adds another three counties, the marshal's certification being 7 March 1822. Given these delays in completing the 1820 federal census in Alabama, we infer that the Jefferson and Marion returns did not reach Washington, D.C., in time, if ever taken. See U.S. Congress, *House Documents* no. 4, 17th Cong., 1st sess., serial 63; Marie Bankhead Owen, *Alabama Census Returns 1820* (Baltimore: Genealogical Publishing Co., 1967), reprinted from the *Alabama Historical Quarterly* 6 no. 3 (1944); and Secretary of State, *Census for 1820* (Washington: Gales & Seaton, 1821; reprint, New York: Luther M. Cornwall Co., n.d.).

8. Delaware Laws 1841, ch. 347, p. 401.

9. Clarence E. Carter, *Territorial Papers of the United States,* vol. 7, Territory of Indiana, 1800-1810 (Washington: GPO, 1939), p. 25. Our thanks to James Hansen for this observation.

County Index

A county can be located on the state maps using the zone number, which is keyed to the zone divisions above each map's legend bar. (Remember that a modern county will appear in **white** lettering on a map dated earlier than that county's creation date.) Jurisdictions functioning like counties are also listed below, such as Louisiana civil parishes and 1810 Missouri districts. Other census units, including Indian reservations, numbered judicial districts, and Yellowstone National Park, are not listed below, but they should be easy to locate. Independent cities have "city" after their name. Counties and cities followed by dates appear only on the maps of those dates. This index lists all present-day U.S. counties, plus (as marked by an asterisk and italics) nearly all counties defunct or later renamed. However, in showing only counties displayed in the *Map Guide*, the list omits (1) counties created and dissolved between successive censuses and (2) the original names of any counties renamed before their first federal census.

*Defunct county or obsolete name.

*Defunct county or obsolete name.

IDAHO
pp. 93-98

Ada	10
Adams	7
Alturas 1870-90	9
Bannock	11
Bear Lake	12
Benewah	4
Bingham	10
Blaine	10
Boise	9
Bonner	2
Bonneville	10
Boundary	1
Butte	9
Camas	10
Canyon	9
Caribou	11
Cassia	12
Clark	8
Clearwater	4
Custer	8
Elmore	10
Franklin	12
Fremont	8
Gem	9
Gooding	11
Idaho	6
Jefferson	9
Jerome	11
Kootenai	3
Latah	4
Lemhi	7
Lewis	5
Lincoln	11
Logan 1890	10
Madison	9
Minidoka	11
Nez Perce	5
Oneida	12
Owyhee	11
Payette	9
Power	11
Shoshone	3
Teton	9
Twin Falls	12
Valley	8
Washington	8

ILLINOIS
pp. 99-105

Adams	6
Alexander	12
Bond	8
Boone	2
Brown	6
Bureau	3
Calhoun	8
Carroll	2
Cass	6
Champaign	6
Christian	7
Clark	8
Clay	9
Clinton	8
Coles	7
Cook	3
Crawford	8
Cumberland	8
DeKalb	3
DeWitt	6
Douglas	7
DuPage	3
Edgar	7
Edwards	9
Effingham	8
Fayette	8
Ford	5
Franklin	10
Fulton	5
Gallatin	11
Greene	7
Grundy	4
Hamilton	10
Hancock	5
Hardin	11
Henderson	5
Henry	4
Iroquois	5
Jackson	11
Jasper	8
Jefferson	10
Jersey	8
Jo Daviess	2
Johnson	11
Kane	3
Kankakee	4
Kendall	3
Knox	4
Lake	2
LaSalle	4
Lawrence	9
Lee	3
Livingston	4
Logan	6
McDonough	5
McHenry	2
McLean	6
Macon	8
Macoupin	8
Madison	9
Marion	9
Marshall	4
Mason	6
Massac	12
Menard	6
Mercer	4
Monroe	10
Montgomery	8
Morgan	7
Moultrie	7
Ogle	2
Peoria	5
Perry	10
Piatt	6
Pike	7
Pope	11
Pulaski	12
Putnam	4
Randolph	10
Richland	9
Rock Island	3
St. Clair	9
Saline	11
Sangamon	7
Schuyler	6
Scott	7
Shelby	7
Stark	4
Stephenson	2
Tazewell	5
Union	11
Vermilion	6
Wabash	9
Warren	5
Washington	9
Wayne	9
White	10
Whiteside	3
Will	3
Williamson	11
Winnebago	2
Woodford	5

INDIANA
pp. 106-13

Adams	4
Allen	3
Bartholomew	7
Benton	4
Blackford	4
Boone	5
Brown	7
Carroll	4
Cass	4
Clark	9
Clay	7
Clinton	5
Crawford	9
Daviess	9
Dearborn	7
Decatur	7
DeKalb	2
Delaware	5
Delaware 1820	5
Dubois	9
Elkhart	2
Fayette	6
Floyd	9
Fountain	5
Franklin	7
Fulton	3
Gibson	9
Grant	4
Greene	8
Hamilton	5
Hamilton 1800	7
Now in OH.	
Hancock	6
Harrison	10
Hendricks	6
Henry	6
Howard	4
Huntington	3
Jackson	8
Jasper	3
Jay	4
Jefferson	8
Jennings	8
Johnson	7
Knox	8

Kosciusko	2
LaGrange	2
Lake	2
LaPorte	2
Lawrence	8
Madison	5
Marion	6
Marshall	2
Martin	9
Miami	4
Monroe	7
Montgomery	5
Morgan	7
Newton	3
Noble	2
Ohio	8
Orange	9
Owen	7
Parke	6
Perry	10
Pike	9
Porter	2
Posey	10
Pulaski	3
Putnam	6
Randolph	5
Randolph, see IL 1800	10
Ripley	8
Rush	6
St. Clair, see IL 1800	8
St. Joseph	2
Scott	9
Shelby	7
Spencer	10
Starke	2
Steuben	2
Sullivan	7
Switzerland	8
Tippecanoe	4
Tipton	5
Union	6
Vanderburgh	10
Vermillion	6
Vigo	7
Wabash	3
Wabash 1820	5
Warren	4
Warrick	10
Washington	9

INDIAN TERRITORY
See Oklahoma 1860 and 1890-1900.

IOWA
pp. 114-17

Adair	4
Adams	4
Allamakee	9
Appanoose	7
Audubon	4
Benton	8
Black Hawk	7
Boone	5
Bremer	5
Buchanan	8
Buena Vista	3
Buncombe 1860	2
Butler	7
Calhoun	4
Carroll	4
Cass	4
Cedar	9
Cerro Gordo	6
Cherokee	3
Chickasaw	7
Clarke	5
Clay	4
Clayton	9
Clinton	10
Crawford	3
Dallas	5
Davis	7
Decatur	6
Delaware	9
Des Moines	9
Dickinson	3
Dubuque	9
Emmet	4
Fayette	8
Floyd	7
Franklin	6
Fremont	3

Greene	4
Grundy	7
Guthrie	4
Hamilton	5
Hancock	5
Hardin	6
Harrison	2
Henry	9
Howard	7
Humboldt	5
Ida	3
Iowa	8
Jackson	10
Jasper	6
Jefferson	8
Johnson	8
Jones	9
Keokuk	8
Kossuth	5
Lee	9
Linn	8
Louisa	9
Lyon	2
Madison	5
Mahaska	7
Marion	6
Marshall	6
Mills	3
Mitchell	5
Monona	2
Monroe	7
Montgomery	3
Muscatine	9
O'Brien	3
Osceola	2
Page	3
Palo Alto	4
Plymouth	2
Pocahontas	4
Polk	6
Pottawattamie	3
Poweshiek	7
Ringgold	5
Sac	3
Scott	10
Shelby	3
Sioux	2
Story	6
Tama	7
Taylor	4

Union	5
Van Buren	8
Wapello	7
Warren	6
Washington	8
Wayne	6
Webster	5
Winnebago	5
Winneshiek	8
Woodbury	2
Worth	6
Wright	5

KANSAS
pp. 118-21

Allen	11
Anderson	11
Arapahoe, see CO 1860	8
Arapahoe 1880	3
Atchison	11
Barber	6
Barton	6
Bourbon	11
Breckinridge 1860	9
Brown	10
Buffalo 1880	4
Butler	9
Chase	9
Chautauqua	9
Cherokee	11
Cheyenne	2
Clark	4
Clay	8
Cloud	7
Coffey	10
Comanche	5
Cowley	9
Crawford	11
Davis 1860-80	9
Decatur	4
Dickinson	8
Doniphan	11
Dorn 1860	11
Douglas	11
Edwards	5
Elk	9
Ellis	5
Ellsworth	7
Finney	3

*Defunct county or obsolete name.

*Defunct county or obsolete name.

MICHIGAN
continued

Hillsdale........11
Houghton.........2
Huron..........11
*Huron 1810.....11
Ingham.........10
Ionia.............9
Iosco...........10
Iron.............3
Isabella..........9
*Isle Royale 1880-90.........1
Jackson.........10
Kalamazoo.......9
Kalkaska.........8
Kent.............9
Keweenaw........2
Lake.............8
Lapeer..........11
Leelanau.........7
Lenawee........11
Livingston.......11
Luce.............6
Mackinac.........7
Macomb.........12
Manistee.........7
*Manitou 1860-90...7
Marquette........4
Mason............7
Mecosta..........8
Menominee.......4
*Michilimackinac 1810-60.........8
Now Mackinac.
Midland..........9
Missaukee........8
Monroe.........12
Montcalm.........9
Montmorency.....9
Muskegon........8
Newaygo.........8
Oakland........11
Oceana..........7
Ogemaw.........9
Ontonagon.......2
Osceola..........8
Oscoda..........9
Otsego..........8
Ottawa..........8

Presque Isle......9
Roscommon......9
Saginaw.........10
St. Clair.........12
St. Joseph........9
Sanilac.........11
Schoolcraft.......5
Shiawassee.....10
Tuscola.........11
Van Buren........9
Washtenaw......11
Wayne...........12
Wexford.........8

MINNESOTA
pp. 169-78

Aitkin............5
Anoka............6
Becker...........3
Beltrami.........4
Benton...........5
*Big Sioux, see 1857, Map C....p. 259
Big Stone........2
Blue Earth.......5
*Breckenridge 1860...2
Brown...........4
*Buchanan 1857-60......6
Carlton..........6
Carver...........5
Cass.............5
Chippewa........3
Chippewa 1830....3
Now in MI.
Chisago..........6
Clay.............2
Clayton 1840.....5
Now in IA.
Clearwater.......3
Cook.............8
Cottonwood......4
Crawford 1830....6
Now in WI.
Crow Wing......5
Dakota...........6
Dodge...........6
Douglas..........3
Faribault.........5
Fillmore.........7

Freeborn.........5
Goodhue.........6
Grant............3
Hennepin.........5
Houston.........8
Hubbard.........4
Isanti...........6
Itasca...........5
Jackson..........4
Kanabec.........6
Kandiyohi........4
Kittson..........2
Koochiching......5
Lac qui Parle.....3
*Lac qui Parle 1870.........3
Lake.............8
Lake of the Woods...4
LeSueur.........5
Lincoln..........2
Lyon.............3
McLeod..........5
*Mahkahta 1850....4
Mahnomen........3
*Manomin 1857-60...6
Marshall.........2
Martin...........4
*Medway, see 1857, Map C......p. 259
Meeker..........4
Mille Lacs........5
*Monongalia 1860-70.........4
Morrison.........5
Mower...........6
Murray..........3
Nicollet..........4
Nobles...........3
Norman..........2
Olmstead.........7
Otter Tail........3
*Pembina 1850-70...2
Pennington.......3
*Pierce 1857-60....4
Pine.............6
Pipestone........2
*Pipestone 1857-60...4
Polk.............3
Pope.............3
Ramsey..........6
Red Lake.........3

Redwood.........3
Renville.........4
Rice.............6
Rock.............2
*Rock 1857-60.....2
Roseau..........3
St. Croix 1840.....6
Now in WI.
St. Louis.........6
Scott............5
Sherburne........5
Sibley...........5
Stearns..........4
Steele...........6
Stevens..........3
Swift............3
Todd............4
*Toombs 1860.....2
Traverse.........2
Wabasha.........7
Wadena..........4
*Wahnahta 1850....2
Waseca..........5
Washington.......6
Watonwan.......3
Wilkin...........2
Winona..........7
Wright...........5
Yellow Medicine...3

MISSISSIPPI
pp. 179-90

Adams...........9
Alcorn...........2
Amite............9
Attala...........5
Baldwin, see AL 1810.........9
Benton...........2
Bolivar..........4
Calhoun..........4
Carroll...........5
Chickasaw........4
Choctaw.........5
Claiborne.........8
Clarke...........8
Clay.............4
Coahoma.........3
Copiah...........8
Covington........8

DeSoto..........2
Forrest..........9
Franklin..........9
George.........10
Greene...........9
Grenada.........4
Hancock.........11
Harrison.........11
Hinds............7
Holmes..........5
Humphreys.......5
Issaquena........6
Itawamba........3
Jackson.........11
Jasper...........8
Jefferson.........8
Jefferson Davis....9
Jones............8
Kemper..........3
Lafayette.........3
Lamar...........9
Lauderdale.......7
Lawrence.........9
Leake............6
Lee.............3
Leflore..........4
Lincoln..........9
Lowndes.........5
Madison..........6
Madison, see AL 1810.........2
Marion...........9
Marshall.........2
Monroe..........4
Montgomery......5
Neshoba.........6
Newton..........7
Noxubee.........8
Oktibbeha........5
Panola...........3
Pearl River......10
Perry............9
*Pickering 1800....8
Pike.............9
Pontotoc.........3
Prentiss.........2
Quitman.........3
Rankin..........7
Scott............7
Sharkey.........6
Simpson.........8

Smith............8
Stone..........10
*Sumner 1880.....4
Sunflower........4
Tallahatchie......4
Tate.............2
Tippah...........2
Tishomingo.......2
Tunica...........2
Union............2
Walthall..........9
Warren...........7
Washington.......5
Washington, see AL 1800-10.....8
Wayne...........8
Webster..........4
Wilkinson.........9
Winston..........5
Yalobusha........3
Yazoo...........6

MISSOURI
pp. 191-98

Adair............6
Andrew..........3
Arkansas, see AR 1810......9
Atchison.........2
Audrain..........7
Barry............4
Barton...........3
Bates............3
Benton...........5
Bollinger.........9
Boone...........6
Buchanan........3
Butler...........9
Caldwell.........4
Callaway.........7
Camden..........6
Cape Girardeau...10
Carroll...........5
Carter...........8
Cass.............3
Cedar............4
Chariton.........5
Christian.........5
Clark............7
Clay.............3

Clinton..........3
Cole.............6
Cooper..........5
Crawford.........8
Dade............4
Dallas...........4
Daviess..........4
DeKalb..........3
Dent.............7
*Dodge 1850......5
Douglas..........6
Dunklin..........9
Franklin..........8
Gasconade.......7
Gentry...........3
Greene...........5
Grundy..........4
Harrison.........4
Henry............4
Hickory..........5
Holt.............2
Howard..........6
Howell...........7
Iron.............6
Jackson..........3
Jasper...........3
Jefferson.........9
Johnson..........4
Knox............6
Laclede..........6
Lafayette.........4
Lawrence.........4
Lewis............7
Lincoln..........8
Linn.............5
Livingston........4
McDonald........3
Macon...........6
Madison..........9
Maries...........7
Marion...........7
Mercer...........4
Miller...........6
Mississippi......10
Moniteau.........6
Monroe..........7
Montgomery......7
Morgan..........5
New Madrid.....10
Newton..........3
Nodaway.........3

Oregon...........7
Osage............7
Ozark............6
Pemiscot........10
Perry...........10
Pettis............5
Phelps...........7
Pike.............8
Platte............3
Polk.............5
Pulaski...........6
Putnam..........5
Ralls............7
Randolph.........6
Ray.............4
Reynolds.........8
Ripley...........8
*Rives 1840.......4
St. Charles........8
St. Clair..........4
St. Francois.......9
St. Louis.........9
St. Louis, city 1880-1920.......9
Ste. Genevieve....9
Saline...........5
Schuyler.........6
Scotland.........6
Scott...........10
Shannon.........7
Shelby...........6
Stoddard.........9
Stone............9
Sullivan.........5
Taney............5
Texas............7
*Van Buren 1840....3
Vernon..........3
Warren...........8
Washington.......8
Wayne...........9
Webster..........5
Worth............3
Wright...........6

MONTANA
pp. 199-205

Beaverhead.......3
Big Horn.........9
*Big Horn 1870....10

*Defunct county or obsolete name.

*Defunct county or obsolete name.

*Defunct county or obsolete name.

*Defunct county or obsolete name.

*Defunct county or obsolete name.

Date Due

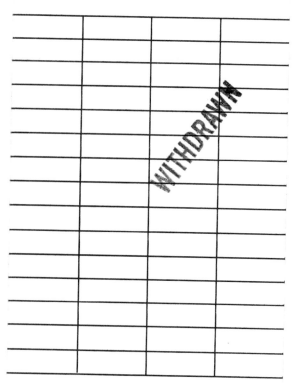